Cover by Sefer Press 2015

Book Format by Sefer Press 2015

Hebrew:Modern Hebrew Text Form
Greek:Majority Text (Byzantine) Text Form

Commentary Editing by Al Garza PhD

For Questions Contact A.G. Ben Shlomo At
BenShlomo@Israelmail.com

Sefer Press
Publishing House

JOHN

A RABBINIC JEWISH SOURCE

COMMENTARY

AND LANGUAGE STUDY BIBLE

Volume 4

KJV-GREEK-HEBREW

WITH TRANSLITERATION

Greek Majority Text And Modern Hebrew

PUBLISHED BY SEFER PRESS PUBLISHING HOUSE©2015

TABLE OF CONTENTS

TITLE: Gospel of John

AUTHOR: John The Beloved; According to Early Greek and Latin Fathers

DATE: 50AD TO 90AD

LANGUAGE: Hebrew and Published into Greek

WRITTEN TO: 1ST Century Jewish Believers

THEME: Demonstrate Yeshua/Jesus as Son of God

PaRDeS: Sod- "Secret" ("Mystery/Hidden") or the esoteric/mystical meaning, as given through inspiration or revelation. This is the "S" in PaRDeS. This understanding is the hidden, secret or mystic meaning of a text.

THE GOSPEL ACCORDING TO
ST JOHN

John, Chapter 1

1. In the beginning was the Word, and the Word was with God, and the Word was God.

Greek/Transliteration

1. Ἐν ἀρχῇ ἦν ὁ λόγος, καὶ ὁ λόγος ἦν πρὸς τὸν θεόν, καὶ θεὸς ἦν ὁ λόγος.

1. En archei ein 'o logos, kai 'o logos ein pros ton theon, kai theos ein 'o logos.

Hebrew/Transliteration

‏א. בְּרֵאשִׁית הָיָה הַדָּבָר וְהַדָּבָר הָיָה אֶת-הָאֱלֹהִים וְהוּא הַדָּבָר הָיָה אֱלֹהִים:

1. Be•re•sheet ha•ya ha•da•var ve•ha•da•var ha•ya et - ha•Elohim ve•hoo ha•da•var ha•ya Elohim.

TaNaKh-Old Testament/Rabbinic Jewish Commentary

"After these things the *Word of YAHWEH* came to Abram in a vision, saying, Do not fear, Abram; I am a shield to you, your reward will increase greatly. And *Abram said, Adonai YAHWEH*, what will You give to me? I am going childless and the son of the inheritance of my house is Eleazar of Damascus?...And He said to him, *I am YAHWEH* who caused you to come out of Ur of the Chaldeans, to give you this land to inherit it." (Genesis 15:1-2;7) **NOTE**: This is the first time in the Bible that *The Word* of YHWH appears, according to Moses.

The phrase, מימרא דיי, "*The Word of the LORD*", so frequently used by the Targumists, is well known: and it is to be observed, that the same things which John here says of the word, they say likewise, as will be observed on the several clauses; from whence it is more likely, that John should take this phrase, since the paraphrases of Onkelos and Jonathan ben Uzziel were written before his time, than that he should borrow it from the writings of Plato, or his followers, as some have thought; with whose philosophy, Ebion and Cerinthus are said to be acquainted; wherefore John, the more easily to gain upon them, uses this phrase, when that of the Son of God would have been disagreeable to them: that there is some likeness between the Evangelist John and Plato in their sentiments concerning *The Word*, will not be denied. Amelius (f), a Platonic philosopher, who lived after the times of John, manifestly refers to these words of his, in agreement with his master's doctrine: his words are these,

"And this was truly "Logos", or *The Word*, by whom always existing, the things that are made, were made, as also Heraclitus thought; and who, likewise that Barbarian (meaning the Evangelist John) reckons was in the order and dignity of the beginning, constituted with God, and was God, by whom all things are entirely made; in whom, whatsoever is made, lives, and has life, and being; and who entered into bodies, and was clothed with flesh, and appeared a man;

So not with standing, that he showed forth the majesty of his nature; and after his dissolution, he was again deified, and was God, as he was before he descended into a body, flesh and man.

Wherefore it is more probable, that the evangelist received this phrase of *The Word*, as a divine person, from the Targums, where there is such frequent mention made of it; or however, there is a very great agreement between what he and these ancient writings of the Jews say of *The Word*, as will be hereafter shown. Moreover, the phrase is frequently used in like manner, in the writings of Philo the Jew; from whence it is manifest, that the name was well known to the Jews, and may be the reason of the evangelist's using it.

Philo the Jew often calls the Logos, or *Word*, the eternal *Word*, the most ancient *Word*, and more ancient than any thing that is made (p). The eternity of the Messiah is acknowledged by the ancient Jews: Mic_5:2 is a full proof of it; which by them (q) is thus paraphrased,

"Out of thee, before me, shall come forth the Messiah, that he may exercise dominion over Israel; whose name is said from eternity, from the days of old".

Jarchi only mentions Psa_72:17 which is rendered by the Targum on the place, before the sun his name was prepared; it may be translated, "before the sun his name was Yinnon"; that is, the Son, namely the Son of God; and Aben Ezra interprets it, יקרא בן, "he shall be called the son"; and to this agrees what the Talmudisis say (r), that the name of the Messiah was before the world was created.

And the Word was with God; The Targum of Jonathan (e), or Chaldee paraphrases; Psa_110:1 "the LORD said to my Lord", is rendered, "the LORD said to his *Word*"; where he is manifestly distinguished from YHWH, that speaks to him; and in Hos_1:7 the LORD promises to "have mercy on the house of Judah", and "save them by the LORD their God". The Targum is, "I will redeem them by *The Word* of the LORD their God"; where *The Word* of the LORD, who is spoken of as a Redeemer and Saviour, is distinguished from the LORD, who promises to save by him. This distinction of YHWH and his *Word*, may be observed in multitudes of places, in the Chaldee paraphrases, and in the writings of Philo the Jew; and this phrase, of "*The Word*" being "with God", is in the Targumim expressed by, מימר מן קדם, "*The Word* from before the LORD", or "Which is before the LORD": being always in his presence, and the messenger of it; so Onkelos paraphrases Gen_31:22 "And *The Word* from before the LORD, came to Laban", and Exo_20:19 thus, "And let not *The Word* from before the LORD speak with us, lest we die".

and the Word was God; the Jews often use *The Word* of the LORD for YHWH, and call him God. Thus the words in Gen_28:20 are paraphrased by Onkelos,

"If "*The Word* of the LORD" will be my help, and will keep me, then "*The Word* of the LORD" shall be, לי לאלהא, "my God":

Again, Lev_26:12 is paraphrased, by the Targum ascribed to Jonathan Ben Uzziel, thus,

"I will cause the glory of my Shekinah to dwell among you, and my *Word* shall "be your God", the Redeemer;

Once more, Deu_26:17 is rendered by the Jerusalem Targum after this manner,

"Ye have made "*The Word* of the LORD" king over you this day, that he may be your God:

And this is frequent with Philo the Jew, who says, the name of God is his *Word*, and calls him, my YHWH, the divine *Word*; and affirms, that the most ancient *Word* is God (s),

(e) De Cathol. Arean. Ver. l. 3. c. 5. & l. 8. c. 24. (f) Apud Euseb. Prepar. Evangel. l. 11. c. 19. (p) De Leg. Alleg. l. 2. p. 93. de Plant. Noe, p. 217. de Migrat. Abraham, p. 389. de Profugis, p. 466. quis. rer. divin. Haeres. p. 509. (q) Targum Jon. in loc. (r) T. Bab. Pesachim, fol. 54. 1. & Nedarim, fol. 39. 2. Pirke Eliezer, c. 3. (s) De Allegor. l. 2. p. 99, 101. & de Somniis, p. 599.

---

2. The same was in the beginning with God.

Greek/Transliteration
2. Οὗτος ἦν ἐν ἀρχῇ πρὸς τὸν θεόν.

2. 'Outos ein en archei pros ton theon.

Hebrew/Transliteration
‫ב. הוּא הָיָה מֵראשׁ אֶת-הָאֱלֹהִים:‬

2. Hoo ha•ya me•rosh et - ha•Elohim.

---

3. All things were made by him; and without him was not any thing made that was made.

Greek/Transliteration
3. Πάντα δι' αὐτοῦ ἐγένετο, καὶ χωρὶς αὐτοῦ ἐγένετο οὐδὲ ἓν ὃ γέγονεν.

3. Panta di autou egeneto, kai choris autou egeneto oude 'en 'o gegonen.

Hebrew/Transliteration
‫ג. כָּל-הַמַּעֲשִׂים נִהְיוּ עַל-יָדוֹ וְאֵין דָּבָר אֲשֶׁר נַעֲשָׂה מִבַּלְעָדָיו:‬

3. Kol - ha•ma•a•sim ni•hi•yoo al - ya•do ve•eyn da•var asher na•a•sa mi•bal•a•dav.

Rabbinic Jewish Commentary

The Targumists attribute the creation of man, in particular, to *The Word* of God: it is said in Gen_1:27. "God created man in his own image": the Jerusalem Targum of it is,

"And *The Word* of YHWH created man in his likeness.

And Gen_3:22 "And the Lord God said, behold the man is become as one of us", the same Targum paraphrases thus,

"And *The Word* of the LORD God said, behold the man whom I have created, is the only one in the world.

Also in the same writings, the creation of all things in general is ascribed to *The Word*: the passage in Deu_33:27 "The eternal God is thy refuge, and underneath are the everlasting arms", is paraphrased by Onkelos,

"The eternal God is an habitation, by whose *Word* the world was made.

In Isa_48:13 it is said, "Mine hand also hath laid the foundation of the earth". The Targum of Jonathan ben Uzziah on it is,

"Yea, by my *Word* I have founded the earth:

Which agrees with what is said in Heb_11:3, and the same says Philo the Jew, who not only calls him the archetype, and exemplar of the world, but the power that made it: he often ascribes the creation of the heavens, and the earth unto him, and likewise the creation of man after whose image, he says, he was made (t). The Ethiopic version adds, at the end of this verse, "And also that which is made is for himself",

(t) De Mundi Opificio, p. 4, 5, 31, 32. De Alleg. l. 1. p. 44. De Sacrificiis Abel & Cain, p. 131. De Profugis, p. 464. & de Monarch. p. 823.

---

4. In him was life; and the life was the light of men.

Greek/Transliteration
4. Ἐν αὐτῷ ζωὴ ἦν, καὶ ἡ ζωὴ ἦν τὸ φῶς τῶν ἀνθρώπων,

4. En auto zoei ein, kai 'ei zoei ein to phos ton anthropon,

Hebrew/Transliteration
‏ד. בּוֹ נִמְצָא חַיִּים וְהַחַיִּים הֵם אוֹר הָאָדָם‎:

---

4. Bo nim•tza cha•yim ve•ha•cha•yim hem or ha•a•dam.

---

5. And the light shineth in darkness; and the darkness comprehended it not.

Greek/Transliteration
5. καὶ τὸ φῶς ἐν τῇ σκοτίᾳ φαίνει, καὶ ἡ σκοτία αὐτὸ οὐ κατέλαβεν.

5. kai to phos en tei skotia phainei, kai 'ei skotia auto ou katelaben.

Hebrew/Transliteration
ה. וְהָאוֹר זֹרֵחַ בַּחֹשֶׁךְ וְהַחֹשֶׁךְ לֹא יְכִילֻּוּ:

5. Ve•ha•or zo•re•ach ba•cho•shech ve•ha•cho•shech lo ye•chi•le•noo.

Rabbinic Jewish Commentary
Rashi says,"The King Messiah, who is compared to light, as it is stated, "I have set up a lamp for my anointed," and Elijah the prophet, who is true, a faithful prophet. (Rashi on Psalm 43:3, Judaica Press.)

Midrash Tanchuma says, "...After this it is written, 'oil for the light' – this is King Messiah, as it says, "I will make the horn of David grow, I will prepare a lamp for My Anointed." (Psalm 132:17) (Midrash Tanchuma, Parashat T'rumah 7, Cited in Concealed Light, Dr. TsviSadan, Vine of David, pg. 232)

The book of Daniel says,
"He reveals the deep and secret things, he knows what is in the darkness, and the light dwells with him. (Daniel 2:22)

The Midrash Rabbah comments on this passage,
"R. Abba of Serungayya said: And the light dwells with him "alludes to the royal Messiah." (Genesis Rabbah 1:6, Soncino Press Edition)

The Midrash Rabbah identifies the name of the Messiah as the Nehirah, Light, "The School of R. Jannai said: His name is *Yinnon*, for it is written, E'er the sun was, his name is *Yinnon* (Ps. 72:17). R. Biba of Sergunieh said: His name is *Nehirah(LIGHT)*, as it is stated, And the light (nehorah) dwelleth with Him (Dan. 2:22) . . .R. Judah b. R. Simon said in the name of R. Samuel b. R. Isaac: King Messiah, whether he be of those still living or of those who are dead, bears the name of David." (Lamentations Rabbah 1:51, Soncino Press Edition)

Pesikta Rabbai makes an incredible statement, "What is meant by *'in Thy light do we see light (Psalm 36:9)?'* What light is it that the congregation of Israel looks for as from a watchtower? It is the light of Messiah, of which it is said, *'And God saw the light that it was good'* (Gen 1:4). This verse proves that the Holy One, blessed be He, contemplated the Messiah and his works before the world was created, and then under His throne of glory put away His Messiah until the time of the generation in which he will appear. Satan asked the Holy One, blessed be He, for whom is the light which is put away under Thy throne of glory? God replied: For him who will turn thee back and put thee to utter shame. Satan said: Master of the universe, show him to me. God replied: Come and see him. And when he saw him, Satan was shaken, and he fell upon his face and said: Surely this is the Messiah who will cause me and all the counterparts in heaven of the princes of the earth's nations to be swallowed up in Gehenna... in that hour all the princely counterparts of the nations, in agitation, will say to Him: Master of the universe, who is this through whose power we are to be swallowed up? What is his name? What kind of being is he? (Pesikta Rabbati 36.1, Yale University Press, pg. 677-678)

Thus the light that is sown is Messiah,
"Light is sown for the righteous, and gladness for the upright in heart."
(Psalms 97:11)

---

6. There was a man sent from God, whose name was John.

Greek/Transliteration
6. Ἐγένετο ἄνθρωπος ἀπεσταλμένος παρὰ θεοῦ, ὄνομα αὐτῷ Ἰωάννης.

6. Egeneto anthropos apestalmenos para theou, onoma auto Yoanneis.

Hebrew/Transliteration
ו. אִישׁ הָיָה בָאָרֶץ יוֹחָנָן שְׁמוֹ אֲשֶׁר שְׁלָחוֹ אֱלֹהִים:

6. Eesh ha•ya va•a•retz Yo•cha•nan sh`mo asher sh`la•cho Elohim.

---

7. The same came for a witness, to bear witness of the Light, that all men through him might believe.

Greek/Transliteration
7. Οὗτος ἦλθεν εἰς μαρτυρίαν, ἵνα μαρτυρήσῃ περὶ τοῦ φωτός, ἵνα πάντες πιστεύσωσιν δι᾽ αὐτοῦ.

7. 'Outos eilthen eis marturian, 'ina martureisei peri tou photos, 'ina pantes pisteusosin di autou.

Hebrew/Transliteration
ז. הוּא בָא לְעֵדוּת לְהָעִיד עַל-הָאוֹר לְמַעַן יַאֲמִינוּ כֻלָּם עַל-יָדוֹ:

7. Hoo va le•e•doot le•ha•eed al - ha•or le•ma•an ya•a•mi•noo choo•lam al - ya•do.

10

Rabbinic Jewish Commentary

This was one of the names of the Messiah with the Jews; of whom they say (u), נהירא שמו, "light is his name"; as it is said in Dan_2:22 and the light dwelleth with him; on which they have (w) elsewhere this gloss, this is the King Messiah; and so they interpret Psa_43:3 of him (x). (y) Philo the Jew often speaks of the Logos, or Word, as light, and calls him the intelligible light; the universal light, the most perfect light; represents him as full of divine light; and says, he is called the sun.

(u) Echa Rabbati, fol. 50. 2. (w) Bereshit Rabba, fol. 1. 3. (x) Jarchi in ib. (y) De Maudi Opificio, p. 6. De Allegor. l. 2. p. 80. & de Somniis, p. 576, 578.

---

8. He was not that Light, but was sent to bear witness of that Light.

Greek/Transliteration

8. Οὐκ ἦν ἐκεῖνος τὸ φῶς, ἀλλ᾽ ἵνα μαρτυρήσῃ περὶ τοῦ φωτός.

8. Ouk ein ekeinos to phos, all 'ina martureisei peri tou photos.

Hebrew/Transliteration

ח. וְלֹא הוּא הָיָה הָאוֹר כִּי אִם-בָּא לְהָעִיד עַל-הָאוֹר הַהוּא:

8. Ve•lo hoo ha•ya ha•or ki eem - ba le•ha•eed al - ha•or ha•hoo.

---

9. That was the true Light, which lighteth every man that cometh into the world.

Greek/Transliteration

9. ᾮν τὸ φῶς τὸ ἀληθινόν, ὃ φωτίζει πάντα ἄνθρωπον ἐρχόμενον εἰς τὸν κόσμον.

9. Ein to phos to aleithinon, 'o photizei panta anthropon erchomenon eis ton kosmon.

Hebrew/Transliteration

ט. הוּא אוֹר אֱמֶת אֲשֶׁר בָּא לָעוֹלָם לְהָאִיר לְכָל-אָדָם:

9. Hoo or emet asher ba la•o•lam le•ha•eer le•chol - adam.

---

10. He was in the world, and the world was made by him, and the world knew him not.

10. Ἐν τῷ κόσμῳ ἦν, καὶ ὁ κόσμος δι᾽ αὐτοῦ ἐγένετο, καὶ ὁ κόσμος αὐτὸν οὐκ ἔγνω.

10. En to kosmo ein, kai 'o kosmos di autou egeneto, kai 'o kosmos auton ouk egno.

י. הוּא הָיָה בָעוֹלָם וְהָעוֹלָם נִהְיָה עַל-יָדוֹ וְהָעוֹלָם אֹתוֹ לֹא יָדָע:

10. Hoo ha•ya va•o•lam ve•ha•olam ni•hi•ya al - ya•do ve•ha•olam o•to lo ya•da.

Rabbinic Jewish Commentary

Kol HaTor says,"Yosef recognized his brothers, but they did not recognize him — This is one of the traits of Yosef not only in his own generation, but in every generation, i.e., that *Mashiach ben Yosef* recognizes his brothers, but they do not recognize him. This is the work of Satan, who hides the characteristics of *Mashiach ben Yosef* so that the footsteps of the *Mashiach* are not recognized and are even belittled because of our many sins. Otherwise, our troubles would already have ended. Were Israel to recognize Yosef, that is, the footsteps of ben Yosef the *Mashiach* which is the ingathering of the exiles etc., then we would already have been redeemed with a complete redemption."
(Kol HaTor 2:39, translated by R' Yechiel Bar Lev and K. Skaist, pg. 37)

Kol HaTor notes something incredible, even the scholars will be struck with blindness,"How strong is the force of the *Sitra Achra* that he managed to hide from the eyes of our holy forefathers the danger of the *klipot* layers: from the eyes of our forefather Abraham, the *klipa* of Ismael; from the eyes of our forefather Isaac, the *klipa* of Esau; and from the eyes of our forefather Jacob, the *klipa* of the *terafim*. During the footsteps of the *Mashiach*, the *Sitra Achra* becomes even stronger, in order to strike Biblical scholars with blindness."
(Kol HaTor 5, translated by R' Yechiel bar Lev and K. Skaist, pg. 122)

---

11. He came unto his own (the Jews), and his own (the Jews) received him not.

11. Εἰς τὰ ἴδια ἦλθεν, καὶ οἱ ἴδιοι αὐτὸν οὐ παρέλαβον.

11. Eis ta idya eilthen, kai 'oi idioi auton ou parelabon.

יא. הוּא בָא אֶל-עַמּוֹ שֶׁלוֹ וְעַמּוֹ שֶׁלוֹ לֹא הֶחֱזִיקוּ-בּוֹ:

11. Hoo va el - amo she•lo ve•a•mo she•lo lo he•che•zi•koo - vo.

Rabbinic Jewish Commentary

The Baal Shem Tov (BeShT), R' Yisrael ben Eliezer (circa 1700-1760 CE), says, "It is written: "The path of the righteous is as the gleam of sunlight, that shines ever brighter until the height of the day" (Proverbs 4:18). That is, the sun in itself shines in its place equally, both at the onset of the day and in the middle. The only thing that obstructs it is the earth, which stands between us and the sun. Therefore, its light does not shine so brightly at dawn – only a little bit – until it spreads across the earth. The same holds true of the Tzaddik [Messiah]. In himself, he is always shining: the blockage is only on the part of the receivers. This too is due to the obstruction of the earth – that is, this world. For people are sunk in this world, and are unable to receive the light of the Tzaddik [Messiah]." (Baal Shem Tov, Rabbi Yisrael ben Eliezer on Devarim, translated by Rabbi Eliezer Shore, pg. 118)

There is a tradition in a text called the *Secrets of R' Shimon bar Yochai*, that Mashiach will be concealed and rejected,

"The Messiah of the lineage of Ephraim shall die there, and Israel shall mourn for him. After this the Holy One blessed be He will reveal to them the Messiah of the lineage of David, but *Israel will wish to stone him*, and they will say to him: 'You speak a lie, for the Messiah has already been slain, and there is no other Messiah destined to arise.' *They will scorn him*, as Scripture says: 'despised and abandoned (by) men' (Isa 53:3). He shall withdraw and be hidden from them, as Scripture continues: 'like one hiding faces from us' (ibid.). But in Israel's great distress, they will turn and cry out from (their) hunger and thirst, and the Holy One, blessed be He, will be revealed to them in His glory, as Scripture promises: 'together all flesh will see' (Isa 40:5). And the King Messiah will sprout up there, as Scripture says: 'and behold with the clouds of heaven etc.' (Dan 7:13), and it is written after it 'and authority was given to him' (Dan 7:14). He shall blow (his breath) at that wicked Armilos and kill him, as Scripture forecasts: 'he will slay the wicked one with the breath of his lips' (Isa 11:4).
(Nistarot ben Shimon bar Yochai, translated by John C. Reeves [8])-

---

12. But as many as received him, to them gave he power to become the sons of God, even to them that believe on his name:

Greek/Transliteration
12. Ὅσοι δὲ ἔλαβον αὐτόν, ἔδωκεν αὐτοῖς ἐξουσίαν τέκνα θεοῦ γενέσθαι, τοῖς πιστεύουσιν εἰς τὸ ὄνομα αὐτοῦ·

12. 'Osoi de elabon auton, edoken autois exousian tekna theou genesthai, tois pisteuousin eis to onoma autou.

Hebrew/Transliteration
יב. וְאֵלֶּה אֲשֶׁר הֶחֱזִיקוּ-בוֹ נָתַן בְּיָדָם לִהְיוֹת בָּנִים לֵאלֹהִים הֲלֹא הֵם הַמַּאֲמִינִים בִּשְׁמוֹ:

12. Ve•e•le asher he•che•zi•koo - vo na•tan - ko•ach be•ya•dam li•hee•yot ba•nim le•Elohim ha•lo hem ha•ma•a•mi•nim bish•mo.

---

13. Which were born, not of blood, nor of the will of the flesh, nor of the will of man, but of God.

Greek/Transliteration
13. οἳ οὐκ ἐξ αἱμάτων, οὐδὲ ἐκ θελήματος σαρκός, οὐδὲ ἐκ θελήματος ἀνδρός, ἀλλ᾽ ἐκ θεοῦ ἐγεννήθησαν.

13. 'oi ouk ex 'aimaton, oude ek theleimatos sarkos, oude ek theleimatos andros, all ek theou egenneitheisan.

Hebrew/Transliteration
יג. אֲשֶׁר לֵדָתָם לֹא מִדָּם וְלֹא מִתַּאֲוַת בָּשָׂר וְלֹא מֵרוּחַ גָּבֶר כִּי אִם-מֵאֱלֹהִים:

13. Asher le•da•tam lo mi•dam ve•lo mi•ta•a•vat ba•sar ve•lo me•roo•ach ga•ver ki eem - me•Elohim.

Rabbinic Jewish Commentary
Now this is owing not to blood, or bloods; not to the blood of circumcision; or of the passover, which the Jews had an high opinion of, and ascribe life and salvation to, and to which notion this may be opposed: so their commentators (f) on Eze_16:6 where the word "live" is twice used, observe on the first "live", by the blood of the passover, on the second "live", by the blood of circumcision; but, alas! these contribute nothing to the life of the new creature: nor is regeneration owing to the blood of ancestors, to natural descent, as from Abraham, which the Jews valued themselves upon.

nor of the will of man... So with the Jews, אִישׁ, "a man", signifies a great man, in opposition to "Adam", or "Enosh", which signify a mean, weak, frail man; and our translators have observed this distinction, in Isa_2:9 and the mean man (Adam) boweth down, and the great man (Ish) "humbleth himself": on which Jarchi has this note, "Adam boweth down", i.e. little men; "and a man humbleth himself", i.e. princes, and mighty men, men of power: and so Kimchi on Psa_4:2. "O ye sons of men", observes, that the Psalmist calls them the sons of men, with respect to the great men of Israel; for there were with Absalom the sons of great men. Though sometimes the Jews say (g), Adam is greater than any of the names of men, as Geber, Enosh, Ish. But now our evangelist observes, let a man be ever so great, or good, or eminent, for gifts and grace, he cannot communicate grace to another, or to whom he will; none are born again of any such will.

(f) Jarchi & Kimchi in loc. Shemot Rabba, sect. 19. fol. 103. 2. & 104. 4. & Mattanot Cehuna in Vajikra Rabba, sect. 23. fol. 164. 2. Zohar in Lev. fol. 39. 2.
(g) Zohar in Lev. fol. 20. 2.

---

14. And the Word was made flesh, and dwelt among us, (and we beheld his glory, the glory as of the only begotten of the Father,) full of grace and truth.

Greek/Transliteration
14. Καὶ ὁ λόγος σὰρξ ἐγένετο, καὶ ἐσκήνωσεν ἐν ἡμῖν- καὶ ἐθεασάμεθα τὴν δόξαν αὐτοῦ, δόξαν ὡς μονογενοῦς παρὰ πατρός- πλήρης χάριτος καὶ ἀληθείας.

14. Kai 'o logos sarx egeneto, kai eskeinosen en 'eimin- kai etheasametha tein doxan autou, doxan 'os monogenous para patros- pleireis charitos kai aleitheias.

Hebrew/Transliteration
‏:יד. וְהַדָּבָר לָבַשׁ בָּשָׂר וַיִּשְׁכֹּן בְּתוֹכֵנוּ וְאֶת-כְּבוֹדוֹ רָאִינוּ כִּכְבוֹד בֶּן יָחִיד לְאָבִיו מָלֵא חֶסֶד וֶאֱמֶת

14. Ve•ha•da•var la•vash ba•sar va•yish•kon be•to•che•noo ve•et - k`vo•do ra•ee•noo kich•vod Ben ya•chid le•Aviv ma•le che•sed ve•e•met.

Rabbinic Jewish Commentary

Michael Munk elucidates the concept of the Torah in the Wisdom of the Hebrew Alef-bet,"The sum total of human knowledge derives from the Torah because the universe is a product of Torah which is the blueprint of the world…When His Ineffable Word took physical form, heaven and earth became the clothing for the Word of God which infuses Creation, and without which Creation would not continue to exist. The spiritual Torah which preceded the world became clothed in ink and parchment…the wisdom of God took for the form of the 613 commandments. But the precepts are not isolated phenomena; they are all interrelated aspects of a single Torah, like the organs and vessels of a single human body to which the totality of the commandments are likened."
(The Wisdom in the Hebrew Alphabet, Artscroll, Michael L. Munk, pg. 47)

The Targumists sometimes speak of the Shekinah of the *Word* dwelling among the Israelites: so Onkelos in Num_11:20 where the Israelites are threatened with flesh, until they loath it; because, says the paraphrast,

"Ye have loathed "the Word of the LORD", whose Shekinah dwelleth among you.

Jonathan ben Uzziel, on the same place, expresses it thus,

"Because ye have loathed the Word of the LORD, the glory of whose Shekinah dwelleth among you.

The Jews speak of the glory of the Messiah to be seen in the world to come. They say (h),

"If a man is worthy of the world to come, (i.e. the times of the Messiah,) he shall "see the glory" of the King Messiah.

And of Moses, they say (i),

"There was (or will be) no generation like that in which he lived, until the generation in which the King Messiah comes, which shall "behold the glory" of the holy, blessed God, as he.

(h) Gloss. in T. Bab. Beracot, fol. 58. 1. (i) Zohar in Lev. fol. 9. 4.

---

15. John bare witness of him, and cried, saying, This was he of whom I spake, He that cometh after me is preferred before me: for he was before me.

Greek/Transliteration
15. Ἰωάννης μαρτυρεῖ περὶ αὐτοῦ, καὶ κέκραγεν λέγων, Οὗτος ἦν ὃν εἶπον, Ὁ ὀπίσω μου ἐρχόμενος ἔμπροσθέν μου γέγονεν· ὅτι πρῶτός μου ἦν.

15. Yoanneis marturei peri autou, kai kekragen legon, 'Outos ein 'on eipon, 'O opiso mou erchomenos emprosthen mou gegonen. 'oti protos mou ein.

Hebrew/Transliteration
טו. וְיוֹחָנָן הֵעִיד עָלָיו וַיִּקְרָא לֵאמֹר זֶה הוּא אֲשֶׁר אָמַרְתִּי עָלָיו כִּי הוּא בָא אַחֲרַי וְהִנֵּה הוּא לְפָנַי כִּי רִאשׁוֹן-לִי:הָיָה

15. Ve•Yo•cha•nan he•eed alav va•yik•ra le•mor ze hoo asher amar•ti alav ki hoo va a•cha•rai ve•hee•ne hoo le•fa•nai ki ri•shon - li ha•ya.

---

16. And of his fulness have all we received, and grace for grace.

Greek/Transliteration
16. Καὶ ἐκ τοῦ πληρώματος αὐτοῦ ἡμεῖς πάντες ἐλάβομεν, καὶ χάριν ἀντὶ χάριτος.

16. Kai ek tou pleiromatos autou 'eimeis pantes elabomen, kai charin anti charitos.

Hebrew/Transliteration
טז. כִּי מִמְּלֹאוֹ נָשָׂאנוּ כֻלָּנוּ חֶסֶד עַל-חָסֶד:

16. Ki mim•lo•o na•sa•noo choo•la•noo che•sed al - cha•sed.

Rabbinic Jewish Commentary
The phraseology is the same with this Jewish one (k), טיבו על ההוא טיבו, "goodness upon that goodness", an additional goodness; so here, grace upon grace, an abundance of it, an addition to it, and an increase of it: so חדו על חדו (l), joy upon joy, is an abundance of joy, a large measure of it; and "holiness upon holiness"

(m), abundance of it,

(k) Zohar in Exod. fol. 45. 1. (l) lb. in Lev. fol. 28. 1. & in Num. fol. 69. 2. & 71. 2. (m) lb. fol. 40. 3. & in Num. fol. 61. 1.

---

17. For the law was given by Moses, but grace and truth came by Jesus Christ.

Greek/Transliteration
17. Ὅτι ὁ νόμος διὰ Μωσέως ἐδόθη, ἡ χάρις καὶ ἡ ἀλήθεια διὰ Ἰησοῦ χριστοῦ ἐγένετο.

17. 'Oti 'o nomos dya Moseos edothei, 'ei charis kai 'ei aleitheya dya Yeisou christou egeneto.

Hebrew/Transliteration
יז. כִּי הַתּוֹרָה נְתוּנָה בְּיַד-מֹשֶׁה וְחֶסֶד וֶאֱמֶת מִמְּקוֹר יֵשׁוּעַ הַמָּשִׁיחַ יָצָאוּ:

17. Ki ha•Torah n`too•na be•yad - Moshe ve•che•sed ve•e•met mim•kor Yeshua ha•Ma•shiach ya•tza•oo.

---

18. No man hath seen God at any time; the only begotten Son, which is in the bosom of the Father, he hath declared him.

Greek/Transliteration
18. Θεὸν οὐδεὶς ἑώρακεν πώποτε· ὁ μονογενὴς υἱός, ὁ ὢν εἰς τὸν κόλπον τοῦ πατρός, ἐκεῖνος ἐξηγήσατο.

18. Theon oudeis 'eoraken popote. 'o monogeneis 'wios, 'o on eis ton kolpon tou patros, ekeinos exeigeisato.

Hebrew/Transliteration
יח. אֶת הָאֱלֹהִים לֹא-רָאָה אָדָם מֵעוֹלָם וְהַבֵּן הַיָּחִיד בְּחֵיק הָאָב הוּא הִגִּיד תְּכוּנָתוֹ:

18. Et ha•Elohim lo - ra•ah adam me•o•lam ve•ha•Ben ha•ya•chid be•cheyk ha•Av hoo hi•gid t`choo•na•to.

Rabbinic Jewish Commentary
To see God, figuratively meaning to know Him, be acquainted with Him, know His character, only in John's writings (Joh_1:18; Joh_6:46; Joh_14:7, Joh_14:9; Joh_15:24; 1Jn_3:6; 1Jn_4:20; 3Jn_1:11). In these cases, it is equivalent to blépō (G991), to see (cf. 1Ki_10:8).

"God never revealed his glory or splendor to anyone. The very bosom and soul of Elohim is reserved for only those within Elohim (they, God) to experience. This is why, in the New Testament, John said in chapter 1 verse 18.

"No one has known Elohim at anytime; the only begotten Elohim who is in the bosom of the Father, He has made him known."

The Hebrew and Jewish understanding of John is that it was the unique Word of God within Elohim (they, God) who knew the very soul and splendor by being in the very bosom of Elohim (they, God). The relationship between them was only experienced by them and no one else."(From YHWH to Elohim to Messiah, pg.47)

The Jerusalem Targum on Gen_3:22 says almost the same of *the Word* of the LORD, as here, where it introduces him saying,

"the *Word* of the LORD God said, lo, the man whom I created, the only one in my world, even as I am, יחידי, "the only one", (or, as the word is sometimes rendered, "the only begotten",) in the highest heavens.

And to the same purpose the Targum of Jonathan, and also Jarchi, on the same place. The Syriac version, P66 and P75 here renders it, "the only unique, God which is in the bosom of the Father"; clearly showing, that he is the only unique, as he is God.

Somewhat like this the Jews (n) say of the Messiah,

"There is none that can declare the name of his Father, and that knows him; but this is hid from the eyes of the multitude, until he comes, ויגידהו, "and he shall declare him".

He is come, and has declared him: so Philo speaks of the "Logos", or Word, as the interpreter of the mind of God, and a teacher of men (o),

(n) R. Moses Haddarsan in Psal. 85. 11. apud Galatin. de Arcan, Cathol. ver. l. 8. c. 2. (o) De nominum mutat. p. 1047.

---

19. And this is the record of John, when the Jews sent priests and Levites from Jerusalem to ask him, Who art thou?

Greek/Transliteration
19. Καὶ αὕτη ἐστὶν ἡ μαρτυρία τοῦ Ἰωάννου, ὅτε ἀπέστειλαν οἱ Ἰουδαῖοι ἐξ Ἱεροσολύμων ἱερεῖς καὶ Λευΐτας ἵνα ἐρωτήσωσιν αὐτόν, Σὺ τίς εἶ;

19. Kai 'autei estin 'ei marturia tou Yoannou, 'ote apesteilan 'oi Youdaioi ex 'Yerosolumon 'iereis kai Leuitas 'ina eroteisosin auton, Su tis ei?

:יט. וְזֹאת עֵדוּת יוֹחָנָן בִּשְׁלֹחַ הַיְּהוּדִים כֹּהֲנִים וּלְוִיִּם מִירוּשָׁלַיִם לִשְׁאֹל אֹתוֹ מִי הוּא

19. Ve•zot e•doot Yo•cha•nan bish•lo•ach ha•Ye•hoo•dim Co•ha•nim ool•vi•yim mi•Ye•roo•sha•la•yim lish•ol o•to mee hoo.

Rabbinic Jewish Commentary

The Jews that sent were the great sanhedrim that sat at Jerusalem, whose business it was to inquire into, examine, and try prophets, whether true or false (p) The persons sent were very likely of their own body, since priests and Levites were in that council. For it is said (q),

"They do not constitute, or appoint in the sanhedrim but priests, Levites, and Israelites, who have their genealogies---and it is commanded, that there should be in the great sanhedrim priests and Levites, as it is said, Deu_17:9 "and thou shalt come unto the priests, the Levites", and if they are not to be found, though they are all Israelites, (not of the tribe of Levi,) it is right.

(p) Misn. Sanhedrin, c. 1. sect. 5. (q) Maimon. Hilch. Sanhedrin, c. 2. sect. 1, 2.

---

20. And he confessed, and denied not; but confessed, I am not the Christ.

Greek/Transliteration

20. Καὶ ὡμολόγησεν, καὶ οὐκ ἠρνήσατο· καὶ ὡμολόγησεν ὅτι Οὐκ εἰμὶ ἐγὼ ὁ χριστός.

20. Kai 'omologeisen, kai ouk eirneisato. kai 'omologeisen 'oti Ouk eimi ego 'o christos.

Hebrew/Transliteration

:כ. וְהוּא הוֹדָה וְלֹא כִחֵד כִּי הִגִּיד לֵאמֹר אָנֹכִי אֵינֶנִּי הַמָּשִׁיחַ

20. Ve•hoo ho•da ve•lo chiched ki hi•gid le•mor ano•chi ey•ne•ni ha•Ma•shi•ach.

---

21. And they asked him, What then? Art thou Elias? And he saith, I am not. Art thou that prophet? And he answered, No.

Greek/Transliteration

21. Καὶ ἠρώτησαν αὐτόν, Τί οὖν; Ἠλίας εἶ σύ; Καὶ λέγει, Οὐκ εἰμί. Ὁ προφήτης εἶ σύ; Καὶ ἀπεκρίθη, Οὔ.

21. Kai eiroteisan auton, Ti oun? Eilias ei su? Kai legei, Ouk eimi. 'O propheiteis ei su? Kai apekrithei, Ou.

:כא. וַיִּשְׁאֲלוּ אֹתוֹ מִי אֵפוֹא אַתָּה הַאַתָּה אֵלִיָּהוּ וַיֹּאמֶר אֵינֶנִּי אֵלִיָּהוּ הַאֵם הַנָּבִיא אַתָּה וַיַּעַן לֹא

21. Va•yish•a•loo o•to mee e•fo ata ha•a•ta Eli•ya•hoo va•yo•mer ey•ne•ni
Eli•ya•hoo ha•eem ha•na•vee ata va•ya•an lo.

Rabbinic Jewish Commentary

The Jews had a notion that that prophet would come in person a little before the coming of the Messiah; See "A Rabbinic Source Commentary" of Matthew on Mat_17:10 wherefore these messengers inquire, that since he had so fully satisfied them that he was not the Messiah, that he would as ingenuously answer to this question, if he was Elias, or not.

Art thou that prophet? Jeremiah, whom some of the Jews (t) have thought to be the prophet Moses spoke of, in Deu_18:15 and expected that he would appear about the times of the Messiah; see Mat_16:14 or any one of the ancient prophets risen from the dead, which they also had a notion of, Luk_9:8 or, as it may be rendered, "art thou a prophet?" for prophecy had long ceased with them.

(t) Baal Hatturim in Deut. xviii. 15. Tzeror Hammor, fol. 127. 4. & 143. 4. Siphre in Jarchi in Jer. i. 5.

---

22. Then said they unto him, Who art thou? that we may give an answer to them that sent us. What sayest thou of thyself?

Greek/Transliteration
22. Εἶπον οὖν αὐτῷ, Τίς εἶ; Ἵνα ἀπόκρισιν δῶμεν τοῖς πέμψασιν ἡμᾶς. Τί
λέγεις περὶ σεαυτοῦ;

22. Eipon oun auto, Tis ei? 'Yna apokrisin domen tois pempsasin 'eimas. Ti
legeis peri seautou?

Hebrew/Transliteration
:כב. וַיֹּאמְרוּ אֵלָיו וּמִי אֵפוֹא אַתָּה כִּי עָלֵינוּ לְהָשִׁיב דָּבָר אֶת-שֹׁלְחֵינוּ מַה-תֹּאמַר עַל-נַפְשֶׁךָ

22. Va•yom•roo elav oo•mi e•fo ata ki aley•noo le•ha•shiv da•var et -
shol•chey•noo ma - to•mar al - naf•she•cha?

---

23. He said, I am the voice of one crying in the wilderness, Make straight the way of the Lord, as said the prophet Esaias.

Greek/Transliteration
23. Ἔφη, Ἐγὼ φωνὴ βοῶντος ἐν τῇ ἐρήμῳ, Εὐθύνατε τὴν ὁδὸν κυρίου,
καθὼς εἶπεν Ἡσαΐας ὁ προφήτης.

23. Ephei, Ego phonei boontos en tei ereimo, Euthunate tein 'odon kuriou, kathos eipen Eisaias 'o propheiteis.

Hebrew/Transliteration

כג. וַיֹּאמֶר אָנֹכִי קוֹל קוֹרֵא בַּמִּדְבָּר פַּנּוּ דֶּרֶךְ יְהֹוָה כַּאֲשֶׁר דִּבֶּר יְשַׁעְיָהוּ הַנָּבִיא:

23. Va•yo•mar ano•chi kol ko•re ba•mid•bar pa•noo de•rech Adonai ka•a•sher di•ber Ye•sha•a•ya•hoo ha•na•vee.

Rabbinic Jewish Commentary

The Jews give a different interpretation of the words; though one of their celebrated commentators (u) owns, that the comforts spoken of in the preceding verses are what will be in the days of the King Messiah: one of them (w) interprets, "the voice", of the Holy Ghost; and so far it may be true, as John was filled with the Holy Ghost, and he spake by him in his ministry: and another (x), of the resurrection of the dead, or the voice that will be heard then, which will be the voice of the archangel: though another of (y) them better explains it by, הם המבשרים, "they are they that bring glad tidings", or good news; such are Gospel preachers; only it should have been in the singular number: for the text speaks but of one voice; of one person crying; and of John the Baptist, who brought the good news, and glad tidings, that the Messiah was coming, yea, that he was already come, and that the kingdom of heaven was at hand. The Hebrew writers generally understand the passage, of the return of the Jews from the Babylonish captivity, and of removing all obstructions in their way to Jerusalem; to which sense the Targum on the place inclines, which paraphrases it thus,

"The voice of him that crieth in the wilderness, prepare the way before the people of the LORD, make in the plain, paths before the congregation of our God."

(u) Kimchi in Isa. xl. 1. (w) Jarchi in Isa xl. 3. (x) Zohar in Gen. fol. 70. 4. (y) Aben Ezra in Isa. ib.

---

24. And they which were sent were of the Pharisees.

Greek/Transliteration
24. Καὶ οἱ ἀπεσταλμένοι ἦσαν ἐκ τῶν Φαρισαίων.

24. Kai 'oi apestalmenoi eisan ek ton Pharisaion.

Hebrew/Transliteration
כד. וְהַשְּׁלוּחִים הָאֵלֶּה הָיוּ מִן-הַפְּרוּשִׁים:

24. Ve•hash•loo•chim ha•e•le ha•yoo min - ha•P`roo•shim.

---

25. And they asked him, and said unto him, Why baptizest thou then, if thou be not that Christ, nor Elias, neither that prophet?

Greek/Transliteration
25. Καὶ ἠρώτησαν αὐτόν, καὶ εἶπον αὐτῷ, Τί οὖν βαπτίζεις, εἰ σὺ οὐκ εἶ ὁ χριστός, οὔτε Ἠλίας, οὔτε ὁ προφήτης;

25. Kai eiroteisan auton, kai eipon auto, Ti oun baptizeis, ei su ouk ei 'o christos, oute Eilias, oute 'o propheiteis?

Hebrew/Transliteration
כה. וַיִּשְׁאָלוּ וַיֹּאמְרוּ אֵלָיו אִם-אֵינְךָ הַמָּשִׁיחַ וְלֹא אֵלִיָּהוּ וְלֹא הַנָּבִיא לָמָה-זֶה מְטַבֵּל הִנֶּךְ:

25. Va•yish•a•loo va•yom•roo elav eem - eyn•cha ha•Ma•shi•ach ve•lo Eli•ya•hoo ve•lo ha•na•vee la•ma - ze me•ta•bel hi•ne•cha.

Rabbinic Jewish Commentary
From hence it appears, that the Jews expected that baptism would be administered in the times of the Messiah, and his forerunner; but from whence they had this notion, it is not easy to say, whether from Zec_13:1 as Grotius, or from Eze_36:25; nor do they speak contemptibly of it, but rather consider it as a very solemn affair, to be performed only by great personages: and this may teach modern ones to think and speak more respectfully of this ordinance than they do, who have given themselves great liberties, and have treated it with much contempt and virulence; calling it by the names of uncleanness, abomination, filthy water, and a devoting of persons to Satan (z): likewise, it is clear from hence, that they expected that this ordinance would be first administered by some person of very great note, either some very famous prophet, as Elias, whom they looked for before the coming of the Messiah, or else the Messiah himself, and not by a common teacher, or any ordinary person; wherefore this rite, as performed by John, could have no likeness with any thing that was in common use among them: besides, it was expressly done in the name of the Messiah, Act_19:5 therefore they conclude he, or his forerunner, must be come; and that John must be one, or other of them, otherwise, why did he administer it? and it is also evident from hence, that no such practice had obtained before among them, or they would not have been alarmed at it, as they were; nor would they have troubled themselves to have sent after John, and inquire of him who he was, that should practise in this manner.

(z) Vet. Nizzachon, p. 56, 62, 64, 70, 74, 77, 148, 191, 193.

---

26. John answered them, saying, I baptize with water: but there standeth one among you, whom ye know not;

Greek/Transliteration
26. Ἀπεκρίθη αὐτοῖς ὁ Ἰωάννης λέγων, Ἐγὼ βαπτίζω ἐν ὕδατι· μέσος δὲ ὑμῶν ἕστηκεν ὃν ὑμεῖς οὐκ οἴδατε.

26. Apekrithei autois 'o Yoanneis legon, Ego baptizo en 'udati. mesos de 'umon 'esteiken 'on 'umeis ouk oidate.

Hebrew/Transliteration

:כו. וַיַּעַן אֹתָם יוֹחָנָן וַיֹּאמַר אָנֹכִי מְטַבֵּל בַּמַּיִם אַךְ אִישׁ עֹמֵד בְּתוֹכְכֶם אֲשֶׁר לֹא יְדַעְתֶּם אֹתוֹ

26. Va•ya•an o•tam Yo•cha•nan va•yo•mar ano•chi me•ta•bel ba•ma•yim ach eesh o•med be•to•che•chem asher lo ye•da•a•tem o•to.

---

27. He it is, who coming after me is preferred before me, whose shoe's latchet I am not worthy to unloose.

Greek/Transliteration
27. Αὐτός ἐστιν ὁ ὀπίσω μου ἐρχόμενος, ὃς ἔμπροσθέν μου γέγονεν· οὗ ἐγὼ οὐκ εἰμὶ ἄξιος ἵνα λύσω αὐτοῦ τὸν ἱμάντα τοῦ ὑποδήματος.

27. Autos estin 'o opiso mou erchomenos, 'os emprosthen mou gegonen. 'ou ego ouk eimi axios 'ina luso autou ton 'imanta tou 'upodeimatos.

Hebrew/Transliteration
:כז. זֶה הַבָּא אַחֲרֵי אֲשֶׁר הָיָה לְפָנַי וַאֲנִי קַלֹּתִי מֵהַתֵּר-לוֹ שְׂרוֹךְ נְעָלָיו

27. Ze ha•ba a•cha•rai asher ha•ya le•fa•nai va•a•ni ka•lo•ti me•ha•ter - lo s`roch n`a•lav.

Rabbinic/Jewish Commentary
In the Talmud (e) it is asked, "What is the manner of possessing of servants? or what is their service? He buckles his (master's) shoes; he "unlooses his shoes", and "carries them before him to the bath.""

Or, as is elsewhere (f) said, "he unlooses his shoes, or carries after him his vessels (whatever he wants) to the bath; he unclothes him, he washes him, he anoints him, he rubs him, he clothes him, he buckles his shoes, and lifts him up."

This was such a servile work, that it was thought too mean for a scholar or a disciple to do; for it is (g) said,

"All services which a servant does for his master, a disciple does for his master, חוץ מהתרת לו מנעל, "except unloosing his shoes"."

The gloss on it says, "he that sees it, will say, he is a "Canaanitish servant":"

For only a Canaanitish, not an Hebrew servant (h), might be employed in, or obliged to such work; for it was reckoned not only, mean and servile, but even base and reproachful. It is one of their (i) canons;

"If thy brother is become poor, and is sold unto thee, thou shalt not make him do the work of a servant; that is, עבורת של נגאי, any reproachful work; such as to buckle his shoes, or unloose them, or carry his instruments (or necessaries) after him to the bath."

(e) T. Hieros. Kiddushin, fol. 59. 4. Maimon. & T. Bartenora in Misu. Kiddushin, c. 1. sect. 3. (f) T. Bab. Kiddushin, fol. 22. 2. Maimon. Hilch. Mechirah, c. 2. sect. 2. (g) T. Bab. Cetubot, fol. 96. 1. Maimon. Talmud Torn, c. 5. sect. 8. (h) Maimon. Hilch. Abadim, c. 1. sect. 7. (i) Moses Kotzensis Mitzvot Torah, precept. neg. 176.

---

28. These things were done in Bethabara beyond Jordan, where John was baptizing.

Greek/Transliteration
28. Ταῦτα ἐν Βηθανίᾳ ἐγένετο πέραν τοῦ Ἰορδάνου, ὅπου ἦν Ἰωάννης βαπτίζων.

28. Tauta en Beithania egeneto peran tou Yordanou, 'opou ein Yoanneis baptizon.

Hebrew/Transliteration
‏:כח. זֹאת הָיְתָה בְּבֵית הָעֲרָבָה מֵעֵבֶר לַיַּרְדֵּן אֲשֶׁר יוֹחָנָן הָיָה מְטַבֵּל שָׁמָּה

28. Zot hai•ta be•Veit ha•Ara•va me•e•ver la•Yarden asher Yo•cha•nan ha•ya me•ta•bel sha•ma.

---

29. The next day John seeth Jesus coming unto him, and saith, Behold the Lamb of God, which taketh away the sin of the world.

Greek/Transliteration
29. Τῇ ἐπαύριον βλέπει τὸν Ἰησοῦν ἐρχόμενον πρὸς αὐτόν, καὶ λέγει, Ἴδε ὁ ἀμνὸς τοῦ θεοῦ, ὁ αἴρων τὴν ἁμαρτίαν τοῦ κόσμου.

29. Tei epaurion blepei ton Yeisoun erchomenon pros auton, kai legei, Yde 'o amnos tou theou, 'o airon tein 'amartian tou kosmou.

Hebrew/Transliteration
‏:כט. וַיְהִי מִמָּחֳרָת וַיַּרְא אֶת-יֵשׁוּעַ בָּא אֵלָיו וַיֹּאמֶר הִנֵּה שֵׂה הָאֱלֹהִים הַנֹּשֵׂא אֶת-חַטַּאת הָעוֹלָם

29. Vay•hi mi•mo•cho•rat va•yar et - Yeshua ba elav va•yo•mar hee•ne Seh ha•Elohim ha•no•se et - cha•tat ha•o•lam.

Rabbinic Jewish Commentary

One part of the work of Elias, which the Jews assign unto him, and the precise time of his doing it, exactly agree with this account of John the Baptist; they say (c), that his work is

"To bring to them (the Israelites) the good news of the coming of the Redeemer; and this shall be, יום אחד, "one day", before the coming of the, Messiah; and this is that which is written, "behold I will send you Elijah the prophet, before the coming of the great and dreadful day of the Lord". Mal_4:5.

The Jewish Rabbi's say (d), that "the morning daily sacrifice made atonement for the iniquities done in the night; and the evening sacrifice made atonement for the iniquities that were by day. And Yeshua is styled the Lamb "of God", in allusion to the same, whom the Cabalistic Jews (e) call the secret of the mystery, and כבשי רחמנא, "the Lambs of God".

(c) R. Abraham ben David in Misn. Ediot, c. 8. sect. 7. (d) R. Menachem, fol. 115. apud Ainsworth, in Exod. xxix. 39. (e) Raya Mehimna, in Zohar in Lev. fol. 33. 2.

---

30. This is he of whom I said, After me cometh a man which is preferred before me: for he was before me.

Greek/Transliteration

30. Οὗτός ἐστιν περὶ οὗ ἐγὼ εἶπον, Ὀπίσω μου ἔρχεται ἀνὴρ ὃς ἔμπροσθέν μου γέγονεν, ὅτι πρῶτός μου ἦν.

30. 'Outos estin peri 'ou ego eipon, Opiso mou erchetai aneir 'os emprosthen mou gegonen, 'oti protos mou ein.

Hebrew/Transliteration

ל: וְהוּא אֲשֶׁר אָמַרְתִּי עָלָיו הִנֵּה אִישׁ בָּא אַחֲרַי וְהִנֵּה הוּא לְפָנַי כִּי רִאשׁוֹן-לִי הָיָה.

30. Ve•hoo asher amar•ti alav hee•ne eesh ba a•cha•rai ve•hee•ne hoo le•fa•nai ki ri•shon - li ha•ya.

---

31. And I knew him not: but that he should be made manifest to Israel, therefore am I come baptizing with water.

Greek/Transliteration

31. Κἀγὼ οὐκ ᾔδειν αὐτόν· ἀλλ᾿ ἵνα φανερωθῇ τῷ Ἰσραήλ, διὰ τοῦτο ἦλθον ἐγὼ ἐν τῷ ὕδατι βαπτίζων.

31. Kago ouk eidein auton. all 'ina phanerothei to Ysraeil, dya touto eilthon ego en to 'udati baptizon.

Hebrew/Transliteration

לא. וַאֲנִי לֹא יָדַעְתִּי אֹתוֹ אַךְ לְמַעַן יִגָּלֶה לְיִשְׂרָאֵל בָּאתִי אֲנִי לִטְבֹּל בַּמָּיִם:

31. Va•a•ni lo ya•da•a•ti o•to ach le•ma•an yi•ga•le le•Israel ba•ti ani lit•bol ba•ma•yim.

---

32. And John bare record, saying, I saw the Spirit descending from heaven like a dove, and it abode upon him.

Greek/Transliteration

32. Καὶ ἐμαρτύρησεν Ἰωάννης λέγων ὅτι Τεθέαμαι τὸ πνεῦμα καταβαῖνον ὡσεὶ περιστερὰν ἐξ οὐρανοῦ, καὶ ἔμεινεν ἐπ᾽ αὐτόν.

32. Kai emartureisen Yoanneis legon 'oti Tetheamai to pneuma katabainon 'osei peristeran ex ouranou, kai emeinen ep auton.

Hebrew/Transliteration

לב. וַיָּעַד יוֹחָנָן לֵאמֹר רָאִיתִי אֶת-הָרוּחַ כְּיוֹנָה יֹרֶדֶת מִן-הַשָּׁמַיִם וַתָּנַח עָלָיו:

32. Va•ya•ad Yo•cha•nan le•mor ra•ee•ti et - ha•Roo•ach ke•yo•na yo•re•det min - ha•sha•ma•yim va•ta•nach alav.

Rabbinic Jewish Commentary

the Jews (r) so often call רוח המשיח מלד של, "the Spirit of the king Messiah, and the spirit of the Messiah". The descent of him was in a "bodily shape", as Luke says in Luk_3:22 or like in the shape of a dove, which is a very fit emblem of the Spirit of God who descended, and the fruits thereof, such as simplicity, meekness, love and also of the dove-like innocence, humility, and affection of Yeshua, on whom he lighted.

However, who can read this account without thinking of Noah's dove, which brought in its mouth the olive leaf, a token of peace and reconciliation, when the waters were abated from off the earth? Give me leave to transcribe a passage I have met with in the book of Zohar (s);

"A door shall be opened, and out of it shall come forth the dove which Noah sent out in the days of the flood, as it is written, "and he sent forth the dove", that famous dove; but the ancients speak not of it, for they knew not what it was, only from whence it came, and did its message; as it is written, "it returned not again unto him any more": no man knows whither it went, but it returned to its place, and was hid within this door; and it shall take a crown in its mouth, and put it upon the head of the king Messiah."

(r) Bereshit Rabba, fol. 2. 4. & 6. 3. Vajikra Rabba, fol. 156. 4. Zohar in Gen. fol. 107. 3. & 128. 3. Baal Hatturim in Gen. i. 2. Caphtor Uperah, fol. 113. 2. (s) In Num. fol. 68. 3, 4.

33. And I knew him not: but he that sent me to baptize with water, the same said unto me, Upon whom thou shalt see the Spirit descending, and remaining on him, the same is he which baptizeth with the Holy Ghost.

Greek/Transliteration

33. Κἀγὼ οὐκ ᾔδειν αὐτόν· ἀλλ᾽ ὁ πέμψας με βαπτίζειν ἐν ὕδατι, ἐκεῖνός μοι εἶπεν, Ἐφ᾽ ὃν ἂν ἴδῃς τὸ πνεῦμα καταβαῖνον καὶ μένον ἐπ᾽ αὐτόν, οὗτός ἐστιν ὁ βαπτίζων ἐν πνεύματι ἁγίῳ.

33. Kago ouk eidein auton. all 'o pempsas me baptizein en 'udati, ekeinos moi eipen, Eph 'on an ideis to pneuma katabainon kai menon ep auton, 'outos estin 'o baptizon en pneumati 'agio.

Hebrew/Transliteration

לג. וַאֲנִי לֹא יָדַעְתִּי אֹתוֹ אַךְ הַשֹּׁלֵחַ אֹתִי לִטְבֹּל בַּמַּיִם אָמַר אֵלַי אֶת-הַלָּז אֲשֶׁר תִּרְאֶה הָרוּחַ יֹרֶדֶת וְתָנוּחַ עָלָיו:זֶה הוּא אֲשֶׁר יִטְבֹּל בְּרוּחַ הַקֹּדֶשׁ

33. Va•a•ni lo ya•da•a•ti o•to ach ha•sho•le•ach o•ti lit•bol ba•ma•yim amar e•lai et - ha•laz asher tir•eh ha•Roo•ach yo•re•det ve•ta•noo•ach alav ze hoo asher yit•bol be•Roo•ach ha•Ko•desh.

Rabbinic Jewish Commentary
See John 1:32 for commentary.

---

34. And I saw, and bare record that this is the Son of God.

Greek/Transliteration
34. Κἀγὼ ἑώρακα, καὶ μεμαρτύρηκα ὅτι οὗτός ἐστιν ὁ υἱὸς τοῦ θεοῦ.

34. Kago 'eoraka, kai memartureika 'oti 'outos estin 'o 'wios tou theou.

Hebrew/Transliteration
:לד. וַאֲנִי רָאִיתִי וָאָעִיד כִּי-זֶה הוּא בֶן-הָאֱלֹהִים

34. Va•a•ni ra•ee•ti va•a•eed ki - ze hoo Ben - ha•Elohim.

Rabbinic Jewish Commentary
Son of God (ben Elohim) is one of the names of the Messiah and comes from Psalm_2:7, "YHWH has said to Me, 'You are My Son'". Messiah Son of God is expected to be not just a righteous person but *the* Righteous Person. Yet to fulfill such a feat, it seems the Messiah would have to be superhuman. So it is not suprising to find interpretations that attribute to Messiah divine qualities.

The Zohar explains that in order for the Messiah to accomplish his task, he must be clothed with divine attributes (binah). The Zohar also implies that this Son of God has two sides, Son of David and Son of Joseph. The Son of Joseph has less authority and will be killed but the Son of David will have the power to resurrect him from the dead. This interpretation show that Son of God, Son of Joseph and Son of David are different manifestations of the same person.

(Perush HaSullam, 203b, Balak, 341; The Concealed Light, Tsvi Sadan, pg.20)

---

35. Again the next day after John stood, and two of his disciples;

Greek/Transliteration
35. Τῇ ἐπαύριον πάλιν εἰστήκει ὁ Ἰωάννης, καὶ ἐκ τῶν μαθητῶν αὐτοῦ δύο·

35. Tei epaurion palin 'eisteikei 'o Yoanneis, kai ek ton matheiton autou duo.

Hebrew/Transliteration
לה. וַיְהִי מִמָּחֳרַת וַיַּעֲמֹד יוֹחָנָן עוֹד עִם-שְׁנַיִם מִתַּלְמִידָיו:

35. Vay•hi mi•mo•cho•rat va•ya•a•mod Yo•cha•nan od eem - sh`na•yim mi•tal•mi•dav.

---

36. And looking upon Jesus as he walked, he saith, Behold the Lamb of God!

Greek/Transliteration
36. καὶ ἐμβλέψας τῷ Ἰησοῦ περιπατοῦντι, λέγει, Ἴδε ὁ ἀμνὸς τοῦ θεοῦ.

36. kai emblepsas to Yeisou peripatounti, legei, Yde 'o amnos tou theou.

Hebrew/Transliteration
לו. וַיַּרְא אֶת-יֵשׁוּעַ מִתְהַלֵּךְ וַיֹּאמַר הִנֵּה שֵׂה הָאֱלֹהִים:

36. Va•yar et - Yeshua mit•ha•lech va•yo•mar hee•ne Seh ha•Elohim.

Rabbinic Jewish Commentary
See John 1:29 for commentary

---

37. And the two disciples heard him speak, and they followed Jesus.

Greek/Transliteration
37. Καὶ ἤκουσαν αὐτοῦ οἱ δύο μαθηταὶ λαλοῦντος, καὶ ἠκολούθησαν τῷ Ἰησοῦ.

37. Kai eikousan autou 'oi duo matheitai lalountos, kai eikoloutheisan to Yeisou.

לז. וַיִּשְׁמְעוּ שְׁנֵי תַלְמִידָיו אֶת-אֲשֶׁר דִּבֵּר וַיֵּלְכוּ אַחֲרֵי יֵשׁוּעַ:

37. Va•yish•me•oo sh`ney tal•mi•dav et - asher di•ber va•yel•choo a•cha•rey Yeshua.

---

38. Then Jesus turned, and saw them following, and saith unto them, What seek ye? They said unto him, Rabbi, (which is to say, being interpreted, Master,) where dwellest thou?

Greek/Transliteration
38. Στραφεὶς δὲ ὁ Ἰησοῦς καὶ θεασάμενος αὐτοὺς ἀκολουθοῦντας, λέγει αὐτοῖς, Τί ζητεῖτε; Οἱ δὲ εἶπον αὐτῷ, Ῥαββί- ὃ λέγεται ἑρμηνευόμενον, Διδάσκαλε- ποῦ μένεις;

38. Strapheis de 'o Yeisous kai theasamenos autous akolouthountas, legei autois, Ti zeiteite? 'Oi de eipon auto, 'Rabbi- 'o legetai 'ermeineuomenon, Didaskale- pou meneis?

Hebrew/Transliteration
לח. וַיִּפֶן יֵשׁוּעַ וַיִּרְאֵם הֹלְכִים אַחֲרָיו וַיֹּאמֶר אֲלֵיהֶם מַה-תְּבַקֵּשׁוּן וַיֹּאמְרוּ אֵלָיו רַבִּי אֲשֶׁר יֵאָמֵר מוֹרִי אַיֵּה מְקוֹם:מוֹשָׁבֶךָ

38. Va•yi•fen Yeshua va•yir•em hol•chim a•cha•rav va•yo•mer aley•hem ma - te•va•ke•shoon va•yom•roo elav Rabbi asher ye•a•mer Mori a•ye me•kom mo•sha•ve•cha?

Rabbinic Jewish Commentary
The repetition of the word Rabbi, is not made in the Vulgate Latin, nor in the Syriac, Arabic, Persic, and Ethiopic versions, nor in Munster's Hebrew Gospel, but is in all the Greek copies, and very justly; since it was usual in the salutations of them, to double the word. It is reported (f) of R. Eleazar ben Simeon, of Migdal Gedur, that having reproached a deformed man he met in the road; when he came to the city where the man lived,

"The citizens came out to meet him, and said to him, peace be upon thee, רבי רבי מורי מורי, "Rabbi, Rabbi, Master, Master"; he (Eleazar) said to them, who do you call "Rabbi, Rabbi?" They replied to him, he who followed thee: he said unto them, if this be a Rabbi, let there not be many such in Israel."

The Jews pretend, that king Jehoshaphat used to salute the Rabbi's with these titles; though they forget that they were not in use in his time, as will be hereafter observed: they say (g),

"Whenever he saw a disciple of the wise men, he rose from his throne, and embraced and kissed him, and called him, אבי אבי רבי רבי מרי מרי, "Father, Father,

Rabbi, Rabbi, Master, Master"."

Where you have the three different words used by Yeshua in this and the following verses, by which these men loved to be called, and he inveighed against; nay, they not only suggest, that kings gave them these honourable titles, and they expected them from them, but even they liked to be called kings themselves. It is said (h) of R. Hona arid R. Chasda, that as they were sitting together, one passed by them,

"And said to them, "peace be to you kings", שלמא עליכו מלכי, "peace be to you kings": they said to him, from whence does it appear to thee, that the Rabbins are called kings? He replied to them, from what is written, "by me kings reign", &c. They said to him, from whence hast thou it, that we are to double or repeat peace, or salutation to kings? He answered them, that R. Judah said, that Rab said from hence, 1Ch_12:18. "Then the spirit came upon Amasai".

This title began but to be in use in the time of our Lord, or a very little while before: none of the prophets had it, nor Ezra the Scribe, nor the men of the great synagogue, nor Simeon the Just, the last of them; nor Antigonus, a man of Socho, a disciple of his: and it is observed by the Jews themselves (i), that

"The five couple are never called by the name of Rabban, nor by the name of Rabbi, only by their own name."

By whom are meant, Joseph ben Joezer, and Joseph ben Jochanan; Joshua ben Perachia, said to be the master of Yeshua of Nazareth, and Nittai the Arbelite; Judah ben Tabai, and Simeon ben Shetach; Shemaiah and Abtalion; Hillell and Shammai. The sons, or disciples of the two last, first took these titles. Rabban Simeon, the son of Hillell, thought by some to be the same Simeon that had Yeshua in his arms, is (k) said to be the first that was called by this name; and it is also observed by them (l), that Rabban was a name of greater honour than Rabbi, or Rab, and that Rabbi was more honourable than Rab; and to be called by a man's own name, was more honourable than any of them. The Karaite Jews make much the same complaint, and give much the same account of the pride and vanity of the Rabbinical Rabbi's, as Yeshua here does; for so one of them says (m);

"The Karaites do not use to act according to the custom of the wise men among the Rabbans, to make to themselves gods of silver, and guides of gold, with this view, להקרא רב, "to be called Rab"; and also to gather wealth and food to fulness."

(f) T. Bab. Taanith, fol. 20. 2. (g) T. Bab. Maccot, fol. 24. 1. & Cetubot, fol. 103. 2. (h) T. Bab. Gittin, fol. 62. 1. (i) Ganz. Tzemach David, par. 1. fol. 21. 1. (k) Ganz. Tzemach David, par. 1. fol. 25. 1. (l) Ib. (m) Eliahu Adderet, c. 6. apud Trigland. de. Sect. Kar. c. 10. p. 164.

39. He saith unto them, Come and see. They came and saw where he dwelt, and abode with him that day: for it was about the tenth hour.

Greek/Transliteration
39. Λέγει αὐτοῖς, Ἔρχεσθε καὶ ἴδετε. Ἦλθον καὶ εἶδον ποῦ μένει· καὶ παρ᾽ αὐτῷ ἔμειναν τὴν ἡμέραν ἐκείνην· ὥρα ἦν ὡς δεκάτη.

39. Legei autois, Erchesthe kai idete. Eilthon kai eidon pou menei. kai par auto emeinan tein 'eimeran ekeinein. 'ora ein 'os dekatei.

Hebrew/Transliteration
לט. וַיֹּאמֶר אֲלֵיהֶם בֹּאוּ וּרְאוּ וַיָּבֹאוּ וַיִּרְאוּ אֶת-מְקוֹם מוֹשָׁבוֹ וַיֵּשְׁבוּ אִתּוֹ בַּיּוֹם הַהוּא וְהָעֵת הָיְתָה כְּשָׁעָה הָעֲשִׂירִית:

39. Va•yo•mer aley•hem bo•oo oor•oo va•ya•vo•oo va•yir•oo et - me•kom mo•sha•vo va•yesh•voo ee•to ba•yom ha•hoo ve•ha•et hai•ta ka•sha•ah ha•a•si•rit.

Rabbinic Jewish Commentary
for it was about the tenth hour; which, according to the Roman way of reckoning, must be ten o'clock in the morning; so that there was a considerable part of the day before them; but according to the Jewish way of reckoning, who reckon twelve hours to a day, it must be four o'clock in the afternoon, when there were but two hours to night: and this being; about the time when the lamb of the daily sacrifice of the evening was offered up, very seasonably did John point unto them, at this time, Yeshua the Lamb of God, the antitype of that sacrifice; for the daily evening sacrifice was slain at eight and a half, and was offered at nine and a half (f), or between the ninth and tenth hours of the day. The Ethiopic version renders it,

"They remained with him that day unto the tenth hour",

(f) Misn. Pesachim, c. 5. sect. 1.

---

40. One of the two which heard John speak, and followed him, was Andrew, Simon Peter's brother.

Greek/Transliteration
40. Ἦν Ἀνδρέας ὁ ἀδελφὸς Σίμωνος Πέτρου εἷς ἐκ τῶν δύο τῶν ἀκουσάντων παρὰ Ἰωάννου καὶ ἀκολουθησάντων αὐτῷ.

40. Ein Andreas 'o adelphos Simonos Petrou 'eis ek ton duo ton akousanton para Yoannou kai akoloutheisanton auto.

Hebrew/Transliteration
מ. וְאֶחָד מִן-הַשְּׁנַיִם אֲשֶׁר שָׁמְעוּ מֵאֵת יוֹחָנָן וְהָלְכוּ אַחֲרָיו הָיָה אַנְדְּרַי אֲחִי שִׁמְעוֹן פֶּטְרוֹס:

40. Ve•e•chad min - hash•na•yim asher sham•oo me•et Yo•cha•nan ve•hal•choo a•cha•rav ha•ya An•de•rai achi Shimon Petros.

---

41. He first findeth his own brother Simon, and saith unto him, We have found the Messias, which is, being interpreted, the Christ.

Greek/Transliteration

41. Εὑρίσκει οὗτος πρῶτος τὸν ἀδελφὸν τὸν ἴδιον Σίμωνα, καὶ λέγει αὐτῷ, Εὑρήκαμεν τὸν Μεσίαν- ὅ ἐστιν μεθερμηνευόμενον, Χριστός.

41. 'Euriskei 'outos protos ton adelphon ton idion Simona, kai legei auto, 'Eureikamen ton Mesian- 'o estin methermeineuomenon, Christos.

Hebrew/Transliteration

:מא. הוּא מָצָא אֶת-אָחִיו אֶת-שִׁמְעוֹן וַיֹּאמֶר אֵלָיו מָצָאנוּ אֶת-הַמָּשִׁיחַ אֲשֶׁר בִּלְשׁוֹן יָוָן כְּרִיסְטוֹס

41. Hoo ma•tza et - a•chiv et - Shimon va•yo•mer elav ma•tza•noo et - ha•Ma•shi•ach asher bil•shon Ya•van Kristos.

Rabbinic Jewish Commentary

This name, Messiah, was well known among the Jews, for that who was promised, and they expected as a Saviour and Redeemer; though it is not very often mentioned in the books of the Old Testament, chiefly in the following places, Psa_2:2; but is very much used in the Chaldee paraphrases: Elias Levita (g) says, he found it in more than fifty verses; and Buxtorf (h) has added others to them, and the word appears in "seventy one" places, which he takes notice of, and are worthy of regard; for they show the sense of the ancient synagogue, concerning the passages of the Old Testament, respecting the Messiah: this Hebrew word is interpreted by the Greek word, "Christ"; and both signify "anointed", and well agree with the person to whom they belong, to which there is an allusion in Son_1:3, "thy name is as ointment poured forth": he is so called, because he was anointed from everlasting, to be prophet, priest, and king; see Psa_2:6 Pro_8:22, and he was anointed as man, with the oil of gladness, with the graces of the Spirit, without measure, Psa_45:7.

The phrase of "finding" a person, twice used in this text, and hereafter in some following verses, is frequent in Talmudic and Rabbinic writings; as

"he went, אשכחיה לרב, "and found him with Rab" (i).

(g) Prefat ad Methurgemen, & in voce משח. (h) Lexicon Talmud p. 1268. (i) T. Bab. Sabbat, fol. 108. 1. Zohar in Lev. fol. 15. 3.

---

42. And he brought him to Jesus. And when Jesus beheld him, he said, Thou art Simon the son of Jona: thou shalt be called Cephas, which is by interpretation, A stone.

Greek/Transliteration

42. Καὶ ἤγαγεν αὐτὸν πρὸς τὸν Ἰησοῦν. Ἐμβλέψας αὐτῷ ὁ Ἰησοῦς εἶπεν, Σὺ εἶ Σίμων ὁ υἱὸς Ἰωνᾶ· σὺ κληθήσῃ Κηφᾶς- ὃ ἑρμηνεύεται Πέτρος.

42. Kai eigagen auton pros ton Yeisoun. Emblepsas auto 'o Yeisous eipen, Su ei Simon 'o 'wios Yona. su kleitheisei Keiphas- 'o 'ermeineuetai Petros.

Hebrew/Transliteration

מב. וַיְבִיאֵהוּ אֶל-יֵשׁוּעַ וַיִּרְאֵהוּ יֵשׁוּעַ וַיֹּאמֶר אַתָּה שִׁמְעוֹן בַּר-יוֹנָה לְךָ יִקָּרֵא כֵיפָא וּבִלְשׁוֹן יָוָן פֶּטְרוֹס:

42. Va•y`vi•e•hoo el - Yeshua va•yir•e•hoo Yeshua va•yo•mar ata Shimon Bar – Yona le•cha yi•ka•re Chey•fa oo•vil•shon Ya•van Petros.

Rabbinic Jewish Commentary

Peter as it should rather be rendered; and as it is in the Vulgate Latin, and Ethiopic versions; and as "Cepha", or "Cephas", in the Syriac and Chaldee languages signifies a stone, or rock (k), so does "Peter" in Greek: hence, the Syriac version here gives no interpretation of the word. Yeshua not only calls Simon by his present name, at first sight of him, but tells him what his future name should be; and which imports, not only that he should be a lively stone in the spiritual building, the assembly, but should have a considerable hand in that work, and abide firm and steadfast to Yeshua, and his interest, notwithstanding his fall; and continue constant and immoveable until death, as he did. The Jews also, in their writings, call him Simeon Kepha (l),

(k) Vid. Targum in Psal. xl. 3. & Prov. xvii. 8. T. Bab. Ceritot, fol. 6. 1. & Gloss. in ib. Tzeror Hammor, fol. 63. 2. (l) Toldos Jesu, p. 20, 21, 22, 23.

---

43. The day following Jesus would go forth into Galilee, and findeth Philip, and saith unto him, Follow me.

Greek/Transliteration

43. Τῇ ἐπαύριον ἠθέλησεν ἐξελθεῖν εἰς τὴν Γαλιλαίαν, καὶ εὑρίσκει Φίλιππον, καὶ λέγει αὐτῷ ὁ Ἰησοῦς, Ἀκολούθει μοι.

43. Tei epaurion eitheleisen exelthein eis tein Galilaian, kai 'curiskci Philippon, kai legei auto 'o Yeisous, Akolouthei moi.

Hebrew/Transliteration

מג. וַיְהִי מִמָּחֳרָת וַיּוֹאֶל לָלֶכֶת הַגָּלִילָה וַיִּמְצָא אֶת-פִילִפּוֹס וַיֹּאמֶר אֵלָיו יֵשׁוּעַ לֵךְ אַחֲרָי:

43. Vay•hi mi•mo•cho•rat va•yo•el la•le•chet ha•Ga•li•la va•yim•tza et –
Pilipos va•yo•mer elav Yeshua lech a•cha•rai.

---

44. Now Philip was of Bethsaida, the city of Andrew and Peter.

Greek/Transliteration
44. Ἦν δὲ ὁ Φίλιππος ἀπὸ Βηθσαϊδά, ἐκ τῆς πόλεως ᾿Ανδρέου καὶ Πέτρου.

44. Ein de 'o Philippos apo Beithsaida, ek teis poleos Andreou kai Petrou.

Hebrew/Transliteration
מד. וּפִילִפּוֹס הָיָה מִבֵּית-צָיְדָה עִיר אַנְדְּרַי וּפֶטְרוֹס:

44. Oo•Filipos ha•ya mi•Beit - Tzai•da eer An•de•rai oo•Fetros.

Rabbinic Jewish Commentary
the city of Andrew and Peter; or "Simon", as read the Syriac and Persic versions:
three apostles were called out of this place, as mean, and wicked, as it was; see
Mat_11:21; which was no small honour to it: it is a saying of the Jews (n), that

"A man's place (his native place) does not honour him, but a man honours his
place."

This was the case here. (n) T. Bab. Taanith, fol. 21. 2.

---

45. Philip findeth Nathanael, and saith unto him, We have found him, of
whom Moses in the law, and the prophets, did write, Jesus of Nazareth, the
son of Joseph.

Greek/Transliteration
45. Εὑρίσκει Φίλιππος τὸν Ναθαναήλ, καὶ λέγει αὐτῷ, ῝Ον ἔγραψεν Μωσῆς ἐν
τῷ νόμῳ καὶ οἱ προφῆται εὑρήκαμεν, ᾿Ιησοῦν τὸν υἱὸν τοῦ ᾿Ιωσὴφ τὸν ἀπὸ
Ναζαρέτ.

45. 'Euriskei Philippos ton Nathanaeil, kai legei auto, 'On egrapsen Moseis en
to nomo kai 'oi propheitai 'eureikamen, Yeisoun ton 'wion tou Yoseiph ton
apo Nazaret.

Hebrew/Transliteration
מה. וַיִּמְצָא פִילִפּוֹס אֶת-נְתַנְאֵל אֵלָיו מְצָאנוּ אֹתוֹ אֲשֶׁר כָּתַב עָלָיו מֹשֶׁה בַּתּוֹרָה וְהַנְּבִיאִים
אֶת-יֵשׁוּעַ בֶּן:יוֹסֵף מִנְּצָרֶת -

45. Va•yim•tza Pilipos et - N`tan•el va•yo•mer elav ma•tza•noo o•to asher ka•tav alav Moshe ba•To•rah ve•ha•n`vi•eem et - Yeshua ben - Yo•sef mi•Ne•tza•ret.

Rabbinic Jewish Commentary

Moses, in the Torah, or Pentateuch, in the five books written by him, frequently speaks of the Messiah as the seed of the woman, that should break the serpent's head; as the seed of Abraham, in whom all nations should be blessed; and as the Shiloh to whom the gathering of the people should be; and as the great prophet, like to himself, God would raise up among the children of Israel, to whom they were to hearken: and as for the prophets, they wrote of his birth of a virgin; of the place of his birth, Bethlehem; of his sufferings, and the glory, that should follow; of his resurrection from the dead, his ascension to heaven, and session at the right hand of God; and of many things relating to his person, and office, and work. And Philip having given this general account of him, proceeds to name him particularly.

---

46. And Nathanael said unto him, Can there any good thing come out of Nazareth? Philip saith unto him, Come and see.

Greek/Transliteration

46. Καὶ εἶπεν αὐτῷ Ναθαναήλ, Ἐκ Ναζαρὲτ δύναταί τι ἀγαθὸν εἶναι; Λέγει αὐτῷ Φίλιππος, Ἔρχου καὶ ἴδε.

46. Kai eipen auto Nathanaeil, Ek Nazaret dunatai ti agathon einai? Legei auto Philippos, Erchou kai ide.

Hebrew/Transliteration

מו. וַיֹּאמֶר אֵלָיו נְתַנְאֵל הֲכִי מִנְּצֶרֶת יָבֹא טוֹב וַיֹּאמֶר אֵלָיו פִּילפּוֹס בֹּא וּרְאֵה:

46. Va•yo•mer elav N`tan•el ha•chi mi•N`tze•ret ya•vo tov va•yo•mer elav Pilipos bo oor•eh.

Rabbinic Jewish Commentary

The whole country of Galilee was had in contempt with the Jews; but Nazareth was so mean a place, that it seems it was even despised by its neighbours, by the Galilaeans themselves; for Nathanael was a Galilean, that said these words. It was so miserable a place that he could hardly think that any sort of good thing, even any worldly good thing, could come from thence; and it was so wicked, as appears from their murderous designs upon Yeshua, that he thought no good man could arise from hence; and still less, any prophet, any person of great note; and still least of all, that that good thing, or person, the Messiah, should spring from it: so that his objection, and prejudice, proceeded not only upon the oracle in Mic_5:2, which points out Bethlehem as the birthplace of the Messiah; but upon the wickedness, and meanness, and obscurity of Nazareth.

The phrase, תא חזי, "come, see", is often used in the book of Zohar (q): so it is, and likewise, בא וראה, "come and see", in the Talmudic writings (r),

(q) In Gen. fol. 13. 1. & 14. 3. & 16. 1, 2. & in Exod. fol. 83. 4. & passim. (r) T. Bab. Taanith, fol. 8. 1. & 23. 2. & 24. 1. Kiddushin, fol. 20. 1. & 33. 1. & Sota, fol. 5. 1, 2. & passim.

---

47. Jesus saw Nathanael coming to him, and saith of him, Behold an Israelite indeed, in whom is no guile!

Greek/Transliteration

47. Εἶδεν ὁ Ἰησοῦς τὸν Ναθαναὴλ ἐρχόμενον πρὸς αὐτόν, καὶ λέγει περὶ αὐτοῦ, Ἴδε ἀληθῶς Ἰσραηλίτης, ἐν ᾧ δόλος οὐκ ἔστιν.

47. Eiden 'o Yeisous ton Nathanaeil erchomenon pros auton, kai legei peri autou, Yde aleithos Ysraeiliteis, en 'o dolos ouk estin.

Hebrew/Transliteration

מז. וַיַּרְא יֵשׁוּעַ אֶת-נְתַנְאֵל בָּא לִקְרָאתוֹ וַיֹּאמֶר עָלָיו אוּלָם זֶה הוּא יִשְׂרָאֵלִי אֲשֶׁר אֵין-בּוֹ רְמִיָּה:

47. Va•yar Yeshua et - N`tan•el ba lik•ra•to va•yo•mer alav oo•lam ze hoo Is•re•eli asher eyn - bo r`mi•ya.

Rabbinic Jewish Commentary

behold an Israelite indeed! a son of Israel, as the Syriac and Persic versions read; a true son of Jacob's; an honest, plain hearted man, like him; one that was an Israelite at heart; inwardly so; not one after the flesh only, but after the Spirit; and which was a rare thing at that time; and therefore a note of admiration is prefixed to it; for all were not Israel, that were of Israel; and indeed but a very few then: and so, בן ישראל, "a son of Israel", and ישראל גמור, "a perfect Israelite", are (s) said of such who have regard to the articles of the Jewish faith, though not even of the seed of Israel.

(s) Addareth Eliahu apud Trigland de Sect. Karaeorum, c. 10. p. 175, 176.

---

48. Nathanael saith unto him, Whence knowest thou me? Jesus answered and said unto him, Before that Philip called thee, when thou wast under the fig tree, I saw thee.

Greek/Transliteration

48. Λέγει αὐτῷ Ναθαναήλ, Πόθεν με γινώσκεις; Ἀπεκρίθη Ἰησοῦς καὶ εἶπεν αὐτῷ, Πρὸ τοῦ σε Φίλιππον φωνῆσαι, ὄντα ὑπὸ τὴν συκῆν, εἶδόν σε.

48. Legei auto Nathanaeil, Pothen me ginoskeis? Apekrithei Yeisous kai eipen auto, Pro tou se Philippon phoneisai, onta 'upo tein sukein, eidon se.

Hebrew/Transliteration

מח. וַיֹּאמֶר אֵלָיו נְתַנְאֵל מֵאַיִן יָדַעְתָּ אֹתִי וַיַּעַן יֵשׁוּעַ וַיֹּאמֶר אֵלָיו טֶרֶם קָרָא לְךָ פִּילִפּוֹס בִּהְיוֹתְךָ
תַּחַת הַתְּאֵנָה:רְאִיתִיךָ

48. Va•yo•mer elav N`tan•el me•a•yin ya•da•ata o•ti va•ya•an Yeshua va•yo•mer elav te•rem ka•ra le•cha Pilipos bi•hi•yot•cha ta•chat ha•te•e•na r`ee•ti•cha.

Rabbinic Jewish Commentary

It was usual with the Rabbis to read, and study in the Torah, under fig trees, and sometimes, though rarely, to pray there. It is said (t),

"R. Jacob, and his companions, were "sitting", studying in the law, תחות חדא תאינה, "under a certain fig tree".

And the rule they give about praying, on, or under one, is thus (u):

"He that prays on the top of an olive tree, or on the top of a "fig tree", or on any other trees, must come down, and "pray below".

It is said of Nathanael, in the Syriac dictionary (x); that his mother laid him under a fig tree, when the infants were slain, i.e. at Bethlehem; which, if it could be depended upon, must be to Nathanael a surprising and undeniable proof of the deity of Yeshua, and of his being the true Messiah; since, at that time, he was an infant of days himself, and was the person Herod was seeking to destroy, as the Messiah, and king of the Jews,

(t) T. Hieros. Beracot, fol. 5. 3. Vid. Shirhashirim Rabba, fol. 16. 4. (u) Ib col. 1. & T. Bab. Beracot, fol. 16. 1. (x) Bar Bahluli apud Castell. Lexic. Polyglott. col. 8437.

---

49. Nathanael answered and saith unto him, Rabbi, thou art the Son of God; thou art the King of Israel.

Greek/Transliteration
49. Ἀπεκρίθη Ναθαναήλ καὶ λέγει αὐτῷ, Ῥαββί, σὺ εἶ ὁ υἱὸς τοῦ θεοῦ, σὺ εἶ ὁ βασιλεὺς τοῦ Ἰσραήλ.

49. Apekrithei Nathanaeil kai legei auto, 'Rabbi, su ei 'o 'wios tou theou, su ci 'o basileus tou Ysraeil.

Hebrew/Transliteration
מט. וַיַּעַן אֹתוֹ נְתַנְאֵל רַבִּי אַתָּה הוּא בֶּן-הָאֱלֹהִים אַתָּה הוּא מֶלֶךְ יִשְׂרָאֵל:

49. Va•ya•an o•to N`tan•el Rabbi ata hoo Ben - ha•Elohim ata hoo Me•lech Israel.

TaNaKh-Old Testament/Rabbinic Jewish Commentary
"Yea, I have set My king on My holy mount on Zion." (Psalm_2:6)

thou art the King of Israel; having in view, no doubt, the passage in Psa_2:6, where the characters of Son of God, and King of Zion, meet in the same person: not King of Israel, in a literal sense; though he was the son of David, and a descendant of his in a right line, and was of the royal line, and had a legal right to the throne of Israel.

---

50. Jesus answered and said unto him, Because I said unto thee, I saw thee under the fig tree, believest thou? thou shalt see greater things than these.

Greek/Transliteration
50. Ἀπεκρίθη Ἰησοῦς καὶ εἶπεν αὐτῷ, Ὅτι εἶπόν σοι, εἶδόν σε ὑποκάτω τῆς συκῆς, πιστεύεις; Μείζω τούτων ὄψει.

50. Apekrithei Yeisous kai eipen auto, 'Oti eipon soi, eidon se 'upokato teis sukeis, pisteueis? Meizo touton opsei.

Hebrew/Transliteration
נ. וַיַּעַן יֵשׁוּעַ וַיֹּאמֶר אֵלָיו יַעַן אֲשֶׁר הֶאֱמַנְתָּ בִּי בַּעֲבוּר אָמְרִי לְךָ תַּחַת הַתְּאֵנָה רְאִיתִיךָ לָכֵן גְּדֹלוֹת מֵאֵלֶּה תִּרְאֶה:

50. Va•ya•an Yeshua va•yo•mer elav ya•an asher he•e•man•ta bi ba•a•voor om•ri le•cha ta•chat ha•te•e•na r`ee•ti•cha la•chen ge•do•lot me•e•le tir•eh.

---

51. And he saith unto him, Verily, verily, I say unto you, Hereafter ye shall see heaven open, and the angels of God ascending and descending upon the Son of man.

Greek/Transliteration
51. Καὶ λέγει αὐτῷ, Ἀμὴν ἀμὴν λέγω ὑμῖν, ἀπ' ἄρτι ὄψεσθε τὸν οὐρανὸν ἀνεῳγότα, καὶ τοὺς ἀγγέλους τοῦ θεοῦ ἀναβαίνοντας καὶ καταβαίνοντας ἐπὶ τὸν υἱὸν τοῦ ἀνθρώπου.

51. Kai legei auto, Amein amein lego 'umin, ap arti opsesthe ton ouranon aneogota, kai tous angelous tou theou anabainontas kai katabainontas epi ton 'wion tou anthropou.

Hebrew/Transliteration

נא. וַיֹּאמֶר אֵלָיו אָמֵן אָמֵן אֲנִי אֹמֵר לָכֶם כִּי תִרְאוּ אֶת-הַשָּׁמַיִם פְּתוּחִים וּמַלְאֲכֵי אֱלֹהִים עֹלִים וְיֹרְדִים עַל בֶּן-הָאָדָם:

51. Va•yo•mer elav Amen Amen ani o•mer la•chem ki tir•oo et - ha•sha•ma•yim p`too•chim oo•mal•a•chey Elohim o•lim ve•yor•dim al Ben - ha•Adam.

Rabbinic Jewish Commentary

It is observable, that some of the Jewish writers (y) understand the ascent, and descent of the messengers, in Gen_28:12, to be, not upon the ladder, but upon Jacob; which makes the phrase there still more agreeable to this; and so they render עליו, in Gen_28:13, not "above it", but "above him".

(y) Bereshit Rabba, sect. 68. fol. 61. 2. & sect. 69. fol. 61. 3, 4.

"R. Hiyya the Elder and R. Jannai disagreed. One maintained: They were ASCENDING AND DESCENDING the ladder; while the other said: they were ASCENDING AND DESCENDING on Jacob.
(Genesis Rabbah 68:12, SoncinoPress Edition)

The passage in Genesis 28:12 says that the messengers were ascending and descending "BO." The word 'bo' here literally means 'on him'. The question is, who is the "him" referring too?

Ladder (sullam) is another name for Messiah and is taken from Jacob's dream. HaGra, in his book Kol HaTor, applies this image to Messiah when he says,

"This is the quality of Joseph [Messiah]…that all his deeds which awake [redemption] from below [earth] are supported from above [heaven]"
(Kol HaTor 62, par.97.)

It is clear that this image of Messiah as Ladder understands him to be the means which gives access to heaven. If one seeks to reach heaven, he can only do so by climbing the Ladder. (The Concealed Light; Tsvi Sadan, pg.168)

John, Chapter 2

1. And the third day there was a marriage in Cana of Galilee; and the mother of Jesus was there:

Greek/Transliteration

1. Καὶ τῇ ἡμέρᾳ τῇ τρίτῃ γάμος ἐγένετο ἐν Καν τῆς Γαλιλαίας, καὶ ἦν ἡ μήτηρ τοῦ Ἰησοῦ ἐκεῖ·

1. Kai tei 'eimera tei tritei gamos egeneto en Kan teis Galilaias, kai ein 'ei meiteir tou Yeisou ekei.

Hebrew/Transliteration

א. וּבַיּוֹם הַשְּׁלִישִׁי הָיְתָה חֲתֻנָּה בְּקָנָה אֲשֶׁר לַגָּלִיל וְאֵם יֵשׁוּעַ הָיְתָה שָׁמָּה:

1. Oo•va•yom hash•li•shi hai•ta cha•too•na be•Kana asher la•Ga•lil ve•em Yeshua hai•ta sha•ma.

Rabbinic Jewish Commentary

There is much dispute, and many rules with the Jews about the times, and days of marriage:

"A virgin, (they say (z),) marries on the fourth day (of the week), and a widow on the fifth, because the sanhedrim sit in the cities twice in the week, on the second, and on the fifth days; so that if there is any dispute about virginity, he (the husband) may come betimes to the sanhedrim."

This was a law that obtained since the times of Ezra; for it is said (a),

"Before the order of Ezra, a woman might be married on any day;"

But in after times, feast days, and sabbath days, were particularly excepted. One of their canons is (b).

"They do not marry women on a feast day, neither virgins, nor widows:"

The reason of it was, that they might not mix one joy with another; and lest a man should leave the joy of the feast, for the joy of his wife. The account Maimonides (c) gives of these several things is this;

"It is lawful to espouse on any common day, even on the ninth of Ab, whether in the day, or in the night; but they do not marry wives neither on the evening of the sabbath, nor on the first of the week: the decree is, lest the sabbath should be profaned by preparing the feast; for the bridegroom is employed about the feast: and there is no need to say, that it is unlawful to marry a wife on the sabbath day; and even on the common day of a feast they do not marry wives, as we have explained; because they do not mix one joy with another, as it is said in Gen_29:27, "fulfil her week, and we will give thee this also": but on the rest of the days it is lawful to marry a wife, any day a man pleases; for he must be employed in the marriage feast three days before the marriage. A place in which the sanhedrim do not sit, but on the second and fifth days only, a virgin is married on the fourth day; that if there is any objection to her virginity, he (her husband) may come betimes to the sanhedrim: and it is a custom of the wise men, that he that marries one that has been married, he may marry her on the fifth day, that so he may rejoice with her on the fifth day, and on the evening of the sabbath, (i.e. the sixth,) and on the sabbath day, and may go forth to his work on the first day."

But elsewhere it is said (d), that

"Now they are used to marry on the "sixth day of the week"."

Yea (e), that

"It is lawful to marry, and to make the feast on the sabbath day."

But whether this marriage was of a virgin, or a widow, cannot be known; nor with certainty can it be said on what day of the week it was: if that day was a sabbath day on which the disciples abode with Yeshua, then it must be on the first day that Yeshua went into Galilee, and found Philip, and conversed with Nathanael; and if this third day is reckoned from John's second testimony, it must be on a Tuesday, the third day of the week; but if from Yeshua's going into Galilee, then it must be on a Wednesday, the fourth day of the week, the day fixed by the Jewish canon for the marriage of a virgin.

---

2. And both Jesus was called, and his disciples, to the marriage.

Greek/Transliteration
2. ἐκλήθη δὲ καὶ ὁ Ἰησοῦς καὶ οἱ μαθηταὶ αὐτοῦ εἰς τὸν γάμον.

2. ekleithei de kai 'o Yeisous kai 'oi matheitai autou eis ton gamon.

Hebrew/Transliteration
‎:ב. וְגַם-יֵשׁוּעַ וְתַלְמִידָיו הָיוּ מִן-קְרוּאֵי הַחֲתֻנָּה

2. Ve•gam - Yeshua ve•tal•mi•dav ha•yoo min - ke•roo•ey ha•cha•too•na.

Rabbinic Jewish Commentary
Yeshua, and his five disciples, made six of the ten, which were always necessary to be present at, the benediction of bridegrooms: for so runs the canon (m);

"They do not bless the blessing of bridegrooms, but with ten principal and free men; and the bridegroom may be one of the number."

To attend a wedding, was reckoned, with the Jews, an act of beneficence and kindness (n). According to the Jewish cations (o), a disciple of a wise man might not partake of any feast, but what was according to the commandment, as the feast of espousals, and of marriage; and such a feast was this, which Yeshua and his disciples were at; and so not to be condemned for it, according to their own maxims.

(m) Maimon. Hilch. Ishot, c. 10. sect. 5. Pirke Eliezer, c. 19. Shirhashirim Rabba, fol. 9. 3. (n) Maimon in Misn. Peah, c. 1. sect. 1. (o) T. Bab. Pesachim, fol. 49. 1. & Maimon. Hilchot Deyot, c. 5. sect. 2.

---

3. And when they wanted wine, the mother of Jesus saith unto him, They have no wine.

Greek/Transliteration
3. Καὶ ὑστερήσαντος οἴνου, λέγει ἡ μήτηρ τοῦ Ἰησοῦ πρὸς αὐτόν, Οἶνον οὐκ ἔχουσιν.

3. Kai 'ustereisantos oinou, legei 'ei meiteir tou Yeisou pros auton, Oinon ouk echousin.

Hebrew/Transliteration
ג. וְאַחֲרֵי אֲשֶׁר תַּם הַיַּיִן אָמְרָה אֵם יֵשׁוּעַ אֵלָיו הִנֵּה אֵין לָהֶם יָיִן:

3. Ve•a•cha•rey asher tam ha•ya•yin am•ra em Yeshua elav hee•ne eyn la•hem ya•yin.

---

4. Jesus saith unto her, Woman, what have I to do with thee? mine hour is not yet come.

Greek/Transliteration
4. Λέγει αὐτῇ ὁ Ἰησοῦς, Τί ἐμοὶ καὶ σοί, γύναι; Οὔπω ἥκει ἡ ὥρα μου.

4. Legei autei 'o Yeisous, Ti emoi kai soi, gunai? Oupo 'eikei 'ei 'ora mou.

Hebrew/Transliteration
ד. וַיֹּאמֶר אֵלֶיהָ יֵשׁוּעַ מַה-לִּי וָלָךְ אִשָּׁה עוֹד לֹא-בָאָה עִתִּי:

4. Va•yo•mer e•le•ha Yeshua ma - li va•lach ee•sha od lo - va•ah ee•ti.

Rabbinic Jewish Commentary
what have I to do with thee? The Jews (r) objects to this sense of the words, but gives a very weak reason for it:

"But I say, (says he,) who should be concerned but the master of the feast? and he was the master of the feast:"

Whereas it is a clear case that he was one of the guests, one that was invited, Joh_2:2, and that there was a governor or ruler of the feast, who might be more properly called the master of it than Yeshua, Joh_2:8. However, since Yeshua afterwards did concern himself in it, it looks as if this was not his meaning. Others render it to the sense we do, "what have I with thee?" as the Ethiopic version; or "what business hast thou with me?" as the Persic version; and is the same with, מה לי ולך, "what have I to do with thee?" used in 1Ki_17:18, where the Septuagint use the same phrase as here; and such a way of speaking is common with Jewish writers (s): hereby signifying, that though, as man, and a son of hers, he had been subject to her, in which he had set an example of obedience to parents; yet, as God, he had a Father in heaven, whose business he came to do; and in that, and in his office, as Mediator, she had nothing to do with him; nor was he to be directed by her in that work; or to be told, or the least hint given when a miracle should be wrought, by him in confirmation of his mission and doctrine.

(r) Vet. Nizzachon, p. 223. (s) Vid. Kimchi in Psal. ii. 12. Bechinat Olam, p. 70.

---

5. His mother saith unto the servants, Whatsoever he saith unto you, do it.

Greek/Transliteration
5. Λέγει ἡ μήτηρ αὐτοῦ τοῖς διακόνοις, Ὅ τι ἂν λέγῃ ὑμῖν, ποιήσατε.

5. Legei 'ei meiteir autou tois dyakonois, 'O ti an legei 'umin, poieisate.

Hebrew/Transliteration
ה. וַתֹּאמֶר אִמּוֹ אֶל-הַמְשָׁרְתִים אֶת-אֲשֶׁר יֹאמַר לָכֶם תַּעֲשׂוּ:

5. Va•to•mer ee•mo el - ha•me•shar•tim et - asher yo•mar la•chem ta•a•soo.

---

6. And there were set there six waterpots of stone, after the manner of the purifying of the Jews, containing two or three firkins apiece.

Greek/Transliteration
6. Ἦσαν δὲ ἐκεῖ ὑδρίαι λίθιναι ἓξ κείμεναι κατὰ τὸν καθαρισμὸν τῶν Ἰουδαίων, χωροῦσαι ἀνὰ μετρητὰς δύο ἢ τρεῖς.

6. Eisan de ekei 'udriai lithinai 'ex keimenai kata ton katharismon ton Youdaion, chorousai ana metreitas duo ei treis.

Hebrew/Transliteration

ו. וְשָׁם נִמְצְאוּ שֵׁשׁ כַּדֵּי-אֶבֶן עֲרֻכוֹת לְטַהֵר אֶת-אֲשֶׁר לֹא טָהוֹר בֵּין הַיְּהוּדִים כַּמִּשְׁפָּט שְׁתַּיִם אוֹ-
שָׁלֹשׁ בַּתִּים:תָּכִיל כָּל-כָּד

6. Ve•sham nim•tze•oo shesh ka•dey - even a•roo•chot le•ta•her et - asher lo
ta•hor bein ha•Ye•hoo•dim ka•mish•pat sh`ta•yim oh - sha•losh ba•tim ta•chil
kol - kad.

Rabbinic Jewish Commentary

To distinguish them from other vessels made of different matter: for the Jews had

"Vessels made of dust, and the dung of beasts, כלי אבנים, "vessels of stone",
vessels of earth, vessels made of shells, vessels of nitre, vessels made of the bones
and skins of fishes (t)."

And as these vessels were very likely for washing of hands, such were used for
that purpose: their rule is (u),

"They may put water for the hands in all sorts of vessels; in vessels of dung, in
stone vessels, and in vessels of earth."

At a wedding were set vessels of various sizes to wash hands and feet in; there was
one vessel called משיכלא, which the gloss says was a large pitcher, or basin, out of
which the whole company washed their hands and their feet; and there was another
called משיכלתא, which was a lesser and beautiful basin, which was set alone for
the more honourable persons, as for the bride, and for any gentlewoman (w); and
such might be these six stone jars, or pots.

(t) Misn. Celim. c. 10. sect. 1. & Maimon. & Bartenora in ib. (u) Misn. Yadaim, c.
1. sect. 2. (w) Gloss in T. Bab. Sabbat, fol. 77. 2.

---

7. Jesus saith unto them, Fill the waterpots with water. And they filled them
up to the brim.

Greek/Transliteration

7. Λέγει αὐτοῖς ὁ Ἰησοῦς, Γεμίσατε τὰς ὑδρίας ὕδατος. Καὶ ἐγέμισαν αὐτὰς
ἕως ἄνω.

7. Legei autois 'o Yeisous, Gemisate tas 'udrias 'udatos. Kai egemisan autas
'eos ano.

Hebrew/Transliteration

ז. וַיֹּאמֶר אֲלֵיהֶם יֵשׁוּעַ מַלְאוּ אֶת-הַכַּדִּים מַיִם וַיְמַלְאוּן עַד-הַשָּׂפָה:

7. Va•yo•mer aley•hem Yeshua mal•oo et - ha•ka•dim ma•yim vay•mal•oon ad
- ha•sa•fa.

8. And he saith unto them, Draw out now, and bear unto the governor of the feast. And they bare it.

Greek/Transliteration
8. Καὶ λέγει αὐτοῖς, Ἀντλήσατε νῦν, καὶ φέρετε τῷ ἀρχιτρικλίνῳ. Καὶ ἤνεγκαν.

8. Kai legei autois, Antleisate nun, kai pherete to architriklino. Kai einegkan.

Hebrew/Transliteration
:ח. וַיֹּאמֶר שַׁאֲבוּ-נָא עַתָּה וְהָבִיאוּ אֶל-פְּקִיד הַמִּשְׁתֶּה וַיָּבִיאוּ

8. Va•yo•mer sha•a•voo - na ata ve•ha•vi•oo el - pe•kid ha•mish•te va•ya•vi•oo.

Rabbinic Jewish Commentary
Since there were six or seven benedictions to be pronounced; and particularly a blessing was said over the cup of wine; for if there was any wine, a cup of it was brought, and he blessed over it first, and ordered every thing concerning the cup: and this made up seven blessings at such a time (y); and therefore was a very fit person to bear the wine to first.

(y) Maimon. Hilchot Ishot, c. 10. sect. 3, 4.

---

9. When the ruler of the feast had tasted the water that was made wine, and knew not whence it was: (but the servants which drew the water knew;) the governor of the feast called the bridegroom,

Greek/Transliteration
9. Ὡς δὲ ἐγεύσατο ὁ ἀρχιτρίκλινος τὸ ὕδωρ οἶνον γεγενημένον, καὶ οὐκ ᾔδει πόθεν ἐστίν- οἱ δὲ διάκονοι ᾔδεισαν οἱ ἠντληκότες τὸ ὕδωρ- φωνεῖ τὸν νυμφίον ὁ ἀρχιτρίκλινος,

9. 'Os de egeusato 'o architriklinos to 'udor oinon gegeneimenon, kai ouk eidei pothen estin- 'oi de dyakonoi eideisan 'oi eintleikotes to 'udor- phonei ton numphion 'o architriklinos,

Hebrew/Transliteration
ט. וַיִּטְעַם פְּקִיד הַמִּשְׁתֶּה אֶת-הַמַּיִם אֲשֶׁר נֶהְפְּכוּ לְיַיִן מִבְּלִי דַעַת מֵאַיִן בָּא רַק הַמְשָׁרְתִים אֲשֶׁר- שָׁאֲבוּ אֶת-הַמַּיִם יָדְעוּ וַיִּקְרָא רַב בֵּית הַמִּשְׁתֶּה אֶל-הֶחָתָן

9. Va•yit•am pe•kid ha•mish•te et - ha•ma•yim asher ne•hef•choo le•ya•yin mi•b`li da•at me•a•yin ba rak ha•me•shar•tim asher - sha•a•voo et - ha•ma•yim ya•da•oo va•yik•ra rav beit ha•mish•te el - he•cha•tan.

10. And saith unto him, Every man at the beginning doth set forth good wine; and when men have well drunk, then that which is worse: but thou hast kept the good wine until now.

Greek/Transliteration

10. καὶ λέγει αὐτῷ, Πᾶς ἄνθρωπος πρῶτον τὸν καλὸν οἶνον τίθησιν, καὶ ὅταν μεθυσθῶσιν, τότε τὸν ἐλάσσω· σὺ τετήρηκας τὸν καλὸν οἶνον ἕως ἄρτι.

10. kai legei auto, Pas anthropos proton ton kalon oinon titheisin, kai 'otan methusthosin, tote ton elasso. su teteireikas ton kalon oinon 'eos arti.

Hebrew/Transliteration

י. וַיֹּאמֶר אֵלָיו כָּל-אִישׁ יָשִׂים יַיִן טוֹב רִאשׁוֹנָה וְאַחֲרֵי שָׁתוּ הַקְּרֻאִים לְרָוָיָה יָשִׂים יַיִן שְׁפַל-עֵרֶךְ לִפְנֵיהֶם וְאַתָּה:צָפַנְתָּ אֶת-הַיַּיִן הַטּוֹב עַד-לָאַחֲרֹנָה

10. Va•yo•mer elav kol - eesh ya•sim ya•yin tov ri•sho•na ve•a•cha•rey sha•too hak•roo•eem lar•va•ya ya•sim ya•yin sh`fal - e•rech lif•ney•hem ve•a•ta tza•fan•ta et - ha•ya•yin ha•tov ad - la•a•cha•ro•na.

Rabbinic Jewish Commentary

then that which is worse; not bad wine, but τον ελασσω, "that which is lesser"; a weaker bodied wine, that is lowered, and of less strength, and not so intoxicating, and which is fittest for the guests. So Martial (z) advises Sextilianus, after he had drank the tenth cup, not to drink the best wine, but to ask his host for wine of Laletania, which was a weaker and lower sort of wine.

(z) A Caupone tibi faex Laletana petatur Si plus quam decics, Sextiliane, bibis. L. 1. Ep. 25.

---

11. This beginning of miracles did Jesus in Cana of Galilee, and manifested forth his glory; and his disciples believed on him.

Greek/Transliteration

11. Ταύτην ἐποίησεν τὴν ἀρχὴν τῶν σημείων ὁ Ἰησοῦς ἐν Καν τῆς Γαλιλαίας, καὶ ἐφανέρωσεν τὴν δόξαν αὐτοῦ· καὶ ἐπίστευσαν εἰς αὐτὸν οἱ μαθηταὶ αὐτοῦ.

11. Tautein epoieisen tein archein ton seimeion 'o Yeisous en Kan teis Galilaias, kai ephanerosen tein doxan autou. kai episteusan eis auton 'oi matheitai autou.

Hebrew/Transliteration

יא. זֹאת רֵאשִׁית הָאֹתוֹת אֲשֶׁר עָשָׂה יֵשׁוּעַ בְּקָנָה אֲשֶׁר לַגָּלִיל וְשָׁם גִּלָּה כְבוֹדוֹ וַיַּאֲמִינוּ בוֹ תַּלְמִידָיו:

11. Zot re•sheet ha•o•tot asher asa Yeshua be•Kana asher la•Ga•lil ve•sham gila che•vo•do va•ya•a•mi•noo vo tal•mi•dav.

Rabbinic Jewish Commentary

This was the first "passover" after Yeshua's baptism, which is generally thought to have been about half a year before; though so much time cannot be made out from the scriptural account; for from his baptism, to his return out of the wilderness to John, were forty days; and from thence, to his coming to Cana, four or, five days more; and perhaps he might be seven days in Cana; for so long a wedding was usually kept; and his stay at Capernaum was but a few days; all which do not amount to above eight or nine weeks at most: the second passover after this, is, by some, thought to be the feast mentioned in Joh_5:1, and the third in Joh_6:4, and the fourth and last, at which he suffered, in Joh_18:28. The Evangelist John is the only writer that gives an account of the passovers after Yeshua entered on his public ministry; by which is known the duration of it, which is generally thought to be about three years and a half. "Three years and a half", the Jews say (a), the Shekinah sat upon the Mount of Olives, expecting that the Israelites would repent, but they did not; and this seems to be the term of time for disciples to learn of their masters: it is said (b), one came from Athens to Jerusalem, and he served "three years and a half" to learn the doctrine of wisdom, and he learned it not.

(a) Praefat. Echa Rabbati, fol. 40. 4. (b) Echa Rabbati, fol. 44. 4.

---

12. After this he went down to Capernaum, he, and his mother, and his brethren, and his disciples: and they continued there not many days.

Greek/Transliteration
12. Μετὰ τοῦτο κατέβη εἰς Καπερναούμ, αὐτὸς καὶ ἡ μήτηρ αὐτοῦ, καὶ οἱ ἀδελφοὶ αὐτοῦ, καὶ οἱ μαθηταὶ αὐτοῦ· καὶ ἐκεῖ ἔμειναν οὐ πολλὰς ἡμέρας.

12. Meta touto katebei eis Kapernaoum, autos kai 'ei meiteir autou, kai 'oi adelphoi autou, kai 'oi matheitai autou. kai ekei emeinan ou pollas 'eimeras.

Hebrew/Transliteration
יב. וְאַחֲרֵי-כֵן יָרַד אֶל-כְּפַר נַחוּם הוּא וְאִמּוֹ וְאֶחָיו וְתַלְמִידָיו וַיֵּשְׁבוּ שָׁם יָמִים לֹא רַבִּים:

12. Ve•a•cha•rey - chen ya•rad el - K`far Na•choom hoo ve•ee•mo ve•e•chav ve•tal•mi•dav va•yesh•voo sham ya•mim lo ra•bim.

---

13. And the Jews' passover was at hand, and Jesus went up to Jerusalem,

Greek/Transliteration
13. Καὶ ἐγγὺς ἦν τὸ Πάσχα τῶν Ἰουδαίων, καὶ ἀνέβη εἰς Ἱεροσόλυμα ὁ Ἰησοῦς.

13. Kai engus ein to Pascha ton Youdaion, kai anebei eis 'Yerosoluma 'o Yeisous.

Hebrew/Transliteration

יג. וַיִּקְרַב חַג-הַפֶּסַח לַיְּהוּדִים וַיַּעַל יֵשׁוּעַ יְרוּשָׁלָיְמָה:

13. Va•yik•rav chag - ha•Pe•sach la•Ye•hoo•dim va•ya•al Yeshua Ye•roo•sha•lai•ma.

Rabbinic Jewish Commentary

The Evangelist John is the only writer that gives an account of the passovers after Yeshua entered on his public ministry; by which is known the duration of it, which is generally thought to be about three years and a half. "Three years and a half", the Jews say (a), the Shekinah sat upon the Mount of Olives, expecting that the Israelites would repent, but they did not; and this seems to be the term of time for disciples to learn of their masters: it is said (b), one came from Athens to Jerusalem, and he served "three years and a half" to learn the doctrine of wisdom, and he learned it not.

(a) Praefat. Echa Rabbati, fol. 40. 4. (b) Echa Rabbati, fol. 44. 4.

---

14. And found in the temple those that sold oxen and sheep and doves, and the changers of money sitting:

Greek/Transliteration

14. Καὶ εὗρεν ἐν τῷ ἱερῷ τοὺς πωλοῦντας βόας καὶ πρόβατα καὶ περιστεράς, καὶ τοὺς κερματιστὰς καθημένους.

14. Kai 'euren en to 'iero tous polountas boas kai probata kai peristeras, kai tous kermatistas katheimenous.

Hebrew/Transliteration

יד. וַיִּמְצָא בַמִּקְדָּשׁ מֹכְרֵי בָקָר וָצֹאן וְיוֹנִים וְאֶת מְחַלִיפֵי-כֶסֶף יוֹשְׁבִים שָׁם:

14. Va•yim•tza ba•mik•dash moch•rey ba•kar va•tzon ve•yo•nim ve•et mach•li•fey che•sef yosh•vim sham.

Rabbinic Jewish Commentary

those that sold oxen, and sheep, and doves: the oxen, or bullocks, were for the Chagigah, or feast kept on the second day of the passover; and the sheep, or lambs, as the Persic version reads, for the passover supper; and the doves were for the offerings of the poorer sort of new mothers: with these they were supplied from the Mount of Olives.

It is said (c), "there were two cedar trees on the Mount of Olives, and under one of them were four shops of them that sold things for purification; and out of one of them they brought forty bushels of young doves every month: and out of them the Israelites had enough for the nests, or the offerings of turtle doves;"

(c) Echa Rabbati, fol. 52. 4.

---

15. And when he had made a scourge of small cords, he drove them all out of the temple, and the sheep, and the oxen; and poured out the changers' money, and overthrew the tables;

Greek/Transliteration

15. Καὶ ποιήσας φραγέλλιον ἐκ σχοινίων πάντας ἐξέβαλεν ἐκ τοῦ ἱεροῦ, τά τε πρόβατα καὶ τοὺς βόας· καὶ τῶν κολλυβιστῶν ἐξέχεεν τὸ κέρμα, καὶ τὰς τραπέζας ἀνέστρεψεν·

15. Kai poieisas phragellion ek schoinion pantas exebalen ek tou 'ierou, ta te probata kai tous boas. kai ton kollubiston execheen to kerma, kai tas trapezas anestrepsen.

Hebrew/Transliteration

טו. וַיִּקַּח חֲבָלִים וְיִשְׂרַג אֹתָם לְמַלְקָה בְּיָדוֹ וַיְגָרֶשׁ אֶת-כֻּלָּם אֶל-מְחוּץ לַמִּקְדָּשׁ גַּם אֶת-הַצֹּאן גַּם אֶת-הַבָּקָר:וַיַּשְׁלֵךְ אֶת-כֶּסֶף הַמְחַלְפִים אַרְצָה וְאֶת-שֻׁלְחֲנֹתֵיהֶם הָפָךְ

15. Va•yi•kach cha•va•lim ve•y•sa•reg o•tam le•mal•ka be•ya•do va•y`ga•resh et - koo•lam el - mi•choo•tz la•mik•dash gam et - ha•tzon gam et - ha•ba•kar va•yash•lech et - ke•sef ham•chal•fim ar•tza ve•et - shool•cha•no•tey•hem ha•fach.

Rabbinic Jewish Commentary

The reason given why Yeshua made use of a whip, or scourge, rather than a staff, is, because it was contrary to a Jewish canon (d) to go into the mountain of the house, or temple, with a staff in the hand; and yet the man of the mountain of the house, or the master of it, who used to go about every ward with torches burning before him, if he found a Levite asleep in his ward (e), struck him במקלו, with his staff, and had power to burn his clothes.

(d) Misn. Beracot, c. 9. sect. 5. (e) Misn. Middot, c. 1. sect. 2.

---

16. And said unto them that sold doves, Take these things hence; make not my Father's house an house of merchandise.

Greek/Transliteration

16. καὶ τοῖς τὰς περιστερὰς πωλοῦσιν εἶπεν, Ἄρατε ταῦτα ἐντεῦθεν· μὴ ποιεῖτε τὸν οἶκον τοῦ πατρός μου οἶκον ἐμπορίου.

16. kai tois tas peristeras polousin eipen, Arate tauta enteuthen. mei poieite
ton oikon tou patros mou oikon emporiou.

Hebrew/Transliteration
:טז. וְאֶל-מֹכְרֵי הַיּוֹנִים אָמַר הוֹצִיאוּ אֶת-אֵלֶּה מִזֶּה וְלֹא תַעֲשׂוּ אֶת-בֵּית אָבִי לְבֵית מִקָּח וּמִמְכָּר

16. Ve•el - moch•rey ha•yo•nim amar ho•tzi•oo et - ele mi•ze ve•lo ta•a•soo et -
beit Avi le•veit mi•kach oo•mim•kar.

Rabbinic Jewish Commentary
This instance of Yeshua now coming into the temple as a public minister, and
which was the first time of his entrance into it, after he had taken this character,
was a further accomplishment of Mal_3:1, for he now went into it, as the Lord and
proprietor of it; and which this action of his in driving out the merchants, with
their cattle, shows; and was a surprising instance of his divine power; and is equal
to other miracles of his, that a single person, a stranger, one of no power and
authority in the government, unassisted and unarmed, with only a scourge of small
cords, should carry such awe and majesty with him, and inject such terror into, and
drive such a number of men before him, who were selling things for religious uses,
and were supported in it by the priests and sanhedrim of the nation.

---

17. And his disciples remembered that it was written, The zeal of thine house
hath eaten me up.

Greek/Transliteration
17. Ἐμνήσθησαν δὲ οἱ μαθηταὶ αὐτοῦ ὅτι γεγραμμένον ἐστίν, Ὁ ζῆλος τοῦ
οἴκου σου καταφάγεταί με.

17. Emneistheisan de 'oi matheitai autou 'oti gegrammenon estin, 'O zeilos
tou oikou sou kataphagetai me.

Hebrew/Transliteration
:יז. אָז זָכְרוּ תַלְמִידָיו אֶת אֲשֶׁר-כָּתוּב קִנְאַת בֵּיתְךָ אֲכָלָתְנִי

17. Az zach•roo tal•mi•dav et asher - ka•toov kin•at beit•cha acha•lat•ni.

Rabbinic Jewish Commentary
The Jews themselves seem to be under some conviction, that Psalm 69 has respect
to him; for Aben Ezra, a noted commentator of theirs, on the last words of the
Psalm, has this note;

"The sense is, they and their children shall inherit it in the days of David, or in the
days of the Messiah."

It appears from hence, that the disciples of Yeshua were acquainted with the sacred writings, and had diligently read them, and searched into them, and had made them their study; and upon this wonderful action of Yeshua, called to mind, and reflected upon the following passage of Scripture, which they judged very proper and pertinent to him:

the zeal of thine house hath eaten me up. This passage, so far as it is cited, agrees exactly, word for word, with the original text in Psa_69:9, wherefore it is very strange that Surenhusius (f) should remark a difference, and give himself a good deal of trouble to reconcile it: he observes, that in the Hebrew text, it is read, יהוה קנאת, "the zeal of the LORD", in the third person; whereas it is there, קנאת ביתך, "the zeal of thine house", as here, in the second person: indeed, the word כי, "for", is left out, as he remarks, there being no need of it in the citation.

(f) Biblos Katallages, p. 347.

---

18. Then answered the Jews and said unto him, What sign shewest thou unto us, seeing that thou doest these things?

Greek/Transliteration
18. Ἀπεκρίθησαν οὖν οἱ Ἰουδαῖοι καὶ εἶπον αὐτῷ, Τί σημεῖον δεικνύεις ἡμῖν, ὅτι ταῦτα ποιεῖς;

18. Apekritheisan oun 'oi Youdaioi kai eipon auto, Ti seimeion deiknueis 'eimin, 'oti tauta poieis?

Hebrew/Transliteration
יח. וַיַּעֲנוּ הַיְּהוּדִים וַיֹּאמְרוּ אֵלָיו מָה אוֹת הֶרְאֵיתָ לָּנוּ כִּי תַעֲשֶׂה כָּזֹאת:

18. Va•ya•a•noo ha•Ye•hoo•dim va•yom•roo elav ma ot her•eyta la•noo ki ta•a•se ka•zot.

Rabbinic Jewish Commentary
what sign shewest thou unto us, seeing thou dost these things? they argued, that either he did these things of himself, by his own authority, and then they must be deemed rash and unjustifiable; or he did it by the authority of others: they knew it was not by theirs, who were the great council of the nation, from whom he should have had his instructions and orders, if he acted by human authority; and if he pretended to a divine authority, as they supposed he did, then they insisted upon a sign or miracle to be wrought, to prove that God was his Father, as he suggested; and that he was the proprietor and owner of the temple, and had a right to purge it, as he had done; see 1Co_1:22.

"For indeed Jews ask for signs and Greeks search for wisdom;"

51

19. Jesus answered and said unto them, Destroy this temple, and in three days I will raise it up.

Greek/Transliteration
19. Ἀπεκρίθη Ἰησοῦς καὶ εἶπεν αὐτοῖς, Λύσατε τὸν ναὸν τοῦτον, καὶ ἐν τρισὶν ἡμέραις ἐγερῶ αὐτόν.

19. Apekrithei Yeisous kai eipen autois, Lusate ton naon touton, kai en trisin 'eimerais egero auton.

Hebrew/Transliteration
יט. וַיַּעַן יֵשׁוּעַ וַיֹּאמֶר אֲלֵיהֶם הִרְסוּ אֶת-הַהֵיכָל הַזֶּה וַאֲנִי בִּשְׁלֹשֶׁת יָמִים אֲקִימֶנּוּ:

19. Va•ya•an Yeshua va•yo•mer aley•hem hir•soo et - ha•hey•chal ha•ze va•a•ni bish•lo•shet ya•mim aki•me•noo.

Rabbinic Jewish Commentary
JERUSALEM — A three-foot-tall tablet with 87 lines of Hebrew that scholars believe dates from the decades just before the birth of Jesus is causing a quiet stir in biblical and archaeological circles, especially because it may speak of a messiah who will rise from the dead after three days. The tablet, probably found near the Dead Sea in Jordan according to some scholars who have studied it, is a rare example of a stone with ink writings from that era — in essence, a Dead Sea Scroll on stone.

Mr. Knohl focuses especially on line 80, which begins clearly with the words "L'shloshet yamin," meaning "in three days." Two more hard-to-read words come later, and Mr. Knohl said he believed that he had deciphered them as well, so that the line reads, "In three days you shall live, I, Gabriel, command you."

Mr. Knohl contends that the stone's writings are about the death of a leader of the Jews who will be resurrected in three days.

Mr. Knohl said that it was less important whether Simon was the messiah of the stone than the fact that it strongly suggested that a savior who died and rose after three days was an established concept at the time of Jesus. He notes that in the Gospels, Jesus makes numerous predictions of his suffering and New Testament scholars say such predictions must have been written in by later followers because there was no such idea present in his day.

But there was, he said, and "Gabriel's Revelation" shows it.

"His mission is that he has to be put to death by the Romans to suffer so his blood will be the sign for redemption to come," Mr. Knohl said. "This is the sign of the son of Joseph. This is the conscious view of Jesus himself. This gives the Last Supper an absolutely different meaning. To shed blood is not for the sins of people but to bring redemption to Israel." (a)

(a) *Israel Knohl*, an iconoclastic professor of Bible studies at Hebrew University in Jerusalem, article taken from the New York Times, By Ethan Bronner Published: July 6, 2008.

---

20. Then said the Jews, Forty and six years was this temple in building, and wilt thou rear it up in three days?

Greek/Transliteration

20. Εἶπον οὖν οἱ Ἰουδαῖοι, Τεσσαράκοντα καὶ ἓξ ἔτεσιν ᾠκοδομήθη ὁ ναὸς οὗτος, καὶ σὺ ἐν τρισὶν ἡμέραις ἐγερεῖς αὐτόν;

20. Eipon oun 'oi Youdaioi, Tessarakonta kai 'ex etesin okodomeithei 'o naos 'outos, kai su en trisin 'eimerais egereis auton?

Hebrew/Transliteration

כ. וַיֹּאמְרוּ הַיְּהוּדִים אַרְבָּעִים שָׁנָה וְשֵׁשׁ שָׁנִים נִבְנָה הַהֵיכָל הַזֶּה וְאַתָּה תְּקִימֶנּוּ בִּשְׁלֹשֶׁת יָמִים:

20. Va•yom•roo ha•Ye•hoo•dim ar•ba•eem sha•na ve•shesh sha•nim niv•na ha•hey•chal ha•ze ve•a•ta te•ki•me•noo bish•lo•shet ya•mim.

Rabbinic Jewish Commentary

The Jews call, בניין הורדוס, "the building of Herod" (g); and say of it, that

"He who has not seen Herod's building, never saw a beautiful building."

And this, according to Josephus (h), was begun in the "eighteenth" year of his reign, in the "thirty fifth" of which Yeshua was born, who was now "thirty" years of age: so that reckoning either the eighteenth year of Herod, or the thirtieth of Yeshua, the present year exclusively, just forty six years had run out, since the rebuilding or reparations were first begun; and which were not yet finished; for some years after this, the above writer observes (i), the temple was finished, even in the times of Nero and Agrippa: and agreeably to this, the words may be rendered, "forty six years has this temple been building"

(g) T. Bab. Bava Bathra, fol. 4. 1. (h) Antiqu. Jud. l. 15. c. 14. (i) Antiqu. Jud. l. 20. c. 8.

---

21. But he spake of the temple of his body.

Greek/Transliteration

21. Ἐκεῖνος δὲ ἔλεγεν περὶ τοῦ ναοῦ τοῦ σώματος αὐτοῦ.

21. Ekeinos de elegen peri tou naou tou somatos autou.

כא. וְהוּא דִבֶּר דְּבָרוֹ עַל-הֵיכַל גְּוִיָּתוֹ:

21. Ve•hoo di•ber de•va•ro al - hey•chal ge•vi•yato.

---

22. When therefore he was risen from the dead, his disciples remembered that he had said this unto them; and they believed the scripture, and the word which Jesus had said.

Greek/Transliteration

22. Ὅτε οὖν ἠγέρθη ἐκ νεκρῶν, ἐμνήσθησαν οἱ μαθηταὶ αὐτοῦ ὅτι τοῦτο ἔλεγεν· καὶ ἐπίστευσαν τῇ γραφῇ, καὶ τῷ λόγῳ ᾧ εἶπεν ὁ Ἰησοῦς.

22. 'Ote oun eigerthei ek nekron, emneistheisan 'oi matheitai autou 'oti touto elegen. Kai episteusan tei graphei, kai to logo 'o eipen 'o Yeisous.

Hebrew/Transliteration

כב. עַל-כֵּן אַחֲרֵי תְקוּמָתוֹ מִן-הַמֵּתִים זָכְרוּ תַלְמִידָיו כִּי-כֹה אָמַר לָהֶם וַיַּאֲמִינוּ בַכָּתוּב וּבִדְבַר יֵשׁוּעַ אֲשֶׁר דִּבֶּר:

22. Al - ken a•cha•rey te•koo•ma•to min - ha•me•tim zach•roo tal•mi•dav ki - cho amar la•hem va•ya•a•mi•noo va•ka•toov oo•vid•var Yeshua asher di•ber.

Rabbinic Jewish Commentary

and they believed the Scripture; that spoke of his resurrection, Psa_16:10, and on the third day, Hos_6:2.

"For You will not leave My soul in Sheol; You will not give Your Holy One to see corruption." Psa_16:10

The Jews (i) say, that

"For three days the soul/body goes to the grave, thinking the body may return; but when it sees the figure of the face changed, it goes away, and leaves it, as it is said, Job_14:22."

So of Jonah's being three days and three nights in the whale's belly, they say (k),

"These are the three days a man is in the grave, and his bowels burst; and after three days that defilement is turned upon his face."

(i) Bereshit Rabba, sect. 100. fol. 88. 2. & T. Hieros. Moed Katon, fol. 82. 2. (k) Zohar in Exod. fol. 78. 2.

---

23. Now when he was in Jerusalem at the passover, in the feast day, many believed in his name, when they saw the miracles which he did.

23. Ὡς δὲ ἦν ἐν τοῖς Ἱεροσολύμοις ἐν τῷ Πάσχα, ἐν τῇ ἑορτῇ, πολλοὶ ἐπίστευσαν εἰς τὸ ὄνομα αὐτοῦ, θεωροῦντες αὐτοῦ τὰ σημεῖα ἃ ἐποίει.

23. 'Os de ein en tois 'Yerosolumois en to Pascha, en tei 'eortei, polloi episteusan eis to onoma autou, theorountes autou ta seimeia 'a epoiei.

Hebrew/Transliteration

כג. וַיְהִי בִּהְיוֹתוֹ בִירוּשָׁלַיִם בְּחַג-הַפֶּסַח וַיַּאֲמִינוּ רַבִּים בִּשְׁמוֹ כִּי רָאוּ אֶת-הָאֹתוֹת אֲשֶׁר עָשָׂה לְעֵינֵיהֶם:

23. Vay•hi bi•hee•yo•to vi•Ye•roo•sha•la•yim be•chag - ha•Pe•sach va•ya•a•mi•noo ra•bim bish•mo ki ra•oo et - ha•o•tot asher asa le•ey•ne•hem.

Rabbinic Jewish Commentary

in the feast day; either on the day the Chagigah was eaten, which was sometimes emphatically called "the feast", as in Num_28:16, "and in the fourteenth day of the first month, is the passover of the LORD; and in the fifteenth day of this month, *is* the feast"; the passover lamb was eaten on the fourteenth day of the month "Nisan", and the "Chagigah" was on the fifteenth; in the former only a lamb was eaten, in the other, cattle out of the herds; hence mention is made, both of flocks and herds, for the keeping the passover, Deu_16:2. Jarchi's note upon the place is, that the herds were for the Chagigah, with which the Talmud (l) agrees; and Jonathan ben Uzziel paraphrases the words thus,

"And ye shall slay the passover before the Lord your God, between the evenings, and the sheep and oxen on the morrow, in that very day, for the joy of the feast;"

For it was observed with great joy and mirth: and the rather this is here meant, since the "Chagigah" is not only called "the feast", but this here is distinguished from the passover, as that is in the passage above cited, Num_28:16. For the passover here, seems to be the general name for the whole seven days of the festival; and the feast to be the particular feast of the first day of it, which was the fifteenth; to which may be added, that on this day all the males made their appearance in court. (m)

(l) Pesachim, fol. 70. 2. (m) Maimon. Hilch. Chagigah, c. 1. sect. 1.

---

24. But Jesus did not commit himself unto them, because he knew all men,

Greek/Transliteration

24. Αὐτὸς δὲ ὁ Ἰησοῦς οὐκ ἐπίστευεν ἑαυτὸν αὐτοῖς, διὰ τὸ αὐτὸν γινώσκειν πάντας,

24. Autos de 'o Yeisous ouk episteuen 'eauton autois, dya to auton ginoskein pantas,

Hebrew/Transliteration

כד. וְיֵשׁוּעַ לֹא הֶאֱמִין לָהֶם יַעַן יָדַע אֶת-יֵצֶר כֻּלָם:

24. Ve•Yeshua lo he•e•min la•hem ya•an ya•da et - ye•tzer koo•lam.

Rabbinic Jewish Commentary

For he knew not only all persons, but παντα, "all things", as some copies read here.

---

25. And needed not that any should testify of man: for he knew what was in man.

Greek/Transliteration

25. καὶ ὅτι οὐ χρείαν εἶχεν ἵνα τις μαρτυρήσῃ περὶ τοῦ ἀνθρώπου· αὐτὸς γὰρ ἐγίνωσκεν τί ἦν ἐν τῷ ἀνθρώπῳ.

25. kai 'oti ou chreian eichen 'ina tis martureisei peri tou anthropou. autos gar eginosken ti ein en to anthropo.

Hebrew/Transliteration

כה. וּבְיַעַן לֹא בִקֵּשׁ עֵדוּת אִישׁ בְּאִישׁ כִּי אֶת-מַחְשְׁבוֹת אָדָם הוּא הָיָה מֵבִין:

25. Oov•ya•an lo vi•kesh e•doot eesh be•eesh ki et - mach•she•vot adam hoo ha•ya me•vin.

Rabbinic Jewish Commentary

Of this or the other man, that he was a good or a bad man; he needed no proofs to be made, or testimonies bore, or evidence given of men's characters and actions; he was of quick understanding, and could distinguish at once between a wicked man and a good man; and so had the characteristic which the Jews require of the Messiah; for they rejected Bar Cozba from being the Messiah, and slew him, because he could not smell, referring to Isa_11:3, or discern a bad man from a good man (n); but this Yeshua could do, without any external evidence.

for he knew what was in man; which none but the spirit of a man can know; his inward thoughts, the secrets of the heart; thus Yeshua knew the thoughts of the Scribes and Pharisees, Mat_9:4, being a discerner of the thoughts, and intents of the heart, Heb_4:12.

This Apollonius Tyaneus, the ape of Yeshua, ascribed to himself (o); but is what is peculiar to God; and Yeshua being God, knows all that is in man.

(n) T. Bab. Sanhedrin, fol. 93. 2. (o) Philostrat. Vit. Apollonii, l. 1. c. 13.

John, Chapter 3

1. There was a man of the Pharisees, named Nicodemus, a ruler of the Jews:

Greek/Transliteration
1. Ἦν δὲ ἄνθρωπος ἐκ τῶν Φαρισαίων, Νικόδημος ὄνομα αὐτῷ, ἄρχων τῶν Ἰουδαίων·

1. Ein de anthropos ek ton Pharisaion, Nikodeimos onoma auto, archon ton Youdaion.

Hebrew/Transliteratioin
א. וַיְהִי אִישׁ מִן-הַפְּרוּשִׁים וּשְׁמוֹ נַקְדִּימוֹן קְצִין הַיְּהוּדִים:

1. Vay•hi eesh min - ha•P`roo•shim oo•sh`mo Nak•di•mon k`tzin ha•Ye•hoo•dim.

Rabbinic Jewish Commentary
"Nicodemon ben Gorion", the brother of Josephus ben Gorion (p), the writer of the Wars and Antiquities of the Jews; and there are some things which make it probable, that he was the same with this Nicodemus; for the Nicodemon the Jews speak so much of, lived in this age; as appears, not only from his being the brother of Josephus, but also from his being contemporary with R. Jochanan ben Zaccai, who lived in this time, and until the destruction of the temple; since these two are said (q) to be together at a feast, made for the circumcision of a child. Moreover, he is represented as very rich, and is said to be one of the three rich men in Jerusalem (r), and who was able to have maintained מדינה, a city ten years (s); and they speak of his daughter, as exceeding rich

The Jewish Encyclopedia says,

"Prominent member of the Sanhedrin, and a man of wealth; lived in Jerusalem in the first century C.E. . . .That the man brought into such prominence in the fourth Gospel must have been a well-known figure of Jewish society at the time is evident. In all probability he is identical with the Talmudical Nicodemus ben Gorion, a popular saint noted for his miraculous powers; and this would explain also the reference to "heavenly things" in Yeshua' arguments with him (John iii. 12). (*Jewish Encyclopedia, Nicodemus*)

(p) Ganz Tzemach David, par. 1. fol. 25. 1. Shalshalet Hakabala, fol. 19. 1. (q) Pirke Eliezer, c. 2. & Juchasin, fol. 23. 2. (r) T. Bab. Gittin, fol. 56. 1. (s) Midrash Kohelet, fol. 75. 4.

---

2. The same came to Jesus by night, and said unto him, Rabbi, we know that thou art a teacher come from God: for no man can do these miracles that thou doest, except God be with him.

Greek/Transliteration

2. οὗτος ἦλθεν πρὸς αὐτὸν νυκτός, καὶ εἶπεν αὐτῷ, Ῥαββί, οἴδαμεν ὅτι ἀπὸ θεοῦ ἐλήλυθας διδάσκαλος· οὐδεὶς γὰρ ταῦτα τὰ σημεῖα δύναται ποιεῖν ἃ σὺ ποιεῖς, ἐὰν μὴ ᾖ ὁ θεὸς μετ᾽ αὐτοῦ.

2. 'outos eilthen pros auton nuktos, kai eipen auto, 'Rabbi, oidamen 'oti apo theou eleiluthas didaskalos. oudeis gar tauta ta seimeia dunatai poiein 'a su poieis, ean mei ei 'o theos met autou.

Hebrew/Transliteration

ב. הוּא בָא אֶל-יֵשׁוּעַ לַיְלָה וַיֹּאמֶר אֵלָיו רַבִּי יָדַעְנוּ כִּי מֵאֵת אֱלֹהִים בָּאתָ לְמוֹרֶה לָנוּ כִּי אֵין לְאֵל יַד-אִישׁ:לַעֲשׂוֹת אֶת-הָאֹתוֹת אֲשֶׁר אַתָּה עֹשֶׂה בִּלְתִּי אִם-אֱלֹהִים עִמּוֹ

2. Hoo va el - Yeshua lai•la va•yo•mer elav Rabbi ya•da•a•noo ki me•et Elohim ba•ta le•mo•re la•noo ki eyn le•el yad - eesh la•a•sot et - ha•o•tot asher ata o•se bil•tee eem - Elohim ee•mo.

Rabbinic Jewish Commentary

It was very common with the Jewish Rabbi's, to meet and converse together, and study the law in the night.

"R. Aba rose, בפלגות ליליא, "in the middle of the night", and the rest of the companions, to study in the law (e)."

And it is often (f) said of R. Simeon ben Joehal, and Eleazar his son, that they sat in the night and laboured in the law; and it was reckoned very commendable so to do, and highly pleasing to God: it is said (g),

"Whoever studies in the law in the night, the holy blessed God draws a thread of mercy upon him in the day:"

And likewise (h), that

"Every one that studies in the law in the night, the Shekinah is over against him."

But it seems, the Babylonian Jews did not study in the law in the night (i): it might seem a needless question to ask, whether Nicodemus came alone, or not, were it not that according to the Jewish canon (k) a scholar might not go out in the night alone, because of suspicion.

Salutations among the Jews, were forbidden in the night (l);

"Says R. Jochanan, it is forbidden a man to salute his neighbour in the night, lest it should be a demon:"

we know that thou art a teacher come from God; the Jews expected the Messiah as a teacher, which they might learn from many prophecies, as from Isa_2:2. Upon the first of which, and on that passage in it, "he will teach us of his ways",

A noted commentator (m) of theirs has this remark; המורה, "the teacher", he is the King Messiah."

And the Targum on Joe_2:23 paraphrases the words thus:

"O ye children of Zion, rejoice and be glad in the word of the Lord your God, for he will return ית מלפכון, "your teacher" to you."

(e) Zohar in Exod. fol. 84. 1. (f) Ib. fol. 8S. 2. in Lev. fol. 5. 3, 4. & 10. 1. & passim. (g) T. Bab. Chagiga, fol. 12. 2. Avoda Zara, fol. 3. 2. Maimon. Hilch. Talmud Tora, c. 3. sect. 13. (h) T. Bab. Tamid. foi. 32. 2. (i) T. Bab. Taanith, fol. 9. 2. (k) T. Bab. Cholin, fol. 91. 1. Piske Tosephot Pesach, art. 12. & Maimon. Hilch, Deyot. c. 5. sect. 9. (l) T. Bab. Sanhedrin, fol. 44. 1. & Megilla, fol. 3. 1. & Piske Tosephot Megilla, art. 4. & in Yebamot, art. 238. (m) R David Kimchi in loc.

---

3. Jesus answered and said unto him, Verily, verily, I say unto thee, Except a man be born again, he cannot see the kingdom of God.

Greek/Transliteration
3. Ἀπεκρίθη ὁ Ἰησοῦς καὶ εἶπεν αὐτῷ, Ἀμὴν ἀμὴν λέγω σοι, ἐὰν μή τις γεννηθῇ ἄνωθεν, οὐ δύναται ἰδεῖν τὴν βασιλείαν τοῦ θεοῦ.

3. Apekrithei 'o Yeisous kai eipen auto, Amein amein lego soi, ean mei tis genneithei anothen, ou dunatai idein tein basileian tou theou.

Hebrew/Transliteration
ג. וַיַּעַן יֵשׁוּעַ וַיֹּאמֶר אֵלָיו אָמֵן אָמֵן אֲנִי אֹמֵר לָךְ אִם-לֹא יִוָּלֵד אִישׁ מִמָּקוֹר עַל לֹא-יוּכַל לִרְאוֹת אֶת-מַלְכוּת הָאֱלֹהִים:

3. Va•ya•an Yeshua va•yo•mer elav Amen amen ani o•mer lach eem - lo yi•va•led eesh mim•kor al lo - yoo•chal lir•ot et - mal•choot ha•Elohim.

Rabbinic Jewish Commentary
The Jews have a frequent saying (p), that

"One that is made a proselyte, כקטון שנולד דמי, "Is like a child new born".

(p) T. Bab. Yebamot, fol. 22. 1. 48. 2. 62. 1. & 97. 2.

---

4. Nicodemus saith unto him, How can a man be born when he is old? can he enter the second time into his mother's womb, and be born?

---

4. Λέγει πρὸς αὐτὸν ὁ Νικόδημος, Πῶς δύναται ἄνθρωπος γεννηθῆναι γέρων ὤν; Μὴ δύναται εἰς τὴν κοιλίαν τῆς μητρὸς αὐτοῦ δεύτερον εἰσελθεῖν καὶ γεννηθῆναι;

4. Legei pros auton 'o Nikodeimos, Pos dunatai anthropos genneitheinai geron on? Mei dunatai eis tein koilian teis meitros autou deuteron eiselthein kai genneitheinai?

ד. וַיֹּאמֶר אֵלָיו נַקְדִּימוֹן אֵיכָה יוּכַל אִישׁ לְהִוָּלֵד וְהוּא זָקֵן הֲכִי יוּכַל לָשׁוּב לְרֶחֶם אִמּוֹ וּלְהִוָּלֵד שֵׁנִית:

4. Va•yo•mer elav Nak•di•mon ey•cha yoo•chal eesh le•hi•va•led ve•hoo za•ken ha•chi yoo•chal la•shoov le•re•chem ee•mo ool•hi•va•led she•nit?

Rabbinic Jewish Commentary
"They asked the Rabbi of Lublin: "Why is it that in the holy Book of Splendor, the turning to God which corresponds to the emanation 'understanding' is called 'Mother'? He explained: "when a man confesses and repents, when his heart accepts Understanding and is converted to it, he becomes like a new-born child, and his own turning to God is his mother."
(*Tales of the Hasidim, Early Masters, Martin Buber, Schocken Books, pg. 314*)

---

5. Jesus answered, Verily, verily, I say unto thee, Except a man be born of water and of the Spirit, he cannot enter into the kingdom of God.

Greek/Transliteration
5. ᾿Απεκρίθη ᾿Ιησοῦς, ᾿Αμὴν ἀμὴν λέγω σοι, ἐὰν μή τις γεννηθῇ ἐξ ὕδατος καὶ πνεύματος, οὐ δύναται εἰσελθεῖν εἰς τὴν βασιλείαν τοῦ θεοῦ.

5. Apekrithei Yeisous, Amein amein lego soi, ean mei tis genneithei ex 'udatos kai pneumatos, ou dunatai eiselthein eis tein basileian tou theou.

Hebrew/Transliteration
ה. וַיַּעַן יֵשׁוּעַ אָמֵן אָמֵן אֲנִי אֹמֵר לָךְ אִם-לֹא יִוָּלֵד אִישׁ מִן-הַמַּיִם וּמִן-הָרוּחַ לֹא-יוּכַל לָבֹא אֶל-מַלְכוּת הָאֱלֹהִים:

5. Va•ya•an Yeshua Amen amen ani o•mer lach eem - lo yi•va•led eesh min - ha•ma•yim oo•min - ha•Roo•ach lo - yoo•chal la•vo el - mal•choot ha•Elohim.

Rabbinic Jewish Commentary
The Vulgate Latin and Ethiopic versions read, "the Holy Spirit", and so Nonnus; and who doubtless is intended: by "water", is not meant material water, or baptismal water; for water baptism is never expressed by water only, without some additional word, which shows, that the ordinance of water baptism is intended.

6. That which is born of the flesh is flesh; and that which is born of the Spirit is spirit.

Greek/Transliteration
6. Τὸ γεγεννημένον ἐκ τῆς σαρκὸς σάρξ ἐστιν· καὶ τὸ γεγεννημένον ἐκ τοῦ πνεύματος πνεῦμά ἐστιν.

6. To gegenneimenon ek teis sarkos sarx estin. kai to gegenneimenon ek tou pneumatos pneuma estin.

Hebrew/Transliteration
:ו. הַנּוֹלָד מִן-הַבָּשָׂר בָּשָׂר הוּא וְהַנּוֹלָד מִן-הָרוּחַ רוּחַ הוּא

6. Ha•no•lad min - ha•ba•sar ba•sar hoo ve•ha•no•lad min - ha•Roo•ach Roo•ach hoo.

---

7. Marvel not that I said unto thee, Ye must be born again.

Greek/Transliteration
7. Μὴ θαυμάσῃς ὅτι εἶπόν σοι, Δεῖ ὑμᾶς γεννηθῆναι ἄνωθεν.

7. Mei thaumaseis 'oti eipon soi, Dei 'umas genneitheinai anothen.

Hebrew/Transliteration
:ז. אַל-תִּתְמַהּ עַל-אֲשֶׁר אָמַרְתִּי לָךְ כִּי נָכוֹן לָכֶם לְהִוָּלֵד מִמְּקוֹר עַל

7. Al - tit•ma al - asher amar•ti lach ki na•chon la•chem le•hi•va•led mim•kor al.

Rabbinic Jewish Commentary
"This day have I given birth to you" (Ps. 2:7). These words refer to Mashiach who is in a realm beyond time. There everything finds healing. Time past is annulled completely... There is only today. Today you were born. Literally! All that is wrong with the world is a part of the "Evil work that is done beneath the sun" in the time-bound world. . . what remedy is there for all the days and years, all the time that [one] wasted in wrongdoing? His only hope is in the realm beyond time. From there comes all healing. It will be as if he were born again today. So long as you have faith – in God, in the World to Come, and in the Messiah who is beyond time – you have eternal hope."
(Rebbe Nachman of Breslov, Meshivat Nefesh, Restore My Soul, Translated by Avraham Greenbaum, Breslov Research Institute, pg. 88-89)

---

8. The wind bloweth where it listeth, and thou hearest the sound thereof, but canst not tell whence it cometh, and whither it goeth: so is every one that is born of the Spirit.

Greek/Transliteration
8. Τὸ πνεῦμα ὅπου θέλει πνεῖ, καὶ τὴν φωνὴν αὐτοῦ ἀκούεις, ἀλλ᾽ οὐκ οἶδας πόθεν ἔρχεται καὶ ποῦ ὑπάγει· οὕτως ἐστὶν πᾶς ὁ γεγεννημένος ἐκ τοῦ πνεύματος.

8. To pneuma 'opou thelei pnei, kai tein phonein autou akoueis, all ouk oidas pothen erchetai kai pou 'upagei. 'outos estin pas 'o gegenneimenos ek tou pneumatos.

Hebrew/Transliteration
ח. הָרוּחַ נֹשֶׁבֶת אֶל-אֲשֶׁר תַּחְפֹּץ וְאַתָּה שֹׁמֵעַ אֶת-קוֹלָהּ וְלֹא תֵדַע מֵאַיִן בָּאָה וְאָן הִיא הֹלֶכֶת כְּמוֹ כֵן כָּל-הַנּוֹלָד:מִן-הָרוּחַ

8. Ha•roo•ach no•she•vet el - asher tach•potz ve•a•ta sho•me•a et - ko•la ve•lo te•da me•a•yin ba•ah ve•an hee ho•le•chet k`mo chen kol - ha•no•lad min - ha•Roo•ach.

Rabbinic Jewish Commentary
The beauty and propriety of this simile will more appear by observing, that the same Hebrew word, רוח, (Ruach) is used both for the wind, and for the Spirit of God; it is used for the "wind", in Gen_3:8; and in other places, and for the Spirit of God, in Gen_1:2, and elsewhere: and so likewise the Greek word πνευμα, is used for them both, for the wind in this place, and often for the Holy Ghost: and it may be observed, that the Holy Spirit, because of his powerful, comfortable, and quickening influences, is compared to the wind, especially to the south wind, in some passages of the Old Testament, which Christ might have in view, Son_4:16.

---

9. Nicodemus answered and said unto him, How can these things be?

Greek/Transliteration
9. Ἀπεκρίθη Νικόδημος καὶ εἶπεν αὐτῷ, Πῶς δύναται ταῦτα γενέσθαι;

9. Apekrithei Nikodeimos kai eipen auto, Pos dunatai tauta genesthai?

Hebrew/Transliteration
:ט. וַיַּעַן נַקְדִּימוֹן וַיֹּאמֶר אֵלָיו אֵיכָה תִקְרֶינָה כָּאֵלֶּה

9. Va•ya•an Nak•di•mon va•yo•mer elav ey•cha tik•re•na ka•e•le?

---

10. Jesus answered and said unto him, Art thou a master of Israel, and knowest not these things?

Greek/Transliteration
10. Ἀπεκρίθη Ἰησοῦς καὶ εἶπεν αὐτῷ, Σὺ εἶ ὁ διδάσκαλος τοῦ Ἰσραήλ, καὶ ταῦτα οὐ γινώσκεις;

10. Apekrithei Yeisous kai eipen auto, Su ei 'o didaskalos tou Ysraeil, kai tauta ou ginoskeis?

Hebrew/Transliteration
י. וַיַּעַן יֵשׁוּעַ וַיֹּאמֶר אֵלָיו הֲגִדְּ מוֹרֶה בְיִשְׂרָאֵל וְאֶת-אֵלֶּה לֹא יָדָעְתָּ:

10. Va•ya•an Yeshua va•yo•mer elav hin•cha mo•re ve•Israel ve•et - ele lo ya•da•ata.

Rabbinic Jewish Commentary
art thou a master in Israel? or "of Israel", as all the Oriental versions render it, as it literally may be rendered he was one of the חכמי ישראל, "wise men", or "Rabbi's of Israel" (r), so often mentioned by the Jews. One of the Jewish Rabbi's was answered, by a boy, just in such language as is here used; who, not understanding the direction he gave him about the way into the city, said to him, אתה הוא חכם של ישראל, "art thou he, a Rabbi?", or "master of Israel?" did not I say to thee so? (s). He was not a common teacher; not a teacher of babes, nor a teacher in their synagogues, or in their "Midrashim", or divinity schools, but in their great Sanhedrim.

What Nicodemus should have understood, about what Yeshua was saying, comes right out of Ezek_36:25-27

"Then will I sprinkle clean water upon you, and ye shall be clean: from all your filthiness, and from all your idols, will I cleanse you. A new heart also will I give you, and a new spirit will I put within you: and I will take away the stony heart out of your flesh, and I will give you an heart of flesh. And I will put my spirit within you, and cause you to walk in my statutes, and ye shall keep my judgments, and do them"

Kimchi and Jarchi interpret of purification by atonement; and the Targum is,

"I will forgive your sins, as one is cleansed by the water of sprinkling, and the ashes of a heifer, which is for a sin offering:"

The Targum paraphrases it,

"A heart fearing, and a spirit fearing;"

This is interpreted, in the Talmud (n), of the evil imagination, or corruption of nature; and is one of the names of it, a stone; and it refers, it is said (o), to the time or world to come, the days of the Messiah.

(n) T. Bab. Succah, fol. 52. 1. (o) Debarim Rabba, fol. 242. 2. & Shirhashirim Rabba, fol. 3. 2. (r) Derech Eretz, fol. 18. 1. (s) Echa Rabbati, fol. 44. 4.

---

11. Verily, verily, I say unto thee, We speak that we do know, and testify that we have seen; and ye receive not our witness.

Greek/Transliteration
11. Ἀμὴν ἀμὴν λέγω σοι ὅτι ὃ οἴδαμεν λαλοῦμεν, καὶ ὃ ἑωράκαμεν μαρτυροῦμεν· καὶ τὴν μαρτυρίαν ἡμῶν οὐ λαμβάνετε.

11. Amein amein lego soi 'oti 'o oidamen laloumen, kai 'o 'eorakamen marturoumen. kai tein marturian 'eimon ou lambanete.

Hebrew/Transliteration
יא. אָמֵן אָמֵן אֲנִי אֹמֵר לָךְ כִּי אֶת אֲשֶׁר-יָדַעְנוּ נְדַבֵּר וְאֶת אֲשֶׁר-רָאִינוּ נָעִיד וְאַתֶּם לֹא תִשְׁמְעוּ לְעֵדוּתֵנוּ:

11. Amen amen ani o•mer lach ki et asher - ya•da•a•noo n`da•ber ve•et asher - ra•ee•noo na•eed ve•a•tem lo tish•me•oo le•e•doo•te•noo.

---

12. If I have told you earthly things, and ye believe not, how shall ye believe, if I tell you of heavenly things?

Greek/Transliteration
12. Εἰ τὰ ἐπίγεια εἶπον ὑμῖν καὶ οὐ πιστεύετε, πῶς, ἐὰν εἴπω ὑμῖν τὰ ἐπουράνια, πιστεύσετε;

12. Ei ta epigeya eipon 'umin kai ou pisteuete, pos, ean eipo 'umin ta epouranya, pisteusete?

Hebrew/Transliteration
יב. אִם בִּדְבָרִים שְׁפָלִים לֹא הֶאֱמַנְתֶּם לִי אֵיךְ תַּאֲמִינוּ לִי כִּי אַגִּיד רָאמוֹת:

12. Eem bid•va•rim sh`fa•lim lo he•e•man•tem li eych ta•a•mi•noo li ki agid ra•mot?

---

13. And no man hath ascended up to heaven, but he that came down from heaven, even the Son of man which is in heaven.

13. Καὶ οὐδεὶς ἀναβέβηκεν εἰς τὸν οὐρανόν, εἰ μὴ ὁ ἐκ τοῦ οὐρανοῦ καταβάς, ὁ υἱὸς τοῦ ἀνθρώπου ὁ ὢν ἐν τῷ οὐρανῷ.

13. Kai oudeis anabebeiken eis ton ouranon, ei mei 'o ek tou ouranou katabas, 'o 'wios tou anthropou 'o on en to ourano.

יג. וְאִישׁ לֹא-עָלָה לַמָּרוֹם בִּלְתִּי הוּא אֲשֶׁר-יָרַד מִמָּרוֹם הֲלֹא הוּא בֶּן-הָאָדָם אֲשֶׁר בַּשָּׁמָיִם:

13. Ve•eesh lo - ala la•ma•rom bil•tee hoo asher - ya•rad mi•ma•rom ha•lo hoo Ben - ha•adam asher ba•sha•ma•yim.

---

14. And as Moses lifted up the serpent in the wilderness, even so must the Son of man be lifted up:

14. Καὶ καθὼς Μωσῆς ὕψωσεν τὸν ὄφιν ἐν τῇ ἐρήμῳ, οὕτως ὑψωθῆναι δεῖ τὸν υἱὸν τοῦ ἀνθρώπου·

14. Kai kathos Moseis 'upsosen ton ophin en tei ereimo, 'outos 'upsotheinai dei ton 'wion tou anthropou.

יד. וְכַאֲשֶׁר נִשָּׂא מֹשֶׁה בַּמִּדְבָּר אֶת-הַנָּחָשׁ עַל-הַנֵּס כֵּן יִנָּשֵׂא בֶּן-הָאָדָם:

14. Ve•cha•a•sher ni•sa Moshe ba•mid•bar et - ha•na•chash al - ha•nes ken yi•na•se Ben - ha•adam.

Rabbinic Jewish Commentary

It is certain, that the Jews had a notion that the brazen serpent was symbolical and figurative: Philo the Jew makes it to be a symbol of fortitude and temperance (t); and the author of the apocryphal book of Wisdom (u), calls it "a sign of salvation". They thought there was something mysterious in it: hence they say (w),

"In four places it is said, "make thee". In three places it is explained, viz. Gen_6:14, and one is not explained, Num_21:8, "make thee a fiery serpent", לֹא פֵּירֵשׁ, is not explained."

And elsewhere (x) they ask,

"And could the serpent kill, or make alive? But at the time that Israel looked up, and served with their hearts their Father which is in heaven, they were healed; but if not, they were brought low."

So that the look was not merely to the brazen serpent, but to God in heaven; yea, to the word of God, his essential Logos, as say the Targumists on Num_21:9. The Jerusalem Targum paraphrases the words thus:

"And Moses made a serpent of brass, and put it upon a high place, and whoever was bitten by the serpents, and lift up his face, in prayer, to his Father which is in heaven, and looked upon the serpent of brass, lived."

And Jonathan ben Uzziel paraphrases them thus:

"And Moses made a serpent of brass, and put it upon a high place; and it was, when a serpent had bitten any man, and he looked to the serpent of brass, "and directed his heart", לשום מימרא דיי, "to the name of the word of the Lord", he lived."

And this healing they understand not only of bodily healing, but of the healing of the soul: for they observe (y), that

"As soon as they said, "we have sinned", immediately their iniquity was expiated; and they had the good news brought them "of the healing of the soul", as it is written, "make thee a seraph"; and he does not say a serpent; and this is it: "and it shall come to pass, that every one that is bitten, when he looketh upon it, shall live", רפואת הנפש, "through the healing of the soul":"

Yea, they compare the Messiah to a serpent; for so the Targum on Isa_14:29 paraphrases that passage:

"The Messiah shall come forth from Jesse's children's children; and his works shall be among you as a "flying serpent"."

And who else can be designed by the "other serpent of life" (z), and the "holy serpent" (a) they speak of, in opposition to the evil serpent that seduced Eve? And it is well known, that נחש, "a serpent", and משיח, "Messiah", are numerically, or by gematry, the same, 358; a way of interpretation, and explanation, often in use with the Jews. Now, as this serpent was lifted up on a pole on high, that every one that was bitten with the fiery serpent might look to it, and be healed;

(t) De Agricult. p. 202. & Allegor. l. 3. p. 1101, 1102, 1103, 1104. (u) C. 16. v. 6. (w) T. Hieros. Roshhashanah, fol. 59. 1. (x) Misn. Roshhashanah, c. 3. sect. 3. (y) Tzeror Hammor, fol. 123. 2. (z) Zohar in Gen fol. 36. 2. (a) Tikkune Zohar in Jetzira, p. 134.

---

15. That whosoever believeth in him should not perish, but have eternal life.

Greek/Transliteration
15. ἵνα πᾶς ὁ πιστεύων εἰς αὐτὸν μὴ ἀπόληται, ἀλλ᾽ ἔχῃ ζωὴν αἰώνιον.

---

15. 'ina pas 'o pisteuon eis auton mei apoleitai, all echei zoein aionion.

Hebrew/Transliteration
טו. לְמַעַן אֲשֶׁר לֹא יֹאבַד כָּל-הַמַּאֲמִין בּוֹ כִּי אִם יִמְצָא בּוֹ חַיֵּי עוֹלָם:

15. Le•ma•an asher lo yo•vad kol - ha•ma•a•min bo ki eem yim•tza vo cha•yey o•lam.

---

16. For God so loved the world, that he gave his only begotten Son, that whosoever believeth in him should not perish, but have everlasting life.

Greek/Transliteration
16. Οὕτως γὰρ ἠγάπησεν ὁ θεὸς τὸν κόσμον, ὥστε τὸν υἱὸν αὐτοῦ τὸν μονογενῆ ἔδωκεν, ἵνα πᾶς ὁ πιστεύων εἰς αὐτὸν μὴ ἀπόληται, ἀλλ᾽ ἔχῃ ζωὴν αἰώνιον.

16. 'Outos gar eigapeisen 'o theos ton kosmon, 'oste ton 'wion autou ton monogenei edoken, 'ina pas 'o pisteuon eis auton mei apoleitai, all echei zoein aionion.

Hebrew/Transliteration
טז. כִּי-כֵן אֹהֵב אֱלֹהִים אֶת-הָעוֹלָם עַד-אֲשֶׁר נָתַן בַּעֲדוֹ אֶת-בְּנוֹ אֶת-יְחִידוֹ וְכָל-הַמַּאֲמִין בּוֹ לֹא-יֹאבַד כִּי בוֹ:יִמְצָא חַיֵּי עוֹלָם

16. Ki - chen o•hev Elohim et - ha•o•lam ad - asher na•tan ba•a•do et - B`no et - ye•chi•do ve•chol - ha•ma•a•min bo lo - yo•vad ki vo yim•tza cha•yey o•lam.

Rabbinic Jewish Commentary
The Jews had the same distinction we have now, the church and the world; the former they took to themselves, and the latter they gave to all the nations around: hence we often meet with this distinction, Israel, and the nations of the world; on those words,

"Let them bring forth their witness", that they may be justified, Isa_43:9 (say (b) the Rabbi's) these are Israel; "or let them hear and say it is truth", these are "the nations of the world"."

And again (c), "The holy, blessed God said to Israel, when I judge Israel, I do not judge them as "the nations of the world":"

And so in a multitude of places: and it should be observed, that Yeshua was now discoursing with a Jewish Rabbi, and that he is opposing a commonly received notion of theirs, that when the Messiah came, the Gentiles should have no benefit or advantage by him, only the Israelites; so far should they be from it, that, according to their sense, the most dreadful judgments, calamities, and curses, should befall them; yea, hell and eternal damnation.

"There is a place (they say (d),) the name of which is "Hadrach", Zec_9:1. This is the King Messiah, who is, חד ורך, "sharp and tender"; sharp to "the nations", and tender to "Israel"."

And so of the "Sun of righteousness", in Mal_4:2, they say (e), "There is healing for the Israelites in it: but the idolatrous nations shall be burnt by it."

And that (f). "There is mercy for Israel, but judgment for the rest of the nations." And on those words in Isa_21:12, "The morning cometh", and also the night, they observe (g),

"The morning is for the righteous, and the night for the wicked; the morning is for Israel, and the night for "the nations of the world"."

And again (h), "In the time to come, (the times of the Messiah,) the holy, blessed God will bring "darkness" upon "the nations", and will enlighten Israel, as it is said, Isa_60:2."

Once more (i), "In the time to come, the holy, blessed God will bring the nations of the world, and will cast them into the midst of hell under the Israelites, as it is said, Isa_43:3."

To which may be added that denunciation of theirs (k). "woe to the nations of the world, who perish, and they know not that they perish: in the time that the sanctuary was standing, the altar atoned for them; but now who shall atone for them?"

Now, in opposition to such a notion, Yeshua addresses this Jew; and it is as if he had said, you Rabbi's say, that when the Messiah comes, only the Israelites, the peculiar favourites of God, shall share in the blessings that come by, and with him; and that the Gentiles shall reap no advantage by him, being hated of God, and rejected of him: but I tell you, God has so loved the Gentiles, as well as the Jews.

(b) T. Bab. Avoda Zara, fol. 2. 1. (c) Ib. fol. 4. 1. Vid. T. Bab. Sanhedrin, fol. 91. 2. & Bereshit Rabba, fol. 11. 3. (d) Shirhashirim Rabba, fol. 24. 1. Jarchi & Kimchi in Zech. ix. 1. (e) Zohar in Gen. fol. 112. 2. (f) Zohar in Exod. fol. 15. 1, 2. (g) T. Hieros. Taaniot, fol. 64. 1. (h) Shemot Rabba, sect. 14. fol. 99. 4. (i) Ib sect. 11. fol. 98. 3. (k) T. Bab. Succa, fol. 55. 2.

---

17. For God sent not his Son into the world to condemn the world; but that the world through him might be saved.

Greek/Transliteration
17. Οὐ γὰρ ἀπέστειλεν ὁ θεὸς τὸν υἱὸν αὐτοῦ εἰς τὸν κόσμον ἵνα κρίνῃ τὸν κόσμον, ἀλλ᾽ ἵνα σωθῇ ὁ κόσμος δι᾽ αὐτοῦ.

---

17. Ou gar apesteilen 'o theos ton 'wion autou eis ton kosmon 'ina krinei ton kosmon, all 'ina sothei 'o kosmos di autou.

Hebrew/Transliteration

יז. כִּי לֹא-שָׁלַח אֱלֹהִים אֶת-בְּנוֹ אֶל-הָעוֹלָם לְהַרְשִׁיעוֹ בְּהִשָּׁפְטוֹ כִּי אִם-לְמַעַן יִוָּשַׁע בּוֹ הָעוֹלָם:

17. Ki lo - sha•lach Elohim et - B`no el - ha•o•lam le•har•shi•o be•hi•shaf•to ki eem - le•ma•an yi•va•sha bo ha•o•lam.

TaNaKh-Old Testament

"And he said, It is a light thing that thou shouldest be my servant to raise up the tribes of Jacob, and to restore the preserved of Israel: I will also give thee for a light to the Gentiles, that thou mayest be my salvation (Yeshua) unto the end of the earth."

---

18. He that believeth on him is not condemned: but he that believeth not is condemned already, because he hath not believed in the name of the only begotten Son of God.

Greek/Transliteration

18. Ὁ πιστεύων εἰς αὐτὸν οὐ κρίνεται· ὁ δὲ μὴ πιστεύων ἤδη κέκριται, ὅτι μὴ πεπίστευκεν εἰς τὸ ὄνομα τοῦ μονογενοῦς υἱοῦ τοῦ θεοῦ.

18. 'O pisteuon eis auton ou krinetai. 'o de mei pisteuon eidei kekritai, 'oti mei pepisteuken eis to onoma tou monogenous 'wiou tou theou.

Hebrew/Transliteration

יח. הַמַּאֲמִין בּוֹ לֹא יֶאְשַׁם וַאֲשֶׁר לֹא-יַאֲמִין בּוֹ אַשְׁמָתוֹ עָלָיו מִנִּי אָז כִּי לֹא-הֶאֱמִין בְּשֵׁם הַבֵּן הַיָּחִיד לֵאלֹהִים:

18. Ha•ma•a•min bo lo ye•e•sham va•a•sher lo - ya•a•min bo ash•ma•to alav mi•ni az ki lo - he•e•min be•shem ha•Ben ha•ya•chid le•Elohim.

---

19. And this is the condemnation, that light is come into the world, and men loved darkness rather than light, because their deeds were evil.

Greek/Transliteration

19. Αὕτη δέ ἐστιν ἡ κρίσις, ὅτι τὸ φῶς ἐλήλυθεν εἰς τὸν κόσμον, καὶ ἠγάπησαν οἱ ἄνθρωποι μᾶλλον τὸ σκότος ἢ τὸ φῶς· ἦν γὰρ πονηρὰ αὐτῶν τὰ ἔργα.

19. 'Autei de estin 'ei krisis, 'oti to phos eleiluthen eis ton kosmon, kai eigapeisan 'oi anthropoid mallon to skotos ei to phos. ein gar poneira auton ta erga.

Hebrew/Transliteration

יט. וְזֶה הוּא הַמִּשְׁפָּט כִּי הָאוֹר בָּא אֶל־הָעוֹלָם וּבְנֵי הָאָדָם אָהֲבוּ אֶת־הַחשֶׁךְ מִן־הָאוֹר כִּי רָעִים מַעֲשֵׂיהֶם:

19. Ve•ze hoo ha•mish•pat ki ha•or ba el - ha•o•lam oov•ney ha•a•dam a•ha•voo et - ha•cho•shech min - ha•or ki ra•eem ma•a•sey•hem.

Rabbinic Jewish Commentary

The Old Testament, which speak of him under the metaphor of the sun, as Psa_84:11, and represent him as the light; and the Jews (t) themselves say, that light is one of the names of the Messiah; and God himself is called by them, the light of the world (u): and likewise he may have regard to those pompous titles and characters, which the Jewish Rabbi's assumed arrogantly to themselves, and oppose himself to them; for they not only called Moses their master, אור העולם, "the light of the world" (w), and also the law of Moses (x), but their Rabbi and Rabbi's.

The Jews, the greater part of them, preferred the darkness of the ceremonial law, and the Mosaic dispensation, and even the traditions of their elders, before the clear Gospel revelation made by Yeshua.

(t) Bereshit Rabba, fol. 1. 3. Echa Rabbati, fol. 50. 2. & Jarchi in Psal xliii. 3. (u) Bemidbar Rabba, sect. 15. fol. 217. 2. (w) Tzeror Hammor, fol. 114. 3. (x) T. Bab. Bava Bathra, fol. 4. 1.

---

20. For every one that doeth evil hateth the light, neither cometh to the light, lest his deeds should be reproved.

Greek/Transliteration

20. Πᾶς γὰρ ὁ φαῦλα πράσσων μισεῖ τὸ φῶς, καὶ οὐκ ἔρχεται πρὸς τὸ φῶς, ἵνα μὴ ἐλεγχθῇ τὰ ἔργα αὐτοῦ.

20. Pas gar 'o phaula prasson misei to phos, kai ouk erchetai pros to phos, 'ina mei elegchthei ta erga autou.

Hebrew/Transliteration

כ. כִּי כָל־פֹּעֵל אָוֶן שֹׂנֵא הוּא אֶת־הָאוֹר וְלֹא יָבֹא אֶל־הָאוֹר לִבְלִי יִבָּחֲנוּ מַעֲשָׂיו:

20. Ki chol - po•el aven so•ne hoo et - ha•or ve•lo ya•vo el - ha•or liv•li yi•ba•cha•noo ma•a•sav.

---

21. But he that doeth truth cometh to the light, that his deeds may be made manifest, that they are wrought in God.

21. Ὁ δὲ ποιῶν τὴν ἀλήθειαν ἔρχεται πρὸς τὸ φῶς, ἵνα φανερωθῇ αὐτοῦ τὰ ἔργα, ὅτι ἐν θεῷ ἐστιν εἰργασμένα.

21. 'O de poion tein aleitheyan erchetai pros to phos, 'ina phanerothei autou ta erga, 'oti en theo estin eirgasmena.

כא. אֲבָל פֹּעֵל אֱמֶת יָבֹא אֶל-הָאוֹר לְמַעַן יִוָּדְעוּ מַעֲשָׂיו אֲשֶׁר עָשָׂה לִפְנֵי הָאֱלֹהִים:

21. Aval po•el emet ya•vo el - ha•or le•ma•an yi•vad•oo ma•a•sav asher asa lif•ney ha•Elohim.

---

22. After these things came Jesus and his disciples into the land of Judaea; and there he tarried with them, and baptized.

22. Μετὰ ταῦτα ἦλθεν ὁ Ἰησοῦς καὶ οἱ μαθηταὶ αὐτοῦ εἰς τὴν Ἰουδαίαν γῆν· καὶ ἐκεῖ διέτριβεν μετ' αὐτῶν καὶ ἐβάπτιζεν.

22. Meta tauta eilthen 'o Yeisous kai 'oi matheitai autou eis tein Youdaian gein. kai ekei dietriben met auton kai ebaptizen.

כב. אַחַר הַדְּבָרִים הָאֵלֶּה הָלַךְ יֵשׁוּעַ וְתַלְמִידָיו אֶל-אֶרֶץ יְהוּדָה וַיֵּשֶׁב עִמָּהֶם וַיִּטַּבֵּל שָׁם:

22. Achar ha•d`va•rim ha•e•le ha•lach Yeshua ve•tal•mi•dav el - e•retz Yehooda va•ye•shev ee•ma•hem vay•ta•bel sham.

Rabbinic Jewish Commentary
came Jesus and his disciples, into the land of Judea; or "into Judea the country", having been in Jerusalem, the city part or chief city in Judea; so that the country is distinguished from, and opposed to the city. And thus, a countryman, and a Jerusalemite, or citizen of Jerusalem, are distinguished (l);

"If, הקרתני, "A countryman", (one that lives in the country any where in the land of Israel out of Jerusalem (m),) receives a field, מירושלמי, "from a man of Jerusalem", the second tithes belong to the Jerusalemite; but the wise men say, the countryman may bring them up, and eat them at Jerusalem."

Or, it may be, because that Jerusalem was part of it in the tribe of Benjamin, and the other in the tribe of Judah; therefore, when Yeshua, and his disciples, left Jerusalem, they might more properly be said to come into the land of Judea. Indeed, it is commonly said by the Jews (n), that Jerusalem was not divided among the tribes, and that it did not belong to any tribe; and if so, then with greater propriety still might Yeshua be said to come into the land of Judea, when he departed from Jerusalem; unless it should be thought, that he went into Galilee, and after that came into the land of Judea.

(l) Misn. Demai, c. 6. sect. 4. (m) Maimon. Bartenora in ib. (n) T. Bab. Yoma, fol. 12. 1, & Megilla, fol. 26. 1.

---

23. And John also was baptizing in Aenon near to Salim, because there was much water there: and they came, and were baptized.

Greek/Transliteration
23. Ἦν δὲ καὶ Ἰωάννης βαπτίζων ἐν Αἰνὼν ἐγγὺς τοῦ Σαλήμ, ὅτι ὕδατα πολλὰ ἦν ἐκεῖ· καὶ παρεγίνοντο καὶ ἐβαπτίζοντο.

23. Ein de kai Yoanneis baptizon en Ainon engus tou Saleim, 'oti 'udata polla ein ekei. Kai pareginonto kai ebaptizonto.

Hebrew/Transliteration
כג. וְגַם-יוֹחָנָן הָיָה מְטַבֵּל בָּעֵת הַהִיא בְּעֵנוֹן בְּאָכָה שָׁלֵם כִּי מַיִם רַבִּים נִמְצְאוּ שָׁם וְהַבָּאִים נִטְבָּלוּ:

23. Ve•gam - Yo•cha•nan ha•ya me•ta•bel ba•et ha•hee be•Enon bo•a•cha sha•lem ki ma•yim ra•bim nim•tze•oo sham ve•ha•ba•eem nit•ba•loo.

---

24. For John was not yet cast into prison.

Greek/Transliteration
24. Οὔπω γὰρ ἦν βεβλημένος εἰς τὴν φυλακὴν ὁ Ἰωάννης.

24. Oupo gar ein bebleimenos eis tein phulakein 'o Yoanneis.

Hebrew/Transliteration
כד. כִּי עוֹד לֹא-נִתַּן יוֹחָנָן אֶל-בֵּית הַכֶּלֶא:

24. Ki od lo - ni•tan Yo•cha•nan el - beit ha•ke•le.

---

25. Then there arose a question between some of John's disciples and the Jews about purifying.

Greek/Transliteration
25. Ἐγένετο οὖν ζήτησις ἐκ τῶν μαθητῶν Ἰωάννου μετὰ Ἰουδαίου περὶ καθαρισμοῦ.

25. Egeneto oun zeiteisis ek ton matheiton Yoannou meta Youdaiou peri katharismou.

:כה. וַיְהִי-רִיב בֵּין תַּלְמִידֵי יוֹחָנָן וּבֵין אַחַד הַיְּהוּדִים עַל-דְּבַר הַטָּהֳרָה

25. Vay•hi - riv bein tal•mi•dey Yo•cha•nan oo•vein achad ha•Ye•hoo•dim al - de•var ha•ta•ha•ra.

Rabbinic Jewish Commentary

about purifying; either about the ceremonial purifications, and ablutions commanded in the law of Moses; or concerning the various washings of persons, and vessels, according to the traditions of the elders, which the Jews in common were very tenacious of; and which they thought were brought into neglect, and contempt, by the baptism of John: and this seems to have been occasioned by the baptism of Yeshua; which the Jew might improve against the disciple of John, and urge, that since another, besides his master, had set up baptizing, who could tell which was most right and safest to follow? and therefore it would have been much better, if no such rite at all had been used by any, but that the purifications required by the law of Moses, and by their elders, had been strictly and solely attended to.

---

26. And they came unto John, and said unto him, Rabbi, he that was with thee beyond Jordan, to whom thou barest witness, behold, the same baptizeth, and all men come to him.

Greek/Transliteration

26. Καὶ ἦλθον πρὸς τὸν Ἰωάννην καὶ εἶπον αὐτῷ, Ῥαββί, ὃς ἦν μετὰ σοῦ πέραν τοῦ Ἰορδάνου, ᾧ σὺ μεμαρτύρηκας, ἴδε οὗτος βαπτίζει, καὶ πάντες ἔρχονται πρὸς αὐτόν.

26. Kai eilthon pros ton Yoannein kai eipon auto, 'Rabbi, 'os ein meta sou peran tou Yordanou, 'o su memartureikas, ide 'outos baptizei, kai pantes erchontai pros auton.

Hebrew/Transliteration

כו. וַיָּבֹאוּ אֶל-יוֹחָנָן וַיֹּאמְרוּ אֵלָיו רַבֵּנוּ הָאִישׁ אֲשֶׁר הָיָה עִמְּךָ בְּעֵבֶר הַיַּרְדֵּן אֲשֶׁר הַעִידֹתָ לּוֹ הִנֵּה הוּא מְטַבֵּל:וְכֻלָּם בָּאִים אֵלָיו

26. Va•ya•vo•oo el - Yo•cha•nan va•yom•roo elav Ra•be•noo ha•eesh asher ha•ya eem•cha be•e•ver ha•Yarden asher ha•ee•dota lo hee•ne hoo me•ta•bel ve•choo•lam ba•eem elav.

Rabbinic Jewish Commentary

That he should baptize, gave them great offence; and that he was so followed, raised their envy; and his being so near to John, might add to their uneasiness. It is a rule with the Jews, that

"It is not lawful for a disciple to teach the constitutions, or sentences of the law, before his master; but must be twelve miles distant from him, as the camp of Israel."

And they say, that "A disciple that teaches before, or in the presence of his master, is guilty of death (r)." (r) T. Hieros. Sheviith, fol. 37. 3.

---

27. John answered and said, A man can receive nothing, except it be given him from heaven.

Greek/Transliteration
27. Ἀπεκρίθη Ἰωάννης καὶ εἶπεν, Οὐ δύναται ἄνθρωπος λαμβάνειν οὐδέν, ἐὰν μὴ ᾖ δεδομένον αὐτῷ ἐκ τοῦ οὐρανοῦ.

27. Apekrithei Yoanneis kai eipen, Ou dunatai anthropos lambanein ouden, ean mei ei dedomenon auto ek tou ouranou.

Hebrew/Transliteration
כז. וַיַּעַן יוֹחָנָן וַיֹּאמֶר לֹא-יוּכַל אִישׁ לָקַחַת דָּבָר אִם לֹא נִתַּן-לוֹ מִמָּרוֹם:

27. Va•ya•an Yo•cha•nan va•yo•mar lo - yoo•chal eesh la•ka•chat da•var eem lo ni•tan - lo mi•ma•rom.

Rabbinic Jewish Commentary
The Jews to call God by the name of "heaven": in this sense it is used by them, when they say (b), that such have no part in the world to come, who affirm, that the law is not מן השמים, "from heaven", that is, from God; which is exactly the phrase here: and when they observe (c), that care should be taken that a man does not pronounce שם שמים, "the name of heaven", that is, God, in vain: and when they tell (d) us of a certain man that built large buildings by the way side, and put food and drink there, so that everyone that came went in and eat, and drank, וברך לשמים, "and blessed heaven"; that is blessed, or gave thanks to God; and when they speak of (e) מיתה לשמים, "death by heaven"; that is, death which is immediately inflicted by God.

(b) T. Hieros. Sanhedrin, fol. 27. 3. Vid. ib. fol. 19. 3. T. Bab. Sanhedrin, fol. 99. 1. (c) T. Bab. Megilla, fol. 3. 1. (d) Abot. R. Nathan, c. 7. fol. 3. 2. (e) Ib. c. 11. fol. 4. 1. Vid. ib. c. 14. fol. 4. 4. & 5. 1. & c. 27. fol. 7. 1.

---

28. Ye yourselves bear me witness, that I said, I am not the Christ, but that I am sent before him.

---

28. Αὐτοὶ ὑμεῖς μαρτυρεῖτε ὅτι εἶπον, Οὐκ εἰμὶ ἐγὼ ὁ χριστός, ἀλλ᾽ ὅτι
᾽Απεσταλμένος εἰμὶ ἔμπροσθεν ἐκείνου.

28. Autoi 'umeis martureite 'oti eipon, Ouk eimi ego 'o christos, all 'oti
Apestalmenos eimi emprosthen ekeinou.

Hebrew/Transliteration
כח. אַתֶּם עֵדַי אֲשֶׁר הִגַּדְתִּי כִּי לֹא-אָנֹכִי הַמָּשִׁיחַ כִּי אִם-שָׁלוּחַ לְפָנָיו:

28. Atem e•dai asher hi•ga•d`ti ki lo - ano•chi ha•Ma•shi•ach ki eem -
sha•loo•ach le•fa•nav.

---

29. He that hath the bride is the bridegroom: but the friend of the
bridegroom, which standeth and heareth him, rejoiceth greatly because of the
bridegroom's voice: this my joy therefore is fulfilled.

Greek/Transliteration
29. Ὁ ἔχων τὴν νύμφην, νυμφίος ἐστίν· ὁ δὲ φίλος τοῦ νυμφίου, ὁ ἑστηκὼς
καὶ ἀκούων αὐτοῦ, χαρᾷ χαίρει διὰ τὴν φωνὴν τοῦ νυμφίου· αὕτη οὖν ἡ χαρὰ
ἡ ἐμὴ πεπλήρωται.

29. 'O echon tein numphein, numphios estin. 'o de philos tou numphiou, 'o
'esteikos kai akouon autou, chara chairei dya tein phonein tou numphiou.
'autei oun 'ei chara 'ei emei pepleirotai.

Hebrew/Transliteration
כט. מִי אֲשֶׁר-לוֹ הַכַּלָּה הוּא הֶחָתָן וְאֹהֵב הֶחָתָן בְּעָמְדוֹ וּכְשָׁמְעוֹ אֹתוֹ שׂוֹשׂ יָשִׂישׂ לְקוֹל הֶחָתָן עַל-כֵּן
מָלְאָה שִׂמְחָתִי:

29. Mee asher - lo ha•ka•la hoo he•cha•tan ve•o•hev he•cha•tan be•om•do
ooch•shom•oh o•to sos ya•sis le•kol he•cha•tan al - ken mal•ah sim•cha•ti.

Rabbinic Jewish Commentary
The allusion is to a custom among the Jews, who, at their marriages, used to have
persons both on the side of the bride, and of the bridegroom, as companions that
attended each, and were called their friends; see Jdg_14:20. Such one is called by
the Rabbi's, שושבין; and this word is interpreted by אוהב, "a lover", or "friend", the
same as here; and by רעהו, "his" (the bridegroom's) "friend" in the time of his
marriage (s). There were two of these, one for the bride, and another for the
bridegroom; for so it is said (t), formerly they appointed two שושבינין,

"Friends", one for him (the bridegroom), and one for her (the bride), that they
might minister to the bridegroom, and do all things at their entrance into the
marriage chamber. --And formerly, these friends slept where the bridegroom and
bride slept."

And so as John is here represented as the friend of Yeshua, the bridegroom of the church; the Jews speak of Moses as the friend of God, the bridegroom of the people of Israel. So one of their writers (u), having delivered a parable concerning a certain king going into a far country, and leaving his espoused wife with his maid-servants, who raising an evil report on her, his friend tore in pieces the matrimonial contract, thus applies it:

"The king, this is the holy, blessed God; the maidens, these are the mixed multitude; and השושבין, "the friend", this is Moses; and the spouse of the holy, blessed God is Israel." The Jews say (w), that Michael and Gabriel were the שושבנין, "bridal friends" to the first Adam.

It was usual for the friend of the bridegroom to carry provisions with him, and eat and drink with the bridegroom, and rejoice with him; and this rejoicing was mutual. Hence those words,

"Give me שושביני, "My friend", that I may rejoice with him:"

The gloss upon it is, "And eat at his marriage, even as he also rejoiced, and ate at my marriage (y)." To this rejoicing the allusion is here.

(s) Misn. Sanhedrin, c. 3. sect. 5. & Bartenora in ib. (t) T. Bab. Cetubot, fol. 12. 1. (u) Jarchi in Exod. xxxiv. 1. Vid. Shemot Rabba, sect. 46. fol. 142. 2. (w) Bereshit Rabba, sect. 8. fol. 8. 2. (x) Jarchi in ib. (y) T. Bab. Bava Bathra, fol. 144. 2. & 145. 1.

---

30. He must increase, but I must decrease.

Greek/Transliteration
30. Ἐκεῖνον δεῖ αὐξάνειν, ἐμὲ δὲ ἐλαττοῦσθαι.

30. Ekeinon dei auxanein, eme de elattousthai.

Hebrew/Transliteration
ל. הוּא יֵלֵךְ הָלוֹךְ וָרָב וַאֲנִי אֵלֵךְ הָלוֹךְ וְחָסוֹר:

30. Hoo ye•lech ha•loch va•rav va•a•ni e•lech ha•loch ve•cha•sor.

---

31. He that cometh from above is above all: he that is of the earth is earthly, and speaketh of the earth: he that cometh from heaven is above all.

Greek/Transliteration
31. Ὁ ἄνωθεν ἐρχόμενος ἐπάνω πάντων ἐστίν. Ὁ ὢν ἐκ τῆς γῆς, ἐκ τῆς γῆς ἐστιν, καὶ ἐκ τῆς γῆς λαλεῖ· ὁ ἐκ τοῦ οὐρανοῦ ἐρχόμενος ἐπάνω πάντων ἐστίν.

31. 'O anothen erchomenos epano panton estin. 'O on ek teis geis, ek teis geis estin, kai ek teis geis lalei. 'o ek tou ouranou erchomenos epano panton estin.

לא. הַבָּא מִמָּרוֹם רָם הוּא מִכֹּל וְהַבָּא מֵאֶרֶץ מֵעָפָר הוּא וְעַל-עָפָר יְדַבֵּר הַבָּא מִשָּׁמַיִם רָם הוּא עַל-
כֹּל:

31. Ha•ba mi•ma•rom ram hoo mi•kol ve•ha•ba me•e•retz me•a•far hoo ve•al – afar ye•da•ber ha•ba mi•sha•ma•yim ram hoo al - kol.

Rabbinic Jewish Commentary
"For like as the ground is given unto the wood, and the sea to his floods: even so they that dwell upon the earth may understand nothing but that which is upon the earth: and he that dwelleth above the heavens may only understand the things that are above the height of the heavens." (2 Esdras 4:21)

---

32. And what he hath seen and heard, that he testifieth; and no man receiveth his testimony.

Greek/Transliteration
32. Καὶ ὃ ἑώρακεν καὶ ἤκουσεν, τοῦτο μαρτυρεῖ· καὶ τὴν μαρτυρίαν αὐτοῦ οὐδεὶς λαμβάνει.

32. Kai 'o 'eoraken kai eikousen, touto marturei. kai tein marturian autou oudeis lambanei.

Hebrew/Transliteration
לב. וְכַאֲשֶׁר רָאָה וְשָׁמַע כֵּן יִתֵּן עֵדוּתוֹ וּלְעֵדוּתוֹ אֵין שֹׁמֵעַ:

32. Ve•cha•a•sher ra•ah ve•sha•ma ken yi•ten e•doo•to ool•e•doo•to eyn sho•me•a.

---

33. He that hath received his testimony hath set to his seal that God is true.

Greek/Transliteration
33. Ὁ λαβὼν αὐτοῦ τὴν μαρτυρίαν ἐσφράγισεν ὅτι ὁ θεὸς ἀληθής ἐστιν.

33. 'O labon autou tein marturian esphragisen 'oti 'o theos aleitheis estin.

Hebrew/Transliteration
לג. וְהַשֹּׁמֵעַ לְעֵדוּתוֹ יַחְתֹּם בְּחוֹתַם יָדוֹ כִּי הָאֱלֹהִים אֱמֶת:

33. Ve•ha•sho•mea le•e•doo•to yach•tom be•cho•tam ya•do ki ha•Elohim emet.

Rabbinic Jewish Commentary

The Jews have a saying (z) that "the seal of the blessed God is truth". The Arabic version renders it, "he is already sealed, because God is true"; and the Ethiopic version, "God hath sealed him, because he is true"; namely, with his holy Spirit.

(z) T. Hieros.Sanhedrin, fol.18.1. & T. Bab. Sanhedrin, fol.64.1.&Yoma, fol.69.2.

34. For he whom God hath sent speaketh the words of God: for God giveth not the Spirit by measure unto him.

Greek/Transliteration

34. Ὃν γὰρ ἀπέστειλεν ὁ θεός, τὰ ῥήματα τοῦ θεοῦ λαλεῖ· οὐ γὰρ ἐκ μέτρου δίδωσιν ὁ θεὸς τὸ πνεῦμα.

34. 'On gar apesteilen 'o theos, ta 'reimata tou theou lalei. ou gar ek metrou didosin 'o theos to pneuma.

Hebrew/Transliteration

לד. כִּי הוּא אֲשֶׁר שְׁלָחוֹ אֱלֹהִים דִּבְרֵי אֱלֹהִים הוּא מְדַבֵּר כִּי-לֹא בִמְשׂוּרָה נָתַן אֶת-רוּחוֹ:

34. Ki hoo asher sh`la•cho Elohim div•rey Elohim hoo me•da•ber ki - lo vim•soo•ra na•tan et - roo•cho.

Rabbinic Jewish Commentary

To which agrees what the Jews say (a) of the Holy Spirit, and his gifts.

"Says R. Joden bar R. Simeon, even the waters which descend from above are not given, but, במדה, "in measure".--Says R. Acha, even the Holy Spirit, which dwells upon the prophets, does not dwell, but במשקל, "in weight".

(a) Vajikra Rabba, sect. 15. fol. 157. 3.

---

35. The Father loveth the Son, and hath given all things into his hand.

Greek/Transliteration

35. Ὁ πατὴρ ἀγαπᾷ τὸν υἱόν, καὶ πάντα δέδωκεν ἐν τῇ χειρὶ αὐτοῦ.

35. 'O pateir agapa ton 'wion, kai panta dedoken en tei cheiri autou.

Hebrew/Transliteration

לה. הָאָב אֹהֵב אֶת-הַבֵּן וְאֶת-כָּל נָתַן בְּיָדוֹ:

35. Ha•Av o•hev et - ha•Ben ve•et - kol na•tan be•ya•do.

---

36. He that believeth on the Son hath everlasting life: and he that believeth not the Son shall not see life; but the wrath of God abideth on him.

Greek/Transliteration

36. Ὁ πιστεύων εἰς τὸν υἱὸν ἔχει ζωὴν αἰώνιον· ὁ δὲ ἀπειθῶν τῷ υἱῷ, οὐκ ὄψεται ζωήν, ἀλλ᾽ ἡ ὀργὴ τοῦ θεοῦ μένει ἐπ᾽ αὐτόν.

36. 'O pisteuon eis ton 'wion echei zoein aionion. 'o de apeithon to 'wio, ouk opsetai zoein, all 'ei orgei tou theou menei ep auton.

Hebrew/Transliteration

לוֹ. מִי אֲשֶׁר יַאֲמִין בַּבֵּן יֶשׁ-לוֹ חַיֵּי עוֹלָם וּמִי אֲשֶׁר לֹא יַאֲמִין בַּבֵּן לֹא יִרְאֶה חַיִּים כִּי אִם-חֲרוֹן אַף אֱלֹהִים עָלָיו:יָחוּל

36. Mee asher ya•a•min ba•Ben yesh - lo cha•yey o•lam oo•mi asher lo ya•a•min ba•Ben lo yir•eh cha•yim ki eem - cha•ron af Elohim alav ya•chool.

Rabbinic Jewish Commentary

Very remarkable are the following words of the Jews (b) concerning the Messiah, whom they call the latter Redeemer:

"Whosoever believes in him "shall" live; but he that believes not in him shall go to the nations of the world, and they shall kill him."

(b) Midrash Ruth, fol. 33. 2.

John, Chapter 4

1. When therefore the Lord knew how the Pharisees had heard that Jesus made and baptized more disciples than John,

Greek/Transliteration

1. Ὡς οὖν ἔγνω ὁ κύριος ὅτι ἤκουσαν οἱ Φαρισαῖοι ὅτι Ἰησοῦς πλείονας μαθητὰς ποιεῖ καὶ βαπτίζει ἢ Ἰωάννης-

1. 'Os oun egno 'o kurios 'oti eikousan 'oi Pharisaioi 'oti Yeisous pleionas matheitas poiei kai baptizei ei Yoanneis-

Hebrew/Transliteration

א. וְכַאֲשֶׁר נוֹדַע לָאָדוֹן כִּי הַפְּרוּשִׁים שָׁמְעוּ לֵאמֹר יֵשׁוּעַ הֶעֱמִיד וְטִבֵּל תַּלְמִידִים רַבִּים מִיּוֹחָנָן:

1. Ve•cha•a•sher no•da la•Adon ki ha•P`roo•shim sham•oo le•mor Yeshua he•e•mid ve•ti•bel tal•mi•dim ra•bim mi•Yo•cha•nan.

---

2. (Though Jesus himself baptized not, but his disciples,)

Greek/Transliteration

2. καίτοιγε Ἰησοῦς αὐτὸς οὐκ ἐβάπτιζεν, ἀλλ᾽ οἱ μαθηταὶ αὐτοῦ-

2. kaitoige Yeisous autos ouk ebaptizen, all 'oi matheitai autou-

Hebrew/Transliteration

ב. אַף כִּי-יֵשׁוּעַ לֹא טִבֵּל אֹתָם רַק תַּלְמִידָיו:

2. Af ki - Yeshua lo ti•bel o•tam rak tal•mi•dav.

---

3. He left Judaea, and departed again into Galilee.

Greek/Transliteration

3. ἀφῆκεν τὴν Ἰουδαίαν, καὶ ἀπῆλθεν εἰς τὴν Γαλιλαίαν.

3. apheiken tein Youdaian, kai apeilthen eis tein Galilaian.

Hebrew/Transliteration

ג. וַיַּעֲזֹב אֶת-יְהוּדָה וַיָּשָׁב וַיִּסַּע הַגָּלִילָה:

3. Va•ya•a•zov et - Yehooda va•ya•shov va•yi•sa ha•Ga•li•la.

---

4. And he must needs go through Samaria.

4. Ἔδει δὲ αὐτὸν διέρχεσθαι διὰ τῆς Σαμαρείας.

4. Edei de auton dierchesthai dya teis Samareias.

ד. וְהָיָה נָכוֹן לוֹ לַעֲבֹר דֶּרֶךְ שֹׁמְרוֹן:

4. Ve•ha•ya na•chon lo la•a•vor de•rech Shom•ron.

---

5. Then cometh he to a city of Samaria, which is called Sychar, near to the parcel of ground that Jacob gave to his son Joseph.

5. Ἔρχεται οὖν εἰς πόλιν τῆς Σαμαρείας λεγομένην Συχάρ, πλησίον τοῦ χωρίου ὃ ἔδωκεν Ἰακὼβ Ἰωσὴφ τῷ υἱῷ αὐτοῦ·

5. Erchetai oun eis polin teis Samareias legomenein Suchar, pleision tou choriou 'o edoken Yakob Yoseiph to 'wio autou.

ה. וַיָּבֹא אֶל-עִיר בְּאֶרֶץ שֹׁמְרוֹן וּשְׁמָהּ סוֹכַר מִמּוּל חֶלְקַת הַשָּׂדֶה אֲשֶׁר-נָתַן יַעֲקֹב לִבְנוֹ לְיוֹסֵף:

5. Va•ya•vo el - eer be•e•retz Shom•ron oosh•ma Soo•char mi•mool chel•kat ha•sa•de asher - na•tan Yaakov liv•no le•Yosef.

Rabbinic Jewish Commentary
Now called Neapolis (d); the same with "Sichem", or "Shechem", as appears from its situation. Hence "Sychar Sichem", is "drunken Sichem"; mention is made in the Talmud (e), of a place called סיכרא, "Sichra". The "parcel of ground", or of a "field", as in Gen_33:19, is in the Persic version, called "a vineyard"; and so Nonnus renders it, "a field planted with vines"; and which may serve to confirm the above conjecture, concerning "Sychar" being a nickname.

(d) Hieron. Epitaph. Paulae, Tom. I. fol. 59. & R. Benjamin Itin. p. 38. (e) T. Bab. Bava Metzia, foi. 42. 1. & 83. 1. & Cholin, fol. 94.

---

6. Now Jacob's well was there. Jesus therefore, being wearied with his journey, sat thus on the well: and it was about the sixth hour.

6. ἦν δὲ ἐκεῖ πηγὴ τοῦ Ἰακώβ. Ὁ οὖν Ἰησοῦς κεκοπιακὼς ἐκ τῆς ὁδοιπορίας ἐκαθέζετο οὕτως ἐπὶ τῇ πηγῇ. Ὥρα ἦν ὡσεὶ ἕκτη.

6. ein de ekei peigei tou Yakob. 'O oun Yeisous kekopyakos ek teis 'odoiporias ekathezeto 'outos epi tei peigei. 'Ora ein 'osei 'ektei.

Hebrew/Transliteration
:ו. וְשָׁם בְּאֵר יַעֲקֹב וְיֵשׁוּעַ עָיְפָה נַפְשׁוֹ בַּדֶּרֶךְ וַיֵּשֶׁב-לוֹ עַל-הַבְּאֵר כְּשָׁעָה הַשִּׁשִׁית

6. Ve•sham be•er Yaakov ve•Yeshua ay•fa naf•sho va•de•rech va•ye•shev - lo al - ha•b`er ke•sha•ah ha•shi•sheet.

Rabbinic Jewish Commentary
In the Talmud (f) there is mention made, of עין סוכר, "the fountain of Sochar"; and may not improperly be rendered, "the well of Sychar": but whether the same with this, is not certain; that appears to be a great way from Jerusalem, as this also was, even forty miles:

and it was about the sixth hour; about twelve o'clock at noon. The Ethiopic version adds by way of explanation, and "it was then noon"; and all the Oriental versions omit ωσει, "about"; rendering it, "it was the sixth hour".

(f) T. Hieron. Shekalim, fol. 48. 4. T. Bab. Bava Kama, fol. 82. 2. & Menachot, fol. 64. 2. & Gloss. in Sanhedrin, fol. 11. 2.

---

7. There cometh a woman of Samaria to draw water: Jesus saith unto her, Give me to drink.

Greek/Transliteration
7. Ἔρχεται γυνὴ ἐκ τῆς Σαμαρείας ἀντλῆσαι ὕδωρ· λέγει αὐτῇ ὁ Ἰησοῦς, Δός μοι πιεῖν.

7. Erchetai gunei ek teis Samareias antleisai 'udor. legei autei 'o Yeisous, Dos moi piein.

Hebrew/Transliteration
:ז. וְהִנֵּה אִשָּׁה שֹׁמְרֹנִית בָּאָה לִשְׁאָב-מַיִם וַיֹּאמֶר אֵלֶיהָ יֵשׁוּעַ תְּנִי-נָא לִי לִשְׁתּוֹת

7. Ve•hee•ne ee•sha Shom•ro•nit ba•ah lish•ov - ma•yim va•yo•mer e•le•ha Yeshua t`ni - na li lish•tot.

---

8. (For his disciples were gone away unto the city to buy meat.)

Greek/Transliteration
8. Οἱ γὰρ μαθηταὶ αὐτοῦ ἀπεληλύθεισαν εἰς τὴν πόλιν, ἵνα τροφὰς ἀγοράσωσιν.

---

8. 'Oi gar matheitai autou apeleilutheisan eis tein polin, 'ina trophas agorasosin.

Hebrew/Transliteration

ח. כִּי תַלְמִידָיו הָלְכוּ הָעִירָה לִשְׁבֹּר לָהֶם אֹכֶל:

8. Ki tal•mi•dav hal•choo ha•ee•ra lish•bor la•hem o•chel.

Rabbinic Jewish Commentary

For though it is said, in the following verse, that the Jews have no dealings with the Samaritans; yet this is not to be understood in the strictest sense; for they had dealings with them in some respects, as will be seen hereafter; particularly their food, eatables, and drinkables, were lawful to be bought of them, and used: it is said by R. Juda bar Pazi, in the name of R. Ame (g),

"A roasted egg of the Cuthites (or Samaritans), lo, this is lawful: says R. Jacob bar Acha, in the name of R. Lazar, the boiled victuals of the Cuthites (Samaritans), lo, these are free; this he says concerning boiled food, because it is not their custom to put wine and vinegar into it," For these were forbidden:

Hence it is often said (h), that "the unleavened bread of the Cuthites (or Samaritans), is lawful, and that a man is allowed the use of it at the passover."

And there was a time when their wine was lawful; for one of their canons runs thus (i);

"He that buys wine of the Cuthites (Samaritans), says, the two logs that I shall separate, lo, they are first fruits"

It is indeed said in one place, R. Eliezer (k). "That, he that eats the bread of the Cuthites (or Samaritans), is as if he eat flesh; to when (who reported this) says (R. Akiba) be silent, I will not tell you what R. Eliezer thinks concerning it."

Upon which the commentators serve (l), that this is not to be understood strictly; cause he that eats bread of the Samaritans, does deserve stripes according to the law, but according to the constitutions of the wise men; but these, Yeshua and his disciples had no regard to.

(g) T. Hieros. Avoda Zara, fol. 44. 4. (h) T. Bab. Gittin, fol. 10. 1. & Cholin, fol. 4. 1. & Kiddushin, fol. 76. 1. (i) Misn. Demai, c. 7. sect. 4. Vid. Bartenora in ib. (k) Misna Sheviith, c. 8. sect. 10. Pirke Eliezer, c. 38. (l) Maimon. & Bartenora in Misn. ib.

---

9. Then saith the woman of Samaria unto him, How is it that thou, being a Jew, askest drink of me, which am a woman of Samaria? for the Jews have no dealings with the Samaritans.

Greek/Transliteration

9. Λέγει οὖν αὐτῷ ἡ γυνὴ ἡ Σαμαρεῖτις, Πῶς σὺ Ἰουδαῖος ὢν παρ' ἐμοῦ πιεῖν αἰτεῖς, οὔσης γυναικὸς Σαμαρείτιδος;- Οὐ γὰρ συγχρῶνται Ἰουδαῖοι Σαμαρείταις.

9. Legei oun auto 'ei gunei 'ei Samareitis, Pos su Youdaios on par emou piein aiteis, ouseis gunaikos Samareitidos?- Ou gar sugchrontai Youdaioi Samareitais.

Hebrew/Transliteration

ט. וַתֹּאמֶר אֵלָיו הָאִשָּׁה הַשֹּׁמְרֹנִית הֲלֹא יְהוּדִי אַתָּה וְאֵיךְ תִּשְׁאַל מִמֶּנִּי לִשְׁתּוֹת וַאֲנִי אִשָּׁה שֹׁמְרֹנִית כִּי-אֵין דָּבָר:לַיְהוּדִים עִם-הַשֹּׁמְרֹנִים

9. Va•to•mer elav ha•ee•sha ha•Shom•ronit ha•lo Ye•hoo•di ata ve•eych tish•al mi•me•ni lish•tot va•a•ni ee•sha Shom•ro•nit ki - eyn da•var la•Ye•hoo•dim eem - ha•Shom•ro•nim.

Rabbinic Jewish Commentary

Not that the waters of Samaria were unlawful for a Jew to drink of; for as

"The land of the Cuthites (or Samaritans), was pure, or clean, so, מקותיה, "their collections of water", and their habitations, and their ways were clean (m),"

And might be used; but because the Jews used no familiarity with the Samaritans, nor would they receive any courtesy or kindness from them.

That discourse of the Samaritans with a Jewish Rabbi (n).

"The Cuthites (or Samaritans) inquired of R. Abhu, your fathers, היו מסתפקין, "used to deal with us" (or minister to us, or supply us with necessaries), wherefore do not ye deal with us? (or take a supply from us;) he replied unto them, your fathers did not corrupt their works, you have corrupted your works."

They might not use their wine and vinegar, nor admit them to their tables; they say of a man (o),

"Because the Cuthites (or Samaritans) ate at his table, it was the reason why his children went into captivity--and further add, that whoever invites a Cuthite (or Samaritan) into his house, and ministers to him, is the cause of captivity to his children."

And they forbid a man to enter into partnership with a Cuthite (or Samaritan (p)): and particularly,

"Three days before the feasts of idolaters (for such they reckoned the Samaritans, as well as others), it is forbidden to have any commerce with them, to borrow of them, or lend to them (q)."

They might go into their cities and buy food of them, as the disciples did, Joh_4:8; they might send their wheat to a Samaritan miller, to be ground (r); and as it appears from the above citations, their houses and habitations were clean, and might be lodged in, with which compare Luk_9:52; the poor of the Samaritans were maintained with the poor of Israel (s)

(m) T. Hieros. Avoda Zara, fol. 44. 4. (n) Ib. (o) T. Bab. Sanhedrin, fol. 104. 1. (p) T. Bab. Becorot, fol. 7. 2. Piske Toseph. ib. art. 4. & in Megilla, art 102. (q) Misna Avoda Zara, c. 1. sect. 1. (r) Misua Demai, c. 3. sect. 4. (s) Piske Tosephot Yoma, art. 63.

---

10. Jesus answered and said unto her, If thou knewest the gift of God, and who it is that saith to thee, Give me to drink; thou wouldest have asked of him, and he would have given thee living water.

Greek/Transliteration
10. Ἀπεκρίθη Ἰησοῦς καὶ εἶπεν αὐτῇ, Εἰ ἤδεις τὴν δωρεὰν τοῦ θεοῦ, καὶ τίς ἐστιν ὁ λέγων σοι, Δός μοι πιεῖν, σὺ ἂν ᾔτησας αὐτόν, καὶ ἔδωκεν ἄν σοι ὕδωρ ζῶν.

10. Apekrithei Yeisous kai eipen autei, Ei eideis tein dorean tou theou, kai tis estin 'o legon soi, Dos moi piein, su an eiteisas auton, kai edoken an soi 'udor zon.

Hebrew/Transliteration
י. וַיַּעַן יֵשׁוּעַ וַיֹּאמֶר אֵלֶיהָ לוּ יָדַעַתְּ אֶת-מַתַּת אֱלֹהִים וּמִי הָאֹמֵר לָךְ תְּנִי לִי לִשְׁתּוֹת אָז שָׁאַלְתְּ אַתְּ מִמֶּנּוּ וְנָתַן:לָךְ מַיִם חַיִּים

10. Va•ya•an Yeshua va•yo•mer e•le•ha loo ya•da•at et - ma•tat Elohim oo•mi ha•o•mer lach t`ni li lish•tot az sha•alt at mi•me•noo ve•na•tan lach ma•yim cha•yim.

Rabbinic Jewish Commentary
For the allusion is to spring water, that bubbles up in a fountain, and is ever running; for such water the Jews call "living water"; as in Gen_26:19; where in the Hebrew text it is "living water"; which we, and also the Chaldee paraphrase, render "springing water". So living waters with them, are said to be always flowing, and never cease (t).

(t) Bartenora in Misn. Negaim, c. 14. sect. 1.

---

11. The woman saith unto him, Sir, thou hast nothing to draw with, and the well is deep: from whence then hast thou that living water?

Greek/Transliteration

11. Λέγει αὐτῷ ἡ γυνή, Κύριε, οὔτε ἄντλημα ἔχεις, καὶ τὸ φρέαρ ἐστὶν βαθύ· πόθεν οὖν ἔχεις τὸ ὕδωρ τὸ ζῶν;

11. Legei auto 'ei gunei, Kurie, oute antleima echeis, kai to phrear estin bathu. pothen oun echeis to 'udor to zon?

Hebrew/Transliteration

יא. וַתֹּאמֶר אֵלָיו הָאִשָּׁה אֲדֹנִי הֵן אֵין-לְךָ בַּמֶּה לִשְׁאֹב וְהַבְּאֵר עֲמֻקָּה וּמֵאַיִן לְךָ אֵפוֹא מַיִם חַיִּים:

11. Va•to•mer elav ha•ee•sha Adoni hen eyn - le•cha ba•me lish•ov ve•ha•b`er a•moo•ka oo•me•ayin le•cha e•fo ma•yim cha•yim?

Rabbinic Jewish Commentary

Though it is strange there was not one; since, according to common usage, and even of the Jews (u),

"A public well had, קול, "a bucket", or pitcher; but a private well had no bucket:"

(u) T. Hieros. Erubin, fol. 20. 2.

---

12. Art thou greater than our father Jacob, which gave us the well, and drank thereof himself, and his children, and his cattle?

Greek/Transliteration

12. Μὴ σὺ μείζων εἶ τοῦ πατρὸς ἡμῶν Ἰακώβ, ὃς ἔδωκεν ἡμῖν τὸ φρέαρ, καὶ αὐτὸς ἐξ αὐτοῦ ἔπιεν, καὶ οἱ υἱοὶ αὐτοῦ, καὶ τὰ θρέμματα αὐτοῦ;

12. Mei su meizon ei tou patros 'eimon Yakob, 'os edoken 'eimin to phrear, kai autos ex autou epien, kai 'oi 'wioi autou, kai ta thremmata autou?

Hebrew/Transliteration

יב. הֲגָדוֹל אַתָּה מִיַּעֲקֹב אָבִינוּ אֲשֶׁר נָתַן-לָנוּ הַבְּאֵר הַזֹּאת אֲשֶׁר מִמֶּנָּה שָׁתָה הוּא וּבָנָיו וּבְעִירוֹ:

12. Ha•ga•dol ata mi•Ya•a•kov avi•noo asher na•tan - la•noo ha•b`er ha•zot asher mi•me•na sha•ta hoo oo•va•nav oov•ee•ro?

Rabbinic Jewish Commentary

A person of greater worth and character than he, who was content to drink of this water; or wiser and more knowing than he, who could find out no better fountain of water in all these parts? she calls Jacob the father of them, according to the common notion and boasting of these people, when it served their turn; otherwise they were not the descendants of Jacob; for after the ten tribes were carried away captive by the king of Assyria, he placed in their room, in the cities of Samaria, men from Babylon, Cuthah Ava, Hamath, and Sepharvaim, Heathenish and idolatrous people; see 2Ki_17:24. And from these, the then Samaritans sprung;

Only upon Sanballat's building a temple on Mount Gerizzim, for Manasseh his son-in-law, when put away from the priesthood by the Jews, for his marriage of his daughter, several wicked persons of the like sort, came out of Judea, and joined themselves to the Samaritans: and such a mixed medley of people were they at this time, though they boasted of Jacob as their father, as this woman did; and so to this day, they draw their genealogy from Abraham, Isaac, and Jacob; and particularly call Joseph their father, and say, from whence are we, but from the tribe of Joseph the just, from Ephraim (w)? as they formerly did (x);

"R. Meir saw a Samaritan, he said to him, from whence comest thou? (that is, from what family;) he answered, from the (tribe) of Joseph."

(w) Epist. Samar. ad Scaliger. in Antiqu. Eccl. Oriental. p. 123, 124, 126. (x) Bereshit Rabba, sect. 94. fol. 82. 1.

---

13. Jesus answered and said unto her, Whosoever drinketh of this water shall thirst again:

Greek/Transliteration
13. Ἀπεκρίθη Ἰησοῦς καὶ εἶπεν αὐτῇ, Πᾶς ὁ πίνων ἐκ τοῦ ὕδατος τούτου, διψήσει πάλιν·

13. Apekrithei Yeisous kai eipen autei, Pas 'o pinon ek tou 'udatos toutou, dipseisei palin.

Hebrew/Transliteration
יג. וַיַּעַן יֵשׁוּעַ וַיֹּאמֶר אֵלֶיהָ כָּל-הַשֹּׁתֶה מִן-הַמַּיִם הָאֵלֶּה יִצְמָא עוֹד:

13. Va•ya•an Yeshua va•yo•mer e•le•ha kol - ha•sho•te min - ha•ma•yim ha•e•le yitz•ma od.

---

14. But whosoever drinketh of the water that I shall give him shall never thirst; but the water that I shall give him shall be in him a well of water springing up into everlasting life.

Greek/Transliteration
14. ὃς δ᾽ ἂν πίῃ ἐκ τοῦ ὕδατος οὗ ἐγὼ δώσω αὐτῷ, οὐ μὴ διψήσῃ εἰς τὸν αἰῶνα· ἀλλὰ τὸ ὕδωρ ὃ δώσω αὐτῷ γενήσεται ἐν αὐτῷ πηγὴ ὕδατος ἁλλομένου εἰς ζωὴν αἰώνιον.

14. 'os d an piei ek tou 'udatos 'ou ego doso auto, ou mei dipseisei eis ton aiona. alla to 'udor 'o doso auto geneisetai en auto peigei 'udatos 'allomenou eis zoein aionion.

Hebrew/Transliteration

יד. וְכָל-אֲשֶׁר יִשְׁתֶּה מִן-הַמַּיִם אֲשֶׁר אֲנִי נֹתֵן לוֹ לֹא יִצְמָא לְעוֹלָם כִּי הַמַּיִם אֲשֶׁר אֲנִי נֹתֵן יִהְיוּ בוֹ
לִמְקוֹר מַיִם:נֹבְעִים לְחַיֵּי עוֹלָם

14. Ve•chol - asher yish•te min - ha•ma•yim asher ani no•ten lo lo yitz•ma
le•o•lam ki ha•ma•yim asher ani no•ten yi•hee•yoo vo lim•kor ma•yim
nov•eem le•cha•yey o•lam.

TaNaKh-Old Testaement/Rabbinic Jewish Commentary

"Behold, El is Y'shua (My salvation)! I will trust and not be afraid, for my strength and song is Yah YAHWEH; yea, He has become to me Y'shua. And you shall draw waters out of the wells of salvation with joy. And in that day you shall say, Praise YAHWEH! Call on His name; declare His doings among the peoples; make mention that His name is exalted. Sing to YAHWEH, for He has done majestically; this is known in all the earth. Cry and shout, O dweller of Zion! For great is the Holy One of Israel in your midst." (Isa_12:2-6)

But more especially Yeshua is meant, who is the "fountain of gardens, and well of living water", Son_4:15 in whom salvation is, and in no other: the words may be rendered, "the wells" or "fountains of the Saviour" (r), yea, of Yeshua; and which are no other than the fulness of grace in him: the phrase denotes the abundance of grace in Yeshua, much of which is given out in conversion; an abundance of it is received with the free gift of righteousness for justification; and a large measure of it in the pardon of sins, and in all the after supplies, through the wilderness of this world, till the saints come to glory; and which is vouchsafed to a great number, to all the elect angels and elect men, to all the churches, and the members thereof, in all ages; and this always has been and ever will be communicating to them.

The Targum is, "And ye shall receive a new doctrine from the chosen, the righteous;"

Or of the righteous; which is true of the doctrine of the Gospel, received by the hands of chosen men, the apostles of Yeshua. The Jews (s) make use of this passage, in confirmation of the ceremony of drawing of water at the feast of tabernacles; and say (t) it signifies the drawing of the Holy Ghost; that is, his grace.

(r) ממעיני הישועה "de fontibus Salvatoris", V. L.; Vatablus. (s) T. Bab. Succa, fol. 48. 2. & 50. 2. (t) Bereshit Rabba, sect. 70. fol. 62. 3. T. Hieros. Succa, fol. 55. 1.

---

15. The woman saith unto him, Sir, give me this water, that I thirst not, neither come hither to draw.

Greek/Transliteration
15. Λέγει πρὸς αὐτὸν ἡ γυνή, Κύριε, δός μοι τοῦτο τὸ ὕδωρ, ἵνα μὴ διψῶ, μηδὲ ἔρχομαι ἐνθάδε ἀντλεῖν.

---

15. Legei pros auton 'ei gunei, Kurie, dos moi touto to 'udor, 'ina mei dipso, meide erchomai enthade antlein.

Hebrew/Transliteration

טו. וַתֹּאמֶר אֵלָיו הָאִשָּׁה תְּנָה-לִי אֲדֹנִי אֶת-הַמַּיִם הָהֵם וְלֹא-אֶצְמָא עוֹד וְלֹא אָבֹא הֵנָּה לִשְׁאֹב׃

15. Va•to•mer elav ha•ee•sha te•na - li Adoni et - ha•ma•yim ha•hem ve•lo - etz•ma od ve•lo avo he•na lish•ov.

---

16. Jesus saith unto her, Go, call thy husband, and come hither.

Greek/Translitration
16. Λέγει αὐτῇ ὁ Ἰησοῦς, Ὕπαγε, φώνησον τὸν ἄνδρα σοῦ, καὶ ἐλθὲ ἐνθάδε.

16. Legei autei 'o Yeisous, 'Upage, phoneison ton andra sou, kai elthe enthade.

Hebrew/Transliteration
טז. וַיֹּאמֶר אֵלֶיהָ יֵשׁוּעַ לְכִי קִרְאִי לְאִישֵׁךְ וּבֹאִי הֵנָּה׃

16. Va•yo•mer e•le•ha Yeshua le•chi kir•ee le•ee•shech oo•vo•ee he•na.

---

17. The woman answered and said, I have no husband. Jesus said unto her, Thou hast well said, I have no husband:

Greek/Transliteration
17. Ἀπεκρίθη ἡ γυνὴ καὶ εἶπεν, Οὐκ ἔχω ἄνδρα. Λέγει αὐτῇ ὁ Ἰησοῦς, Καλῶς εἶπας ὅτι Ἄνδρα οὐκ ἔχω·

17. Apekrithei 'ei gunei kai eipen, Ouk echo andra. Legei autei 'o Yeisous, Kalos eipas 'oti Andra ouk echo.

Hebrew/Transliteration
יז. וַתַּעַן הָאִשָּׁה וַתֹּאמֶר אֵלָיו אֵין-לִי אִישׁ וַיֹּאמֶר אֵלֶיהָ יֵשׁוּעַ כֵּן דִּבַּרְתְּ כִּי אֵין-לָךְ אִישׁ׃

17. Va•ta•an ha•ee•sha va•to•mer elav eyn - li eesh va•yo•mer e•le•ha Yeshua ken di•bart ki eyn - lach eesh.

---

18. For thou hast had five husbands; and he whom thou now hast is not thy husband: in that saidst thou truly.

Greek/Transliteration
18. πέντε γὰρ ἄνδρας ἔσχες, καὶ νῦν ὃν ἔχεις οὐκ ἔστιν σου ἀνήρ· τοῦτο ἀληθὲς εἴρηκας.

18. pente gar andras esches, kai nun 'on echeis ouk estin sou aneir. touto
aleithes eireikas.

Hebrew/Transliteration

יח. חֲמִשָּׁה בְעָלִים הָיוּ לָךְ וְהוּא אֲשֶׁר עִמָּךְ כַּיּוֹם אֵינֶנּוּ בַעְלֵךְ וּבְזֹאת אֱמֶת דִּבַּרְתְּ:

18. Cha•mi•sha ve•a•lim ha•yoo lach ve•hoo asher ee•mech ka•yom ey•ne•noo
va•a•lech oo•va•zot emet di•bart.

Rabbinic Jewish Commentary

Which she either had had lawfully, and had buried one after another; and which
was no crime, and might be: the Sadducees propose a case to Yeshua, in which a
woman is said to have had seven husbands successively, in a lawful manner,
Mat_22:25. Or rather, she had had so many, and had been divorced from everyone
of them, for adultery; for no other cause it should seem did the Samaritans divorce;
seeing that they only received the law of Moses, and rejected, at least, many of the
traditions of the elders; and since they are particularly said (y).

"Not to be expert in the Torah of marriages and divorces:"

(y) T. Bab. Kiddushin, fol 76. 1.

---

19. The woman saith unto him, Sir, I perceive that thou art a prophet.

Greek/Transliteration
19. Λέγει αὐτῷ ἡ γυνή, Κύριε, θεωρῶ ὅτι προφήτης εἶ σύ.

19. Legei auto 'ei gunei, Kurie, theoro 'oti propheiteis ei su.

Hebrew/Transliteration

יט. וַתֹּאמֶר אֵלָיו הָאִשָּׁה אֲדֹנִי רֹאָה אָנֹכִי כִּי נָבִיא אָתָּה:

19. Va•to•mer elav ha•ee•sha Adoni ro•ah ano•chi ki na•vi ata.

**20. Our fathers worshipped in this mountain; and ye say, that in Jerusalem is
the place where men ought to worship.**

Greek/Transliteration
20. Οἱ πατέρες ἡμῶν ἐν τῷ ὄρει τούτῳ προσεκύνησαν· καὶ ὑμεῖς λέγετε ὅτι ἐν
Ἱεροσολύμοις ἐστὶν ὁ τόπος ὅπου δεῖ προσκυνεῖν.

20. 'Oi pateres 'eimon en to orei touto prosekuneisan. kai 'umeis legete 'oti en
'Yerosolumois estin 'o topos 'opou dei proskunein.

כ. אֲבֹתֵינוּ הִשְׁתַּחֲווּ בָּהָר הַזֶּה וְאַתֶּם אֹמְרִים כִּי יְרוּשָׁלַיִם הַמָּקוֹם לְהִשְׁתַּחֲוֹת:

20. Avo•tey•noo hish•ta•cha•voo ba•har ha•ze ve•a•tem om•rim ki Ye•roo•sha•la•yim ha•ma•kom le•hish•ta•cha•vot.

Rabbinic Jewish Commentary

This temple, we are told (b), was built about forty years after the second temple at Jerusalem: and stood two hundred years, and then was destroyed by Jochanan, the son of Simeon, the son of Mattathiah, who was called Hyrcanus, and so says Josephus (c); it might now be rebuilt: however, this did not put a stop to worship in this place, about which there were great contentions, between the Jews and the Samaritans; of which we have some instances, in the writings of the former: it is said (d), that

"R. Jonathan went to pray in Jerusalem, and passed by that mountain (the gloss says, Mount Gerizim), and a certain Samaritan saw him, and said to him, whither art thou going? he replied, that he was going to pray at Jerusalem; he said to him, is it not better for thee to pray in this blessed mountain, and not in that dunghill house? he replied, why is it blessed? he answered, because it was not overflowed by the waters of the flood; the thing was hid from the eyes of R. Jonathan, and he could not return an answer."

This story is told elsewhere (e), with a little variation, and more plainly as to the place, thus;

"It happened to R. Jonathan, that he went to Neapolis, of the Cuthites, or Samaritans, (i.e. to Sichem, for Sichem is now called Naplous,) and he was riding upon an ass, and an herdsman with him; a certain, Samaritan joined himself to them: when they came to Mount Gerizim, the Samaritan said to R. Jonathan, how came it to pass that we are come to this holy mountain? R. Jonathan replied, whence comes it to be holy? the Samaritan answered him, because it was not hurt by the waters of the flood."

Much the same story is told of R. Ishmael bar R. Jose (f). It is to be observed in this account, that the Samaritans call this mountain the holy mountain, they imagined there was something sacred in it; and the blessed mountain, or the mountain of blessing; no doubt, because the blessings were pronounced upon it; though a very poor reason is given by them in the above passages. And they not only urged the above instances of the worship or the patriarchs at, or about this place, which this woman refers to; but even falsified a passage in the Pentateuch, as is generally thought, in favour of this mount; for in Deu_27:4, instead of Mount Ebal, in the Samaritan Pentateuch Mount Gerizim is inserted. So stood the ease on one side of the question; on the other hand, the Jews pleaded for the temple at Jerusalem.

So the Targumist on 2Ch_3:1 enlarges on this head;

"And Solomon began to build the sanctuary of the Lord in Jerusalem, on Mount Moriah, in the place where Abraham worshipped and prayed in the name of the Lord: הוא אתר ארע פולחנא, "this place is the land of worship"; for there all generations worshipped before the Lord; and there Abraham offered up his son Isaac, for a burnt offering, and the word of the Lord delivered him, and a ram was appointed in his stead; there Jacob prayed when he fled from Esau his brother; there the angel of the Lord appeared to David, when he disposed the sacrifice in the place he bought of Ornan, in the floor of Ornan the Jebusite."

And since, now there were so many things to be said on each side of the question, this woman desires, that seeing Yeshua was a prophet, he would be pleased to give her his sense of the matter, and inform her which was the right place of worship.

(z) Misna Sota, c. 7. sect. 5. T. Bab. Sota, fol. 33. 2. (a) Antiqu. l. 12. c. 1. Vid. Juchasin, fol. 14. 2. (b) Juchasin, fol. 14. 2. & 15. 1. (c) Antiqu. l. 13. c. 17. (d) Bereshit Rabba, sect. 32. fol. 27. 4. & Shirhashirim Rabba, fol. 16. 3. (e) Debarim Rabba, sect. 3. fol. 238. 2. (f) Bereshit Rabba, sect. 81. fol. 71. 1.

---

21. Jesus saith unto her, Woman, believe me, the hour cometh, when ye shall neither in this mountain, nor yet at Jerusalem, worship the Father.

Greek/Transliteration
21. Λέγει αὐτῇ ὁ Ἰησοῦς, Γύναι, πίστευσόν μοι, ὅτι ἔρχεται ὥρα, ὅτε οὔτε ἐν τῷ ὄρει τούτῳ οὔτε ἐν Ἱεροσολύμοις προσκυνήσετε τῷ πατρί.

21. Legei autei 'o Yeisous, Gunai, pisteuson moi, 'oti erchetai 'ora, 'ote oute en to orei touto oute en 'Yerosolumois proskuneisete to patri.

Hebrew/Transliteration
כא. וַיֹּאמֶר אֵלֶיהָ יֵשׁוּעַ הַאֲמִינִי לִי אִשָּׁה כִּי תָבֹא עֵת אֲשֶׁר לֹא-בָּהָר הַזֶּה וְלֹא בִירוּשָׁלַיִם תִּשְׁתַּחֲוּוּ לָאָב:

21. Va•yo•mer e•le•ha Yeshua ha•a•mi•ni li ee•sha ki ta•vo et asher lo - ba•har ha•ze ve•lo vi•Ye•roo•sha•la•yim tish•ta•cha•voo la•Av.

---

22. Ye worship ye know not what: we know what we worship: for salvation is of the Jews.

Greek/Transliteration
22. Ὑμεῖς προσκυνεῖτε ὃ οὐκ οἴδατε· ἡμεῖς προσκυνοῦμεν ὃ οἴδαμεν· ὅτι ἡ σωτηρία ἐκ τῶν Ἰουδαίων ἐστίν.

22. 'Umeis proskuneite 'o ouk oidate. 'eimeis proskunoumen 'o oidamen. 'oti 'ei soteiria ek ton Youdaion estin.

Hebrew/Transliteration

כב. אַתֶּם מִשְׁתַּחֲוִים אֶל-אֲשֶׁר לֹא תֵדְעוּן וַאֲנַחְנוּ מִשְׁתַּחֲוִים אֶל-אֲשֶׁר נֵדָע כִּי הַיְשׁוּעָה בָּאָה מִמְּקוֹר הַיְּהוּדִים:

22. Atem mish•ta•cha•vim el - asher lo ted•oon va•a•nach•noo mish•ta•cha•vim el – asher ne•da ki ha•Y`shoo•ah va•ah mim•kor ha•Ye•hoo•dim.

Rabbinic Jewish Commentary

Sometimes they say (g) the Cuthites, or Samaritans, worshipped fire; and at other times, and which chiefly prevails with them, they assert (h), that their wise men, upon searching, found that they worshipped the image of a dove on Mount Gerizim; and sometimes they say (i), they worshipped the idols, the strange gods, or Teraphim, which Jacob hid under the oak in Sichem; which last, if true, may serve to illustrate these words of Yeshua, that they worshipped they knew not what, since they worshipped idols hid in the mount.

"R. Ishmael bar Jose, they say (k) went to Neapolis, (Sichem, called Naplous,) the Cuthites, or Samaritans came to him (to persuade him to worship with them in their mountain); he said unto them, I will show you that ye do not "worship at this mountain", but "the images which are hid under it"; for it is written, Gen_35:4; "and Jacob hid them" under the oak which was by Shechem."

And elsewhere (l) it is reported of the same Rabbi, that he went to Jerusalem to pray, as before related on Joh_4:20, and after what passed between him, and the Samaritan he met with at Mount Gerizim, before mentioned, he added;

"And said to him, I will tell you what ye are like, (ye are like) to a dog that lusts after carrion; so because ye know the idols are hid under it, (the mountain,) as it is written, Gen_35:4 and Jacob hid them, therefore ye lust after it: they said--this man knows that idols are hid here, and perhaps he will take them away; and they consulted together to kill him: he arose, and made his escape in the night."

(g) T. Bab. Taanith, fol. 5. 2. (h) Maimon. in Misn. Beracot, c. 8. sect. 8. & Bartenora in ib. c. 7. sect. 1. & in Nidda, c. 4. sect. 1. (i) Shalshelet Hakkabala, fol. 15. 2. (k) T. Hieros. Avoda Zara, fol. 44. 4. (l) Bereshit Rabba, sect. 81. fol. 71. 1.

---

23. But the hour cometh, and now is, when the true worshippers shall worship the Father in spirit and in truth: for the Father seeketh such to worship him.

Greek/Transliteration

23. Ἀλλ᾽ ἔρχεται ὥρα καὶ νῦν ἐστιν, ὅτε οἱ ἀληθινοὶ προσκυνηταὶ προσκυνήσουσιν τῷ πατρὶ ἐν πνεύματι καὶ ἀληθείᾳ· καὶ γὰρ ὁ πατὴρ τοιούτους ζητεῖ τοὺς προσκυνοῦντας αὐτόν.

23. All erchetai 'ora kai nun estin, 'ote 'oi aleithinoi proskuneitai proskuneisousin to patri en pneumati kai aleitheia. kai gar 'o pateir toioutous zeitei tous proskunountas auton.

Hebrew/Transliteration

כג. אַךְ תָּבֹא עֵת וְגַם-הִיא בָאָה וְהַמִּשְׁתַּחֲוִים הַנֶּאֱמָנִים יִשְׁתַּחֲווּ לָאָב בְּרוּחַ וּבֶאֱמֶת כִּי בְּמִשְׁתַּחֲוִים כָּאֵלֶה חָפֵץ:הָאָב

23. Ach ta•vo et ve•gam - hee va•ah ve•ha•mish•ta•cha•vim ha•ne•e•ma•nim yish•ta•cha•voo la•Av ba•roo•ach oo•va•e•met ki be•mish•ta•cha•vim ka•e•le cha•fetz ha•Av.

Rabbinic Jewish Commentary

Enoch is said, פלח בקושטא, "To worship in truth", before the LORD, in the Targums of Jonathan and Jerusalem, in Gen_5:24.

---

24. God is a Spirit: and they that worship him must worship him in spirit and in truth.

Greek/Transliteration

24. Πνεῦμα ὁ θεός· καὶ τοὺς προσκυνοῦντας αὐτόν, ἐν πνεύματι καὶ ἀληθείᾳ δεῖ προσκυνεῖν.

24. Pneuma 'o theos. kai tous proskunountas auton, en pneumati kai aleitheia dei proskunein.

Hebrew/Transliteration

:כד. הָאֱלֹהִים הוּא רוּחַ וְהַמִּשְׁתַּחֲוִים לוֹ עֲלֵיהֶם לְהִשְׁתַּחֲוֹת בְּרוּחַ וּבֶאֱמֶת

24. Ha•Elohim hoo Roo•ach ve•ha•mish•ta•cha•vim lo aley•hem le•hish•ta•cha•vot be•roo•ach oo•ve•e•met.

---

25. The woman saith unto him, I know that Messias cometh, which is called Christ: when he is come, he will tell us all things.

Greek/Transliteration

25. Λέγει αὐτῷ ἡ γυνή, Οἶδα ὅτι Μεσίας ἔρχεται· ὁ λεγόμενος χριστός· ὅταν ἔλθῃ ἐκεῖνος, ἀναγγελεῖ ἡμῖν πάντα.

25. Legei auto 'ei gunei, Oida 'oti Mesias erchetai- 'o legomenos christos. 'otan elthei ekeinos, anangelei 'eimin panta.

Hebrew/Transliteration

:כה. וַתֹּאמֶר אֵלָיו הָאִשָּׁה יָדַעְתִּי כִּי-יָבֹא מָשִׁיחַ הַנִּקְרָא כְּרִיסְטוֹס וְכַאֲשֶׁר יָבֹא לָנוּ יַגִּיד לָנוּ אֶת-כֹּל

25. Va•to•mer elav ha•ee•sha ya•da•a•ti ki - ya•vo Mashi•ach ha•nik•ra Chris•tos ve•cha•a•sher ya•vo ya•gid la•noo et - kol.

Rabbinic Jewish Commentary

It is certain, that the Samaritans to this day do expect a Messiah, though they know not his name, unless it be השהב; the meaning of which they do not understand (m) to me it seems to be an abbreviation of השהבא, or הוא אשר הבא, "he that is to come"; by which, in a way, the Jews understand the Messiah; and to which this Samaritan woman seems to have some respect.

The times of the Messiah would be times of great knowledge, founded on several prophecies, as Isa_2:3, and which they sometimes express in the following manner (n):

"In the days of the Messiah, even the little children in the world shall find out the hidden things of wisdom, and know in it the ends and computations (of times), and at that time he shall be made manifest unto all."

And again (o),

"Says R. Judah, the holy blessed God will reveal the deep mysteries of the law in the times of the King Messiah; for "the earth shall be filled with the knowledge of the LORD" and it is written, "they shall not teach every man his brother."

And elsewhere (p),

"The whole world shall be filled with the words of the Messiah, and with the words of the Torah, and with the words of the commandments; and these things shall extend to the isles afar off; to many people, the uncircumcised in heart, and the uncircumcised in flesh; and they shall deal in the secrets of the Torah.--And there shall be no business in the world, but to know the T only; wherefore the Israelites shall be exceeding wise, and know secret things, and comprehend the knowledge of their Creator, as much as is possible for a man to do, as it is said,

"The earth shall be filled with the knowledge of YHWH."

Accordingly, the Messiah is come, who lay in the bosom of the Father, and has made known all things to his disciples, he hath heard of him; he has declared him to them, his love, grace, and mercy. God has spoken all he has to say that appertains to his own worship, and the salvation of the children of men by his Son Yeshua the Messsiah.

(m) 1 Epist. Samar. ad Scaliger, in Antiq. Eccl. Oriental, p. 125. (n) Zohar in Gen. fol, 74. 1. (o) Zohar in Lev. x. 1. (p) Maimon. Hilch. Melachim, c. 11. sect. 4. & 12. 5.

26. Jesus saith unto her, I that speak unto thee am he.

Greek/Transliteration
26. Λέγει αὐτῇ ὁ Ἰησοῦς, Ἐγώ εἰμι, ὁ λαλῶν σοι.

26. Legei autei 'o Yeisous, Ego eimi, 'o lalon soi.

Hebrew/Transliteration
:כו. וַיֹּאמֶר אֵלֶיהָ יֵשׁוּעַ אֲנִי הוּא הַמְדַבֵּר אֵלָיִךְ

26. Va•yo•mer e•le•ha Yeshua ani hoo ha•me•da•ber ela•yich.

---

27. And upon this came his disciples, and marvelled that he talked with the woman: yet no man said, What seekest thou? or, Why talkest thou with her?

Greek/Transliteration
27. Καὶ ἐπὶ τούτῳ ἦλθον οἱ μαθηταὶ αὐτοῦ, καὶ ἐθαύμασαν ὅτι μετὰ γυναικὸς ἐλάλει· οὐδεὶς μέντοι εἶπεν, Τί ζητεῖς; ἤ, Τί λαλεῖς μετ᾽ αὐτῆς;

27. Kai epi touto eilthon 'oi matheitai autou, kai ethaumasan 'oti meta gunaikos elalei. Oudeis mentoi eipen, Ti zeiteis? ei, Ti laleis met auteis?

Hebrew/Transliteration
כז. עוֹד דְּבָרוֹ בְּפִיו וְתַלְמִידָיו בָּאוּ וַיִּתְמְהוּ עַל-דַּבְּרוֹ עִם-אַשָּׁה אַךְ אִישׁ לֹא אָמַר מַה-תְּבַקֵּשׁ אוֹ לָמָה תְדַבֵּר:אֵלֶיהָ

27. Od de•va•ro be•fiv ve•tal•mi•dav ba•oo va•yit•me•hoo al - dab•ro eem - ee•sha ach eesh lo amar ma? - te•va•kesh oh la•ma te•da•ber e•le•ha?

Rabbinic Jewish Commentary
Their rule is this, "Do not multiply discourse with a woman, with his wife they say, much less with his neighbour's wife: hence the wise men say, at whatsoever time a man multiplies discourse with a woman, he is the cause of evil to himself, and ceases from the words of the law, and at last shall go down into sheol (q)."

And especially this was thought to be very unseemly in any public place, as in an inn, or in the street: hence that direction (r),

"Let not a man talk with a woman in the streets, even with his wife; and there is no need to say with another man's wife."

And particularly it was thought very unbecoming a religious man, a doctor, or scholar, or a disciple of a wise man so to do. This is one of the six things which are a reproach to a scholar, "to talk with a woman in the street" (s). And it is even said, (t), "let him not talk with a woman in the street, though she is his wife, or his sister, or his daughter."

Now this shows the reverence the disciples had for Yeshua, and the great opinion they entertained of him, that whatever he did was well, and wisely done, though it might seem strange to them, and they could not account for it: however, they did not think that he, who was their Lord and master, was accountable to them for what he did; and they doubted not but he had good reasons for his conduct.

(q) Pirke Abot, c. 1. sect. 5. Abot R, Nathan, c. 7. fol. 3. 3. & Derech Eretz, fol. 17. 3. (r) Bemidbar Rabba, sect 10. fol. 200. 2. (s) T. Bab. Beracot, fol. 43. 2. (t) Maimon. Hilch. Dayot, c. 5. sect. 7.

---

28. The woman then left her waterpot, and went her way into the city, and saith to the men,

Greek/Transliteration
28. ᾿Αφῆκεν οὖν τὴν ὑδρίαν αὐτῆς ἡ γυνή, καὶ ἀπῆλθεν εἰς τὴν πόλιν, καὶ λέγει τοῖς ἀνθρώποις,

28. Apheiken oun tein 'udrian auteis 'ei gunei, kai apeilthen eis tein polin, kai legei tois anthropois,

Hebrew/Transliteration
כח. וְהָאִשָּׁה עָזְבָה אֶת-כַּדָּהּ וַתֵּלֶךְ הָעִירָה וַתֹּאמֶר אֶל-הָעָם:

28. Ve•ha•ee•sha az•va et - ka•da va•te•lech ha•ee•ra va•to•mer el - ha•am.

Rabbinic Jewish Commentary
and saith to the men. The Ethiopic version adds, "of her house"; no doubt the men of the place in general are meant; not only those of her family, but the inhabitants of the city. The Syriac version leaves out the words, "to the men". The Jews will not allow the Cuthites, or Samaritans, to be called "men"; this they peculiarly ascribe to priests, Levites, and Israelites (u).

(u) T. Bab. Yebamot, fol. 61. 1. & Tosephot in ib.

---

29. Come, see a man, which told me all things that ever I did: is not this the Christ?

Greek/Transliteration
29. Δεῦτε, ἴδετε ἄνθρωπον, ὃς εἶπέν μοι πάντα ὅσα ἐποίησα· μήτι οὗτός ἐστιν ὁ χριστός;

29. Deute, idete anthropon, 'os eipen moi panta 'osa epoieisa. meiti 'outos estin 'o christos?

Hebrew/Transliteration
:כט. בֹּאוּ וּרְאוּ אִישׁ אֲשֶׁר הִגִּיד לִי כָּל-אֲשֶׁר עָשִׂיתִי הַאֵין זֶה הוּא הַמָּשִׁיחַ

29. Bo•oo oor•oo eesh asher hi•gid li kol - asher a•si•ti ha•ein ze hoo
ha•Ma•shi•ach.

---

30. Then they went out of the city, and came unto him.

Greek/Transliteration
30. Ἐξῆλθον ἐκ τῆς πόλεως, καὶ ἤρχοντο πρὸς αὐτόν.

30. Exeilthon ek teis poleos, kai eirchonto pros auton.

Hebrew/Transliteration
:ל. וַיֵּצְאוּ מִן-הָעִיר לָבֹא אֵלָיו

30. Va•yetz•oo min - ha•eer la•vo elav.

---

31. In the mean while his disciples prayed him, saying, Master, eat.

Greek/Transliteration
31. Ἐν δὲ τῷ μεταξὺ ἠρώτων αὐτὸν οἱ μαθηταί, λέγοντες, Ῥαββί, φάγε.

31. En de to metaxu eiroton auton 'oi matheitai, legontes, 'Rabbi, phage.

Hebrew/Transliteration
:לא. וַיְהִי עַד-כֹּה וְעַד כֹּה וַיֹּאמְרוּ אֵלָיו תַּלְמִידָיו רַבִּי אֱכֹל

31. Vay•hi ad - ko ve•ad ko va•yom•roo elav tal•mi•dav Rabbi e•chol.

---

32. But he said unto them, I have meat to eat that ye know not of.

Greek/Transliteration
32. Ὁ δὲ εἶπεν αὐτοῖς, Ἐγὼ βρῶσιν ἔχω φαγεῖν ἣν ὑμεῖς οὐκ οἴδατε.

32. 'O de eipen autois, Ego brosin echo phagein 'ein 'umeis ouk oidate.

Hebrew/Transliteration
:לב. וַיֹּאמֶר אֲלֵיהֶם אֲנִי יֶשׁ-לִי לֶאֱכֹל אֹכֶל אֲשֶׁר לֹא יְדַעְתֶּם

32. Va•yo•mer aley•hem ani yesh - li le•e•chol o•chel asher lo ye•da•a•tem.

33. Therefore said the disciples one to another, Hath any man brought him ought to eat?

33. Ἔλεγον οὖν οἱ μαθηταὶ πρὸς ἀλλήλους, Μή τις ἤνεγκεν αὐτῷ φαγεῖν;

33. Elegon oun 'oi matheitai pros alleilous, Mei tis einegken auto phagein?

Hebrew/Transliteration
‏לג. וַיֹּאמְרוּ הַתַּלְמִידִים אִישׁ אֶל-רֵעֵהוּ הַאִם הֵבִיא לוֹ אִישׁ מַאֲכָל לְאָכְלָה:

33. Va•yom•roo ha•tal•mi•dim eesh el - re•e•hoo ha•eem he•vi lo eesh ma•a•chal le•och•la?

---

34. Jesus saith unto them, My meat is to do the will of him that sent me, and to finish his work.

Greek/Transliteration
34. Λέγει αὐτοῖς ὁ Ἰησοῦς, Ἐμὸν βρῶμά ἐστιν, ἵνα ποιῶ τὸ θέλημα τοῦ πέμψαντός με, καὶ τελειώσω αὐτοῦ τὸ ἔργον.

34. Legei autois 'o Yeisous, Emon broma estin, 'ina poio to theleima tou pempsantos me, kai teleioso autou to ergon.

Hebrew/Transliteration
‏לד. וַיֹּאמֶר אֲלֵיהֶם יֵשׁוּעַ מַאֲכָלִי הוּא עֲשׂוֹת רְצוֹן שֹׁלְחִי וּלְכַלּוֹת אֶת-פָּעֳלוֹ:

34. Va•yo•mer aley•hem Yeshua ma•a•cha•li hoo asot r`tzon shol•chi ool•cha•lot et - pa•o•lo.

---

35. Say not ye, There are yet four months, and then cometh harvest? behold, I say unto you, Lift up your eyes, and look on the fields; for they are white already to harvest.

Greek/Transliteration
35. Οὐχ ὑμεῖς λέγετε ὅτι Ἔτι τετράμηνός ἐστιν, καὶ ὁ θερισμὸς ἔρχεται; Ἰδού, λέγω ὑμῖν, ἐπάρατε τοὺς ὀφθαλμοὺς ὑμῶν, καὶ θεάσασθε τὰς χώρας, ὅτι λευκαί εἰσιν πρὸς θερισμὸν ἤδη.

35. Ouch 'umeis legete 'oti Eti tetrameinos estin, kai 'o therismos erchetai? Ydou, lego 'umin, eparate tous ophthalmous 'umon, kai theasasthe tas choras, 'oti leukai eisin pros therismon eidei.

99

Hebrew/Transliteration

לה. הֵן אַתֶּם אֹמְרִים עוֹד אַרְבָּעָה חֳדָשִׁים טֶרֶם יָבֹא הַקָּצִיר וַאֲנִי אֹמֵר לָכֶם שְׂאוּ אֶת-עֵינֵיכֶם וּרְאוּ אֶל-הַשָּׂדוֹת:אֲשֶׁר הִלְבִּינוּ לַקָּצִיר

35. Hen atem om•rim od ar•ba•ah cho•da•shim te•rem ya•vo ha•ka•tzir va•a•ni o•mer la•chem s`oo et - ey•ne•chem oor•oo el - ha•sa•dot asher hil•bi•noo la•ka•tzir.

Rabbinic Jewish Commentary
The wheat was sown before this time, and the barley a good while after.

"Half Tisri, Marcheshvan, and half Cisleu, were, זרע, seed time (w)"

The earliest they sowed their wheat was in Tisri, which answers to our September and October; i.e. to half one, and half the other. The month of Marcheshvan, which answers to October and November, was the principal month for sowing it (x): hence that paraphrase on Ecc_11:2,

"Give a good part of thy seed to thy field in Tisri, and do not refrain from sowing even in Cisleu."

As for the barley, that was sown in the months of Shebet and Adar, and usually in the latter (y); the former of which answers to January and February, and the latter to February and March. And we read (z) of their sowing seventy days before the passover, which was within six weeks of the beginning of barley harvest.

for they are white already to harvest; alluding to the corn fields, which, when ripe, and near harvest, look white: hence we read (a) of שדה הלבן, "the white field": which the Jews say is a field sown with wheat or barley, and so called to distinguish it from a field planted with trees; though it may be rather, that it is so called from its white look when ripe. So the three Targums paraphrase Gen_49:12,

"His hills (his valleys, or fields, as Onkelos) יחוורן, "are white" with corn, and flocks of sheep."

(w) T. Bab. Bava Metzia, fol. 106. 2. (x) Gloss in T. Bab. Roshhashana, fol. 16. 1. (y) Gloss in Bava Metzia & in Roshhashana ib. (z) Misn. Menachot, c. 8. sect. 2. (a) Misn. Sheviith, c. 2. sect. 1. & Moed Katon, c. 1. sect. 4.

---

36. And he that reapeth receiveth wages, and gathereth fruit unto life eternal: that both he that soweth and he that reapeth may rejoice together.

Greek/Transliteration
36. Καὶ ὁ θερίζων μισθὸν λαμβάνει, καὶ συνάγει καρπὸν εἰς ζωὴν αἰώνιον· ἵνα καὶ ὁ σπείρων ὁμοῦ χαίρῃ καὶ ὁ θερίζων.

---

36. Kai 'o therizon misthon lambanei, kai sunagei karpon eis zoein aionion. 'ina kai 'o speiron 'omou chairei kai 'o therizon.

Hebrew/Transliteration

:לו. הַקּוֹצֵר יִמְצָא שְׂכָרוֹ וּתְבוּאָה יֶאֱסֹף לְחַיֵּי עוֹלָם וְהַזֹּרֵעַ וְהַקּוֹצֵר יִשְׂמְחוּ יַחְדָּו

36. Ha•ko•tzer yim•tza s`cha•ro oot•voo•ah ye•e•sof le•cha•yey o•lam ve•ha•zo•rea ve•ha•ko•tzer yis•me•choo yach•dav.

---

37. And herein is that saying true, One soweth, and another reapeth.

Greek/Transliteration

37. Ἐν γὰρ τούτῳ ὁ λόγος ἐστὶν ὁ ἀληθινός, ὅτι Ἄλλος ἐστὶν ὁ σπείρων, καὶ ἄλλος ὁ θερίζων.

37. En gar touto 'o logos estin 'o aleithinos, 'oti Allos estin 'o speiron, kai allos 'o therizon.

Hebrew/Transliteration

:לז. לְמַלֹּאת דְּבַר הַמָּשָׁל אֶחָד זֹרֵעַ וְאַחֵר קֹצֵר

37. Le•ma•lot de•var ha•m a•shal e•chad zo•re•a ve•a•cher ko•tzer.

---

38. I sent you to reap that whereon ye bestowed no labour: other men laboured, and ye are entered into their labours.

Greek/Transliteration

38. Ἐγὼ ἀπέστειλα ὑμᾶς θερίζειν ὃ οὐχ ὑμεῖς κεκοπιάκατε· ἄλλοι κεκοπιάκασιν, καὶ ὑμεῖς εἰς τὸν κόπον αὐτῶν εἰσεληλύθατε.

38. Ego apesteila 'umas therizein 'o ouch 'umeis kekopyakate. alloi kekopyakasin, kai 'umeis eis ton kopon auton eiseleiluthate.

Hebrew/Transliteration

:לח. אָנֹכִי שָׁלַחְתִּי אֶתְכֶם לִקְצֹר בְּמָקוֹם לֹא עֲמַלְתֶּם שָׁם אֲחֵרִים עָמְלוּ וְאַתֶּם בָּאתֶם עַל-עֲמָלָם

38. Ano•chi sha•lach•ti et•chem lik•tzor be•ma•kom lo amal•tem sham a•che•rim am•loo ve•a•tem ba•tem al - ama•lam.

---

39. And many of the Samaritans of that city believed on him for the saying of the woman, which testified, He told me all that ever I did.

39. Ἐκ δὲ τῆς πόλεως ἐκείνης πολλοὶ ἐπίστευσαν εἰς αὐτὸν τῶν Σαμαρειτῶν διὰ τὸν λόγον τῆς γυναικὸς μαρτυρούσης ὅτι Εἶπέν μοι πάντα ὅσα ἐποίησα.

39. Ek de teis poleos ekeineis polloi episteusan eis auton ton Samareiton dya ton logon teis gunaikos marturouseis 'oti Eipen moi panta 'osa epoieisa.

לט. וְרַבִּים מִן-הַשֹּׁמְרֹנִים בָּעִיר הַהִיא הֶאֱמִינוּ בוֹ בַּעֲבוּר דְּבַר הָאִשָּׁה אֲשֶׁר הֵעִידָה לֵאמֹר הוּא הִגִּיד לִי אֶת:כָּל-אֲשֶׁר עָשִׂיתִי -

39. Ve•ra•bim min - ha•Shom•ro•nim ba•eer ha•hee he•e•mi•noo vo ba•a•voor de•var ha•ee•sha asher he•ee•da le•mor hoo hi•gid li et - kol - asher a•si•ti.

---

40. So when the Samaritans were come unto him, they besought him that he would tarry with them: and he abode there two days.

40. Ὡς οὖν ἦλθον πρὸς αὐτὸν οἱ Σαμαρεῖται, ἠρώτων αὐτὸν μεῖναι παρ' αὐτοῖς· καὶ ἔμεινεν ἐκεῖ δύο ἡμέρας.

40. 'Os oun eilthon pros auton 'oi Samareitai, eiroton auton meinai par autois. kai emeinen ekei duo 'eimeras.

מ. וַיָּבֹאוּ אֵלָיו הַשֹּׁמְרֹנִים וַיִּקְרְאוּ לוֹ לָשֶׁבֶת אִתָּם וַיֵּשֶׁב שָׁם יוֹמָיִם:

40. Va•ya•vo•oo elav ha•Shom•ro•nim va•yik•re•oo lo la•she•vet ee•tam va•ye•shev sham yo•ma•yim.

---

41. And many more believed because of his own word;

41. Καὶ πολλῷ πλείους ἐπίστευσαν διὰ τὸν λόγον αὐτοῦ,

41. Kai pollo pleious episteusan dya ton logon autou,

מא. וְעוֹד רַבִּים מֵהֵמָּה הֶאֱמִינוּ בוֹ בַּעֲבוּר דִּבְרֵי פִיהוּ:

41. Ve•od ra•bim me•he•ma he•e•mi•noo vo ba•a•voor div•rey fi•hoo.

---

42. And said unto the woman, Now we believe, not because of thy saying: for we have heard him ourselves, and know that this is indeed the Christ, the Saviour of the world.

Greek/Transliteration
42. τῇ τε γυναικὶ ἔλεγον ὅτι Οὐκέτι διὰ τὴν σὴν λαλιὰν πιστεύομεν· αὐτοὶ γὰρ ἀκηκόαμεν, καὶ οἴδαμεν ὅτι οὗτός ἐστιν ἀληθῶς ὁ σωτὴρ τοῦ κόσμου, ὁ χριστός.

42. tei te gunaiki elegon 'oti Ouketi dya tein sein lalyan pisteuomen. autoi gar akeikoamen, kai oidamen 'oti 'outos estin aleithos 'o soteir tou kosmou, 'o christos.

Hebrew/Transliteration
מב. וַיֹּאמְרוּ אֶל-הָאִשָּׁה עַתָּה אֲנַחְנוּ מַאֲמִינִים בּוֹ לֹא-בַעֲבוּר דְּבָרֵךְ כִּי גַּם-אֲנַחְנוּ שָׁמַעְנוּ וַנֵּדַע כִּי- אָמֵן זֶה הוּא:הַמָּשִׁיחַ מוֹשִׁיעַ הָעוֹלָם

42. Va•yom•roo el - ha•ee•sha ata a•nach•noo ma•a•mi•nim bo lo - va•a•voor d`va•rech ki gam - a•nach•noo sha•ma•a•noo va•ne•da ki - amen ze hoo ha•Ma•shi•ach Mo•shi•a ha•o•lam.

Rabbinic Jewish Commentary
The Jews (b) do call the Messenger in Exo_23:20 פרוקא דעלמא, "the Saviour", or "Redeemer of" the world. And this the Samaritans might know from the writings of Moses, as from Gen_22:18 their present knowledge of Yeshua was not a mere notional, speculative, and general one, but was special, spiritual, and saving, which they had from the spirit of wisdom and revelation in the knowledge of Yeshua; they approved of him as their Saviour; they trusted in him as such; they had an experimental acquaintance with him, and practically owned him; and which they attained to by hearing him.

(b) Zohar in Gen. fol. 124. 4.

---

43. Now after two days he departed thence, and went into Galilee.

Greek/Transliteration
43. Μετὰ δὲ τὰς δύο ἡμέρας ἐξῆλθεν ἐκεῖθεν, καὶ ἀπῆλθεν εἰς τὴν Γαλιλαίαν.

43. Meta de tas duo 'eimeras exeilthen ekeithen, kai apeilthen eis tein Galilaian.

Hebrew/Transliteration
:מג. וַיְהִי אַחֲרֵי שְׁנַיִם יָמִים וַיִּסַּע לְמַסָּעָיו הַגָּלִילָה

43. Vay•hi a•cha•rey sh`na•yim ya•mim va•yi•sa le•ma•sa•av ha•Ga•li•la.

44. For Jesus himself testified, that a prophet hath no honour in his own country.

Greek/Transliteration
44. Αὐτὸς γὰρ ὁ Ἰησοῦς ἐμαρτύρησεν ὅτι προφήτης ἐν τῇ ἰδίᾳ πατρίδι τιμὴν οὐκ ἔχει.

44. Autos gar 'o Yeisous emartureisen 'oti propheiteis en tei idia patridi timein ouk echei.

Hebrew/Transliteration
מד. אַף כִּי הִגִּיד יֵשׁוּעַ כִּי אֵין-כָּבוֹד לְנָבִיא בְּאֶרֶץ מוֹלַדְתּוֹ:

44. Af ki hi•gid Yeshua ki eyn - ka•vod le•na•vi be•e•retz mo•la•d`to.

---

45. Then when he was come into Galilee, the Galilaeans received him, having seen all the things that he did at Jerusalem at the feast: for they also went unto the feast.

Greek/Transliteration
45. Ὅτε οὖν ἦλθεν εἰς τὴν Γαλιλαίαν, ἐδέξαντο αὐτὸν οἱ Γαλιλαῖοι, πάντα ἑωρακότες ἃ ἐποίησεν ἐν Ἱεροσολύμοις ἐν τῇ ἑορτῇ· καὶ αὐτοὶ γὰρ ἦλθον εἰς τὴν ἑορτήν.

45. 'Ote oun eilthen eis tein Galilaian, edexanto auton 'oi Galilaioi, panta 'eorakotes 'a epoieisen en 'Yerosolumois en tei 'eortei. kai autoi gar eilthon eis tein 'eortein.

Hebrew/Transliteration
מה. וַיָּבֹא אֶל-הַגָּלִיל וַיַּחֲזִיקוּ-בוֹ הַגְּלִילִים כִּי רָאוּ אֶת כָּל-אֲשֶׁר עָשָׂה בִירוּשָׁלַיִם בִּימֵי הֶחָג כִּי גַם-הֵם חָגְגוּ:שָׁם אֶת-הֶחָג הַהוּא

45. Va•ya•vo el - ha•Galil va•ya•cha•zi•koo - vo ha•Ga•li•lim ki ra•oo et kol - asher asa vi•Ye•roo•sha•la•yim bi•mey he•chag ki gam - hem cha•ge•goo sham et - ha•chag ha•hoo.

Rabbinic Jewish Commentary
for they also went unto the feast; as well as Yeshua and his disciples: they kept the feast of the passover, and went yearly to Jerusalem on that account: so Josephus speaks of the Galilaeans going to the Jewish festivals at Jerusalem, when he says (c);

"It was the custom, or usual with the Galilaeans, when they went to the holy city at the festivals, to go through the country of the Samaritans;"

(c) Antiqu. Jud. l. 20. c. 5.

46. So Jesus came again into Cana of Galilee, where he made the water wine. And there was a certain nobleman, whose son was sick at Capernaum.

Greek/Transliteration
46. Ἦλθεν οὖν πάλιν ὁ Ἰησοῦς εἰς τὴν Κανᾶ τῆς Γαλιλαίας, ὅπου ἐποίησεν τὸ ὕδωρ οἶνον. Καὶ ἦν τις βασιλικός, οὗ ὁ υἱὸς ἠσθένει ἐν Καπερναούμ.

46. Eilthen oun palin 'o Yeisous eis tein Kana teis Galilaias, 'opou epoieisen to 'udor oinon. Kai ein tis basilikos, 'ou 'o 'wios eisthenei en Kapernaoum.

Hebrew/Transliteration
מו. וַיָּבֹא יֵשׁוּעַ עוֹד הַפַּעַם אֶל-קָנָה בַּגָּלִיל אֲשֶׁר הָפַךְ שָׁם הַמַּיִם לְיָיִן וְאִישׁ הָיָה מֵעַבְדֵי הַמֶּלֶךְ וּבְנוֹ - חֹלֶה בִּכְפַר:נַחוּם

46. Va•ya•vo Yeshua od ha•pa•am el - Kana ba•Ga•lil asher ha•fach sham ha•ma•yim le•ya•yin ve•eesh ha•ya me•av•dey ha•me•lech oov•no cho•le bi•Ch`far - Na•choom.

---

47. When he heard that Jesus was come out of Judaea into Galilee, he went unto him, and besought him that he would come down, and heal his son: for he was at the point of death.

Greek/Transliteration
47. Οὗτος ἀκούσας ὅτι Ἰησοῦς ἥκει ἐκ τῆς Ἰουδαίας εἰς τὴν Γαλιλαίαν, ἀπῆλθεν πρὸς αὐτόν, καὶ ἠρώτα αὐτὸν ἵνα καταβῇ καὶ ἰάσηται αὐτοῦ τὸν υἱόν· ἔμελλεν γὰρ ἀποθνήσκειν.

47. 'Outos akousas 'oti Yeisous 'eikei ek teis Youdaias eis tein Galilaian, apeilthen pros auton, kai eirota auton 'ina katabei kai iaseitai autou ton 'wion. emellen gar apothneiskein.

Hebrew/Transliteration
מז. וְכַאֲשֶׁר שָׁמַע כִּי-בָא יֵשׁוּעַ מִיהוּדָה לַגָּלִיל וַיֵּלֶךְ אֵלָיו וַיִּפְצַר-בּוֹ לָרֶדֶת אִתּוֹ וְלִרְפֹּא אֶת-בְּנוֹ אֲשֶׁר נָטָה לָמוּת:

47. Ve•cha•a•sher sha•ma ki - va Yeshua mi•Y`hoo•da la•Ga•lil va•ye•lech elav va•yif•tzar - bo la•re•det ee•to ve•lir•po et - b`no asher na•ta la•moot.

---

48. Then said Jesus unto him, Except ye see signs and wonders, ye will not believe.

Greek/Transliteration
48. Εἶπεν οὖν ὁ Ἰησοῦς πρὸς αὐτόν, Ἐὰν μὴ σημεῖα καὶ τέρατα ἴδητε, οὐ μὴ πιστεύσητε.

48. Eipen oun 'o Yeisous pros auton, Ean mei seimeia kai terata ideite, ou mei pisteuseite.

Hebrew/Transliteration
:מח. וַיֹּאמֶר אֵלָיו יֵשׁוּעַ אִם-לֹא תִרְאוּ אֹתוֹת וּמֹפְתִים לֹא תַאֲמִינוּ

48. Va•yo•mer elav Yeshua eem - lo tir•oo o•tot oo•mof•tim lo ta•a•mi•noo.

---

49. The nobleman saith unto him, Sir, come down ere my child die.

Greek/Transliteration
49. Λέγει πρὸς αὐτὸν ὁ βασιλικός, Κύριε, κατάβηθι πρὶν ἀποθανεῖν τὸ παιδίον μου.

49. Legei pros auton 'o basilikos, Kurie, katabeithi prin apothanein to paidion mou.

Hebrew/Transliteration
:מט. וַיֹּאמֶר אֵלָיו הָאִישׁ רְדָה-נָּא אֲדֹנִי בְּטֶרֶם יָמוּת בְּנִי

49. Va•yo•mer elav ha•eesh r`da - na Adoni be•te•rem ya•moot b`ni.

---

50. Jesus saith unto him, Go thy way; thy son liveth. And the man believed the word that Jesus had spoken unto him, and he went his way.

Greek/Transliteration
50. Λέγει αὐτῷ ὁ Ἰησοῦς, Πορεύου· ὁ υἱός σου ζῇ. Καὶ ἐπίστευσεν ὁ ἄνθρωπος τῷ λόγῳ ᾧ εἶπεν αὐτῷ ὁ Ἰησοῦς, καὶ ἐπορεύετο.

50. Legei auto 'o Yeisous, Poreuou. 'o 'wios sou zei. Kai episteusen 'o anthropos to logo 'o eipen auto 'o Yeisous, kai eporeueto.

Hebrew/Transliteration
:נ. וַיֹּאמֶר אֵלָיו יֵשׁוּעַ לֵךְ לְדַרְכְּךָ בִּנְךָ חָי וְהָאִישׁ הֶאֱמִין בַּדָּבָר אֲשֶׁר-דִּבֶּר יֵשׁוּעַ וַיֵּלַךְ

50. Va•yo•mer elav Yeshua lech le•dar•ke•cha bin•cha chai ve•ha•eesh he•e•min ba•da•var asher - di•ber Yeshua va•ye•lech.

---

51. And as he was now going down, his servants met him, and told him, saying, Thy son liveth.

51. Ἤδη δὲ αὐτοῦ καταβαίνοντος, οἱ δοῦλοι αὐτοῦ ἀπήντησαν αὐτῷ, καὶ ἀπήγγειλαν λέγοντες ὅτι Ὁ παῖς σου ζῇ.

51. Eidei de autou katabainontos, 'oi douloi autou apeinteisan auto, kai apeingeilan legontes 'oti 'O pais sou zei.

נא. וַיְהִי בְּלֶכְתּוֹ וַיִּפְגְּעוּ-בוֹ עֲבָדָיו וַיַּגִּידוּ לוֹ לֵאמֹר בִּנְךָ חָי:

51. Vay•hi be•lech•to va•yif•ge•oo - vo ava•dav va•ya•gi•doo lo le•mor bin•cha chai.

---

52. Then inquired he of them the hour when he began to amend. And they said unto him, Yesterday at the seventh hour the fever left him.

52. Ἐπύθετο οὖν παρ᾽ αὐτῶν τὴν ὥραν ἐν ᾗ κομψότερον ἔσχεν. Καὶ εἶπον αὐτῷ ὅτι Χθὲς ὥραν ἑβδόμην ἀφῆκεν αὐτὸν ὁ πυρετός.

52. Eputheto oun par auton tein 'oran en 'ei kompsoteron eschen. Kai eipon auto 'oti Chthes 'oran 'ebdomein apheiken auton 'o puretos.

נב. וַיִּדְרֹשׁ מֵהֶם אֶת-הַשָּׁעָה אֲשֶׁר הֵחֵל לְהֵרָפֵא מֵחָלְיוֹ וַיֹּאמְרוּ אֵלָיו אֶתְמוֹל בַּשָּׁעָה הַשְּׁבִיעִית סָרָה מִמֶּנּוּ:הַקַּדָּחַת.

52. Va•yid•rosh me•hem et - ha•sha•ah asher he`chel le•he•ra•fe me•chol•yo va•yom•roo elav et•mol ba•sha•ah hash•vi•eet sa•ra mi•me•noo ha•ka•da•chat.

---

53. So the father knew that it was at the same hour, in the which Jesus said unto him, Thy son liveth: and himself believed, and his whole house.

53. Ἔγνω οὖν ὁ πατὴρ ὅτι ἐν ἐκείνῃ τῇ ὥρᾳ, ἐν ᾗ εἶπεν αὐτῷ ὁ Ἰησοῦς ὅτι Ὁ υἱός σου ζῇ· καὶ ἐπίστευσεν αὐτὸς καὶ ἡ οἰκία αὐτοῦ ὅλη.

53. Egno oun 'o pateir 'oti en ekeinei tei 'ora, en eipen auto 'o Yeisous 'oti 'O 'wios sou zei. Kai episteusen autos kai 'ei oikia autou 'olei.

נג. וַיֵּדַע אָבִיו כִּי הָיָה בַּשָּׁעָה הַהִיא אֲשֶׁר הִגִּיד-לוֹ יֵשׁוּעַ בִּנְךָ חָי וַיַּאֲמֵן הוּא וְכָל-בֵּיתוֹ:

53. Va•ye•da aviv ki ha•ya ba•sha•ah ha•hee asher hi•gid - lo Yeshua bin•cha chai va•ya•a•men hoo ve•chol - bei•to.

Rabbinic Jewish Commentary

There is a story, told by the Jews, and which seems somewhat like to this (d);

"It is reported concerning R. Chanina ben Dosa, that when he prayed for the sick, he used to say, **זה חי,** "this liveth", and this dies; it was said to him, whence knowest thou this? he replied, if my prayer be ready in my mouth, I know that he is accepted (of God, i.e. the sick man for whom he prayed); but if not, I know that he will be snatched away (by the disease):"

Upon which the Gemarists give the following relation (e);

"It happened that the son of Rabban Gamaliel (the Apostle Paul's master) was sick, he sent two disciples to R. Chanina ben Dosa, to ask mercy for him; when he saw them, he went up to a chamber, and sought mercy for him; and when he came down, he said unto them, **לכו שחלצתו חמה,** "go your way, for the fever has left him"; they said unto him, art thou a prophet? he replied, I am not a prophet, nor the son of a prophet; but so I have received, that if my prayer is ready in my mouth, I know that he is accepted; and if not, I know that he shall be snatched away; and they sat and wrote and observed "the very hour"; and when they came to Rabban Gamaliel, he said unto them, this service ye have not been wanting in, nor abounded in; but so the thing was, that in that hour the fever left him, and he asked of us water to drink."

Which story perhaps is told, to vie with this miracle of Yeshua, and to obscure the glory of it.

(d) Misn. Beracot, c. 5. sect. 5. (e) T. Bab. Beracot, fol. 34. 2.

---

54. This is again the second miracle that Jesus did, when he was come out of Judaea into Galilee.

Greek/Transliteration

54. Τοῦτο πάλιν δεύτερον σημεῖον ἐποίησεν ὁ Ἰησοῦς, ἐλθὼν ἐκ τῆς Ἰουδαίας εἰς τὴν Γαλιλαίαν.

54. Touto palin deuteron seimeion epoieisen 'o Yeisous, elthon ek teis Youdaias eis tein Galilaian.

Hebrew/Transliteration

נד. זֶה הוּא הָאוֹת הַשֵּׁנִי אֲשֶׁר עָשָׂה יֵשׁוּעַ בַּגָּלִיל בְּשׁוּבוֹ מִיהוּדָה:

54. Ze hoo ha•ot ha•she•ni asher asa Yeshua ba•Ga•lil be•shoo•vo mi•Y`hoo•da.

John, Chapter 5

1. After this there was a feast of the Jews; and Jesus went up to Jerusalem.

Greek/Transliteration

1. Μετὰ ταῦτα ἦν ἡ ἑορτὴ τῶν Ἰουδαίων, καὶ ἀνέβη ὁ Ἰησοῦς εἰς Ἱεροσόλυμα.

1. Meta tauta ein 'ei 'eortei ton Youdaion, kai anebei 'o Yeisous eis 'Yerosoluma.

Hebrew/Transliteration

א: וְאַחֲרֵי-כֵן בָּא מוֹעֵד חַג הַיְּהוּדִים וַיַּעַל יֵשׁוּעַ יְרוּשָׁלָיְמָה

1. Ve•a•cha•rey - chen ba mo•ed chag ha•Ye•hoo•dim va•ya•al Yeshua Ye•roo•sha•lai•ma.

---

2. Now there is at Jerusalem by the sheep market a pool, which is called in the Hebrew tongue Bethesda, having five porches.

Greek/Transliteration

2. Ἔστιν δὲ ἐν τοῖς Ἱεροσολύμοις ἐπὶ τῇ προβατικῇ κολυμβήθρα, ἡ ἐπιλεγομένη Ἑβραϊστὶ Βηθεσδά, πέντε στοὰς ἔχουσα.

2. Estin de en tois 'Yerosolumois epi tei probatikei kolumbeithra, 'ei epilegomenei 'Ebraisti Beithesda, pente stoas echousa.

Hebrew/Transliteration

ב. וּבִירוּשָׁלַיִם בְּרֵכַת מַיִם עַל-יַד שַׁעַר הַצֹּאן אֲשֶׁר קָרְאוּ לָהּ בְּלָשׁוֹן עִבְרִית בֵּית-חַסְדָּא וְלָהּ חֲמִשָּׁה אֶלָמוֹת:

2. Oo•vi•ye•roo•sha•la•yim b`re•chat ma•yim al - yad sha•ar ha•tzon asher kar•oo la be•la•shon Eev•rit Beit - Chasda ve•la cha•mi•sha oo•la•mot.

Rabbinic Jewish Commentary

The Vulgate Latin and Ethiopic versions read, "there is at Jerusalem a sheep pool"; and so it is interpreted in the Arabic version, and Jerom calls it the "cattle pool" (f). The Targumist on Jer_31:39 speaks of a pool called בריכה עגלה, "the calf", or "heifer pool"; though the translations of it, both in the London Polyglott, and in the king of Spain's Bible, interpret it "the round pool". This pool of Bethesda, is thought by some, to be the same which the Jews call the great pool in Jerusalem; they say (g),

"Between Hebron and Jerusalem, is the fountain Etham, from whence the waters come by way of pipes, unto the great pool, which is in Jerusalem."

And R. Benjamin (h) speaks of a pool, which is to be seen to this day, where the ancients slew their sacrifices, and all the Jews write their names on the wall: and some think it was so called, because the sheep that were offered in sacrifice, were there washed; which must be either before, or after they were slain; not before, for it was not required that what was to be slain for sacrifice should be washed first; and afterwards, only the entrails of a beast were washed; and for this there was a particular place in the temple, called לשכת המדיחין "the washing room"; where, they say (i), they washed the inwards of the holy sacrifices. This pool here, therefore, seems rather to have been a bath for unclean persons; and having this miraculous virtue hereafter spoken of, diseased persons only, at certain times, had recourse to it. The Syriac and Persic versions call it, "a place of a baptistery"; and both leave out the clause, "by the sheep market", or "gate": it is not easy to say where and what it was.

which is called in the Hebrew tongue, Bethesda; The Vulgate Latin and Ethiopic versions read Bethsaida, very wrongly; and it is called by Tertullian (l) the pool of Bethsaida. The Hebrew tongue here mentioned is כתב של עבר הנהר, "the language of those beyond the river" (m), i.e. the river Euphrates; which is the Chaldee language, as distinct from the Assyrian language, which is called the holy and blessed language; the former is what the Cuthites, or Samaritans used; the latter, that in which the book of the law was written (n).

(f) De Locis Hebraicis, p. 89. L. Tom. III. (g) Cippi Hebraici, p. 10. (h) Itinerar. p. 43. (i) Misn. Middot, c. 5. sect. 2. Maimon. Beth Habbechira, c. 5. sect. 17. (k) De Excidio, l. 2. c. 15. (l) Adv. Judaeos, c. 13. (m) De Semente, p. 345. Tom. I. (n) In Chambers' Dictionary, in the word "Piscina".

---

3. In these lay a great multitude of impotent folk, of blind, halt, withered, waiting for the moving of the water.

Greek/Transliteration
3. Ἐν ταύταις κατέκειτο πλῆθος πολὺ τῶν ἀσθενούντων, τυφλῶν, χωλῶν, ξηρῶν, ἐκδεχομένων τὴν τοῦ ὕδατος κίνησιν.

3. En tautais katekeito pleithos polu ton asthenounton, tuphlon, cholon, xeiron, ekdechomenon tein tou 'udatos kineisin.

Hebrew/Transliteration
ג. וְשָׁם שָׁכְבוּ רַבִּים חוֹלִים עִוְרִים פִּסְחִים וִיבֵשֵׁי-כֹּחַ וְהֵם מְיַחֲלִים שָׁם לִתְנוּעַת הַמָּיִם:

3. Ve•sham shach•voo ra•bim cho•lim eev•rim pis•chim vi•ve•shey - cho•ach ve•hem me•ya•cha•lim sham lit•noo•at ha•ma•yim.

---

4. For an angel went down at a certain season into the pool, and troubled the water: whosoever then first after the troubling of the water stepped in was made whole of whatsoever disease he had.

Greek/Transliteration

4. Ἄγγελος γὰρ κατὰ καιρὸν κατέβαινεν ἐν τῇ κολυμβήθρᾳ, καὶ ἐτάρασσεν τὸ ὕδωρ· ὁ οὖν πρῶτος ἐμβὰς μετὰ τὴν ταραχὴν τοῦ ὕδατος, ὑγιὴς ἐγίνετο, ᾧ δήποτε κατείχετο νοσήματι.

4. Angelos gar kata kairon katebainen en tei kolumbeithra, kai etarassen to 'udor. 'o oun protos embas meta tein tarachein tou 'udatos, 'ugieis egineto, 'o deipote kateicheto noseimati.

Hebrew/Transliteration

ד. כִּי לְעַד מִן-הָעִתִּים יֵרֵד מַלְאָךְ אֶל-הַבְּרֵכָה וְהִרְתִּיחַ אֶת-הַמַּיִם וְהָיָה הָרִאשׁוֹן הַיֹּרֵד שָׁם אַחֲרֵי אֲשֶׁר רְתְחוּ׃הַמַּיִם וְרָפָא לוֹ מִכָּל-מַחֲלָה אֲשֶׁר דָּבְקָה-בּוֹ

4. Ki le•ad min - ha•ee•tim ye•red mal•ach el - hab•re•cha ve•hir•ti•ach et - ha•ma•yim ve•ha•ya ha•ri•shon ha•yo•red sham a•cha•rey asher root•choo ha•ma•yim ve•ra•fa lo mi•kol - ma•cha•la asher dav•ka - bo.

Rabbinic Jewish Commentary

This messenger was "The Messenger of the LORD", as the Vulgate Latin, and two of Beza's copies read; and so the Ethiopic version reads, "The Messenger of God"; who either in a visible form came down from heaven, and went into the pool, the Ethiopic version very wrongly renders it, "was washed in the pool"; or it was concluded by the people, from the unusual agitation of the water, and the miraculous virtue which ensued upon it, that an angel did descend into it; and this was not at all times, but at a certain time; either once a year, as Tertullian thought, at the time of the feast of the passover, or every sabbath, as this was now the sabbath day; or it may be there was no fixed period for it, but at some times and seasons in the year so it was, which kept the people continually waiting for it.

The Jews have a notion of spirits troubling waters; they speak of a certain fountain where a spirit resided, and an evil spirit attempted to come in his room; upon which a contest arose, and they saw ערבוביא דמייא, "the waters troubled", and think drops of blood upon them (q): the Syriac (r) writers have a tradition, that

"Because the body of Isaiah the prophet was hid in Siloah, therefore a messenger descended and moved the waters."

From whence it seems, that only one person at a season received a cure, by going in first into the water, so Tertullian thought (s): the Jews ascribe an healing virtue to the well of Miriam; they say,

"A certain ulcerous person went to dip himself in the sea of Tiberias, and it happened at that time, that the well of Miriam flowed, and he washed, ואיתסי, and was healed (t)."

(q) Vajikra Rabba, sect. 24. fol. 165. 2. (r) Vid. Hackspan. Interpr. Errabund. sect. 20. (s) De Baptismo, c. 5. (t) Midrash Kohelet, fol. 71. 4.

---

5. And a certain man was there, which had an infirmity thirty and eight years.

Greek/Transliteration
5. Ἦν δέ τις ἄνθρωπος ἐκεῖ τριάκοντα ὀκτὼ ἔτη ἔχων ἐν τῇ ἀσθενείᾳ.

5. Ein de tis anthropos ekei tryakonta okto etei echon en tei astheneia.

Hebrew/Transliteration
‏ה. וְאִישׁ הָיָה שָׁם אֲשֶׁר חָלָה אֶת-חָלְיוֹ שְׁמֹנֶה וּשְׁלֹשִׁים שָׁנָה:

5. Ve•eesh ha•ya sham asher cha•la et - chol•yo sh`mo•ne oosh•lo•shim sha•na.

Rabbinic Commentary
Tertullian says (u), that there was in Judea a medicinal lake, before Yeshua's time; and that the pool of Bethsaida (it should be Bethesda) was useful in curing the diseases of the Israelites; but ceased from yielding any benefit, when the name of the LORD was blasphemed by them, through their rage and fury, and continuance in it (w); but in what year it began, and the precise time it ceased, he says not. The Persic version here adds, "and was reduced to such a state that he could not move".

(u) De Anima, c. 50. (w) Adv. Judaeos, c. 13.

---

6. When Jesus saw him lie, and knew that he had been now a long time in that case, he saith unto him, Wilt thou be made whole?

Greek/Transliteration
6. Τοῦτον ἰδὼν ὁ Ἰησοῦς κατακείμενον, καὶ γνοὺς ὅτι πολὺν ἤδη χρόνον ἔχει, λέγει αὐτῷ, Θέλεις ὑγιὴς γενέσθαι;

6. Touton idon 'o Yeisous katakeimenon, kai gnous 'oti polun eidei chronon echei, legei auto, Theleis 'ugieis genesthai?

Hebrew/Transliteration
‏ו. וַיַּרְא אֹתוֹ יֵשׁוּעַ שֹׁכֵב עַל-מִשְׁכָּבוֹ וַיֵּדַע כִּי שָׁכַב כֵּן יָמִים רַבִּים וַיֹּאמֶר אֵלָיו הֶחָפֵץ אַתָּה לְהֵרָפֵא:

6. Va•yar o•to Yeshua sho•chev al - mish•ka•vo va•ye•da ki sha•chav ken ya•mim ra•bim va•yo•mer elav he•cha•fetz ata le•he•ra•fe?

---

7. The impotent man answered him, Sir, I have no man, when the water is troubled, to put me into the pool: but while I am coming, another steppeth down before me.

Greek/Transliteration

7. Ἀπεκρίθη αὐτῷ ὁ ἀσθενῶν, Κύριε, ἄνθρωπον οὐκ ἔχω ἵνα, ὅταν ταραχθῇ τὸ ὕδωρ, βάλη με εἰς τὴν κολυμβήθραν· ἐν ᾧ δὲ ἔρχομαι ἐγώ, ἄλλος πρὸ ἐμοῦ καταβαίνει.

7. Apekrithei auto 'o asthenon, Kurie, anthropon ouk echo 'ina, 'otan tarachthei to 'udor, balei me eis tein kolumbeithran. en 'o de erchomai ego, allos pro emou katabainei.

Hebrew/Transliteration

ז. וַיַּעַן אֹתוֹ הַחוֹלֶה אֲדֹנִי אֵין לִי אִישׁ אֲשֶׁר יוֹרִידֵנִי אֶל-הַבְּרֵכָה לְעֵת רְגְשַׁת הַמַּיִם וַאֲנִי טֶרֶם אֵרֵד וְיָרַד אַחֵר לְפָנָי:

7. Va•ya•an o•to ha•cho•le Adoni eyn li eesh asher yo•ri•de•ni el - hab•re•cha le•et rig•shat ha•ma•yim va•a•ni te•rem ered ve•ya•rad a•cher le•fa•nai.

---

8. Jesus saith unto him, Rise, take up thy bed, and walk.

Greek/Transliteration

8. Λέγει αὐτῷ ὁ Ἰησοῦς, Ἔγειραι, ἆρον τὸν κράββατόν σου, καὶ περιπάτει.

8. Legei auto 'o Yeisous, Egeirai, aron ton krabbaton sou, kai peripatei.

Hebrew/Transliteration

ח. וַיֹּאמֶר אֵלָיו יֵשׁוּעַ קוּם שָׂא אֶת-מִשְׁכָּבְךָ וְהִתְהַלֵּךְ:

8. Va•yo•mer elav Yeshua koom sa et - mish•kav•cha ve•hit•ha•lech.

---

9. And immediately the man was made whole, and took up his bed, and walked: and on the same day was the Sabbath.

Greek/Transliteration

9. Καὶ εὐθέως ἐγένετο ὑγιὴς ὁ ἄνθρωπος, καὶ ἦρεν τὸν κράββατον αὐτοῦ καὶ περιεπάτει. Ἦν δὲ σάββατον ἐν ἐκείνῃ τῇ ἡμέρᾳ.

9. Kai eutheos egeneto 'ugieis 'o anthropos, kai eiren ton krabbaton autou kai periepatei. Ein de sabbaton en ekeinei tei 'eimera.

Hebrew/Transliteration

ט. וּפִתְאֹם שָׁב הָאִישׁ לְאֵיתָנוֹ וַיִּשָּׂא אֶת-מִשְׁכָּבוֹ וַיֵּלֶךְ:

9. Oo•fit•om shav ha•eesh le•ey•ta•no va•yi•sa et - mish•ka•vo va•ye•lech.

---

10. The Jews therefore said unto him that was cured, It is the Sabbath day: it is not lawful for thee to carry thy bed.

Greek/Transliteration

10. Ἔλεγον οὖν οἱ Ἰουδαῖοι τῷ τεθεραπευμένῳ, Σάββατόν ἐστιν· οὐκ ἔξεστίν σοι ἆραι τὸν κράββατον.

10. Elegon oun 'oi Youdaioi to tetherapeumeno, Sabbaton estin. ouk exestin soi arai ton krabbaton.

Hebrew/Transliteration

י. וְהַיּוֹם הַהוּא הָיָה יוֹם הַשַּׁבָּת וַיֹּאמְרוּ הַיְּהוּדִים אֶל-הָאִישׁ הַנִּרְפָּא הֲלֹא שַׁבָּת הַיּוֹם וְאֵין לְךָ לָשֵׂאת אֶת:הַמִּשְׁכָּב -

10. Ve•ha•yom ha•hoo ha•ya yom ha•Sha•bat va•yom•roo ha•Ye•hoo•dim el - ha•eesh ha•nir•pa ha•lo Sha•bat ha•yom ve•eyn le•cha la•set et - ha•mish•kav.

Rabbinic Jewish Commentary

It was forbid by the law, to carry any burden on the sabbath day; see Neh_13:15; for

"Carrying out and bringing in anything, from one place to another, is said (x) to be work, and one of the principal works;"

And therefore forbid by the law, which says, "thou shall not do any work"; and one of the traditions of the elders is this (y),

"Whoever carries anything out (i.e. on the sabbath day), whether in his right hand, or in his left, in his bosom, or עַל כְּתֵפוֹ, "on his shoulder", is guilty; for so carried the Kohathites."

And particularly it is said (z), that

"He that rolls up a bed of the brasiers or tinkers (i.e. on the sabbath day) is bound to a sin offering."

Which was a fold up bed, such as tinkers, and those that went from city to city to work, had; and who carried their beds with them, as the gloss observes; and were so far from being lawful to be carried by them, on the sabbath, that they might not fold them up.

(x) Maimon. Hilchot Sabbat, c. 12. sect. 6. (y) Misn. Sabbat, c. 10. sect. 3. (z) T. Bab. Sabbat, fol. 47. 1. & 138. 1.

11. He answered them, He that made me whole, the same said unto me, Take up thy bed, and walk.

Greek/Transliteration
11. Ἀπεκρίθη αὐτοῖς, Ὁ ποιήσας με ὑγιῆ, ἐκεῖνός μοι εἶπεν, Ἆρον τὸν κράββατόν σου καὶ περιπάτει.

11. Apekrithei autois, 'O poieisas me 'ugiei, ekeinos moi eipen, Aron ton krabbaton sou kai peripatei.

Hebrew/Transliteration
יא. וַיַּעַן אֹתָם לֵאמֹר הָרֹפֵא אֹתִי הוּא אָמַר אֵלַי שָׂא אֶת-מִשְׁכָּבְךָ וְהִתְהַלֵּךְ:

11. Va•ya•an o•tam le•mor ha•ro•fe o•ti hoo amar e•lai sa et - mish•kav•cha ve•hit•ha•lech.

---

12. Then asked they him, What man is that which said unto thee, Take up thy bed, and walk?

Greek/Transliteration
12. Ἠρώτησαν οὖν αὐτόν, Τίς ἐστιν ὁ ἄνθρωπος ὁ εἰπών σοι, Ἆρον τὸν κράββατόν σου καὶ περιπάτει;

12. Eiroteisan oun auton, Tis estin 'o anthropos 'o eipon soi, Aron ton krabbaton sou kai peripatei?

Hebrew/Transliteration
יב. וַיִּשְׁאָלֻהוּ מִי הוּא הָאִישׁ אֲשֶׁר אָמַר אֵלֶיךָ שָׂא אֶת-מִשְׁכָּבְךָ וְהִתְהַלֵּךְ:

12. Va•yish•a•loo•hoo mee hoo ha•eesh asher amar e•le•cha sa et - mish•kav•cha ve•hit•ha•lech?

Rabbinic Jewish Commentary
And so the Jews since, though they cannot find fault with the cure, which they put an "if" upon, yet are highly displeased with the order, to take up his bed and carry it:

"If (say they (a)) he wrought a cure, lo, that is good, but why did he bid him take up his bed?"

The answer may be, to show that he was cured.

(a) Vet. Nizzachon, p. 207.

---

13. And he that was healed wist not who it was: for Jesus had conveyed himself away, a multitude being in that place.

Greek/Transliteration
13. Ὁ δὲ ἰαθεὶς οὐκ ᾔδει τίς ἐστιν· ὁ γὰρ Ἰησοῦς ἐξένευσεν, ὄχλου ὄντος ἐν τῷ τόπῳ.

13. 'O de iatheis ouk eidei tis estin. 'o gar Yeisous exeneusen, ochlou ontos en to topo.

Hebrew/Transliteration
יג. וְהַנִּרְפָּא לֹא יָדַע מִי הוּא כִּי יֵשׁוּעַ הָלַךְ-לוֹ בְּהִתְאַסֵּף עַם-רָב בַּמָּקוֹם הַהוּא:

13. Ve•ha•nir•pa lo ya•da mee hoo ki Yeshua ha•lach - lo be•hit•a•sef am - rav ba•ma•kom ha•hoo.

---

14. Afterward Jesus findeth him in the temple, and said unto him, Behold, thou art made whole: sin no more, lest a worse thing come unto thee.

Greek/Transliteration
14. Μετὰ ταῦτα εὑρίσκει αὐτὸν ὁ Ἰησοῦς ἐν τῷ ἱερῷ, καὶ εἶπεν αὐτῷ, Ἴδε ὑγιὴς γέγονας· μηκέτι ἁμάρτανε, ἵνα μὴ χεῖρόν τί σοι γένηται.

14. Meta tauta 'euriskei auton 'o Yeisous en to 'iero, kai eipen auto, Yde 'ugieis gegonas. Meiketi 'amartane, 'ina mei cheiron ti soi geneitai.

Hebrew/Transliteration
יד. אַחֲרֵי-כֵן מָצָא אֹתוֹ יֵשׁוּעַ בְּבֵית הַמִּקְדָּשׁ וַיֹּאמֶר אֵלָיו רְאֵה כִּי נִרְפֵּאתָ אַל-תּוֹסֶף לַחֲטֹא פֶּן-תְּאֻנֶּה אֵלֶיךָ רָעָה:גְּדוֹלָה מִזֹּאת

14. A•cha•rey - chen ma•tza o•to Yeshua be•veit ha•mik•dash va•yo•mer elav r`•eh ki nir•pe•ta al - to•sef la•cha•to pen - te•oo•ne e•le•cha ra•ah ge•do•la mi•zot.

---

15. The man departed, and told the Jews that it was Jesus, which had made him whole.

Greek/Transliteration
15. Ἀπῆλθεν ὁ ἄνθρωπος, καὶ ἀνήγγειλεν τοῖς Ἰουδαίοις ὅτι Ἰησοῦς ἐστιν ὁ ποιήσας αὐτὸν ὑγιῆ.

15. Apeilthen 'o anthropos, kai aneingeilen tois Youdaiois 'oti Yeisous estin 'o poieisas auton 'ugiei.

טו. וַיֵּלֶךְ הָאִישׁ וַיַּגֵּד לַיְּהוּדִים כִּי-יֵשׁוּעַ הוּא אֲשֶׁר רְפָאוֹ:

15. Va•ye•lech ha•eesh va•ya•ged la•Ye•hoo•dim ki - Yeshua hoo asher rip•oh.

---

16. And therefore did the Jews persecute Jesus, and sought to slay him, because he had done these things on the Sabbath day.

Greek/Transliteration
16. Καὶ διὰ τοῦτο ἐδίωκον τὸν Ἰησοῦν οἱ Ἰουδαῖοι, καὶ ἐζήτουν αὐτὸν ἀποκτεῖναι, ὅτι ταῦτα ἐποίει ἐν σαββάτῳ.

16. Kai dya touto ediokon ton Yeisoun 'oi Youdaioi, kai ezeitoun auton apokteinai, 'oti tauta epoiei en sabbato.

Hebrew/Transliteration
טז. וְעַל-כֵּן רָדְפוּ הַיְּהוּדִים אֶת-יֵשׁוּעַ וַיְבַקְשׁוּ הֲמִיתוֹ עֵקֶב אֲשֶׁר עָשָׂה זֹאת בַּשַּׁבָּת:

16. Ve•al - ken rad•foo ha•Ye•hoo•dim et - Yeshua vay•vak•shoo ha•mi•to e•kev asher asa zot ba•Sha•bat.

---

17. But Jesus answered them, My Father worketh hitherto, and I work.

Greek/Transliteation
17. Ὁ δὲ Ἰησοῦς ἀπεκρίνατο αὐτοῖς, Ὁ πατήρ μου ἕως ἄρτι ἐργάζεται, κἀγὼ ἐργάζομαι.

17. 'O de Yeisous apekrinato autois, 'O pateir mou 'eos arti ergazetai, kago ergazomai.

Hebrew/Transliteration
יז. וַיַּעַן אֹתָם יֵשׁוּעַ אָבִי פֹּעֵל פְּעֻלָּתוֹ עַד-עָתָּה וְגַם-אֲנִי פֹּעֵל הִנֵּנִי:

17. Va•ya•an o•tam Yeshua Avi po•el pe•oo•la•to ad - ata ve•gam - ani po•el hi•ne•ni.

Rabbinic Jewish Commentary
and I work; or "also I work"; as the Syriac and Arabic version reads; i.e. in conjunction with him, as a co-efficient cause in the works of providence, in the government of the world, in upholding all things in it, in bearing up the pillars of the earth, in holding things together, and sustaining all creatures: or I also work in imitation of him, in doing good both to the bodies and souls of men on the sabbath day, being the LORD of it: I do but what my Father does, and therefore, as he is not to be blamed for his works on that day, as none will say he is, no more am I.

Philo the Jew says (b), "God never ceases to work; but as it is the property of fire to burn, and of snow to cool, so of God to work."

And what most men call fortune, he calls the divine Logos, or *Word,* to whom he ascribes all the affairs of providence (c).

(b) Leg. Ailegor. l. 1. p. 41. (c) Quod Deus sit Immutab. p. 318.

---

18. Therefore the Jews sought the more to kill him, because he not only had broken the Sabbath, but said also that God was his Father, making himself equal with God.

Greek/Transliteration

18. Διὰ τοῦτο οὖν μᾶλλον ἐζήτουν αὐτὸν οἱ Ἰουδαῖοι ἀποκτεῖναι, ὅτι οὐ μόνον ἔλυεν τὸ σάββατον, ἀλλὰ καὶ πατέρα ἴδιον ἔλεγεν τὸν θεόν, ἴσον ἑαυτὸν ποιῶν τῷ θεῷ.

18. Dya touto oun mallon ezeitoun auton 'oi Youdaioi apokteinai, 'oti ou monon eluen to sabbaton, alla kai patera idion elegen ton theon, ison 'eauton poion to theo.

Hebrew/Transliteration

יח. וּבַעֲבוּר זֹאת בִּקְשׁוּ הַיְּהוּדִים בְּחֵפֶץ יֶתֶר לְהָרְגוֹ כִּי לֹא רַק אֶת-יוֹם הַשַּׁבָּת חִלֵּל כִּי אִם גַּם-אָמַר עַל-אֱלֹהִים:כִּי הוּא אָבִיו וְכִי הוּא דוֹמֶה לֵאלֹהִים

18. Oo•va•a•voor zot bik•shoo ha•Ye•hoo•dim be•che•fetz ye•ter le•hor•go ki lo rak et – yom ha•Sha•bat chi•lel ki eem gam - amar al - Elohim ki hoo Aviv ve•chi hoo do•me le•Elohim.

Rabbinic Jewish Commentary

making himself to be equal with God; to be of the same nature, and have the same perfections, and do the same works; for by saying that God was His Father, and so that he was the Son of God, a phrase, which, with them, signified a divine person, as they might learn from Psa_2:7, and by ascribing the same operations to himself, as to his Father, they rightly understood him, that he asserted his equality with him; for had he intended no more, and had they imagined that he intended no more by calling God his Father, than that he was so by creation, as he is to all men, or by adoption, as he was to the Jews, they would not have been so angry with him; for the phrase, in this sense, they used themselves: but they understood him otherwise, as asserting his proper deity, and perfect equality with the Father; and therefore to the charge of sabbath breaking, add that of blasphemy, and on account of both, sought to put him to death; for according to their canons, both the sabbath breaker, and the blasphemer, were to be stoned (d).

(d) Misn. Sanhedrin, c. 7. sect. 4.

---

19. Then answered Jesus and said unto them, Verily, verily, I say unto you, The Son can do nothing of himself, but what he seeth the Father do: for what things soever he doeth, these also doeth the Son likewise.

Greek/Transliteration

19. Ἀπεκρίνατο οὖν ὁ Ἰησοῦς καὶ εἶπεν αὐτοῖς, Ἀμὴν ἀμὴν λέγω ὑμῖν, οὐ δύναται ὁ υἱὸς ποιεῖν ἀφ᾽ ἑαυτοῦ οὐδέν, ἐὰν μή τι βλέπῃ τὸν πατέρα ποιοῦντα· ἃ γὰρ ἂν ἐκεῖνος ποιῇ, ταῦτα καὶ ὁ υἱὸς ὁμοίως ποιεῖ.

19. Apekrinato oun 'o Yeisous kai eipen autois, Amein amein lego 'umin, ou dunatai 'o 'wios poiein aph 'eautou ouden, ean mei ti blepei ton patera poiounta. 'a gar an ekeinos poiei, tauta kai 'o 'wios 'omoios poiei.

Hebrew/Transliteration

יט. וַיַּעַן יֵשׁוּעַ וַיֹּאמֶר אֲלֵיהֶם אָמֵן אָמֵן אֲנִי אֹמֵר לָכֶם הַבֵּן לֹא-יוּכַל לַעֲשׂוֹת דָּבָר מִלִּבּוֹ בִּלְתִּי אֶת אֲשֶׁר-רֹאֶה:מַה-פֹּעַל הָאָב כִּי אֶת-אֲשֶׁר הוּא עֹשֶׂה עֹשֶׂה גַם-הַבֵּן כָּמֹהוּ

19. Va•ya•an Yeshua va•yo•mer aley•hem Amen amen ani o•mer la•chem ha•Ben lo - yoo•chal la•a•sot da•var mi•li•bo bil•tee et asher - ro•eh ma - po•el ha•Av ki et – asher hoo o•se o•se gam - ha•Ben ka•mo•hoo.

Rabbinic Jewish Commentary

Philo the Jew (e) says of the "Father's most ancient Son, whom he otherwise calls the firstborn; that being begotten, he imitates the Father, and seeing, or looking to his exemplars and archetypes, forms species;"

That is, being conversant with the original and eternal ideas of things in the divine mind, acts according to them, which he could not do if he was not of the same nature with, and equal to his Father. Moreover, the Son sees what the Father does by co-operating with him, and so does no other than what he sees the Father do, in conjunction with him: to which may be added, that the phrase shows, that the Son does nothing but in wisdom, and with knowledge; and that as the Father, so he does all things after the counsel of his will.

(e) De Confus. Ling. p. 329.

---

20. For the Father loveth the Son, and sheweth him all things that himself doeth: and he will shew him greater works than these, that ye may marvel.

Greek/Transliteration

20. Ὁ γὰρ πατὴρ φιλεῖ τὸν υἱόν, καὶ πάντα δείκνυσιν αὐτῷ ἃ αὐτὸς ποιεῖ· καὶ μείζονα τούτων δείξει αὐτῷ ἔργα, ἵνα ὑμεῖς θαυμάζητε.

20. 'O gar pateir philei ton 'wion, kai panta deiknusin auto 'a autos poiei. kai meizona touton deixei auto erga, 'ina 'umeis thaumazeite.

Hebrew/Transliteration

כ. כִּי הָאָב אֹהֵב אֶת-הַבֵּן וּמַרְאֶה אֹתוֹ אֶת-כֹּל אֲשֶׁר הוּא עֹשֶׂה וּגְדֹלוֹת מֵאֵלֶּה יַרְאֶנּוּ לִהְיוֹת לְפֶלֶא בְּעֵינֵיכֶם:

20. Ki ha•Av o•hev et - ha•Ben oo•mar•eh o•to et - kol asher hoo o•se
oog•do•lot me•e•le yar•e•noo li•hee•yot le•fe•le be•ey•ne•chem.

---

21. For as the Father raiseth up the dead, and quickeneth them; even so the Son quickeneth whom he will.

Greek/Transliteration

21. Ὥσπερ γὰρ ὁ πατὴρ ἐγείρει τοὺς νεκροὺς καὶ ζῳοποιεῖ, οὕτως καὶ ὁ υἱὸς οὓς θέλει ζῳοποιεῖ.

21. 'Osper gar 'o pateir egeirei tous nekrous kai zoopoiei, 'outos kai 'o 'wios 'ous thelei zoopoiei.

Hebrew/Transliteration

כא. כִּי כַּאֲשֶׁר הָאָב מַעֲלֶה וּמְחַיֶּה אֶת-הַמֵּתִים כֵּן יְחַיֶּה גַּם-הַבֵּן אֶת-אֲשֶׁר חָפֵץ בּוֹ:

21. Ki ka•a•sher ha•Av ma•a•le oom•cha•ye et - ha•me•tim ken ye•cha•ye gam - ha•Ben et - asher cha•fetz bo.

Rabbinic Jewish Commentary

Now as the quickening of the dead is an act of almighty power, and this being exercised by the Son in a sovereign way, as is by his Father, it shows his proper deity, and full equality with the Father. The resurrection of the dead is here expressed by "quickening", as it frequently is by the Jews, who often speak of תחיית המתים, "the quickening the dead", for the resurrection; so the Targumist on Zec_3:8, "in the quickening of the dead", אחינך, "I will quicken thee"; see the Jerusalem Targum on Gen_29:26.

---

22. For the Father judgeth no man, but hath committed all judgment unto the Son:

Greek/Transliteration

22. Οὐδὲ γὰρ ὁ πατὴρ κρίνει οὐδένα, ἀλλὰ τὴν κρίσιν πᾶσαν δέδωκεν τῷ υἱῷ·

22. Oude gar 'o pateir krinei oudena, alla tein krisin pasan dedoken to 'wio.

Hebrew/Transliteration

כב. וְהָאָב לֹא-יִשְׁפֹּט אִישׁ אַךְ כָּל-מִשְׁפָּטוֹ נָתַן בְּיַד הַבֵּן:

22. Ve•ha•Av lo - yish•pot eesh ach kol - mish•pa•to na•tan be•yad ha•Ben.

The Jews had an officer in their Sanhedrim, whom they called Ab Beth Din, or "the father of the house of judgment", to whom belonged the trying of causes, and of judging and determining them. Hence the Targumist on Son_7:4 says,

ואב בית דינא, "and the father of the house of judgment", who judgeth thy judgments, or determines thy causes, is mighty over thy people."

Whether there may not be some allusion here to this officer, I leave to be considered.

---

23. That all men should honour the Son, even as they honour the Father. He that honoureth not the Son honoureth not the Father which hath sent him.

Greek/Transliteration
23. ἵνα πάντες τιμῶσιν τὸν υἱόν, καθὼς τιμῶσιν τὸν πατέρα. Ὁ μὴ τιμῶν τὸν υἱόν, οὐ τιμᾷ τὸν πατέρα τὸν πέμψαντα αὐτόν.

23. 'ina pantes timosin ton 'wion, kathos timosin ton patera. 'O mei timon ton 'wion, ou tima ton patera ton pempsanta auton.

Hebrew/Transliteration
כג. לְמַעַן יְכַבְּדוּ כֻלָּם אֶת-הַבֵּן כַּאֲשֶׁר יְכַבְּדוּ אֶת-הָאָב מִי אֲשֶׁר לֹא-יְכַבֵּד אֶת-הַבֵּן אֵינֶנּוּ מְכַבֵּד אֶת הָאָב אֲשֶׁר:שְׁלָחוּ

23. Le•ma•an ye•chab•doo choo•lam et - ha•Ben ka•a•sher ye•chab•doo et - ha•Av mee asher lo - ye•cha•bed et - ha`Ben ey•ne•noo me•cha•bed et ha•Av asher sh`la•cho.

Rabbinic Jewish Commentary
Honor is a name for Messiah in "His glory is great in Your salvation; honor and majesty You have placed upon him" (Psalm 21:5). In Psalm 21 it says that God will bestow honor and majesty upon "him." Before considering that "him" is Messiah, the sages wondered why God was called "the King of glory" (Psalm 24:10). One answer says that the psalmist called God "King of glory" because he shares his glory with those who fear him:

"Consider how for an earthly king, no one rides his horses and no one sits on his throne, but God set Solomon on his throne, as it says, 'Solomon sat on the throne of the LORD as king' (1 Chronicles 29:23) … No one uses the scepter of an earthly king, but God gave his scepter to Moses, as it says, 'Moses carried the staff of God in his hand' (Exodus 4:20)" (Exodus Rabbah 8:1).

The verse about Solomon is particularly striking, since in other words it can be said that here for the first time, the son of David is found to be sitting as king on God's throne. This suggests that Messiah will surely be worthy of such honor.

Continuing in the same train of thought, since Messiah is esteemed higher than Moses, Solomon, or anyone else, it is only logical to conclude that Psalm 21:5 speaks of Messiah, since only he is truly worthy to be thoroughly outfitted with God's belongings— crown, scepter, and garment included. That such honor is given to Messiah is described in another Midrash: "No one is allowed to wear the crown of an earthly king, but God gives his crown to King Messiah, as it says, 'You set a crown of pure gold upon his head' (Psalm 21:3).

No one is allowed to be clothed with the garment of an earthly king, but God gave it to King Messiah, as it says, 'Honor and majesty You have placed upon him' (Psalm 21:5). No earthly king's deputy is called by the king's name, but God ... calls King Messiah by his name, as it says, 'This is His name by which He will be called: YHWH Our Righteousness' (Jeremiah 23:6)" (Midrash Tehillim, Psalm 21). Honor is therefore a fitting name for Messiah. Commenting on "You shall give some of your authority (hod) to him" (Numbers 27:20), based on the Hebrew "honor" instead of "authority," Rabbi Judah bar Nachman says, "You shall give him [Joshua] some of your honor but not all of your honor; [but] great is the honor of King Messiah who was given the honor of a rabbi and the majesty of a disciple" (Yalkut Shim'oni, Pinchas , par. 771). *The Conealed Light; Tsvi Sadad, pg.54*

---

24. Verily, verily, I say unto you, He that heareth my word, and believeth on him that sent me, hath everlasting life, and shall not come into condemnation; but is passed from death unto life.

Greek/Transliteration
24. Ἀμὴν ἀμὴν λέγω ὑμῖν ὅτι ὁ τὸν λόγον μου ἀκούων, καὶ πιστεύων τῷ πέμψαντί με, ἔχει ζωὴν αἰώνιον· καὶ εἰς κρίσιν οὐκ ἔρχεται, ἀλλὰ μεταβέβηκεν ἐκ τοῦ θανάτου εἰς τὴν ζωήν.

24. Amein amein lego 'umin 'oti 'o ton logon mou akouon, kai pisteuon to pempsanti me, echei zoein aionion. kai eis krisin ouk erchetai, alla metabebeiken ek tou thanatou eis tein zoein.

Hebrew/Transliteration
כד. אָמֵן אָמֵן אֲנִי אֹמֵר לָכֶם הַמַּקְשִׁיב לִדְבָרַי וּמַאֲמִין בְּשֹׁלְחִי יֶשׁ-לוֹ חַיֵּי עוֹלָם וְלֹא יָבֹא לְהִשָּׁפֵט כִּי- עָבַר מִמָּוֶת:לַחַיִּים

24. Amen amen ani o•mer la•chem ha•mak•shiv lid•va•rai oo•ma•a•min be•shol•chi yesh - lo cha•yey o•lam ve•lo ya•vo le•hi•sha•fet ki - avar mi•ma•vet la•cha•yim.

---

25. Verily, verily, I say unto you, The hour is coming, and now is, when the dead shall hear the voice of the Son of God: and they that hear shall live.

Greek/Transliteration

25. Ἀμὴν ἀμὴν λέγω ὑμῖν ὅτι ἔρχεται ὥρα καὶ νῦν ἐστιν, ὅτε οἱ νεκροὶ ἀκούσονται τῆς φωνῆς τοῦ υἱοῦ τοῦ θεοῦ, καὶ οἱ ἀκούσαντες ζήσονται.

25. Amein amein lego 'umin 'oti erchetai 'ora kai nun estin, 'ote 'oi nekroi akousontai teis phoneis tou 'wiou tou theou, kai 'oi akousantes zeisontai.

Hebrew/Transliteration

כה. אָמֵן אָמֵן אֲנִי אֹמֵר לָכֶם כִּי-תָבֹא עֵת וְכִי גַם-בָּאָה וְהַמֵּתִים יִשְׁמְעוּ אֶת-קוֹל בֶּן-הָאֱלֹהִים וְהַשֹּׁמְעִים חָיֹה:יִחְיוּ

25. Amen amen ani o•mer la•chem ki - ta•vo et ve•chi gam - ba•ah ve•ha•me•tim yish•me•oo et - kol Ben - ha•Elohim ve•ha•shom•eem cha•yo yich•yoo.

---

26. For as the Father hath life in himself; so hath he given to the Son to have life in himself;

Greek/Transliteration

26. Ὥσπερ γὰρ ὁ πατὴρ ἔχει ζωὴν ἐν ἑαυτῷ, οὕτως ἔδωκεν καὶ τῷ υἱῷ ζωὴν ἔχειν ἐν ἑαυτῷ·

26. 'Osper gar 'o pateir echei zoein en 'eauto, 'outos edoken kai to 'wio zoein echein en 'eauto.

Hebrew/Transliteration

כו. כִּי כַּאֲשֶׁר חַיֵּי הָאָב מִמְּקוֹר עַצְמוֹ כֵּן נָתַן לַבֵּן לִהְיוֹת-לוֹ חַיָּיו מִמְּקוֹר עַצְמוֹ:

26. Ki ka•a•sher cha•yey ha•Av mim•kor atz•mo ken ni•tan la•Ben li•hee•yot – lo cha•yav mim•kor atz•mo.

---

27. And hath given him authority to execute judgment also, because he is the Son of man.

Greek/Transliteration

27. καὶ ἐξουσίαν ἔδωκεν αὐτῷ καὶ κρίσιν ποιεῖν, ὅτι υἱὸς ἀνθρώπου ἐστίν.

27. kai exousian edoken auto kai krisin poiein, 'oti 'wios anthropou estin.

Hebrew/Transliteration

כז. וְגַם-כֹּחַ נָתַן בְּיָדוֹ לַעֲשׂוֹת מִשְׁפָּט כִּי בֶן-הָאָדָם הוּא:

27. Ve•gam - ko•ach na•tan be•ya•do la•a•sot mish•pat ki Ven - ha•adam hoo.

Rabbinic Jewish Commentary

because he is the son of man; truly and properly man; because though he was in the form of God, and equal to him, yet became man, and was in the form of a servant: and so reads the Ethiopic version, "because the Son of God is the son of man"; and therefore the authority of executing judgment, according to the council and covenant of peace, is committed to him; or that men might have a visible judge, or be judged by one in their own nature: agreeably the Persic version renders it, "because the Son himself is he who judges the sons of men"; or rather because he is that son of man spoken of in prophecy, especially in Dan_7:13; by whom is meant the Messiah, as the Jews themselves allow (f), and who was not a mere man, but the man God's fellow; and so being omniscient and omnipotent, was equal to such a work, which otherwise he would not have been. The Syriac version joins this clause to the beginning of Joh_5:28, and reads it thus, "because he is the son of man, marvel not at this"; let this be no obstruction to your faith of his quickening the dead, and having authority to execute judgment on all; since, though the son of man, he is not a mere man, but God over all, as what is next ascribed to him manifestly shows.

(f) Zohar in Gen. fol. 85. 4. Bemidbar Rabba, sect. 13. fol. 209. 4. Jarchi & Saadiah Gaon in Dan. vii. 13. & R. Jeshuah in Aben Ezra in ib.

---

28. Marvel not at this: for the hour is coming, in the which all that are in the graves shall hear his voice,

Greek/Transliteration
28. Μὴ θαυμάζετε τοῦτο· ὅτι ἔρχεται ὥρα, ἐν ᾗ πάντες οἱ ἐν τοῖς μνημείοις ἀκούσονται τῆς φωνῆς αὐτοῦ,

28. Mei thaumazete touto. 'oti erchetai 'ora, en pantes 'oi en tois mneimeiois akousontai teis phoneis autou,

Hebrew/Transliteration
כח. עַל-זֹאת אַל-תִּתַּמְּהוּ תָמֹהַּ כִּי הִנֵּה יוֹם בָּא וְכָל-שֹׁכְנֵי קֶבֶר יִשְׁמְעוּ אֶת-קֹלוֹ וְיַעֲלוּ:

28. Al - zot al - ti•tam•hoo ta•mo•ha ki hee•ne yom ba ve•chol - shoch•ney kever yish•me•oo et - ko•lo ve•ya•a•loo.

Rabbinic Jewish Commentary
The Jews observe (g), that "There are three things which do not come into the world but "by voices"; there is the voice of a living creature, as it is written, Gen_3:16, "in sorrow thou shalt bring forth children", and as it is written, Gen_30:22, "and God hearkened to her"; and there is the voice of rains, as it is

written, 1Ki_18:41, "for there is a voice of abundance of rain", and it is written, Psa_29:3, "The voice of the LORD is upon the waters"; and קול תהיית המתים, "There is the voice of the resurrection of the dead", as it is written, Isa_40:3, "The voice of him that crieth in the wilderness";"

But that was the voice of John the Baptist. It will be the voice of the Son of God that will quicken and raise the dead.

(g) Zohar in Gen. fol. 70. 4.

---

29. And shall come forth; they that have done good, unto the resurrection of life; and they that have done evil, unto the resurrection of damnation.

Greek/Transliteration
29. καὶ ἐκπορεύσονται, οἱ τὰ ἀγαθὰ ποιήσαντες, εἰς ἀνάστασιν ζωῆς· οἱ δὲ τὰ φαῦλα πράξαντες, εἰς ἀνάστασιν κρίσεως.

29. kai ekporeusontai, 'oi ta agatha poieisantes, eis anastasin zoeis. 'oi de ta phaula praxantes, eis anastasin kriseos.

Hebrew/Transliteration
כט. הָעֹשִׂים טוֹב יַעַמְדוּ לַחַיִּים וְהָעֹשִׂים רָע יַעַמְדוּ לַמִּשְׁפָּט:

29. Ha•o•sim tov ya•am•doo la•cha•yim ve•ha•o•sim ra ya•am•doo la•mish•pat.

TaNaKh-Old Testament
"And many of those sleeping in the earth's dust shall awake, some to everlasting life, and some to reproaches and to everlasting loathing." (Dan_12:2)

---

30. I can of mine own self do nothing: as I hear, I judge: and my judgment is just; because I seek not mine own will, but the will of the Father which hath sent me.

Greek/Transliteration
30. Οὐ δύναμαι ἐγὼ ποιεῖν ἀπ᾽ ἐμαυτοῦ οὐδέν· καθὼς ἀκούω, κρίνω· καὶ ἡ κρίσις ἡ ἐμὴ δικαία ἐστίν· ὅτι οὐ ζητῶ τὸ θέλημα τὸ ἐμόν, ἀλλὰ τὸ θέλημα τοῦ πέμψαντός με πατρός.

30. Ou dunamai ego poiein ap emautou ouden. kathos akouo, krino. kai 'ei krisis 'ei emei dikaia estin. 'oti ou zeito to theleima to emon, alla to theleima tou pempsantos me patros.'

Hebrew/Transliteration

ל. לֹא אוּכַל לַעֲשׂוֹת דָּבָר מִלִּבִּי כַּאֲשֶׁר אֶשְׁמַע כֵּן אֶשְׁפֹּט וּמִשְׁפָּטִי מִשְׁפַּט-צֶדֶק כִּי לֹא רְצוֹנִי אֲנִי מְבַקֵּשׁ כִּי אִם:רְצוֹן הָאָב אֲשֶׁר שְׁלָחִי -

30. Lo oo•chal la•a•sot da•var mi•li•bi ka•a•sher esh•ma ken esh•pot oo•mish•pa•ti mish•pat - tze•dek ki lo r`tzo•ni ani me•va•kesh ki eem - r`tzon ha•Av asher shol•chi.

Rabbinic Jewish Commentary

Hearing here signifies perfect knowledge, and understanding of a cause; and so it is used in the Jewish writings, in matters of difficulty, that come before a court of judicature (h):

"There were three courts of judicature; one that sat at the gate of the mountain of the house; and one that sat at the gate of the court; and another that sat in the paved chamber: they go (first) to that which is at the gate of the mountain of the house, and say, so have I expounded, and so have the companions expounded; so have I taught, and so have the companions (or colleagues) taught: אם שמעו, "if they hear", they say; (i.e. as one of their commentators explains it (i), if they know the law, and hear, or understand the sense of the law; in such a case they declare what they know;) if not, they go to them that are at the gate of the court, and say (as before).--And, "if they hear", they tell them; but if not, they go to the great Sanhedrim in the paved chamber, from whence goes forth the law to all Israel."

(h) Misn. Sanhedrin, c. 10. sect. 2. (i) Maimon. in ib.

---

31. If I bear witness of myself, my witness is not true.

Greek/Transliteration
31. Ἐὰν ἐγὼ μαρτυρῶ περὶ ἐμαυτοῦ, ἡ μαρτυρία μου οὐκ ἔστιν ἀληθής.

31. Ean ego marturo peri emautou, 'ei marturia mou ouk estin aleitheis.

Hebrew/Transliteration
:לֹא. אִם-אֲנִי לְבַדִּי מֵעִיד עָלַי לֹא נֶאֶמְנָה עֵדוּתִי

31. Eem - ani le•va•di me•eed a•lai lo ne•em•na e•doo•ti.

Rabbinic Jewish Commentary

According to the Jewish canons, a man might not be a witness for his wife, because she was reckoned as himself.

"An husband is not to be believed in bearing witness for his wife, that had been carried captive, that she is not defiled, שאין אדם מעיד לעצמו, "for no man witness of himself" (k)."

So likewise they say (l), "A city that is subdued by an army, all the priestesses (or priests' daughters) that are found in it are rejected (from the priesthood, as defiled); but if they have witnesses, whether a servant, or an handmaid, lo, they are to be believed; but no man is to be believed for himself: says R. Zechariah ben Hakatzah, by this habitation (swearing by the temple) her hand was not removed from my hand, from the time the Gentiles entered Jerusalem, till they went out: they replied to him, "no man bears witness of himself"."

my witness is not true, **לֹא נֶאֱמָן,** not to be believed, or admitted as an authentic testimony: and so the Ethiopic version renders it, "is not credible"; not valid in law, or in such a court of judicature in which Yeshua now was; for, as according to the Jewish law, no man was admitted a witness for himself, so neither was anything established by a single testimony, but by the mouth of two or three witnesses, Deu_19:15.

(k) Maimon. Issure Bia, c. 18. sect. 19. (l) Misn. Cetubot, c. 2. sect. 9. T. Bab. Cetubot, fol. 27. 2. Juchasin, fol. 56. 1.

---

32. There is another that beareth witness of me; and I know that the witness which he witnesseth of me is true.

Greek/Transliteration
32. Ἄλλος ἐστὶν ὁ μαρτυρῶν περὶ ἐμοῦ, καὶ οἶδα ὅτι ἀληθής ἐστιν ἡ μαρτυρία ἣν μαρτυρεῖ περὶ ἐμοῦ.

32. Allos estin 'o marturon peri emou, kai oida 'oti aleitheis estin 'ei marturia 'ein marturei peri emou.

Hebrew/Transliteration
לב. אַךְ יֵשׁ עֵד אַחֵר לִי וְיָדַעְתִּי כִּי עֵדוּתוֹ אֲשֶׁר-הוּא מֵעִיד עָלַי נֶאֱמָנָה:

32. Ach yesh ed a•cher li ve•ya•da•a•ti ki e•doo•to asher - hoo me•eed a•lai ne•e•ma•na.

---

33. Ye sent unto John, and he bare witness unto the truth.

Greek/Transliteration
33. Ὑμεῖς ἀπεστάλκατε πρὸς Ἰωάννην, καὶ μεμαρτύρηκεν τῇ ἀληθείᾳ.

33. 'Umeis apestalkate pros Yoannein, kai memartureiken tei aleitheia.

Hebrew/Transliteration
לג. אַתֶּם שְׁלַחְתֶּם אֶל-יוֹחָנָן וְהוּא הֵעִיד עֵדוּת אֱמֶת:

33. Atem sh`lach•tem el - Yo•cha•nan ve•hoo he•eed e•doot emet.

---

34. But I receive not testimony from man: but these things I say, that ye might be saved.

Greek/Transliteration
34. Ἐγὼ δὲ οὐ παρὰ ἀνθρώπου τὴν μαρτυρίαν λαμβάνω, ἀλλὰ ταῦτα λέγω ἵνα ὑμεῖς σωθῆτε.

34. Ego de ou para anthropou tein marturian lambano, alla tauta lego 'ina 'umeis sotheite.

Hebrew/Transliteration
לד. וַאֲנִי לֹא מֵאָדָם אֶקַּח לִי עֵדוּת אַךְ הַדְּבָרִים הָאֵלֶּה דִּבַּרְתִּי לְמַעַן אַתֶּם תִּוָּשֵׁעוּן:

34. Va•a•ni lo me•a•dam e•kach li e•doot ach ha•d`va•rim ha•e•le di•bar•ti le•ma•an atem ti•va•she•oon.

---

35. He was a burning and a shining light: and ye were willing for a season to rejoice in his light.

Greek/Transliteration
35. Ἐκεῖνος ἦν ὁ λύχνος ὁ καιόμενος καὶ φαίνων, ὑμεῖς δὲ ἠθελήσατε ἀγαλλιαθῆναι πρὸς ὥραν ἐν τῷ φωτὶ αὐτοῦ.

35. Ekeinos ein 'o luchnos 'o kaiomenos kai phainon, 'umeis de eitheleisate agallyatheinai pros 'oran en to photi autou.

Hebrew/Transliteration
לה. הוּא הָיָה לַפִּיד בֹּעֵר וּמֵאִיר וּבְאוֹרוֹ הוֹאַלְתֶּם לְהִתְעַלֵּם עַד-אַרְגִּיעָה:

35. Hoo ha•ya la•pid bo•er oo•me•eer oov•o•ro ho•al•tem le•hit•a•lem ad - ar•gi•ah.

Rabbinic Jewis Commentary
It was common with the Jews to call their Rabbis, who were famous for their knowledge, and holiness of life, lights, burning lights, and shining lights; or in words which amount to the same. So R. Simeon ben Jochai is often called in the book of Zohar, בוצינא קדישא, "the holy light"; and particularly it is said of him (m),

"R. Simeon, כבוצינא דשרגא דאדליק, is as "The lamp of light which burns above", and "burns" below; and by the light which burns below all the children of the world are enlightened: woe to the world, when the light below ascends to the light above."

So R. Abhu is called בוצינא דנהורא, "The lamp of light" (n): and it is (o) said of Shuah, Judah's father-in-law, that he was בוצינא דאתרא, "the light of the place"; that is, where he lived. The gloss on the place says, he was a man of note in the city, and enlightened their eyes; and it is very frequent with them still, when they are praising any of their Rabbis, to say of him, he was המאור הגדול, "a great light", who enlightened the eyes of Israel, and in whose light the people walked (p); so among the philosophers, Xenophon, and Plato, are called duo lumina (q), "two lights"

(m) Zohar in Exod. fol. 79. 1. (n) T. Bab. Cetubot, fol. 17. 1. (o) Bereshit Rabba, sect. 85. fol. 74. 4. & Mattanot Cehunah in ib. (p) Vid. R. David Ganz Tzemach David, par. 1. fol. 38. 1. 41. 1. 44. 2. 45. 1. 46. 2. & 47. 1. (q) A. Gell. Noct. Attic. l. 14. c. 3.

---

36. But I have greater witness than that of John: for the works which the Father hath given me to finish, the same works that I do, bear witness of me, that the Father hath sent me.

Greek/Transliteration

36. Ἐγὼ δὲ ἔχω τὴν μαρτυρίαν μείζω τοῦ Ἰωάννου· τὰ γὰρ ἔργα ἃ ἔδωκέν μοι ὁ πατὴρ ἵνα τελειώσω αὐτά, αὐτὰ τὰ ἔργα ἃ ἐγὼ ποιῶ, μαρτυρεῖ περὶ ἐμοῦ ὅτι ὁ πατήρ με ἀπέσταλκεν.

36. Ego de echo tein marturian meizo tou Yoannou. ta gar erga 'a edoken moi 'o pateir 'ina teleioso auta, auta ta erga 'a ego poio, marturei peri emou 'oti 'o pateir me apestalken.

Hebrew/Transliteration

לו. וְלִי עֵדוּת גְּדוֹלָה מֵעֵדוּת יוֹחָנָן כִּי הַמַּעֲשִׂים אֲשֶׁר נָתַן-לִי אָבִי לְכַלּוֹתָם הַמַּעֲשִׂים הָאֵלֶּה אֲנִי עֹשֶׂה וְהֵם:מְעִידִים עָלַי כִּי שְׁלָחַנִי הָאָב

36. V•li e•doot ge•do•la me•e•doot Yo•cha•nan ki ha•ma•a•sim asher na•tan - li Avi le•cha•lo•tam ha•ma•a•sim ha•e•le ani o•se ve•hem me•ee•dim a•lai ki sh`la•cha•ni ha•Av.

---

37. And the Father himself, which hath sent me, hath borne witness of me. Ye have neither heard his voice at any time, nor seen his shape.

Greek/Transliteration

37. Καὶ ὁ πέμψας με πατήρ, αὐτὸς μεμαρτύρηκεν περὶ ἐμοῦ. Οὔτε φωνὴν αὐτοῦ ἀκηκόατε πώποτε, οὔτε εἶδος αὐτοῦ ἑωράκατε.

37. Kai 'o pempsas me pateir, autos memartureiken peri emou. Oute phonein autou akeikoate popote, oute eidos autou 'eorakate.

Hebrew/Transliteration

לז. וְהָאָב אֲשֶׁר שְׁלָחַנִי הוּא הֵעִיד עָלָי וְאַתֶּם אֶת-קֹלוֹ לֹא-שְׁמַעְתֶּם מֵעוֹלָם וְאֶת-תְּאָרוֹ לֹא רְאִיתֶם:

37. Ve•ha•Av asher sh`la•cha•ni hoo he•eed a•lai ve•a•tem et - ko•lo lo - sh`ma•a•tem me•o•lam ve•et - to•o•ro lo r`ee•tem.

Rabbinic Jewish Commentary

"In the gospel of John we have another passage of Scripture that some have used to say that nobody can see God. In John 5:37-38 we read Jesus telling the Jewish leaders, who just accused him of calling God his own father and making himself equal to God, that *"You (Jewish leaders) have neither heard His voice at any time nor seen His form."* Jesus is not speaking about the prophets in the Hebrew Scriptures. He is telling the wicked Jewish leaders why they have not seen or heard from the father. They reject the testimony of the witnesses that speak of Jesus. Read…chapter 5:1-47 for the full context."
(From YHWH To Elohim To Messiah; by A.G. Shlomo, pg.48)

---

38. And ye have not his word abiding in you: for whom he hath sent, him ye believe not.

Greek/Transliteration

38. Καὶ τὸν λόγον αὐτοῦ οὐκ ἔχετε μένοντα ἐν ὑμῖν, ὅτι ὃν ἀπέστειλεν ἐκεῖνος, τούτῳ ὑμεῖς οὐ πιστεύετε.

38. Kai ton logon autou ouk echete menonta en 'umin, 'oti 'on apesteilen ekeinos, touto 'umeis ou pisteuete.

Hebrew/Transliteration

לח. וְאֵין דְּבָרוֹ שֹׁכֵן בְּקִרְבְּכֶם כִּי אֹתוֹ אֲשֶׁר שָׁלַח לֹא תַאֲמִינוּ בוֹ:

38. Ve•eyn de•va•ro sho•chen be•kir•be•chem ki o•to asher sha•lach lo ta•a•mi•noo vo.

---

39. Search the scriptures; for in them ye think ye have eternal life: and they are they which testify of me.

Greek/Transliteration

39. Ἐρευνᾶτε τὰς γραφάς, ὅτι ὑμεῖς δοκεῖτε ἐν αὐταῖς ζωὴν αἰώνιον ἔχειν, καὶ ἐκεῖναί εἰσιν αἱ μαρτυροῦσαι περὶ ἐμοῦ·

39. Ereunate tas graphas, 'oti 'umeis dokeite en autais zoein aionion echein, kai ekeinai eisin 'ai marturousai peri emou.

Hebrew/Transliteration

:לט. אַתֶּם דֹּרְשִׁים מֵעַל-כִּתְבֵי הַקֹּדֶשׁ כִּי בָהֶם אַתֶּם אֹמְרִים חַיֵּי עוֹלָם לָכֶם וְהֵם הֵמָּה הַמְּעִידִים עָלָי

39. Atem dor•shim me•al - kit•vey ha•ko•desh ki ba•hem atem om•rim
cha•yey o•lam la•chem ve•hem he•ma ham•ee•dim a•lai.

Rabbinic Jewish Commentary

The meaning here is, that they imagined, by having these writings in their hands, and by their reading them, and hearing them expounded every sabbath day, they should obtain and inherit everlasting life: hence they call (r) the Torah eternal life, and say (s) concerning the reading of it, that

"He that begins to read in the book of the Torah is obliged to bless after this manner: blessed be he that has chosen us above all nations, and hath given us his Torah.--And he that finishes blesses after him in this manner: blessed is he who hath given us his Torah, the Torah of truth, and has planted "eternal life" in the midst of us."

This was an opinion of theirs: so the Persic version reads, "for such is your opinion"; and though this was a very vain one, yet it shows what a very high opinion they had of the Scriptures: and now to these Yeshua appeals as witnesses for him, and against which they could not object, upon their own principles:

(r) Zohar in Gen. fol. 100. 3. (s) Maimon. in Misn. Megilla, c. 4. sect. 1.

---

40. And ye will not come to me, that ye might have life.

Greek/Traansliteration
40. καὶ οὐ θέλετε ἐλθεῖν πρός με, ἵνα ζωὴν ἔχητε.

40. kai ou thelete elthein pros me, 'ina zoein echeite.

Hebrew/Transliteration
:מ. וְלֹא אֲבִיתֶם לָבֹא אֵלַי לִהְיוֹת לָכֶם חַיִּים

40. Ve•lo avi•tem la•vo e•lai li•hee•yot la•chem cha•yim.

41. I receive not honour from men.

Greek/Transliteration
41. Δόξαν παρὰ ἀνθρώπων οὐ λαμβάνω·

41. Doxan para anthropon ou lambano.

Hebrew/Transliteration
:מא. כָּבוֹד לֹא-אֶקַּח מִבְּנֵי אָדָם

41. Ka•vod lo - e•kach mi•b`ney adam.

---

42. But I know you, that ye have not the love of God in you.

Greek/Transliteration
42. ἀλλ᾽ ἔγνωκα ὑμᾶς, ὅτι τὴν ἀγάπην τοῦ θεοῦ οὐκ ἔχετε ἐν ἑαυτοῖς.

42. all egnoka 'umas, 'oti tein agapein tou theou ouk echete en 'eautois.

Hebrew/Transliteration
מב. וְאֶתְכֶם יָדַעְתִּי כִּי אֵין-אַהֲבַת אֱלֹהִים בְּקִרְבְּכֶם:

42. Ve•et•chem ya•da•a•ti ki eyn - a•ha•vat Elohim be•kir•be•chem.

---

43. I am come in my Father's name, and ye receive me not: if another shall come in his own name, him ye will receive.

Greek/Transliteration
43. Ἐγὼ ἐλήλυθα ἐν τῷ ὀνόματι τοῦ πατρός μου, καὶ οὐ λαμβάνετέ με· ἐὰν ἄλλος ἔλθῃ ἐν τῷ ὀνόματι τῷ ἰδίῳ, ἐκεῖνον λήψεσθε.

43. Ego eleilutha en to onomati tou patros mou, kai ou lambanete me. ean allos elthei en to onomati to idio, ekeinon leipsesthe.

Hebrew/Transliteration
מג. אָנֹכִי הִנֵּה בָאתִי בְּשֵׁם אָבִי וְלֹא הֶחֱזַקְתֶּם בִּי וְאִם-יָבֹא אַחֵר בְּשֵׁם עַצְמוֹ בּוֹ תַחֲזִיקוּן:

43. Ano•chi hee•ne va•ti be•shem Avi ve•lo he•che•zak•tem bi ve•eem - ya•vo a•cher be•shem atz•mo bo ta•cha•zi•koon.

Rabbinic Jewish Commentary
The Ethiopic version reads, "if another shall come in my name"; saying he is Christ, or the Messiah:

him ye will receive; as thousands of them did receive Barchocab, the false Messiah, who rose up some years after in Adrian's time; and even some of their greatest Rabbins, as particularly the famous R. Akiba, who was his armour bearer: and it is easy to observe, that though they were so backward to receive, and so much prejudiced against the true Messiah, they were always forward enough to embrace a false one: and indeed to follow any, that set up himself for a temporal deliverer of them; as the instances of Theudas, and Judas of Galilee, with others, show; see Act_5:36. And the true reason why they rejected Yeshua was, because he did not appear in outward pomp and glory, nor set up a temporal kingdom, or give out that he would deliver them from the Roman yoke.

44. How can ye believe, which receive honour one of another, and seek not the honour that cometh from God only?

Greek/Transliteration
44. Πῶς δύνασθε ὑμεῖς πιστεῦσαι, δόξαν παρὰ ἀλλήλων λαμβάνοντες, καὶ τὴν δόξαν τὴν παρὰ τοῦ μόνου θεοῦ οὐ ζητεῖτε;

44. Pos dunasthe 'umeis pisteusai, doxan para alleilon lambanontes, kai tein doxan tein para tou monou theou ou zeiteite?

Hebrew/Transliteration
מד. אֵיךְ תּוּכְלוּ לְהַאֲמִין אַחֲרֵי אֲשֶׁר תִּרְדְּפוּ כָבוֹד אִישׁ מֵרֵעֵהוּ וְאֶת-הַכָּבוֹד הַבָּא מֵאֵת הָאֱלֹהִים הָאֶחָד לֹא:תְבַקֵּשׁוּן

44. Eych tooch•loo le•ha•a•min a•cha•rey asher tir•de•foo cha•vod eesh me•re•e•hoo ve•et - ha•ka•vod ha•ba me•et ha•Elohim ha•e•chad lo te•va•ke•shoon?

---

45. Do not think that I will accuse you to the Father: there is one that accuseth you, even Moses, in whom ye trust.

Greek/Transliteration
45. Μὴ δοκεῖτε ὅτι ἐγὼ κατηγορήσω ὑμῶν πρὸς τὸν πατέρα· ἔστιν ὁ κατηγορῶν ὑμῶν, Μωσῆς, εἰς ὃν ὑμεῖς ἠλπίκατε.

45. Mei dokeite 'oti ego kateigoreiso 'umon pros ton patera. estin 'o kateigoron 'umon, Moseis, eis 'on 'umeis eilpikate.

Hebrew/Transliteratioin
מה. אַל-תְּחַשְׁבוּ כִּי אֲנִי אָבִיא שִׂטְנָה עֲלֵיכֶם לִפְנֵי הָאָב יֵשׁ אֶחָד מֵבִיא שִׂטְנָה עֲלֵיכֶם מֹשֶׁה אֲשֶׁר בְּטַחְתֶּם בּוֹ:

45. Al - te•chash•voo ki ani avi sit•na aley•chem lif•ney ha•Av yesh e•chad me•vi sit•na aley•chem Moshe asher be•tach•tem bo.

Rabbinic Jewish Commentary
The Jews have a notion, that when the Messiah comes, there will be accusations lodged against their Rabbis and wise men (t).

"R. Zeira says, that R. Jeremiah bar Aba said, that in the generation in which the son of David shall come, there will be קטיגוריא בתלמידי חכמים, "accusations against the disciples of the wise men".

And one of their writers (u) thus interprets, Dan_12:1,

"And at that time "shall Michael stand up"; he shall be as silent as a dumb man, when he shall see the holy blessed God contending with him, and saying, how shall I destroy a nation so great as this, for the sake of Israel? "and there shall be a time of trouble" in the family above, and there shall be "accusations" against the disciples of the wise men."

However, there was no need for Yeshua to accuse them.

The Torah of Moses in which they trust for life, will rise up in judgment, and be a swift witness against them: so the Jews sometimes speak of the Torah of Moses, as witnessing against the people of Israel (w).

(t) T. Bab. Cetubot, fol. 112. 2. (u) Jarchi in Dan xii. 1. Vid. Abkath Rocel, par. 2. p. 265. (w) Prefat. Echa Rabbati, fol. 40. 1.

---

46. For had ye believed Moses, ye would have believed me: for he wrote of me.

Greek/Transliteration
46. Εἰ γὰρ ἐπιστεύετε Μωσῇ, ἐπιστεύετε ἂν ἐμοί· περὶ γὰρ ἐμοῦ ἐκεῖνος ἔγραψεν.

46. Ei gar episteuete Mosei, episteuete an emoi. peri gar emou ekeinos egrapsen.

Hebrew/Transliteration
מו. כִּי לוּ הֶאֱמַנְתֶּם בְּמֹשֶׁה הֶאֱמַנְתֶּם גַּם-בִּי כִּי עָלַי הוּא כָתַב:

46. Ki loo he•e•man•tem be•Moshe he•e•man•tem gam - bi ki a•lai hoo cha•tav.

Rabbinic Jewish Commentary
In the Torah written by him, Messiah is spoken of, as the seed of the woman, that should bruise the serpent's head; as the seed of Abraham, in whom all nations of the earth should be blessed; as the Shiloh, to whom the gathering of the people should be; and as that prophet, who should be like unto himself, to whom the people of Israel should hearken; and he wrote many things typically of Messiah; and indeed, the whole Mosaic economy was typical of Messiah, as the epistle to the Hebrews shows: and therefore disbelieving Yeshua, was disbelieving Moses; who therefore would be an accuser of them, and a witness against them.

---

47. But if ye believe not his writings, how shall ye believe my words?

Greek/Transliteration
47. Εἰ δὲ τοῖς ἐκείνου γράμμασιν οὐ πιστεύετε, πῶς τοῖς ἐμοῖς ῥήμασιν πιστεύσετε;

47. Ei de tois ekeinou grammasin ou pisteuete, pos tois emois 'reimasin pisteusete?

Hebrew/Transliteration
מז. אַךְ אִם-בִּכְתָבָיו לֹא תַאֲמִינוּ אֵיךְ תַאֲמִינוּ בִּדְבָרָי:

47. Ach eem - bich•ta•vav lo ta•a•mi•noo eych ta•a•mi•noo bid•va•rai?

John, Chapter 6

1. After these things Jesus went over the sea of Galilee, which is the sea of Tiberias.

Greek/Transliteration
1. Μετὰ ταῦτα ἀπῆλθεν ὁ Ἰησοῦς πέραν τῆς θαλάσσης τῆς Γαλιλαίας, τῆς Τιβεριάδος.

1. Meta tauta apeilthen 'o Yeisous peran teis thalasseis teis Galilaias, teis Tiberyados.

Hebrew/Transliteration
א. וַיְהִי אַחֲרֵי-כֵן וַיַּעֲבֹר יֵשׁוּעַ אֶל-עֵבֶר יַם-הַגָּלִיל הוּא יַם טִיבַרְיָה:

1. Vay•hi a•cha•rey - chen va•ya•a•vor Yeshua el - ever yam - ha•Galil hoo yam Ti•var•ya.

Rabbinic Jewish Commentary
which is the sea of Tiberias; and is frequently so called by the Jewish writers (x), who often make mention of טבריה ימה של, "the sea of Tiberias"; and by other writers, it is called the lake of Tiberias (y); Pliny, who calls it the lake of Genesara (z), says,

"It was sixteen miles long, and six broad, and was beset with very pleasant towns; on the east were Julias and Hippo, and on the south Tarichea, by which name some call the lake, and on the west Tiberias, wholesome for the hot waters."

And these are the waters which the Jews call דימוסין דטבריא, or, חמי, the hot baths of Tiberias (a); and from the city of Tiberias built by Herod, and called so in honour of Tiberius Caesar, the sea took its name.

(x) T. Bab. Bava Kama, fol. 81. 2. & Bava Bathra, fol. 74. 2. Becorot, fol. 55. 1. Megilla, fol. 5. 2. & 6. 1. Moed. Katon, fol. 18. 2. & T. Hieros. Kilaim, fol. 32. 3. & Erubin, fol. 25. 2. (y) Solin, c. 48. Pausan. l. 5. p. 298. (z) Lib. 5. c. 15. (a) T. Hieros. Peah, fol 21. 2. & Sheviith, fol. 38. 4. Kiddushin, fol. 61. 1. R. Benj. Itinerar. p. 53.

---

2. And a great multitude followed him, because they saw his miracles which he did on them that were diseased.

Greek/Transliteration
2. Καὶ ἠκολούθει αὐτῷ ὄχλος πολύς, ὅτι ἑώρων αὐτοῦ τὰ σημεῖα ἃ ἐποίει ἐπὶ τῶν ἀσθενούντων.

2. Kai eikolouthei auto ochlos polus, 'oti 'eoron autou ta seimeia 'a epoiei epi ton asthenounton.

:ב. וַהֲמוֹן עַם-רָב הָלְכוּ אַחֲרָיו כִּי רָאוּ אֶת-הָאֹתוֹת אֲשֶׁר עָשָׂה לְחוֹלִים

2. Va•ha•mon am - rav hal•choo a•cha•rav ki ra•oo et - ha•o•tot asher asa le•cho•lim.

---

3. And Jesus went up into a mountain, and there he sat with his disciples.

Greek/Transliteration
3. Ἀνῆλθεν δὲ εἰς τὸ ὄρος ὁ Ἰησοῦς, καὶ ἐκεῖ ἐκάθητο μετὰ τῶν μαθητῶν αὐτοῦ.

3. Aneilthen de eis to oros 'o Yeisous, kai ekei ekatheito meta ton matheiton autou.

Hebrew/Transliteration
:ג. וַיַּעַל יֵשׁוּעַ אֶל-הָהָר וַיֵּשֶׁב-שָׁם עִם-תַּלְמִידָיו

3. Va•ya•al Yeshua el - ha•har va•ye•shev - sham eem - tal•mi•dav.

---

4. And the passover, a feast of the Jews, was nigh.

Greek/Transliteration
4. Ἦν δὲ ἐγγὺς τὸ Πάσχα, ἡ ἑορτὴ τῶν Ἰουδαίων.

4. Ein de engus to Pascha, 'ei 'eortei ton Youdaion.

Hebrew/Transliteration
:ד. וּמוֹעֵד הַפֶּסַח חַג הַיְּהוּדִים קָרֵב לָבוֹא

4. Oo•mo•ed ha•Pe•sach chag ha•Ye•hoo•dim ka•rav la•vo.

Rabbinic Jewish Commentary
This was the third passover, since Yeshua's baptism, and entrance on his public ministry; see Joh_2:13. Whether Yeshua went up to this feast is not certain; some think he did not; but from what is said in Joh_7:1, it looks as if he did: how nigh it was to the feast, cannot well be said. Thirty days before the feast, they began to talk about it; and especially in the last fifteen days, they made preparations for it, as being at hand (b); and if there was now so long time to it, there was time enough for Yeshua to go to it.

(b) T. Bab. Pesach. fol. 6. 1. Maimon. & Bartenora in Misn. Shekalim, c. 3. sect. 1.

5. When Jesus then lifted up his eyes, and saw a great company come unto him, he saith unto Philip, Whence shall we buy bread, that these may eat?

Greek/Transliteration
5. Ἐπάρας οὖν ὁ Ἰησοῦς τοὺς ὀφθαλμούς, καὶ θεασάμενος ὅτι πολὺς ὄχλος ἔρχεται πρὸς αὐτόν, λέγει πρὸς τὸν Φίλιππον, Πόθεν ἀγοράσομεν ἄρτους, ἵνα φάγωσιν οὗτοι;

5. Eparas oun 'o Yeisous tous ophthalmous, kai theasamenos 'oti polus ochlos erchetai pros auton, legei pros ton Philippon, Pothen agorasomen artous, 'ina phagosin 'outoi?

Hebrew/Transliteration
ה. וַיִּשָׂא יֵשׁוּעַ אֶת-עֵינָיו וַיַּרְא הָמוֹן עַם-רָב בָּא אֵלָיו וַיֹּאמֶר אֶל-פִילִפּוֹס מֵאַיִן נִשְׁבֹּר לָהֶם לֶחֶם לֶאֱכֹל:

5. Va•yi•sa Yeshua et - ey•nav va•yar ha•mon am - rav ba elav va•yo•mer el – Pilipos me•a•yin nish•bor la•hem le•chem le•e•chol?

---

6. And this he said to prove him: for he himself knew what he would do.

Greek/Transliteration
6. Τοῦτο δὲ ἔλεγεν πειράζων αὐτόν· αὐτὸς γὰρ ᾔδει τί ἔμελλεν ποιεῖν.

6. Touto de elegen peirazon auton. autos gar eidei ti emellen poiein.

Hebrew/Transliteration
ו. וְהוּא דִבֶּר כָּזֹאת לְנַסּוֹתוֹ כִּי הוּא יָדַע אֶת-אֲשֶׁר יַעֲשֶׂה:

6. Ve•hoo di•ber ka•zot le•na•so•to ki hoo ya•da et - asher ya•a•se.

---

7. Philip answered him, Two hundred pennyworth of bread is not sufficient for them, that every one of them may take a little.

Greek/Transliteration
7. Ἀπεκρίθη αὐτῷ Φίλιππος, Διακοσίων δηναρίων ἄρτοι οὐκ ἀρκοῦσιν αὐτοῖς, ἵνα ἕκαστος αὐτῶν βραχύ τι λάβῃ.

7. Apekrithei auto Philippos, Dyakosion deinarion artoi ouk arkousin autois, 'ina 'ekastos auton brachu ti labei.

Hebrew/Transliteration
ז. וַיַּעַן אֹתוֹ פִילִפּוֹס מָאתַיִם דִּינָר לֶחֶם לֹא-יִשְׂפֹּק לָהֶם לֶאֱכֹל מִמְּנוּ אִישׁ אִישׁ פַּת קְטַנָּה:

7. Va•ya•an o•to Pilipos ma•ta•yim di•nar le•chem lo - yis•pok la•hem
le•e•chol mi•me•noo eesh eesh pat ke•ta•na.

---

8. One of his disciples, Andrew, Simon Peter's brother, saith unto him,

Greek/Transliteration
8. Λέγει αὐτῷ εἷς ἐκ τῶν μαθητῶν αὐτοῦ, Ἀνδρέας ὁ ἀδελφὸς Σίμωνος
Πέτρου,

8. Legei auto 'eis ek ton matheiton autou, Andreas 'o adelphos Simonos
Petrou,

Hebrew/Transliteration
ח. וְאֶחָד מִתַּלְמִידָיו אַנְדְרִי אֲחִי שִׁמְעוֹן פֶּטְרוֹס אָמַר אֵלָיו לֵאמֹר:

8. Ve•e•chad mi•tal•mi•dav An•de•rai achi Shimon Petros amar elav le•mor.

---

9. There is a lad here, which hath five barley loaves, and two small fishes: but
what are they among so many?

Greek/Transliteration
9. Ἔστιν παιδάριον ἓν ὧδε, ὃ ἔχει πέντε ἄρτους κριθίνους καὶ δύο ὀψάρια·
ἀλλὰ ταῦτα τί ἐστιν εἰς τοσούτους;

9. Estin paidarion 'en 'ode, 'o echei pente artous krithinous kai duo opsarya.
alla tauta ti estin eis tosoutous?

Hebrew/Transliteration
ט. יֶשְׁנוֹ פֹּה נַעַר אֶחָד וְלוֹ חֲמִשָּׁה לֶחֶם שְׂעֹרִים וְדָגִים שְׁנָיִם אַךְ מָה אֵלֶּה לְעַם-רָב כָּזֶה:

9. Yesh•no po na•ar e•chad ve•lo cha•mi•sha le•chem s`o•rim ve•da•gim
sh`na•yim ach ma ele le•am - rav ka•ze?

Rabbinic Jewish Commentary
and two small fishes; there were but "two", and these "small"; it is amazing, that
five thousand persons should everyone have something of them, and enough: these
fishes seem to be what the Jews (c) call מוניני, and which the gloss interprets
"small fishes": and by the word which is used of them, they seem to be salted, or
pickled fishes, and such it is very probable these were; Nonnus calls them, ιχθυας
οπταλεους, "fishes which were broiled", or perhaps dried in the sun.

(c) T. Bab. Cetubot, fol. 60. 2. & Sanhedrin, fol. 49. 1.

---

10. And Jesus said, Make the men sit down. Now there was much grass in the place. So the men sat down, in number about five thousand.

Greek/Transliteration
10. Εἶπεν δὲ ὁ Ἰησοῦς, Ποιήσατε τοὺς ἀνθρώπους ἀναπεσεῖν. Ἦν δὲ χόρτος πολὺς ἐν τῷ τόπῳ. Ἀνέπεσον οὖν οἱ ἄνδρες τὸν ἀριθμὸν ὡσεὶ πεντακισχίλιοι.

10. Eipen de 'o Yeisous, Poieisate tous anthropous anapesein. Ein de chortos polus en to topo. Anepeson oun 'oi andres ton arithmon 'osei pentakischilioi.

Hebrew/Transliteration
י. וַיֹּאמֶר יֵשׁוּעַ הוֹשִׁיבוּ אֶת-הָאֲנָשִׁים וַיֵּשְׁבוּ כַּחֲמֵשֶׁת אֲלָפִים אִישׁ לְמִסְפָּרָם בִּנְאוֹת דֶּשֶׁא אֲשֶׁר נִמְצָא שָׁם לְמַכְבִּיר:

10. Va•yo•mer Yeshua ho•shi•voo et - ha•a•na•shim va•yesh•voo ka•cha•me•shet ala•fim eesh le•mis•pa•ram bin•ot de•she asher nim•tza sham le•mach•bir.

---

11. And Jesus took the loaves; and when he had given thanks, he distributed to the disciples, and the disciples to them that were set down; and likewise of the fishes as much as they would.

Greek/Transliteration
11. Ἔλαβεν δὲ τοὺς ἄρτους ὁ Ἰησοῦς, καὶ εὐχαριστήσας διέδωκεν τοῖς μαθηταῖς, οἱ δὲ μαθηταὶ τοῖς ἀνακειμένοις· ὁμοίως καὶ ἐκ τῶν ὀψαρίων ὅσον ἤθελον.

11. Elaben de tous artous 'o Yeisous, kai eucharisteisas diedoken tois matheitais, 'oi de matheitai tois anakeimenois. 'omoios kai ek ton opsarion 'oson eithelon.

Hebrew/Transliteration
יא. וַיִּקַּח יֵשׁוּעַ אֶת-כִּכְּרוֹת הַלֶּחֶם וַיְבָרֶךְ וַיְחַלֵּק לְתַלְמִידָיו וְהַתַּלְמִידִים לְכָל-הַיּשְׁבִים שָׁמָּה וְגַם מִן-הַדָּגִים נָתַן לָהֶם כְּאַוַּת נַפְשָׁם:

11. Va•yi•kach Yeshua et - kik•rot ha•le•chem vay•va•rech vay•cha•lek le•tal•mi•dav ve•ha•tal•mi•dim le•chol - ha•yosh•vim sha•ma ve•gam min - ha•da•gim na•tan la•hem ke•a•vat naf•sham.

---

12. When they were filled, he said unto his disciples, Gather up the fragments that remain, that nothing be lost.

Greek/Transliteration
12. Ὡς δὲ ἐνεπλήσθησαν, λέγει τοῖς μαθηταῖς αὐτοῦ, Συναγάγετε τὰ περισσεύσαντα κλάσματα, ἵνα μή τι ἀπόληται.

12. 'Os de enepleistheisan, legei tois matheitais autou, Sunagagete ta perisseusanta klasmata, 'ina mei ti apoleitai.

Hebrew/Transliteration

יב. וְאַחֲרֵי אֲשֶׁר שָׂבְעוּ אָמַר אֶל-תַּלְמִידָיו אִסְפוּ אֶת-הַפְּתוֹתִים הַנּוֹתָרִים לִבְלִי יֹאבַד מְאוּמָה:

12. Ve•a•cha•rey asher sav•oo amar el - tal•mi•dav ees•foo et - hap•to•tim ha•no•ta•rim liv•li yo•vad me•oo•ma.

---

13. Therefore they gathered them together, and filled twelve baskets with the fragments of the five barley loaves, which remained over and above unto them that had eaten.

Greek/Transliteration

13. Συνήγαγον οὖν, καὶ ἐγέμισαν δώδεκα κοφίνους κλασμάτων ἐκ τῶν πέντε ἄρτων τῶν κριθίνων, ἃ ἐπερίσσευσεν τοῖς βεβρωκόσιν.

13. Suneigagon oun, kai egemisan dodeka kophinous klasmaton ek ton pente arton ton krithinon, 'a eperisseusen tois bebrokosin.

Hebrew/Transliteration

יג. וַיַּאַסְפוּ וַיְמַלְאוּ שְׁנֵים-עָשָׂר סַלִּים פְּתוֹתִים אֲשֶׁר הוֹתִירוּ הָאֹכְלִים מִן-חֲמֵשָׁה לַחְמֵי הַשְּׂעֹרִים:

13. Va•ya•as•foo vay•mal•oo sh`neym - asar sa•lim pe•to•tim asher ho•ti•roo ha•och•lim min - cha•mi•sha lach•mey has•o•rim.

---

14. Then those men, when they had seen the miracle that Jesus did, said, This is of a truth that prophet that should come into the world.

Greek/Transliteration

14. Οἱ οὖν ἄνθρωποι ἰδόντες ὃ ἐποίησεν σημεῖον ὁ Ἰησοῦς, ἔλεγον ὅτι Οὗτός ἐστιν ἀληθῶς ὁ προφήτης ὁ ἐρχόμενος εἰς τὸν κόσμον.

14. 'Oi oun anthropoi idontes 'o epoieisen seimeion 'o Yeisous, elegon 'oti 'Outos estin aleithos 'o propheiteis 'o erchomenos eis ton kosmon.

Hebrew/Transliteration

יד. וַיְהִי כִּרְאוֹת הָעָם אֶת-הָאוֹת הַזֶּה אֲשֶׁר עָשָׂה יֵשׁוּעַ וַיֹּאמְרוּ אָמְנָם זֶה הוּא הַנָּבִיא הַבָּא לְתֵבֵל אָרְצָה:

14. Vay•hi kir•ot ha•am et - ha•ot ha•ze asher asa Yeshua va•yom•roo om•nam ze hoo ha•na•vee ha•ba le•te•vel ar•tza.

Rabbinic Jewish Commentary

said, this is of a truth that prophet that should come into the world; meaning that prophet, that Moses spoke of, in Deu_18:15; for the ancient Jews understood this passage of the Messiah, though the modern ones apply it to others; And these men concluded that Yeshua was that prophet, or the true Messiah, from the miracle he wrought; in which he appeared, not only to be like to Moses, but greater than he.

"YAHWEH your Elohim shall raise up to you a prophet from among you, of your brothers, one like me [by the Holy Spirit]; you shall listen to him," (Deut_18:15)

The Targum of Jonathan adds,"by the Holy Spirit;"which he received without measure, and in respect of which was superior to Moses, or any of the prophets: he was like to Moses in the faithful discharge of his office, in his familiar converse with God, in the miracles which he wrought; as well as in his being a Mediator, and the Redeemer of his people, as Moses was a mediator between God and the people of Israel, and the deliverer of them out of Egypt; and it is a saying of the Jews (p) themselves,"as was the first redeemer, so is the second:"

(p) Midrash Kohelet, fol. 63. 2.

---

15. When Jesus therefore perceived that they would come and take him by force, to make him a king, he departed again into a mountain himself alone.

Greek/Transliteration

15. Ἰησοῦς οὖν γνοὺς ὅτι μέλλουσιν ἔρχεσθαι καὶ ἁρπάζειν αὐτόν, ἵνα ποιήσωσιν αὐτὸν βασιλέα, ἀνεχώρησεν εἰς τὸ ὄρος αὐτὸς μόνος.

15. Yeisous oun gnous 'oti mellousin erchesthai kai 'arpazein auton, 'ina poieisosin auton basilea, anechoreisen eis to oros autos monos.

Hebrew/Transliteration

טו. וַיֵּדַע יֵשׁוּעַ כִּי-יָבֹאוּ וְתָפְשׂוּ-בוֹ לַעֲשׂוֹתוֹ לְמֶלֶךְ עַל-כֵּן חָלַץ מֵהֶם עוֹד הַפַּעַם אֶל-הָהָר לְבַדּוֹ:

15. Va•ye•da Yeshua ki - ya•vo•oo ve•taf•soo - vo la•a•sho•to le•me•lech al - ken cha•latz me•hem od ha•pa•am el - ha•har le•va•do.

---

16. And when even was now come, his disciples went down unto the sea,

Greek/Transliteration

16. Ὡς δὲ ὀψία ἐγένετο, κατέβησαν οἱ μαθηταὶ αὐτοῦ ἐπὶ τὴν θάλασσαν,

16. 'Os de opsia egeneto, katebeisan 'oi matheitai autou epi tein thalassan,

:טז. וַיְהִי לְעֵת עֶרֶב וַיֵּלְכוּ תַלְמִידָיו אֶל-הַיָּם

16. Vay•hi le•et erev va•yel•choo tal•mi•dav el - ha•yam,

---

17. And entered into a ship, and went over the sea toward Capernaum. And it was now dark, and Jesus was not come to them.

Greek/Transliteration

17. καὶ ἐμβάντες εἰς τὸ πλοῖον, ἤρχοντο πέραν τῆς θαλάσσης εἰς Καπερναούμ. Καὶ σκοτία ἤδη ἐγεγόνει, καὶ οὐκ ἐληλύθει πρὸς αὐτοὺς ὁ Ἰησοῦς.

17. kai embantes eis to ploion, eirchonto peran teis thalasseis eis Kapernaoum. Kai skotia eidei egegonei, kai ouk eleiluthei pros autous 'o Yeisous.

Hebrew/Transliteration

:יז. וַיֵּרְדוּ בָאֳנִיָּה וַיַּעַבְרוּ אֶל-עֵבֶר הַיָּם אֶל-כְּפַר נַחוּם וְהִנֵּה חֹשֶׁךְ בָּא וְיֵשׁוּעַ עוֹד לֹא-בָא אֲלֵיהֶם

17. Va•yer•doo va•o•ni•ya va•ya•av•roo el - ever ha•yam el - K`far Na•choom ve•hee•ne cho•shech ba ve•Yeshua od lo - va aley•hem.

---

18. And the sea arose by reason of a great wind that blew.

Greek/Transliteration

18. Ἥ τε θάλασσα ἀνέμου μεγάλου πνέοντος διηγείρετο.

18. 'Ei te thalassa anemou megalou pneontos dieigeireto.

Hebrew/Transliteration

:יח. וַיְהִי סַעַר גָּדוֹל עֹבֵר וְהַיָּם הֹלֵךְ וְסֹעֵר

18. Vay•hi sa•ar ga•dol o•ver ve•ha•yam ho•lech ve•so•er.

---

19. So when they had rowed about five and twenty or thirty furlongs, they see Jesus walking on the sea, and drawing nigh unto the ship: and they were afraid.

19. Ἐληλακότες οὖν ὡς σταδίους εἴκοσι πέντε ἢ τριάκοντα, θεωροῦσιν τὸν Ἰησοῦν περιπατοῦντα ἐπὶ τῆς θαλάσσης, καὶ ἐγγὺς τοῦ πλοίου γινόμενον· καὶ ἐφοβήθησαν.

19. Eleilakotes oun 'os stadious eikosi pente ei tryakonta, theorousin ton Yeisoun peripatounta epi teis thalasseis, kai engus tou ploiou ginomenon. kai ephobeitheisan.

Hebrew/Transliteration

יט. וַיַּחְתְּרוּ כְמֵרְחַק עֶשְׂרִים וְחָמֵשׁ אוֹ שְׁלֹשִׁים מֵעֲנוֹת וַיִּרְאוּ אֶת-יֵשׁוּעַ הוֹלֵךְ עַל-פְּנֵי הַיָּם הָלוֹךְ
וְקָרֵב אֶל-הָאֳנִיָּה וַיִּירָאוּ -

19. Va•yach•te•roo ke•mer•chak es•rim ve•cha•mesh oh sh`lo•shim ma•a•not va•yir•oo et - Yeshua ho•lech al - p`ney ha•yam ha•loch ve•ka•rev el - ha•o•ni•ya va•yi•ra•oo.

Rabbinic/TaNaKh-Old Testament Commentary

walking upon the sea; as on dry land: though it was so stormy and boisterous, that the disciples, though in a ship, were in the utmost danger, yet he upon the waves, was in none at all; by which action he showed himself to be the Lord of the sea, and to be truly and properly God; whose character is, that he "...stretching out the heavens by Himself, and *walking on the waves of the sea*;..." Job 9:8.

The Jews, especially the sect of the Pharisees, had a notion, from whom the disciples might have their's, of spirits, apparitions, and demons, being to be seen in the night; hence that rule (u), "it is forbidden a man to salute his friend in the night, for we are careful, lest שד הוא, "it should be a demon"."

They say a great many things of one לילית, "Lilith", that has its name from לילה, "the night", a she demon, that used to appear in the night, with an human face, and carry off young children, and kill them. Some such frightful notions had possessed the minds of the disciples: demons are, by the Jews, called מזיקין, "hurtful", or "hurting", all their study being to do hurt to men; and the same word is here used in Munster's Hebrew Gospel: (u) T. Bab. Megilla, fol. 3. 1. Sanhedrim, fol. 44. 1.

---

20. But he saith unto them, It is I; be not afraid.

Greek/Transliteration
20. Ὁ δὲ λέγει αὐτοῖς, Ἐγώ εἰμι· μὴ φοβεῖσθε.

20. 'O de legei autois, Ego eimi. mei phobeisthe.

Hebrew/Transliteration
כ. וַיֹּאמֶר אֲלֵיהֶם אֲנִי הוּא אַל-תִּירָאוּ:

20. Va•yo•mer aley•hem ani hoo al - ti•ra•oo.

---

21. Then they willingly received him into the ship: and immediately the ship was at the land whither they went.

Greek/Transliteration
21. Ἤθελον οὖν λαβεῖν αὐτὸν εἰς τὸ πλοῖον· καὶ εὐθέως τὸ πλοῖον ἐγένετο ἐπὶ τῆς γῆς εἰς ἣν ὑπῆγον.

21. Eithelon oun labein auton eis to ploion. kai eutheos to ploion egeneto epi teis geis eis 'ein 'upeigon.

Hebrew/Transliteration
כא. וַיּוֹאִילוּ לָקַחַת אֹתוֹ אֶל-הָאֳנִיָה וְהִנֵּה פִתְאֹם הִגִּיעָה הָאֳנִיָה אֶל-הַיַּבָּשָׁה אֶל-מְחוֹז חֶפְצָם:

21. Va•yo•ee•loo la•ka•chat o•to el - ha•o•ni•ya ve•hee•ne pit•om hi•gi•ah ha•o•ni•ya el - ha•ya•ba•sha el - me•choz chef•tzam.

---

22. The day following, when the people which stood on the other side of the sea saw that there was none other boat there, save that one whereinto his disciples were entered, and that Jesus went not with his disciples into the boat, but that his disciples were gone away
alone;

Greek/Transliteration
22. Τῇ ἐπαύριον ὁ ὄχλος ὁ ἑστηκὼς πέραν τῆς θαλάσσης, ἰδὼν ὅτι πλοιάριον ἄλλο οὐκ ἦν ἐκεῖ εἰ μὴ ἓν ἐκεῖνο εἰς ὃ ἐνέβησαν οἱ μαθηταὶ αὐτοῦ, καὶ ὅτι οὐ συνεισῆλθεν τοῖς μαθηταῖς αὐτοῦ ὁ Ἰησοῦς εἰς τὸ πλοιάριον, ἀλλὰ μόνοι οἱ μαθηταὶ αὐτοῦ ἀπῆλθον-

22. Tei epaurion 'o ochlos 'o 'esteikos peran teis thalasseis, idon 'oti ployarion allo ouk ein ekei ei mei 'en ekeino eis 'o enebeisan 'oi matheitai autou, kai 'oti ou suneiseilthen tois matheitais autou 'o Yeisous eis to ployarion, alla monoi 'oi matheitai autou apeilthon-

Hebrew/Transliteration
כב. וַיְהִי מִמָּחֳרָת וַיַּרְא הָעָם הֲמוֹן הָעָם הָעֹמֵד מֵעֵבֶר לַיָּם כִּי מִבַּלְעֲדֵי הָאֳנִיָה הָאֳנִיָה לֹא הָיְתָה שָׁם אֳנִיָּה אַחֶרֶת כִּי אִם:אַחַת אֲשֶׁר יָרְדוּ-בָה תַּלְמִידָיו וְכִי לֹא-יָרַד יֵשׁוּעַ בָּה עִם-תַּלְמִידָיו כִּי אִם-תַּלְמִידָיו עָבְרוּ - לְבַדָּם

22. Vay•hi mi•mo•cho•rat va•yar ha•mon ha•am ha•o•med me•e•ver la•yam ki mi•bal•a•dey ha•o•ni•ya lo hai•ta sham o•ni•ya a•che•ret ki eem - a•chat asher yar•doo - va tal•mi•dav ve•chi lo - ya•rad Yeshua ba eem - tal•mi•dav ki eem - tal•mi•dav av•roo le•va•dam.

---

23. (Howbeit there came other boats from Tiberias nigh unto the place where they did eat bread, after that the Lord had given thanks:)

Greek/Transliteration
23. ἄλλα δὲ ἦλθεν πλοιάρια ἐκ Τιβεριάδος ἐγγὺς τοῦ τόπου ὅπου ἔφαγον τὸν ἄρτον, εὐχαριστήσαντος τοῦ κυρίου-

23. alla de eilthen ployarya ek Tiberyados engus tou topou 'opou ephagon ton arton, eucharisteisantos tou kuriou-

Hebrew/Transliteration
כג. רַק אֳנִיּוֹת אֲחֵרוֹת הִגִּיעוּ מִטִּיבֶרְיָה מִקָּרוֹב לַמָּקוֹם אֲשֶׁר אָכְלוּ-שָׁם אֶת-הַלֶּחֶם כַּאֲשֶׁר בֵּרַךְ הָאָדוֹן:

23. Rak o•ni•yot a•che•rot hi•gi•oo mi•Ti•var•ya mi•ka•rov la•ma•kom asher ach•loo - sham et - ha•le•chem ka•a•sher be•rach ha•Adon.

Rabbinic Jewish Commentary
A city by the sea side, built by Herod, and called so in honour of Tiberius Caesar; though the Jews give a different etymology of it; they say, it is the same with Rakkath, Jos_19:35, and that it was a fortified place from the days of Joshua, and that on one side, ימה חומתה, "the sea was its wall" (d): and so Jonathan the Targumist on Deu_3:17 says, that Tiberias was near the sea of salt: this place became famous for many of the wise men that lived here; here was a famous university, and here the Misna and Jerusalem Talmud were written; and here the Sanhedrim sat, after it removed from Jerusalem.

---

24. When the people therefore saw that Jesus was not there, neither his disciples, they also took shipping, and came to Capernaum, seeking for Jesus.

Greek/Transliteration
24. ὅτε οὖν εἶδεν ὁ ὄχλος ὅτι Ἰησοῦς οὐκ ἔστιν ἐκεῖ οὐδὲ οἱ μαθηταὶ αὐτοῦ, ἐνέβησαν αὐτοὶ εἰς τὰ πλοῖα, καὶ ἦλθον εἰς Καπερναούμ, ζητοῦντες τὸν Ἰησοῦν.

24. 'ote oun eiden 'o ochlos 'oti Yeisous ouk estin ekei oude 'oi matheitai autou, enebeisan autoi eis ta ploia, kai eilthon eis Kapernaoum, zeitountes ton Yeisoun.

Hebrew/Transliteration
כד. וְעַל-כֵּן בִּרְאוֹת הֲמוֹן הָעָם כִּי יֵשׁוּעַ אֵינֶנּוּ שָׁם וְאַף-לֹא תַלְמִידָיו וַיֵּרְדוּ גַם-הֵמָּה בָּאֳנִיּוֹת הָאֵלֶּה - וַיָּבֹאוּ כְּפַר-נַחוּם לְבַקֵּשׁ אֶת-יֵשׁוּעַ:

24. Ve•al - ken bir•ot ha•mon ha•am ki Yeshua ey•ne•noo sham ve•af - lo tal•mi•dav va•yer•doo gam - he•ma ba•o•ni•yot ha•e•le va•ya•vo•oo K`far - Na•choom le•va•kesh et - Yeshua.

25. And when they had found him on the other side of the sea, they said unto him, Rabbi, when camest thou hither?

Greek/Transliteration
25. Καὶ εὑρόντες αὐτὸν πέραν τῆς θαλάσσης, εἶπον αὐτῷ, ῾Ραββί, πότε ὧδε γέγονας;

25. Kai 'eurontes auton peran teis thalasseis, eipon auto, 'Rabbi, pote 'ode gegonas?

Hebrew/Transliteration
כה. וַיִּמְצָאֻהוּ מֵעֵבֶר לַיָּם וַיֹּאמְרוּ אֵלָיו רַבֵּנוּ מָתַי בָּאתָ הֵנָּה:

25. Va•yim•tza•oo•hoo me•e•ver la•yam va•yom•roo elav Ra•be•noo ma•tai ba•ta he•na?

---

26. Jesus answered them and said, Verily, verily, I say unto you, Ye seek me, not because ye saw the miracles, but because ye did eat of the loaves, and were filled.

Greek/Transliteration
26. ᾽Απεκρίθη αὐτοῖς ὁ ᾽Ιησοῦς καὶ εἶπεν, ᾽Αμὴν ἀμὴν λέγω ὑμῖν, ζητεῖτέ με, οὐχ ὅτι εἴδετε σημεῖα, ἀλλ᾽ ὅτι ἐφάγετε ἐκ τῶν ἄρτων καὶ ἐχορτάσθητε.

26. Apekrithei autois 'o Yeisous kai eipen, Amein amein lego 'umin, zeiteite me, ouch 'oti eidete seimeia, all 'oti ephagete ek ton arton kai echortastheite.

Hebrew/Transliteration
כו. וַיַּעַן אֹתָם יֵשׁוּעַ לֵאמֹר אָמֵן אָמֵן אֲנִי אֹמֵר לָכֶם הֵן לֹא בִקַּשְׁתֶּם אֹתִי יַעַן אֲשֶׁר רְאִיתֶם אֶת- אֹתוֹתַי כִּי אִם-יַעַן מִכִּכְּרוֹת הַלֶּחֶם אֲכַלְתֶּם וַשְׂבַעְתֶּם -

26. Va•ya•an o•tam Yeshua le•mor Amen amen ani o•mer la•chem hen lo vi•kash•tem o•ti ya•an asher r`ee•tem et - o•to•tai ki eem - ya•an mi•kik•rot ha•le•chem achal•tem oos•va•a•tem.

---

27. Labour not for the meat which perisheth, but for that meat which endureth unto everlasting life, which the Son of man shall give unto you: for him hath God the Father sealed.

Greek/Transliteration
27. ᾽Εργάζεσθε μὴ τὴν βρῶσιν τὴν ἀπολλυμένην, ἀλλὰ τὴν βρῶσιν τὴν μένουσαν εἰς ζωὴν αἰώνιον, ἣν ὁ υἱὸς τοῦ ἀνθρώπου ὑμῖν δώσει· τοῦτον γὰρ ὁ πατὴρ ἐσφράγισεν, ὁ θεός.

27. Ergazesthe mei tein brosin tein apollumenein, alla tein brosin tein menousan eis zoein aionion, 'ein 'o 'wios tou anthropou 'umin dosei. touton gar 'o pateir esphragisen, 'o theos.

כז. אַל-תַּעַמְלוּ בְּעַד אֹכֶל אֹבֵד כִּי אִם-בְּעַד לֶחֶם עֹמֵד לְחַיֵּי עוֹלָם אֲשֶׁר בֶּן-הָאָדָם יִתֵּן לָכֶם כִּי-עָלָיו חָתַם:הָאֱלֹהִים הָאָב אֶת-חֹתָמוֹ

27. Al - ta•am•loo be•ad o•chel o•ved ki eem - be•ad le•chem o•med le•cha•yey o•lam asher Ben - ha•adam yi•ten la•chem ki - alav cha•tam ha•Elohim ha•Av et - cho•ta•mo.

---

28. Then said they unto him, What shall we do, that we might work the works of God?

Greek/Transliteration
28. Εἶπον οὖν πρὸς αὐτόν, Τί ποιῶμεν, ἵνα ἐργαζώμεθα τὰ ἔργα τοῦ θεοῦ;

28. Eipon oun pros auton, Ti poiomen, 'ina ergazometha ta erga tou theou?

Hebrew/Transliteration
:כח. וַיֹּאמְרוּ אֵלָיו מַה-נַּעֲשֶׂה אֲשֶׁר נִפְעַל פְּעֻלּוֹת אֱלֹהִים

28. Va•yom•roo elav ma - na•a•se asher nif•al pe•oo•lot Elohim?

---

29. Jesus answered and said unto them, This is the work of God, that ye believe on him whom he hath sent.

Greek/Transliteration
29. Ἀπεκρίθη Ἰησοῦς καὶ εἶπεν αὐτοῖς, Τοῦτό ἐστιν τὸ ἔργον τοῦ θεοῦ, ἵνα πιστεύσητε εἰς ὃν ἀπέστειλεν ἐκεῖνος.

29. Apekrithei Yeisous kai eipen autois, Touto estin to ergon tou theou, 'ina pisteuseite eis 'on apesteilen ekeinos.

Hebrew/Transliteration
:כט. וַיַּעַן יֵשׁוּעַ וַיֹּאמֶר אֲלֵיהֶם זֹאת פְּעֻלַּת אֱלֹהִים כִּי-תַאֲמִינוּ בָאִישׁ אֲשֶׁר שְׁלָחוֹ אֲלֵיכֶם

29. Va•ya•an Yeshua va•yo•mer aley•hem zot pe•oo•lat Elohim ki - ta•a•mi•noo va•eesh asher sh`la•cho aley•chem.

Rabbinic Jewish Commentary
This, as a principle, is purely God's work; as it is an act, or as it is exercised under the influence of divine grace, it is man's act: "that ye believe"; the object of it is

Yeshua, as sent by the Father, as the Mediator between God and men, as appointed by him to be the Saviour and Redeemer; and believing in Yeshua, is believing in God that sent him. The Jews reduce all the six hundred and thirteen precepts of the Torah, for so many they say there are, to this one, "the just shall live by his faith", Hab_2:4. (e).

(e) T. Bab. Maccot, fol. 23. 2. & 24. 1.

---

30. They said therefore unto him, What sign shewest thou then, that we may see, and believe thee? what dost thou work?

Greek/Transliteration
30. Εἶπον οὖν αὐτῷ, Τί οὖν ποιεῖς σὺ σημεῖον, ἵνα ἴδωμεν καὶ πιστεύσωμέν σοι; Τί ἐργάζῃ;

30. Eipon oun auto, Ti oun poieis su seimeion, 'ina idomen kai pisteusomen soi? Ti ergazei?

Hebrew/Transliteration
לְ. וַיֹּאמְרוּ אֵלָיו וּמֶה-הָאוֹת אֲשֶׁר תַּעֲשֶׂה כִּי נִרְאֶה וְנַאֲמִין בָּךְ מַה-תִּפְעָל:

30. Va•yom•roo elav oo•me - ha•ot asher ta•a•se ki nir•eh ve•na•a•min bach ma - tif•al?

---

31. Our fathers did eat manna in the desert; as it is written, He gave them bread from heaven to eat.

Greek/Transliteration
31. Οἱ πατέρες ἡμῶν τὸ μάννα ἔφαγον ἐν τῇ ἐρήμῳ, καθώς ἐστιν γεγραμμένον, Ἄρτον ἐκ τοῦ οὐρανοῦ ἔδωκεν αὐτοῖς φαγεῖν.

31. 'Oi pateres 'eimon to manna ephagon en tei ereimo, kathos estin gegrammenon, Arton ek tou ouranou edoken autois phagein.

Hebrew/Transliteration
לֹא. אֲבוֹתֵינוּ אָכְלוּ אֶת-הַמָּן בַּמִּדְבָּר כַּכָּתוּב לֶחֶם שָׁמַיִם נָתַן-לָמוֹ לֶאֱכֹל:

31. Avo•tey•noo ach•loo et - ha•man ba•mid•bar ka•ka•toov le•chem sha•ma•yim na•tan - la•mo le•e•chol.

Rabbinic Jewish Commentary
Which was a sort of food prepared by messengers in the air, and rained down from thence about the tents of the Israelites; it was a small round thing, as small as the hoar frost on the ground; it was like a coriander seed, and the colour of it was the

colour of bdellium: it was so called, either from מנה, "to prepare", because it was prepared, and got ready for the Israelites; or from the first words that were spoken upon sight of it, מן הו, "what is it?" for they knew not what it was: and this the Jewish fathers fed upon all the while they were in the wilderness, till they came to Canaan's land, and they only; it was food peculiar to them: "our fathers did eat"; and so the Jews (f) observe on those words in Exo_16:35,

"And the children of Israel did eat manna forty years"; the children of Israel, ולא אחרא, "not another". And the children of Israel saw, and said, what is it? and not the rest of the mixed multitude."

as it is written; In Psa_78:24, or rather in Exo_16:15; and perhaps both places may be respected:

he gave them bread from heaven to eat; they leave out the word Lord, being willing it should be understood of Moses, to whom they ascribed it, as appears from the following words of Yeshua, who denies that Moses gave it; and add the phrase "from heaven", to set forth the excellent nature of it, which is taken from Exo_16:4, where the manna, as here, is called "bread from heaven".

(f) Zohar in Exod. fol. 75. 2.

---

32. Then Jesus said unto them, Verily, verily, I say unto you, Moses gave you not that bread from heaven; but my Father giveth you the true bread from heaven.

Greek/Transliteration
32. Εἶπεν οὖν αὐτοῖς ὁ Ἰησοῦς, Ἀμὴν ἀμὴν λέγω ὑμῖν, οὐ Μωσῆς δέδωκεν ὑμῖν τὸν ἄρτον ἐκ τοῦ οὐρανοῦ· ἀλλ᾽ ὁ πατήρ μου δίδωσιν ὑμῖν τὸν ἄρτον ἐκ τοῦ οὐρανοῦ τὸν ἀληθινόν.

32. Eipen oun autois 'o Yeisous, Amein amein lego 'umin, ou Moseis dedoken 'umin ton arton ek tou ouranou. all 'o pateir mou didosin 'umin ton arton ek tou ouranou ton aleithinon.

Hebrew/Transliteration
לב. וַיֹּאמֶר אֲלֵיהֶם יֵשׁוּעַ אָמֵן אָמֵן אֲנִי אֹמֵר לָכֶם מֹשֶׁה לֹא נָתַן לָכֶם לֶחֶם שָׁמַיִם כִּי אִם-אָבִי נֹתֵן לָכֶם לֶחֶם:אֱמֶת מִן-הַשָּׁמָיִם

32. Va•yo•mer aley•hem Yeshua Amen amen ani o•mer la•chem Moshe lo na•tan la•chem le•chem sha•ma•yim ki eem - Avi no•ten la•chem le•chem emet min - ha•sha•ma•yim.

Rabbinic Jewish Commentary
Moses had no hand in it; he did not so much as pray for it, much less procure it, or prepare it: it was promised and prepared by God, and rained by him, and who

directed to the gathering and use of it. This stands opposed to a notion of the Jews, that the manna was given by means of Moses, for his sake, and on account of his merits: for they say (g),

"There arose up three good providers, or pastors for Israel, and they are these, Moses, and Aaron, and Miriam; and three good gifts were given by their means, and they are these, the well, the cloud, and the manna; the well by the merits of Miriam; the pillar of cloud by the merits of Aaron; מן בזכות משה, "the manna, by the merits of Moses"." This Yeshua denies; and affirms,

Philo the Jew says (h), the heavenly food of the soul, which is called "manna", the divine *Word* distributes alike to all that ask.

(g) T. Bab. Taanith, fol. 9. 1. Seder Olam Rabba, p. 28. (h) Quis rer. divin.

---

33. For the bread of God is he which cometh down from heaven, and giveth life unto the world.

Greek/Transliteration
33. Ὁ γὰρ ἄρτος τοῦ θεοῦ ἐστιν ὁ καταβαίνων ἐκ τοῦ οὐρανοῦ καὶ ζωὴν διδοὺς τῷ κόσμῳ.

33. 'O gar artos tou theou estin 'o katabainon ek tou ouranou kai zoein didous to kosmo.

Hebrew/Transliteration
לג. כִּי-לֶחֶם אֱלֹהִים הוּא הַיֹּרֵד מִן-הַשָּׁמַיִם וְהַנּוֹתֵן חַיִּים לָעוֹלָם:

33. Ki - le•chem Elohim hoo ha•yo•red min - ha•sha•ma•yim ve•ha•no•ten cha•yim la•o•lam.

---

34. Then said they unto him, Lord, evermore give us this bread.

Greek/Transliteration
34. Εἶπον οὖν πρὸς αὐτόν, Κύριε, πάντοτε δὸς ἡμῖν τὸν ἄρτον τοῦτον.

34. Eipon oun pros auton, Kurie, pantote dos 'eimin ton arton touton.

Hebrew/Transliteration
לד. וַיֹּאמְרוּ אֵלָיו אֲדֹנֵינוּ תְּנָה-לָנוּ אֶת-הַלֶּחֶם הַזֶּה תָּמִיד:

34. Va•yom•roo elav Ado•ney•noo te•na - la•noo et - ha•le•chem ha•ze ta•mid.

Rabbinic Jewish Commentary

Josephus (i) says of the "manna", which was a type of this bread, that there was such a divine quality in it, that whoever tasted of it needed nothing else: and the Jews also say (k), that

"In the manna were all kinds of tastes, and everyone of the Israelites tasted all that he desired; for so it is written in Deu_2:7, "these forty years the LORD thy God hath been with thee, thou hast lacked nothing", or "not wanted anything"; what is anything? when he desired to eat anything, and said with his mouth, O that I had fat to eat, immediately there was in his mouth the taste of fat.--Young men tasted the taste of bread, old men the taste of honey, and children the taste of oil."

Yea, they say (l), "Whoever desired flesh, he tasted it, and whoever desired fish, he tasted it, and whoever desired fowl, chicken, pheasant, or pea hen, so he tasted whatever he desired."

And to this agrees what is said in the apocryphal book of Wisdom, 16:20,21:

"Thou feddest thine own people with messengers food, and didst send them from heaven bread, prepared without their labour, able to content every man's delight, and agreeing to every taste; for thy sustenance (or manna) declared thy sweetness unto thy children, and serving to the appetite of the eater, tempered itself to every man's liking."

(i) Antiqu. l. 3. c. 1. sect. 6. (k) Shemot Rabba, sect. 25. fol. 108. 4. (l) Bemidbar Rabba, sect. 7. fol. 188. 1.

---

35. And Jesus said unto them, I am the bread of life: he that cometh to me shall never hunger; and he that believeth on me shall never thirst.

Greek/Transliteration

35. Εἶπεν δὲ αὐτοῖς ὁ Ἰησοῦς, Ἐγώ εἰμι ὁ ἄρτος τῆς ζωῆς· ὁ ἐρχόμενος πρός με οὐ μὴ πεινάσῃ· καὶ ὁ πιστεύων εἰς ἐμὲ οὐ μὴ διψήσῃ πώποτε.

35. Eipen de autois 'o Yeisous, Ego eimi 'o artos teis zoeis. 'o erchomenos pros me ou mei peinasei. kai 'o pisteuon eis eme ou mei dipseisei popote.

Hebrew/Transliteration

לה. וַיֹּאמֶר אֲלֵיהֶם יֵשׁוּעַ אָנֹכִי הוּא לֶחֶם הַחַיִּים כָּל-הַבָּא אֵלַי לֹא יִרְעָב וְכָל-הַמַּאֲמִין בִּי לֹא יִצְמָא עוֹד לְעוֹלָם:

35. Va•yo•mer aley•hem Yeshua ano•chi hoo le•chem ha•cha•yim kol - ha•ba e•lai lo yir•av ve•chol - ha•ma•a•min bi lo yitz•ma od le•o•lam.

---

36. But I said unto you, That ye also have seen me, and believe not.

Greek/Transliteration
36. Ἀλλ᾽ εἶπον ὑμῖν ὅτι καὶ ἑωράκατέ με, καὶ οὐ πιστεύετε.

36. All eipon 'umin 'oti kai 'eorakate me, kai ou pisteuete.

Hebrew/Transliteration
:לו. וַאֹמַר אֲלֵיכֶם אֲשֶׁר רְאִיתֶם אֹתִי וְלֹא הֶאֱמַנְתֶּם בִּי

36. Va•o•mar aley•chem asher r`ee•tem o•ti ve•lo he•e•man•tem bi.

---

37. All that the Father giveth me shall come to me; and him that cometh to me I will in no wise cast out.

Greek/Transliteration
37. Πᾶν ὃ δίδωσίν μοι ὁ πατὴρ πρὸς ἐμὲ ἥξει· καὶ τὸν ἐρχόμενον πρός με οὐ μὴ ἐκβάλω ἔξω.

37. Pan 'o didosin moi 'o pateir pros eme 'eixei. kai ton erchomenon pros me ou mei ekbalo exo.

Hebrew/Transliteration
:לז. כָּל-אִישׁ אֲשֶׁר אֹתוֹ יִתֶּן-לִי הָאָב יָבֹא אֵלַי וְהַבָּא אֵלַי לֹא אֲגָרְשֶׁנּוּ מִפָּנָי

37. Kol - eesh asher o•to yi•ten - li ha•Av ya•vo e•lai ve•ha•ba e•lai lo agar•she•noo mi•pa•nai.

---

38. For I came down from heaven, not to do mine own will, but the will of him that sent me.

Greek/Transliteration
38. Ὅτι καταβέβηκα ἐκ τοῦ οὐρανοῦ, οὐχ ἵνα ποιῶ τὸ θέλημα τὸ ἐμόν, ἀλλὰ τὸ θέλημα τοῦ πέμψαντός με.

38. 'Oti katabebeika ek tou ouranou, ouch 'ina poio to theleima to emon, alla to theleima tou pempsantos me.

Hebrew/Transliteration
:לח. כִּי יָרַדְתִּי מִן-הַשָּׁמַיִם לֹא לַעֲשׂוֹת רְצוֹנִי כִּי אִם-רְצוֹן הָאָב אֲשֶׁר שְׁלָחִי

38. Ki ya•ra•de•ti min - ha•sha•ma•yim lo la•a•sot r`tzo•ni ki eem - r`tzon ha•Av asher shol•chi.

Rabbinic Jewish Commentary

The Jew (m) objects to this, and says, "If this respects the descent of the soul, the soul of every man descended from thence; but if it respects the body, the rest of the evangelists contradict his words, particularly Luke, when he says, Luk_2:7 that his mother brought him forth at Bethlehem."

What the above Jewish writer (n) objects to this part of the text is of very little moment: whose words are;

"Moreover, what he says, "Not to do mine own will, but the will of him that sent me", shows, that he that sent, is not one and the same with him that is sent, seeing the will of him that is sent, is not as the will of him that sends."

But this descent regards neither his soul nor body, but his divine Spirit, which always was in heaven, and not any local descent of that, see John 1:1.

(m) R. Isaac Chizzuk Emuna, par. 2. c. 44. p. 434. (n) R. Chizzuk Emmuna, par. 2. c. 44. p. 434.

---

39. And this is the Father's will which hath sent me, that of all which he hath given me I should lose nothing, but should raise it up again at the last day.

Greek/Transliteration
39. Τοῦτο δέ ἐστιν τὸ θέλημα τοῦ πέμψαντός με πατρός, ἵνα πᾶν ὃ δέδωκέν μοι, μὴ ἀπολέσω ἐξ αὐτοῦ, ἀλλὰ ἀναστήσω αὐτὸ τῇ ἐσχάτῃ ἡμέρᾳ.

39. Touto de estin to theleima tou pempsantos me patros, 'ina pan 'o dedoken moi, mei apoleso ex autou, alla anasteiso auto tei eschatei 'eimera.

Hebrew/Transliteration
לט. וְזֶה רְצוֹן הָאָב אֲשֶׁר שְׁלָחִי כִּי אֶת-אֲשֶׁר נָתַן לִי לֹא-יֹאבַד לִי אַף אֶחָד כִּי אֲקִימֶנּוּ בַּיּוֹם הָאַחֲרוֹן:

39. Ve•ze r`tzon ha•Av asher shol•chi ki et - asher na•tan li lo - yo•vad li af e•chad ki aki•me•noo ba•yom ha•a•cha•ron.

Rabbinic Jewish Commentary
The Jews (o), speaking of the resurrection, and making mention of that passage in Num_23:10, "Who shall count the dust of Jacob?" add,

"and he (i.e. God) shall order it all, ולא יתאביד כלום, "and not anything shall be lost", but all shall rise again; for, lo, it is said, Dan_12:2, "and many of them that sleep in the dust".

(o) Zohar in Exod. fol. 43. 4.

---

40. And this is the will of him that sent me, that every one which seeth the Son, and believeth on him, may have everlasting life: and I will raise him up at the last day.

Greek/Transliteration
40. Τοῦτο δέ ἐστιν τὸ θέλημα τοῦ πέμψαντός με, ἵνα πᾶς ὁ θεωρῶν τὸν υἱὸν καὶ πιστεύων εἰς αὐτόν, ἔχῃ ζωὴν αἰώνιον, καὶ ἀναστήσω αὐτὸν ἐγὼ τῇ ἐσχάτῃ ἡμέρᾳ.

40. Touto de estin to theleima tou pempsantos me, 'ina pas 'o theoron ton 'wion kai pisteuon eis auton, echei zoein aionion, kai anasteiso auton ego tei eschatei 'eimera.

Hebrew/Transliteration
מ. כִּי זֶה רְצוֹן אָבִי מִי אֲשֶׁר רֹאֶה אֶת-הַבֵּן וּמַאֲמִין בּוֹ יִהְיוּ-לוֹ חַיֵּי עוֹלָם וַאֲנִי אֲקִימְּוּ בַּיּוֹם הָאַחֲרוֹן:

40. Ki ze r`tzon Avi mee asher ro•eh et - ha•Ben oo•ma•a•min bo yi•hee•yoo – lo cha•yey o•lam va•a•ni aki•me•noo ba•yom ha•a•cha•ron.

Rabbinic Jewish Commmentary
The Jewish notion, that the resurrection of the dead would be at the Messiah's coming: it will be at his second coming, but was not to be at his first; there was indeed then a resurrection of some particular persons, but not a general one of all the saints: that the Jews expect the resurrection of the dead when the Messiah comes, appears from their Targums, Talmuds, and other writers; so the Targumist on Hos_14:8,

"They shall be gathered from their captivity, they shall sit under the shadow of their Messiah, "and the dead shall live", and good shall be multiplied in the land."

And in the Talmud (p) it is said,

"The holy blessed God will quicken the righteous, and they shall not return to their dust."

The gloss upon it is,

"The holy blessed God will quicken them "in the days of the Messiah."

And so the land of the living is said to be,

"The land, whose dead live first in the days of the Messiah (q)."

And hence R. Jeremiah desired to he buried with his clothes and shoes on, and staff in his hand, that when the Messiah came, he might be ready (r) with which agree others of the more modern writers; so Kimchi on Isa_66:5.

"They shall live at the resurrection of the dead, in the days of the Messiah."

And the same writer on Jer_23:20 observes it is said,

"ye" shall consider, and not "they" shall consider; which intimates the "resurrection of the dead in the days of the Messiah"."

And says Aben Ezra on Dan_12:2,

"The righteous which die in captivity shall live, when the Redeemer comes;"

Though some of their writers differ in this point, and will not allow the days of the Messiah, and the resurrection of the dead, to be one and the same (s).

(p) T. Bab. Sanhedrin, fol. 92. 1. (q) T. Hieros. Kilaim, fol. 32. 3. (r) T. Hieros. Kilaim, foi. 32. 3. col. 2. (s) Zohar in Gen. fol. 82. 4.

---

41. The Jews then murmured at him, because he said, I am the bread which came down from heaven.

Greek/Transliteration
41. Ἐγόγγυζον οὖν οἱ Ἰουδαῖοι περὶ αὐτοῦ, ὅτι εἶπεν, Ἐγώ εἰμι ὁ ἄρτος ὁ καταβὰς ἐκ τοῦ οὐρανοῦ.

41. Egonguzon oun 'oi Youdaioi peri autou, 'oti eipen, Ego eimi 'o artos 'o katabas ek tou ouranou.

Hebrew/Transliteration
מא. וַיִּלֹּנוּ עָלָיו הַיְּהוּדִים עַל כִּי-אָמַר אָנֹכִי הוּא לֶחֶם הַיֹּרֵד מִן-הַשָּׁמָיִם:

41. Va•yi•lo•noo alav ha•Ye•hoo•dim al ki - amar ano•chi hoo le•chem ha•yo•red min - ha•sha•ma•yim.

---

42. And they said, Is not this Jesus, the son of Joseph, whose father and mother we know? how is it then that he saith, I came down from heaven?

Greek/Transliteration
42. Καὶ ἔλεγον, Οὐχ οὗτός ἐστιν Ἰησοῦς ὁ υἱὸς Ἰωσήφ, οὗ ἡμεῖς οἴδαμεν τὸν πατέρα καὶ τὴν μητέρα; Πῶς οὖν λέγει οὗτος ὅτι Ἐκ τοῦ οὐρανοῦ καταβέβηκα;

42. Kai elegon, Ouch 'outos estin Yeisous 'o 'wios Yoseiph, 'ou 'eimeis oidamen ton patera kai tein meitera? Pos oun legei 'outos 'oti Ek tou ouranou katabebeika?

מב. וַיֹּאמְרוּ הֲלֹא זֶה הוּא יֵשׁוּעַ בֶּן-יוֹסֵף אֲשֶׁר יָדַעְנוּ אֶת-אָבִיו וְאֶת-אִמּוֹ וְאֵיךְ יֹאמַר הוּא מִן-
הַשָּׁמַיִם יָרָדְתִּי:

42. Va•yom•roo ha•lo ze hoo Yeshua ben - Yo•sef asher ya•da•a•noo et - aviv
ve•et - ee•mo ve•eych yo•mar hoo min - ha•sha•ma•yim ya•ra•de•ti?

---

43. Jesus therefore answered and said unto them, Murmur not among
yourselves.

Greek/Transliteration
43. Ἀπεκρίθη οὖν ὁ Ἰησοῦς καὶ εἶπεν αὐτοῖς, Μὴ γογγύζετε μετ᾽ ἀλλήλων.

43. Apekrithei oun 'o Yeisous kai eipen autois, Mei gonguzete met alleilon.

Hebrew/Transliteration
מג. וַיַּעַן יֵשׁוּעַ וַיֹּאמֶר אֲלֵיהֶם אַל-נָא תְהִי תְלוּנָה בֵּינֵיכֶם:

43. Va•ya•an Yeshua va•yo•mer aley•hem al - na te•hi t`loo•na bey•ney•chem.

---

44. No man can come to me, except the Father which hath sent me draw him:
and I will raise him up at the last day.

Greek/Transliteration
44. Οὐδεὶς δύναται ἐλθεῖν πρός με, ἐὰν μὴ ὁ πατὴρ ὁ πέμψας με ἑλκύσῃ αὐτόν,
καὶ ἐγὼ ἀναστήσω αὐτὸν ἐν τῇ ἐσχάτῃ ἡμέρᾳ.

44. Oudeis dunatai elthein pros me, ean mei 'o pateir 'o pempsas me 'elkusei
auton, kai ego anasteiso auton en tei eschatei 'eimera.

Hebrew/Transliteration
מד. לֹא-יוּכַל אִישׁ לָבֹא אֵלַי בִּלְתִּי אִם-יִמְשְׁכֵהוּ הָאָב אֲשֶׁר שְׁלָחָנִי וַאֲנִי אֲקִימֶנּוּ בַּיּוֹם הָאַחֲרוֹן:

44. Lo - yoo•chal eesh la•vo e•lai bil•tee eem - yim•she•che•hoo ha•Av asher
sh`la•cha•ni va•a•ni aki•me•noo ba•yom ha•a•cha•ron.

Rabbinic Jewish Commentary
The Jews have a saying (t), that the proselytes, in the days of the Messiah, shall be
all of them, גרים גרורים, "proselytes drawn": that is, such as shall freely and
voluntarily become proselytes, as those who are drawn by the Father are.

(t) T. Bab. Avoda Zara, fol. 3. 2. & 24. 1.

---

45. It is written in the prophets, And they shall be all taught of God. Every man therefore that hath heard, and hath learned of the Father, cometh unto me.

Greek/Transliteration

45. Ἔστιν γεγραμμένον ἐν τοῖς προφήταις, Καὶ ἔσονται πάντες διδακτοὶ θεοῦ. Πᾶς οὖν ὁ ἀκούων παρὰ τοῦ πατρὸς καὶ μαθών, ἔρχεται πρός με.

45. Estin gegrammenon en tois propheitais, Kai esontai pantes didaktoi theou. Pas oun 'o akouon para tou patros kai mathon, erchetai pros me.

Hebrew/Transliteration

מה. הֲלֹא כָתוּב בַּנְּבִיאִים וְכָל-בָּנַיִךְ לִמּוּדֵי יְהוָֹה כָּל-הַשֹּׁמֵעַ מִן-הָאָב וְלֹמֵד מִמֶּנּוּ יָבֹא אֵלָי:

45. Ha•lo cha•toov van•vi•eem ve•chol - ba•na•yich li•moo•dey Adonai kol - ha•sho•me•a min - ha•Av ve•lo•med mi•me•noo ya•vo e•lai.

Rabbinic Jewish Commentary

In Isa_54:13; so the Syriac version reads, "in the prophet". The Targum paraphrases it, "all thy children shall learn in the Torah of the LORD."

The Jews themselves acknowledge the prophecy belongs to the times of the Messiah, to which they expressly apply (u) the words in Isa_54:5, "Thy Maker is thy husband". And one of their modern commentators allows (w), that this very passage, "all thy children shall be taught of God", refers, לעתיד, "to the time to come"; that is, to the times of the Messiah, for so they say (x),

"They are truly taught of God from whom prophecy comes, which does not to all the world, but to Israel only, of whom it is written, "and all thy children are taught of God"."

(u) Shemot Rabba, sect. 15. fol. 102. 4. (w) Kimichi in loc. (x) Zohar in Exod. fol. 70. 1.

---

46. Not that any man hath seen the Father, save he which is of God, he hath seen the Father.

Greek/Transliteration

46. Οὐχ ὅτι τὸν πατέρα τις ἑώρακεν, εἰ μὴ ὁ ὢν παρὰ τοῦ θεοῦ, οὗτος ἑώρακεν τὸν πατέρα.

46. Ouch 'oti ton patera tis 'eoraken, ei mei 'o on para tou theou, 'outos 'eoraken ton patera.

Hebrew/Transliteration

מו. וְלֹא כִי-רָאָה אָדָם אֶת-הָאָב כִּי רַק זֶה אֲשֶׁר מֵאֵת יְהוָֹה הוּא רָאָה אֶת-הָאָב:

46. Ve•lo ki - ra•ah adam et - ha•Av ki rak ze asher me•et Adonai hoo ra•ah et - ha•Av.

Rabbinic Jewish Commentary
See John 1:18 for the explainaiton of "no man has seen the Father or God".

---

47. Verily, verily, I say unto you, He that believeth on me hath everlasting life.

Greek/Transliteration
47. Ἀμὴν ἀμὴν λέγω ὑμῖν, ὁ πιστεύων εἰς ἐμέ, ἔχει ζωὴν αἰώνιον.

47. Amein amein lego 'umin, 'o pisteuon eis eme, echei zoein aionion.

Hebrew/Transliteration
מז. אָמֵן אָמֵן אֲנִי אֹמֵר לָכֶם כָּל-הַמַּאֲמִין בִּי יֵשׁ-לוֹ חַיֵּי עוֹלָם:

47. Amen amen ani o•mer la•chem kol - ha•ma•a•min bi yesh - lo cha•yey o•lam.

---

48. I am that bread of life.

Greek/Transliteration
48. Ἐγώ εἰμι ὁ ἄρτος τῆς ζωῆς.

48. Ego eimi 'o artos teis zoeis.

Hebrew/Transliteration
מח. אֲנִי הוּא לֶחֶם הַחַיִּים:

48. Ani hoo le•chem ha•cha•yim.

Rabbinic Jewish Commentary
The Rabbi's say concerning the meaning of "in the sweat of your face you shall eat bread" (Gen.3:19), the following explanation is given: "This hints about the Torah which is called bread, as it says, 'Come, eat of my bread' (Prov.9:5). Because of Adam's sin, the Torah could not be fully explained until the days of Messiah…who is able to reveal the full and complete meaning of the Torah, which gives life. (Panim Yafot, Breshit 3; The Concealed Light pg.136, Tsvi Sadan)

---

49. Your fathers did eat manna in the wilderness, and are dead.

Greek/Transliteration
49. Οἱ πατέρες ὑμῶν ἔφαγον τὸ μάννα ἐν τῇ ἐρήμῳ, καὶ ἀπέθανον.

49. 'Oi pateres 'umon ephagon to manna en tei ereimo, kai apethanon.

Hebrew/Transliteration
מט. אֲבוֹתֵיכֶם אָכְלוּ אֶת-הַמָּן בַּמִּדְבָּר וַיָּמֻתוּ:

49. Avo•tei•chem ach•loo et - ha•man ba•mid•bar va•ya•moo•too.
50. This is the bread which cometh down from heaven, that a man may eat thereof, and not die.

Greek/Transliteration
50. Οὗτός ἐστιν ὁ ἄρτος ὁ ἐκ τοῦ οὐρανοῦ καταβαίνων, ἵνα τις ἐξ αὐτοῦ φάγῃ καὶ μὴ ἀποθάνῃ.

50. 'Outos estin 'o artos 'o ek tou ouranou katabainon, 'ina tis ex autou phagei kai mei apothanei.

Hebrew/Transliteration
נ. וְזֶה הוּא הַלֶּחֶם הַיֹּרֵד מִן-הַשָּׁמַיִם לְבַעֲבוּר יֹאכַל-אָדָם מִמֶּנּוּ וְלֹא יָמוּת:

50. Ve•ze hoo ha•le•chem ha•yo•red min - ha•sha•ma•yim le•va•a•voor yo•chal – adam mi•me•noo ve•lo ya•moot.

---

51. I am the living bread which came down from heaven: if any man eat of this bread, he shall live for ever: and the bread that I will give is my flesh, which I will give for the life of the world.

Greek/Transliteration
51. Ἐγώ εἰμι ὁ ἄρτος ὁ ζῶν, ὁ ἐκ τοῦ οὐρανοῦ καταβάς· ἐάν τις φάγῃ ἐκ τούτου τοῦ ἄρτου, ζήσεται εἰς τὸν αἰῶνα. Καὶ ὁ ἄρτος δὲ ὃν ἐγὼ δώσω, ἡ σάρξ μου ἐστίν, ἣν ἐγὼ δώσω ὑπὲρ τῆς τοῦ κόσμου ζωῆς.

51. Ego eimi 'o artos 'o zon, 'o ek tou ouranou katabas. ean tis phagei ek toutou tou artou, zeisetai eis ton aiona. Kai 'o artos de 'on ego doso, 'ei sarx mou estin, 'ein ego doso 'uper teis tou kosmou zoeis.

Hebrew/Transliteration
נא. אָנֹכִי לֶחֶם חַיִּים הַיֹּרֵד מִן-הַשָּׁמַיִם אָדָם כִּי-יֹאכַל מִלֶּחֶם הַזֶּה וְחַי לְעוֹלָם וְהַלֶּחֶם אֲשֶׁר אֲנִי נֹתֵן בְּשָׂרִי הוּא:אֲשֶׁר אֶתְּנֶנּוּ בְּעַד חַיֵּי הָעוֹלָם

51. Ano•chi le•chem cha•yim ha•yo•red min - ha•sha•ma•yim adam ki - yo•chal mi•le•chem ha•ze va•chai le•o•lam ve•ha•le•chem asher ani no•ten be•sa•ri hoo asher et•ne•noo be•ad cha•yey ha•o•lam.

Rabbinic Jewish Commentary
See John 6:32;34 commentary on the manna from heaven.

---

52. The Jews therefore strove among themselves, saying, How can this man give us his flesh to eat?

Greek/Transliteration

52. Ἐμάχοντο οὖν πρὸς ἀλλήλους οἱ Ἰουδαῖοι λέγοντες, Πῶς δύναται οὗτος ἡμῖν δοῦναι τὴν σάρκα φαγεῖν;

52. Emachonto oun pros alleilous 'oi Youdaioi legontes, Pos dunatai 'outos 'eimin dounai tein sarka phagein?

Hebrew/Transliteration

נב. וַיֵּרָגְנוּ הַיְּהוּדִים בֵּינֵיהֶם לֵאמֹר אֵיכָה יוּכַל זֶה לָתֶת-לָנוּ אֶת-בְּשָׂרוֹ לֶאֱכֹל:

52. Va•ye•rag•noo ha•Ye•hoo•dim bey•ne•hem le•mor ey•cha yoo•chal ze la•tet - la•noo et - be•sa•ro le•e•chol?

---

53. Then Jesus said unto them, Verily, verily, I say unto you, Except ye eat the flesh of the Son of man, and drink his blood, ye have no life in you.

Greek/Transliteration

53. Εἶπεν οὖν αὐτοῖς ὁ Ἰησοῦς, Ἀμὴν ἀμὴν λέγω ὑμῖν, ἐὰν μὴ φάγητε τὴν σάρκα τοῦ υἱοῦ τοῦ ἀνθρώπου καὶ πίητε αὐτοῦ τὸ αἷμα, οὐκ ἔχετε ζωὴν ἐν ἑαυτοῖς.

53. Eipen oun autois 'o Yeisous, Amein amein lego 'umin, ean mei phageite tein sarka tou 'wiou tou anthropou kai pieite autou to 'aima, ouk echete zoein en 'eautois.

Hebrew/Transliteration

נג. וַיֹּאמֶר אֲלֵיהֶם יֵשׁוּעַ אָמֵן אָמֵן אֲנִי אֹמֵר לָכֶם אִם-לֹא תֹאכְלוּ מִבְּשַׂר בֶּן-הָאָדָם וּמִדָּמוֹ לֹא תִשְׁתּוּ לֹא יִהְיוּ:לָכֶם חַיִּים בְּעַצְמוֹתֵיכֶם

53. Va•yo•mer aley•hem Yeshua Amen amen ani o•mer la•chem eem - lo toch•loo mib•sar Ben - ha•adam oo•mi•da•mo lo tish•too lo yi•hee•yoo la•chem cha•yim be•atz•mo•tey•chem.

---

54. Whoso eateth my flesh, and drinketh my blood, hath eternal life; and I will raise him up at the last day.

Greek/Transliteration

54. Ὁ τρώγων μου τὴν σάρκα καὶ πίνων μου τὸ αἷμα, ἔχει ζωὴν αἰώνιον, καὶ ἐγὼ ἀναστήσω αὐτὸν τῇ ἐσχάτῃ ἡμέρᾳ.

54. 'O trogon mou tein sarka kai pinon mou to 'aima, echei zoein aionion, kai ego anasteiso auton tei eschatei 'eimera.

Hebrew/Transliteration

נד. הָאֹכֵל מִבְּשָׂרִי וְהַשֹּׁתֶה מִדָּמִי יֶשׁ-לוֹ חַיֵּי עוֹלָם וַאֲנִי אֲקִימֶנּוּ בַּיּוֹם הָאַחֲרוֹן:

54. Ha•o•chel mib•sa•ri ve•ha•sho•te mi•da•mi yesh - lo cha•yey o•lam va•a•ni aki•me•noo ba•yom ha•a•cha•ron.

---

55. For my flesh is meat indeed, and my blood is drink indeed.

Greek/Transliteration

55. Ἡ γὰρ σάρξ μου ἀληθῶς ἐστιν βρῶσις, καὶ τὸ αἷμά μου ἀληθῶς ἐστιν πόσις.

55. 'Ei gar sarx mou aleithos estin brosis, kai to 'aima mou aleithos estin posis.

Hebrew/Transliteration

נה. כִּי בְשָׂרִי הוּא אֹכֶל אֱמֶת וְדָמִי שִׁקּוּי אֱמֶת:

55. Ki ve•sa•ri hoo o•chel emet ve•da•mee shi•kooy emet.

---

56. He that eateth my flesh, and drinketh my blood, dwelleth in me, and I in him.

Greek/Transliteration

56. Ὁ τρώγων μου τὴν σάρκα καὶ πίνων μου τὸ αἷμα, ἐν ἐμοὶ μένει, κἀγὼ ἐν αὐτῷ.

56. 'O trogon mou tein sarka kai pinon mou to 'aima, en emoi menei, kago en auto.

Hebrew/Transliteration

נו. הָאֹכֵל אֶת-בְּשָׂרִי וְהַשֹּׁתֶה אֶת-דָּמִי הוּא יִשְׁכָּן-בִּי וַאֲנִי בוֹ:

56. Ha•o•chel et - be•sa•ri ve•ha•sho•te et - da•mi hoo yish•kan - bi va•a•ni vo.

---

57. As the living Father hath sent me, and I live by the Father: so he that eateth me, even he shall live by me.

Greek/Transliteration
57. Καθὼς ἀπέστειλέν με ὁ ζῶν πατήρ, κἀγὼ ζῶ διὰ τὸν πατέρα· καὶ ὁ τρώγων με, κἀκεῖνος ζήσεται δι᾽ ἐμέ.

57. Kathos apesteilen me 'o zon pateir, kago zo dya ton patera. kai 'o trogon me, kakeinos zeisetai di eme.

Hebrew/Transliteration
נז. כִּי כְּמוֹ הָאָב הַחַי שְׁלָחַנִי וְאָנֹכִי חַי בִּגְלָלוֹ כֵּן הָאֹכֵל אֹתִי גַּם-הוּא יִחְיֶה בִּגְלָלִי:

57. Ki k`mo ha•Av ha•chai sh`la•cha•ni ve•a•no•chi chai big•la•lo ken ha•o•chel o•ti gam - hoo yich•ye big•la•li.

Rabbinic Jewish Commentary
The phrase of eating the Messiah was a familiar one, and well known to the Jews; though these Capernaites cavilled at it, and called it an hard saying.

"Says Rab, the Israelites shall "eat" the years of the Messiah: (the gloss on it is, the fulness which the Israelites shall have in those days:) says R. Joseph, it is certainly so; but who shall "eat him?" shall Chellek and Billek (two judges in Sodom) אכלי לה, "eat him?" contrary to the words of R. Hillell, who says, Israel shall have no Messiah, for אכלוהו, "they ate him" in the days of Hezekiah (y);"

That is, they enjoyed him then; for he thought that Hezekiah was the Messiah; but that was the Rabbi's mistake. The Messiah now was, and to be enjoyed and eaten by faith in a spiritual sense, and everyone that does so, shall live.

(y) T. Bab. Sanhedrin, fol. 98. 2. & 99. 1.

---

58. This is that bread which came down from heaven: not as your fathers did eat manna, and are dead: he that eateth of this bread shall live for ever.

Greek/Transliteration
58. Οὗτός ἐστιν ὁ ἄρτος ὁ ἐκ τοῦ οὐρανοῦ καταβάς· οὐ καθὼς ἔφαγον οἱ πατέρες ὑμῶν τὸ μάννα, καὶ ἀπέθανον· ὁ τρώγων τοῦτον τὸν ἄρτον, ζήσεται εἰς τὸν αἰῶνα.

58. 'Outos estin 'o artos 'o ek tou ouranou katabas. ou kathos ephagon 'oi pateres 'umon to manna, kai apethanon. 'o trogon touton ton arton, zeisetai eis ton aiona.

Hebrew/Transliteration
נח. זֶה הוּא הַלֶּחֶם הַיֹּרֵד מִן-הַשָּׁמַיִם לֹא כְמוֹ אֲשֶׁר אָכְלוּ אֲבוֹתֵיכֶם וַיָּמֻתוּ הָאֹכֵל מִן-הַלֶּחֶם הַזֶּה יִחְיֶה לְעוֹלָם:

58. Ze hoo ha•le•chem ha•yo•red min - ha•sha•ma•yim lo cha•man asher ach•loo avo•tei•chem va•me•too ha•o•chel min - ha•le•chem ha•ze yich•ye le•o•lam.

---

59. These things said he in the synagogue, as he taught in Capernaum.

Greek/Transliteration

59. Ταῦτα εἶπεν ἐν συναγωγῇ διδάσκων ἐν Καπερναούμ.

59. Tauta eipen en sunagogei didaskon en Kapernaoum.

Hebrew/Transliteration

‎:נט. כַּדְּבָרִים הָאֵלֶּה דִּבֶּר בְּלַמְּדוֹ בְּבֵית הַכְּנֶסֶת בִּכְפַר-נַחוּם

59. Ka•d`va•rim ha•e•le di•ber be•lam•do be•veit ha•k`ne•set bi•Ch`far - Na•choom.

---

60. Many therefore of his disciples, when they had heard this, said, This is an hard saying; who can hear it?

Greek/Transliteration

60. Πολλοὶ οὖν ἀκούσαντες ἐκ τῶν μαθητῶν αὐτοῦ εἶπον, Σκληρός ἐστιν οὗτος ὁ λόγος· τίς δύναται αὐτοῦ ἀκούειν;

60. Polloi oun akousantes ek ton matheiton autou eipon, Skleiros estin 'outos 'o logos. Tis dunatai autou akouein?

Hebrew/Transliteration

‎:ס. וְרַבִּים מִתַּלְמִידָיו שָׁמְעוּ וַיֹּאמְרוּ קָשֶׁה הַדָּבָר הַזֶּה מִי יוּכַל לְשָׁמְעוֹ

60. Ve•ra•bim mi•tal•mi•dav sham•oo va•yom•roo ka•she ha•da•var ha•ze mee yoo•chal le•shom•oh?

Rabbinic Jewish Commentary

said, this is an hard saying; or it is to be objected to; so קשיא, "an hard thing", the word here used in the Syriac version, and קשה הוא עלי, "it is to me a hard thing", are phrases used to express an objection in the Talmudic writings, where they are often met with: or it is difficult to be understood and received; so הדבר הקשה, "an hard saying", or "an hard cause", is a cause difficult to be tried and determined, Exo_18:26, and is used of that which seems incredible and absurd, and is surprising and unaccountable: so it is said (z), that

"It happened to a certain woman, that she came before R. Abika: she said to him, I have seen a spot; he said to her, perhaps there is a wound in thee; she answered him, yes, and it is healed; he replied, perhaps it may be opened, and the blood brought out; she answered him, yes; and he pronounced her clean. R. Abika saw his disciples look upon one another; and he said unto them, מה הדבר קשה, "is this an hard saying with you?"

Is it a difficult thing with you? does it seem absurd to you? or are you surprised at it? anything difficult, or which seems irreconcilable, is so called: so the slaying the passover between the two evenings is called by Aben Ezra, in Exo_12:6, מלה קשה, "an hard saying". In like sense the phrase is used here; and the allusion may be to food that is hard of digestion, since Yeshua had been speaking of himself under the metaphors of bread and meat.

(z) Misn. Nidda, c. 8, sect. 3.

---

61. When Jesus knew in himself that his disciples murmured at it, he said unto them, Doth this offend you?

Greek/Transliteration
61. Εἰδὼς δὲ ὁ Ἰησοῦς ἐν ἑαυτῷ ὅτι γογγύζουσιν περὶ τούτου οἱ μαθηταὶ αὐτοῦ, εἶπεν αὐτοῖς, Τοῦτο ὑμᾶς σκανδαλίζει;

61. Eidos de 'o Yeisous en 'eauto 'oti gonguzousin peri toutou 'oi matheitai autou, eipen autois, Touto 'umas skandalizei?

Hebrew/Transliteration
סא. וְיֵשׁוּעַ יָדַע בְּנַפְשׁוֹ כִּי תַלְמִידָיו מַלִּינִים עַל-זֶה וַיֹּאמֶר אֲלֵיהֶם הֲזֶה הָיָה לָכֶם לְמוֹקֵשׁ:

61. Ve•Yeshua ya•da be•naf•sho ki tal•mi•dav ma•li•nim al - ze va•yo•mer aley•hem ha•ze ha•ya la•chem le•mo•kesh?

---

62. What and if ye shall see the Son of man ascend up where he was before?

Greek/Transliteration
62. Ἐὰν οὖν θεωρῆτε τὸν υἱὸν τοῦ ἀνθρώπου ἀναβαίνοντα ὅπου ἦν τὸ πρότερον;

62. Ean oun theoreite ton 'wion tou anthropou anabainonta 'opou ein to proteron?

Hebrew/Transliteration
סב. וּמַה-יִּהְיֶה כִּי-תִרְאוּ אֶת-בֶּן-הָאָדָם עֹלֶה אֶל-אֲשֶׁר הָיָה-שָׁם לְפָנִים:

62. Oo•ma - yi•hee•ye ki - tir•oo et - Ben - ha•adam o•le el - asher ha•ya - sham le•fa•nim?

---

63. It is the spirit that quickeneth; the flesh profiteth nothing: the words that
I speak unto you, they are spirit, and they are life.

Greek/Transliteration
63. Τὸ πνεῦμά ἐστιν τὸ ζῳοποιοῦν, ἡ σὰρξ οὐκ ὠφελεῖ οὐδέν· τὰ ῥήματα ἃ
ἐγὼ λαλῶ ὑμῖν, πνεῦμά ἐστιν καὶ ζωή ἐστιν.

63. To pneuma estin to zoopoioun, 'ei sarx ouk ophelei ouden. ta 'reimata 'a
ego lalo 'umin, pneuma estin kai zoei estin.

Hebrew/Transliteration
סג. הָרוּחַ הוּא הַמְחַיֶּה וְהַבָּשָׂר לֹא-יִצְלַח לְכֹל הַדְּבָרִים אֲשֶׁר דִּבַּרְתִּי אֲלֵיכֶם רוּחַ הֵם וְחַיִּים:

63. Ha•roo•ach hoo ham•cha•ye ve•ha•ba•sar lo - yitz•lach la•kol ha•d`va•rim
asher di•bar•ti aley•chem roo•ach hem ve•cha•yim.

---

64. But there are some of you that believe not. For Jesus knew from the
beginning who they were that believed not, and who should betray him.

Greek/Transliteration
64. Ἀλλ᾽ εἰσὶν ἐξ ὑμῶν τινες οἳ οὐ πιστεύουσιν. ᾔδει γὰρ ἐξ ἀρχῆς ὁ Ἰησοῦς,
τίνες εἰσὶν οἱ μὴ πιστεύοντες, καὶ τίς ἐστιν ὁ παραδώσων αὐτόν.

64. All eisin ex 'umon tines 'oi ou pisteuousin. dei gar ex archeis 'o Yeisous,
tines eisin 'oi mei pisteuontes, kai tis estin 'o paradoson auton.

Hebrew/Transliteration
סד. אַךְ-יֵשׁ אֲנָשִׁים בָּכֶם אֲשֶׁר אֵין אֵמֻן בָּם כִּי יֵשׁוּעַ יָדַע מֵרֹאשׁ מִי אֵלֶּה אֲשֶׁר לֹא יַאֲמִינוּ וּמִי הוּא
אֲשֶׁר:יַסְגִּירֵהוּ

64. Ach - yesh a•na•shim ba•chem asher eyn emoon bam chi Yeshua ya•da
me•rosh mee ele asher lo ya•a•mi•noo oo•mi hoo asher yas•gi•re•hoo.

---

65. And he said, Therefore said I unto you, that no man can come unto me,
except it were given unto him of my Father.

Greek/Transliteration
65. Καὶ ἔλεγεν, Διὰ τοῦτο εἴρηκα ὑμῖν, ὅτι οὐδεὶς δύναται ἐλθεῖν πρός με, ἐὰν
μὴ ᾖ δεδομένον αὐτῷ ἐκ τοῦ πατρός μου.

65. Kai elegen, Dya touto eireika 'umin, 'oti oudeis dunatai elthein pros me,
ean mei ei dedomenon auto ek tou patros mou.

Hebrew/Transliteration

:סה. וַיֹּאמֶר בַּעֲבוּר זֶה הִגַּדְתִּי לָכֶם כִּי לֹא-יוּכַל אִישׁ לָבֹא אֵלַי בִּלְתִּי אִם-נָתוּן-לוֹ מֵאֵת הָאָב

65. Va•yo•mar ba•a•voor ze hi•ga•d`ti la•chem ki lo - yoo•chal eesh la•vo e•lai
bil•tee eem - na•toon - lo me•et ha•Av.

Rabbinic Jewish Commentary
See John 6:44-45 for commentary on *coming* or *drawing* to God.

---

66. From that time many of his disciples went back, and walked no more with
him.

Greek/Transliteration
66. Ἐκ τούτου πολλοὶ ἀπῆλθον τῶν μαθητῶν αὐτοῦ εἰς τὰ ὀπίσω, καὶ οὐκέτι
μετ᾽ αὐτοῦ περιεπάτουν.

66. Ek toutou polloi apeilthon ton matheiton autou eis ta opiso, kai ouketi met
autou periepatoun.

Hebrew/Transliteration

:סו. וּבַעֲבוּר הַדָּבָר הַזֶּה שָׁבוּ אָחוֹר רַבִּים מִתַּלְמִידָיו וְלֹא הָלְכוּ עוֹד עִמּוֹ

66. Oo•va•a•voor ha•da•var ha•ze sha•voo achor ra•bim mi•tal•mi•dav ve•lo
hal•choo od ee•mo.

---

67. Then said Jesus unto the twelve, Will ye also go away?

Greek/Transliteration
67. Εἶπεν οὖν ὁ Ἰησοῦς τοῖς δώδεκα, Μὴ καὶ ὑμεῖς θέλετε ὑπάγειν;

67. Eipen oun 'o Yeisous tois dodeka, Mei kai 'umeis thelete 'upagein?

Hebrew/Transliteration

:סז. וַיֹּאמֶר יֵשׁוּעַ אֶל-שְׁנֵים הֶעָשָׂר הֲיֵשׁ אֶת-לִבְכֶם לָשׁוּב מֵאַחֲרַי גַּם-אַתֶּם

67. Va•yo•mer Yeshua el - sh`neym he•a•sar ha•yesh et - lib•chem la•shoov
me•a•cha•rai gam – atem?

---

68. Then Simon Peter answered him, Lord, to whom shall we go? thou hast
the words of eternal life.

68. Ἀπεκρίθη οὖν αὐτῷ Σίμων Πέτρος, Κύριε, πρὸς τίνα ἀπελευσόμεθα;
Ῥήματα ζωῆς αἰωνίου ἔχεις.

68. Apekrithei oun auto Simon Petros, Kurie, pros tina apeleusometha?
'Reimata zoeis aioniou echeis.

סח. וַיַּעַן אֹתוֹ שִׁמְעוֹן פֶּטְרוֹס אֲדֹנִי אֶל-מִי נֵלֵךְ וְדִבְרֵי חַיֵּי עוֹלָם עִמָּךְ:

68. Va•ya•an o•to Shimon Petros Adoni el - mee ne•lech ve•div•rey cha•yey
o•lam ee•mach.

---

69. And we believe and are sure that thou art that Christ, the Son of the living
God.

69. Καὶ ἡμεῖς πεπιστεύκαμεν καὶ ἐγνώκαμεν ὅτι σὺ εἶ ὁ χριστὸς ὁ υἱὸς τοῦ
θεοῦ τοῦ ζῶντος.

69. Kai 'eimeis pepisteukamen kai egnokamen 'oti su ei 'o christos 'o 'wios tou
theou tou zontos.

סט. וַאֲנַחְנוּ הֶאֱמַנּוּ וְגַם-יָדַעְנוּ כִּי אַתָּה הוּא הַמָּשִׁיחַ בֶּן-אֵל חָי:

69. Va•a•nach•noo he•e•ma•noo ve•gam - ya•da•a•noo ki ata hoo
ha•Ma•shi•ach Ben – El chai.

---

70. Jesus answered them, Have not I chosen you twelve, and one of you is a
devil?

70. Ἀπεκρίθη αὐτοῖς ὁ Ἰησοῦς, Οὐκ ἐγὼ ὑμᾶς τοὺς δώδεκα ἐξελεξάμην, καὶ
ἐξ ὑμῶν εἷς διάβολός ἐστιν;

70. Apekrithei autois 'o Yeisous, Ouk ego 'umas tous dodeka exelexamein, kai
ex 'umon 'eis dyabolos estin?

ע. וַיַּעַן אֹתָם יֵשׁוּעַ הֲלֹא שְׁנֵים עָשָׂר בָּחַרְתִּי בָכֶם וְאֶחָד מִכֶּם שָׂטָן הוּא:

70. Va•ya•an o•tam Yeshua ha•lo sh`neym asar ba•char•ti va•chem ve•e•chad mi•kem Satan hoo?

Rabbinic Jewish Commentary

The Syriac, Persic, and Ethiopic versions read, "is Satan"; which name, if given to Peter, as it once was on a certain occasion, Mat_16:23, might very well be given to Judas.

---

71. He spake of Judas Iscariot the son of Simon: for he it was that should betray him, being one of the twelve.

Greek/Transliteration

71. Ἔλεγεν δὲ τὸν Ἰούδαν Σίμωνος Ἰσκαριώτην· οὗτος γὰρ ἔμελλεν αὐτὸν παραδιδόναι, εἷς ὢν ἐκ τῶν δώδεκα.

71. Elegen de ton Youdan Simonos Yskariotein. 'outos gar emellen auton paradidonai, 'eis on ek ton dodeka.

Hebrew/Transliteration

עא. וְזֹאת דִּבֶּר עַל-יְהוּדָה בֶּן-שִׁמְעוֹן אִישׁ-קְרִיּוֹת כִּי זֶה נָכוֹן הָיָה לְהַסְגִּירוֹ וְהוּא אֶחָד מִשְׁנֵים הֶעָשָׂר:

71. Ve•zot di•ber al - Yehooda ben - Shimon Eesh - K`ri•yot ki ze na•chon ha•ya le•has•gi•ro ve•hoo e•chad mi•sh`neim he•a•sar.

John, Chapter 7

1. After these things Jesus walked in Galilee: for he would not walk in Jewry (Judea), because the Jews sought to kill him.

Greek/Transliteration

1. Καὶ περιεπάτει ὁ Ἰησοῦς μετὰ ταῦτα ἐν τῇ Γαλιλαίᾳ· οὐ γὰρ ἤθελεν ἐν τῇ Ἰουδαίᾳ περιπατεῖν, ὅτι ἐζήτουν αὐτὸν οἱ Ἰουδαῖοι ἀποκτεῖναι.

1. Kai periepatei 'o Yeisous meta tauta en tei Galilaia. ou gar eithelen en tei Youdaia peripatein, 'oti ezeitoun auton 'oi Youdaioi apokteinai.

Hebrew/Transliteration

א. אַחֲרֵי-כֵן נָסַע יֵשׁוּעַ הֵנָּה וָהֵנָּה בַּגָּלִיל כִּי לֹא אָבָה לִנְסֹעַ בִּיהוּדָה אַחֲרֵי-אֲשֶׁר בִּקְשׁוּ הַיְּהוּדִים לְהָרְגוֹ:

1. A•cha•rey - chen na•sa Yeshua he•na va•he•na ba•Ga•lil ki lo ava lin•so•a bi•Y`hoo•da a•cha•rey - asher bik•shoo ha•Ye•hoo•dim le•hor•go.

---

2. Now the Jews' feast of tabernacles was at hand.

Greek/Transliteration

2. Ἦν δὲ ἐγγὺς ἡ ἑορτὴ τῶν Ἰουδαίων ἡ Σκηνοπηγία.

2. Ein de engus 'ei 'eortei ton Youdaion 'ei Skeinopeigia.

Hebrew/Transliteration

ב. וַיִּקְרַב חַג הַיְּהוּדִים חַג הַסֻּכּוֹת:

2. Va•yik•rav chag ha•Ye•hoo•dim chag ha•Sookot.

Rabbinic Jewish Commentary

Which began on the fifteenth day of the month Tisri, which answers to part of our September; when the Jews erected tents or booths, in which they dwelt, and ate their meals during this festival; and which was done, in commemoration of the Israelites dwelling in booths in the wilderness; and was typical of Yeshua's tabernacling in human nature; and an emblem of the saints dwelling in the earthly houses and tabernacles of their bodies, in this their wilderness and pilgrimage state. Some assign other reasons of this feast, as that it was appointed in commemoration of the divine command, for building the tabernacle; and others, that it was instituted in memory of the protection of the people of Israel under the cloud, as they travelled through the wilderness; by which they were preserved, as in a tent or booth; and to this inclines the Targum of Onkelos, on Lev_23:43, which paraphrases the words thus, "That your generations may know, that in the shadow of the clouds, I caused the children of Israel to dwell, when I brought them out of the land of Egypt": and one of the Jewish commentators (a) suggests, that the reason why the first place the Israelites pitched at, when they came out of Egypt, was called Succoth, which signifies "tents", or "tabernacles", is, because there they were covered with the clouds of glory: but the true reason of this feast is that which is first given, as is clear from Lev_23:43, and because they were obliged to dwell in tents, as soon as they came out of Egypt, therefore the first place they encamped at, was called "Succoth", or tabernacles, Exo_12:37. This feast was not kept at the time of year the people came out of Egypt; for that was at the time of the passover; but was put off, as it seems, to a colder season of the year; and which was not so convenient for dwelling in booths; lest it should be thought they observed this feast for the sake of pleasure and recreation, under the shade of these bowers; which, as appears from Neh_8:15, were made of olive, pine, myrtle, and palm branches, and branches of thick trees; and were fixed, some on the roofs of their houses, others in their courts, and in the courts of the house of God; and others in the streets: an account of the sacrifices offered at this feast, is given in Num_29:13, in which may be observed, that on the first day thirteen young bullocks were offered; on the second, twelve; on the third, eleven; on the fourth, ten; on the fifth, nine; on the sixth, eight; and on the seventh, seven; and on the eighth, but one. The Jews, in their Misna, have a treatise called "Succa", or the "Tabernacle", in which they treat of this feast; and which contains various traditions, concerning their booths, their manner of living in them, and other rites and usages observed by them, during this festival: they are very particular about the measure and form, and covering of their booths; a booth might not be higher than twenty cubits, nor lower than ten hands' breadth; and its breadth might not be less than seven hands' breadth by seven; but it might he carried out as wide as they pleased (b), provided it had three sides: they might not cover their booths with anything, but what grew out of the earth, or was rooted up from thence; nor with anything that received uncleanness, or was of an ill smell, or anything that was fallen and faded (c): into these booths they brought their best goods, their best bedding, and all their drinking vessels, &c. and left their houses empty; for here was their fixed dwelling; they only occasionally went into their houses (d); for here they were obliged to dwell day and night, and eat all their meals, during the seven days of the feast; and however, it was reckoned praiseworthy, and he was accounted the most religious, who ate nothing out of his booth (e); they were indeed excused when it was rainy weather, but as soon as the rain was over, they were obliged to return again (f) and besides, their dwelling and sleeping, and eating and drinking, in their booths, there were various other rites which were performed by them; as particularly, the carrying of palm tree branches in their hands, or what they call the "Lulab"; which was made up of branches of palm tree, myrtle, and willow, bound up together in a bundle, which was carried in the right hand, and a pome citron in the left; and as they carried them, they waved them three times towards the several quarters of the world; and every day they went about the altar once, with these in their hands, saying the words in Psa_118:25, "Save now, I beseech thee, O Lord, O Lord I beseech thee, send now prosperity": and on the seventh day, they went about the altar seven times (g): also there were great illuminations in the temple; at the going out of the first day of the feast, they went down to the court of the women; they made a great preparation (i.e. as Bartenora explains it, they set benches round it, and set the women above, and the men below); and there were golden candlesticks there, and at the head of them four golden basins, and four ladders to every candlestick; and four young priests had four pitchers of oil, that held a hundred and twenty logs, which they put into each basin; and of the old breeches and girdles of the priests, they made wicks, and with them lighted them; and there was not a court in Jerusalem, which was not lighted with that light; and religious men, and men of good works, danced before them, with lighted torches in their hands, singing songs and hymns of praise (h); and this continued the six nights following (i): there was also, on everyone of these days, another custom observed; which was that of fetching water from the pool of Siloah, and pouring it with wine upon the altar, which was attended with great rejoicing; of which; to which may be added, the music that was used during the performance of these rites; at the illumination in the court of the women, there were harps, psalteries, cymbals, and other instruments of music, playing all the while; and two priests with trumpets, who sounded, when they had the signal; and on every day, as they brought water from Siloah to the altar, they sounded with trumpets, and shouted; the great "Hallel", or hymn, was sung all the eight days, and the pipe was blown, sometimes five days, and sometimes six (k); and even on all the eight days; and the whole was a feast of rejoicing, according to Lev_23:40.

(a) Baal Hatturim in Numb. xxxiii. 5. (b) Misn. Succa, c. 1. sect. 1. Maimon. Hilch. Succa, c. 4. sect. 1. (c) Misn. Succa, sect. 4, 5, 6. Maimon. ib. c. 5. sect. 1, 2, &c. (d) Maimon. ib. c. 6. sect. 5. (e) Misn. ib. c. 2. sect. 5, 6. Maimon. ib. sect. 6, 7. (f) Maimon. ib. sect. 10. (g) Misn. ib. c. 4. sect. 1, 2, 3, 4, 5. Maimon. Hilch. Lulab, c. 7. sect. 5, 6, 9, 23. (h) Misn. Succa, c. 5. sect 2, 3, 4. (i) Maimon. ib. c. 8. sect. 12. (k) Misn. ib. c. 4. sect. 8, 9. & c. 5. 1, 4, 5. & Eracin, c. 2. sect. 3.

---

3. His brethren therefore said unto him, Depart hence, and go into Judaea, that thy disciples also may see the works that thou doest.

Greek/Transliteration
3. Εἶπον οὖν πρὸς αὐτὸν οἱ ἀδελφοὶ αὐτοῦ, Μετάβηθι ἐντεῦθεν, καὶ ὕπαγε εἰς τὴν Ἰουδαίαν, ἵνα καὶ οἱ μαθηταί σου θεωρήσωσιν τὰ ἔργα σου ἃ ποιεῖς.

3. Eipon oun pros auton 'oi adelphoi autou, Metabeithi enteuthen, kai 'upage eis tein Youdaian, 'ina kai 'oi matheitai sou theoreisosin ta erga sou 'a poieis.

Hebrew/Transliteration
ג. וַיֹּאמְרוּ אֵלָיו אֶחָיו עֲלֵה מִזֶּה וְלֶךְ-לְךָ אֶל-אֶרֶץ יְהוּדָה לְמַעַן יִרְאוּ תַלְמִידֶיךָ גַּם-שָׁם אֶת-הָעֲלִילֹת אֲשֶׁר-אַתָּה:עֹשֶׂה

3. Va•yom•roo elav echav a•le mi•ze ve•lech - le•cha el - e•retz Yehooda le•ma•an yir•oo tal•mi•de•cha gam - sham et - ha•a•li•lot asher - ata o•se.

Rabbinic Jewish Commentary
That is, the brethren of Yeshua, as the Syriac and Persic versions express it; who were not James and Joses, and Simon and Judas, the sons of Alphaeus, the brother

of Joseph, the husband of Mary, so called, Mat_13:55, for some of these were of the number of the twelve; and all of them believers in Yeshua; whereas these his brethren were not. The Jew (l) therefore is mistaken, who supposed the above persons are here intended; and objects this their unbelief to Yeshua, as if they knew him too well to give him any credit; whereas they did believe in him, and abode by him to the last; and some of them, if not all, suffered death for his sake. They therefore are to be understood of some distant relations of Mary or Joseph, that dwelt at Nazareth, or Capernaum, or in some of those parts; and the feast of tabernacles being at hand, they put him upon going up to it, being willing to be rid of him.

(l) R. Isaac Chizzuk Emuna, par. 2. c. 45. p. 434, 435.

4. For there is no man that doeth any thing in secret, and he himself seeketh to be known openly. If thou do these things, shew thyself to the world.

Greek/Transliteration
4. Οὐδεὶς γὰρ ἐν κρυπτῷ τι ποιεῖ, καὶ ζητεῖ αὐτὸς ἐν παρρησίᾳ εἶναι. Εἰ ταῦτα ποιεῖς, φανέρωσον σεαυτὸν τῷ κόσμῳ.

4. Oudeis gar en krupto ti poiei, kai zeitei autos en parreisia einai. Ei tauta poieis, phaneroson seauton to kosmo.

Hebrew/Transliteration
ד. כִּי אֵין-אִישׁ עֹשֶׂה דָבָר בַּסֵּתֶר וּמְבַקֵּשׁ הוּא לְהִוָּדַע נֶגֶד הַשָּׁמֶשׁ וְאִם כֵּן אַתָּה עֹשֶׂה קוּם הִוָּדַע בָּאָרֶץ:

4. Ki eyn - eesh o•se da•var ba•se•ter oom•va•kesh hoo le•hi•va•da ne•ged ha•sha•mesh ve•eem ken ata o•se koom hi•va•da ba•a•retz.

5. For neither did his brethren believe in him.

Greek/Transliteration
5. Οὐδὲ γὰρ οἱ ἀδελφοὶ αὐτοῦ ἐπίστευον εἰς αὐτόν.

5. Oude gar 'oi adelphoi autou episteuon eis auton.

Hebrew/Transliteration
ה. כִּי-אֶחָיו גַּם-הֵם לֹא הֶאֱמִינוּ בּוֹ:

5. Ki - echav gam - hem lo he•e•mi•noo vo.

6. Then Jesus said unto them, My time is not yet come: but your time is always ready.

Greek/Transliteration
6. Λέγει οὖν αὐτοῖς ὁ Ἰησοῦς, Ὁ καιρὸς ὁ ἐμὸς οὔπω πάρεστιν, ὁ δὲ καιρὸς ὁ ὑμέτερος πάντοτέ ἐστιν ἕτοιμος.

6. Legei oun autois 'o Yeisous, 'O kairos 'o emos oupo parestin, 'o de kairos 'o 'umeteros pantote estin 'etoimos.

Hebrew/Transliteration
ו. וַיֹּאמֶר אֲלֵיהֶם יֵשׁוּעַ עוֹד לֹא-בָאָה עִתִּי עַד-הֵנָּה וְעִתְּכֶם הִיא אִתְּכֶם תָּמִיד:

6. Va•yo•mer aley•hem Yeshua od lo - va•ah ee•ti ad - he•na ve•eet•chem hee eet•chem ta•mid.

---

7. The world cannot hate you; but me it hateth, because I testify of it, that the works thereof are evil.

Greek/Transliteration
7. Οὐ δύναται ὁ κόσμος μισεῖν ὑμᾶς· ἐμὲ δὲ μισεῖ, ὅτι ἐγὼ μαρτυρῶ περὶ αὐτοῦ, ὅτι τὰ ἔργα αὐτοῦ πονηρά ἐστιν.

7. Ou dunatai 'o kosmos misein 'umas. eme de misei, 'oti ego marturo peri autou, 'oti ta erga autou poneira estin.

Hebrew/Transliteration
ז. הָעוֹלָם לֹא-תוּכַל לִשְׂנֹא אֶתְכֶם וְאֹתִי תִשְׂנָא עֵקֶב עֵדוּתִי בָהּ כִּי רָעִים מַעֲשֶׂיהָ:

7. Ha•o•lam lo - too•chal lis•no et•chem ve•o•ti tis•na e•kev e•doo•ti va ki ra•eem ma•a•se•ha.

---

8. Go ye up unto this feast: I go not up yet unto this feast; for my time is not yet full come.

Greek/Transliteration
8. Ὑμεῖς ἀνάβητε εἰς τὴν ἑορτὴν ταύτην· ἐγὼ οὔπω ἀναβαίνω εἰς τὴν ἑορτὴν ταύτην, ὅτι ὁ καιρὸς ὁ ἐμὸς οὔπω πεπλήρωται.

8. 'Umeis anabeite eis tein 'eortein tautein. ego oupo anabaino eis tein 'eortein tautein, 'oti 'o kairos 'o emos oupo pepleirotai.

Hebrew/Transliteration
ח. עֲלוּ אַתֶּם לְעֵת הֶחָג וַאֲנִי לֹא אֶעֱלֶה לְעֵת הֶחָג עַתָּה כִּי לֹא מָלְאָה עִתִּי עַד-כֹּה:

8. A•loo atem le•et he•chag va•a•ni lo e•e•le le•et he•chag ata ki lo mal•ah ee•ti ad - ko.

---

9. When he had said these words unto them, he abode still in Galilee.

Greek/Transliteration
9. Ταῦτα δὲ εἰπὼν αὐτοῖς, ἔμεινεν ἐν τῇ Γαλιλαίᾳ.

9. Tauta de eipon autois, emeinen en tei Galilaia.

Hebrew/Transliteration
ט. כַּדְּבָרִים הָאֵלֶּה דִּבֶּר וַיִּתְמַהְמַהּ בַּגָּלִיל:

9. Ka•d`va•rim ha•e•le di•ber va•yit•ma•ha•ma ba•Ga•lil.

---

10. But when his brethren were gone up, then went he also up unto the feast, not openly, but as it were in secret.

Greek/Transliteration
10. Ὡς δὲ ἀνέβησαν οἱ ἀδελφοὶ αὐτοῦ, τότε καὶ αὐτὸς ἀνέβη εἰς τὴν ἑορτήν, οὐ φανερῶς, ἀλλ᾽ ὡς ἐν κρυπτῷ.

10. 'Os de anebeisan 'oi adelphoi autou, tote kai autos anebei eis tein 'eortein, ou phaneros, all 'os en krupto.

Hebrew/Transliteration
י. וְאַחֲרֵי אֲשֶׁר עָלוּ אֶחָיו לְעֵת הֶחָג עָלָה גַּם-הוּא לֹא בַגָּלוּי כִּי אִם-כְּמִסְתַּתֵּר:

10. Ve•a•cha•rey asher a•loo echav le•et he•chag ala gam - hoo lo va•ga•looy ki eem - ke•mis•ta•ter.

Rabbinic Jewish Commentary
The Ethiopic version reads, "he went up that day"; which is very likely, and no ways contrary to what is said, in Joh_7:14; for though he did not go up to the temple to teach, till the middle of the feast, he might be up at the feast sooner: and according to the law, it was necessary that he should be there on the first and second days, and keep the Chagigah, and make his appearance in the court; though there was a provision made for such that failed, the canon runs thus (m);

"He that does not make his festival sacrifice, on the first good day of the feast, may make it throughout the whole feast, and on the last good day of the feast; and if the feast passes, and he has not made the festival sacrifice, he is not obliged to a compensation; and of this it is said, Ecc_1:15, "That which is crooked cannot be made straight".

But however, whatever day he went on, he went up,

not openly, but as it were in secret: as he was made under the law, and came to fulfil all righteousness, it was necessary that he should observe every precept, and fulfil the whole law: and therefore he went up to this feast; yet in the most private manner, that he might escape those who would lie in wait for him, and sought to kill him: and this he did, not through fear of death, but because his hour was not yet come; this was not the feast he was to suffer at, but the passover following; which when near at hand, he went up to it, and entered Jerusalem in the most public manner.

(m) Misn. Chagiga, c. 1. sect. 6. Maimon. Hilch. Chagiga, c. 2. sect. 4, 5, 6, 7.

---

11. Then the Jews sought him at the feast, and said, Where is he?

Greek/Transliteration
11. Οἱ οὖν Ἰουδαῖοι ἐζήτουν αὐτὸν ἐν τῇ ἑορτῇ, καὶ ἔλεγον, Ποῦ ἐστιν ἐκεῖνος;

11. 'Oi oun Youdaioi ezeitoun auton en tei 'eortei, kai elegon, Pou estin ekeinos?

Hebrew/Transliteration
יא. וַיְבַקְשׁוּ אֹתוֹ הַיְּהוּדִים בֶּחָג וַיֹּאמְרוּ אַיֵּה אֵיפֹא הוּא:

11. Vay•vak•shoo o•to ha•Ye•hoo•dim be•chag va•yom•roo a•ye ey•fo hoo?

---

12. And there was much murmuring among the people concerning him: for some said, He is a good man: others said, Nay; but he deceiveth the people.

Greek/Transliteration
12. Καὶ γογγυσμὸς πολὺς περὶ αὐτοῦ ἦν ἐν τοῖς ὄχλοις· οἱ μὲν ἔλεγον ὅτι Ἀγαθός ἐστιν· ἄλλοι ἔλεγον, Οὔ, ἀλλὰ πλανᾷ τὸν ὄχλον.

12. Kai gongusmos polus peri autou ein en tois ochlois. 'oi men elegon 'oti Agathos estin. Alloi elegon, Ou, alla plana ton ochlon.

Hebrew/Transliteration
יב. וַיְהִי הָעָם נָדוֹן הַרְבֵּה אֵלֶּה אֹמְרִים כִּי-טוֹב הוּא וְאֵלֶּה אֹמְרִים לֹא כִּי-מַתְעֶה הוּא אֶת-הָעָם:

12. Vay•hi ha•am na•don har•be ele om•rim ki - tov hoo ve•e•le om•rim lo ki - mat•eh hoo et - ha•am.

---

13. Howbeit no man spake openly of him for fear of the Jews.

Greek/Transliteration
13. Οὐδεὶς μέντοι παρρησίᾳ ἐλάλει περὶ αὐτοῦ διὰ τὸν φόβον τῶν Ἰουδαίων.

13. Oudeis mentoi parreisia elalei peri autou dya ton phobon ton Youdaion.

Hebrew/Transliteration
יג. אֶפֶס אֵין-אִישׁ מְדַבֵּר עָלָיו בַּגָּלוּי מִפְּנֵי יִרְאַת הַיְּהוּדִים:

13. E•fes eyn - eesh me•da•ber alav ba•ga•looy mip•ney yir•at ha•Ye•hoo•dim.

---

14. Now about the midst of the feast Jesus went up into the temple, and taught.

Greek/Transliteration
14. Ἤδη δὲ τῆς ἑορτῆς μεσούσης, ἀνέβη ὁ Ἰησοῦς εἰς τὸ ἱερόν, καὶ ἐδίδασκεν.

14. Eidei de teis 'eorteis mesouseis, anebei 'o Yeisous eis to 'ieron, kai edidasken.

Hebrew/Transliteration
יד. וַיְהִי בְּתוֹךְ יְמֵי הֶחָג וַיַּעַל יֵשׁוּעַ וַיְלַמֵּד בְּבֵית הַמִּקְדָּשׁ:

14. Vay•hi be•toch ye•mey he•chag va•ya•al Yeshua vay•la•med be•veit ha•mik•dash.

Rabbinic Jewish Commentary
About the fourth day of it, for it lasted eight days; this might be on the sabbath day, which sometimes was בתוך החג, "in the middle of the feast" (n)

(n) Misa. Succa, c. 5. sect. 5.

---

15. And the Jews marvelled, saying, How knoweth this man letters, having never learned?

Greek/Transliteration
15. Καὶ ἐθαύμαζον οἱ Ἰουδαῖοι λέγοντες, Πῶς οὗτος γράμματα οἶδεν, μὴ μεμαθηκώς;

15. Kai ethaumazon 'oi Youdaioi legontes, Pos 'outos grammata oiden, mei mematheikos?

Hebrew/Transliteration
:טו. וְהַיְּהוּדִים תָּמָהוּ לֵאמֹר מֵאַיִן יֹדֵעַ זֶה סֵפֶר וְהוּא לֹא לֻמֶּד

15. Ve•haye•hoo•dim tam•hoo le•mor me•a•yin yo•de•a ze se•fer ve•hoo lo loo•mad?

Rabbinic Jewish Commentary

saying, how knoweth this man letters? or "the Scriptures", as the Arabic and Persic versions render it; which are called "holy letters", 2Ti_3:15; according to which, the sense is, that they were surprised at his knowledge of the Scriptures, that he should be conversant with them, and be able to interpret them, and give the sense and meaning of them, in so full and clear a manner, as he did: or else the sense is, how came this man to be such a learned man? whence has he this wisdom, and all this learning which he shows? as in Mat_13:54. So a learned man is in Isa_29:11, said to be one that יודע הספר, επισταμενος γραμματα, "knows letters", as the Septuagint there translate the Hebrew text; but how Yeshua should know them, or be a learned man,

having never learned, was surprising to them: that is, he had not had a liberal education, but was brought up to a trade; he was not trained up at the feet of any of their Rabbi's, in any of their universities, or schools of learning; and in which they were certainly right. Modern Jews pretend to say he had a master, whom they sometimes call Elchanan (o), but most commonly they make him to be R. Joshua ben Perachiah (p): with whom they say, he fled into Alexandria in Egypt, for fear of Jannai the king: and one of their writers (q), on this account, charges the evangelist with a falsehood: but who are we to believe, the Jews who lived at the same time with Yeshua, and knew his education and manner of life, or those that have lived ages since?

(o) Toldos Jesu, p. 5. (p) Juchasin, fol. 159. 1. Ganz Tzemach David, par. 1, fol. 21. 1. & 24. (q) R. Isaac Chizzuk Emuna, par. 2. c. 46. p. 435.

---

16. Jesus answered them, and said, My doctrine is not mine, but his that sent me.

Greek/Transliteration
16. Ἀπεκρίθη οὖν αὐτοῖς ὁ Ἰησοῦς καὶ εἶπεν, Ἡ ἐμὴ διδαχὴ οὐκ ἔστιν ἐμή, ἀλλὰ τοῦ πέμψαντός με.

16. Apekrithei oun autois 'o Yeisous kai eipen, 'Ei emei didachei ouk estin emei, alla tou pempsantos me.

Hebrew/Transliteration
:טז. וַיַּעַן אֹתָם יֵשׁוּעַ וַיֹּאמֶר לֹא תוֹרָתִי שֶׁלִּי אֲנִי מוֹרֶה כִּי אִם-תּוֹרַת שֹׁלְחִי

16. Va•ya•an o•tam Yeshua va•yo•mar lo to•ra•ti she•li ani mo•re ki eem - to•rat shol•chi.

---

17. If any man will do his will, he shall know of the doctrine, whether it be of God, or whether I speak of myself.

Greek/Transliteration
17. Ἐάν τις θέλῃ τὸ θέλημα αὐτοῦ ποιεῖν, γνώσεται περὶ τῆς διδαχῆς, πότερον ἐκ τοῦ θεοῦ ἐστιν, ἢ ἐγὼ ἀπ᾽ ἐμαυτοῦ λαλῶ.

17. Ean tis thelei to theleima autou poiein, gnosetai peri teis didacheis, poteron ek tou theou estin, ei ego ap emautou lalo.

Hebrew/Transliteration
יז. מִי הָאִישׁ הֶחָפֵץ לַעֲשׂוֹת רְצוֹנוֹ הוּא יֵדַע תּוֹרָתִי אִם-מֵאֵת אֱלֹהִים הִיא אוֹ מִלִּבִּי אֲנִי מוֹרֶה:

17. Mee ha•eesh he•cha•fetz la•a•sot r`tzo•no hoo ye•da to•ra•ti eem - me•et Elohim hee oh mi•li•bi ani mo•re.

---

18. He that speaketh of himself seeketh his own glory: but he that seeketh his glory that sent him, the same is true, and no unrighteousness is in him.

Greek/Transliteration
18. Ὁ ἀφ᾽ ἑαυτοῦ λαλῶν, τὴν δόξαν τὴν ἰδίαν ζητεῖ· ὁ δὲ ζητῶν τὴν δόξαν τοῦ πέμψαντος αὐτόν, οὗτος ἀληθής ἐστιν, καὶ ἀδικία ἐν αὐτῷ οὐκ ἔστιν.

18. 'O aph 'eautou lalon, tein doxan tein idian zeitei. 'o de zeiton tein doxan tou pempsantos auton, 'outos aleitheis estin, kai adikia en auto ouk estin.

Hebrew/Transliteration
יח. הַמּוֹרֶה מִלִּבּוֹ אֶת-כְּבוֹדוֹ הוּא מְבַקֵּשׁ וְהַמְבַקֵּשׁ כְּבוֹד שֹׁלְחוֹ נֶאֱמָן הוּא וְלֹא עַוְלָתָה בּוֹ:

18. Ha•mo•re mi•li•bo et - k`vo•do hoo me•va•kesh ve•ham•va•kesh k`vod shol•cho ne•e•man hoo ve•lo av•la•ta bo.

---

19. Did not Moses give you the law, and yet none of you keepeth the law? Why go ye about to kill me?

Greek/Transliteration
19. Οὐ Μωσῆς δέδωκεν ὑμῖν τὸν νόμον, καὶ οὐδεὶς ἐξ ὑμῶν ποιεῖ τὸν νόμον; Τί με ζητεῖτε ἀποκτεῖναι;

19. Ou Moseis dedoken 'umin ton nomon, kai oudeis ex 'umon poiei ton nomon? Ti me zeiteite apokteinai?

Hebrew/Transliteration

יט. הֲלֹא מֹשֶׁה נָתַן לָכֶם אֶת-הַתּוֹרָה וְאֵין-אִישׁ מִכֶּם שֹׁמֵר אֶת-הַתּוֹרָה מַדּוּעַ תְּבַקְשׁוּ לְהָרְגֵנִי:

19. Ha•lo Moshe na•tan la•chem et - ha•Torah ve•eyn - eesh mi•kem sho•mer et - ha•Torah ma•doo•a te•vak•shoo le•hor•ge•ni?

---

20. The people answered and said, Thou hast a devil: who goeth about to kill thee?

Greek/Transliteration

20. Ἀπεκρίθη ὁ ὄχλος καὶ εἶπεν, Δαιμόνιον ἔχεις· τίς σε ζητεῖ ἀποκτεῖναι;

20. Apekrithei 'o ochlos kai eipen, Daimonion echeis. tis se zeitei apokteinai?

Hebrew/Transliteration

כ. וַיַּעַן הָעָם וַיֹּאמַר רוּחַ רָעָה בָּךְ מִי אֵיפֹא מְבַקֶּשׁ לְהָרְגֶךָ:

20. Va•ya•an ha•am va•yo•mar roo•ach ra•ah bach mee ey•fo me•va•kesh le•hor•ge•cha?

---

21. Jesus answered and said unto them, I have done one work, and ye all marvel.

Greek/Transliteration

21. Ἀπεκρίθη Ἰησοῦς καὶ εἶπεν αὐτοῖς, Ἓν ἔργον ἐποίησα, καὶ πάντες θαυμάζετε.

21. Apekrithei Yeisous kai eipen autois, 'En ergon epoieisa, kai pantes thaumazete.

Hebrew/Transliteration

כא. וַיַּעַן יֵשׁוּעַ וַיֹּאמֶר אֲלֵיהֶם פְּעֻלָּה אַחַת פָּעַלְתִּי וְכֻלְּכֶם תִּתַּמָּהוּ:

21. Va•ya•an Yeshua va•yo•mer aley•hem pe•oo•la a•chat pa•al•ti ve•chool•chem ti•ta•ma•hoo.

---

22. Moses therefore gave unto you circumcision; (not because it is of Moses, but of the fathers;) and ye on the Sabbath day circumcise a man.

---

22. Διὰ τοῦτο Μωσῆς δέδωκεν ὑμῖν τὴν περιτομήν- οὐχ ὅτι ἐκ τοῦ Μωσέως ἐστίν, ἀλλ᾽ ἐκ τῶν πατέρων- καὶ ἐν σαββάτῳ περιτέμνετε ἄνθρωπον.

22. Dya touto Moseis dedoken 'umin tein peritomein- ouch 'oti ek tou Moseos estin, all ek ton pateron- kai en sabbato peritemnete anthropon.

Hebrew/Transliteration

כב. הֵן מֹשֶׁה נָתַן לָכֶם אֶת-הַמּוּלֹת אַף כִּי-לֹא מִמֹּשֶׁה הִיא כִּי אִם מִן-הָאָבֹת וְעַל-כֵּן בַּשַׁבָּת תָּמוּלוּ בֶּן-זָכָר:

22. Hen Moshe na•tan la•chem et - ha•moo•lot af ki - lo mi•Moshe hee ki eem min - ha•a•vot ve•al - ken ba•Sha•bat ta•moo•loo ben - za•char.

Rabbinic Jewish Commentary

Abraham, Isaac, and Jacob, to whom it was enjoined by God, and who practised it before the times of Moses; so that this command was in force before him, and obligatory upon the descendants of Abraham, before he delivered it; and would have been, if he had never mentioned it; though the Jews say (r),

"We do not circumcise because Abraham our father, on whom be peace, circumcised himself and his household, but because the holy blessed God commanded us by Moses, that we should be circumcised, as Abraham our father was circumcised."

But no doubt it would have been binding on them, if Moses had said nothing about it; the command to Abraham is so express, for the circumcision of his male offspring, Gen_17:10; however, it being both of Moses and of the fathers, laid a very great obligation on the Jews to observe it.

and ye on the sabbath day, circumcise a man; a male child, as they did, when the eighth day fell on a sabbath day; for the law of circumcision was before the law of the sabbath, and therefore was not to be made void by it, nor was it made void by it; and so much is intimated by Yeshua's observing, that it was not of Moses, but of the fathers; and this is the reason which the Karaite Jews give for circumcision on the sabbath day: for (s)

"Say they, because it is a former command, from the time of Abraham our father, on whom be peace, before the giving of the law of the sabbath, היו מלים בשבת, "they circumcise on the sabbath day", and when the command of the sabbath afterwards took place, it was not possible it should disannul circumcision on the sabbath day; and for the same reason, they also allow the sacrifice of the passover to be done on the sabbath day, because it is a command which went before the command of the sabbath."

And this was also the sense and practice of the other Jews: thus citing the law of Moses in Lev_12:3. "And in the eighth day, the flesh of his foreskin shall be circumcised", by way of gloss upon it add, ואפילו בשבת, "and even on the sabbath day" (t); and on the same text another writer observes (u), that by Gematry, every day is fit for circumcision. R. Jose says (w),

"They do all things necessary to circumcision, on the sabbath day."

R. Abika says (x),

"All work that can be done on the evening of the sabbath, does not drive away the sabbath; but circumcision, which cannot be done on the evening of the sabbath, drives away the sabbath: they do all things necessary to circumcision; they circumcise, and make bare, and suck, and put (on the wound) a plaster and cummin; and which, if not bruised on the evening of the sabbath, they may chew with their teeth."

Also it is allowed of (y), to "wash the infant on the third day of circumcision, which happens to be on the sabbath."

Moreover, a case is put after this manner (z);

"If a man has two infants, one to be circumcised after the sabbath, and the other to be "circumcised on the sabbath", and forgets, and circumcises that, that was to be after the sabbath, on the sabbath, he is guilty of sin; if one is to be circumcised in the evening of the sabbath, and the other on the sabbath, and he forgets, and circumcises that which should be on the evening of the sabbath, on the sabbath, R. Eliezer pronounces him guilty, but R, Joshua absolves him."

And we have an instance (a) of

"R. Sheshana, the son of R. Samuel bar Abdimo, that when he was to be circumcised, it was the sabbath day, and they forgot the razor; and they inquired of R. Meni and R. Isaac ben Eleazar, and it was drove off to another day."

From all which it appears, that circumcision on the sabbath day, was a common practice, and which confirms the assertion of Yeshua.

(r) Maimon. in Misn. Cholin, c. 7. sect. 6. (s) R. Eliaha in Adderet apud Trigland. de Sect. Karaeorum, c. 9. p. 134. (t) T. Bab. Sabbat, fol. 132. 1. Mitzvot Tora, pr. Affirm. 28. (u) Baal Hatturim in Lev. xii. 3. (w) Misna Sabbat, c. 18. sect. 3. (x) Misna Sabbat, c. 19. sect. 1, 2. T. Bab. Pesachim, fol. 69. 2. Maimon. Hilchot Milah, c. 2. sect. 6, 7. (y) Ib. sect. 3. Bereshit Rabba, sect. 8. fol. 70. 3. Maimon. ib. sect. 6. (z) Ib. sect. 4. T. Bab. Ceritot, fol. 19. 2. (a) Juchasin, fol. 105. 2.

---

23. If a man on the Sabbath day receive circumcision, that the law of Moses should not be broken; are ye angry at me, because I have made a man every whit whole on the Sabbath day?

Greek/Transliteration

23. Εἰ περιτομὴν λαμβάνει ἄνθρωπος ἐν σαββάτῳ, ἵνα μὴ λυθῇ ὁ νόμος Μωσέως, ἐμοὶ χολᾶτε ὅτι ὅλον ἄνθρωπον ὑγιῆ ἐποίησα ἐν σαββάτῳ;

23. Ei peritomein lambanei anthropos en sabbato, 'ina mei luthei 'o nomos Moseos, emoi cholate 'oti 'olon anthropon 'ugiei epoieisa en sabbato?

Hebrew/Tranliteration

כג. וְעַתָּה אִם-בַּשַּׁבָּת הַמּוֹל יִמּוֹל בֶּן-זָכָר לְבַעֲבוּר לֹא תוּפַר תּוֹרַת מֹשֶׁה לָמָה-זֶּה תִּתְעַבְּרוּ-בִי עַל כִּי-רְפָאתִי:אִישׁ כֻּלוֹ בַּשַּׁבָּת

23. Ve•a•ta eem - ba•Sha•bat hi•mol yi•mol ben - za•char le•va•a•voor lo too•far to•rat Moshe la•ma - ze tit•ab•roo - vi al ki - ri•pe•ti eesh koo•lo ba•Sha•bat?

Rabbinic Jewish Commentary

because I have made a man every whit whole on the sabbath day? or "a man that was whole, sound on the sabbath day"; who was wholly, or all over disordered, every limb of whom shook with the palsy: or as some think the sense is, he was made every whit whole, both in soul and body; and then the argument is, if it was, no breach of the sabbath to make a wound, and lay a plaster on it, as in circumcision; it would be no violation of it, nor ought any to be offended with it, that Yeshua should heal a diseased man, who was so in every part of his body, and restore health to his soul likewise and nothing is more common with the Jews than to say, the danger of life, and פיקוח נפש, "the preservation of the soul", or life, drive away the sabbath (b).

(b) T. Bab. Sabbat, fol. 132. 1.

---

24. Judge not according to the appearance, but judge righteous judgment.

Greek/Transliteration

24. Μὴ κρίνετε κατ᾽ ὄψιν, ἀλλὰ τὴν δικαίαν κρίσιν κρίνατε.

24. Mei krinete kat opsin, alla tein dikaian krisin krinate.

Hebrew/Transliteration

כד. אַל-תִּשְׁפְּטוּ לַעֵינָיִם כִּי אִם-מִשְׁפַּט-צֶדֶק שְׁפֹטוּ:

24. Al - tish•pe•too la•ey•na•yim ki eem - mish•pat - tze•dek sh`fo•too.

---

25. Then said some of them of Jerusalem, Is not this he, whom they seek to kill?

25. Ἔλεγον οὖν τινες ἐκ τῶν Ἱεροσολυμιτῶν, Οὐχ οὗτός ἐστιν ὃν ζητοῦσιν ἀποκτεῖναι;

25. Elegon oun tines ek ton 'Yerosolumiton, Ouch 'outos estin 'on zeitousin apokteinai?

Hebrew/Transliteration
:כה. וַיֹּאמְרוּ אֲחָדִים מִיֹּשְׁבֵי יְרוּשָׁלַיִם הֲלֹא זֶה הוּא אֲשֶׁר הֵם מְבַקְשִׁים לַהֲמִיתוֹ

25. Va•yom•roo a•cha•dim mi•yosh•vey Ye•roo•sha•la•yim ha•lo ze hoo asher hem me•vak•shim la•ha•mi•to?

Rabbinic Jewish Commentary
Who were inhabitants of Jerusalem, and so are distinguished from the people, Joh_7:20, who came up out of the country to the feast; so Jose ben Jochanan is called איש ירושלים, "a man of Jerusalem" (c); that is, an inhabitant of it: now these men living in the city, knew more of the temper and disposition, the designs and attempts, of the chief priests, Scribes, and elders, to take away the life of Yeshua.

(c) Pirke Abot, c. 1. sect. 4, 5.

---

26. But, lo, he speaketh boldly, and they say nothing unto him. Do the rulers know indeed that this is the very Christ?

Greek/Transliteration
26. Καὶ ἴδε παρρησίᾳ λαλεῖ, καὶ οὐδὲν αὐτῷ λέγουσιν. Μήποτε ἀληθῶς ἔγνωσαν οἱ ἄρχοντες ὅτι οὗτός ἐστιν ἀληθῶς ὁ χριστός;

26. Kai ide parreisia lalei, kai ouden auto legousin. Meipote aleithos egnosan 'oi archontes 'oti 'outos estin aleithos 'o christos?

Hebrew/Transliteration
כו. וְהִנֵּה הוּא מְדַבֵּר בָּרַבִּים וְהֵם אֵינָם אֹמְרִים לוֹ דָבָר הַאַף אֻמְנָם הִכִּירוּ שָׂרֵינוּ כִּי-בֶאֱמֶת הוּא הַמָּשִׁיחַ:

26. Ve•hee•ne hoo me•da•ber ba•ra•bim ve•hem ey•nam om•rim lo da•var ha•af oom•nam hi•ki•roo sa•rey•noo ki - be•e•met hoo ha•Ma•shi•ach?

---

27. Howbeit we know this man whence he is: but when Christ cometh, no man knoweth whence he is.

Greek/Transliteration
27. Ἀλλὰ τοῦτον οἴδαμεν πόθεν ἐστίν· ὁ δὲ χριστὸς ὅταν ἔρχηται, οὐδεὶς γινώσκει πόθεν ἐστίν.

27. Alla touton oidamen pothen estin. 'o de christos 'otan ercheitai, oudeis ginoskei pothen estin.

Hebrew/Transliteration

כז. אַךְ אֶת-הָאִישׁ הַזֶּה יָדַעְנוּ מֵאַיִן הוּא אֲבָל הַמָּשִׁיחַ בְּבֹאוֹ לֹא-יֵדַע אָדָם מֵאַיִן בָּא:

27. Ach et - ha•eesh ha•ze ya•da•a•noo me•a•yin hoo aval ha•Ma•shi•ach be•vo•o lo - ye•da adam me•a•yin ba.

Rabinic Jewish Commentary

Jews used to call him the seed which comes from another place; not from the place from whence seed ordinarily comes, from the loins of men, but from some other place they knew not where: their words are very remarkable on that passage in Gen_4:25, "and she called his name Seth, for God hath appointed me another seed". This observation is made by R. Tanchuma, in the name of R. Samuel (d); says he,

"She has respect to that seed, which is he that comes, ממקום אחר, "from another place", and what is this? this is the King Messiah."

And elsewhere (e), the same Rabbi observes on those words in Gen_19:32, "that we may preserve seed of our father": it is not written, "that we may preserve a son of our father", but "that we may preserve seed of our father"; that seed which is he that comes from "another place"; and what is this? this is the King Messiah. The modern Jews (f) endeavour to explain away the sense of this phrase, "another seed", as if it regarded strange seed; and that the sense of the expression is only, that the Messiah should spring from the family of Moab, and from Ruth the Moabitess: nor is their sense what Aquinas (g) at tributes to the Jewish Rabbi's,

"That the more noble part of that mass, of which Adam was made, remained untouched (by sin), and was afterwards transfused into Seth; and so through all descending from him, unto Joakim, or Eliakim, or Heli, the father of the virgin, out of which the body of the blessed Virgin was made:"

Which is no other than a Popish device, fathered upon the Jews, and made for the sake of the, Virgin Mary, rather than for the sake of Yeshua. But their meaning is, that Yeshua should not begotten of man, or come into the world in the ordinary way of generation, but should be born of a virgin; and so it could not be known, and accounted for from whence he was, or from whence that seed was of which he was made. The messenger gives the best account of this in Luk_1:35, a body was prepared for Messiah by the LORD; it was conceived by the power of the Holy Ghost; his birth of a virgin was miraculous; it is beyond the comprehension of men, and cannot explained by any mortal; from whence he is it cannot be said; no man can be pointed to as his father; all that can be said is, he was made of a woman, a virgin.

(d) Bereshit Rabba, sect. 23. fol. 20. 4. Midrash Ruth, fol. 36. 1. (e) Bereshit Rabba, sect. 51. fol. 46. 1. Midrash Ruth, fol. 35. 4. (f) Mattanot Cehunah & Jade Moseh in ib. (g) In 3 sent distinct. 3. art. 2.

---

28. Then cried Jesus in the temple as he taught, saying, Ye both know me, and ye know whence I am: and I am not come of myself, but he that sent me is true, whom ye know not.

Greek/Transliteration

28. Ἔκραξεν οὖν ἐν τῷ ἱερῷ διδάσκων ὁ Ἰησοῦς καὶ λέγων, Κἀμὲ οἴδατε, καὶ οἴδατε πόθεν εἰμί· καὶ ἀπ᾽ ἐμαυτοῦ οὐκ ἐλήλυθα, ἀλλ᾽ ἔστιν ἀληθινὸς ὁ πέμψας με, ὃν ὑμεῖς οὐκ οἴδατε.

28. Ekraxen oun en to 'iero didaskon 'o Yeisous kai legon, Kame oidate, kai oidate pothen eimi. kai ap emautou ouk eleilutha, all estin aleithinos 'o pempsas me, 'on 'umeis ouk oidate.

Hebrew/Transliteration

כח. אָז יְלַמֵּד יֵשׁוּעַ בַּמִּקְדָּשׁ וַיִּקְרָא לֵאמֹר אָכֵן יְדַעְתֶּם אֹתִי גַּם-יְדַעְתֶּם מֵאַיִן אָנֹכִי אַךְ מִלִּבִּי לֹא-בָאתִי כִּי יֵשׁ:נֶאֱמָן אֲשֶׁר שְׁלָחַנִי וְאַתֶּם לֹא יְדַעְתֶּם אֹתוֹ

28. Az ye•la•med Yeshua ba•mik•dash va•yik•ra le•mor a•chen ye•da•a•tem o•ti gam - ye•da•a•tem me•a•yin ano•chi ach mi•li•bi lo - va•ti ki yesh ne•e•man asher sh`la•cha•ni ve•a•tem lo ye•da•a•tem o•to.

---

29. But I know him: for I am from him, and he hath sent me.

Greek/Transliteration

29. Ἐγὼ οἶδα αὐτόν, ὅτι παρ᾽ αὐτοῦ εἰμι, κἀκεῖνός με ἀπέστειλεν.

29. Ego oida auton, 'oti par autou eimi, kakeinos me apesteilen.

Hebrew/Transliteration

כט. וַאֲנִי יָדַעְתִּי אֹתוֹ כִּי מֵאִתּוֹ אָנֹכִי וְהוּא שְׁלָחָנִי:

29. Va•a•ni ya•da•a•ti o•to ki me•ee•to ano•chi ve•hoo sh`la•cha•ni.

---

30. Then they sought to take him: but no man laid hands on him, because his hour was not yet come.

Greek/Transliteration

30. Ἐζήτουν οὖν αὐτὸν πιάσαι. Καὶ οὐδεὶς ἐπέβαλεν ἐπ᾽ αὐτὸν τὴν χεῖρα, ὅτι οὔπω ἐληλύθει ἡ ὥρα αὐτοῦ.

30. Ezeitoun oun auton pyasai. Kai oudeis epebalen ep auton tein cheira, 'oti oupo eleiluthei 'ei 'ora autou.

Hebrew/Transliteration

ל. וַיְבַקְשׁוּ לְתָפְשׂוֹ וְאִישׁ לֹא-שָׁלַח בּוֹ יָד כִּי עוֹד לֹא-בָאָה עִתּוֹ:

30. Vay•vak•shoo le•tof•so ve•eesh lo - sha•lach bo yad ki od lo - va•ah ee•to.

Rabbinic Jewish Commentary

because his hour was not yet come; to suffer and die, to depart out of this world, and go to the Father: there was a precise time fixed for this in the council and covenant of God, by mutual compact, called "due time"; as his coming into the world is called "the fulness of time"; nor could he die before that time, and therefore no man was suffered to lay hands on him, whatever good will he had to it. And there is a time for every man's death, nor can any man die before that time, or live beyond it; see Ecc_3:2; and this is the sense of the ancient Jews; for they say (h),

"A man before his years, or his time, does not die;"

That is, before he comes to the years appointed for him: and they ask (i),

"Who is there that goes before his time? i.e. dies before his time?"

And it is said (k) of a certain person who was in his house, and מטא זמניה, "his time was come"; and he died without sickness: though it must be owned some of them were otherwise minded, and say (l), that death, by the hand of heaven, or God, shortens a man's years; and that there are some reasons for which righteous men depart out of this world before their time is come; and particularly of Enoch they say, God took him before his time was come (m).

(h) T. Bab. Yebamot, fol. 114. 2. & Sanhedrin, fol. 29. 1. & Bava Metzia, fol. 85. 1. (i) T. Bab. Chagiga, fol. 4. 2. (k) Zohar in Exod. fol. 71. 4. (l) Piske Tosephot. Sabbat, art. 113. (m) Zohar in Exod. fol. 4. 4.

---

31. And many of the people believed on him, and said, When Christ cometh, will he do more miracles than these which this man hath done?

Greek/Transliteration

31. Πολλοὶ δὲ ἐκ τοῦ ὄχλου ἐπίστευσαν εἰς αὐτόν, καὶ ἔλεγον ὅτι Ὁ χριστὸς ὅταν ἔλθῃ, μήτι πλείονα σημεῖα τούτων ποιήσει ὧν οὗτος ἐποίησεν;

31. Polloi de ek tou ochlou episteusan eis auton, kai elegon 'oti 'O christos 'otan elthei, meiti pleiona seimeia touton poieisei 'on 'outos epoieisen?

Hebrew/Transliteration

לֹא. וְרַבִּים מִן-הָעָם הֶאֱמִינוּ-בֹו וַיֹּאמְרוּ הֲכִי הַמָּשִׁיחַ בְּבֹאוֹ יַעֲשֶׂה אֹתֹות רַבִּים מֵאֲשֶׁר הוּא עֹשֶׂה:

31. Ve•ra•bim min - ha•am he•e•mi•noo - vo va•yom•roo ha•chi ha•Ma•shi•ach be•vo•o ya•a•se o•tot ra•bim me•a•sher hoo o•se?

Rabbinic Jewish Commentary

The Jews expected many miracles to be wrought by the Messiah when he came, and they had good reason for it from Isa_35:5. To these Christ sends John the Baptist, and the Jews, for proofs of his being the Messiah, Mat_11:4; and by these he was approved of God as such, Act_2:23. And it is certain that the ancient Jews expected miracles in the days of the Messiah.

"Says R. Simeon to Eleazar his son, Eleazar, at the time that the King Messiah is raised up, how many "signs and other wonders" will be done in the world? a little after, from that day all the signs, and "wonders", and "mighty works", which the holy blessed God did in Egypt, he will do to the Israelites, as it is said, Mic_7:15, "according to the days of thy coming out of the land of Egypt, will I show unto him marvellous things" (n)."

So the Targumist on Isa_53:8 paraphrases thus,

"From afflictions and punishment he will deliver our captivity, and "the wonderful things" which shall be done for us in his days, who can tell?"

It is true indeed that the modern Jews have laid aside such expectations, and pretend they were not looked for formerly. Maimonides says (o),

"Let it not enter into thy heart, that the King Messiah hath need to do signs and wonders (as that he shall renew things in the world, or raise the dead, and the like; these are things which fools speak of); the thing is not so."

And he instances in Ben Coziba, who set up for the Messiah, of whom R. Akiba, and the rest of the wise men of that age, did not require a sign or miracle: yet this same writer elsewhere says (p), that

"All nations shall make peace with the Messiah, and serve him, because of his great righteousness, and the miracles which shall be done by him."

(n) Zohar in Exod. fol. 3. 4. & 4. 2. (o) Hilchot Melakim, c. 11. sect. 3. (p) In Misn. Sanhedrin, c. 11. sect. 1.

---

32. The Pharisees heard that the people murmured such things concerning him; and the Pharisees and the chief priests sent officers to take him.

32. Ἤκουσαν οἱ Φαρισαῖοι τοῦ ὄχλου γογγύζοντος περὶ αὐτοῦ ταῦτα· καὶ ἀπέστειλαν ὑπηρέτας οἱ Φαρισαῖοι καὶ οἱ ἀρχιερεῖς ἵνα πιάσωσιν αὐτόν.

32. Eikousan 'oi Pharisaioi tou ochlou gonguzontos peri autou tauta. kai apesteilan 'upeiretas 'oi Pharisaioi kai 'oi archiereis 'ina pyasosin auton.

לב. וַיִּשְׁמְעוּ הַפְּרוּשִׁים כִּי הָעָם מִתְלַחֲשִׁים כָּזֹאת עַל-אֹדוֹתָיו וַיִּשְׁלְחוּ רָאשֵׁי הַכֹּהֲנִים וְהַפְּרוּשִׁים מְשָׁרְתִים:לְתָפְשׂוֹ

32. Va•yish•me•oo ha•P`roo•shim ki ha•am mit•la•cha•shim ka•zot al - o•do•tav va•yish•le•choo ra•shey ha•ko•ha•nim ve•haP`roo•shim me•shar•tim le•tof•so.

---

33. Then said Jesus unto them, Yet a little while am I with you, and then I go unto him that sent me.

33. Εἶπεν οὖν ὁ Ἰησοῦς, Ἔτι μικρὸν χρόνον μεθ᾽ ὑμῶν εἰμι, καὶ ὑπάγω πρὸς τὸν πέμψαντά με.

33. Eipen oun 'o Yeisous, Eti mikron chronon meth 'umon eimi, kai 'upago pros ton pempsanta me.

לג. וַיֹּאמֶר אֲלֵיהֶם יֵשׁוּעַ עוֹד מְעַט מִזְעָר אֶהְיֶה עִמָּכֶם וְאֵלֵךְ לִי אֶל-שֹׁלְחִי:

33. Va•yo•mer aley•hem Yeshua od me•at miz•ar e•he•ye ee•ma•chem ve•e•lech li el - shol•chi.

---

34. Ye shall seek me, and shall not find me: and where I am, thither ye cannot come.

34. Ζητήσετέ με, καὶ οὐχ εὑρήσετε· καὶ ὅπου εἰμὶ ἐγώ, ὑμεῖς οὐ δύνασθε ἐλθεῖν.

34. Zeiteisete me, kai ouch 'eureisete. kai 'opou cimi cgo, 'umeis ou dunasthe elthein.

לד. תְּבַקְשֻׁנִי וְלֹא תִמְצָאֻנִי וּבַאֲשֶׁר אֶהְיֶה אֲנִי לֹא תוּכְלוּ אַתֶּם לָבֹא שָׁמָּה:

34. Te`vak•shoo•ni ve•lo tim•tza•oo•ni oo•va•a•sher e•he•ye ani lo tooch•loo atem la•vo sha•ma.

---

35. Then said the Jews among themselves, Whither will he go, that we shall not find him? will he go unto the dispersed among the Gentiles, and teach the Gentiles?

Greek/Transliteration

35. Εἶπον οὖν οἱ Ἰουδαῖοι πρὸς ἑαυτούς, Ποῦ οὗτος μέλλει πορεύεσθαι ὅτι ἡμεῖς οὐχ εὑρήσομεν αὐτόν; Μὴ εἰς τὴν διασπορὰν τῶν Ἑλλήνων μέλλει πορεύεσθαι, καὶ διδάσκειν τοὺς Ἕλληνας;

35. Eipon oun 'oi Youdaioi pros 'eautous, Pou 'outos mellei poreuesthai 'oti 'eimeis ouch 'eureisomen auton? Mei eis tein dyasporan ton 'Elleinon mellei poreuesthai, kai didaskein tous 'Elleinas?

Hebrew/Transliteration

לה. וַיֹּאמְרוּ הַיְּהוּדִים אִישׁ אֶל-אָחִיו אָנָה יֵלֵךְ זֶה כִּי לֹא נִמְצָא אֹתוֹ הֲיֵלֵךְ אֶל-הַנְּפוֹצִים בְּאֶרֶץ יָוָן וּלְלַמֵּד אֶת:הַיְּוָנִים -

35. Va•yom•roo ha•Ye•hoo•dim eesh el - a•chiv ana ye•lech ze ki lo nim•tza o•to ha•ye•lech el - ha•ne•fo•tzim be•e•retz Ya•van oo•le•la•med et - ha•Y`va•nim?

---

36. What manner of saying is this that he said, Ye shall seek me, and shall not find me: and where I am, thither ye cannot come?

Greek/Transliteration

36. Τίς ἐστιν οὗτος ὁ λόγος ὃν εἶπεν, Ζητήσετέ με, καὶ οὐχ εὑρήσετε· καὶ ὅπου εἰμὶ ἐγώ, ὑμεῖς οὐ δύνασθε ἐλθεῖν;

36. Tis estin 'outos 'o logos 'on eipen, Zeiteisete me, kai ouch 'eureisete. kai 'opou eimi ego, 'umeis ou dunasthe elthein?

Hebrew/Transliteration

לו. מָה-הַדָּבָר הַזֶּה אֲשֶׁר אָמַר תְּבַקְשֻׁנִי וְלֹא תִמְצָאֻנִי וּבַאֲשֶׁר אֲנִי אֶהְיֶה אֲנִי לֹא תוּכְלוּ אַתֶּם לָבֹא שָׁמָּה:

36. Ma - ha•da•var ha•ze asher amar te•vak•shoo•ni ve•lo tim•tza•oo•ni oo•va•a•sher e•he•ye ani lo tooch•loo atem la•vo sha•ma?

---

37. In the last day, that great day of the feast, Jesus stood and cried, saying, If any man thirst, let him come unto me, and drink.

Greek/Transliteration

37. Ἐν δὲ τῇ ἐσχάτῃ ἡμέρᾳ τῇ μεγάλῃ τῆς ἑορτῆς εἱστήκει ὁ Ἰησοῦς καὶ ἔκραξεν, λέγων, Ἐάν τις διψᾷ, ἐρχέσθω πρός με καὶ πινέτω.

37. En de tei eschatei 'eimera tei megalei teis 'eorteis 'eisteikei 'o Yeisous kai ekraxen, legon, Ean tis dipsa, erchestho pros me kai pineto.

Hebrew/Transliteration

לז. וַיְהִי בַּיּוֹם הָאַחֲרוֹן הַגָּדוֹל בֶּחָג וַיַּעֲמֹד יֵשׁוּעַ וַיִּקְרָא הוֹי כָּל-צָמֵא לְכוּ אֵלַי וּשְׁתוּ:

37. Vay•hi ba•yom ha•a•cha•ron ha•ga•dol be•chag va•ya•a•mod Yeshua va•yik•ra hoy kol - tza•me le•choo e•lai oosh•too.

Rabbinic Jewish Commentary

That is, of tabernacles, as appears from Joh_7:2, which was usually called חג, "the feast", in distinction from the passover and Pentecost (q); and the eighth day of it was called הרגל האחרון, "the last day of the feast" (r), as here: and it was a "great day", being, as is said in Lev_23:36, an holy convocation, a solemn assembly, in which no servile work was done, and in which an offering was made by fire unto the LORD.

According to the traditions of the Jews, fewer sacrifices were offered on this day than on the rest; for on the first day they offered thirteen bullocks, and lessened one every day; so that on the seventh, day, there was but seven offered, and on the eighth day but one, when the priests returned to their lots, as at other feasts (s); but notwithstanding the Jews make out this to be the greater day for them, since the seventy bullocks offered on the other seven days, were for the seventy nations of the world; but the one bullock, on the eighth day, was peculiarly for the people of Israel (t): and besides, they observe, that there were several things peculiar on this day, as different from the rest; as the casting of lots, the benediction by itself, a feast by itself, an offering by itself, a song by itself, and a blessing by itself (u): and on this day they had also the ceremony of drawing and pouring water, attended with the usual rejoicings as on other days; the account of which is this (w):

"The pouring out of water was after this manner; a golden pot, which held three logs, was tilled out of Siloah, and when they came to the water gate, they blew (their trumpets) and shouted, and blew; (then a priest) went up by the ascent of the altar, and turned to the left hand, (where) were two silver basins--that on the west side was filled with water, and that on the east with wine; he poured the basin of water into that of wine, and that of wine into that of water."

At which time there were great rejoicing, piping, and dancing, by the most religious and sober people among the Jews; insomuch that it is said (x), that

"He that never saw the rejoicing of the place of drawing of water, never saw any rejoicing in his life."

And this ceremony, they say (y), is a tradition of Moses from Mount Sinai, and refers to some secret and mysterious things; yea, they plainly say, that it has respect to the pouring forth of the Holy Ghost (z).

"Says R. Joshua ben Levi, why is its name called the place of drawing water? because, from thence שואבים רוח הקודש, "they draw the Holy Ghost", as it is said, "and ye shall draw water with joy out of the wells of salvation", Isa_12:3."

Moreover, it was on this day they prayed for the rains for the year ensuing: it is asked (a),

"From what time do they make mention of the powers of the rains (which descend by the power of God)? R. Eliezer says, from the first good day of the feast (of tabernacles); R. Joshua says, from the last good day of the feast.--They do not pray for the rains, but near the rains;"

That is, the time of rains; and which, one of their commentators says (b), is the eighth day of the feast of tabernacles; for from the feast of tabernacles, thenceforward is the time of rains. The Jews have a notion, that at this feast the rains of the ensuing year were fixed: hence they say (c), that

"At the feast of tabernacles judgment is made concerning the waters;"

Or a decree or determination is made concerning them by God. Upon which the Gemara (d) has these words,

"Wherefore does the law say pour out water on the feast of tabernacles? Says the holy blessed God, pour out water before me, that the rains of the year may be blessed unto you."

Now when all these things are considered, it will easily be seen with what pertinency Yeshua expresses himself on this day, with respect to the effusion of the gifts and graces of the Spirit of God.

(q) Shirshashirim Rabba, fol. 5. 3. & 7. 3. (r) Misn. Bava Metzia, c. 7. sect. 6. & Maimon. in ib. (s) Bartenora in Misn. Succa, c. 5. sect. 6. (t) T. Bab. Succa, fol. 55. 2. Bemidbar Rabba, sect. 21. fol. 231. 1. (u) T. Bab. Succa, fol. 48. 1. (w) Misn. Succa, c. 4. sect. 9. (x) Misn. Succa, c. 5. sect. 1, 4. (y) T. Zebachim, fol. 110. 2. Maimon. in Misn. Succa, c. 4. sect. 9. & Hilthot Tamidin, c. 10. sect. 6. (z) T. Hieros. Succa, fol. 55. 1. Bereshit Rabba, sect. 70. fol. 62. 3. & Midrash Ruth, fol. 32. 2. Caphtor, fol. 52. 1. (a) Misn. Taanith, c. 1. sect. 1, 2. (b) Bartenora, in ib. (c) Misn. Roshhashana, c. 1. sect. 2. (d) T. Bab. Roshhashana, fol. 16. 1.

---

38. He that believeth on me, as the scripture hath said, out of his belly shall flow rivers of living water.

Greek/Transliteration

38. Ὁ πιστεύων εἰς ἐμέ, καθὼς εἶπεν ἡ γραφή, ποταμοὶ ἐκ τῆς κοιλίας αὐτοῦ ῥεύσουσιν ὕδατος ζῶντος.

38. 'O pisteuon eis eme, kathos eipen 'ei graphei, potamoi ek teis koilias autou 'reusousin 'udatos zontos.

Hebrew/Transliteration

לח. הַמַּאֲמִין בִּי כִּדְבַר הַכָּתוּב מִקִּרְבּוֹ יִזְלוּ נַחֲלֵי מַיִם חַיִּים:

38. Ha•ma•a•min bi ki•d`var ha•ka•toov mi•kir•bo yiz•loo na•cha•ley ma•yim cha•yim.

Rabbinic Jewish Commentary

The Jews ought not to find fault with Yeshua's using such expressions, mystically understood, since they, comparing Moses and the Messiah together, say,

"As the first Redeemer caused a well to spring up, so the last Redeemer shall cause waters to spring up, according to Joe_3:18 (e)."

(e) Midrash Kohelet, fol. 63. 2.

---

39. (But this spake he of the Spirit, which they that believe on him should receive: for the Holy Ghost was not yet given; because that Jesus was not yet glorified.)

Greek/Transliteration

39. Τοῦτο δὲ εἶπεν περὶ τοῦ πνεύματος οὗ ἔμελλον λαμβάνειν οἱ πιστεύοντες εἰς αὐτόν· οὔπω γὰρ ἦν πνεῦμα ἅγιον, ὅτι Ἰησοῦς οὐδέπω ἐδοξάσθη.

39. Touto de eipen peri tou pneumatos 'ou emellon lambanein 'oi pisteuontes eis auton. Oupo gar ein pneuma 'agion, 'oti Yeisous oudepo edoxasthei.

Hebrew/Transliteration

לט. כָּזֹאת דִּבֶּר עַל-הָרוּחַ אֲשֶׁר תְּנַח עַל-הַמַּאֲמִינִים בּוֹ כִּי עוֹד לֹא-נִשְׁפַּךְ רוּחַ הַקֹּדֶשׁ בְּטֶרֶם לֶקַח יֵשׁוּעַ אַחַר:כָּבוֹד

39. Ka•zot di•ber al - ha•Roo•ach asher ta•nach al - ha•ma•a•mi•nim bo ki od lo - nish•pach Roo•ach ha•Ko•desh be•te•rem loo•kach Yeshua achar cha•vod.

Rabbinic Jewish Commentary

The Arabic version renders it, "for the Holy Ghost was not yet come"; he was; he was in being as a divine person, equal with the Father and Son, so he was from everlasting; and he had been bestowed in his grace upon the Old Testament saints, and rested in his gifts upon the prophets of that dispensation; but, as the Jews themselves confess (f),

"After the death of the latter prophets, Haggai, Zachariah, and Malachi, the Holy Ghost removed from Israel."

And they expressly say, be was not there in the time of the second temple. Maimonides says (g),

"They made the Urim and Thummim in the second temple, to complete the eight garments (of the priests) though they did not inquire by them; and why did they not inquire by them? because the Holy Ghost was not there; and every priest that does not speak by the Holy Ghost, and the Shekinah, does not dwell upon him, they do not inquire by him."

They observe (h) there were five things in the first temple which were not in the second, and they are these,

"The ark with the mercy seat, and cherubim, the fire (from heaven), and the Shekinah, וְרוּחַ הַקֹּדֶשׁ, "and the Holy Spirit", and the Urim and Thummim."

(f) T. Bab. Yoma, fol. 9. 2. Sota, fol. 48. 2. & Sanhedrin, fol. 11. 1. (g) Hilchot Cele Hamikdash, c. 10. sect. 10. Vid. T. Bab. Yoma, fol. 73. 2. (h) T. Bab. Yoma, fol. 21. 2. Vid. Jarchi & Kimchi in Hagg. i. 8.

---

40. Many of the people therefore, when they heard this saying, said, Of a truth this is the Prophet.

Greek/Transliteration
40. Πολλοὶ οὖν ἐκ τοῦ ὄχλου ἀκούσαντες τὸν λόγον ἔλεγον, Οὗτός ἐστιν ἀληθῶς ὁ προφήτης.

40. Polloi oun ek tou ochlou akousantes ton logon elegon, 'Outos estin aleithos 'o propheiteis.

Hebrew/Transliteration
מ. וְיֵשׁ מִן-הָעָם כְּשָׁמְעָם אֶת-הַדְּבָרִים הָאֵלֶּה אָמְרוּ אָכֵן זֶה הוּא הַנָּבִיא:

40. Ve•yesh min - ha•am ke•shom•am et - ha•d`va•rim ha•e•le am•roo a•chen ze hoo ha•na•vee.

---

41. Others said, This is the Christ. But some said, Shall Christ come out of Galilee?

Greek/Transliteration
41. Ἄλλοι ἔλεγον, Οὗτός ἐστιν ὁ χριστός. Ἄλλοι ἔλεγον, Μὴ γὰρ ἐκ τῆς Γαλιλαίας ὁ χριστὸς ἔρχεται;

41. Alloi elegon, 'Outos estin 'o christos. Alloi elegon, Mei gar ek teis Galilaias 'o christos erchetai?

Hebrew/Transliteration
מא. וְיֵשׁ אֲשֶׁר אָמְרוּ זֶה הוּא הַמָּשִׁיחַ וַאֲחֵרִים אָמְרוּ הֲמִן-הַגָּלִיל יָבֹא הַמָּשִׁיחַ:

41. Ve•yesh asher am•roo ze hoo ha•Ma•shi•ach va•a•che•rim am•roo ha•min - ha•Galil ya•vo ha•Ma•shi•ach?

Rabbinic Jewish Commentary
"The glory of his majesty" refers to the Messiah when he shall reveal himself in the land of Galilee; for in this part of the Holy Land the desolation first began, and therefore he will manifest himself there first . . . and when the Messiah shall have manifested himself, a star shall come forth from the East variegated in hue and shining brilliantly, and seven other stars shall surround it, and make war on it from all sides, three times a day for seventy days, before the eyes of the whole world. The one star shall fight against the seven with rays of fire flashing on every side, and it shall smite them until they are extinguished, evening after evening. . . . After the seventy days the one star shall vanish."
(Zohar, Volume II, Shemot 7b, Soncino Press Edition, pg. 21)

For if they did not mean this, according to their own accounts, the Messiah was to be in Galilee, and to be first revealed there; for they affirm (i) this in so many words, that יתגלי מלכא משיחא בארעא דגליל, "the King Messiah shall be revealed in the land of Galilee"; accordingly Yeshua, the true Messiah, as he was brought up in Galilee, though not born there, so he first preached there, and there wrought his first miracle; here he chiefly was, unless at the public feasts; and here he manifested himself to his disciples after his resurrection.

(i) Zohar in Gen. fol. 74. 3. & in Exod. fol. 3. 3. & 4. 1.

---

42. Hath not the scripture said, That Christ cometh of the seed of David, and out of the town of Bethlehem, where David was?

Greek/Transliteration
42. Οὐχὶ ἡ γραφὴ εἶπεν ὅτι ἐκ τοῦ σπέρματος Δαυίδ, καὶ ἀπὸ Βηθλεέμ, τῆς κώμης ὅπου ἦν Δαυίδ, ὁ χριστὸς ἔρχεται;

42. Ouchi 'ei graphei eipen 'oti ek tou spermatos Dauid, kai apo Beithle'em, teis komeis 'opou ein Dauid, 'o christos erchetai?

Hebrew/Transliteration

מ״ב. הֲלֹא הַכָּתוּב אֹמֵר כִּי מִזֶּרַע דָּוִד מִבֵּית-לֶחֶם הָעִיר חָנָה דָּוִד מִשָּׁם יֵצֵא הַמָּשִׁיחַ:

42. Ha•lo ha•ka•toov o•mer ki mi•ze•ra David mi•Beit - Le•chem ha•eer chana David mi•sham ye•tze ha•Ma•shi•ach?

Rabbinic Jewish Commentary

that Christ cometh out of the seed of David; that he should be a rod out of the stem of Jesse, and a branch out of his roots; that he should be one out of David's loins, and of the fruit of his body, referring to Isa_11:1, which was very true, and what was commonly known, and expected among the Jews, that the Messiah should be David's son, as Jesus of Nazareth was.

"And there shall come forth a rod out of the stem of Jesse, and a Branch shall grow out of his roots" (Isa_11:1)

By which is meant, not Hezekiah, as R. Moses (o) the priest, and others, since he was now born, and must be at least ten or twelve years of age; but the Messiah, as both the text and context show, and as is owned by many Jewish writers (p), ancient and modern: and he is called a "rod", either because of his unpromising appearance, arising "out of the stem of Jesse"; from him, in the line of David, when that family was like a tree cut down, and its stump only left in the ground, which was the case when Yeshua was born of it.

Targum agrees, paraphrasing the words thus, "and a King shall come forth from the sons of Jesse:"

The Targum, "and the Messiah shall be anointed (or exalted) from his children's children."

The branch is a well known name of the Messiah; the word Netzer, here used, is the name of the city of Nazareth (q); which perhaps was so called, from the trees, plants, and grass, which grew here; and so our Lord's dwelling here fulfilled a prophecy, that he should be called a Nazarene; or an inhabitant of Netzer, Mat_2:23.

And the passage they had in view, is Mic_5:2. Now these very things they object to Yeshua being the Messiah, were what were fulfilled in him, and proved him to be the person; for his supposed father, and real mother Mary, were of the house and lineage of David; and though he was conceived at Nazareth, and brought up there, yet by a remarkable providence, which brought Joseph and Mary to Bethlehem, he was born there.

(o) Apud Aben Ezra in loc. (p) Bereshit Rabba, sect. 85. fol. 75. 1. Midrash Tillim in Psal. lxxii. 1. Apud Yalkut Simeoni, par. 2. fol. 112. 2. Abarbinel, Mashmia Jeshua, fol. 8. 4. Aben Ezra, Jarchi, & Kimchi, in loc. Nachman. Disputat. cum Fratre Paulo, p. 53. (q) David de Pomis Lexic. p. 141.

43. So there was a division among the people because of him.

Greek/Transliteration
43. Σχίσμα οὖν ἐν τῷ ὄχλῳ ἐγένετο δι᾽ αὐτόν.

43. Schisma oun en to ochlo egeneto di auton.

Hebrew/Transliteration
מג. וַיֵּחָלֵק הָעָם בְּהַצּוֹתָם עָלָיו:

43. Va•ye•cha•lek ha•am be•ha•tzo•tam alav.

---

44. And some of them would have taken him; but no man laid hands on him.

Greek/Translitertation
44. Τινὲς δὲ ἤθελον ἐξ αὐτῶν πιάσαι αὐτόν, ἀλλ᾽ οὐδεὶς ἐπέβαλεν ἐπ᾽ αὐτὸν τὰς χεῖρας.

44. Tines de eithelon ex auton pyasai auton, all oudeis epebalen ep auton tas cheiras.

Hebrew/Transliteration
מד. וְיֵשׁ מֵהֶם אֲשֶׁר רָצוּ לְתָפְשׂוֹ וְאִישׁ לֹא-שָׁלַח בּוֹ יָדוֹ:

44. Ve•yesh me•hem asher ra•tzoo le•tof•so ve•eesh lo - sha•lach bo ya•do.

---

45. Then came the officers to the chief priests and Pharisees; and they said unto them, Why have ye not brought him?

Greek/Transliteration
45. ῞Ηλθον οὖν οἱ ὑπηρέται πρὸς τοὺς ἀρχιερεῖς καὶ Φαρισαίους· καὶ εἶπον αὐτοῖς ἐκεῖνοι, Διὰ τί οὐκ ἠγάγετε αὐτόν;

45. Eilthon oun 'oi 'upeiretai pros tous archiereis kai Pharisaious. kai eipon autois ekeinoi, Dya ti ouk eigagete auton?

Hebrew/Transliteration
מה. וַיָּשׁוּבוּ הַמְשָׁרְתִים אֶל-רָאשֵׁי הַכֹּהֲנִים וְהַפְּרוּשִׁים וְהֵם אָמְרוּ אֲלֵיהֶם מַדּוּעַ לֹא-הֲבֵאתֶם אֹתוֹ:

45. Va•ya•shoo•voo ha•me•shar•tim el - ra•shey ha•ko•ha•nim ve•haP`roo•shim ve•hem am•roo aley•hem ma•doo•a lo - ha•ve•tem o•to?

---

46. The officers answered, Never man spake like this man.

Greek/Transliteration
46. Ἀπεκρίθησαν οἱ ὑπηρέται, Οὐδέποτε οὕτως ἐλάλησεν ἄνθρωπος, ὡς οὗτος ὁ ἄνθρωπος.

46. Apekritheisan 'oi 'upeiretai, Oudepote 'outos elaleisen anthropos, 'os 'outos 'o anthropos.

Hebrew/Transliteration
מו. וַיַּעֲנוּ הַמְשָׁרְתִים לֵאמֹר מֵעוֹלָם לֹא-דִבֶּר אָדָם כָּמֹהוּ:

46. Va•ya•a•noo ha•me•shar•tim le•mor me•o•lam lo - di•ber adam ka•mo•hoo.

---

47. Then answered them the Pharisees, Are ye also deceived?

Greek/Transliteration
47. Ἀπεκρίθησαν οὖν αὐτοῖς οἱ Φαρισαῖοι, Μὴ καὶ ὑμεῖς πεπλάνησθε;

47. Apekritheisan oun autois 'oi Pharisaioi, Mei kai 'umeis peplaneisthe?

Hebrew/Transliteration
מז. וַיֹּאמְרוּ אֲלֵיהֶם הַפְּרוּשִׁים הֲכִי נִדַּחְתֶּם גַּם-אַתֶּם:

47. Va•yom•roo aley•hem ha•P`roo•shim ha•chi ni•dach•tem gam – atem?

---

48. Have any of the rulers or of the Pharisees believed on him?

Greek/Transliteration
48. Μή τις ἐκ τῶν ἀρχόντων ἐπίστευσεν εἰς αὐτόν, ἢ ἐκ τῶν Φαρισαίων;

48. Mei tis ek ton archonton episteusen eis auton, ei ek ton Pharisaion?

Hebrew/Transliteration
מח. הֲכִי הֶאֱמִין בּוֹ אַחַד הַשָּׂרִים אוֹ אַחַד הַפְּרוּשִׁים:

48. Ha•chi he•e•min bo achad ha•sa•rim oh achad ha•P`roo•shim?

---

49. But this people who knoweth not the law are cursed.

Greek/Transliteration
49. Ἀλλ᾽ ὁ ὄχλος οὗτος ὁ μὴ γινώσκων τὸν νόμον ἐπικατάρατοί εἰσιν.

49. All 'o ochlos 'outos 'o mei ginoskon ton nomon epikataratoi eisin.

Hebrew/Transliteration

מט. לְבַד הֶהָמוֹן הַזֶּה אֲשֶׁר אֵינָם יֹדְעִים אֶת-הַתּוֹרָה אֲרוּרִים הֵמָּה:

49. Le•vad he•ha•mon ha•ze asher ey•nam yod•eem et - ha•Torah a•roo•rim he•ma.

Rabbinic Jewish Commentary

With great contempt they style the followers of Jesus "this people"; the common people, the dregs of them, the refuse of the earth; and whom they call, עם הארץ, "the people of the earth", in distinction from the wise men, and their disciples: and when they speak the best of them, their account is this (p);

"One of the people of the earth is one that has moral excellencies, but not intellectual ones; that is, there is in him common civility, but the law is not in him;"

As here, "who knoweth not the law": they always reckon them very ignorant. Says one (q) of their writers,

"They that are without knowledge are the multitude."

And elsewhere it is said (r),

"The old men of the people of the earth, when they grow old their knowledge is disturbed (or is lost), as it is said, Job_12:20, but so it is not with the old men of the law, when they grow old, their knowledge rests upon them, as it is said, Job_12:12, "with the ancient is wisdom"."

Upon which one of the commentators (s) has this gloss;

"These are the disciples of the wise men; for the people of the earth, what wisdom is there in them?"

The oral law is here intended, which they pretended was given by word of mouth to Moses, and handed down to posterity from one to another; and this lay among the doctors: they tell us (t), that Moses received it at Sinai, and delivered it to Joshua, and Joshua to the elders, and the elders to the prophets, and the prophets to the men of the great synagogue (Ezra's), the last of which was Simeon the just: Antigonus, a man of Socho, received it from him; and Jose ben Joezer, and Jose ben Jochanan, received it from him; and Joshua ben Perachia, (whom they sometimes say was the master of Yeshua of Nazareth,) and Nittai the Arbelite, received it from them; by whom it was delivered to Judah ben Tabia, and Simeon ben Shetach; and from them it was received by Shemaiah, and Abtalion, who delivered it to Hillell, and Shammai; who, or whose scholars, were, at this time, when these words were spoken, the present possessors of it, and taught it their disciples in their schools: and thus it was handed down from one to another, until the times of R. Judah, who collected the whole of the traditions of the elders together, and published it under the title of the Misna; and then, as Maimonides says (u), it was revealed to all Israel; whereas before it was but in a few hands, who instructed others in it; but as for the common people, they knew little of it, especially of the nice distinctions and decisions of it; and these people were always had in great contempt by the wise men: they would not receive a testimony from them, nor give one for them, nor deliver a secret to them, nor proclaim anything of theirs that was lost, nor walk with them in the way, nor make a guardian of any of them (w). The people of the earth were not reckoned holy or religious (x), but generally profane and wicked; that they were abandoned to sin, rejected of God, and to be cast off by men; yea, they will not allow that they shall rise again at the last day, unless it be for the sake of some wise men they are allied unto, or have done some service for. They say (y).

"Whoever ministers in the light of the law, the light of the law will quicken him; but whoever does not minister in the light of the law, the light of the law will not quicken him--though it is possible for such an one to cleave to the Shekinah--for everyone that marries his daughter to a scholar of a wise man, or makes merchandise for the disciples of the wise men, and they receive any advantage from his goods, this brings on him what is written, as if he cleaved to the Shekinah."

(p) Maimon. in Pirke Abot, c. 2. sect. 5. & c. 5. sect. 7. (q) Abarbinel in proph. post. fol. 473. (r) Misn. Kenim, c. 3. sect. 6. Vid. T. Bab. Sabbat, fol. 152. 1. (s) Bartenora in Misn. ib. (t) Pirke Abot, c. 1. sect. 1-12. (u) Praefat. ad Yad Hazaka. (w) Buxtorf. Lex. Talmud. col. 1626. (x) Ib. Florileg. Heb. p. 276. (y) T. Bab. Cetubot, fol. 111. 2.

---

50. Nicodemus saith unto them, (he that came to Jesus by night, being one of them,)

Greek/Transliteration
50. Λέγει Νικόδημος πρὸς αὐτούς- ὁ ἐλθὼν νυκτὸς πρὸς αὐτόν, εἷς ὢν ἐξ αὐτῶν-

50. Legei Nikodeimos pros autous- 'o elthon nuktos pros auton, 'eis on ex auton-

Hebrew/Transliteration
נ. וַיֹּאמֶר אֲלֵיהֶם נַקְדִּימוֹן הוּא אֲשֶׁר-בָּא אֵלָיו לְפָנִים וְהוּא אֶחָד מִן-הַפְּרוּשִׁים:

50. Va•yo•mer aley•hem Nak•di•mon hoo asher - ba elav le•fa•nim ve•hoo e•chad min - ha•P`roo•shim.

---

51. Doth our law judge any man, before it hear him, and know what he doeth?

51. Μὴ ὁ νόμος ἡμῶν κρίνει τὸν ἄνθρωπον, ἐὰν μὴ ἀκούσῃ παρ᾽ αὐτοῦ πρότερον καὶ γνῷ τί ποιεῖ;

51. Mei 'o nomos 'eimon krinei ton anthropon, ean mei akousei par autou proteron kai gno ti poiei?

נא. הֲכִי תִשְׁפֹּט תּוֹרָתֵנוּ אֶת-הָאָדָם בְּטֶרֶם יִשְׁמַע מַה-בְּפִיו וּבְטֶרֶם יֵדַע מֶה-עָשָׂה:

51. Ha•chi tish•pot To•ra•te•noo et - ha•a•dam be•te•rem yi•sha•ma ma - be•fiv oov•te•rem yi•va•da me – asa?

---

52. They answered and said unto him, Art thou also of Galilee? Search, and look: for out of Galilee ariseth no prophet.

52. Ἀπεκρίθησαν καὶ εἶπον αὐτῷ, Μὴ καὶ σὺ ἐκ τῆς Γαλιλαίας εἶ; Ἐρεύνησον καὶ ἴδε ὅτι προφήτης ἐκ τῆς Γαλιλαίας οὐκ ἐγήγερται.

52. Apekritheisan kai eipon auto, Mei kai su ek teis Galilaias ei? Ereuneison kai ide 'oti propheiteis ek teis Galilaias ouk egeigertai.

נב. וַיַּעֲנוּ וַיֹּאמְרוּ אֵלָיו הֲמִן-הַגָּלִיל גַּם-אַתָּה דְּרֹשׁ וַחֲקֹר כִּי לֹא-קָם נָבִיא מִן-הַגָּלִיל:

52. Va•ya•a•noo va•yom•roo elav ha•min - ha•Galil gam? - ata d`rosh va•cha•kor ki lo – kam na•vi min - ha•Galil.

Rabbinic Jewish Commentary

for out of Galilee ariseth no prophet; but this is false, for Jonah the prophet was of Gathhepher, which was in the tribe of Zebulun, which tribe was in Galilee; see 2Ki_14:25. And the Jews (z) themselves say, that Jonah, the son of Amittai, was, מזבולון, of "Zebulun", and that his father was of Zebulun, and his mother was of Asher (a); both which tribes were in Galilee: and if no prophet had, as yet, arose from thence, it did not follow that no one should arise: besides, there is a prophecy in which it was foretold, that a prophet, and even the Messiah, the great light, should arise in Galilee; and they themselves say, that the Messiah should be revealed in Galilee; See John 7:41

(z) T. Hieros. Succa, fol. 55. 1, (a) Bereshit Rabba, sect. 98. fol. 85. 4.

53. And every man went unto his own house.

Greek/Transliteration
53. Καὶ ἐπορεύθη ἕκαστος εἰς τὸν οἶκον αὐτοῦ·

53. Kai eporeuthei 'ekastos eis ton oikon autou.

Hebrew/Transliteration
נג. וַיֵּלְכוּ אִישׁ אִישׁ לְבֵיתוֹ:

53. Va•yel•choo eesh eesh le•vey•to.

Rabbinic Jewish Commentary
The officers not bringing Yeshua with them, and the Sanhedrim being posed with Nicodemus, broke up without doing any business, and every member of it went home: this we may suppose was about the time of the evening sacrifice: for

"The great sanhedrim sat from the time of the morning daily sacrifice, to the time of the evening daily sacrifice (b):"

And it is said (c), that "After the evening daily sacrifice, the Sanhedrim went, לבי־תאם, "to their own houses";"

As they now did, and not to their booths, the feast of tabernacles being now over.

(b) Maimon. Hilchot Sanhedrin, c. 3. sect. 1. (c) Piske Tosephot Sanhedrin, art. 35.

John, Chapter 8

1. Jesus went unto the mount of Olives.

Greek/Transliteration
1. Ἰησοῦς δὲ ἐπορεύθη εἰς τὸ ὄρος τῶν Ἐλαιῶν.

1. Yeisous de eporeuthei eis to oros ton Elaion.

Hebrew/Transliteration
א. וַיֵּלְכוּ אִישׁ אִישׁ לְבֵיתוֹ וְיֵשׁוּעַ הָלַךְ אֶל-הַר הַזֵּיתִים:

1. Va•yel•choo eesh eesh le•vey•to ve•Yeshua ha•lach el - Har ha•Zey•tim.

---

2. And early in the morning he came again into the temple, and all the people came unto him; and he sat down, and taught them.

Greek/Transliteration
2. Ὄρθρου δὲ πάλιν παρεγένετο εἰς τὸ ἱερόν, καὶ πᾶς ὁ λαὸς ἤρχετο· καὶ καθίσας ἐδίδασκεν αὐτούς.

2. Orthrou de palin paregeneto eis to 'ieron, kai pas 'o laos eircheto. kai kathisas edidasken autous.

Hebrew/Transliteration
ב. וַיְהִי בַבֹּקֶר וַיָּבֹא עוֹד אֶל-הַמִּקְדָּשׁ וְכָל-הָעָם בָּאוּ אֵלָיו וַיֵּשֶׁב וַיְלַמְּדֵם:

2. Vay•hi ba•bo•ker va•ya•vo od el - ha•mik•dash ve•chol - ha•am ba•oo elav va•ye•shev vay•lam•dem.

---

3. And the scribes and Pharisees brought unto him a woman taken in adultery; and when they had set her in the midst,

Greek/Transliteration
3. Ἄγουσιν δὲ οἱ γραμματεῖς καὶ οἱ Φαρισαῖοι πρὸς αὐτὸν γυναῖκα ἐν μοιχείᾳ καταληφθεῖσαν· καὶ στήσαντες αὐτὴν ἐν μέσῳ,

3. Agousin de 'oi grammateis kai 'oi Pharisaioi pros auton gunaika en moicheia kataleiphtheisan. kai steisantes autein en meso,

Hebrew/Transliteration
ג. וְהַסּוֹפְרִים וְהַפְּרוּשִׁים הֵבִיאוּ לְפָנָיו אִשָּׁה אֲשֶׁר נִתְפְּשָׂה בְנַאֲפוּפֶיהָ וַיַּעֲמִדוּהָ בַּתָּוֶךְ:

3. Ve•ha•sof•rim ve•haP`roo•shim he•vi•oo le•fa•nav ee•sha asher nit•pe•sa be•na•a•foo•fe•ha va•ya•a•mi•doo•ha ba•ta•vech.

Rabbinic Jewish Commentary

Who this woman was, is not material to know; what is pretended to be taken out of the annals of the Spanish Jews, is no doubt a fable; that she was the wife of one Manasseh of Jerusalem, an old man, whose name was Susanna (d).

This history of the woman taken in adultery, is not in the Alexandrian copy, and in other ancient copies; nor is it in Nonnus, Chrysostom, and Theophylact; nor in any of the editions of the Syriac version, until it was restored by De Dieu, from a copy of Archbishop Usher's; but was in the Arabic and Ethiopic versions, and in the Harmonies of Tatian and Ammonius; the former of which lived about the year 160, and so within 60 years, or thereabouts, of the death of the Evangelist John, and the other about the year 230; it was also in Stephens's sixteen ancient Greek copies, and in all Beza's seventeen, excepting one; nor need the authenticness of it be doubted of; Eusebius (e) says, it is in the Gospel according to the Hebrews; nor should its authority be called in question.

(d) Vid. Selden. Uxor Hebr. l. 3. c. 11. p. 377. (e) Hist. Ecless. l. 3. c. 39.

---

4. They say unto him, Master, this woman was taken in adultery, in the very act.

Greek/Transliteration

4. λέγουσιν αὐτῷ, πειράζοντες, Διδάσκαλε, αὕτη ἡ γυνὴ κατελήφθη ἐπ᾽ αὐτοφόρῳ μοιχευομένη.

4. legousin auto, peirazontes, Didaskale, 'autei 'ei gunei kateleiphthei ep autophoro moicheuomenei.

Hebrew/Transliteration

:ד. וַיֹּאמְרוּ אֵלָיו רַבֵּנוּ הָאִשָּׁה הַזֹּאת נִתְפְּשָׂה בְנַאֲפוּפֶיהָ כְּגַנָּב בַּמַּחְתָּרֶת

4. Va•yom•roo elav Ra•be•noo ha•ee•sha ha•zot nit•pe•sa be•na•a•foo•fe•ha ke•ga•nav ba•mach•ta•ret.

Rabbinic Jewish Commentary

By two persons at least, who could be witnesses of it; otherwise the accusation was not legal; see Deu_19:15; though in the case of a wife suspected of adultery, they admitted a single witness as valid (f):

in the very act; or "in the theft itself", for adultery is a theft; it is an unlawful use of another's property;

(f) Maimon. Hilchot Eduth, c. 5. sect. 2.

---

5. Now Moses in the law commanded us, that such should be stoned: but what sayest thou?

Greek/Transliteration
5. Ἐν δὲ τῷ νόμῳ Μωσῆς ἡμῖν ἐνετείλατο τὰς τοιαύτας λιθοβολεῖσθαι· σὺ οὖν τί λέγεις;

5. En de to nomo Moseis 'eimin eneteilato tas toyautas lithoboleisthai. su oun ti legeis?

Hebrew/Transliteration
ה. וּבַתּוֹרָה צִוָּה-לָנוּ מֹשֶׁה לִסְקֹל בָּאֲבָנִים אִשָּׁה כָזֹאת וּמַה-תֹּאמַר אָתָה:

5. Oo•va•to•rah tzi•va - la•noo Moshe lis•kol ba•a•va•nim ee•sha cha•zot oo•ma - to•mar ata?

Rabbinic Jewish Commentary
Not in Lev_20:10; for though according to the law there, an adulteress, one that was a married woman, and so an adulterer, that was a married man, were to be put to death; yet the death was not stoning, but strangling; for it is a rule with the Jews (g), that where death is simply mentioned (without restraining it to any particular kind) strangling is intended, and which rule they apply to this law: and accordingly in their Misna, or oral law, one that lies with another man's wife, is reckoned among those that are to be strangled (h): Kimchi indeed says (i), that adulteresses, according to the law, are to be stoned with stones; but then this must be understood of such as are betrothed, but not married; and such a person, Moses has commanded in the law, to be stoned, Deu_22:23. And with this agree the traditions of the Jews (k);

"A daughter of Israel must be stoned, who is ארוסה ולא נשואה, "betrothed, but not married"."

And such an one we must believe this woman was; she was betrothed to a man, but not married to him, and therefore to be stoned: the Jews (l) have also a saying, that

"If all adulterers were punished with stoning, according to the law, the stones would be consumed; but they would not be consumed;"

Adultery was so common with that people:

but what sayest thou? dost thou agree with Moses, or not?

(g) Maimon. Hilchot Issure Bia, c. 1. sect. 6. (h) Misn. Sanhedrin, c. 10. sect. 1. (i) In Ezek. xvi. 40. (k) T. Bab. Sanhedrin, fol. 51. 2. (l) Apud Castell. Lex. Polyglott, col. 2180.

6. This they said, tempting him, that they might have to accuse him. But Jesus stooped down, and with his finger wrote on the ground, as though he heard them not.

Greek/Transliteration
6. Τοῦτο δὲ ἔλεγον πειράζοντες αὐτόν, ἵνα ἔχωσιν κατηγορεῖν αὐτοῦ. Ὁ δὲ Ἰησοῦς κάτω κύψας, τῷ δακτύλῳ ἔγραφεν εἰς τὴν γῆν, μὴ προσποιούμενος.

6. Touto de elegon peirazontes auton, 'ina echosin kateigorein autou. 'O de Yeisous kato kupsas, to daktulo egraphen eis tein gein, mei prospoioumenos.

Hebrew/Transliteration
ו: וְכָזֹאת אָמְרוּ לְנַסּוֹתוֹ לִמְצֹא עָלָיו דָּבָר לְשִׂטְנוֹ וַיִּשְׁתּוֹחַח יֵשׁוּעַ וַיִּכְתָּו בְּאֶצְבָּעוֹ עַל-הָאָרֶץ

6. Ve•cha•zot am•roo le•na•so•to lim•tzo alav da•var le•sit•no va•yish•to•chach Yeshua vay•tav be•etz•ba•o al - ha•a•retz.

Rabbinic Jewish Commentary
(See Jer_17:13, "They that depart from me shall be written in the earth". It could be that Yeshua was writing their names in the earth, thus fulfilling this prophecy in Jeremiah. They knew the Old Testament and this passage, and were convicted in their hearts. Editor.)

---

7. So when they continued asking him, he lifted up himself, and said unto them, He that is without sin among you, let him first cast a stone at her.

Greek/Transliteration
7. Ὡς δὲ ἐπέμενον ἐρωτῶντες αὐτόν, ἀνακύψας εἶπεν πρὸς αὐτούς, Ὁ ἀναμάρτητος ὑμῶν, πρῶτον ἐπ᾿ αὐτὴν τὸν λίθον βαλέτω.

7. 'Os de epemenon erotontes auton, anakupsas eipen pros autous, 'O anamarteitos 'umon, proton ep autein ton lithon baleto.

Hebrew/Transliteration
ז: וְכַאֲשֶׁר הוֹסִיפוּ לִשְׁאֹל אֹתוֹ וַיָּקָם וַיֹּאמֶר אֲלֵיהֶם מִי-בָכֶם נָקִי מֵעָוֹן יַדֶּה-בָּהּ אֶבֶן רִאשׁוֹנָה

7. Ve•cha•a•sher ho•si•foo lish•ol o•to va•ya•kom va•yo•mer aley•hem mee - va•chem na•ki me•avon ya•de - ba even ri•sho•na.

Rabbinic Jewish Commentary
Adultery increased to such a degree in this age, that they were obliged to leave off the trial of suspected wives, because their husbands were generally guilty this way; and the waters would have no effect, if the husband was criminal also: so the Jews say (q), "when adulterers increased, the bitter waters ceased; and Rabban Jochanan ben Zaccai (who was now living) caused them to cease."

In vindication of which, he cited the passage in Hos_4:14; and this agrees with their own account of the times of the Messiah, and the signs thereof, among which stands this (r);

"In the age in which the son of David comes, the house of assembly (the gloss interprets it the place where the disciples of the wise men meet to learn the law) shall become, לזונות, "a brothel house"."

And that this sin so greatly prevailed, Yeshua well knew; and perhaps none of those Scribes and Pharisees were free from it, in one shape or another; and therefore bids him that was.

Another problem arises here because they failed to bring the male as well, Lev_20:10. Moses commands both to be put to death.

"And a man who commits adultery with a man's wife, who commits adultery with the wife of his neighbor, the adulterer and the adulteress dying shall die."

The Targum: and the Jews say (b), strangling was thus performed; they that were strangled were fixed up to their knees in dung, and then they put a hard napkin within a soft one, and rolled it about his neck, and one drew it to him this way, and another drew it to him that way, until he expired: and there is no unlawful copulation punished with strangling, according to Maimonides (c), but lying with another man's wife; and who observes, that the death which is spoken of in the law absolutely, that is, without specifying any kind of death, is strangling; but stoning seems rather meant, agreeably to Deu_22:24.

(q) Misn. Sota, c. 9. sect. 9. (r) Misn. ib c. 9. sect. 15. T. Bab. Sanhedrin, fol. 97. 1. (b) Misn. Sanhedrin, c. 7. sect. 3. (c) Hilchot lssure Biah, c. 1. sect. 6.

---

8. And again he stooped down, and wrote on the ground.

Greek/Transliteration
8. Καὶ πάλιν κάτω κύψας ἔγραφεν εἰς τὴν γῆν.

8. Kai palin kato kupsas egraphen eis tein gein.

Hebrew/Transliteration
ח. וַיִּשְׁתּוֹחַח שֵׁנִית וַיָּתָר עוֹד עַל-הָאָרֶץ:

8. Va•yish•to•chach she•nit vay•tav od al - ha•a•retz.

---

9. And they which heard it, being convicted by their own conscience, went out one by one, beginning at the eldest, even unto the last: and Jesus was left alone, and the woman standing in the midst.

Greek/Transliteration

9. Οἱ δέ, ἀκούσαντες, καὶ ὑπὸ τῆς συνειδήσεως ἐλεγχόμενοι, ἐξήρχοντο εἷς καθ᾽ εἷς, ἀρξάμενοι ἀπὸ τῶν πρεσβυτέρων· καὶ κατελείφθη μόνος ὁ Ἰησοῦς, καὶ ἡ γυνὴ ἐν μέσῳ οὖσα.

9. 'Oi de, akousantes, kai 'upo teis suneideiseos elegchomenoi, exeirchonto 'eis kath 'eis, arxamenoi apo ton presbuteron. kai kateleiphthei monos 'o Yeisous, kai 'ei gunei en meso ousa.

Hebrew/Transliteration

ט. וְהֵם כְּשָׁמְעָם אֶת־זֹאת וַיַּךְ לִבָּם אֹתָם יָצְאוּ אִישׁ אִישׁ מִזָּקֵן וְעַד־צָעִיר וַיִּוָּתֵר יֵשׁוּעַ לְבַדּוֹ וְהָאִשָּׁה עֹמֶדֶת בְּתָוֶךְ:

9. Ve•hem ke•shom•am et - zot va•yach li•bam o•tam yatz•oo eesh eesh mi•za•ken ve•ad - tza•eer va•yi•va•ter Yeshua le•va•do ve•ha•ee•sha o•me•det ba•ta•vech.

---

10. When Jesus had lifted up himself, and saw none but the woman, he said unto her, Woman, where are those thine accusers? hath no man condemned thee?

Greek/Transliteration

10. Ἀνακύψας δὲ ὁ Ἰησοῦς, καὶ μηδένα θεασάμενος πλὴν τῆς γυναικός, εἶπεν αὐτῇ, Ποῦ εἰσιν ἐκεῖνοι οἱ κατήγοροί σου; Οὐδείς σε κατέκρινεν;

10. Anakupsas de 'o Yeisous, kai meidena theasamenos plein teis gunaikos, eipen autei, Pou eisin ekeinoi 'oi kateigoroi sou? Oudeis se katekrinen?

Hebrew/Transliteration

י. וַיָּקָם יֵשׁוּעַ וַיַּרְא כִּי אֵין אִישׁ בִּלְתִּי הָאִשָּׁה לְבַדָּהּ וַיֹּאמֶר אִשָּׁה אַיֵּה הֵם שֹׂטְנַיִךְ הֲכִי לֹא הִרְשִׁיעֵךְ אִישׁ:

10. Va•ya•kom Yeshua va•yar ki eyn eesh bil•tee ha•ee•sha le•va•da va•yo•mar ee•sha a•ye hem sit•na•yich ha•chi lo hir•shi•ech eesh?

---

11. She said, No man, Lord. And Jesus said unto her, Neither do I condemn thee: go, and sin no more.

Greek/Transliteration

11. Ἡ δὲ εἶπεν, Οὐδείς, κύριε. Εἶπεν δὲ ὁ Ἰησοῦς, Οὐδὲ ἐγώ σε κρίνω· πορεύου καὶ μηκέτι ἁμάρτανε.

11. 'Ei de eipen, Oudeis, kurie. Eipen de 'o Yeisous, Oude ego se krino.
poreuou kai meiketi 'amartane.

Hebrew/Transliteration

יא. וַתֹּאמֶר אֵין גַּם-אֶחָד אָדֹנִי וַיֹּאמֶר אֵלֶיהָ יֵשׁוּעַ גַּם-אֲנִי לֹא אַרְשִׁיעֵךְ לְכִי לְבֵיתֵךְ וְאַל-תֶּחֱטָאִי
עוֹד:

11. Va•to•mer eyn gam - e•chad Adoni va•yo•mer e•le•ha Yeshua gam - ani lo
ar•shi•ech le•chi le•vey•tech ve•al - te•chet•ee od.

---

12. Then spake Jesus again unto them, saying, I am the light of the world: he
that followeth me shall not walk in darkness, but shall have the light of life.

Greek/Transliteration
12. Πάλιν οὖν αὐτοῖς ὁ Ἰησοῦς ἐλάλησεν λέγων, Ἐγώ εἰμι τὸ φῶς τοῦ
κόσμου· ὁ ἀκολουθῶν ἐμοὶ οὐ μὴ περιπατήσῃ ἐν τῇ σκοτίᾳ, ἀλλ᾽ ἕξει τὸ φῶς
τῆς ζωῆς.

12. Palin oun autois 'o Yeisous elaleisen legon, Ego eimi to phos tou kosmou.
'o akolouthon emoi ou mei peripateisei en tei skotia, all 'exei to phos teis zoeis.

Hebrew/Transliteration
יב. וַיּוֹסֶף יֵשׁוּעַ וַיְדַבֵּר אֲלֵיהֶם לֵאמֹר אָנֹכִי אוֹר הָעוֹלָם הַהֹלֵךְ אַחֲרַי לֹא יֵלֵךְ בַּחֹשֶׁךְ כִּי-לוֹ אוֹר
הַחַיִּים:

12. Va•yo•sef Yeshua va•y`da•ber aley•hem le•mor ano•chi or ha•o•lam
ha•ho•lech a•cha•rai lo ye•lech ba•cho•shech ki - lo or ha•cha•yim.

Rabbinic Jewish Commentary
Which is אור העולם, "the light of the world", as Aben Ezra in Psa_19:8 rightly calls
it: thus on occasion of the water in Jacob's well, he discoursed of living water; and
upon the Jews at Capernaum mentioning the manna, he treated at large concerning
himself as the bread of life: and he might also make use of this character, and
apply it to himself, with a view to some passages in the Old Testament, which
speak of him under the metaphor of the sun, as Psa_84:11, and represent him as
the light; and the Jews (t) themselves say, that light is one of the names of the
Messiah; and God himself is called by them, the light of the world (u): and
likewise he may have regard to those pompous titles and characters, which the
Jewish Rabbi's assumed arrogantly to themselves, and oppose himself to them; for
they not only called Moses their master, אור העולם, "the light of the world" (w),
and also the law of Moses (x), but their Rabbi's as well.

Also we read, "It was taught: The light which was created in the six days of
Creation cannot illumine by day, because it would eclipse the light of the sun, nor
by night, because it was created only to illumine by day. Then where is it? It is
stored up for the righteous in the Messianic future, as it says, 'Moreover the light

of the moon shall be as the light of the sun, and the light of the sun shall be sevenfold, as the light of the seven days (Isaiah 30:26)."
(Genesis Rabbah 3:6, Soncino Press Edition)

The Midrash Rabbah identifies Messiah as "Yinnon",
"The School of R. Jannai said: His name is *Yinnon*, for it is written, Before the sun was, his name is *Yinnon* (Ps. 72:17).
(Lamentations Rabbah 1:51, Soncino Press Edition)

The Midrash Rabbah identifies Micah 4:2 as Messianic,
"Moses asked: 'shall they remain in pledge forever?' G-d replied: 'No, only Until the sun appears', that is, till the coming of the Messiah; for it says, *But unto you that fear My name shall the sun of righteousness arise with healing in its wings.*"
(Exodus Rabbah 31:10, Soncino Press Edition)

Rashi says, "The King Messiah, who is compared to light, as it is stated "I have set up a lamp for my anointed," and Elijah the prophet, who is true, a faithful prophet.
(Rashi on Psalm 43:3, Judaica Press)

The book of Daniel says,
"He reveals the deep and secret things, he knows what is in the darkness, and the light dwells with him. (Daniel 2:22)

The Midrash Rabbah comments on this passage,
"R. Abba of Serungayya said: And the light dwells with him "alludes to the royal Messiah. " (Genesis Rabbah 1:6, Soncino Press Edition)

The Midrash Rabbah identifies the name of the Messiah as the Nehirah, Light,
"The School of R. Jannai said: His name is *Yinnon*, for it is written, E'er the sun was, his name is *Yinnon* (Ps. 72:17). R. Biba of Sergunieh said: His name is *Nehirah (LIGHT)*, as it is stated, And the light (nehorah) dwelleth with Him (Dan. 2:22) . . .R. Judah b. R. Simon said in the name of R. Samuel b. R. Isaac: King Messiah, whether he be of those still living or of those who are dead, bears the name of David." (Lamentations Rabbah 1:51, Soncino Press Edition)

Pesikta Rabbai makes an incredible statement,
"What is meant by *'in Thy light do we see light'*? What light is it that the congregation of Israel looks for as from a watchtower? It is the light of Messiah, of which it is said, *'And God saw the light that it was good'* (Gen 1:4). This verse proves that the Holy One, blessed be He, contemplated the Messiah and his works before the world was created, and then under His throne of glory put away His Messiah until the time of the generation in which he will appear. Satan asked the Holy One, blessed be He, for whom is the light which is put away under Thy throne of glory? God replied: For him who will turn thee back and put thee to utter shame. Satan said: Master of the universe, show him to me. God replied: Come and see him. And when he saw him, Satan was shaken, and he fell upon his face and said: Surely this is the Messiah who will cause me and all the counterparts in heaven of the princes of the earth's nations to be swallowed up in Gehenna...in

that hour all the princely counterparts of the nations, in agitation, will say to Him: Master of the universe, who is this through whose power we are to be swallowed up? What is his name? What kind of being is he?"
(Pesikta Rabbati 36.1, Yale University Press, pg. 677-678)

Hanukkah is a time of light piercing the darkness. This is the time to shine, to go against the flow, to withstand the forces around us pressuring us to conform to the pattern of this world. This is the time to re-dedicate our lives and our bodies to be Temples for HaShem, to cleanse it from all impurity. We are called to be the Moon, reflecting the Light of the Messiah to a dark world. R' Tzvi Elimelech Shapira says,

"Each Chanukkah at the time of the lighting the candles, the concealed light of Messiah is revealed . . ."
(Benei Issachar, Kislev-Tevet 2, 16, cited in The Concealed Light, Tsvi Sadan, Vine of David, pg. 159)

(t) Bereshit Rabba, fol. 1. 3. Echa Rabbati, fol. 50. 2. & Jarchi in Psal xliii. 3. (u) Bemidbar Rabba, sect. 15. fol. 217. 2. (w) Tzeror Hammor, fol. 114. 3. (x) T. Bab. Bava Bathra, fol. 4. 1.

---

13. The Pharisees therefore said unto him, Thou bearest record of thyself; thy record is not true.

Greek/Transliteration
13. Εἶπον οὖν αὐτῷ οἱ Φαρισαῖοι, Σὺ περὶ σεαυτοῦ μαρτυρεῖς· ἡ μαρτυρία σου οὐκ ἔστιν ἀληθής.

13. Eipon oun auto 'oi Pharisaioi, Su peri seautou martureis. 'ei marturia sou ouk estin aleitheis.

Hebrew/Transliteration
:יג. וַיֹּאמְרוּ אֵלָיו הַפְּרוּשִׁים אַתָּה מֵעִיד עֵדוּת לְנַפְשֶׁךָ עֵדוּתְךָ לֹא נֶאֱמָנָה

13. Va•yom•roo elav ha•P`roo•shim ata me•eed e•doot le•naf•she•cha e•doot•cha lo ne•e•ma•na.

---

14. Jesus answered and said unto them, Though I bear record of myself, yet my record is true: for I know whence I came, and whither I go; but ye cannot tell whence I come, and whither I go.

Greek/Transliteration
14. Ἀπεκρίθη Ἰησοῦς καὶ εἶπεν αὐτοῖς, Κἂν ἐγὼ μαρτυρῶ περὶ ἐμαυτοῦ, ἀληθής ἐστιν ἡ μαρτυρία μου· ὅτι οἶδα πόθεν ἦλθον, καὶ ποῦ ὑπάγω· ὑμεῖς δὲ οὐκ οἴδατε πόθεν ἔρχομαι, καὶ ποῦ ὑπάγω.

14. Apekrithei Yeisous kai eipen autois, Kan ego marturo peri emautou, aleitheis estin 'ei marturia mou. 'oti oida pothen eilthon, kai pou 'upago. 'umeis de ouk oidate pothen erchomai, kai pou 'upago.

יד. וַיַּעַן יֵשׁוּעַ וַיֹּאמֶר אֲלֵיהֶם אַף אִם-אֲנִי מֵעִיד לְנַפְשִׁי עֵדוּתִי נֶאֱמָנָה כִּי-יָדַעְתִּי מֵאַיִן בָּאתִי וּלְאָן אֲנִי הֹלֵךְ וְאַתֶּם אֵינְכֶם יֹדְעִים מֵאַיִן בָּאתִי וּלְאָן אֲנִי הֹלֵךְ:

14. Va•ya•an Yeshua va•yo•mer aley•hem af eem - ani me•eed le•naf•shi e•doo•ti ne•e•ma•na ki - ya•da•a•ti me•a•yin ba•ti ool•an ani ho•lech ve•a•tem eyn•chem yod•eem me•a•yin ba•ti ool•an ani ho•lech.

Rabbinic Jewish Commentary
See John 5:31 for commentary on this passage.

---

15. Ye judge after the flesh; I judge no man.

Greek/Transliteration
15. Ὑμεῖς κατὰ τὴν σάρκα κρίνετε· ἐγὼ οὐ κρίνω οὐδένα.

15. 'Umeis kata tein sarka krinete. ego ou krino oudena.

Hebrew/Transliteration
טו. אַתֶּם דָּנִים לְעֵינֵי בָשָׂר וַאֲנִי אֵינֶנִּי דָן אַף לֹא-לְאֶחָד:

15. Atem da•nim le•ei•ney va•sar va•a•ni ey•ne•ni dan af lo - la•e•chad.

---

16. And yet if I judge, my judgment is true: for I am not alone, but I and the Father that sent me.

Greek/Transliteration
16. Καὶ ἐὰν κρίνω δὲ ἐγώ, ἡ κρίσις ἡ ἐμὴ ἀληθής ἐστιν· ὅτι μόνος οὐκ εἰμί, ἀλλ᾿ ἐγὼ καὶ ὁ πέμψας με πατήρ.

16. Kai ean krino de ego, 'ei krisis 'ei emei aleitheis estin. 'oti monos ouk eimi, all ego kai 'o pempsas me pateir.

Hebrew/Transliteration
טז. וְאַף לוּ-דָן הָיִיתִי דִינִי דִין אֱמֶת כִּי אֵינֶנִּי לְבַדִּי כִּי אִם-אֲנִי וְהָאָב אֲשֶׁר שְׁלָחָנִי:

16. Ve•af loo - dan ha•yi•ti di•ni din emet ki ey•ne•ni le•va•di ki eem - ani ve•ha•Av asher sh`la•cha•ni.

---

17. It is also written in your law, that the testimony of two men is true.

Greek/Transliteration
17. Καὶ ἐν τῷ νόμῳ δὲ τῷ ὑμετέρῳ γέγραπται ὅτι δύο ἀνθρώπων ἡ μαρτυρία ἀληθής ἐστιν.

17. Kai en to nomo de to 'umetero gegraptai 'oti duo anthropon 'ei marturia aleitheis estin.

Hebrew/Transliteration
יז. וְגַם בְּתוֹרַתְכֶם כָּתוּב כִּי עַל-פִּי שְׁנַיִם עֵדִים יָקוּם דָּבָר:

17. Ve•gam be•to•rat•chem ka•toov ki al - pi sh`na•yim e•dim ya•koom da•var.

Rabbinic Jewish Commentary
The Torah of Moses, which was given unto them, and they boasted of; the passage referred to is in Deu_19:15; see also Deu_17:6; where though what follows is not to be found in so many words, yet the sense is there expressed.

Concerning which the Jewish writers say (y),

"They used not to determine any judiciary matter by the mouth of one witness, neither pecuniary causes, nor causes of life and death, as it is said, Deu_17:6. It is asked (z) in their oral law, if the testimony of two men stand, why does the Scripture particularly mention three? (for no other reason) but to compare or equal three with two, that as three convict two of a falsehood, two may also convict three."

On which one of their commentators (a) has this observation, taking notice of Deu_19:18, which speaks of a single witness;

"Mar (a Rabbi) says, wherever it is said a "witness", it is to be understood of two, unless the Scripture particularly specifies one."

In the case of a wife suspected of adultery, and in the business of striking off the neck of the heifer in case of murder, they admitted of one witness (b).

(y) Maimon. Hilchot Eduth. c. 5. sect. 1. (z) Misn. Maccot. c. 1. sect. 7. (a) Bartenora in ib. (b) Maimon. Hilchot Eduth, ib. sect. 2.

---

18. I am one that bear witness of myself, and the Father that sent me beareth witness of me.

Greek/Transliteration
18. Ἐγώ εἰμι ὁ μαρτυρῶν περὶ ἐμαυτοῦ, καὶ μαρτυρεῖ περὶ ἐμοῦ ὁ πέμψας με πατήρ.

18. Ego eimi 'o marturon peri emautou, kai marturei peri emou 'o pempsas me pateir.

Hebrew/Transliteration

:יח. אֲנִי הוּא הַמֵּעִיד עֵדוּת לְנַפְשִׁי וְאָבִי אֲשֶׁר שְׁלָחַנִי גַם-הוּא לִי לְעֵד

18. Ani hoo ha•me•eed e•doot le•naf•shi ve•Avi asher sh`la•cha•ni gam - hoo li le•ed.

---

19. Then said they unto him, Where is thy Father? Jesus answered, Ye neither know me, nor my Father: if ye had known me, ye should have known my Father also.

Greek/Transliteration

19. Ἔλεγον οὖν αὐτῷ, Ποῦ ἐστιν ὁ πατήρ σου; Ἀπεκρίθη Ἰησοῦς, Οὔτε ἐμὲ οἴδατε, οὔτε τὸν πατέρα μου· εἰ ἐμὲ ᾔδειτε, καὶ τὸν πατέρα μου ᾔδειτε ἄν.

19. Elegon oun auto, Pou estin 'o pateir sou? Apekrithei Yeisous, Oute eme oidate, oute ton patera mou. ei eme eideite, kai ton patera mou eideite an.

Hebrew/Tranliteration

יט. וַיֹּאמְרוּ אֵלָיו אָבִיךְ אַיּוֹ וַיַּעַן יֵשׁוּעַ לֹא יְדַעְתֶּם גַם-אֹתִי וְגַם-לֹא אֶת-אָבִי לוּ יְדַעְתֶּם אֹתִי אָז יְדַעְתֶּם גַם אֶת:אָבִי -

19. Va•yom•roo elav Avi•cha ayo va•ya•an Yeshua lo ye•da•a•tem gam - o•ti ve•gam – lo et - Avi loo ye•da•a•tem o•ti az ye•da•a•tem gam et - Avi.

---

20. These words spake Jesus in the treasury, as he taught in the temple: and no man laid hands on him; for his hour was not yet come.

Greek/Transliteration

20. Ταῦτα τὰ ῥήματα ἐλάλησεν ὁ Ἰησοῦς ἐν τῷ γαζοφυλακίῳ, διδάσκων ἐν τῷ ἱερῷ· καὶ οὐδεὶς ἐπίασεν αὐτόν, ὅτι οὔπω ἐληλύθει ἡ ὥρα αὐτοῦ.

20. Tauta ta 'reimata elaleisen 'o Yeisous en to gazophulakio, didaskon en to 'iero. kai oudeis epiasen auton, 'oti oupo eleiluthei 'ei 'ora autou.

Hebrew/Transliteration

כ. כַּדְּבָרִים הָאֵלֶּה דִּבֶּר יֵשׁוּעַ בְּבֵית הָאוֹצָר כַּאֲשֶׁר לִמֵּד בַּמִּקְדָּשׁ וְלֹא-תְפָשׂוֹ אִישׁ כִּי עוֹד לֹא-בָּאָה :עִתּוֹ

20. Ka•d`va•rim ha•e•le di•ber Yeshua be•veit ha•o•tzar ka•a•sher li•med ba•mik•dash ve•lo - te•fa•so eesh ki od lo - va•ah ee•to.

214

21. Then said Jesus again unto them, I go my way, and ye shall seek me, and shall die in your sins: whither I go, ye cannot come.

Greek/Transliteration
21. Εἶπεν οὖν πάλιν αὐτοῖς ὁ Ἰησοῦς, Ἐγὼ ὑπάγω, καὶ ζητήσετέ με, καὶ ἐν τῇ ἁμαρτίᾳ ὑμῶν ἀποθανεῖσθε· ὅπου ἐγὼ ὑπάγω, ὑμεῖς οὐ δύνασθε ἐλθεῖν.

21. Eipen oun palin autois 'o Yeisous, Ego 'upago, kai zeiteisete me, kai en tei 'amartia 'umon apothaneisthe. 'opou ego 'upago, 'umeis ou dunasthe elthein.

Hebrew/Transliteration
כא. וַיּוֹסֶף יֵשׁוּעַ וַיֹּאמֶר אֲלֵיהֶם אֲנִי אֵלֵךְ לִי וְאַתֶּם תְּבַקְשׁוּנִי וּבְחַטֹּאתֵיכֶם תָּמוּתוּ וְאֶל-אֲשֶׁר אֲנִי הֹלֵךְ - אַתֶּם לֹא:תוּכְלוּ לָבֹא שָׁמָּה

21. Va•yo•sef Yeshua va•yo•mer aley•hem ani e•lech li ve•a•tem te•vak•shoo•ni oov•cha•to•tey•chem ta•moo•too ve•el - asher ani ho•lech atem lo - tooch•loo la•vo sha•ma.

---

22. Then said the Jews, Will he kill himself? because he saith, Whither I go, ye cannot come.

Greek/Transliteration
22. Ἔλεγον οὖν οἱ Ἰουδαῖοι, Μήτι ἀποκτενεῖ ἑαυτόν, ὅτι λέγει, Ὅπου ἐγὼ ὑπάγω, ὑμεῖς οὐ δύνασθε ἐλθεῖν;

22. Elegon oun 'oi Youdaioi, Meiti apoktenei 'eauton, 'oti legei, 'Opou ego 'upago, 'umeis ou dunasthe elthein?

Hebrew/Transliteration
כב. וַיֹּאמְרוּ הַיְּהוּדִים הֲיְאַבֵּד נַפְשׁוֹ בְּיָדָיִם כִּי אֹמֵר אֶל-אֲשֶׁר אֲנִי הֹלֵךְ אַתֶּם לֹא-תוּכְלוּ לָבֹא שָׁמָּה:

22. Va•yom•roo ha•Ye•hoo•dim hay•a•bed naf•sho be•ya•da•yim ki o•mer el - asher ani ho•lech atem lo - tooch•loo la•vo sha•ma.

---

23. And he said unto them, Ye are from beneath; I am from above: ye are of this world; I am not of this world.

Greek/Transliteration
23. Καὶ εἶπεν αὐτοῖς, Ὑμεῖς ἐκ τῶν κάτω ἐστέ, ἐγὼ ἐκ τῶν ἄνω εἰμί· ὑμεῖς ἐκ τοῦ κόσμου τούτου ἐστέ, ἐγὼ οὐκ εἰμὶ ἐκ τοῦ κόσμου τούτου.

23. Kai eipen autois, 'Umeis ek ton kato este, ego ek ton ano eimi. 'umeis ek tou kosmou toutou este, ego ouk eimi ek tou kosmou toutou.

כג. וַיֹּאמֶר אֲלֵיהֶם אַתֶּם מִשּׁוֹכְנֵי מַטָּה וַאֲנִי מִשּׁוֹכְנֵי מַעְלָה אַתֶּם מִן-הָעוֹלָם הַזֶּה וַאֲנִי אֵינֶנִּי מִן-הָעוֹלָם הַזֶּה:

23. Va•yo•mer aley•hem atem mi•shoch•ney ma•ta va•a•ni mi•shoch•ney ma•a•la atem min - ha•o•lam ha•ze va•a•ni ey•ne•ni min - ha•o•lam ha•ze.

---

24. I said therefore unto you, that ye shall die in your sins: for if ye believe not that I am he, ye shall die in your sins.

24. Εἶπον οὖν ὑμῖν ὅτι ἀποθανεῖσθε ἐν ταῖς ἁμαρτίαις ὑμῶν· ἐὰν γὰρ μὴ πιστεύσητε ὅτι ἐγώ εἰμι, ἀποθανεῖσθε ἐν ταῖς ἁμαρτίαις ὑμῶν.

24. Eipon oun 'umin 'oti apothaneisthe en tais 'amartiais 'umon. ean gar mei pisteuseite 'oti ego eimi, apothaneisthe en tais 'amartiais 'umon.

כד. לָכֵן אָמַרְתִּי לָכֶם כִּי תָמוּתוּ בְּחַטֹּאתֵיכֶם כִּי אִם-לֹא תַאֲמִינוּ-בִי כִּי-אֲנִי הוּא תָּמוּתוּ בְּחַטֹּאתֵיכֶם:

24. La•chen amar•ti la•chem ki ta•moo•too ve•cha•to•tey•chem ki eem - lo ta•a•mi•noo - vi ki - ani hoo ta•moo•too ve•cha•to•tey•chem.

Rabbinic Jewish Commentary
Dying in sin, and dying in Christ, are two widely different things. They that die in faith, die in Yeshua: they that die in unbelief, die in sin; and this is a dreadful dying; see Jos_22:20 where the Targum paraphrases it, "and he, one man", (or alone,) לֹא מוּת בְּחוּבֵיהּ, "did not die in his sins".

---

25. Then said they unto him, Who art thou? And Jesus saith unto them, Even the same that I said unto you from the beginning.

25. Ἔλεγον οὖν αὐτῷ, Σὺ τίς εἶ; Καὶ εἶπεν αὐτοῖς ὁ Ἰησοῦς, Τὴν ἀρχὴν ὅ τι καὶ λαλῶ ὑμῖν.

25. Elegon oun auto, Su tis ei? Kai eipen autois 'o Yeisous, Tein archein 'o ti kai lalo 'umin.

כה. וַיֹּאמְרוּ אֵלָיו וּמִי-זֶה אָתָּה וַיֹּאמֶר אֲלֵיהֶם יֵשׁוּעַ אֲנִי הוּא כַּאֲשֶׁר אָמַרְתִּי אֲלֵיכֶם מֵרֹאשׁ:

25. Va•yom•roo elav oo•mi - ze ata va•yo•mer aley•hem Yeshua ani hoo ka•a•sher amar•ti aley•chem me•rosh.

26. I have many things to say and to judge of you: but he that sent me is true; and I speak to the world those things which I have heard of him.

Greek/Transliteration
26. Πολλὰ ἔχω περὶ ὑμῶν λαλεῖν καὶ κρίνειν· ἀλλ᾽ ὁ πέμψας με ἀληθής ἐστιν, κἀγὼ ἃ ἤκουσα παρ᾽ αὐτοῦ, ταῦτα λέγω εἰς τὸν κόσμον.

26. Polla echo peri 'umon lalein kai krinein. all 'o pempsas me aleitheis estin, kago 'a eikousa par autou, tauta lego eis ton kosmon.

Hebrew/Transliteration
כו. יֶשׁ-לִי רַבּוֹת לְדַבֵּר וְלִשְׁפֹּט עֲלֵיכֶם אָכֵן שֹׁלְחִי נֶאֱמָן הוּא וְאֶת-הַדָּבָר אֲשֶׁר אֶשְׁמַע מִמֶּנּוּ אֹתוֹ אֲדַבֵּר אֶל:הָעוֹלָם -

26. Yesh - li ra•bot le•da•ber ve•lish•pot aley•chem a•chen shol•chi ne•e•man hoo ve•et - ha•da•var asher esh•ma mi•me•noo o•to ada•ber el - ha•o•lam.

---

27. They understood not that he spake to them of the Father.

Greek/Transliteration
27. Οὐκ ἔγνωσαν ὅτι τὸν πατέρα αὐτοῖς ἔλεγεν.

27. Ouk egnosan 'oti ton patera autois elegen.

Hebrew/Transliteration
כז. וְהֵם לֹא הֵבִינוּ זֹאת כִּי עַל-הָאָב דִּבֶּר אֲלֵיהֶם:

27. Ve•hem lo he•vi•noo zot ki al - ha•Av di•ber aley•hem.

---

28. Then said Jesus unto them, When ye have lifted up the Son of man, then shall ye know that I am he, and that I do nothing of myself; but as my Father hath taught me, I speak these things.

Greek/Transliteration
28. Εἶπεν οὖν αὐτοῖς ὁ Ἰησοῦς, Ὅταν ὑψώσητε τὸν υἱὸν τοῦ ἀνθρώπου, τότε γνώσεσθε ὅτι ἐγώ εἰμι, καὶ ἀπ᾽ ἐμαυτοῦ ποιῶ οὐδέν, ἀλλὰ καθὼς ἐδίδαξέν με ὁ πατήρ μου, ταῦτα λαλῶ·

28. Eipen oun autois 'o Yeisous, 'Otan 'upsoseite ton 'wion tou anthropou, tote gnosesthe 'oti ego eimi, kai ap emautou poio ouden, alla kathos edidaxen me 'o pateir mou, tauta lalo.

Hebrew/Transliteration
כח. וַיֹּאמֶר יֵשׁוּעַ כַּאֲשֶׁר תַּגְבִּיהוּ אֶת-בֶּן-הָאָדָם לְמַעְלָה אָז תַּכִּירוּ כִּי-אֲנִי הוּא וְלֹא עָשִׂיתִי מֵאוּמָה מִלִּבִּי כִּי:אִם-הַדָּבָר אֲשֶׁר הוֹרַנִי הָאָב אֹתוֹ אֲנִי מְדַבֵּר

28. Va•yo•mer Yeshua ka•a•sher tag•bi•hoo et - Ben - ha•adam le•ma•a•la az ta•ki•roo ki - ani hoo ve•lo a•si•ti me•oo•ma mi•li•bi ki eem - ha•da•var asher ho•ra•ni ha•Av o•to ani me•da•ber.

---

29. And he that sent me is with me: the Father hath not left me alone; for I do always those things that please him.

Greek/Transliteration
29. καὶ ὁ πέμψας με μετ᾽ ἐμοῦ ἐστιν· οὐκ ἀφῆκέν με μόνον ὁ πατήρ, ὅτι ἐγὼ τὰ ἀρεστὰ αὐτῷ ποιῶ πάντοτε.

29. kai 'o pempsas me met emou estin. ouk apheiken me monon 'o pateir, 'oti ego ta aresta auto poio pantote.

Hebrew/Transliteration
כט. וְשֹׁלְחִי עִמָּדִי הוּא לֹא זָנַח אֹתִי גַּלְמוּד כִּי אֶת-הַטּוֹב בְּעֵינָיו אֲנִי עֹשֶׂה תָּמִיד:

29. Ve•shol•chi ee•ma•di hoo lo za•nach o•ti gal•mood ki et - ha•tov be•ey•nav ani o•se ta•mid.

---

30. As he spake these words, many believed on him.

Greek/Transliteration
30. Ταῦτα αὐτοῦ λαλοῦντος πολλοὶ ἐπίστευσαν εἰς αὐτόν.

30. Tauta autou lalountos polloi episteusan eis auton.

Hebrew/Transliteration
ל. וַיְהִי כְּדַבְּרוֹ אֶת-הַדְּבָרִים הָאֵלֶּה וַיַּאֲמִינוּ-בוֹ רַבִּים:

30. Vay•hi ke•dab•ro et - ha•d`va•rim ha•e•le va•ya•a•mi•noo - vo ra•bim.

---

31. Then said Jesus to those Jews which believed on him, If ye continue in my word, then are ye my disciples indeed;

Greek/Transliteration
31. Ἔλεγεν οὖν ὁ Ἰησοῦς πρὸς τοὺς πεπιστευκότας αὐτῷ Ἰουδαίους, Ἐὰν ὑμεῖς μείνητε ἐν τῷ λόγῳ τῷ ἐμῷ, ἀληθῶς μαθηταί μου ἐστέ·

31. Elegen oun 'o Yeisous pros tous pepisteukotas auto Youdaious, Ean 'umeis meineite en to logo to emo, aleithos matheitai mou este.

לא. וַיֹּאמֶר יֵשׁוּעַ אֶל-הַיְּהוּדִים הַמַּאֲמִינִים בּוֹ אִם-תַּעַמְדוּ בִדְבָרִי אָז תִּהְיוּ תַלְמִידַי בֶּאֱמֶת וּבְתָמִים:

31. Va•yo•mer Yeshua el - ha•Ye•hoo•dim ha•ma•a•mi•nim bo eem -
ta•am•doo bid•va•rai az ti•hi•yoo tal•mi•dai be•e•met oov•ta•mim.

---

32. And ye shall know the truth, and the truth shall make you free.

32. καὶ γνώσεσθε τὴν ἀλήθειαν, καὶ ἡ ἀλήθεια ἐλευθερώσει ὑμᾶς.

32. kai gnosesthe tein aleitheyan, kai 'ei aleitheya eleutherosei 'umas.

לב. כִּי תַשְׂכִּילוּ אֶת-הָאֱמֶת וְהָאֱמֶת תַּעֲשֶׂה אֶתְכֶם חָפְשִׁים:

32. Ki tas•ki•loo et - ha•e•met ve•ha•e•met ta•a•se et•chem chof•shim.

---

33. They answered him, We be Abraham's seed, and were never in bondage
to any man: how sayest thou, Ye shall be made free?

33. Ἀπεκρίθησαν αὐτῷ, Σπέρμα Ἀβραάμ ἐσμεν, καὶ οὐδενὶ δεδουλεύκαμεν
πώποτε· πῶς σὺ λέγεις ὅτι Ἐλεύθεροι γενήσεσθε;

33. Apekritheisan auto, Sperma Abra'am esmen, kai oudeni dedouleukamen
popote. pos su legeis 'oti Eleutheroi geneisesthe?

לג. וַיַּעֲנוּ אֹתוֹ הֵן זֶרַע אַבְרָהָם אֲנַחְנוּ וְלֹא-הָיִינוּ עֲבָדִים לְאָדָם מֵעוֹלָם וְאֵיךְ תֹּאמַר אַתָּה כִּי-חָפְשִׁים
תִּהְיוּ:

33. Va•ya•a•noo o•to hen ze•ra Avraham a•nach•noo ve•lo - ha•yi•noo
a•va•dim le•a•dam me•o•lam ve•eych to•mar ata ki - chof•shim ti•hi•yoo?

Rabbinic Jewish Commentary
This the Jews always valued themselves upon, and reckoned themselves, on this
account, upon a level with the nobles and the princes of the earth.

"Says R. Akiba (c), even the poor of Israel are to be considered as if they were בני
חורין, "noblemen", that are fallen from their substance, because they are the
children of Abraham, Isaac, and Jacob".

(c) Misn. Bava Kama, c. 8. sect. 6. & T. Bab. Bava Kama, fol. 86. 1. & 91. 1.

34. Jesus answered them, Verily, verily, I say unto you, Whosoever committeth sin is the servant of sin.

Greek/Transliteration
34. Ἀπεκρίθη αὐτοῖς ὁ Ἰησοῦς, Ἀμὴν ἀμὴν λέγω ὑμῖν, ὅτι πᾶς ὁ ποιῶν τὴν ἁμαρτίαν δοῦλός ἐστιν τῆς ἁμαρτίας.

34. Apekrithei autois 'o Yeisous, Amein amein lego 'umin, 'oti pas 'o poion tein 'amartian doulos estin teis 'amartias.

Hebrew/Transliteration
:לד. וַיַּעַן אֹתָם יֵשׁוּעַ אָמֵן אָמֵן אֲנִי אֹמֵר לָכֶם כָּל-אִישׁ אֲשֶׁר יַעֲשֶׂה חֵטְא עֶבֶד לַחֵטְא הוּא

34. Va•ya•an o•tam Yeshua Amen amen ani o•mer la•chem kol - eesh asher ya•a•se chet eved la•chet hoo.

Rabbinic Jewish Commentary
Of the Messiah they say,
"This is through the mystic influence of the *Vau*, who is always in readiness to pour on it blessing, and who is the "son of freedom" and "son of Jubilee", who obtains for slaves their freedom. He is a scion of the supernal world, and the author of all life, of all illuminations, and all exalted states."
(Zohar 1:124b, Soncino Press Edition)

---

35. And the servant abideth not in the house for ever: but the Son abideth ever.

Greek/Transliteration
35. Ὁ δὲ δοῦλος οὐ μένει ἐν τῇ οἰκίᾳ εἰς τὸν αἰῶνα· ὁ υἱὸς μένει εἰς τὸν αἰῶνα.

35. 'O de doulos ou menei en tei oikia eis ton aiona. 'o 'wios menei eis ton aiona.

Hebrew/Transliteration
:לה. וְהָעֶבֶד לֹא-יֵשֵׁב בַּבַּיִת עַד-עוֹלָם אַךְ הַבֵּן יֵשֵׁב שָׁם עַד-עוֹלָם

35. Ve•ha•e•ved lo - ye•shev ba•ba•yit ad - o•lam ach ha•Ben ye•shev sham ad - o•lam.

Rabbinic Jewish Commentary
The allusion is to the case of servants in common; and, in a literal sense, it is true both of good and bad servants: good servants do not always continue in their master's house; even an Hebrew servant, that loved his master, and would not go out free at the end of his servitude; and who, after having his ear bored, is said to serve him for ever, Exo_21:6; yet that "for ever" was but until the year of jubilee, whether near or remote, as the Jewish commentators (d) in general explain it;

Nay, if his master died before that time, he went out free: he was not obliged to serve his son or heirs; and so say the Misnic Rabbi's (e):

"One that is bored is obtained by boring, and he possesses himself (or becomes free) by the year of jubilee, and by the death of his master."

And to this agrees what Maimonides (f) says;

"He that has served six years, and will not go out, lo, this is bored, and he serves until the year of jubilee, or until his master dies; and although he leaves a son, he that is bored does not serve the son; which may be learned from the letter of the words, "he shall serve him", not his son, "for ever", until the jubilee: from whence it appears, that he that is bored does not possess himself (or is free) but by the jubilee, and by the death of his master."

And one of their writers (g) observes, that the word rendered, "shall serve him", is by Gematry, and not his son. And among the Romans, good servants were oftentimes made free, and bad ones were turned out, and put into a work house, to grind corn in mills, a sort of bridewell; and such evil servants may more especially be respected, since Yeshua is speaking of servants of sin.

(d) Jarchi, Aben Ezra, & ben Gersom in Exod. xxi. 6. (e) Misn. Kiddushin, c. 1. sect. 1. (f) Hilchot Abadim, c. 3. sect. 6, 7. (g) Baal Hatturim in Exod. xxi. 6.

---

36. If the Son therefore shall make you free, ye shall be free indeed.

Greek/Transliteration
36. Ἐὰν οὖν ὁ υἱὸς ὑμᾶς ἐλευθερώσῃ, ὄντως ἐλεύθεροι ἔσεσθε.

36. Ean oun 'o 'wios 'umas eleutherosei, ontos eleutheroi esesthe.

Hebrew/Transliteration
:לו. לָכֵן אִם-הַבֵּן יַעֲשֶׂה אֶתְכֶם חָפְשִׁים חָפְשִׁים תִּהְיוּ אֶל-נָכוֹן

36. La•chen eem - ha•Ben ya•a•se et•chem chof•shim chof•shim ti•hi•yoo el - na•chon.

Rabbinic Jewish Commentary
Of the Messiah they say,
"This is through the mystic influence of the *Vau*, who is always in readiness to pour on it blessing, and who is the "son of freedom" and "son of Jubilee", who obtains for slaves their freedom. He is a scion of the supernal world, and the author of all life, of all illuminations, and all exalted states."
(Zohar 1:124b, Soncino Press Edition)

The Jews, who were partly servants, and partly free: so it is said (i),

מי שחציו עבד, "He who is half a servant", or partly a servant, and partly free, shall serve his master one day, and himself another."

And such an one, as the commentators (k) say, is one who is a servant of two partners, and is made free by one of them; or who has paid half his price to his master (for his freedom), but the other half is still due: and of one in such circumstances it is said (l), that

"He that is partly a servant, and partly free, may not eat of his master's (lamb at the passover):"

But now those who are made free by Yeshua the Son of God, they are not in part only, but are wholly free, and have a right to all the privileges of his house, to the supper of the Lord, and to every other immunity.

(h) Theophili Antecensor. Institut. Imperat. Justinian. l. 1. tit. 6. sect. 5. p. 38. (i) Misn. Gittin, c. 4. sect. 5. & Ediot, c. 1. sect. 13. (k) Maimonides, Jarchi, & Bartenora in ib. (l) Misn. Pesachim, c. 8. sect. 1.

---

37. I know that ye are Abraham's seed; but ye seek to kill me, because my word hath no place in you.

Greek/Transliteration
37. Οἶδα ὅτι σπέρμα Ἀβραάμ ἐστε· ἀλλὰ ζητεῖτέ με ἀποκτεῖναι, ὅτι ὁ λόγος ὁ ἐμὸς οὐ χωρεῖ ἐν ὑμῖν.

37. Oida 'oti sperma Abra'am este. alla zeiteite me apokteinai, 'oti 'o logos 'o emos ou chorei en 'umin.

Hebrew/Transliteration
לז. יָדַעְתִּי כִּי-זֶרַע אַבְרָהָם אַתֶּם וּבְכָל-זֹאת תְּבַקְשׁוּ אֶת-נַפְשִׁי לְקַחְתָּהּ כִּי לִדְבָרַי אֵין מְסִלּוֹת בִּלְבַבְכֶם:

37. Ya•da•a•ti ki - ze•ra Avraham atem oov•chol - zot te•vak•shoo et - naf•shi le•kach•ta ki lid•va•rai eyn me•si•lot bil•vav•chem.

---

38. I speak that which I have seen with my Father: and ye do that which ye have seen with your father.

Greek/Transliteration
38. Ἐγὼ ὃ ἑώρακα παρὰ τῷ πατρί μου, λαλῶ· καὶ ὑμεῖς οὖν ὃ ἑωράκατε παρὰ τῷ πατρὶ ὑμῶν, ποιεῖτε.

38. Ego 'o 'eoraka para to patri mou, lalo. kai 'umeis oun 'o 'eorakate para to patri 'umon, poieite.

Hebrew/Transliteration

לח. אֲנִי מְדַבֵּר אֵת אֲשֶׁר רָאִיתִי אֵצֶל הָאָב וְאַתֶּם עֹשִׂים אֵת אֲשֶׁר שְׁמַעְתֶּם מֵאֵת אֲבִיכֶם:

38. Ani me•da•ber et asher ra•ee•ti etzel ha•Av ve•a•tem o•sim et asher sh`ma•a•tem me•et avi•chem.

---

39. They answered and said unto him, Abraham is our father. Jesus saith unto them, If ye were Abraham's children, ye would do the works of Abraham.

Greek/Transliteration
39. Ἀπεκρίθησαν καὶ εἶπον αὐτῷ, Ὁ πατὴρ ἡμῶν Ἀβραάμ ἐστιν. Λέγει αὐτοῖς ὁ Ἰησοῦς, Εἰ τέκνα τοῦ Ἀβραὰμ ἦτε, τὰ ἔργα τοῦ Ἀβραὰμ ἐποιεῖτε.

39. Apekritheisan kai eipon auto, 'O pateir 'eimon Abra'am estin. Legei autois 'o Yeisous, Ei tekna tou Abra'am eite, ta erga tou Abra'am epoieite.

Hebrew/Transliteration
לט. וַיַּעֲנוּ וַיֹּאמְרוּ אֵלָיו אָבִינוּ הוּא אַבְרָהָם וַיֹּאמֶר אֲלֵיהֶם יֵשׁוּעַ לוּ הֱיִיתֶם בְּנֵי אַבְרָהָם כְּמַעֲשֵׂי אַבְרָהָם עֲשִׂיתֶם:

39. Va•ya•a•noo va•yom•roo elav avi•noo hoo Avraham va•yo•mer aley•hem Yeshua loo he•yi•tem b`ney Avraham ke•ma•a•sey Avraham asi•tem.

Rabbinic Jewish Commentary
Jesus saith unto them, if ye were Abraham's children, ye would do the works of Abraham; for who should children imitate but their parents? Abraham was a merciful, charitable, and hospitable man, as well as a man of strict justice and integrity; he feared God, believed in him, and was ready to receive every message and revelation which came from him; and they are his genuine children and offspring, who walk in the steps of his faith, charity, justice, and piety: and this is a rule which the Jews themselves give (m), whereby the seed of Abraham may be known:

"whoever is merciful to the creature (man), it is evident that he is of the seed of Abraham, our father; but whoever has not mercy on the creature, it is a clear case that he is not of the seed of Abraham our father."

And if this is a sure rule of judging, these men could not be the seed of Abraham, who were a merciless, barbarous, and cruel generation. Another of their writers (n) has this observation, agreeably to the way of reasoning Yeshua uses;

"A disciple is to be judged of according to his manners; he that walks in the ways of the Lord, he is of the disciples of Abraham, our father, seeing he is used to his manners, and learns of his works; but the disciple who is corrupt in his manners, though he is of the children of Israel, lo, he is not of the "disciples of Abraham", seeing he is not accustomed to his manners."

Whence it appears, that they say these things not to distinguish themselves from other people who claimed a descent from Abraham, as the Ishmaelites or Saracens did; as did also the Spartans or Lacedemonians; for so writes Areus their king, to Onias the high priest of the Jews,

"It is found in writing, that the Lacedemonians and Jews are brethren, and that they are of the stock of Abraham," (1 Maccab. 12:20,21)

But to distinguish those who were religious and virtuous among the Jews themselves, from those that were not; and so Yeshua means not to deny, that the Jews, though they were evil men, were the seed of Abraham, according to the flesh; but that they were not so in a spiritual sense, they did not tread in his steps, or do the works he did. The Persic version reads in the singular number, "ye would do the work of Abraham"; and if any particular work is designed, it is most likely to be the work of faith, since it was that which Abraham was famous for; and the doing of which denominated men, even Gentiles, the children of Abraham, and which the Jews were wanting in, they disbelieving and rejecting the Messiah.

(m) T. Bab. Betza, fol. 82. 2. (n) Abarbinel Naehaleth Abot, fol. 183. 1.

---

40. But now ye seek to kill me, a man that hath told you the truth, which I have heard of God: this did not Abraham.

Greek/Transliteration
40. Νῦν δὲ ζητεῖτέ με ἀποκτεῖναι, ἄνθρωπον ὃς τὴν ἀλήθειαν ὑμῖν λελάληκα, ἣν ἤκουσα παρὰ τοῦ θεοῦ· τοῦτο ᾿Αβραὰμ οὐκ ἐποίησεν.

40. Nun de zeiteite me apokteinai, anthropon 'os tein aleitheyan 'umin lelaleika, 'ein eikousa para tou theou. touto Abra'am ouk epoieisen.

Hebrew/Transliteration
מ. וְאַתֶּם מְבַקְשִׁים אֶת-נַפְשִׁי לְקַחְתָּה בַּאֲשֶׁר אֱמֶת אַגִּיד לָכֶם אֵת אֲשֶׁר שָׁמַעְתִּי מֵאֵת אֱלֹהִים כָּזֹאת לֹא עָשָׂה:אַבְרָהָם

40. Ve•a•tem me•vak•shim et - naf•shi le•kach•ta ba•a•sher emet agid la•chem et asher sha•ma•a•ti me•et Elohim ka•zot lo asa Avraham.

Rabbinic Jewish Commentary
The Jew (o) makes an objection from these words against the deity of Christ;

"You see (says he) that Jesus declares concerning himself that he is not God, but man; and so says Paul concerning him, Rom_5:15; and so Yeshua, in many places, calls himself the son of man: for do we find in any place that he calls himself God, as the Nazarenes believe."

(o) R. Isaac Chizzuk Emuna, par. 2. c. 48. p. 436. & par. 1. c. 10. p. 118.

---

41. Ye do the deeds of your father. Then said they to him, We be not born of fornication; we have one Father, even God.

Greek/Transliteration

41. Ὑμεῖς ποιεῖτε τὰ ἔργα τοῦ πατρὸς ὑμῶν. Εἶπον οὖν αὐτῷ, Ἡμεῖς ἐκ πορνείας οὐ γεγεννήμεθα· ἕνα πατέρα ἔχομεν, τὸν θεόν.

41. 'Umeis poieite ta erga tou patros 'umon. Eipon oun auto, 'Eimeis ek porneias ou gegenneimetha. 'ena patera echomen, ton theon.

Hebrew/Transliteration

מא. כְּמַעֲשֵׂי אֲבִיכֶם אַתֶּם עֹשִׂים וַיֹּאמְרוּ אֵלָיו לֹא יַלְדֵי זְנוּנִים אֲנַחְנוּ יֶשׁ-לָנוּ אָב אֶחָד אֱלֹהִים:

41. Ke•ma•a•sey avi•chem atem o•sim va•yom•roo elav lo yal•dey ze•noo•nim a•nach•noo yesh - la•noo Av e•chad Elohim.

---

42. Jesus said unto them, If God were your Father, ye would love me: for I proceeded forth and came from God; neither came I of myself, but he sent me.

Greek/Transliteration

42. Εἶπεν οὖν αὐτοῖς ὁ Ἰησοῦς, Εἰ ὁ θεὸς πατὴρ ὑμῶν ἦν, ἠγαπᾶτε ἂν ἐμέ· ἐγὼ γὰρ ἐκ τοῦ θεοῦ ἐξῆλθον καὶ ἥκω· οὐδὲ γὰρ ἀπ᾽ ἐμαυτοῦ ἐλήλυθα, ἀλλ᾽ ἐκεῖνός με ἀπέστειλεν.

42. Eipen oun autois 'o Yeisous, Ei 'o theos pateir 'umon ein, eigapate an eme. ego gar ek tou theou exeilthon kai 'eiko. oude gar ap emautou eleilutha, all ekeinos me apesteilen.

Hebrew/Transliteration

מב. וַיֹּאמֶר אֲלֵיהֶם יֵשׁוּעַ אִם אֱלֹהִים אֲבִיכֶם תֶּאֱהָבוּנִי כִּי מֵאֵת אֱלֹהִים יָצָאתִי וּמֵאִתּוֹ בָאתִי וְלֹא-מִלִּבִּי כִּי-הוּא:שְׁלָחָנִי

42. Va•yo•mer aley•hem Yeshua eem Elohim Avi•chem te•e•ha•voo•ni ki me•et Elohim ya•tza•ti oo•me•ee•to va•ti ve•lo - mi•li•bi ki - hoo sh`la•cha•ni.

---

43. Why do ye not understand my speech? even because ye cannot hear my word.

Greek/Transliteration
43. Διὰ τί τὴν λαλιὰν τὴν ἐμὴν οὐ γινώσκετε; Ὅτι οὐ δύνασθε ἀκούειν τὸν λόγον τὸν ἐμόν.

43. Dya ti tein lalyan tein emein ou ginoskete? 'Oti ou dunasthe akouein ton logon ton emon.

Hebrew/Transliteration
מג. מַדּוּעַ לֹא תָבִינוּ נִיב שְׂפָתָי אֵין זֶה כִּי אִם לֹא-תוּכְלוּן לְהַשְׂכִּיל אֶל-תּוֹרָתִי:

43. Ma•doo•a lo ta•vi•noo niv s`fa•tai eyn ze ki eem lo - tooch•loon le•has•kil el - to•ra•ti.

---

44. Ye are of your father the devil, and the lusts of your father ye will do. He was a murderer from the beginning, and abode not in the truth, because there is no truth in him. When he speaketh a lie, he speaketh of his own: for he is a liar, and the father of it.

Greek/Transliteration
44. Ὑμεῖς ἐκ τοῦ πατρὸς τοῦ διαβόλου ἐστέ, καὶ τὰς ἐπιθυμίας τοῦ πατρὸς ὑμῶν θέλετε ποιεῖν. Ἐκεῖνος ἀνθρωποκτόνος ἦν ἀπ᾽ ἀρχῆς, καὶ ἐν τῇ ἀληθείᾳ οὐχ ἕστηκεν, ὅτι οὐκ ἔστιν ἀλήθεια ἐν αὐτῷ. Ὅταν λαλῇ τὸ ψεῦδος, ἐκ τῶν ἰδίων λαλεῖ· ὅτι ψεύστης ἐστὶν καὶ ὁ πατὴρ αὐτοῦ.

44. 'Umeis ek tou patros tou dyabolou este, kai tas epithumias tou patros 'umon thelete poiein. Ekeinos anthropoktonos ein ap archeis, kai en tei aleitheia ouch 'esteiken, 'oti ouk estin aleitheya en auto. 'Otan lalei to pseudos, ek ton idion lalei. 'oti pseusteis estin kai 'o pateir autou.

Hebrew/Transliteration
מד. אַתֶּם מֵאֵת אֲבִיכֶם הַשָּׂטָן הִנְּכֶם וַתִּתְמַכְּרוּ לַעֲשׂוֹת כְּתַאֲוַת אֲבִיכֶם הוּא הָיָה רֹצֵחַ נְפָשׁוֹת מֵרֹאשׁ - וּבְמוֹ:אֱמֶת לֹא עָמַד כִּי אֱמֶת אֵין-בּוֹ כַּאֲשֶׁר יְדַבֵּר כָּזָב מִלִּבּוֹ הוּא דֹבֵר כִּי-מְשַׁקֵּר הוּא וַאֲבִי כָּל-מְשַׁקֵּר

44. Atem me•et avi•chem ha•Satan hin•chem va•tit•mak•roo la•a•sot ke•ta•a•vat avi•chem hoo ha•ya ro•tze•ach n`fa•shot me•rosh oov•mo - emet lo amad ki emet eyn - bo ka•a•sher ye•da•ber ka•zav mi•li•bo hoo do•ver ki - me•sha•ker hoo va•a•vi chol - me•sha•ker.

Rabbinic Jewish Commentary
The Syriac version renders it, "from Bereshith", which is the first word in the Hebrew Bible, and is frequently used by the Jewish Rabbins for the six days of the creation; and if Adam fell, as some think, the same day he was created, it might be

properly said that the devil was a murderer from thence. Philo (p) speaks of Eve's serpent, as ανθρωπου φονωντα, "a murderer of man"; applying to this purpose the text before referred to, Gen_3:15.

for he is a liar, and the father of it; he was a liar, as early as he was a murderer, or rather earlier; it was with a lie he deceived, and so murdered our first parents, and he has continued so ever since; he was the first author of a lie; the first lie that ever was told, was told by him; he was the first inventor of one; he was the first of that trade; in this sense the word "father" is used, Gen_4:20; so the serpent is by the Cabalistic Jews (q) called, the lip of lie, or the lying lip.

(p) De Agricultura, p. 203. (q) Lex. Cabalist. p. 724.

---

45. And because I tell you the truth, ye believe me not.

Greek/Transliteration
45. Ἐγὼ δὲ ὅτι τὴν ἀλήθειαν λέγω, οὐ πιστεύετέ μοι.

45. Ego de 'oti tein aleitheyan lego, ou pisteuete moi.

Hebrew/Transliteration
מה. וַאֲנִי כַּאֲשֶׁר אֱמֶת אֲנִי דֹבֵר לֹא תַאֲמִינוּ לִי:

45. Va•a•ni ka•a•sher emet ani do•ver lo ta•a•mi•noo li.

---

46. Which of you convinceth me of sin? And if I say the truth, why do ye not believe me?

Greek/Transliteration
46. Τίς ἐξ ὑμῶν ἐλέγχει με περὶ ἁμαρτίας; Εἰ δὲ ἀλήθειαν λέγω, διὰ τί ὑμεῖς οὐ πιστεύετέ μοι;

46. Tis ex 'umon elegchei me peri 'amartias? Ei de aleitheyan lego, dya ti 'umeis ou pisteuete moi?

Hebrew/Transliteration
מו. מִי-מִכֶּם יַכְזִיבֵנִי עַל-שֶׁמֶץ דָּבָר וְאִם דֹבֵר אֱמֶת אֲנִי מַדּוּעַ לֹא-תַאֲמִינוּ לִי:

46. Mee - mi•kem yach•zi•ve•ni al - she•metz da•var ve•eem do•ver emet ani ma•doo•a lo - ta•a•mi•noo li?

---

47. He that is of God heareth God's words: ye therefore hear them not, because ye are not of God.

Greek/Transliteration

47. Ὁ ὢν ἐκ τοῦ θεοῦ τὰ ῥήματα τοῦ θεοῦ ἀκούει· διὰ τοῦτο ὑμεῖς οὐκ ἀκούετε, ὅτι ἐκ τοῦ θεοῦ οὐκ ἐστέ.

47. 'O on ek tou theou ta 'reimata tou theou akouei. dya touto 'umeis ouk akouete, 'oti ek tou theou ouk este.

Hebrew/Transliteration

מז. מִי אֲשֶׁר מֵאֵת אֱלֹהִים הוּא יִשְׁמַע דִּבְרֵי אֱלֹהִים וְאַתֶּם לֹא תִשְׁמָעוּנִי כִּי לֹא מֵאֵת אֱלֹהִים אַתֶּם:

47. Mee asher me•et Elohim hoo yish•ma div•rey Elohim ve•a•tem lo tish•ma•oo•ni ki lo me•et Elohim atem.

---

48. Then answered the Jews, and said unto him, Say we not well that thou art a Samaritan, and hast a devil?

Greek/Transliteration

48. Ἀπεκρίθησαν οὖν οἱ Ἰουδαῖοι καὶ εἶπον αὐτῷ, Οὐ καλῶς λέγομεν ἡμεῖς ὅτι Σαμαρείτης εἶ σύ, καὶ δαιμόνιον ἔχεις;

48. Apekritheisan oun 'oi Youdaioi kai eipon auto, Ou kalos legomen 'eimeis 'oti Samareiteis ei su, kai daimonion echeis?

Hebrew/Transliteration

מח. וַיַּעֲנוּ הַיְּהוּדִים וַיֹּאמְרוּ אֵלָיו הֲלֹא הֵיטֵב דִּבַּרְנוּ כִּי שֹׁמְרוֹנִי אַתָּה וְרוּחַ רָעָה בָּךְ:

48. Va•ya•a•noo ha•Ye•hoo•dim va•yom•roo elav ha•lo hei•tev di•bar•noo ki Shom•ro•ni ata ve•roo•ach ra•ah bach?

Rabbinic Jewish Commentary

The Jews had a very ill opinion of the Samaritans, on these accounts and to call a man a Samaritan, was all one as to call him an heretic, an idolater, or an excommunicated person; for such were the Samaritans with the Jews; they charged them with corrupting the Scriptures, and with worshipping idols, which were hid in Mount Gerizim; and they give us a dreadful account of their being anathematized by Ezra, Zorobabel, and Joshua; who, they say (r),

"Gathered the whole congregation into the temple, and brought in three hundred priests, and three hundred children, and three hundred trumpets, and three hundred books of the law, in their hands; they blew the trumpets, and the Levites sung, and they anathematized the Samaritans, by the inexplicable name of God, and by the writing on tables, and with the anathema of the house of judgment, above and below; (saying,) let not any Israelite for ever eat of the fruit, or of the least morsel of a Samaritan; hence they say, whoso eateth the flesh of a Samaritan, it is all one as if he ate swine's flesh; also let not a Samaritan be made a proselyte, nor have a part in the resurrection of the dead; as it is said, "You have nothing to do with to build an house unto our God", Ezr_4:3, neither in this world, nor in the world to come: moreover, also let him have no part in Jerusalem; as it is said, "But you have no portion, nor, right, nor memorial in Jerusalem", Neh_2:20; and they sent this anathema to the Israelites that were in Babylon, and they added thereunto, curse upon curse moreover, king Cyrus added an everlasting anathema to it, as it is said, "And the God that hath caused his name to dwell there, destroy. Ezr_6:12."

And hence, because the Samaritans were had in such abhorrence by the Jews, they would not ask a blessing over food in company with them (s), nor say Amen after they had asked one (t); nor indeed, after the better sort of them had asked, unless the whole blessing was distinctly heard (u), that so they might be sure there was no heresy in it; by all which it appears, how opprobrious this name was, and what a sad character was fixed upon a man that bore it; and as Yeshua was called by the Jews a Samaritan, they having no name more hateful and reproachful to call him by, so the believers are still in their writings called Cuthites, or Samaritans; and it is indeed with them a general name for all Gentiles and idolaters, or whom they esteem such.

(r) Pirke Eliezer, c. 38. (s) Bartenora in Misn. Beracot, c. 7. sect. 1. (t) Elias in Tishbi in voce כות. (u) Misn. Beracot, c. 8. sect. 8. & Maimon. & Bartonera in ib.

---

49. Jesus answered, I have not a devil; but I honour my Father, and ye do dishonour me.

Greek/Transliteration
49. Ἀπεκρίθη Ἰησοῦς, Ἐγὼ δαιμόνιον οὐκ ἔχω, ἀλλὰ τιμῶ τὸν πατέρα μου, καὶ ὑμεῖς ἀτιμάζετέ με.

49. Apekrithei Yeisous, Ego daimonion ouk echo, alla timo ton patera mou, kai 'umeis atimazete me.

Hebrew/Transliteration
מט. וַיַּעַן יֵשׁוּעַ רוּחַ רָעָה אֵין-בִּי כִּי אִם-מְכַבֵּד אֲנִי אֶת-אָבִי וְאַתֶּם תִּבְזֻנִי:

49. Va•ya•an Yeshua roo•ach ra•ah eyn - bi ki eem - me•cha•bed ani et - Avi ve•a•tem tiv•zoo•ni.

---

50. And I seek not mine own glory: there is one that seeketh and judgeth.

Greek/Transliteration
50. Ἐγὼ δὲ οὐ ζητῶ τὴν δόξαν μου· ἔστιν ὁ ζητῶν καὶ κρίνων.

50. Ego de ou zeito tein doxan mou. estin 'o zeiton kai krinon.

נ. וַאֲנִי לֹא אֶת-כְּבוֹדִי אֲנִי מְבַקֵּשׁ יֵשׁ אֶחָד אֲשֶׁר הוּא מְבַקְשׁוֹ וְגַם-יִשְׁפֹּט:

50. Va•a•ni lo et - ke•vo•di ani me•va•kesh yesh e•chad asher hoo me•vak•sho
ve•gam - yish•pot.

---

51. Verily, verily, I say unto you, If a man keep my saying, he shall never see
death.

51. Ἀμὴν ἀμὴν λέγω ὑμῖν, ἐάν τις τὸν λόγον τὸν ἐμὸν τηρήσῃ, θάνατον οὐ μὴ
θεωρήσῃ εἰς τὸν αἰῶνα.

51. Amein amein lego 'umin, ean tis ton logon ton emon teireisei, thanaton ou
mei theoreisei eis ton aiona.

נא. אָמֵן אָמֵן אֲנִי אֹמֵר לָכֶם אִם יִשְׁמֹר אִישׁ אֶת-דְּבָרַי לֹא יִרְאֶה-מָוֶת לְעוֹלָם:

51. Amen amen ani o•mer la•chem eem yish•mor eesh et - d`va•ri lo yir•eh -
ma•vet le•o•lam.

---

52. Then said the Jews unto him, Now we know that thou hast a devil.
Abraham is dead, and the prophets; and thou sayest, If a man keep my
saying, he shall never taste of death.

52. Εἶπον οὖν αὐτῷ οἱ Ἰουδαῖοι, Νῦν ἐγνώκαμεν ὅτι δαιμόνιον ἔχεις. Ἀβραὰμ
ἀπέθανεν καὶ οἱ προφῆται, καὶ σὺ λέγεις, Ἐάν τις τὸν λόγον μου τηρήσῃ, οὐ
μὴ γεύσηται θανάτου εἰς τὸν αἰῶνα.

52. Eipon oun auto 'oi Youdaioi, Nun egnokamen 'oti daimonion echeis.
Abra'am apethanen kai 'oi propheitai, kai su legeis, Ean tis ton logon mou
teireisei, ou mei geuseitai thanatou eis ton aiona.

נב. וַיֹּאמְרוּ אֵלָיו הַיְּהוּדִים עַתָּה יָדַעְנוּ כִּי-רוּחַ רָעָה בָּךְ גַּם-אַבְרָהָם מֵת גַּם-הַנְּבִיאִים וְאַתָּה אָמַרְתָּ
אִם יִשְׁמֹר:אִישׁ אֶת-דְּבָרַי לֹא יִטְעַם-מָוֶת לְעוֹלָם

52. Va•yom•roo elav ha•Ye•hoo•dim ata ya•da•a•noo ki - roo•ach ra•ah bach
gam - Avraham met gam - ha•n`vi•eem ve•a•ta amar•ta eem yish•mor eesh et
- d`va•ri lo yit•am - ma•vet le•o•lam.

53. Art thou greater than our father Abraham, which is dead? and the prophets are dead: whom makest thou thyself?

Greek/Transliteration

53. Μὴ σὺ μείζων εἶ τοῦ πατρὸς ἡμῶν Ἀβραάμ, ὅστις ἀπέθανεν; Καὶ οἱ προφῆται ἀπέθανον· τίνα σεαυτὸν σὺ ποιεῖς;

53. Mei su meizon ei tou patros 'eimon Abra'am, 'ostis apethanen? Kai 'oi propheitai apethanon. tina seauton su poieis?

Hebrew/Transliteration

נג. הֲגָדוֹל אַתָּה מֵאַבְרָהָם אָבִינוּ אֲשֶׁר מֵת וְהַנְּבִיאִים כִּי מֵתוּ מַה תַּעֲשֶׂה בְנַפְשֶׁךָ:

53. Ha•ga•dol ata me•Avraham avi•noo asher met ve•ha•n`vi•eem ki me•too ma ta•a•se ve•naf•she•cha?

Rabbinic Jewish Commentary

The Jews had a mighty opinion of their ancestors, especially of Abraham; and yet they allow the Messiah to be greater than he, as Jesus truly was: so one of their ancient commentators (w) on those words of Isa_52:13 thus paraphrases them,

""Behold my servant shall deal prudently", this is the King Messiah; "he shall be exalted" above Abraham, as it is written, Gen_14:22, "and extolled" above Moses, as it is written, Num_11:12, and he shall be higher than the ministering angels, as it is written, Eze_1:26, for he shall be גדול מן אבות, "greater than the fathers"."

(w) Tachuma apud Huls. p. 321.

---

54. Jesus answered, If I honour myself, my honour is nothing: it is my Father that honoureth me; of whom ye say, that he is your God:

Greek/Transliteration

54. Ἀπεκρίθη Ἰησοῦς, Ἐὰν ἐγὼ δοξάζω ἐμαυτόν, ἡ δόξα μου οὐδέν ἐστιν· ἔστιν ὁ πατήρ μου ὁ δοξάζων με, ὃν ὑμεῖς λέγετε ὅτι θεὸς ἡμῶν ἐστιν,

54. Apekrithei Yeisous, Ean ego doxazo emauton, 'ei doxa mou ouden estin. estin 'o pateir mou 'o doxazon me, 'on 'umeis legete 'oti theos 'eimon estin,

Hebrew/Transliteration

נד. וַיַּעַן יֵשׁוּעַ אִם-אֲנִי אֶתֵּן כָּבוֹד לְנַפְשִׁי כְּבוֹדִי כְאָיִן אַךְ אָבִי הוּא מְכַבְּדֵנִי אֲשֶׁר עָלָיו תֹּאמְרוּן כִּי הוּא אֱלֹהֵיכֶם:

54. Va•ya•an Yeshua eem - ani e•ten ka•vod le•naf•shi ke•vo•di che•a•yin ach Avi hoo me•chab•de•ni asher alav tom•roon ki hoo Elohey•chem.

231

55. Yet ye have not known him; but I know him: and if I should say, I know him not, I shall be a liar like unto you: but I know him, and keep his saying.

Greek/Transliteration
55. καὶ οὐκ ἐγνώκατε αὐτόν· ἐγὼ δὲ οἶδα αὐτόν, καὶ ἐὰν εἴπω ὅτι οὐκ οἶδα αὐτόν, ἔσομαι ὅμοιος ὑμῶν, ψεύστης· ἀλλ᾽ οἶδα αὐτόν, καὶ τὸν λόγον αὐτοῦ τηρῶ.

55. kai ouk egnokate auton. ego de oida auton, kai ean eipo 'oti ouk oida auton, esomai 'omoios 'umon, pseusteis. all oida auton, kai ton logon autou teiro.

Hebrew/Transliteration
נה. וְאַתֶּם לֹא יְדַעְתֶּם אֹתוֹ אַדְ אֲנִי יֹדֵעַ אֹתוֹ וְכִי-אֹמַר לֹא יְדַעְתִּיו אֶהְיֶה מְכַזֵּב כְּמוֹכֶם אָכֵן יְדַעְתִּיו וְאֶת-דְּבָרוֹ:אֲנִי שֹׁמֵר

55. Ve•a•tem lo ye•da•a•tem o•to ach ani yo•de•a o•to ve•chi - o•mar lo ye•da•a•tiv e•he•ye me•cha•zev ke•mo•chem a•chen ye•da•a•tiv ve•et - de•va•ro ani sho•mer.

---

56. Your father Abraham rejoiced to see my day: and he saw it, and was glad.

Greek/Transliteration
56. Ἀβραὰμ ὁ πατὴρ ὑμῶν ἠγαλλιάσατο ἵνα ἴδῃ τὴν ἡμέραν τὴν ἐμήν, καὶ εἶδεν καὶ ἐχάρη.

56. Abra'am 'o pateir 'umon eigallyasato 'ina idei tein 'eimeran tein emein, kai eiden kai echarei.

Hebrew/Transliteration
נו. אַבְרָהָם אֲבִיכֶם שָׂשׂ לִרְאוֹת אֶת-יוֹמִי וַיַּרְא וַיִּשְׂמָח:

56. Av•ra•ham avi•chem sas lir•ot et - yo•mi va•yar va•yis•mach.

Rabbinic Jewish Commentary
Or "he was desirous to see my day", as the Syriac and Arabic versions rightly render the word; or "very desirous", as the Persic version: and indeed, this was what many kings and prophets, and righteous men, were desirous of, even of seeing the Messiah and his day: we often read of ימות המשיח, "the days of the Messiah": and the Jews, in their Talmud (y), dispute much about them, how long they will be; one says forty years, another seventy, another three ages: it is the opinion of some, that they shall be according to the number of the days of the year, three hundred and sixty five years; some say seven thousand years, and others as many as have been from the beginning of the world; and others, as many as from Noah; but we know the day of Messiah better, and how long he was here on earth; and whose whole time here is called his day; this Abraham had a very great desire

to see. This brings to mind what the Jews say at the rejoicing at the Torah, when the book of the Torah is brought out (z).

"Abraham rejoiced with the rejoicing of the Torah, he that cometh shall come, the branch with the joy of the Torah; Isaac, Jacob, Moses, Aaron, Joshua, Samuel, David, Solomon, rejoiced with the joy of the Torah; he that cometh shall come, the branch with the joy of the Torah."

(y) T. Bab. Sanhedrin, fol. 99. 1. (z) Seder Tephillot, fol. 309. 1. Ed. Basil.

---

57. Then said the Jews unto him, Thou art not yet fifty years old, and hast thou seen Abraham?

Greek/Transliteration
57. Εἶπον οὖν οἱ Ἰουδαῖοι πρὸς αὐτόν, Πεντήκοντα ἔτη οὔπω ἔχεις, καὶ Ἀβραὰμ ἑώρακας;

57. Eipon oun 'oi Youdaioi pros auton, Penteikonta etei oupo echeis, kai Abra'am 'eorakas?

Hebrew/Transliteration
נז. וַיֹּאמְרוּ אֵלָיו הַיְּהוּדִים אֵינְךָ עוֹד בֶּן-חֲמִשִּׁים שָׁנָה וְאֶת-אַבְרָהָם רָאִיתָ:

57. Va•yom•roo elav ha•Ye•hoo•dim eyn•cha od ben - cha•mi•shim sha•na ve•et – Avraham ra•ee•ta.

Rabbinic Jewish Commentary
Therefore he could never see Abraham, nor Abraham see him; moreover, this age of fifty, is often spoken of by the Jews, and much observed; at the age of fifty, a man is fit to give counsel, they say (a); hence the Levites were dismissed from service at that age, it being more proper for them then to give advice, than to bear burdens; a Methurgeman, or an interpreter in a congregation, was not chosen under fifty years of age (b); and if a man died before he was fifty, this was called the death of cutting off (c); a violent death, a death inflicted by God, as a punishment; Yeshua lived not to that age, he was now many years short of it.

(a) Pirke Abot, c. 5. sect. 21. (b) T. Bab. Chagiga, fol. 14. 1. Juchasin, fol. 44. 2. (c) T. Hieros. Biccurim, fol. 64. 3. T. Bab. Moed Katon, fol. 28. 1. Macsecheth Semachot, c. 3. sect. 9. Kimchi in Isa. xxxviii. 10.

---

58. Jesus said unto them, Verily, verily, I say unto you, Before Abraham was, I am.

---

58. Εἶπεν αὐτοῖς ὁ Ἰησοῦς, Ἀμὴν ἀμὴν λέγω ὑμῖν, πρὶν Ἀβραὰμ γενέσθαι, ἐγώ εἰμι.

58. Eipen autois 'o Yeisous, Amein amein lego 'umin, prin Abra'am genesthai, ego eimi.

Hebrew/Transliteration

נח. וַיֹּאמֶר אֲלֵיהֶם יֵשׁוּעַ אָמֵן אָמֵן אֲנִי אֹמֵר לָכֶם אֲנִי הָיִיתִי עוֹד עַד לֹא-הָיָה אַבְרָהָם:

58. Va•yo•mer aley•hem Yeshua Amen amen ani o•mer la•chem ani ha•yi•ti od ad lo -ha•ya Avraham.

Rabbinic Jewish Commentary

It was very clear to the Judeans exactly what Yeshua's claim was, because they immediately took up stones to put him to death (Joh_8:59) for blasphemy. Claiming to be God and, specifically, pronouncing God's name (as Yeshua had just done) were punishable by death (Lev_24:15-16 and Mishna Sanhedrin 7:5, "The blasphemer is not guilty until he pronounces the Name.").

---

59. Then took they up stones to cast at him: but Jesus hid himself, and went out of the temple, going through the midst of them, and so passed by.

Greek/Transliteration

59. Ἦραν οὖν λίθους ἵνα βάλωσιν ἐπ᾽ αὐτόν· Ἰησοῦς δὲ ἐκρύβη, καὶ ἐξῆλθεν ἐκ τοῦ ἱεροῦ, διελθὼν διὰ μέσου αὐτῶν· καὶ παρῆγεν οὕτως.

59. Eiran oun lithous 'ina balosin ep auton. Yeisous de ekrubei, kai exeilthen ek tou 'ierou, dielthon dya mesou auton. kai pareigen 'outos.

Hebrew/Transliteration

נט. וַיִּשְׂאוּ אֲבָנִים לִרְגֹּם אֹתוֹ אַךְ יֵשׁוּעַ הִסְתַּתֵּר מֵעֵינֵיהֶם וַיֵּצֵא מִן-הַמִּקְדָּשׁ וַיַּעֲבֹר בְּתֹכָם וַיֵּלֶךְ הָלוֹךְ:

59. Va•yis•oo ava•nim lir•gom o•to ach Yeshua his•ta•ter me•ey•ne•hem va•ye•tze min - ha•mik•dash va•ya•a•vor be•to•cham va•ye•lech ha•loch.

Rabbinic Jewish Commentary

Supposing that he had spoken blasphemy; for they well understood that he, by so saying, made himself to be the eternal God, the unchangeable YHWH. Should it be asked how they came by their stones in the temple? It may be replied, the temple was still building, Joh_2:20, and stones, or pieces of stones, might lie about, with which they furnished themselves, in order to have destroyed Yeshua: and this they attempted, though it was on the sabbath day, as appears from Joh_9:1; and with them, סקילה בשבת, "stoning on the sabbath day" (d) was allowed in some cases. (d) T. Hieros. Yom Tob, fol. 63. 2.

John, Chapter 9

1. And as Jesus passed by, he saw a man which was blind from his birth.

Greek/Transliteration
1. Καὶ παράγων εἶδεν ἄνθρωπον τυφλὸν ἐκ γενετῆς.

1. Kai paragon eiden anthropon tuphlon ek geneteis.

Hebrew/Transliteration
א. וַיְהִי בְּעָבְרוֹ וַיַּרְא אִישׁ אֲשֶׁר נוֹלַד עִוֵּר מֵרֶחֶם אִמּוֹ:

1. Vay•hi be•ov•ro va•yar eesh asher no•lad ee••ver me•re•chem ee•mo.

---

2. And his disciples asked him, saying, Master, who did sin, this man, or his parents, that he was born blind?

Greek/Transliteration
2. Καὶ ἠρώτησαν αὐτὸν οἱ μαθηταὶ αὐτοῦ λέγοντες, ῾Ραββί, τίς ἥμαρτεν, οὗτος ἢ οἱ γονεῖς αὐτοῦ, ἵνα τυφλὸς γεννηθῇ;

2. Kai eiroteisan auton 'oi matheitai autou legontes, 'Rabbi, tis 'eimarten, 'outos ei 'oi goneis autou, 'ina tuphlos genneithei?

Hebrew/Transliteration
ב. וַיִּשְׁאָלֻהוּ תַלְמִידָיו לֵאמֹר רַבֵּנוּ מִי חָטָא הָאִישׁ הַזֶּה אוֹ יֹלְדָיו כִּי נוֹלַד עִוֵּר:

2. Va•yish•a•loo•hoo tal•mi•dav le•mor Ra•be•noo mee cha•ta ha•eesh ha•ze oh yol•dav ki no•lad ee•ver.

Rabbinic Jewish Commentary
This notion, Josephus says (a), was embraced by the Pharisees; though, according to him, it seems, that they only understood it of the souls of good men; and if so, this could lay no foundation for such a question, unless these disciples had given into the Pythagorean notion of a transmigration of all souls, which was to be known by defects, as blindness. (b); or else this question proceeded upon a principle received by the Jews, that an infant might do that which was faulty and criminal, and actually sin in the womb; or on another, which prevailed among them, that there should be neither merit nor demerit in the days of the Messiah; that is, that neither the good deeds, nor bad deeds of their parents, should be imputed to their children, neither the one to their advantage, nor the other to their disadvantage: and therefore since he the Messiah was come, they ask, how this blindness should come to pass? what should be the reason of it?

(a) De Bello Jud. l. 2. c. 8. sect. 14. (b) Sallust. de Diis, c. 20.

3. Jesus answered, Neither hath this man sinned, nor his parents: but that the works of God should be made manifest in him.

Greek/Transliteration
3. Ἀπεκρίθη Ἰησοῦς, Οὔτε οὗτος ἥμαρτεν οὔτε οἱ γονεῖς αὐτοῦ· ἀλλ' ἵνα φανερωθῇ τὰ ἔργα τοῦ θεοῦ ἐν αὐτῷ.

3. Apekrithei Yeisous, Oute 'outos 'eimarten oute 'oi goneis autou. all 'ina phanerothei ta erga tou theou en auto.

Hebrew/Transliteration
:ג. וַיַּעַן יֵשׁוּעַ לֹא הוּא חָטָא וְלֹא יֹלְדָיו אַךְ לְבַעֲבוּר יֵרָאוּ-בוֹ מַעַלְלֵי-אֵל

3. Va•ya•an Yeshua lo hoo cha•ta ve•lo yol•dav ach le•va•a•voor ye•ra•oo - vo ma•a•le•ley - El.

---

4. I must work the works of him that sent me, while it is day: the night cometh, when no man can work.

Greek/Transliteration
4. Ἐμὲ δεῖ ἐργάζεσθαι τὰ ἔργα τοῦ πέμψαντός με ἕως ἡμέρα ἐστίν· ἔρχεται νύξ, ὅτε οὐδεὶς δύναται ἐργάζεσθαι.

4. Eme dei ergazesthai ta erga tou pempsantos me 'eos 'eimera estin. erchetai nux, 'ote oudeis dunatai ergazesthai.

Hebrew/Transliteration
:ד. עָלַי לְעוֹלֵל עֲלֹלוֹת שֹׁלְחִי בְּעוֹד יוֹם כִּי-יָבֹא לַיְלָה וְאָז לֹא-יוּכַל אִישׁ לַעֲשׂוֹת מְאוּמָה

4. A•lai le•o•lel ali•lot shol•chi be•od yom ki - ya•vo lai•la ve•az lo - yoo•chal eesh la•a•sot me•oo•ma.

---

5. As long as I am in the world, I am the light of the world.

Greek/Transliteration
5. Ὅταν ἐν τῷ κόσμῳ ὦ, φῶς εἰμι τοῦ κόσμου.

5. 'Otan en to kosmo o, phos eimi tou kosmou.

Hebrew/Transliteration
:ה. בְּעוֹד אֲנִי בָעוֹלָם אוֹר הָעוֹלָם הִנֶּנִי

5. Be•od ani va•o•lam or ha•o•lam hi•ne•ni.

---

6. When he had thus spoken, he spat on the ground, and made clay of the spittle, and he anointed the eyes of the blind man with the clay,

Greek/Transliteration
6. Ταῦτα εἰπών, ἔπτυσεν χαμαί, καὶ ἐποίησεν πηλὸν ἐκ τοῦ πτύσματος, καὶ ἐπέχρισεν τὸν πηλὸν ἐπὶ τοὺς ὀφθαλμοὺς τοῦ τυφλοῦ,

6. Tauta eipon, eptusen chamai, kai epoieisen peilon ek tou ptusmatos, kai epechrisen ton peilon epi tous ophthalmous tou tuphlou,

Hebrew/Transliteration
:ו. הַדָּבָר יָצָא מִפִּיו וַיָּרֶק רֹק בֶּעָפָר הָאֲדָמָה וַיִּגְבָּל-חֹמֶר וַיִּמְרַח עַל-עֵינָיו

6. Ha•da•var ya•tza mi•piv va•ya•rek rok ba•a•far ha•a•da•ma va•yig•bal -
cho•mer va•yim•rach al - ey•nav.

Rabbinic Jewish Commentary
The Misnic Rabbi's speak (c) of טיט נרוק, "clay that is spitted", or "spittle clay", which their commentators say (d) was a weak, thin clay, like spittle or water; but this here was properly spittle clay, or clay made of spittle, for want of water; or it may be rather, through choice Yeshua spat upon the dust of the earth, and worked it together into a consistence, like clay.

(c) Misn. Mikvaot, c. 7. sect. 1. (d) Jarchi, Maimon. & Bartenora in ib.

---

7. And said unto him, Go, wash in the pool of Siloam, (which is by interpretation, Sent.) He went his way therefore, and washed, and came seeing.

Greek/Transliteration
7. καὶ εἶπεν αὐτῷ, Ὕπαγε νίψαι εἰς τὴν κολυμβήθραν τοῦ Σιλωάμ- ὃ ἑρμηνεύεται, Ἀπεσταλμένος. Ἀπῆλθεν οὖν καὶ ἐνίψατο, καὶ ἦλθεν βλέπων.

7. kai eipen auto, 'Upage nipsai eis tein kolumbeithran tou Siloam- 'o 'ermeineuetai, Apestalmenos. Apeilthen oun kai enipsato, kai eilthen blepon.

Hebrew/Transliteration
:ז. וַיֹּאמֶר אֵלָיו הָלֹךְ וְרָחַצְתָּ בִּבְרֵכַת הַשִּׁלוֹחַ אֲשֶׁר יֵאָמֵר שָׁלוּחַ וַיֵּלֶךְ וַיִּרְחַץ וַיָּבֹא בְעֵינַיִם פְּקֵחוֹת

7. Va•yo•mer elav ha•loch ve•ra•chatz•ta biv•re•chat ha•shi•lo•ach asher ye•a•mer sha•loo•ach va•ye•lech va•yir•chatz va•ya•vo be•ey•na•yim p`koo•chot.

Rabbinic Jewish Commentary

A fountain of this name is called Siloah, Isa_8:6, and according to the Jewish writers, sometimes Gihon (e); and this, they say (f), was without Jerusalem, though near unto it: hither the Jews went at the feast of tabernacles (g), and drew water with great rejoicing, and brought it, and poured it on the altar; the waters thereof also the priests drank for digestion, when they had eaten too much flesh (h); and this was likewise made use of to wash in, in case of uncleanness. It is said (i) of Benaiah, one of David's worthies, that

"One day he set his foot upon a dead toad, and he went down to Siloah, and broke the pieces of hail, (or ice congealed together,) and dipped himself."

This blind man was sent, not to wash himself all over, but only his face or eyes; and so the Arabic and Persic versions read, "wash thy face"; the clay from it: this may be emblematical of the grace of the Spirit, sometimes signified by water and washing, which accompanying the word, makes it effectual to the salvation of souls.

(e) Targum, Jarchi, Kimchi, & Solomon ben Melech in 1 Kings i. 39. (f) Jarchi & Bartenora in Misn. Succa, c. 4. sect. 9. (g) Misn. Succa, c. 4. sect. 9. (h) Abot R. Nathan, c. 35. fol. 8. 3. (i) Targum in 1 Chron. xi. 22.

---

8. The neighbours therefore, and they which before had seen him that he was blind, said, Is not this he that sat and begged?

Greek/Transliteration

8. Οἱ οὖν γείτονες καὶ οἱ θεωροῦντες αὐτὸν τὸ πρότερον ὅτι τυφλὸς ἦν, ἔλεγον, Οὐχ οὗτός ἐστιν ὁ καθήμενος καὶ προσαιτῶν;

8. 'Oi oun geitones kai 'oi theorountes auton to proteron 'oti tuphlos ein, elegon, Ouch 'outos estin 'o katheimenos kai prosaiton?

Hebrew/Transliteration

ח. וַיֹּאמְרוּ שְׁכֵנָיו הַיֹּדְעִים אֹתוֹ מֵאָז הֲלֹא-זֶה הוּא הַיֹּשֵׁב הַמְבַקֵּשׁ נְדָבוֹת:

8. Va•yom•roo sh`che•nav ha•yod•eem o•to me•az ha•lo - ze hoo ha•yo•shev ham•va•kesh n`da•vot?

---

9. Some said, This is he: others said, He is like him: but he said, I am he.

Greek/Transliteration
9. Ἄλλοι ἔλεγον ὅτι Οὗτός ἐστιν· ἄλλοι δὲ ὅτι Ὅμοιος αὐτῷ ἐστιν. Ἐκεῖνος ἔλεγεν ὅτι Ἐγώ εἰμι.

9. Alloi elegon 'oti 'Outos estin. alloi de 'oti 'Omoios auto estin. Ekeinos elegen 'oti Ego eimi.

Hebrew/Transliteration
:ט. אֵלֶּה אָמְרוּ כִּי-זֶה הוּא וְאֵלֶּה לֹא-כֵן רַק דּוֹמֶה-לוֹ וְהוּא אָמַר אֲנִי הוּא

9. Ele am•roo ki - ze hoo ve•e•le lo - chen rak do•me - lo ve•hoo amar ani hoo.

---

10. Therefore said they unto him, How were thine eyes opened?

Greek/Transliteration
10. Ἔλεγον οὖν αὐτῷ, Πῶς ἀνεῴχθησάν σου οἱ ὀφθαλμοί;

10. Elegon oun auto, Pos aneochtheisan sou 'oi ophthalmoi?

Hebrew/Transliteration
:י. וַיֹּאמְרוּ אֵלָיו אֵיכָה אֵיפוֹא נִפְקְחוּ עֵינֶיךָ

10. Va•yom•roo elav ey•cha ey•fo nif•ke•choo ey•ne•cha?

---

11. He answered and said, A man that is called Jesus made clay, and anointed mine eyes, and said unto me, Go to the pool of Siloam, and wash: and I went and washed, and I received sight.

Greek/Transliteration
11. Ἀπεκρίθη ἐκεῖνος καὶ εἶπεν, Ἄνθρωπος λεγόμενος Ἰησοῦς πηλὸν ἐποίησεν, καὶ ἐπέχρισέν μου τοὺς ὀφθαλμούς, καὶ εἶπέν μοι, Ὕπαγε εἰς τὴν κολυμβήθραν τοῦ Σιλωάμ, καὶ νίψαι. Ἀπελθὼν δὲ καὶ νιψάμενος, ἀνέβλεψα.

11. Apekrithei ekeinos kai eipen, Anthropos legomenos Yeisous peilon epoieisen, kai epechrisen mou tous ophthalmous, kai eipen moi, 'Upage eis tein kolumbeithran tou Siloam, kai nipsai. Apelthon de kai nipsamenos, aneblepsa.

Hebrew/Transliteration
יא. וַיַּעַן אִישׁ אֲשֶׁר שְׁמוֹ יֵשׁוּעַ גֶּבֶל חֹמֶר וַיִּמְרַח עַל-עֵינַי וְכֹה אָמַר אֵלַי הָלֹךְ וְרָחַצְתָּ בִּבְרֵכַת הַשִּׁלֹחַ וָאֵלֵךְ וָאֶרְחַץ:וְעֵינַי נִפְקָחוּ

11. Va•ya•an eesh asher sh`mo Yeshua ga•val cho•mer va•yim•rach al - ey•nai ve•cho amar e•lai ha•loch ve•ra•chatz•ta biv•re•chat ha•shi•lo•ach va•e•lech va•er•chatz ve•ey•nai nif•ka•choo.

---

12. Then said they unto him, Where is he? He said, I know not.

Greek/Transliteration
12. Εἶπον οὖν αὐτῷ, Ποῦ ἐστιν ἐκεῖνος; Λέγει, Οὐκ οἶδα.

12. Eipon oun auto, Pou estin ekeinos? Legei, Ouk oida.

Hebrew/Transliteration
יב. וַיֹּאמְרוּ אֵלָיו וְאַיּוֹ וַיֹּאמֶר לֹא יָדָעְתִּי:

12. Va•yom•roo elav ve•a•yo va•yo•mer lo ya•da•a•ti.

---

13. They brought to the Pharisees him that aforetime was blind.

Greek/Transliteration
13. Ἄγουσιν αὐτὸν πρὸς τοὺς Φαρισαίους, τόν ποτε τυφλόν.

13. Agousin auton pros tous Pharisaious, ton pote tuphlon.

Hebrew/Transliteration
יג. וַיָּבִיאוּ אֶת-הָעִוֵּר הָרֹאֶה הַזֶּה אֶל-הַפְּרוּשִׁים:

13. Va•ya•vi•oo et - ha•ee•ver ha•ro•eh ha•ze el - ha•P`roo•shim.

---

14. And it was the Sabbath day when Jesus made the clay, and opened his eyes.

Greek/Transliteration
14. Ἦν δὲ σάββατον ὅτε τὸν πηλὸν ἐποίησεν ὁ Ἰησοῦς, καὶ ἀνέῳξεν αὐτοῦ τοὺς ὀφθαλμούς.

14. Ein de sabbaton 'ote ton peilon epoieisen 'o Yeisous, kai aneoxen autou tous ophthalmous.

Hebrew/Translitaration
יד. וְהַיּוֹם אֲשֶׁר לָשׁ יֵשׁוּעַ אֶת-הַטִּיחַ וְאֶת-עֵינָיו פָּקַח הָיָה יוֹם הַשַּׁבָּת:

14. Ve•ha•yom asher lash Yeshua et - ha•ti•ach ve•et - ey•nav pa•kach ha•ya yom ha•Sha•bat.

_____

15. Then again the Pharisees also asked him how he had received his sight. He said unto them, He put clay upon mine eyes, and I washed, and do see.

Greek/Transliteration

15. Πάλιν οὖν ἠρώτων αὐτὸν καὶ οἱ Φαρισαῖοι, πῶς ἀνέβλεψεν. Ὁ δὲ εἶπεν αὐτοῖς, Πηλὸν ἐπέθηκέν μου ἐπὶ τοὺς ὀφθαλμούς, καὶ ἐνιψάμην, καὶ βλέπω.

15. Palin oun eiroton auton kai 'oi Pharisaioi, pos aneblepsen. 'O de eipen autois, Peilon epetheiken mou epi tous ophthalmous, kai enipsamein, kai blepo.

Hebrew/Transliteration

טו. וַיּוֹסִיפוּ גַם-הַפְּרוּשִׁים לִשְׁאֹל אֹתוֹ אֵיךְ נִתַּן לוֹ אוֹר עֵינָיו וַיַּגֵּד לָהֶם כִּי שָׂם טִיחַ עַל-עֵינַי וָאֶרְחַץ וְהִנֵּה עֵינַי:רֹאוֹת

15. Va•yo•si•foo gam - ha•P`roo•shim lish•ol o•to eych ni•tan lo or ey•nav va•ya•ged la•hem ki sam ti•ach al - ey•nai va•er•chatz ve•hee•ne ey•nai ro•ot.

_____

16. Therefore said some of the Pharisees, This man is not of God, because he keepeth not the Sabbath day. Others said, How can a man that is a sinner do such miracles? And there was a division among them.

Greek/Transliteration

16. Ἔλεγον οὖν ἐκ τῶν Φαρισαίων τινές, Οὗτος ὁ ἄνθρωπος οὐκ ἔστιν παρὰ τοῦ θεοῦ, ὅτι τὸ σάββατον οὐ τηρεῖ. Ἄλλοι ἔλεγον, Πῶς δύναται ἄνθρωπος ἁμαρτωλὸς τοιαῦτα σημεῖα ποιεῖν; Καὶ σχίσμα ἦν ἐν αὐτοῖς.

16. Elegon oun ek ton Pharisaion tines, 'Outos 'o anthropos ouk estin para tou theou, 'oti to sabbaton ou teirei. Alloi elegon, Pos dunatai anthropos 'amartolos toyauta seimeia poiein? Kai schisma ein en autois.

Hebrew/Transliteration

טז. וְיֵשׁ מִן-הַפְּרוּשִׁים אָמְרוּ הָאִישׁ הַזֶּה אֵינֶנּוּ אִישׁ אֱלֹהִים כִּי אֵינֶנּוּ שֹׁמֵר אֶת-הַשַּׁבָּת וְיֵשׁ אָמְרוּ הֲיוּכַל אִישׁ:חֹטֵא לַעֲשׂוֹת מוֹפְתִים כָּאֵלֶּה וַיְהִי מָדוֹן בֵּינֵיהֶם

16. Ve•yesh min - ha•P`roo•shim am•roo ha•eesh ha•ze ey•ne•noo eesh Elohim ki ey•ne•noo sho•mer et - ha•Sha•bat ve•yesh am•roo ha•yoo•chal eesh cho•te la•a•sot mof•tim ka•e•le vay•hi ma•don bey•ne•hem.

_____

Rabbinic Jewish Commentary

because he keepeth not the sabbath day: this they concluded from his making clay of spittle, and spreading it on the blind man's eyes, which was contrary to the traditions of their elders: one of whose rules and canons is (n), that

"It is forbidden to put fasting spittle even on the eyelid on a sabbath day."

An eye salve, or a plaster for the eye, if it was put on for pleasure, was lawful, but not for healing (o): but if it was put on, on the evening of the sabbath, it might continue on the sabbath day (p).

(n) T. Hieros. Sabbat, fol. 14. 4. & Avoda Zara, fol. 40. 4. & T. Bab. Sabbat, fol 108. 2. & Maimon. Hilchot Sabbat, c. 21. sect. 25. (o) Piske Tosephot Sabbat, art. 67. (p) T. Hieros. Sabbat, fol. 3, 4. Maimon. ib.

---

17. They say unto the blind man again, What sayest thou of him, that he hath opened thine eyes? He said, He is a prophet.

Greek/Transliteration

17. Λέγουσιν τῷ τυφλῷ πάλιν, Σὺ τί λέγεις περὶ αὐτοῦ, ὅτι ἤνοιξέν σου τοὺς ὀφθαλμούς; Ὁ δὲ εἶπεν ὅτι Προφήτης ἐστίν.

17. Legousin to tuphlo palin, Su ti legeis peri autou, 'oti einoixen sou tous ophthalmous? 'O de eipen 'oti Propheiteis estin.

Hebrew/Transliteration

:יז. וַיּוֹסִיפוּ וַיֹּאמְרוּ אֶל-הָעִוֵּר וּמַה-תֹּאמַר אַתָּה עָלָיו כִּי פָּקַח אֶת-עֵינֶיךָ וַיֹּאמֶר כִּי נָבִיא הוּא

17. Va•yo•si•foo va•yom•roo el - ha•ee•ver oo•ma - to•mar ata alav ki pa•kach et - ey•ne•cha va•yo•mer ki na•vi hoo.

---

8. But the Jews did not believe concerning him, that he had been blind, and received his sight, until they called the parents of him that had received his sight.

Greek/Transliteration

18. Οὐκ ἐπίστευσαν οὖν οἱ Ἰουδαῖοι περὶ αὐτοῦ, ὅτι τυφλὸς ἦν καὶ ἀνέβλεψεν, ἕως ὅτου ἐφώνησαν τοὺς γονεῖς αὐτοῦ τοῦ ἀναβλέψαντος,

18. Ouk episteusan oun 'oi Youdaioi peri autou, 'oti tuphlos ein kai aneblepsen, 'eos 'otou ephoneisan tous goneis autou tou anablepsantos,

Hebrew/Transliteration

:יח. וְלֹא-הֶאֱמִינוּ לוֹ הַיְּהוּדִים כִּי עִוֵּר הָיָה וְאוֹר עֵינָיו נִתַּן לוֹ עַד-אֲשֶׁר קָרְאוּ לְיֹלְדֵי הָעִוֵּר הָרֹאֶה

18. Ve•lo - he•e•mi•noo lo ha•Ye•hoo•dim ki ee•ver ha•ya ve•or ey•nav ni•tan
lo ad - asher kar•oo le•yol•dey ha•ee•ver ha•ro•eh.

---

19. And they asked them, saying, Is this your son, who ye say was born blind?
how then doth he now see?

Greek/Transliteration

19. καὶ ἠρώτησαν αὐτοὺς λέγοντες, Οὗτός ἐστιν ὁ υἱὸς ὑμῶν, ὃν ὑμεῖς λέγετε
ὅτι τυφλὸς ἐγεννήθη; Πῶς οὖν ἄρτι βλέπει;

19. kai eiroteisan autous legontes, 'Outos estin 'o 'wios 'umon, 'on 'umeis
legete 'oti tuphlos egenneithei? Pos oun arti blepei?

Hebrew/Transliteration

יט. וַיִּשְׁאֲלוּ אֹתָם לֵאמֹר הֲזֶה בִנְכֶם אֲשֶׁר אֲמַרְתֶּם כִּי נוֹלַד עִוֵּר וְאֵיךְ הוּא רֹאֶה עָתָּה:

19. Va•yish•a•loo o•tam le•mor ha•ze vin•chem asher amar•tem ki no•lad
ee•ver ve•eych hoo ro•eh ata?

---

20. His parents answered them and said, We know that this is our son, and
that he was born blind:

Greek/Transliteration

20. Ἀπεκρίθησαν δὲ αὐτοῖς οἱ γονεῖς αὐτοῦ καὶ εἶπον, Οἴδαμεν ὅτι οὗτός
ἐστιν ὁ υἱὸς ἡμῶν, καὶ ὅτι τυφλὸς ἐγεννήθη·

20. Apekritheisan de autois 'oi goneis autou kai eipon, Oidamen 'oti 'outos
estin 'o 'wios 'eimon, kai 'oti tuphlos egenneithei.

Hebrew/Transliteration

כ. וַיַּעֲנוּ אֹתָם יֹלְדָיו וַיֹּאמְרוּ יָדַעְנוּ בְּנֵנוּ הוּא זֶה וְגַם נוֹלַד עִוֵּר:

20. Va•ya•a•noo o•tam yol•dav va•yom•roo ya•da•a•noo be•ne•noo hoo ze
ve•gam no•lad ee•ver.

---

21. But by what means he now seeth, we know not; or who hath opened his
eyes, we know not: he is of age; ask him: he shall speak for himself.

Greek/Transliteration

21. πῶς δὲ νῦν βλέπει, οὐκ οἴδαμεν· ἢ τίς ἤνοιξεν αὐτοῦ τοὺς ὀφθαλμούς,
ἡμεῖς οὐκ οἴδαμεν· αὐτὸς ἡλικίαν ἔχει· αὐτὸν ἐρωτήσατε, αὐτὸς περὶ ἑαυτοῦ
λαλήσει.

21. pos de nun blepei, ouk oidamen. ei tis einoixen autou tous ophthalmous,
'eimeis ouk oidamen. autos 'eilikian echei. auton eroteisate, autos peri 'eautou
laleisei.

כא. אֲבָל לֹא יָדַעְנוּ אֵיךְ הוּא רֹאֶה עַתָּה וְלֹא יָדַעְנוּ מִי פָקַח אֶת-עֵינָיו הֲלֹא בָא בַיָּמִים הוּא שַׁאֲלוּ
אֹתוֹ וְהוּא:בְּפִיו יַגִּיד לָכֶם

21. Aval lo ya•da•a•noo eych hoo ro•eh ata ve•lo ya•da•a•noo mee fa•kach et -
ey•nav ha•lo va va•ya•mim hoo sha•a•loo o•to ve•hoo be•fiv ya•gid la•chem.

Rabbinic Jewish Commentary
he is of age; at man's estate, as, with the Jews, one was, who was at the age of
thirteen years, if he could produce the signs of puberty: and such an one was
allowed a witness in any case, but not under this age; nor if he was arrived to it, if
the above signs could not be produced (q). This man very likely was much older,
as may be thought from the whole of his conduct, his pertinent answers, and just
reasoning: wherefore his parents direct the sanhedrim to him for an answer to their
third question.

(q) Maimon. Hilchot Eduth, c. 9. sect. 7.

---

22. These words spake his parents, because they feared the Jews: for the Jews
had agreed already, that if any man did confess that he was Christ, he should
be put out of the synagogue.

Greek/Translitartion
22. Ταῦτα εἶπον οἱ γονεῖς αὐτοῦ, ὅτι ἐφοβοῦντο τοὺς Ἰουδαίους· ἤδη γὰρ
συνετέθειντο οἱ Ἰουδαῖοι, ἵνα ἐάν τις αὐτὸν ὁμολογήσῃ χριστόν,
ἀποσυνάγωγος γένηται.

22. Tauta eipon 'oi goneis autou, 'oti ephobounto tous Youdaious. eidei gar
sunetetheinto 'oi Youdaioi, 'ina ean tis auton 'omologeisei christon,
aposunagogos geneitai.

כב. כָּזֹאת דִּבְּרוּ יֹלְדָיו מִיִּרְאָתָם אֶת-הַיְּהוּדִים אֲשֶׁר כְּבָר חָרְצוּ לְנַדּוֹת אֶת-כָּל-אֲשֶׁר יוֹדֶה כִּי הוּא
הַמָּשִׁיחַ:

22. Ka•zot dib•roo yol•dav mi•yir•a•tam et - ha•Ye•hoo•dim asher k`var
char•tzoo le•na•dot et - kol - asher yo•de ki hoo ha•Ma•shi•ach.

Rabbinic Jewish Commentary
he should be put out of the synagogue; which was not that sort of
excommunication which they called נדוי, "Niddui", a separation from civil society
for the space of four cubits, and which held but thirty days, if the person repented;

---

if he did not, it was continued to sixty days; and after that, in case of non-repentance, to ninety days; and if no amendment, then they proceeded to another excommunication called חרם, "Cherem", or שמתא, "Shammatha", whereby such were anathematized, and cut off from the whole body of the Jewish church and people, called sometimes the synagogue and congregation of Israel (r); and this struck great terror in the minds of the people; and this was what intimidated the parents of the blind man, being what is intended here. Though these are sometimes put one for another, and signify the same thing; and he that was under the former of those censures, is said to be מובדל מן ציבור, "separated from the congregation" (s), a phrase by which the word here used may be very well rendered: but in some things there was a difference between them; the one was without cursing, the other with; he that was under "Niddui", might teach others the traditions, and they might teach him; he might hire workmen, and be hired himself: but he that was under "Cherem" might neither teach others, nor they teach him; but he might teach himself, that he might not forget his learning; and he might neither hire, nor be hired; and they did not trade with him, nor did they employ him in any business, unless in very little, just to keep him alive (t); yea, the goods which he was possessed of, were confiscated, and which they conclude should be done from (u) Ezr_10:8, which may be compared with this passage; so that this greatly and chiefly affected them in the affairs of civil life, and which made it so terrible: for I do not find that they were obliged to abstain from the temple, or temple worship, or from the synagogue, and the worship of it, and which is the mistake of some learned men: it is certain, they might go into places of worship, though with some difference from others; for it is said (w), that

"All that go into the temple, go in, in the right hand way, and go round, and come out in the left, except such an one to whom anything has befallen him, and he goes about to the left; (and when asked) why dost thou go to the left? (he answers) because I am a mourner; (to whom it is replied) he that dwells in this house comfort thee: (or) שאני מנודה, "because I am excommunicated"; (to whom they say) he that dwells in this house put it into thy heart (that thou mayest hearken to the words of thy friends, as it is afterwards explained) and they may receive thee."

And it is elsewhere said (x), that

"Solomon, when he built the temple, made two gates, the one for bridegrooms, and the other for mourners and excommunicated persons; and the Israelites, when they went in on sabbath days, or feast days, sat between these two gates; and when anyone came in by the gate of the bridegrooms, they knew he was a bridegroom, and said unto him, he that dwells in this house make thee cheerful with sons and daughters: and when anyone came in at the gate of mourners, and his upper lip covered, they knew that he was a mourner, and said unto him, he that dwells in this house comfort thee: and when anyone came in at the gate of mourners, and his upper lip was not covered, they knew שהיה מנודה, "that he was excommunicated"; and said unto him, he that dwells in this house comfort thee, and put it into thy heart to hearken to thy friends."

And it is afterwards also said in the same place, that when the temple was destroyed, it was decreed that such persons should come into synagogues and schools; but then they were not reckoned as members of the Jewish church, but as persons cut off from the people of Israel, and scarce allowed to be of their commonwealth. And it may be further observed, that excommunication with the Jews was not only on religious accounts, but on civil accounts; on account of money, or when a man would not pay his debts, according to the decree of the sanhedrim (y). The twenty four reasons of excommunication, given by Maimonides (z), chiefly respect contempt of the sanhedrim, and of the wise men, and breach of the traditions of the elders; sometimes they excommunicated for immorality, particularly the Essenes, as Josephus relates, who says (a), that such who are taken in grievous sins, they cast them out of their order; and he that is so dealt with commonly dies a miserable death; for being bound by oaths and customs, he cannot eat the food of others, and so starves. The same is reported (b) by R. Abraham Zachuth: and sometimes excommunication was for Epicurism, or heresy, and such they reckoned the belief of Jesus of Nazareth, as the Messiah, on account of which this decree was made, and which continued with them; for not only this blind man was cast out of the synagogue by virtue of it, but our Lord tells his disciples, that they should be so treated by the Jews after his death; and we find it remained in force and practice many hundreds of years afterwards. Athanasius (c) relates of a Jew, that lived in Berytus, a city in Syria, between Tyre and Sidon, that an image of Yeshua being found in his house by another Jew, though unknown to him; and this being discovered to the chief priests and elders of the Jews, they cast him out of the synagogue. Sometimes this sentence was pronounced by word of mouth, and sometimes it was delivered in writing: the form of one is given us by Buxtorf (d), out of an ancient Hebrew manuscript; and a dreadful shocking one it is; and is as follows:

"According to the mind of the LORD of lords, let such an one, the son of such an one, be in "Cherem", or anathematized, in both houses of judgment, of those above, and those below; and with the anathema of the saints on high, with the anathema of the "Seraphim" and "Ophanim", and with the anathema of the whole congregation, great and small; let great and real stripes be upon him, and many and violent diseases; and let his house be an habitation of dragons; and let his star be dark in the clouds; and let him be for indignation, wrath, and anger; and let his carcass be for beasts and serpents; and let those that rise up against him, and his enemies, rejoice over him; and let his silver and his gold be given to others; and let all his children be exposed at the gate of his enemies, and at his day may others be amazed; and let him be cursed from the mouth of Addiriron and Actariel, (names of angels, as are those that follow,) and from the mouth of Sandalphon and Hadraniel, and from the mouth of Ansisiel and Pathchiel, and from the mouth of Seraphiel and Zaganzael, and from the mouth of Michael and Gabriel, and from the mouth of Raphael and Meshartiel; and let him be anathematized from the mouth of Tzabtzabib, and from tile mouth of Habhabib, he is YHWH the Great, and from the mouth of the seventy names of the great king, and from the side of Tzortak the great chancellor; and let him be swallowed up as Korah and his company, with terror, and with trembling; let his soul go out; let the reproof of the Lord kill him; and let him be strangled as Ahithophel in his counsel; and let his leprosy be as the leprosy of Gehazi; and let there be no raising him up from his fall; and in the sepulchres of Israel let not his grave be; and let his wife be given to another; and let others bow upon her at his death: in this anathema, let such an one, the son of such an one be, and let this be his inheritance; but upon me, and upon all Israel, may God extend his peace and his blessing. Amen."

And if he would, he might add these verses in Deu_29:19, "and it come to pass when he heareth the words of this curse, that he bless himself in his heart, saying, I shall have peace, though I walk in the imagination of mine heart, to add drunkenness to thirst: the LORD will not spare him, but then the anger of the LORD, and his jealousy shall smoke against that man, and all the curses that are written in this book shall lie upon him, and the LORD shall blot out his name from under heaven. And the LORD shall separate, him unto evil, out of all the tribes of Israel, according, to all the curses of the covenant, that are written in this book of the Torah". There were many rites and ceremonies, which in process of time were used, when such a sentence was pronounced, as blowing of horns and trumpets, and lighting of candles, and putting them out: hence, trumpets are reckoned (d) a among the instruments of judges. It is said (e) of R. Judah, that being affronted by a certain person, he resented the injury, and brought out the trumpets and excommunicated him: and they tell us (f), that Barak anathematized Meroz, whom they take to be some great person, with four hundred trumpets: and they also say (g), that four hundred trumpets were brought out, and they excommunicated Jesus of Nazareth; though these words are left out in some editions of the Talmud. Now this was done in order to inject terror both into those that were guilty, and also into the whole congregation of the people, that they might hear and fear; for the "Cherem", or that sort of excommunication which goes by that name, was done publicly before the whole synagogue, all the heads and elders of the church being gathered together; and then candles were lighted, and as soon as the form of the curse was finished, they were put out, as a sign that the excommunicated person was unworthy of the heavenly light (h). Very likely the Papists took their horrible custom from hence of cursing with bell, book, and candle.

(r) Vid. Maimon. Talmud Tora, c. 7. sect. 6. Buxtorf. Lex. Rab. col. 1303. & Epist. Heb. Institut. p. 57. (s) Maimon. Hilchod Talmud Tora, c. 7. sect. 4. (t) Ib. sect. 5. (u) T. Bab. Moed Katon, fol. 16. 1. (w) Misn. Middot, c. 2. sect. 2. (x) Pirke Eiiezer, c. 17. (y) T. Bab. Moed Katon, fol. 16. 1. & Gloss in ib. (z) Hilchot Talmud Tora, c. 6. sect. 14. (a) De Bello Jud. l. 2. c. 8. sect. 8. (b) Juchasin, fol. 139. 2. (c) Oper. ejus, Tom. 2. p. 12, 17. Ed. Commelin. (d) Lex Rab. col. 828. (d) T. Bab. Sanhedrin, fol 7. 2. (e) T. Bab. Kiddushin, c. 4. in Beth Israel, fol. 57. 1. (f) T. Bab. Moed Katon, fol. 16. 1. & Shebuot, fol. 36. 1. (g) T. Bab. Sanhedrin, fol. 107. 2. Ed. Venet. (h) Buxtorf. Epist. Heb. Institut. c. 6. p. 56.

---

23. Therefore said his parents, He is of age; ask him.

Greek/Transliteration
23. Διὰ τοῦτο οἱ γονεῖς αὐτοῦ εἶπον ὅτι Ἡλικίαν ἔχει, αὐτὸν ἐρωτήσατε.

---

23. Dya touto 'oi goneis autou eipon 'oti 'Eilikian echei, auton eroteisate.

כג. עַל-כֵּן אָמְרוּ יֹלְדָיו כִּי בָא בַשָּׁנִים הוּא שַׁאֲלוּ אֶת-פִּיהוּ:

23. Al - ken am•roo yol•dav ki va va•sha•nim hoo sha•a•loo et - pi•hoo.

---

24. Then again called they the man that was blind, and said unto him, Give God the praise: we know that this man is a sinner.

Greek/Transliteration

24. Ἐφώνησαν οὖν ἐκ δευτέρου τὸν ἄνθρωπον ὃς ἦν τυφλός, καὶ εἶπον αὐτῷ, Δὸς δόξαν τῷ θεῷ· ἡμεῖς οἴδαμεν ὅτι ὁ ἄνθρωπος οὗτος ἁμαρτωλός ἐστιν.

24. Ephoneisan oun ek deuterou ton anthropon 'os ein tuphlos, kai eipon auto, Dos doxan to theo. 'eimeis oidamen 'oti 'o anthropos 'outos 'amartolos estin.

Hebrew/Transliteration

כד. אָז קָרְאוּ שֵׁנִית לָעִוֵּר הָרֹאֶה אֵלָיו וַיֹּאמְרוּ שִׂים-נָא כָבוֹד לֵאלֹהִים אֲנַחְנוּ יָדַעְנוּ כִּי-הָאִישׁ הַזֶּה חֹטֵא הוּא:

24. Az kar•oo she•nit la•ee•ver ha•ro•eh va•yom•roo elav sim - na ka•vod le•Elohim a•nach•noo ya•da•a•noo ki - ha•eesh ha•ze cho•te hoo.

Rabbinic Jewish Commentary

and said unto him, give God the praise; a phrase used when confession of sin was required; see Jos_7:19; and this may be the meaning of it here; confess this fraud and imposture before the omniscient God, the searcher of hearts, and in so doing glorify that perfection of his. One and the same word, ידה, signifies both to confess the truth of anything, as a sinful action, Pro_28:13, and to give thanks and praise to God for any mercy and blessing, Psa_45:17.

---

25. He answered and said, Whether he be a sinner or no, I know not: one thing I know, that, whereas I was blind, now I see.

Greek/Transliteration

25. Ἀπεκρίθη οὖν ἐκεῖνος καὶ εἶπεν, Εἰ ἁμαρτωλός ἐστιν, οὐκ οἶδα· ἓν οἶδα, ὅτι τυφλὸς ὤν, ἄρτι βλέπω.

25. Apekrithei oun ekeinos kai eipen, Ei 'amartolos estin, ouk oida. 'en oida, 'oti tuphlos on, arti blepo.

Hebrew/Translitaration

כה. וַיַּעַן וַיֹּאמֶר אִם-חֹטֵא הוּא לֹא יָדַעְתִּי רַק אַחַת יָדַעְתִּי כִּי עִוֵּר הָיִיתִי וְעַתָּה הִנְנִי רֹאֶה:

25. Va•ya•an va•yo•mer eem - cho•te hoo lo ya•da•a•ti rak a•chat ya•da•a•ti ki
ee•ver ha•yi•ti ve•a•ta hi•ne•ni ro•eh.

---

26. Then said they to him again, What did he to thee? how opened he thine
eyes?

Greek/Translitaration
26. Εἶπον δὲ αὐτῷ πάλιν, Τί ἐποίησέν σοι; Πῶς ἤνοιξέν σου τοὺς ὀφθαλμούς;

26. Eipon de auto palin, Ti epoieisen soi? Pos einoixen sou tous ophthalmous?

Hebrew/Transliteration
כו. וַיֹּאמְרוּ אֵלָיו מֶה-עָשָׂה לָךְ אֵיךְ פָּקַח אֶת-עֵינֶיךָ:

26. Va•yom•roo elav me - asa lach eych pa•kach et - ey•ne•cha?

---

27. He answered them, I have told you already, and ye did not hear:
wherefore would ye hear it again? will ye also be his disciples?

Greek/Transliteration
27. Ἀπεκρίθη αὐτοῖς, Εἶπον ὑμῖν ἤδη, καὶ οὐκ ἠκούσατε. Τί πάλιν θέλετε
ἀκούειν; Μὴ καὶ ὑμεῖς θέλετε αὐτοῦ μαθηταὶ γενέσθαι;

27. Apekrithei autois, Eipon 'umin eidei, kai ouk eikousate. Ti palin thelete
akouein? Mei kai 'umeis thelete autou matheitai genesthai?

Hebrew/Transliteration
כז. וַיַּעַן אֹתָם הֲלֹא אָמַרְתִּי לָכֶם וְלֹא שְׁמַעְתֶּם וּמַה-לָּכֶם לִשְׁמֹעַ שֵׁנִית הֲגַם אַתֶּם חֲפֵצִים לִהְיוֹת
תַּלְמִידָיו:

27. Va•ya•an o•tam ha•lo amar•ti la•chem ve•lo sh`ma•a•tem oo•ma - la•chem
lish•mo•a she•nit ha•gam atem cha•fe•tzim li•hee•yot tal•mi•dav?

---

28. Then they reviled him, and said, Thou art his disciple; but we are Moses'
disciples.

Greek?Transliteration
28. Ἐλοιδόρησαν αὐτόν, καὶ εἶπον, Σὺ εἶ μαθητὴς ἐκείνου· ἡμεῖς δὲ τοῦ
Μωσέως ἐσμὲν μαθηταί.

28. Eloidoreisan auton, kai eipon, Su ei matheiteis ekeinou. 'eimeis de tou
Moseos esmen matheitai.

Hebrew/Transliteration

כח. וַיְגַדְּפוּ אֹתוֹ וַיֹּאמְרוּ אַתָּה הוּא תַלְמִידוֹ וַאֲנַחְנוּ תַּלְמִידֵי מֹשֶׁה אֲנָחְנוּ:

28. Vay•gad•foo o•to va•yom•roo ata hoo tal•mi•do va•a•nach•noo tal•mi•dey Moshe a•nach•noo.

Rabbinic Jewish Commentary

This was a phrase in use among the Jews: so the Targumist (i) on Num_3:2 says,

"These are the names of they sons of Aaron the priests, תלמידיא דמשה, "the disciples of Moses", the master of the Israelites;"

Particularly the Pharisees, as here, claimed this title to themselves: for it is said,

"All the seven days (before the day of atonement) they delivered to him (the high priest) two of the disciples of the wise men, to instruct him in the service (of that day), who were, מתלמידיו של משה, "of the disciples of Moses", in opposition to the Sadducees:" (k)

From whence it appears, that these disciples of Moses were of the sect of the Pharisees, who assumed this character as peculiar to themselves; sometimes they call themselves the disciples of Abraham, though the description they give of such, by no means belongs to them; They say (l),

"Whoever has three things in him, is מתלמידיו של אברהם, "of the disciples of Abraham" our father, and who has three other things is of the disciples of Balaam the wicked: he that has a good eye, (beneficence, or temperance, or contentment,) a lowly spirit, and an humble soul, he is of "the disciples of Abraham" our father; but he that has evil eye, and a proud spirit, and a large soul (lustful or covetous), is of the disciples of Balaam."

This last character best agrees with those very persons, who would be thought to be the disciples of Abraham and of Moses.

(i) Jonathan ben Uzziel in ib. (k) T. Bab. Yoma, fol. 4. 1. (l) Pirke Abot, c. 5. sect. 19.

---

29. We know that God spake unto Moses: as for this fellow, we know not from whence he is.

Greek/Transliteration

29. Ἡμεῖς οἴδαμεν ὅτι Μωσῇ λελάληκεν ὁ θεός· τοῦτον δὲ οὐκ οἴδαμεν πόθεν ἐστίν.

29. 'Eimeis oidamen 'oti Mosei lelaleiken 'o theos. touton de ouk oidamen pothen estin.

:כט. יָדַעְנוּ כִּי אֶל-מֹשֶׁה דִּבֶּר אֱלֹהִים וְזֶה הָאִישׁ לֹא יָדַעְנוּ מֵאַיִן הוּא

29. Ya•da•a•noo ki el - Moshe di•ber Elohim ve•ze ha•eesh lo ya•da•a•noo
me•a•yin hoo.

---

30. The man answered and said unto them, Why herein is a marvellous thing,
that ye know not from whence he is, and yet he hath opened mine eyes.

Greek/Transliteration
30. Ἀπεκρίθη ὁ ἄνθρωπος καὶ εἶπεν αὐτοῖς, Ἐν γὰρ τούτῳ θαυμαστόν ἐστιν,
ὅτι ὑμεῖς οὐκ οἴδατε πόθεν ἐστίν, καὶ ἀνέῳξέν μου τοὺς ὀφθαλμούς.

30. Apekrithei 'o anthropos kai eipen autois, En gar touto thaumaston estin,
'oti 'umeis ouk oidate pothen estin, kai aneoxen mou tous ophthalmous.

Hebrew/Transliteration
:ל. וַיַּעַן הָאִישׁ וַיֹּאמֶר אֲלֵיהֶם דְּבַר פֶּלֶא הוּא אַתֶּם לֹא יְדַעְתֶּם מֵאַיִן הוּא וְהוּא אֶת-עֵינַי פָּקַח

30. Va•ya•an ha•eesh va•yo•mer aley•hem de•var pe•le hoo atem lo
ye•da•a•tem me•a•yin hoo ve•hoo et - ey•nai pa•kach.

---

31. Now we know that God heareth not sinners: but if any man be a
worshipper of God, and doeth his will, him he heareth.

Greek/Transliteration
31. Οἴδαμεν δὲ ὅτι ἁμαρτωλῶν ὁ θεὸς οὐκ ἀκούει· ἀλλ᾽ ἐάν τις θεοσεβὴς ᾖ,
καὶ τὸ θέλημα αὐτοῦ ποιῇ, τούτου ἀκούει.

31. Oidamen de 'oti 'amartolon 'o theos ouk akouei. all ean tis theosebeis ei,
kai to theleima autou poiei, toutou akouei.

Hebrew/Transliteration
לא. וַאֲנַחְנוּ יָדַעְנוּ כִּי חַטָּאִים לֹא-יִשְׁמַע אֱלֹהִים כִּי אִם-הַיָּרֵא אֶת-הָאֱלֹהִים וְהָעֹשֶׂה אֶת-רְצוֹנוֹ אֹתוֹ
:יִשְׁמָע

31. Va•a•nach•noo ya•da•a•noo ki cha•ta•eem lo - yish•ma Elohim ki eem -
ha•ya•re et - ha•Elohim ve•ha•o•se et - r`tzo•no o•to yish•ma.

Rabbinic Jewish Commentary
This was known from the Scripture, and all experience; see Psa_66:18. The Persic
and Ethiopic versions read, "I know, that God"

"If I had regarded iniquity in my heart, YAHWEH would not have heard."

---

32. Since the world began was it not heard that any man opened the eyes of one that was born blind.

Greek/Transliteration
32. Ἐκ τοῦ αἰῶνος οὐκ ἠκούσθη ὅτι ἤνοιξέν τις ὀφθαλμοὺς τυφλοῦ γεγεννημένου.

32. Ek tou aionos ouk eikousthei 'oti einoixen tis ophthalmous tuphlou gegenneimenou.

Hebrew/Transliteration
:לב. מִי שָׁמַע מֵעוֹדוֹ כִּי-פָקַח אִישׁ אֶת-עֵינֵי הַנּוֹלַד עִוֵּר מֵרָחֶם

32. Mee sha•ma me•o•do ki - fa•kach eesh et - ey•ney ha•no•lad ee•ver me•ra•chem.

Rabbinic Jewish Commentary
Since the world began,.... εκ του αιωνος, "from eternity", or never: the phrase answers to מעולם, frequently used by the Jews (m), for never; and so the Arabic version renders it, "it was never heard". since time was:

was it not heard, that any man opened the eyes of one that was born blind; as not any physician by any natural means, or art, so not any prophet in a miraculous way, no not Moses himself; among all the miracles he wrought, which the Jews say (n) were seventy six, and which were two more than were wrought by all the prophets put together, this is not to be found in the list of them, nor in the catalogue of miracles done by others. Elisha indeed prayed to God to restore sight to an army smitten with blindness; but then they were persons who saw before, and were not blind from their birth. Wherefore it must follow, that Jesus, the author of this miracle, must be greater than any of the prophets, even than Moses himself, and has a greater confirmation of his mission from God, than either he or they had: and as this was a miracle in nature, it is no less a miracle in grace, that one born in the blindness and darkness of sin, ignorance, and infidelity, should have the eyes of his understanding opened, to behold divine and spiritual things.

(m) Abot R. Nathan, c. 35. fol. 8. 2. Maimon. Mechira, c. 20. sect. 8. & Shelchim & Shotaphim, c. 10. sect. 1, 2, 3, 4. & passim. (n) Menasseh ben Israel, Conciliat. in Deut. Quaest. 11. p. 240.

---

33. If this man were not of God, he could do nothing.

Greek/Transliteration
33. Εἰ μὴ ἦν οὗτος παρὰ θεοῦ, οὐκ ἠδύνατο ποιεῖν οὐδέν.

33. Ei mei ein 'outos para theou, ouk eidunato poiein ouden.

Hebrew/Transliteration

לג: לוּלֵא הָיָה זֶה אִישׁ אֱלֹהִים לֹא-יָכֹל עֲשׂוֹת דָּבָר׃

33. Loo•le ha•ya ze eesh Elohim lo - ya•chol asot da•var.

---

34. They answered and said unto him, Thou wast altogether born in sins, and dost thou teach us? And they cast him out.

Greek/Transliteration

34. Ἀπεκρίθησαν καὶ εἶπον αὐτῷ, Ἐν ἁμαρτίαις σὺ ἐγεννήθης ὅλος, καὶ σὺ διδάσκεις ἡμᾶς; Καὶ ἐξέβαλον αὐτὸν ἔξω.

34. Apekritheisan kai eipon auto, En 'amartiais su egenneitheis 'olos, kai su didaskeis 'eimas? Kai exebalon auton exo.

Hebrew/Transliteration

לד. וַיַּעֲנוּ וַיֹּאמְרוּ אֵלָיו הֵן בְּעָוֹן חוֹלַלְתָּ וְאַתָּה תְלַמֵּד אֹתָנוּ וַיְּדְחֲפוּ אֹתוֹ מֵעַל-פְּנֵיהֶם׃

34. Va•ya•a•noo va•yom•roo elav hen be•avon cho•lal•ta ve•a•ta te•la•med o•ta•noo va•yid•cha•foo o•to me•al - p`ney•hem.

---

35. Jesus heard that they had cast him out; and when he had found him, he said unto him, Dost thou believe on the Son of God?

Greek/Transliteration

35. Ἤκουσεν ὁ Ἰησοῦς ὅτι ἐξέβαλον αὐτὸν ἔξω· καὶ εὑρὼν αὐτόν, εἶπεν αὐτῷ, Σὺ πιστεύεις εἰς τὸν υἱὸν τοῦ θεοῦ;

35. Eikousen 'o Yeisous 'oti exebalon auton exo. kai 'euron auton, eipen auto, Su pisteueis eis ton 'wion tou theou?

Hebrew/Transliteration

לה. וְיֵשׁוּעַ שָׁמַע כִּי דָחֲפוּ אֹתוֹ מֵעַל-פְּנֵיהֶם וַיִּפְגְּשֵׁהוּ וַיֹּאמֶר הֲתַאֲמִין בְּבֶן-הָאֱלֹהִים׃

35. Ve•Yeshua sha•ma ki da•cha•foo o•to me•al - p`ney•hem va•yif•ge•she•hoo va•yo•mar ha•ta•a•min be•Ven - ha•Elohim?

---

36. He answered and said, Who is he, Lord, that I might believe on him?

Greek/Transliteration

36. Ἀπεκρίθη ἐκεῖνος καὶ εἶπεν, Καὶ τίς ἐστιν, κύριε, ἵνα πιστεύσω εἰς αὐτόν;

36. Apekrithei ekeinos kai eipen, Kai tis estin, kurie, 'ina pisteuso eis auton?

Hebrew/Transliteration
לו. וַיַּעַן וַיֹּאמַר וּמִי הוּא-זֶה אֲדֹנִי וְאַאֲמִין בּוֹ:

36. Va•ya•an va•yo•mar oo•mi hoo - ze Adoni ve•a•a•min bo?

---

37. And Jesus said unto him, Thou hast both seen him, and it is he that talketh with thee.

Greek/Transliteration
37. Εἶπεν δὲ αὐτῷ ὁ Ἰησοῦς, Καὶ ἑώρακας αὐτόν, καὶ ὁ λαλῶν μετὰ σοῦ ἐκεῖνός ἐστιν.

37. Eipen de auto 'o Yeisous, Kai 'eorakas auton, kai 'o lalon meta sou ekeinos estin.

Hebrew/Transliteration
לז. וַיֹּאמֶר אֵלָיו יֵשׁוּעַ הֲלֹא רָאִיתָ אֹתוֹ וְהִנֵּה הוּא הַמְדַבֵּר אֵלֶיךָ זֶה הוּא:

37. Va•yo•mer elav Yeshua ha•lo ra•ee•ta o•to ve•hee•ne hoo ha•me•da•ber e•le•cha ze hoo.

---

38. And he said, Lord, I believe. And he worshipped him.

Greek/Transliteration
38. Ὁ δὲ ἔφη, Πιστεύω, κύριε· καὶ προσεκύνησεν αὐτῷ.

38. 'O de ephei, Pisteuo, kurie. kai prosekuneisen auto.

Hebrew/Transliteration
לח. וַיֹּאמֶר הִנְנִי מַאֲמִין אֲדֹנִי וַיִּשְׁתַּחוּ לוֹ:

38. Va•yo•mar hi•ne•ni ma•a•min Adoni va•yish•ta•choo lo.

---

39. And Jesus said, For judgment I am come into this world, that they which see not might see; and that they which see might be made blind.

Greek/Transliteration
39. Καὶ εἶπεν ὁ Ἰησοῦς, Εἰς κρίμα ἐγὼ εἰς τὸν κόσμον τοῦτον ἦλθον, ἵνα οἱ μὴ βλέποντες βλέπωσιν, καὶ οἱ βλέποντες τυφλοὶ γένωνται.

39. Kai eipen 'o Yeisous, Eis krima ego eis ton kosmon touton eilthon, 'ina 'oi
mei blepontes bleposin, kai 'oi blepontes tuphloi genontai.

לט. וַיֹּאמֶר יֵשׁוּעַ אֲנִי לָדִין בָּאתִי בָאָרֶץ לְמַעַן הַעִוְרִים יִהְיוּ רֹאִים וְהָרֹאִים יִהְיוּ עִוְרִים:

39. Va•yo•mer Yeshua ani la•din ba•ti va•a•retz le•ma•an ha•eev•rim
yi•hee•yoo ro•eem ve•ha•ro•eem yi•hee•yoo eev•rim.

---

40. And some of the Pharisees which were with him heard these words, and
said unto him, Are we blind also?

Greek/Transliteration
40. Καὶ ἤκουσαν ἐκ τῶν Φαρισαίων ταῦτα οἱ ὄντες μετ᾽ αὐτοῦ, καὶ εἶπον
αὐτῷ, Μὴ καὶ ἡμεῖς τυφλοί ἐσμεν;

40. Kai eikousan ek ton Pharisaion tauta 'oi ontes met autou, kai eipon auto,
Mei kai 'eimeis tuphloi esmen?

Hebrew/Transliteration
מ. וּמִן-הַפְּרוּשִׁים אֲשֶׁר הָיוּ עִמּוֹ וְשָׁמְעוּ אֶת-דְּבָרָיו אָמְרוּ הֲגַם אֲנַחְנוּ עִוְרִים:

40. Oo•min - ha•P`roo•shim asher ha•yoo ee•mo ve•sham•oo et - d`va•rav
am•roo ha•gam a•nach•noo eev•rim?

---

41. Jesus said unto them, If ye were blind, ye should have no sin: but now ye
say, We see; therefore your sin remaineth.

Greek/Transliteration
41. Εἶπεν αὐτοῖς ὁ Ἰησοῦς, Εἰ τυφλοὶ ἦτε, οὐκ ἂν εἴχετε ἁμαρτίαν· νῦν δὲ
λέγετε ὅτι Βλέπομεν· ἡ οὖν ἁμαρτία ὑμῶν μένει.

41. Eipen autois 'o Yeisous, Ei tuphloi eite, ouk an eichete 'amartian. nun de
legete 'oti Blepomen. 'ei oun 'amartia 'umon menei.

Hebrew/Transliteration
מא. וַיֹּאמֶר אֲלֵיהֶם יֵשׁוּעַ לוּ עִוְרִים הֱיִיתֶם לֹא-הָיָה בָכֶם עָוֹן אֲבָל אַתֶּם אֹמְרִים כִּי הִנְּכֶם רֹאִים לָכֵן
נִמְצָא עָוֹן:בָּכֶם

41. Va•yo•mer aley•hem Yeshua loo eev•rim he•yi•tem lo - ha•ya va•chem
a•von aval atem om•rim ki hin•chem ro•eem la•chen nim•tza a•von ba•chem.

John, Chapter 10

1. Verily, verily, I say unto you, He that entereth not by the door into the sheepfold, but climbeth up some other way, the same is a thief and a robber.

Greek/Transliteration
1. Ἀμὴν ἀμὴν λέγω ὑμῖν, ὁ μὴ εἰσερχόμενος διὰ τῆς θύρας εἰς τὴν αὐλὴν τῶν προβάτων, ἀλλὰ ἀναβαίνων ἀλλαχόθεν, ἐκεῖνος κλέπτης ἐστὶν καὶ λῃστής.

1. Amein amein lego 'umin, 'o mei eiserchomenos dya teis thuras eis tein aulein ton probaton, alla anabainon allachothen, ekeinos klepteis estin kai leisteis.

Hebrew/Transliteration
א. אָמֵן אָמֵן אֲנִי אֹמֵר לָכֶם אִישׁ אֲשֶׁר לֹא-יָבֹא דֶרֶךְ הַשַּׁעַר אֶל-מִכְלְאוֹת הַצֹּאן כִּי אִם-יַעֲלֶה בְדֶרֶךְ אַחֵר גַּנָּב:הוּא וְשֹׁדֵד

1. Amen amen ani o•mer la•chem eesh asher lo - ya•vo de•rech ha•sha•ar el - mich•le•ot ha•tzon ki eem - ya•a•le ve•de•rech a•cher ga•nav hoo ve•sho•ded.

Rabbinic Jewish Commentary
The sheepfold, with the Jews, was called דיר; and this, as their writers say (o), was an enclosure sometimes in the manner of a building, and made of stone, and sometimes was fenced with reeds, and in it was a large door, at which the shepherd went in and out, when he led in, or brought out the sheep. At tithing, which was done in the sheepfold, they made a little door, so that two lambs could not come out together; and to this enclosure is the allusion here.

The Persic version renders the words, "whoever does not introduce the sheep through the door of the sheepfold, know that that man is a thief and a robber"; which these men were so far from doing, that they would not suffer those that were entering to go in, Mat_23:13. The difference between a thief and a robber, with the Jews, was, that the former took away a man's property privately, and the latter openly (p).

(o) Maimon & Bartenora in Misn. Becorot, c. 9. sect. 7. (p) Maimon. Hilchot Genuba, c. 1. sect. 3.

---

2. But he that entereth in by the door is the shepherd of the sheep.

Greek/Transliteration
2. Ὁ δὲ εἰσερχόμενος διὰ τῆς θύρας ποιμήν ἐστιν τῶν προβάτων.

2. 'O de eiserchomenos dya teis thuras poimein estin ton probaton.

Hebrew/Transliteration
:ב. וְאִישׁ הַבָּא דֶרֶךְ הַשַּׁעַר הוּא רֹעֵה הַצֹּאן

2. Ve•eesh ha•ba de•rech ha•sha•ar hoo ro•eh ha•tzon.

---

3. To him the porter openeth; and the sheep hear his voice: and he calleth his own sheep by name, and leadeth them out.

Greek/Transliteration
3. Τούτῳ ὁ θυρωρὸς ἀνοίγει, καὶ τὰ πρόβατα τῆς φωνῆς αὐτοῦ ἀκούει, καὶ τὰ ἴδια πρόβατα καλεῖ κατ᾽ ὄνομα, καὶ ἐξάγει αὐτά.

3. Touto 'o thuroros anoigei, kai ta probata teis phoneis autou akouei, kai ta idya probata kalei kat onoma, kai exagei auta.

Hebrew/Transliteration
ג. לוֹ יִפְתַּח הַשֹּׁעֵר וְהַצֹּאן תִּשְׁמַעְנָה בְקֹלוֹ וְהוּא בְּשֵׁמוֹת יִקְרָא אֶל-צֹאנוֹ וְיוֹצִיאָן:

3. Lo yif•tach ha•sho•er ve•ha•tzon tish•ma•a•na ve•ko•lo ve•hoo be•she•mot yik•ra el - tzo•no ve•yo•tzi•en.

---

4. And when he putteth forth his own sheep, he goeth before them, and the sheep follow him: for they know his voice.

Greek/Transliteration
4. Καὶ ὅταν τὰ ἴδια πρόβατα ἐκβάλῃ, ἔμπροσθεν αὐτῶν πορεύεται· καὶ τὰ πρόβατα αὐτῷ ἀκολουθεῖ, ὅτι οἴδασιν τὴν φωνὴν αὐτοῦ.

4. Kai 'otan ta idya probata ekbalei, emprosthen auton poreuetai. kai ta probata auto akolouthei, 'oti oidasin tein phonein autou.

Hebrew/Transliteration
ד. בְּהוֹצִיאוֹ אֶת-כָּל-צֹאנוֹ יַעֲבֹר לִפְנֵיהֶן וְהָלְכוּ אַחֲרָיו הַצֹּאן כִּי יֹדְעוֹת אֶת-קֹלוֹ:

4. Be•ho•tzi•o et - kol - tzo•no ya•a•vor lif•ney•hen ve•hal•choo a•cha•rav ha•tzon ki yod•ot et - ko•lo.

---

5. And a stranger will they not follow, but will flee from him: for they know not the voice of strangers.

Greek/Transliteration
5. Ἀλλοτρίῳ δὲ οὐ μὴ ἀκολουθήσωσιν, ἀλλὰ φεύξονται ἀπ᾽ αὐτοῦ· ὅτι οὐκ οἴδασιν τῶν ἀλλοτρίων τὴν φωνήν.

5. Allotrio de ou mei akoloutheisosin, alla pheuxontai ap autou. 'oti ouk oidasin ton allotrion tein phonein.

Hebrew/Transliteration

:ה. וְאַחֲרֵי זָר לֹא תֵלַכְנָה כִּי תָנוֹסְנָה מִפָּנָיו יַעַן קוֹל זָרִים לֹא יָדָעוּ

5. Ve•a•cha•rey zar lo te•lach•na ki ta•nos•na mi•pa•nav ya•an kol za•rim lo ya•da•oo.

---

6. This parable spake Jesus unto them: but they understood not what things they were which he spake unto them.

Greek/Translitaration

6. Ταύτην τὴν παροιμίαν εἶπεν αὐτοῖς ὁ Ἰησοῦς· ἐκεῖνοι δὲ οὐκ ἔγνωσαν τίνα ἦν ἃ ἐλάλει αὐτοῖς.

6. Tautein tein paroimian eipen autois 'o Yeisous. ekeinoi de ouk egnosan tina ein 'a elalei autois.

Hebrew/Transliteration

:ו. אֶת-הַמָּשָׁל הַזֶּה נָשָׂא עֲלֵיהֶם יֵשׁוּעַ וְהֵם לֹא הֵבִינוּ מַה-זֶּה אֲשֶׁר דִּבֶּר אֲלֵיהֶם

6. Et - ha•ma•shal ha•ze na•sa aley•hem Yeshua ve•hem lo he•vi•noo ma - ze asher di•ber aley•hem.

---

7. Then said Jesus unto them again, Verily, verily, I say unto you, I am the door of the sheep.

Greek/Transliteration

7. Εἶπεν οὖν πάλιν αὐτοῖς ὁ Ἰησοῦς, Ἀμὴν ἀμὴν λέγω ὑμῖν ὅτι ἐγώ εἰμι ἡ θύρα τῶν προβάτων.

7. Eipen oun palin autois 'o Yeisous, Amein amein lego 'umin 'oti ego eimi 'ei thura ton probaton.

Hebrew/Transliteration

:ז. וַיּוֹסֶף יֵשׁוּעַ וַיְדַבֵּר אֲלֵיהֶם אָמֵן אָמֵן אֲנִי אֹמֵר לָכֶם אָנֹכִי שַׁעַר הַצֹּאן

7. Va•yo•sef Yeshua va•y`da•ber aley•hem Amen amen ani o•mer la•chem ano•chi sha•ar ha•tzon.

Rabbinic Jewish Commentary

The ancient Hebrew word picture for the word *door* in Hebrew, "dalet", is "The door of the shepherd leads to the covenant"; *dalet, lamed, taw*. (HWP pg.24)

---

8. All that ever came before me are thieves and robbers: but the sheep did not hear them.

Greek/Transliteration

8. Πάντες ὅσοι ἦλθον κλέπται εἰσὶν καὶ λῃσταί· ἀλλ᾽ οὐκ ἤκουσαν αὐτῶν τὰ πρόβατα.

8. Pantes 'osoi eilthon kleptai eisin kai leistai. all ouk eikousan auton ta probata.

Hebrew/Transliteration

ח. כֹּל אֲשֶׁר בָּאוּ לְפָנַי גַּנָּבִים הֵם וְשֹׁדְדִים וְלֹא-שָׁמְעוּ אֲלֵיהֶם הַצֹּאן:

8. Kol asher ba•oo le•fa•nai ga•na•vim hem ve•sho•de•dim ve•lo - sham•oo aley•hem ha•tzon.

---

9. I am the door: by me if any man enter in, he shall be saved, and shall go in and out, and find pasture.

Greek/Transliteration

9. Ἐγώ εἰμι ἡ θύρα· δι᾽ ἐμοῦ ἐάν τις εἰσέλθῃ, σωθήσεται, καὶ εἰσελεύσεται καὶ ἐξελεύσεται, καὶ νομὴν εὑρήσει.

9. Ego eimi 'ei thura. di emou ean tis eiselthei, sotheisetai, kai eiseleusetai kai exeleusetai, kai nomein 'eureisei.

Hebrew/Transliteration

ט. אָנֹכִי הַשַּׁעַר אִישׁ כִּי-יָבֹא כִּי יְוָשֵׁעַ דֶּרֶךְ בִּי וְיֵצֵא וּבָא וּמָצָא מִרְעֶה:

9. Ano•chi ha•sha•ar eesh ki - ya•vo de•rech bi ye•va•she•a oo•va ve•ye•tze oo•ma•tza mir•eh.

---

10. The thief cometh not, but for to steal, and to kill, and to destroy: I am come that they might have life, and that they might have it more abundantly.

Greek/Transliteration

10. Ὁ κλέπτης οὐκ ἔρχεται εἰ μὴ ἵνα κλέψῃ καὶ θύσῃ καὶ ἀπολέσῃ· ἐγὼ ἦλθον ἵνα ζωὴν ἔχωσιν, καὶ περισσὸν ἔχωσιν.

10. 'O klepteis ouk erchetai ei mei 'ina klepsei kai thusei kai apolesei. ego eilthon 'ina zoein echosin, kai perisson echosin.

Hebrew/Transliteration

י. הַגַּנָּב לֹא יָבֹא כִּי אִם-לִגְנֹב לִשְׁחֹט וּלְהַשְׁמִיד וַאֲנִי בָאתִי לְמַעַן יִמְצְאוּ חַיִּים וְחַצַּת נַפְשָׁם לָרְוָיָה:

10. Ha•ga•nav lo ya•vo ki eem - lig•nov lish•chot ool•hash•mid va•a•ni va•ti le•ma•an yim•tze•oo cha•yim ve•cha•yat naf•sham lar•va•ya.

---

11. I am the good shepherd: the good shepherd giveth his life for the sheep.

Greek/Transliteration

11. Ἐγώ εἰμι ὁ ποιμὴν ὁ καλός· ὁ ποιμὴν ὁ καλὸς τὴν ψυχὴν αὐτοῦ τίθησιν ὑπὲρ τῶν προβάτων.

11. Ego eimi 'o poimein 'o kalos. 'o poimein 'o kalos tein psuchein autou titheisin 'uper ton probaton.

Hebrew/Transliteration

יא. אֲנִי הוּא הָרֹעֶה הַטּוֹב הָרֹעֶה הַטּוֹב יִתֵּן אֶת-נַפְשׁוֹ בְּעַד הַצֹּאן:

11. Ani hoo ha•ro•eh ha•tov ha•ro•eh ha•tov yi•ten et - naf•sho be•ad ha•tzon.

Rabbinic Jewish Commentary

The Ethiopic version renders it, "The good shepherd gives his life for the redemption of his sheep"; so Nonnus paraphrases it, the "ransom price of his own sheep": this belongs to Yeshua's priestly office, and with the Jews priests were sometimes shepherds hence we read (q) of רועים כהנים, "shepherds that were priests". Philo the Jew speaks (r) of God as a shepherd and king; and of his setting his Word, his firstborn Son, over the holy flock, to take care of it: and a good shepherd is thus described by the (s) Jews;

"As רועה טוב, "a good shepherd", delivers the flock from the wolf, and from the lions, so he that leads Israel, if he is good, delivers them from the idolatrous nations, and from judgment below and above, and leads them to the life of the world to come, or eternal life."

Which description agrees with Yeshua, "the good shepherd"; and so the LORD is said to be רועה טוב, "the good shepherd", and merciful, and there is none like him (t).

(q) Misn. Becorot, c. 5. sect. 4. (r) De Agricultura, p. 195. & de nom. mutat. p. 1062. (s) Zohar in Exod. fol. 9. 3. (t) Aben Ezra in Psal. xxiii. 3. & Kimchi in Psal.

---

12. But he that is an hireling, and not the shepherd, whose own the sheep are not, seeth the wolf coming, and leaveth the sheep, and fleeth: and the wolf catcheth them, and scattereth the sheep.

Greek/Transliteration

12. Ὁ μισθωτὸς δέ, καὶ οὐκ ὢν ποιμήν, οὗ οὐκ εἰσὶν τὰ πρόβατα ἴδια, θεωρεῖ τὸν λύκον ἐρχόμενον, καὶ ἀφίησιν τὰ πρόβατα, καὶ φεύγει· καὶ ὁ λύκος ἁρπάζει αὐτά, καὶ σκορπίζει τὰ πρόβατα.

12. 'O misthotos de, kai ouk on poimein, 'ou ouk eisin ta probata idya, theorei ton lukon erchomenon, kai aphieisin ta probata, kai pheugei. kai 'o lukos 'arpazei auta, kai skorpizei ta probata.

Hebrew/Transliteration

יב. וְהַשָּׂכִיר אֲשֶׁר אֵינֶנּוּ רֹעֶה וְלֹא-לוֹ הַצֹּאן יִרְאֶה אֶת-הַזְּאֵב בָּא יַעֲזֹב אֶת-הַצֹּאן וְיָנוּס וְהַזְּאֵב יַחֲטֹף - וְיָפִיץ אֶת:הַצֹּאן

12. Ve•ha•sa•chir asher ey•ne•noo ro•eh ve•lo - lo ha•tzon yir•eh et - ha•z`ev ba ya•a•zov et - ha•tzon ve•ya•noos ve•ha•z`ev ya•cha•tof ve•ya•fitz et - ha•tzon.

Rabbinic Jewish Commentary

The Jews compare Israel to a flock of sheep, and Satan, they say, הוא הזאב, "he is the wolf" (u); or any false prophet, or teacher, who are ravenous wolves; though sometimes in sheep's clothing; or any tyrant, oppressor, or persecutor of the saints.

The Jews have a rule concerning such an hireling shepherd (w), which is this;

"A shepherd that feeds his flock, and leaves it, and goes to the city, and a wolf comes and ravines, and the lion comes and tears in pieces, he is free; but if he leaves by it his staff and his scrip, he is guilty."

Which Maimonides thus (x) expresses and explains;

"A shepherd who can deliver that which is torn, and that which is carried captive, with other shepherds, and with staves, and does not call the other shepherds, nor bring the staves to deliver them, he is guilty: one that keeps freely, and one that keeps for hire; he that keeps freely, calls the shepherds, and brings the staves freely; and if he does not find them, he is not guilty; but he that keeps for hire, is obliged to hire shepherds and staves, in order to deliver them."

(u) Caphtor, fol. 58. 1. (w) T. Bab. Bava Metzia, fol. 41. 1. & 93. 2. & 106. 1. (x) Hilchot Shechirut c. 3. sect. 6.

---

13. The hireling fleeth, because he is an hireling, and careth not for the sheep.

Greek/Transliteration

13. Ὁ δὲ μισθωτὸς φεύγει, ὅτι μισθωτός ἐστιν, καὶ οὐ μέλει αὐτῷ περὶ τῶν προβάτων.

13. 'O de misthotos pheugei, 'oti misthotos estin, kai ou melei auto peri ton probaton.

Hebrew/Transliteration

יג. וְהַשָּׂכִיר נָס כִּי שָׂכִיר הוּא וְלֹא יִדְאַג לַצֹּאן:

13. Ve•ha•sa•chir nas ki sa•chir hoo ve•lo yid•ag la•tzon.

Rabbinic Jewish Commentary

Abarbinel (y) has a note on Isa_40:11 which may serve to illustrate this passage:

""He shall feed his flock like a shepherd"; not as he that feeds the flock of others, for the hire they give him, but as a shepherd that feeds his own flock; who has compassion more abundantly on it, because it is his own flock; and therefore he saith, "behold his reward is with him", for he does not seek a reward from another; "and his work is before him"; for he feeds what is his own, and therefore his eyes and his heart are there."

Which is not the case of the hireling; he does not care for them, he has not their good at heart; but the good shepherd has, such an one as Yeshua is.

(y) Mashmia Jeshua, fol. 20. 4.

---

14. I am the good shepherd, and know my sheep, and am known of mine.

Greek/Transliteration

14. Ἐγώ εἰμι ὁ ποιμὴν ὁ καλός, καὶ γινώσκω τὰ ἐμά, καὶ γινώσκομαι ὑπὸ τῶν ἐμῶν.

14. Ego eimi 'o poimein 'o kalos, kai ginosko ta ema, kai ginoskomai 'upo ton emon.

Hebrew/Transliteration

יד. אֲנִי הוּא הָרֹעֶה הַטּוֹב יָדַעְתִּי אֶת אֲשֶׁר-לִי וְנוֹדַעְתִּי לַאֲשֶׁר לִי:

14. Ani hoo ha•ro•eh ha•tov ya•da•a•ti et asher - li ve•no•da•a•ti la•a•sher li.

---

15. As the Father knoweth me, even so know I the Father: and I lay down my life for the sheep.

Greek/Transliteration

15. Καθὼς γινώσκει με ὁ πατήρ, κἀγὼ γινώσκω τὸν πατέρα· καὶ τὴν ψυχήν μου τίθημι ὑπὲρ τῶν προβάτων.

15. Kathos ginoskei me 'o pateir, kago ginosko ton patera. kai tein psuchein mou titheimi 'uper ton probaton.

Hebrew/Transliteration

טו. כַּאֲשֶׁר גַּם-הָאָב יֹדֵעַ אֹתִי וַאֲנִי יֹדֵעַ אֶת-הָאָב וְאֶת-הָאָב:נַפְשִׁי אֶתֵּן בְּעַד הַצֹּאן

15. Ka•a•sher gam - ha•Av yo•de•a o•ti va•a•ni yo•de•a et - ha•Av ve•et - naf•shi e•ten be•ad ha•tzon.

---

16. And other sheep I have, which are not of this fold: them also I must bring, and they shall hear my voice; and there shall be one fold, and one shepherd.

Greek/Transliteration

16. Καὶ ἄλλα πρόβατα ἔχω, ἃ οὐκ ἔστιν ἐκ τῆς αὐλῆς ταύτης· κἀκεῖνά με δεῖ ἀγαγεῖν, καὶ τῆς φωνῆς μου ἀκούσουσιν· καὶ γενήσεται μία ποίμνη, εἷς ποιμήν.

16. Kai alla probata echo, 'a ouk estin ek teis auleis tauteis. kakeina me dei agagein, kai teis phoneis mou akousousin. kai geneisetai mia poimnei, 'eis poimein.

Hebrew/Transliteration

טז. וְעוֹד צֹאן אֲחֵרוֹת יֶשׁ-לִי אֲשֶׁר אֵינָן מִן-הַמִּכְלָה הַזֹּאת וְעָלַי לִנְהֹג גַּם-אֹתָן וְהֵנָּה בְּקוֹלִי תִשְׁמַעְנָה וְהָיָה:עֵדֶר אֶחָד וְרֹעֶה אֶחָד

16. Ve•od tzon a•che•rot yesh - li asher ey•nan min - ha•mich•la ha•zot ve•a•lai lin•hag gam - o•tan ve•he•na be•ko•li tish•ma•a•na ve•ha•ya eder e•chad ve•ro•eh e•chad.

---

17. Therefore doth my Father love me, because I lay down my life, that I might take it again.

Greek/Transliteration

17. Διὰ τοῦτο ὁ πατήρ με ἀγαπᾷ, ὅτι ἐγὼ τίθημι τὴν ψυχήν μου, ἵνα πάλιν λάβω αὐτήν.

17. Dya touto 'o pateir me agapa, 'oti ego titheimi tein psuchein mou, 'ina palin labo autein.

Hebrew/Transliteration

יז. עַל-כֵּן יֶאֱהָבַנִי הָאָב כִּי אֶת-נַפְשִׁי אֶתֵּן וְאָשִׁיב וְאֶקָּחֶיהָ:

17. Al - ken ye•e•ha•va•ni ha•Av ki et - naf•shi e•ten ve•a•shiv ve•e•ka•che•ha.

18. No man taketh it from me, but I lay it down of myself. I have power to lay it down, and I have power to take it again. This commandment have I received of my Father.

Greek/Transliteration

18. Οὐδεὶς αἴρει αὐτὴν ἀπ᾽ ἐμοῦ, ἀλλ᾽ ἐγὼ τίθημι αὐτὴν ἀπ᾽ ἐμαυτοῦ. Ἐξουσίαν ἔχω θεῖναι αὐτήν, καὶ ἐξουσίαν ἔχω πάλιν λαβεῖν αὐτήν. Ταύτην τὴν ἐντολὴν ἔλαβον παρὰ τοῦ πατρός μου.

18. Oudeis airei autein ap emou, all ego titheimi autein ap emautou. Exousian echo theinai autein, kai exousian echo palin labein autein. Tautein tein entolein elabon para tou patros mou.

Hebrew/Transliteration

יח. אִישׁ לֹא יִקַּח נַפְשִׁי מִמֶּנִּי כִּי אִם-אָנִי אֶתְּנֶנָּה יֶשׁ-לְאֵל יָדִי לְתִתָּהּ וְיֶשׁ-לְאֵל לַהֲשִׁיבָהּ אֵלַי זֹאת הַמִּצְוָה:צֻוֵּיתִי מֵאֵת אָבִי

18. Eesh lo yi•kach naf•shi mi•me•ni chi eem - ani et•ne•na yesh - le•el ya•di le•ti•ta ve•yesh - le•el la•ha•shi•va e•lai zot ha•mitz•va tzoo•vei•ti me•et Avi.

---

19. There was a division therefore again among the Jews for these sayings.

Greek/Transliteration

19. Σχίσμα οὖν πάλιν ἐγένετο ἐν τοῖς Ἰουδαίοις διὰ τοὺς λόγους τούτους.

19. Schisma oun palin egeneto en tois Youdaiois dya tous logous toutous.

Hebrew/Transliteration

יט. וַיֵּחָלְקוּ הַיְּהוּדִים עוֹד הַפַּעַם עַל-הַדְּבָרִים הָאֵלֶּה:

19. Va•ye•chal•koo ha•Ye•hoo•dim od ha•pa•am al - ha•d`va•rim ha•e•le.

---

20. And many of them said, He hath a devil, and is mad; why hear ye him?

Greek/Transliteration

20. Ἔλεγον δὲ πολλοὶ ἐξ αὐτῶν, Δαιμόνιον ἔχει καὶ μαίνεται· τί αὐτοῦ ἀκούετε;

20. Elegon de polloi ex auton, Daimonion echei kai mainetai. ti autou akouete?

Hebrew/Transliteration

כ. רַבִּים מֵהֶם אָמְרוּ רוּחַ רָע בּוֹ וּמְשֻׁגָּע הוּא לָמָה-זֶּה תִּשְׁמְעוּ אֵלָיו:

20. Ra•bim me•hem am•roo roo•ach ra bo oom•shoo•ga hoo la•ma - ze tish•me•oo elav?

Rabbinic Jewish Commentary
It was a notion of the Jews, that madness or distraction was from the devil, and therefore these two are here joined together, having a devil, and being mad: there is a spirit which they call Tazazith, and which, they say (z), is an evil spirit that takes away the understanding of men; and under the influence of such a "demon", the Jews thought Yeshua to be.

(z) R. David Kimchi, Sepher Shorash rad. תזן.

---

21. Others said, These are not the words of him that hath a devil. Can a devil open the eyes of the blind?

Greek/Transliteration
21. Ἄλλοι ἔλεγον, Ταῦτα τὰ ῥήματα οὐκ ἔστιν δαιμονιζομένου· μὴ δαιμόνιον δύναται τυφλῶν ὀφθαλμοὺς ἀνοίγειν;

21. Alloi elegon, Tauta ta 'reimata ouk estin daimonizomenou. mei daimonion dunatai tuphlon ophthalmous anoigein?

Hebrew/Transliteration
כא. וַאֲחֵרִים אָמְרוּ אֵין הַדְּבָרִים הָאֵלֶּה דִּבְרֵי בַעַל רוּחַ רָע הֲיֵשׁ עִם-רוּחַ רָע לִפְקֹחַ עֵינֵי עִוְרִים:

21. Va•a•che•rim am•roo eyn ha•d`va•rim ha•e•le div•rey va•al roo•ach ra ha•yesh eem - roo•ach ra lif•ko•ach ey•ney eev•rim?

---

22. And it was at Jerusalem the feast of the dedication, and it was winter.

Greek/Transliteration
22. Ἐγένετο δὲ τὰ Ἐγκαίνια ἐν Ἱεροσολύμοις, καὶ χειμὼν ἦν·

22. Egeneto de ta Egkainya en 'Yerosolumois, kai cheimon ein.

Hebrew/Transliteration
כב. וַיְהִי בִּימֵי הַחֲנֻכָּה בִּימֵי הַחֹרֶף בִּירוּשָׁלָיִם:

22. Vay•hi bi•mey ha•Cha•nooka bi•mey ha•cho•ref bi•Ye•roo•sha•la•yim.

Rabbinic Jewish Commentary
And it was at Jerusalem the feast of the dedication,.... That is, of the temple; not as built by Solomon, as Nonnus in his paraphrase suggests; or as rebuilt by Zerubabel, for there were no annual feasts appointed in commemoration of either

of these; and besides, they were neither of them in the winter time; the dedication of Solomon's temple was in autumn, at the feast of tabernacles, about September, 1Ki_8:2; and the dedication of the house in Zorobabel's time, was in the spring, about February, Ezr_6:15; but this was the feast of dedication, appointed by Judas Maccabaeus and his brethren, on account of the purging the temple, and renewing the altar, after the profanation of them by Antiochus; which feast lasted eight days, and began on the twenty fifth of the month Cisleu, which answers to part of our December; see the Apocrypha:

"52 Now on the five and twentieth day of the ninth month, which is called the month Casleu, in the hundred forty and eighth year, they rose up betimes in the morning, 56 And so they kept the dedication of the altar eight days and offered burnt offerings with gladness, and sacrificed the sacrifice of deliverance and praise. 59 Moreover Judas and his brethren with the whole congregation of Israel ordained, that the days of the dedication of the altar should be kept in their season from year to year by the space of eight days, from the five and twentieth day of the month Casleu, with mirth and gladness." (1 Maccabees 4)

"5 Now upon the same day that the strangers profaned the temple, on the very same day it was cleansed again, even the five and twentieth day of the same month, which is Casleu. 8 They ordained also by a common statute and decree, That every year those days should be kept of the whole nation of the Jews." (2 Maccabees 10:8)

With which the Jewish writers agree (a): the account Maimonides gives (b) of it is this;

"When the Israelites prevailed over their enemies and destroyed them, it was on the twenty fifth of the month Chisleu; and they went into the temple and could not find any pure oil in the sanctuary, but one vial; and it was not enough to light but one day only, and they lighted lamps of it for eight days, until the olives were squeezed, and they brought forth pure oil: wherefore the wise men of that generation ordered, that those eight days beginning at the twenty fifth of Chisleu, should be days of rejoicing and praise, and they lighted lamps at the doors of their houses; every night of these eight nights, to show and make known the miracle; and these days are called חנוכה "the dedication"; and they are forbidden mourning and fasting, as the days of "purim"; and the lighting of the lamps on them, is a commandment from the Scribes, as is the reading of the book of Esther. How many lamps do they light at the feast of the dedication? the order is, that every house should light one lamp, whether the men of the house be many, or whether there is but one man in it; but he that honours the command, lights up lamps according to the number of the men of the house, a lamp for everyone, whether men or women; and he that honours it more, lights up a lamp for every man the first night, and adds as he goes, every night a lamp; for instance, if there be ten men in the house, the first night he lights up ten lamps, and on the second night twenty, and on the third night thirty; until he comes to the eighth night, when he lights up fourscore lamps."

Wherefore, as Josephus says (c), this feast was called φωτα, "lights"; though he seems to assign another reason of its name, because that prosperity and happiness appeared to them beyond hope, and unexpected: and though this was only an order of Judas and his brethren, and the congregation of Israel, yet the Jews observe it as religiously, as if it was the appointment of God himself, and they do not spare to call it so; for in the service of this feast, they have these words (d);

"Blessed art thou, O LORD our God, the King of the world, who hath sanctified us by his commandments, and hath "commanded" us to light the lamp of the dedication; blessed art thou, O LORD our God, the King of the world, who did wonders for our fathers on those days, at this time; blessed art thou, O LORD our God, the King of the world, who has kept us alive, and preserved us, and brought us to this time; these lamps we light, because of the wonders and marvellous things, and salvations, and wars, thou hast wrought for our fathers on those days at this time, by the hand of thine holy priests.--These lamps are holy, we have no power to use them, but only to behold them, so as to confess and praise thy great name, for thy miracles, and for thy wonders, and for thy salvations."

And though this feast is said to be at Jerusalem, yet it was not confined there, as were the other feasts of the passover, pentecost, and tabernacles, for this might be kept in any part of the land: mention is made of the feast of dedication at Lydda (e), and in other countries; Maimonides (f) says

"It is a common custom in all our cities in Spain, that all the men of the house light up a lamp the first night, and add as they go along, a lamp every night, till he lights up on the eighth night eight lamps, whether the men of the house be many, or there be but one man."

Some have been of opinion, that this feast of dedication was on the account of the victory Judith gained over Holophernes, by cutting off his head; or however, that the commemoration of that victory was a part of this festival: in the Vulgate Latin edition of Judith 16:31 it is said,

"The day of the festivity of this victory is received by the Hebrews into the number of holy days; and is kept by the Jews from that time, to the present day."

And Sigonius (g) asserts, that it is celebrated by the Jews on the twenty fifth day of the month Chisleu; which is the same day the feast began, that was instituted by Judas Maccabaeus, on the above account; and certain it is, that the Jews do make mention of that fact of hers, in the service for the first sabbath of this feast (h); and some of their writers would have this fact to be in the times of the Maccabees, though as one of their chronologers (i) observes, it appears from the history of Judith, to have been in the times of Nebuchadnezzar; and there are some that say it was in the times of Cambyses, son of Cyrus, king of Persia, and was two or three hundred years before the miracle of the dedication: but he serves, that the wise men of that age agreed to comprehend the memorial of that wonderful event, with the miracle of the dedication: and so R. Leo Modena (k) says,

"They have a tradition, that in ordaining this feast to be kept, they had an eve also upon that famous exploit performed by Judith upon Holophernes; although many are of opinion, that this happened not at this time of the year; and that they make a commemoration of that piece of gallantry of hers now, because she was of the stock of the Maccabees."

But that cannot be, since she must be some hundreds of years before them; wherefore others make mention of another Judith, a daughter of one of the Maccabees, who performed a like exploit upon Nicanor, a general of Demetrius's army: to which R. Gedaliah has respect, when he says (l),

"The wise men agreed to comprehend together in the joy of the feast of dedication, the affair of Judith, seeing there was another Judith, from her that killed Holophernes, a daughter of the Maccabees."

But it is not clear that there was any such woman, nor that Nicanor was slain by one; and besides, he was killed on the thirteenth of Adar, and that day was ordained to be kept yearly on that account, in the Apocrypha:

"43 So the thirteenth day of the month Adar the hosts joined battle: but Nicanor's host was discomfited, and he himself was first slain in the battle. 49 Moreover they ordained to keep yearly this day, being the thirteenth of Adar."
(1 Maccabees 7)

"And they ordained all with a common decree in no case to let that day pass without solemnity, but to celebrate the thirtieth day of the twelfth month, which in the Syrian tongue is called Adar, the day before Mardocheus' day."
(2 Maccabees 15:36)

and the month of Adar answers to part of February.

And it was winter; for the month Chisleu answers to our November and December; so that the twenty fifth of that month might be about the tenth of December, and the Jews reckon part of that month winter, and it must be the part in which this feast was; they say (m),

"Half Chisleu, Tebeth, and half Shebet, are חורף, "winter":"

So that the evangelist might with propriety say, according to the sense of the Jewish nation, that it was winter; though it was but just entered, even not more than ten days: the reason why this is observed, may be for what follows.

(a) Ganz Tzemach David, par. 1. fol. 22. 1. Tzeror Hammor, fol. 137. 2. (b) Hilchot Megilla Uchanucha, c. 3. sect. 2, 3. & 4. 1, 2. Vid. T. Bab. Sabbat, fol. 21. 2. (c) Antiqu. l. 12. c. 7. sect. 7. (d) Seder Tephillot, fol. 234. 1, 2. Ed. Amsterd. (e) T. Bab. Roshhashana, fol. 18. 2. (f) Hilchot Chanuca, c. 4. sect. 3. (g) De Repub. Heb. l. 3. c. 17. (h) Seder Tephillot, fol. 133. 2. (i) Ganz Tzemach David, par. 1. fol. 22. 1. (k) History of the Rites of the Jews, c. 9.

23. And Jesus walked in the temple in Solomon's porch.

Greek/Transliteration
23. καὶ περιεπάτει ὁ Ἰησοῦς ἐν τῷ ἱερῷ ἐν τῇ στοᾷ Σολομῶνος.

23. kai periepatei 'o Yeisous en to 'iero en tei stoa Solomonos.

Hebrew/Transliteration
:כג. וַיִּתְהַלֵּךְ יֵשׁוּעַ בְּבֵית הַמִּקְדָּשׁ בְּאוּלָם שְׁלֹמֹה

23. Va•yit•ha•lech Yeshua be•veit ha•mik•dash be•oo•lam Sh`lo•mo.

Rabbinic Jewish Commentary
The account Josephus (n) gives of it is this;

"There was a porch without the temple, overlooking a deep valley, supported by
walls of four hundred cubits, made of four square stone, very white; the length of
each stone was twenty cubits, and the breadth six; the work of king Solomon, who
first founded the whole temple."

Now, though this was not the porch that was built by Solomon, yet as it was built
on the same spot, and in imitation of it, it bore his name.

---

24. Then came the Jews round about him, and said unto him, How long dost thou make us to doubt? If thou be the Christ, tell us plainly.

Greek/Transliteration
24. Ἐκύκλωσαν οὖν αὐτὸν οἱ Ἰουδαῖοι, καὶ ἔλεγον αὐτῷ, Ἕως πότε τὴν
ψυχὴν ἡμῶν αἴρεις; Εἰ σὺ εἶ ὁ χριστός, εἰπὲ ἡμῖν παρρησίᾳ.

24. Ekuklosan oun auton 'oi Youdaioi, kai elegon auto, 'Eos pote tein
psuchein 'eimon aireis? Ei su ei 'o christos, eipe 'eimin parreisia.

Hebrew/Transliteration
כד. וַיָּסֹבּוּ אֹתוֹ הַיְהוּדִים וַיֹּאמְרוּ עַד-אָנָה תִמְשְׁכֵנוּ בְנַפְשֵׁנוּ אִם-אַתָּה הוּא הַמָּשִׁיחַ הַגֶּד-לָנוּ לְעֵין
:הַשָּׁמֶשׁ

24. Va•ya•so•boo o•to ha•Ye•hoo•dim va•yom•roo ad - ana tim•she•che•noo
ve•naf•she•noo eem - ata hoo ha•Ma•shi•ach ha•ged - la•noo le•ein
ha•sha•mesh.

Rabbinic Jewish Commentary

The Vulgate Latin, Syriac, Persic, and Ethiopic versions literally render it, "how long dost thou take away our soul?" that is, deprive us of the knowledge of thee; Nonnus renders it, "wherefore dost thou steal away our minds with words?" so Jacob when he went away privately, without the knowledge of Laban, is said to steal away the heart of Laban, as it is in the Hebrew text, in Gen_31:20 (o). In like manner the Jews charge Yeshua with taking away their soul, or stealing away their heart, or hiding himself from them; not telling them plainly, who he was.

(o) See De Dieu in loc.

---

25. Jesus answered them, I told you, and ye believed not: the works that I do in my Father's name, they bear witness of me.

Greek/Transliteration

25. Ἀπεκρίθη αὐτοῖς ὁ Ἰησοῦς, Εἶπον ὑμῖν, καὶ οὐ πιστεύετε· τὰ ἔργα ἃ ἐγὼ ποιῶ ἐν τῷ ὀνόματι τοῦ πατρός μου, ταῦτα μαρτυρεῖ περὶ ἐμοῦ·

25. Apekrithei autois 'o Yeisous, Eipon 'umin, kai ou pisteuete. ta erga 'a ego poio en to onomati tou patros mou, tauta marturei peri emou.

Hebrew/Transliteration

כה. וַיַּעַן אֹתָם יֵשׁוּעַ הֵן הִגַּדְתִּי לָכֶם וְלֹא הֶאֱמַנְתֶּם בִּי הַמַּעֲשִׂים אֲשֶׁר-אֲנִי עֹשֶׂה בְּשֵׁם אָבִי הֵם לִי לְעֵדוּת:

25. Va•ya•an o•tam Yeshua hen hi•ga•d`ti la•chem ve•lo he•e•man•tem bi ha•ma•a•sim asher - ani o•se be•shem Avi hem li le•e•doot.

---

26. But ye believe not, because ye are not of my sheep, as I said unto you.

Greek/Transliteration

26. ἀλλ᾽ ὑμεῖς οὐ πιστεύετε· οὐ γάρ ἐστε ἐκ τῶν προβάτων τῶν ἐμῶν, καθὼς εἶπον ὑμῖν.

26. all 'umeis ou pisteuete. ou gar este ek ton probaton ton emon, kathos eipon 'umin.

Hebrew/Transliteration

כו. רַק אַתֶּם לֹא תַאֲמִינוּ כִּי לֹא מִצֹּאנִי אַתֶּם כַּאֲשֶׁר אָמַרְתִּי לָכֶם:

26. Rak atem lo ta•a•mi•noo ki lo mi•tzo•ni atem ka•a•sher amar•ti la•chem.

---

27. My sheep hear my voice, and I know them, and they follow me:

Greek/Transliteration
27. Τὰ πρόβατα τὰ ἐμὰ τῆς φωνῆς μου ἀκούει, κἀγὼ γινώσκω αὐτά, καὶ ἀκολουθοῦσίν μοι·

27. Ta probata ta ema teis phoneis mou akouei, kago ginosko auta, kai akolouthousin moi.

Hebrew/Transliteration
כז. צֹאנִי שֹׁמְעוֹת אֶת-קֹלִי וַאֲנִי יֹדֵעַ אֹתָן וְהֵנָּה הֹלְכוֹת אַחֲרָי:

27. Tzo•ni shom•ot et - ko•li va•a•ni yo•de•a o•tan ve•he•na hol•chot a•cha•rai.

---

28. And I give unto them eternal life; and they shall never perish, neither shall any man pluck them out of my hand.

Greek/Transliteration
28. κἀγὼ ζωὴν αἰώνιον δίδωμι αὐτοῖς· καὶ οὐ μὴ ἀπόλωνται εἰς τὸν αἰῶνα, καὶ οὐχ ἁρπάσει τις αὐτὰ ἐκ τῆς χειρός μου.

28. kago zoein aionion didomi autois. kai ou mei apolontai eis ton aiona, kai ouch 'arpasei tis auta ek teis cheiros mou.

Hebrew/Transliteration
כח. וְחַיֵּי עוֹלָם אֶתֵּן לָהֶן לֹא תֹאבַדְנָה לָנֶצַח וְלֹא יַחֲטֹף אֹתָן אִישׁ מִיָּדִי:

28. Ve•cha•yey o•lam e•ten la•hen lo to•vad•na la•ne•tzach ve•lo ya•cha•tof o•tan eesh mi•ya•di.

---

29. My Father, which gave them me, is greater than all; and no man is able to pluck them out of my Father's hand.

Greek/Transliteration
29. Ὁ πατήρ μου ὃς δέδωκέν μοι, μείζων πάντων ἐστίν· καὶ οὐδεὶς δύναται ἁρπάζειν ἐκ τῆς χειρὸς τοῦ πατρός μου.

29. 'O pateir mou 'os dedoken moi, meizon panton estin. kai oudeis dunatai 'arpazein ek teis cheiros tou patros mou.

Hebrew/Transliteration
כט. אָבִי אֲשֶׁר נְתָנָן לִי אַדִּיר הוּא מִכֹּל וְאֵין אִישׁ אֲשֶׁר-יוּכַל לַחֲטֹף אֶתְהֶן מִיַּד הָאָב:

29. Avi asher n`ta•nan li adir hoo mi•kol ve•eyn eesh asher - yoo•chal la•cha•tof et•hen mi•yad ha•Av.

Rabbinic Jewish Commentary
The Apocrypha reads:

"But the souls of the righteous are in the hand of God, and there shall no torment touch them." (Wisdom 3:1).

---

30. I and my Father are one.

Greek/Transliteration
30. Ἐγὼ καὶ ὁ πατὴρ ἕν ἐσμεν.

30. Ego kai 'o pateir 'en esmen.

Hebrew/Transliteration
ל. וַאֲנִי וְהָאָב אֶחָד:

30. Va•a•ni ve•ha•Av e•chad.

Rabbinic Jewish Commentary
From the use of the verb plural, "I and *my* Father", εσμεν, "we are one"; that is, in nature and essence, and perfections, particularly in power.

The Jew (p) objects, that "If the sense of this expression is, that the Father and the Son are one, as the Nazarenes understand and believe it, it will be found that Yeshua himself destroys this saying, as it is written in Mar_13:32, for saith Yeshua, "that day and that hour, there is knoweth, not the angels, nor the Son, but the Father only"; lo, these words show, that the Father and the Son are not one, since the Son does not know what the Father knows."

The Talmud teaches that the son is a limb of his father. Yitzhak Kasdan elucidates the passage, "Indeed, this is the underpinning of the concept in the *g'marah* (Sanhedrin 104a) that "b'ra m'zakeh aba" – a son brings merit to his father through good deeds, learning Torah, etc. He does so because "b'ra kareih d'avuah" (cf. Eruvin70b), a son is considered an extension – literally the leg – of his father, either because the son and father are part and parcel of each other (i.e., are joined together) or because the father is considered the *gorem*, the cause, of his son's actions (i.e., since the son emulates him by following in his footsteps). In other words, the son's actions and accomplishments are considered as the father's and are credited to the father." (Yitzhak Kasdan, Understanding The Mitzvah of Hesped [2])

This subject is spoken by the *Alter Rebbe*, R' Schneur Zalman of Liadi, (1745 CE – 1812 CE) in his epic work, the Tanya. Yanki Tauber of Chabad.org elucidates,

On a deeper level, however, the child remains inseparable from his begetter. In the words of the Talmud, "A son is a limb of his father." At the very heart of the child's consciousness lies an inescapable truth: he is his father's child, an extension of his being, a projection of his personality. In body, they have become two distinct entities; in essence, they are one."
(Yanki Tauber, The Head, Chabad.org [3])

Rebbe Nachman illustrates the unity of father and son,
"This is (Genesis 49:24) "…from there the Shepherd, the evan (the Rock) of Israel." Onkelos translates ["EVaN" as a composite of] AV and BeN (father and son). This is the complete-statement: father and son as one. For a half-statement corresponds to the son alone, but the complete-statement is father and son as one. Everything is encompassed there, and through this one can come to the concept of shepherds, as above. Hence this is the meaning of, "from there the Shepherd, the EVaN of Israel."
(R' Nachman of Breslov, Likutey Moharan I, 22:10, Volume 3, published by the Breslov Research Institute, pg 381)

(p) Isaac Chizzuk Emuna, par. 2. c. 50. p. 438, 439.

---

31. Then the Jews took up stones again to stone him.

Greek/Transliteration
31. Ἐβάστασαν οὖν πάλιν λίθους οἱ Ἰουδαῖοι ἵνα λιθάσωσιν αὐτόν.

31. Ebastasan oun palin lithous 'oi Youdaioi 'ina lithasosin auton.

Hebrew/Transliteration
לֹא. וַיּוֹסִיפוּ הַיְּהוּדִים וַיִּשְׂאוּ אֲבָנִים לְסָקְלוֹ:

31. Va•yo•si•foo ha•Ye•hoo•dim va•yis•oo ava•nim le•sok•lo.

Rabbinic Jewish Commentary
In the Torah, Israel almost stoned Moses Rabbeinu, (Our Rabbi)
"Moses cried to the LORD, saying, What shall I do with these people? They are almost ready to stone me." (Exodus 17:4)

There is a tradition in a text called the Secrets of R' Shimon bar Yochai, that Mashiach will be concealed and rejected,

"The Messiah of the lineage of Ephraim shall die there, and Israel shall mourn for him. After this the Holy One blessed be He will reveal to them the Messiah of the lineage of David, but *Israel will wish to stone him*, and they will say to him: 'You speak a lie, for the Messiah has already been slain, and there is no other Messiah destined to arise.' *They will scorn him*, as Scripture says: 'despised and abandoned (by) men' (Isa 53:3). He shall withdraw and be hidden from them, as

Scripture continues: 'like one hiding faces from us' (ibid.).

But in Israel's great distress, they will turn and cry out from (their) hunger and thirst, and the Holy One, blessed be He, will be revealed to them in His glory, as Scripture promises: 'together all flesh will see' (Isa 40:5). And the King Messiah will sprout up there, as Scripture says: 'and behold with the clouds of heaven etc.' (Dan 7:13), and it is written after it 'and authority was given to him' (Dan 7:14).

He shall blow (his breath) at that wicked Armilos and kill him, as Scripture forecasts: 'he will slay the wicked one with the breath of his lips' (Isa 11:4)."

(Nistarot ben Shimon bar Yochai, translated by John C. Reeves [8])

---

32. Jesus answered them, Many good works have I shewed you from my Father; for which of those works do ye stone me?

Greek/Transliteration

32. Ἀπεκρίθη αὐτοῖς ὁ Ἰησοῦς, Πολλὰ καλὰ ἔργα ἔδειξα ὑμῖν ἐκ τοῦ πατρός μου· διὰ ποῖον αὐτῶν ἔργον λιθάζετέ με;

32. Apekrithei autois 'o Yeisous, Polla kala erga edeixa 'umin ek tou patros mou. dya poion auton ergon lithazete me?

Hebrew/Transliteration

לב. וַיַּעַן אֹתָם יֵשׁוּעַ הֵן מַעֲשִׂים רַבִּים טוֹבִים הֶרְאֵיתִי לָכֶם מֵאֵת הָאָב עַל-אֵי-זֶה מִן-הַמַּעֲשִׂים הָאֵלֶּה תִּסְקְלֻנִי:

32. Va•ya•an o•tam Yeshua hen ma•a•sim ra•bim to•vim her•ei•ti la•chem me•et ha•Av al - ey - ze min - ha•ma•a•sim ha•e•le tis•ke•loo•ni.

---

33. The Jews answered him, saying, For a good work we stone thee not; but for blasphemy; and because that thou, being a man, makest thyself God.

Greek/Transliteration

33. Ἀπεκρίθησαν αὐτῷ οἱ Ἰουδαῖοι λέγοντες, Περὶ καλοῦ ἔργου οὐ λιθάζομέν σε, ἀλλὰ περὶ βλασφημίας, καὶ ὅτι σὺ ἄνθρωπος ὢν ποιεῖς σεαυτὸν θεόν.

33. Apekritheisan auto 'oi Youdaioi legontes, Peri kalou ergou ou lithazomen se, alla peri blaspheimias, kai 'oti su anthropos on poieis seauton theon.

Hebrew/Transliteration

לג. וַיַּעֲנוּ אֹתוֹ הַיְּהוּדִים לֵאמֹר עַל-מַעֲשֶׂה טוֹב לֹא נִסְקְלֶךָ כִּי אִם-עַל-חִלּוּל הַשֵּׁם בַּאֲשֶׁר כִּי אָדָם אַתָּה וְהִנְּךָ אֹמֵר לְנַפְשְׁךָ אֱלֹהִים אָתָּה:

33. Va•ya•a•noo o•to ha•Ye•hoo•dim le•mor al - ma•a•se tov lo nis•ke•le•cha ki eem - al - chi•lool ha•shem ba•a•sher ki adam ata ve•hin•cha o•mer le•naf•she•cha Elohim ata.

Rabbinic Jewish Commentary

but for blasphemy; which required death by stoning, according to Lev_24:16, and according to the Jews' oral law (q).

Two mistakes they seem to be guilty of in this account; one that Yeshua was a mere man, the other that he made himself God, or assumed deity to himself, which did not belong to him, and therefore must be guilty of blasphemy; neither of which were true: the phrase is used by the Jews, of others who have taken upon them the name and title of God; as of Hiram king of Tyre, of whom they say, שעשה עצמו אלוה, "that he made himself God" (r); the same they say of Nebuchadnezzar; and the modern Jews still continue the same charge against Yeshua, as their ancestors did, and express it in the same language, and say of him, that he was a man, and set himself up for God (s).

(q) Misn. Sanhedrin, c. 7. sect. 4. (r) Bereshit Rabba, sect. 96. fol. 83. 4. & Tzeror Hammor, fol. 134. 4. (s) Aben Ezra in Gen. xxvii. 39. & Abarbinel Mashmia Jeshua, fol. 5. 1.

---

34. Jesus answered them, Is it not written in your law, I said, Ye are gods?

Greek/Transliteration
34. Ἀπεκρίθη αὐτοῖς ὁ Ἰησοῦς, Οὐκ ἔστιν γεγραμμένον ἐν τῷ νόμῳ ὑμῶν, Ἐγὼ εἶπα, Θεοί ἐστε;

34. Apekrithei autois 'o Yeisous, Ouk estin gegrammenon en to nomo 'umon, Ego eipa, Theoi este?

Hebrew/Transliteration
לד. וַיַּעַן אֹתָם יֵשׁוּעַ הֲלֹא כָתוּב בְּתוֹרַתְכֶם אֲנִי אָמַרְתִּי אֱלֹהִים אַתֶּם:

34. Va•ya•an o•tam Yeshua ha•lo cha•toov be•to•rat•chem ani amar•ti Elohim atem?

Rabbinic Jewish Commentary
Jesus answered them, is it not written in your law,.... In the torah which was given unto them, of which they boasted, and pretended to understand, and interpret, even in Psa_82:6; for the torah includes not only the Pentateuch, but all the books of the Old Testament: it is an observation of one of the Jewish Rabbi's (t), that

"With the wise men of blessed memory, it is found in many places that the word torah comprehends the Prophets and the Hagiographa."

Among which last stands the book of Psalms; and this may be confirmed by a passage out of the Talmud (u); it is asked,

"From whence does the resurrection of the dead appear, מן התורה, "out of the torah?""

It is answered,

"As it is said in Psa_84:4, "Blessed are they that dwell in thy house, they will still praise thee, Selah; they do praise thee", it is not said, but "they will praise thee"; from hence is a proof of the resurrection of the dead, "out of the torah"."

The same question is again put, and then Isa_52:8 is cited, and the like observation made upon it. Moreover, this is a way of speaking used by the Jews, when they introduce another citing a passage of Scripture thus (w), הלא כתיב בתורתכם, "is it not written in your torah", Deu_4:9, "only take heed to thyself". So here the Scripture follows,

I said, ye are gods? which is spoken to civil magistrates, so called, because of their authority and power; and because they do, in some sort, represent the divine majesty, in the government of nations and kingdoms. Many of the Jewish writers, by "gods", understand "the messengers". The Targum paraphrases the words thus:

"I said ye are accounted as messengers, as the messengers on high, all of you;"

And to this sense some of their commentators interpret it. Jarchi's gloss is, ye are gods; that is, messengers; for when I gave the torah to you, it was on this account, that the messenger of death might not any more rule over you: the note of Aben Ezra is, "and the children of the Most High": as messengers; and the sense is, your soul is as the soul of messengers: hence the (x) Jew charges Yeshua with seeking refuge in words, that will not profit, or be any help to him, when he cites these words, showing that magistrates are called gods, when the sense is only, that they are like to the messengers in respect of their souls:

But let it be observed, that it is not said, "ye are as gods", as in Gen_3:5, but "ye are gods"; not like unto them only, but are in some sense gods; and besides, to say that they are like to messengers, with respect to their souls, which come from above, is to say no more of the judges of the earth, than what may be said of every man: to which may be added, that this objector himself owns, that judges are called אלהים, "gods", as in Exo_22:9; the cause of both parties shall come before אלהים, "the judges"; and that even the word is used in this sense in this very psalm, from whence these words are cited, Psa_82:1, "he judgeth among" אלהים, "the gods"; and both Kimchi and Ben Melech interpret this text itself in the same way, and observe, that judges are called gods, when they judge truly and aright: all which is sufficient to justify Yeshua in the citation of this passage, and the use he makes of it.

(t) R. Azarias in Meor Enayim, c. 7. fol. 47. 1. (u) T. Bab. Sanhedrin, fol. 91. 2. (w) T. Bab. Beracot, fol. 32. 2. (x) R. Isaac Chizzuk Emuna, par. 2. c. 51. p. 440, 441.

35. If he called them gods, unto whom the word of God came, and the scripture cannot be broken;

Greek/Transliteration

35. Εἰ ἐκείνους εἶπεν θεούς, πρὸς οὓς ὁ λόγος τοῦ θεοῦ ἐγένετο- καὶ οὐ δύναται λυθῆναι ἡ γραφή-

35. Ei ekeinous eipen theous, pros 'ous 'o logos tou theou egeneto- kai ou dunatai lutheinai 'ei graphei-

Hebrew/Transliteration

לה. וְעַתָּה אִם-אֲנָשִׁים נִקְרְאוּ אֱלֹהִים אֲשֶׁר תּוֹרַת הָאֱלֹהִים אִתָּם וּדְבַר הַכָּתוּב אֵין לְהָשִׁיב:

35. Ve•a•ta eem - a•na•shim nik•re•oo elohim asher to•rat ha•Elohim ee•tam oo•d`var ha•ka•toov eyn le•ha•shiv.

Rabbinic Jewish Commentary

The Syriac version reads, "because the word of God came to them". This sense is favoured by the Ethiopic version, which renders it, "if he called them gods to whom God appeared, the Word of God was with them": or else the commission from God, authorizing them to act in the capacity of rulers and governors, is here meant; or rather the Word of God, which, in the passage of Scripture cited, calls them so, as it certainly does.

and the Scripture cannot be broken; or be made null and void; whatever that says is true, there is no contradicting it, or objecting to it: it is a Jewish way of speaking, much used in the Talmud (y); when one Rabbi has produced an argument, or instance, in any point of debate, another says, איכא למיפרך, "it may be broken"; or objected to, in such and such a manner, and be refuted: but the Scripture cannot be broken, that is not to be objected to, there can be no confutation of that.

(y) T. Bab. Zebachim, fol. 4. 1. & Becorot, fol. 32. 1. & passim.

---

36. Say ye of him, whom the Father hath sanctified, and sent into the world, Thou blasphemest; because I said, I am the Son of God?

Greek/Transliteration

36. ὃν ὁ πατὴρ ἡγίασεν καὶ ἀπέστειλεν εἰς τὸν κόσμον, ὑμεῖς λέγετε ὅτι Βλασφημεῖς, ὅτι εἶπον, Υἱὸς τοῦ θεοῦ εἰμι;

36. 'on 'o pateir 'eigiasen kai apesteilen eis ton kosmon, 'umeis legete 'oti Blaspheimeis, 'oti eipon, 'Wios tou theou eimi?

Hebrew/Transliteration

לו. אֵיךְ תֹּאמְרוּן עַל-זֶה אֲשֶׁר קִדְּשׁוֹ הָאָב וַיִּשְׁלָחֵהוּ בָאָרֶץ מְגַדֵּף אַתָּה יַעַן אָמַרְתִּי בֶּן-הָאֱלֹהִים אָנִי:

36. Eych tom•roon al - ze asher kid•sho ha•Av va•yish•la•che•hoo va•a•retz me•ga•def ata ya•an amar•ti Ben - ha•Elohim ani.

Rabbinic Jewish Commentary
thou blasphemest, because I said, I am the Son of God; for what he had said in Joh_10:30 is equivalent to it; and in it he was rightly understood by the Jews, and what he here and afterwards says confirms it: the argument is what the Jews call קל וחומר, "from the lesser to the greater", and stands thus; that if mere frail mortal men, and some of them wicked men, being made rulers and judges in the earth are called gods, by God himself, to whom the word of God came in time, and constituted them gods, or governors, but for a time; and this is a fact stands recorded in Scripture, which cannot be denied or disproved, then surely it cannot be blasphemy in Yeshua, to assert himself to be the Son of God, who existed as a divine person from all eternity; and was so early set apart to the office of prophet, priest, and king; and in the fulness of time was sent into this world, to be the author of eternal salvation to the sons of men.

The "lesser to greater" argument is from the Seven Rules of Hillel who established the rules of the interpretation of the Scriptures and the deduction of laws from them in writing before the time of Yeshua.

---

37. **If I do not the works of my Father, believe me not.**

Greek/Transliteration
37. Εἰ οὐ ποιῶ τὰ ἔργα τοῦ πατρός μου, μὴ πιστεύετέ μοι·

37. Ei ou poio ta erga tou patros mou, mei pisteuete moi.

Hebrew/Transliteration
לז. אִם-לֹא עָשִׂיתִי אֶת-מַעֲשֵׂי אָבִי לֹא תַאֲמִינוּ לִי:

37. Eem - lo a•si•ti et - ma•a•sey Avi lo ta•a•mi•noo li.

---

38. **But if I do, though ye believe not me, believe the works: that ye may know, and believe, that the Father is in me, and I in him.**

Greek/Transliteration
38. εἰ δὲ ποιῶ, κἂν ἐμοὶ μὴ πιστεύητε, τοῖς ἔργοις πιστεύσατε· ἵνα γνῶτε καὶ πιστεύσητε ὅτι ἐν ἐμοὶ ὁ πατήρ, κἀγὼ ἐν αὐτῷ.

38. ei de poio, kan emoi mei pisteuete, tois ergois pisteusate. 'ina gnote kai pisteuseite 'oti en emoi 'o pateir, kago en auto.

Hebrew/Transliteration

לח. וְאִם-עָשִׂיתִים אַף כִּי לֹא-אֲבִיתֶם לְהַאֲמִין בִּי הַאֲמִינוּ בְּמַעֲשֵׂי יָדָי לְמַעַן תֵּדְעוּ וְתַאֲמִינוּ כִּי הָאָב
בִּי וַאֲנִי בָּאָב:

38. Ve•eem - asi•tim af ki lo - avi•tem le•ha•a•min bi ha•a•mi•noo be•ma•a•sey
ya•dai le•ma•an ted•oo ve•ta•a•mi•noo ki ha•Av bi va•a•ni ba•Av.

---

39. Therefore they sought again to take him: but he escaped out of their hand,

Greek/Transliteration

39. Ἐζήτουν οὖν πάλιν αὐτὸν πιάσαι· καὶ ἐξῆλθεν ἐκ τῆς χειρὸς αὐτῶν.

39. Ezeitoun oun palin auton pyasai. kai exeilthen ek teis cheiros auton.

Hebrew/Transliteration

לט. וַיּוֹסִיפוּ וַיְבַקְשׁוּ לְתָפְשׂוֹ אַךְ הוּא נִמְלַט מִיָּדָם:

39. Va•yo•si•foo vay•vak•shoo le•tof•so ach hoo nim•lat mi•ya•dam.

---

40. And went away again beyond Jordan into the place where John at first
baptized; and there he abode.

Greek/Transliteration

40. Καὶ ἀπῆλθεν πάλιν πέραν τοῦ Ἰορδάνου εἰς τὸν τόπον ὅπου ἦν Ἰωάννης
τὸ πρῶτον βαπτίζων· καὶ ἔμεινεν ἐκεῖ.

40. Kai apeilthen palin peran tou Yordanou eis ton topon 'opou ein Yoanneis
to proton baptizon. kai emeinen ekei.

Hebrew/Transliteration

מ. וַיֵּצֵא וַיֵּשֶׁב אֶל-עֵבֶר הַיַּרְדֵּן אֶל-הַמָּקוֹם אֲשֶׁר יוֹחָנָן הָיָה מְטַבֵּל שָׁם בַּתְּחִלָּה וַיֵּשֶׁב שָׁם:

40. Va•ye•tze va•ya•shov el - ever ha•Yarden el - ha•ma•kom asher
Yo•cha•nan ha•ya me•ta•bel sham bat•chi•la va•ye•shev sham.

---

41. And many resorted unto him, and said, John did no miracle: but all things
that John spake of this man were true.

Greek/Transliteration

41. Καὶ πολλοὶ ἦλθον πρὸς αὐτόν, καὶ ἔλεγον ὅτι Ἰωάννης μὲν σημεῖον
ἐποίησεν οὐδέν· πάντα δὲ ὅσα εἶπεν Ἰωάννης περὶ τούτου, ἀληθῆ ἦν.

---

41. Kai polloi eilthon pros auton, kai elegon 'oti Yoanneis men seimeion epoieisen ouden. Panta de 'osa eipen Yoanneis peri toutou, aleithei ein.

מא. וַיָּבֹאוּ אֵלָיו רַבִּים וַיֹּאמְרוּ הִנֵּה יוֹחָנָן לֹא-נָתַן מוֹפֵת אֲבָל כָּל-אֲשֶׁר דִּבֶּר עַל-הָאִישׁ הַזֶּה אֱמֶת הוּא:

41. Va•ya•vo•oo elav ra•bim va•yom•roo hee•ne Yo•cha•nan lo - na•tan mo•fet aval kol - asher di•ber al - ha•eesh ha•ze emet hoo.

---

42. And many believed on him there.

Greek/Transliteration
42. Καὶ ἐπίστευσαν πολλοὶ ἐκεῖ εἰς αὐτόν.

42. Kai episteusan polloi ekei eis auton.

Hebrew/Transliteration
מב. וַיַּאֲמִינוּ-בוֹ רַבִּים בַּמָּקוֹם הַהוּא:

42. Va•ya•a•mi•noo - vo ra•bim ba•ma•kom ha•hoo.

John, Chapter 11

1. Now a certain man was sick, named Lazarus, of Bethany, the town of Mary and her sister Martha.

Greek/Transliteration

1. ᾿Ην δέ τις ἀσθενῶν Λάζαρος ἀπὸ Βηθανίας, ἐκ τῆς κώμης Μαρίας καὶ Μάρθας τῆς ἀδελφῆς αὐτῆς.

1. Ein de tis asthenon Lazaros apo Beithanias, ek teis komeis Marias kai Marthas teis adelpheis auteis.

Hebrew/Transliteration

א. וַיְהִי אִישׁ חֹלֶה וּשְׁמוֹ אֶלְעָזָר מִבֵּית-עַנְיָה מְקוֹם מוֹשַׁב מִרְיָם וּמַרְתָא אֲחוֹתָה:

1. Vay•hi eesh cho•le oo•sh`mo El•a•zar mi•Beit - An•ya me•kom mo•shav Mir•yam oo•Marta acho•ta.

---

2. (It was that Mary which anointed the Lord with ointment, and wiped his feet with her hair, whose brother Lazarus was sick.)

Greek/Transliteration

2. ᾿Ην δὲ Μαρία ἡ ἀλείψασα τὸν κύριον μύρῳ, καὶ ἐκμάξασα τοὺς πόδας αὐτοῦ ταῖς θριξὶν αὐτῆς, ἧς ὁ ἀδελφὸς Λάζαρος ἠσθένει.

2. Ein de Maria 'ei aleipsasa ton kurion muro, kai ekmaxasa tous podas autou tais thrixin auteis, 'eis 'o adelphos Lazaros eisthenei.

Hebrew/Transliteration

ב. הִיא מִרְיָם אֲשֶׁר מָשְׁחָה אֶת-הָאָדוֹן בְּשֶׁמֶן רֹקֵחַ וּבְשַׂעֲרֹתֶיהָ נִגְּבָה אֶת-רַגְלָיו וְאֶלְעָזָר הוּא אָחִיהָ אֲשֶׁר חָלָה:

2. Hee Mir•yam asher mash•cha et - ha•Adon be•she•men ro•ke•ach oov•sa•a•ro•te•ha nig•va et - rag•lav ve•El•azar hoo a•chi•ha asher cha•la.

---

3. Therefore his sisters sent unto him, saying, Lord, behold, he whom thou lovest is sick.

Greek/Transliteration

3. ᾿Απέστειλαν οὖν αἱ ἀδελφαὶ πρὸς αὐτὸν λέγουσαι, Κύριε, ἴδε ὃν φιλεῖς ἀσθενεῖ.

3. Apesteilan oun 'ai adelphai pros auton legousai, Kurie, ide 'on phileis asthenei.

ג. וַתִּשְׁלַחְנָה הָאֲחָיוֹת אֵלָיו לֵאמֹר אֲדֹנִי הִנֵּה זֶה אֲשֶׁר נַפְשְׁךָ אֲהַבְתָהוּ חֹלֶה הוּא:

3. Va•tish•lach•na ha•a•cha•yot elav le•mor Adoni hee•ne ze asher
naf•she•cha ahe•vat•hoo cho•le hoo.

---

4. When Jesus heard that, he said, This sickness is not unto death, but for the
glory of God, that the Son of God might be glorified thereby.

Greek/Transliteration
4. Ἀκούσας δὲ ὁ Ἰησοῦς εἶπεν, Αὕτη ἡ ἀσθένεια οὐκ ἔστιν πρὸς θάνατον,
ἀλλ᾽ ὑπὲρ τῆς δόξης τοῦ θεοῦ, ἵνα δοξασθῇ ὁ υἱὸς τοῦ θεοῦ δι᾽ αὐτῆς.

4. Akousas de 'o Yeisous eipen, 'Autei 'ei astheneya ouk estin pros thanaton,
all 'uper teis doxeis tou theou, 'ina doxasthei 'o 'wios tou theou di auteis.

Hebrew/Transliteration
ד. וַיִּשְׁמַע יֵשׁוּעַ וַיֹּאמַר הַמַּחֲלָה הַזֹּאת לֹא לַמָּוֶת כִּי אִם-לִכְבוֹד הָאֱלֹהִים לְמַעַן יִכָּבֵד-בָּהּ בֶּן-
הָאֱלֹהִים:

4. Va•yish•ma Yeshua va•yo•mar ha•ma•cha•la ha•zot lo la•ma•vet ki eem -
lich•vod ha•Elohim le•ma•an yi•ka•ved - ba Ben - ha•Elohim.

Rabbinic Jewish Commentary
The Jews distinguish between sickness and sickness; there are some that are sick,
the greater part of whom are, לחיים, "for life"; and there are others that are "sick",
the greater part of whom are, למיתה, "for death" (z), or are sick unto death, whose
sickness issues in death; but this of Lazarus's was not to be unto death, at least not
finally.

(z) T. Bab. Kiddushin, fol. 71. 2.

---

5. Now Jesus loved Martha, and her sister, and Lazarus.

Greek/Transliteration
5. Ἠγάπα δὲ ὁ Ἰησοῦς τὴν Μάρθαν καὶ τὴν ἀδελφὴν αὐτῆς καὶ τὸν Λάζαρον.

5. Eigapa de 'o Yeisous tein Marthan kai tein adelphein auteis kai ton
Lazaron.

Hebrew/Transliteration
ה. וְיֵשׁוּעַ אָהַב אֶת-מַרְתָּא וְאֶת-אֲחוֹתָהּ וְאֶת-אֶלְעָזָר:

5. Ve•Yeshua ahav et - Marta ve•et - acho•ta ve•et - El•a•zar.

---

6. When he had heard therefore that he was sick, he abode two days still in the same place where he was.

Greek/Transliteration

6. Ὡς οὖν ἤκουσεν ὅτι ἀσθενεῖ, τότε μὲν ἔμεινεν ἐν ᾧ ἦν τόπῳ δύο ἡμέρας.

6. 'Os oun eikousen 'oti asthenei, tote men emeinen en 'o ein topo duo 'eimeras.

Hebrew/Transliteration

‎:ו. וַיְהִי בְּשָׁמְעוֹ כִּי חָלָה וַיִּתְמַהְמַהּ וַיֵּשֶׁב יוֹמַיִם בַּמָּקוֹם אֲשֶׁר-הוּא שָׁם

6. Vay•hi be•shom•oh ki cha•la va•yit•ma•ha•ma va•ye•shev yo•ma•yim ba•ma•kom asher - hoo sham.

---

7. Then after that saith he to his disciples, Let us go into Judaea again.

Greek/Transliteration

7. Ἔπειτα μετὰ τοῦτο λέγει τοῖς μαθηταῖς, Ἄγωμεν εἰς τὴν Ἰουδαίαν πάλιν.

7. Epeita meta touto legei tois matheitais, Agomen eis tein Youdaian palin.

Hebrew/Transliteration

‎:ז. וְאַחֲרֵי-כֵן אָמַר לְתַלְמִידָיו לְכוּ וְנָשׁוּבָה אֶל-אֶרֶץ יְהוּדָה

7. Ve•a•cha•rey - chen amar le•tal•mi•dav le•choo ve•na•shoo•va el - e•retz Yehooda.

---

8. His disciples say unto him, Master, the Jews of late sought to stone thee; and goest thou thither again?

Greek/Transliteration

8. Λέγουσιν αὐτῷ οἱ μαθηταί, Ῥαββί, νῦν ἐζήτουν σε λιθάσαι οἱ Ἰουδαῖοι, καὶ πάλιν ὑπάγεις ἐκεῖ;

8. Legousin auto 'oi matheitai, 'Rabbi, nun ezeitoun se lithasai 'oi Youdaioi, kai palin 'upageis ekei?

Hebrew/Transliteration

‎:ח. וַיֹּאמְרוּ אֵלָיו תַּלְמִידָיו רַבֵּנוּ הֲלֹא זֶה עַתָּה בִּקְשׁוּ הַיְּהוּדִים לְסָקְלְךָ וְאַתָּה עוֹד תָּשׁוּב שָׁמָּה

8. Va•yom•roo elav tal•mi•dav Ra•be•noo ha•lo ze ata bik•shoo ha•Ye•hoo•dim lis•kol•cha ve•a•ta od ta•shoov sha•ma?

---

9. Jesus answered, Are there not twelve hours in the day? If any man walk in the day, he stumbleth not, because he seeth the light of this world.

Greek/Transliteration
9. Ἀπεκρίθη Ἰησοῦς, Οὐχὶ δώδεκά εἰσιν ὧραι τῆς ἡμέρας; Ἐάν τις περιπατῇ ἐν τῇ ἡμέρᾳ, οὐ προσκόπτει, ὅτι τὸ φῶς τοῦ κόσμου τούτου βλέπει.

9. Apekrithei Yeisous, Ouchi dodeka eisin 'orai teis 'eimeras? Ean tis peripatei en tei 'eimera, ou proskoptei, 'oti to phos tou kosmou toutou blepei.

Hebrew/Transliteration
ט. וַיַּעַן יֵשׁוּעַ הֲלֹא שְׁתֵּים-עֶשְׂרֵה שָׁעוֹת בַּיּוֹם אִישׁ הַהֹלֵךְ בַּיּוֹם לֹא יִכָּשֵׁל כִּי יִרְאֶה אוֹר הָעוֹלָם הַזֶּה:

9. Va•ya•an Yeshua ha•lo sh`teim - es•re sha•ot ba•yom eesh ha•ho•lech ba•yom lo yi•ka•shel ki yir•eh or ha•o•lam ha•ze.

Rabbinic Jewish Commentary
So the Jews reckoned, and so they commonly say (a), שתים עשרה שעות הוי היום, "twelve hours are a day", or a day consists of twelve hours, which they divided into four parts, each part consisting of three hours this was a matter well known, and Yeshua puts the question as such, it being what might be easily answered, and at once assented to.

(a) T. Bab Sanhedrin, fol. 88. 2. Avoda Zara, fol. 3. 2. Vid. Philo. de Somniis, p. 1143.

---

10. But if a man walk in the night, he stumbleth, because there is no light in him.

Greek/Transliteration
10. Ἐὰν δέ τις περιπατῇ ἐν τῇ νυκτί, προσκόπτει, ὅτι τὸ φῶς οὐκ ἔστιν ἐν αὐτῷ.

10. Ean de tis peripatei en tei nukti, proskoptei, 'oti to phos ouk estin en auto.

Hebrew/Transliteration
י. אֲבָל הַהֹלֵךְ בַּלַּיְלָה יִכָּשֵׁל כִּי הָאוֹר אֵינֶנּוּ-בוֹ:

10. Aval ha•ho•lech ba•lai•la yi•ka•shel ki ha•or ey•ne•noo - vo.

---

11. These things said he: and after that he saith unto them, Our friend Lazarus sleepeth; but I go, that I may awake him out of sleep.

11. Ταῦτα εἶπεν, καὶ μετὰ τοῦτο λέγει αὐτοῖς, Λάζαρος ὁ φίλος ἡμῶν κεκοίμηται· ἀλλὰ πορεύομαι ἵνα ἐξυπνίσω αὐτόν.

11. Tauta eipen, kai meta touto legei autois, Lazaros 'o philos 'eimon kekoimeitai. Alla poreuomai 'ina exupniso auton.

יא. וְאַחֲרֵי דַבְּרוֹ כָזאת אָמַר אֲלֵיהֶם אֶלְעָזָר יְדִידֵנוּ יָשֵׁן וַאֲנִי הֹלֵךְ לְהָעִיר אֹתוֹ מִשְּׁנָתוֹ:

11. Ve•a•cha•rey dab•ro cha•zot amar aley•hem El•a•zar ye•di•de•noo ya•shen va•a•ni ho•lech le•ha•eer o•to mish•na•to.

Rabinic Jewish Commentary
Meaning, that he was dead; in which sense the word is often used in the Old Testament, and in the common dialect of the Jews, and frequently in their writings; and especially it is so used of good men: and it is an observation of theirs (b), that

"It is usual to say of the righteous, that there is no death in them, אלא שינה, "but sleep". (b) Gloss in T. Hieros. Celaim in En Yaacov, fol. 4. 4.

but I go, that I may awake him out of sleep; that is, to raise him from the dead, for, the resurrection of the dead is expressed by awaking; see Psa_17:15; which for Yeshua to do, was as easy as to awake a man out of natural sleep.

---

12. Then said his disciples, Lord, if he sleep, he shall do well.

12. Εἶπον οὖν οἱ μαθηταὶ αὐτοῦ, Κύριε, εἰ κεκοίμηται, σωθήσεται.

12. Eipon oun 'oi matheitai autou, Kurie, ei kekoimeitai, sotheisetai.

יב. וַיַּעֲנוּ תַלְמִידָיו אֲדֹנִי אִם-יָשֵׁן הוּא שְׁנָתוֹ תַחֲלִימֵהוּ וָחָי:

12. Va•ya•a•noo tal•mi•dav Adoni eem - ya•shen hoo sh`na•to ta•cha•li•me•hoo va•chai.

---

13. Howbeit Jesus spake of his death: but they thought that he had spoken of taking of rest in sleep.

13. Εἰρήκει δὲ ὁ Ἰησοῦς περὶ τοῦ θανάτου αὐτοῦ· ἐκεῖνοι δὲ ἔδοξαν ὅτι περὶ τῆς κοιμήσεως τοῦ ὕπνου λέγει.

13. Eireikei de 'o Yeisous peri tou thanatou autou. ekeinoi de edoxan 'oti peri teis koimeiseos tou 'upnou legei.

Hebrew/Transliteration

יג. וְיֵשׁוּעַ דִּבֶּר כֵּן עַל-מוֹתוֹ וְהֵם חָשְׁבוּ כִּי עַל-מְנוּחָתוֹ בַּשֵּׁנָה הוּא מְדַבֵּר:

13. Ve•Yeshua di•ber ken al - mo•to ve•hem chash•voo ki al - me•noo•cha•to ba•she•na hoo me•da•ber.

---

14. Then said Jesus unto them plainly, Lazarus is dead.

Greek/Transliteration

14. Τότε οὖν εἶπεν αὐτοῖς ὁ Ἰησοῦς παρρησίᾳ, Λάζαρος ἀπέθανεν.

14. Tote oun eipen autois 'o Yeisous parreisia, Lazaros apethanen.

Hebrew/Transliteration

יד. אָז אָמַר אֲלֵיהֶם יֵשׁוּעַ בְּשָׂפָה בְרוּרָה אֶלְעָזָר מֵת:

14. Az amar aley•hem Yeshua be•sa•fa ve•roo•ra El•a•zar met.

---

15. And I am glad for your sakes that I was not there, to the intent ye may believe; nevertheless let us go unto him.

Greek/Transliteration

15. Καὶ χαίρω δι᾽ ὑμᾶς, ἵνα πιστεύσητε, ὅτι οὐκ ἤμην ἐκεῖ· ἀλλὰ ἄγωμεν πρὸς αὐτόν.

15. Kai chairo di 'umas, 'ina pisteuseite, 'oti ouk eimein ekei. alla agomen pros auton.

Hebrew/Transliteration

טו. וַאֲנִי שָׂמֵחַ לְמַעַנְכֶם כִּי לֹא-הָיִיתִי שָׁמָּה לְבַעֲבוּר תַּאֲמִינוּ אַךְ נֵלְכָה-נָּא אֵלָיו:

15. Va•a•ni sa•me•ach le•ma•an•chem ki lo - ha•yi•ti sha•ma le•va•a•voor ta•a•mi•noo ach nel•cha - na elav.

---

16. Then said Thomas, which is called Didymus, unto his fellowdisciples, Let us also go, that we may die with him.

Greek/Transliteration

16. Εἶπεν οὖν Θωμᾶς, ὁ λεγόμενος Δίδυμος, τοῖς συμμαθηταῖς, Ἄγωμεν καὶ ἡμεῖς, ἵνα ἀποθάνωμεν μετ᾽ αὐτοῦ.

16. Eipen oun Thomas, 'o legomenos Didumos, tois summatheitais, Agomen kai 'eimeis, 'ina apothanomen met autou.

Hebrew/Transliteration
:טז. וַיֹּאמֶר תּוֹמָא הַנִּקְרָא דִידוּמוֹס אֶל-חֲבֵרָיו הַתַּלְמִידִים נֵלְכָה-נָּא גַם-אֲנַחְנוּ וְנָמוּתָה עִמּוֹ

16. Va•yo•mer Toma ha•nik•ra Di•doo•mos el - cha•ve•rav ha•tal•mi•dim nel•cha - na gam - a•nach•noo ve•na•moo•ta ee•mo.

---

17. Then when Jesus came, he found that he had lain in the grave four days already.

Greek/Transliteration
17. Ἐλθὼν οὖν ὁ Ἰησοῦς εὖρεν αὐτὸν τέσσαρας ἡμέρας ἤδη ἔχοντα ἐν τῷ μνημείῳ.

17. Elthon oun 'o Yeisous 'euren auton tessaras 'eimeras eidei echonta en to mneimeio.

Hebrew/Transliteration
:יז. וַיָּבֹא יֵשׁוּעַ וַיִּמְצָא כִּי זֶה כְבָר אַרְבָּעָה יָמִים שֹׁכֵב בַּקָּבֶר

17. Va•ya•vo Yeshua va•yim•tza ki ze che•var ar•ba•ah ya•mim sho•chev ba•ka•ver.

---

18. Now Bethany was nigh unto Jerusalem, about fifteen furlongs off:

Greek/Transliteration
18. Ἦν δὲ ἡ Βηθανία ἐγγὺς τῶν Ἰεροσολύμων, ὡς ἀπὸ σταδίων δεκαπέντε·

18. Ein de 'ei Beithania engus ton 'Yerosolumon, 'os apo stadion dekapente.

Hebrew/Transliteration
:יח. וּבֵית-עַנְיָה קְרֹבָה לִירוּשָׁלַיִם כַּחֲמֵשׁ עֶשְׂרֵה מַעֲנוֹת צֶמֶד שָׂדֶה

18. Oo•Veit - An•ya ke•ro•va li•Ye•roo•sha•la•yim ka•cha•mesh es•re ma•a•not tze•med sa•de.

Rabbinic Jewish Commentary
about fifteen furlongs off; that is, about two miles, for seven furlongs and a half made a Jewish mile, as appears from one of their canons (c), which runs thus:

"They do not spread nets for doves, except it be distant from an habitable place, שלשים רים, "thirty furlongs";"

Which the commentators say (d) are "four miles": and still more expressly it is said (e), that

"Between Jerusalem and Zuck, (the place where the scape goat was had,) there were ten tents, and ninety furlongs, שבעה ומחצה לכל מיל "seven and a half to every mile"."

Hence a furlong was called one seventh and a half of a mile (f), which was 266 cubits, and two thirds of one.

(c) Misn. Bava Kama, c. 7. sect. 7. (d) Maimon. Jarchi, & Bartenora in ib. (e) Misn. Yoma, c. 6. sect. 4. (f) T. Bab. Bava Metzia, fol. 33. 1. Maimon. Hilch. Rotzeach, c. 13. sect. 6.

---

19. And many of the Jews came to Martha and Mary, to comfort them concerning their brother.

Greek/Transliteration
19. καὶ πολλοὶ ἐκ τῶν Ἰουδαίων ἐληλύθεισαν πρὸς τὰς περὶ Μάρθαν καὶ Μαρίαν, ἵνα παραμυθήσωνται αὐτὰς περὶ τοῦ ἀδελφοῦ αὐτῶν.

19. kai polloi ek ton Youdaion eleilutheisan pros tas peri Marthan kai Marian, 'ina paramutheisontai autas peri tou adelphou auton.

Hebrew/Transliteration
יט. וִיהוּדִים רַבִּים בָּאוּ אֶל-מַרְתָא וּמִרְיָם לְנַחֲמָן עַל-אֲחִיהֶן:

19. Vi•Yehoo•dim ra•bim ba•oo el - Marta oo•Miryam le•na•cha•man al - achi•hen.

Rabbinic Jewish Commentary
to comfort them concerning their brother; by reason of his death, as was usual with the Jews to do, after the dead was buried; for they did not allow of it before: hence that saying (g) of R. Simeon ben Eleazar,

"Do not comfort him (thy friend) in the time his dead lies before him."

The first office of this kind was done when they returned from the grave; for it is said (h), when they return

"From the grave they make rows round about the mourner, לנחמו, "to comfort him", and they make him to sit, and they stand, and there never were less than ten in a row."

It was an ancient custom for the mourners to stand in their place in a row, and all the people passed by, and every man as he came to the mourner comforted him, and passed on (i). But besides these consolations, there were others administered at their own houses, which were usually done the first week, for it is said (k),

"The mourner the first week does not go out of the door of his house; the second he goes out, but does not sit, or continue in his place; the third he continues in his place, but does not speak; the fourth, lo, he is as every other man. R. Judah says, there is no need to say, the first week he does not go out of the door of his house, for behold, all come to his house, לנחמו, "to comfort him"."

And is was on the third day more particularly on which these consolatory visits were paid (l):

"On the first day he (the mourner) did not wear his phylacteries; on the second, he put them on; on the third day, others come to comfort him."

This rule the Jews here seem to have observed, since Lazarus had been dead four days; and they were come from Jerusalem hither to comfort his sisters on account of his death. The whole of this ceremony is thus related by Maimonides (m),

"How do they comfort mourners? after they have buried the dead, the mourners gather together, and stand on the side of the grave; and all that accompany the dead stand round about them, one row within another: and there is no row less than ten; and the mourners are not of the number; the mourners stand on the left hand of the comforters; and all the comforters go to the mourners, one by one, and say to them, תנוחמו מן השמים, "may ye be comforted from heaven": after that the mourner goes to his house, and every day of the seven days of mourning, men come to comfort him; whether new faces come, or do not, the mourner sits down at the head, (or in the chief place,) and no comforters may sit but upon the floor, as it is said, Job_2:13, "and they sat with him on the ground": nor may they say any thing until the mourner has opened his mouth first, as it is said, Job_2:13, "and none spake a word unto him": and it is written afterwards, Job_3:1, "so opened Job his mouth", &c. and Eliphaz answered, Job_4:1, and when he nods with his head, the comforters may not sit with him any longer, that they may not trouble him more than is necessary. If a man dies, and there are no mourners to be comforted, ten worthy men go and sit in his place all the seven days of mourning; and the rest of the people gather to them; and if there are not ten fixed every day, ten of the rest of the people gather together, and sit in his place:"

For this business of comforting mourners was reckoned an act of great piety and mercy (n); and these Jews here might come, not so much out of respect to the dead, or to his sisters, as because it was thought to be a meritorious act.

(g) Pirke Abot, c. 4. sect. 18. (h) Gloss in Cetubot, fol. 8. 2. & in Beracot, fol. 16. 2. (i) Gloss in T. Bab. Sanhedrin, fol. 19. 1. (k) T. Bab. Moed Katon, fol. 23. 1. (l) Massech. Semachot, c. 6. fol. 14. 3. (m) Hilch. Ebel, c. 13. sect. 1, 2, 3, 4. (n) Maimon. in Misn. Peah, c. 1. sect. 1.

20. Then Martha, as soon as she heard that Jesus was coming, went and met
    him: but Mary sat still in the house.

Greek/Transliteration
20. Ἡ οὖν Μάρθα, ὡς ἤκουσεν ὅτι Ἰησοῦς ἔρχεται, ὑπήντησεν αὐτῷ· Μαρία
    δὲ ἐν τῷ οἴκῳ ἐκαθέζετο.

20. 'Ei oun Martha, 'os eikousen 'oti Yeisous erchetai, 'upeinteisen auto.
    Maria de en to oiko ekathezeto.

Hebrew/Translieration
:כ. וַיְהִי כִשְׁמֹעַ מַרְתָא כִּי יֵשׁוּעַ בָּא וַתֵּצֵא לִקְרָאתוֹ וּמִרְיָם יֹשֶׁבֶת בַּבָּיִת

20. Vay•hi ki•sh`mo•a Marta ki Yeshua ba va•te•tze lik•ra•to oo•Miryam
    yo•she•vet ba•ba•yit.

---

21. Then said Martha unto Jesus, Lord, if thou hadst been here, my brother
    had not died.

Greek/Transliteration
21. Εἶπεν οὖν Μάρθα πρὸς τὸν Ἰησοῦν, Κύριε, εἰ ἦς ὧδε, ὁ ἀδελφός μου οὐκ
    ἂν ἐτεθνήκει.

21. Eipen oun Martha pros ton Yeisoun, Kurie, ei eis 'ode, 'o adelphos mou
    ouk an etethneikei.

Hebrew/Transliteration
:כא. וַתֹּאמֶר מַרְתָא אֶל-יֵשׁוּעַ אֲדֹנִי לוּ הָיִיתָ פֹּה עִמָּנוּ וְלֹא-מֵת אָחִי

21. Va•to•mer Marta el - Yeshua Adoni loo ha•yi•ta po ee•ma•noo ve•lo - met
    achi.

---

22. But I know, that even now, whatsoever thou wilt ask of God, God will give
    it thee.

Greek/Transliteration
22. Ἀλλὰ καὶ νῦν οἶδα ὅτι ὅσα ἂν αἰτήσῃ τὸν θεόν, δώσει σοι ὁ θεός.

22. Alla kai nun oida 'oti 'osa an aiteisei ton theon, dosei soi 'o theos.

Hebrew/Transliteration
:כב. וְגַם-עַתָּה יָדַעְתִּי כִּי כָל-אֲשֶׁר תִּשְׁאַל מֵאֵת הָאֱלֹהִים כֵּן יִתֶּן לְךָ הָאֱלֹהִים

22. Ve•gam - ata ya•da•a•ti ki chol - asher tish•al me•et ha•Elohim ken yi•ten le•cha ha•Elohim.

---

23. Jesus saith unto her, Thy brother shall rise again.

Greek/Transliteration
23. Λέγει αὐτῇ ὁ Ἰησοῦς, Ἀναστήσεται ὁ ἀδελφός σου.

23. Legei autei 'o Yeisous, Anasteisetai 'o adelphos sou.

Hebrew/Transliteration
‎:כג. וַיֹּאמֶר אֵלֶיהָ יֵשׁוּעַ הֲלֹא יָקוּם אָחִיךְ

23. Va•yo•mer e•le•ha Yeshua ha•lo ya•koom a•chi•ch.

---

24. Martha saith unto him, I know that he shall rise again in the resurrection at the last day.

Greek/Transliteration
24. Λέγει αὐτῷ Μάρθα, Οἶδα ὅτι ἀναστήσεται ἐν τῇ ἀναστάσει ἐν τῇ ἐσχάτῃ ἡμέρᾳ.

24. Legei auto Martha, Oida 'oti anasteisetai en tei anastasei en tei eschatei 'eimera.

Hebrew/Translitearation
‎:כד. וַתֹּאמֶר אֵלָיו מַרְתָא יָדַעְתִּי כִּי יָקוּם בְּיוֹם הַתְּקוּמָה בַּיּוֹם הָאַחֲרוֹן

24. Va•to•mer elav Marta ya•da•a•ti ki ya•koom be•yom ha•t`koo•ma ba•yom ha•a•cha•ron.

Rabbinic Jewish Commentary
The Jews were divided about the doctrine of the resurrection, the Sadducees denied it, the Pharisees asserted it; and on this latter side was Martha; she believed there would be a resurrection of the dead; that this would be at the last day, or at the end of the world; and that her brother would rise at that general resurrection: wherefore, if Yeshua meant no more than that, this was what she always believed. The Syriac version renders it, "in the consolation at the last day"; and so the time of the resurrection is, by the Jews, called "the days of consolation" (o).

(o) Targum Jon. in Gen i. 21. & in Hos. vi. 2.

---

25. Jesus said unto her, I am the resurrection, and the life: he that believeth in me, though he were dead, yet shall he live:

Greek/Transliteration

25. Εἶπεν αὐτῇ ὁ Ἰησοῦς, Ἐγώ εἰμι ἡ ἀνάστασις καὶ ἡ ζωή· ὁ πιστεύων εἰς ἐμέ, κἂν ἀποθάνῃ, ζήσεται·

25. Eipen autei 'o Yeisous, Ego eimi 'ei anastasis kai 'ei zoei. 'o pisteuon eis eme, kan apothanei, zeisetai.

Hebrew/Transliteration

כה. וַיֹּאמֶר אֵלֶיהָ יֵשׁוּעַ אָנֹכִי הַתְּקוּמָה וְהַחַיִּים הַמַּאֲמִין בִּי אַף כִּי-הוּא מֵת יָקוּם וָחָי:

25. Va•yo•mer e•le•ha Yeshua ano•chi ha•t`koo•ma ve•ha•cha•yim ha•ma•a•min bi af ki - hoo met ya•koom va•chai.

---

26. And whosoever liveth and believeth in me shall never die. Believest thou this?

Greek/Transliteration

26. καὶ πᾶς ὁ ζῶν καὶ πιστεύων εἰς ἐμέ, οὐ μὴ ἀποθάνῃ εἰς τὸν αἰῶνα. Πιστεύεις τοῦτο;

26. kai pas 'o zon kai pisteuon eis eme, ou mei apothanei eis ton aiona. Pisteueis touto?

Hebrew/Transliteration

כו. וְכָל-חַי אֲשֶׁר יַאֲמִין-בִּי לֹא יָמוּת לְעוֹלָם הֲתַאֲמִינִי זֹאת אָתְּ:

26. Ve•chol - chai asher ya•a•min - bi lo ya•moot le•o•lam ha•ta•a•mi•nee zot at?

---

27. She saith unto him, Yea, Lord: I believe that thou art the Christ, the Son of God, which should come into the world.

Greek/Transliteration

27. Λέγει αὐτῷ, Ναί, κύριε· ἐγὼ πεπίστευκα, ὅτι σὺ εἶ ὁ χριστός, ὁ υἱὸς τοῦ θεοῦ, ὁ εἰς τὸν κόσμον ἐρχόμενος.

27. Legei auto, Nai, kurie. ego pepisteuka, 'oti su ei 'o christos, 'o 'wios tou theou, 'o eis ton kosmon erchomenos.

Hebrew/Transliteration

כז. וַתֹּאמֶר אֵלָיו הֵן אֲדֹנִי הֵן אָנֹכִי הֶאֱמַנְתִּי כִּי-אַתָּה הוּא הַמָּשִׁיחַ בֶּן-הָאֱלֹהִים הַבָּא אֶל-הָעוֹלָם:

---

27. Va•to•mer elav hen Adoni hen ano•chi he•e•man•ti ki - ata hoo
ha•Ma•shi•ach Ben - ha•Elohim ha•ba el - ha•o•lam.

---

28. And when she had so said, she went her way, and called Mary her sister
secretly, saying, The Master is come, and calleth for thee.

Greek/Transliteration

28. Καὶ ταῦτα εἰποῦσα ἀπῆλθεν, καὶ ἐφώνησεν Μαρίαν τὴν ἀδελφὴν αὐτῆς
λάθρα, εἰποῦσα, Ὁ διδάσκαλος πάρεστιν καὶ φωνεῖ σε.

28. Kai tauta eipousa apeilthen, kai ephoneisen Marian tein adelphein auteis
lathra, eipousa, 'O didaskalos parestin kai phonei se.

Hebrew/Transliteration

:כח. וּבְדַבְּרָהּ כָּזֹאת הָלְכָה וְקָרְאָה לְמִרְיָם אֲחוֹתָהּ בַּסֵּתֶר לֵאמֹר הִגֵּה בָא הָרַבִּי וְהוּא קֹרֵא לָךְ

28. Oov•dab•ra ka•zot hal•cha ve•kar•ah le•Mir•yam acho•ta ba•se•ter le•mor
hee•ne ba ha•Rabbi ve•hoo ko•re lach.

---

29. As soon as she heard that, she arose quickly, and came unto him.

Greek/Transliteration

29. Ἐκείνη ὡς ἤκουσεν, ἐγείρεται ταχὺ καὶ ἔρχεται πρὸς αὐτόν.

29. Ekeinei 'os eikousen, egeiretai tachu kai erchetai pros auton.

Hebrew/Transliteration

:כט. וַתִּשְׁמַע וַתָּקָם כְּרֶגַע וַתָּבֹא אֵלָיו

29. Va•tish•ma va•ta•kom ke•re•ga va•ta•vo elav.

---

30. Now Jesus was not yet come into the town, but was in that place where
Martha met him.

Greek/Transliteration

30. Οὔπω δὲ ἐληλύθει ὁ Ἰησοῦς εἰς τὴν κώμην, ἀλλ᾽ ἦν ἐν τῷ τόπῳ ὅπου
ὑπήντησεν αὐτῷ ἡ Μάρθα.

30. Oupo de eleiluthei 'o Yeisous eis tein komein, all ein en to topo 'opou
'upeinteisen auto 'ei Martha.

Hebrew/Transliteration

:ל. וְיֵשׁוּעַ טֶרֶם יָבֹא אֶל-הַכְּפָר כִּי אִם-עוֹדֶנּוּ עֹמֵד בַּמָּקוֹם אֲשֶׁר פָּגְשָׁה-בּוֹ מַרְתָא

---

30. Ve•Yeshua te•rem ya•vo el - ha•k`far ki eem - o•de•noo o•med ba•ma•kom asher pag•sha - bo Marta.

---

31. The Jews then which were with her in the house, and comforted her, when they saw Mary, that she rose up hastily and went out, followed her, saying, She goeth unto the grave to weep there.

Greek/Transliteration
31. Οἱ οὖν Ἰουδαῖοι οἱ ὄντες μετ᾽ αὐτῆς ἐν τῇ οἰκίᾳ καὶ παραμυθούμενοι αὐτήν, ἰδόντες τὴν Μαρίαν ὅτι ταχέως ἀνέστη καὶ ἐξῆλθεν, ἠκολούθησαν αὐτῇ, λέγοντες ὅτι ὑπάγει εἰς τὸ μνημεῖον, ἵνα κλαύσῃ ἐκεῖ.

31. 'Oi oun Youdaioi 'oi ontes met auteis en tei oikia kai paramuthoumenoi autein, idontes tein Marian 'oti tacheos anestei kai exeilthen, eikoloutheisan autei, legontes 'oti 'upagei eis to mneimeion, 'ina klausei ekei.

Hebrew/Transliteration
לא. וְהַיְּהוּדִים אֲשֶׁר-הָיוּ אִתָּהּ-הָיוּ בַּבַּיִת לְנַחֲמָהּ בִּרְאוֹתָם כִּי-קָמָה מִרְיָם וְיָצְאָה פִתְאֹם הָלְכוּ אַחֲרֶיהָ בְּחָשְׁבָם כִּי:לִבְפּוֹת אֶל-הַקֶּבֶר הִיא הֹלָכֶת -

31. Ve•haye•hoo•dim asher - ha•yoo ee•ta ba•ba•yit le•na•cha•ma bir•o•tam ki - ka•ma Mir•yam ve•yatz•ah fit•om hal•choo acha•re•ha be•chosh•vam ki - liv•kot el - ha•ke•ver hee ho•la•chet.

Rabbinic Jewish Commentary
The Jews were wont to go to the graves on different accounts; one was to see whether the persons were dead or not: for so it is said (p),

"They go to the graves and visit until three days."

The Persians also visit the sepulchres of their principal "Imams", or prelates (t); and the Jews were wont to visit the graves of their great men, in honour to them; yea, the disciples of the wise men used to meet there to study the law, thereby showing respect, and doing honour to the deceased. It is said of Hezekiah, 2Ch_32:33, "that all Judah, and the inhabitants of Jerusalem, did him honour at his death"; from whence say the Talmudists (u) we learn, that they fixed a sitting or a school at his grave; the gloss is, a session (or school) of the wise men to study in the law there. So says Maimonides (w), when a king dies they make a sitting at his grave seven days, as it is said, 2Ch_32:33, "they did him honour at his death"; that is, they made a sitting at his grave.

(p) Massech. Semachot. c. 8. fol. 15. 1. (t) Reland de Relig. Mohammed. l. 1. p. 72. (u) T. Bab. Bava Kama, fol. 16. 2. (w) Hilchot Ebel. c. 14. sect. 25.

---

32. Then when Mary was come where Jesus was, and saw him, she fell down at his feet, saying unto him, Lord, if thou hadst been here, my brother had not died.

Greek/Transliteration
32. Ἡ οὖν Μαρία, ὡς ἦλθεν ὅπου ἦν ὁ Ἰησοῦς, ἰδοῦσα αὐτόν, ἔπεσεν αὐτοῦ εἰς τοὺς πόδας λέγουσα αὐτῷ, Κύριε, εἰ ἦς ὧδε, οὐκ ἂν ἀπέθανέν μου ὁ ἀδελφός.

32. 'Ei oun Maria, 'os eilthen 'opou ein 'o Yeisous, idousa auton, epesen autou eis tous podas legousa auto, Kurie, ei eis 'ode, ouk an apethanen mou 'o adelphos.

Hebrew/Transliteration
לב. וּמִרְיָם בָּאָה אֶל-הַמָּקוֹם אֲשֶׁר יֵשׁוּעַ עֹמֵד שָׁם וַתִּרְאֵהוּ וַתִּפֹּל לְרַגְלָיו וַתֹּאמֶר לוֹ אֲדֹנִי לוּ הָיִיתָ פֹּה עִמָּנוּ:וְלֹא-מֵת אָחִי

32. Oo•Mir•yam ba•ah el - ha•ma•kom asher Yeshua o•med sham va•tir•e•hoo va•ti•pol le•rag•lav va•to•mer lo Adoni loo ha•yi•ta po ee•ma•noo ve•lo - met achi.

---

33. When Jesus therefore saw her weeping, and the Jews also weeping which came with her, he groaned in the spirit, and was troubled,

Greek/Transliteration
33. Ἰησοῦς οὖν ὡς εἶδεν αὐτὴν κλαίουσαν, καὶ τοὺς συνελθόντας αὐτῇ Ἰουδαίους κλαίοντας, ἐνεβριμήσατο τῷ πνεύματι, καὶ ἐτάραξεν ἑαυτόν,

33. Yeisous oun 'os eiden autein klaiousan, kai tous sunelthontas autei Youdaious klaiontas, enebrimeisato to pneumati, kai etaraxen 'eauton,

Hebrew/Transliteration
לג. כִּרְאוֹת יֵשׁוּעַ אֹתָהּ בֹּכִיָּה וְאֶת-הַיְּהוּדִים בֹּכִים עִמָּהּ וַיֵּאָנַח רוּחוֹ בְּקִרְבּוֹ וַיִּסָּעֵר לִבּוֹ:

33. Kir•ot Yeshua o•ta bo•chi•ya ve•et - ha•Ye•hoo•dim bo•chim ee•ma va•ye•mar roo•cho be•kir•bo va•yi•sa•er li•bo.

---

34. And said, Where have ye laid him? They said unto him, Lord, come and see.

Greek/Transliteration
34. καὶ εἶπεν, Ποῦ τεθείκατε αὐτόν; Λέγουσιν αὐτῷ, Κύριε, ἔρχου καὶ ἴδε.

34. kai eipen, Pou tetheikate auton? Legousin auto, Kurie, erchou kai ide.

:לד. וַיֹּאמֶר אָן קְבַרְתֶּם אֹתוֹ וַיֹּאמְרוּ אֵלָיו בֹּא אֲדֹנֵינוּ וּרְאֵה

34. Va•yo•mer an ke•var•tem o•to va•yom•roo elav bo Ado•ney•noo oor•eh.

---

35. Jesus wept.

Greek/Transliteration
35. Ἐδάκρυσεν ὁ Ἰησοῦς.

35. Edakrusen 'o Yeisous.

Hebrew/Transliteration
:לה. וַיֵּבְךְּ יֵשׁוּעַ

35. Va•yivch Yeshua.

---

36. Then said the Jews, Behold how he loved him!

Greek/Transliteration
36. Ἔλεγον οὖν οἱ Ἰουδαῖοι, Ἴδε πῶς ἐφίλει αὐτόν.

36. Elegon oun 'oi Youdaioi, Yde pos ephilei auton.

Hebrew/Transliteration
:לו. וַיֹּאמְרוּ הַיְּהוּדִים רְאוּ מַה-נִּפְלָאָה לוֹ אַהֲבָתוֹ

36. Va•yom•roo ha•Ye•hoo•dim r`oo ma - nif•la•ah lo aha•va•to.

---

37. And some of them said, Could not this man, which opened the eyes of the blind, have caused that even this man should not have died?

Greek/Transliteration
37. Τινὲς δὲ ἐξ αὐτῶν εἶπον, Οὐκ ἠδύνατο οὗτος, ὁ ἀνοίξας τοὺς ὀφθαλμοὺς τοῦ τυφλοῦ, ποιῆσαι ἵνα καὶ οὗτος μὴ ἀποθάνῃ;

37. Tines de ex auton eipon, Ouk eidunato 'outos, 'o anoixas tous ophthalmous tou tuphlou, poieisai 'ina kai 'outos mei apothanei?

Hebrew/Transliteration
:לז. וְיֵשׁ מֵהֶם אָמְרוּ הַהוּא אֲשֶׁר פָּקַח עֵינֵי הָעִוֵּר לֹא יָכֹל לַעֲצֹר גַּם אֶת-זֶה מִמָּוֶת

37. Ve•yesh me•hem am•roo ha•hoo asher pa•kach ey•ney ha•ee•ver lo ya•chol la•a•tzor gam et - ze mi•ma•vet?

---

38. Jesus therefore again groaning in himself cometh to the grave. It was a cave, and a stone lay upon it.

Greek/Transliteration

38. Ἰησοῦς οὖν πάλιν ἐμβριμώμενος ἐν ἑαυτῷ ἔρχεται εἰς τὸ μνημεῖον. Ἦν δὲ σπήλαιον, καὶ λίθος ἐπέκειτο ἐπ᾽ αὐτῷ.

38. Yeisous oun palin embrimomenos en 'eauto erchetai eis to mneimeion. Ein de speilaion, kai lithos epekeito ep auto.

Hebrew/Transliteration

לח. וְיֵשׁוּעַ בְּמַר נַפְשׁוֹ בָּא אֶל-הַקֶּבֶר וְהוּא מְעָרָה וְאֶבֶן שׂוּמָה עַל-פִּיהָ:

38. Ve•Yeshua be•mar naf•sho ba el - ha•ka•ver ve•hoo me•a•ra ve•e•ven soo•ma al - pi•ha.

Rabbinic Jewish Commentary

it was a cave; either a natural one, such as were in rocks and mountains, of which sort there were many in Judea, and near Jerusalem being a rocky and mountainous country, of which Josephus (x) makes mention; where thieves and robbers sheltered themselves, and could not easily be come at and where persons in danger fled to for safety, and hid themselves; and the reason why such places were chose to bury in, was because here the bodies were safe from beasts of prey: or this was an artificial cave made out of a rock, in form of one, as was the tomb of Joseph of Arimathea; and it was the common custom of the Jews to make caves and bury in; yea, they were obliged to it by their traditions: thus says Maimonides (y),

"He that sells a place to his friend to make in it a grave or that receives from his friend a place to make in it a grave, עושה מערה, "must make a cave", and open in it eight graves, three on one side and three on another, and two over against the entrance "into the cave": the measure of "the cave" is four cubits by six, and every grave is four cubits long, and six hands broad, and seven high; and there is a space between every grave, on the sides a cubit and a half, and between the two in the middle two cubits."

And elsewhere (z) he observes, that

"They dig מערות, "caves" in the earth, and make a grave in the side "of the cave", and bury him (the dead) in it."

And such caves for burying the dead, were at and near the Mount of Olives; and near the same must be this cave where Lazarus was buried; for Bethany was not far from thence: so in the Cippi Hebraici we read (a), that at the bottom of the

Mount (of Olives) is a very great "cave", said to be Haggai the prophet's; and in it are many caves.--And near it is the grave of Zachariah the prophet, in a "cave" shut up; and frequent mention is made there of caves in which persons were buried; perhaps the custom of burying in them might take its rise from the cave of Machpelah, which Abraham, their father, bought for a buryingplace for his dead.

The sepulchre of Lazarus is pretended (b) to be shown to travellers to this day, over which is built a chapel of marble, very decent, and comely, and stands close by a church built in honour of Martha and Mary, the two sisters of Lazarus, in the place where their house stood; but certain it is, that the grave of Lazarus was out of the town.

and a stone lay upon it. Our version is not so accurate, nor so agreeable to the form of graves with the Jews, nor to this of Lazarus's; their graves were not as ours, dug in the earth and open above, so as to have a stone laid over them, for they often were, as this, caves in rocks, either natural, or hewn out of them by art; and there was a door at the side of them, by which there was an entrance into them; and at this door a stone was laid it would be better rendered here, and "a stone was laid to it"; not "upon it", for it had no opening above, but to it, at the side of it; and accordingly the Syriac and Persic versions read, "a stone was laid at the door of it"; and the Arabic version, "and there was a great stone at the door of it", as was at the door of Yeshua's sepulchre. In the Jewish sepulchres there was חצר, "a court" (c) which was before the entrance into the cave; this was four square; it was six cubits long, and six broad; and here the bearers put down the corpse, and from hence it was carried into the cave, at which there was an entrance, sometimes called פי המערה, "the mouth of the cave" (d); and sometimes, פתח הקבר, "the door of the grave" (e); of its form, measure, and place, there is no express mention in the Jewish writings: it is thought to be about a cubit's breadth, and was on the side of the cave; so that at it, it might be looked into; and at the mouth of the cave was a stone put to stop it up, which was called גולל, from its being rolled there; though that with which the mouth of the cave was shut up, was not always a stone, nor made of stone; Maimonides (f) says, it was made of stone, or wood, or the like matter; and so in the Misna (g) it is said,

גולל לקבר, "The covering for a grave", (or that with which it is stopped up,) if it be made of a piece of timber, whether it stands, or whether it inclines to the side, does not defile, but over against the door only;"

(x) Antiqu. l. 14. c. 15. sect. 5. (y) Hilchot Mecira, c. 21. sect. 6. (z) Hilchot Ebel, c. 4. sect. 4. (a) P. 27, 29. Ed. Hottinger. (b) Itinerar. Bunting. p. 364. (c) Misn. Bava Bathra, c. 6. sect. 8. (d) Misn. ib. (e) Maimon. R. Samson, & Bartenora in Misn. Ohalot, c. 15. sect. 8. (f) In Misn. Ohalot, c. 2. sect. 4. (g) Ib c. 15, sect. 8.

---

39. Jesus said, Take ye away the stone. Martha, the sister of him that was dead, saith unto him, Lord, by this time he stinketh: for he hath been dead four days.

---

39. Λέγει ὁ Ἰησοῦς, Ἄρατε τὸν λίθον. Λέγει αὐτῷ ἡ ἀδελφὴ τοῦ τεθνηκότος Μάρθα, Κύριε, ἤδη ὄζει· τεταρταῖος γάρ ἐστιν.

39. Legei 'o Yeisous, Arate ton lithon. Legei auto 'ei adelphei tou tethneikotos Martha, Kurie, eidei ozei. tetartaios gar estin.

Hebrew/Transliteration

לט. וַיֹּאמֶר יֵשׁוּעַ גֹּלּוּ אֶת-הָאָבֶן וַתֹּאמֶר אֵלָיו מַרְתָא אֲחוֹת הַמֵּת אֲדֹנִי הִנֵּה הוּא נִבְאָשׁ כִּי-זֶה לוֹ יָמִים אַרְבָּעָה:

39. Va•yo•mer Yeshua go•loo et - ha•a•ven va•to•mer elav Marta a•chot ha•met Adoni hee•ne hoo niv•ash ki - ze lo ya•mim ar•ba•ah.

Rabbinic Jewish Commentary

This order was contrary to a rule of the Jews, which forbid the opening of a grave after it was stopped up (h); but a greater than the fathers of the traditions was here, even he who has the keys of sheol, or the grave, and can open, or order it to be opened, when he pleases.

The Jews (i) say, that "for three days the soul goes to the grave, thinking the body may return; but when it sees the figure of the face changed, it goes away, and leaves it, as it is said, Job_14:22."

So of Jonah's being three days and three nights in the whale's belly, they say (k),

"These are the three days a man is in the grave, and his bowels burst; and after three days that defilement is turned upon his face."

Hence, they do not allow anyone to bear witness of one that is dead or killed, that he is such an one, after three days, because then his countenance is changed (l), and he cannot be well known.

(h) Apud Buxtorf Lex. Rab. col. 437. (i) Bereshit Rabba, sect. 100. fol. 88. 2. & T. Hieros. Moed Katon, fol. 82. 2. (k) Zohar in Exod. fol. 78. 2. (l) Misn. Yebamot, c. 16. sect. 3. & Maimon. Jarchi, & Bartenora in ib. & Maimon. Hilchot Gerushim, c. 13. sect. 21. T. Bab. Yebamot, fol. 120. 1. & Gloss. in ib.

---

40. Jesus saith unto her, Said I not unto thee, that, if thou wouldest believe, thou shouldest see the glory of God?

Greek/Transliteration
40. Λέγει αὐτῇ ὁ Ἰησοῦς, Οὐκ εἶπόν σοι, ὅτι ἐὰν πιστεύσῃς, ὄψει τὴν δόξαν τοῦ θεοῦ;

40. Legei autei 'o Yeisous, Ouk eipon soi, 'oti ean pisteuseis, opsei tein doxan tou theou?

Hebrew/Transliteration

מ. וַיֹּאמֶר אֵלֶיהָ יֵשׁוּעַ הֲלֹא אָמַרְתִּי לָךְ אִם-תַּאֲמִינִי אָז תִּרְאִי אֶת-כְּבוֹד הָאֱלֹהִים:

40. Va•yo•mer e•le•ha Yeshua ha•lo amar•ti lach eem - ta•a•mi•ni az tir•ee et - k`vod ha•Elohim?

---

41. Then they took away the stone from the place where the dead was laid. And Jesus lifted up his eyes, and said, Father, I thank thee that thou hast heard me.

Greek/Transliteration

41. Ἦραν οὖν τὸν λίθον, οὗ ἦν ὁ τεθνηκὼς κείμενος. Ὁ δὲ Ἰησοῦς ἦρεν τοὺς ὀφθαλμοὺς ἄνω, καὶ εἶπεν, Πάτερ, εὐχαριστῶ σοι ὅτι ἤκουσάς μου.

41. Eiran oun ton lithon, 'ou ein 'o tethneikos keimenos. 'O de Yeisous eiren tous ophthalmous ano, kai eipen, Pater, eucharisto soi 'oti eikousas mou.

Hebrew/Transliteration

מא. וַיִּגְלוּ אֶת-הָאֶבֶן אֲשֶׁר הַמֵּת הוּשַׂם שָׁם וְיֵשׁוּעַ נָשָׂא אֶת-עֵינָיו לַמָּרוֹם וַיֹּאמַר אוֹדְךָ אָבִי כִּי עֲנִיתָנִי:

41. Va•ya•go•loo et - ha•e•ven asher ha•met hoo•sam sham ve•Yeshua na•sa et - ey•nav la•ma•rom va•yo•mar od•cha Avi ki ani•ta•ni.

---

42. And I knew that thou hearest me always: but because of the people which stand by I said it, that they may believe that thou hast sent me.

Greek/Transliteration

42. Ἐγὼ δὲ ᾔδειν ὅτι πάντοτέ μου ἀκούεις· ἀλλὰ διὰ τὸν ὄχλον τὸν περιεστῶτα εἶπον, ἵνα πιστεύσωσιν ὅτι σύ με ἀπέστειλας.

42. Ego de eidein 'oti pantote mou akoueis. alla dya ton ochlon ton periestota eipon, 'ina pisteusosin 'oti su me apesteilas.

Hebrew/Transliteration

מב. וַאֲנִי יָדַעְתִּי כִּי מִדֵּי אַדַבֵּר אַתָּה תַעֲנֶה אֶפֶס בַּעֲבוּר הָעָם הָעֹמֵד עָלַי דִּבַּרְתִּי כֵן לְבַעֲבוּר יַאֲמִינוּ כִּי אַתָּה:שְׁלַחְתָּנִי

42. Va•a•ni ya•da•a•ti ki mee•dey ada•ber ata ta•a•ne e•fes ba•a•voor ha•am ha•o•med a•lai di•bar•ti chen le•va•a•voor ya•a•mi•noo ki ata sh`lach•ta•ni.

43. And when he thus had spoken, he cried with a loud voice, Lazarus, come forth.

Greek/Transliteration

43. Καὶ ταῦτα εἰπών, φωνῇ μεγάλῃ ἐκραύγασεν, Λάζαρε, δεῦρο ἔξω.

43. Kai tauta eipon, phonei megalei ekraugasen, Lazare, deuro exo.

Hebrew/Transliteration

מג. כְּכַלֹּתוֹ לְדַבֵּר כֵּן וַיִּקְרָא בְקוֹל גָּדוֹל אֶלְעָזָר עוּרָה וְצֵאָה:

43. Ke•cha•lo•to le•da•ber ken va•yik•ra ve•kol ga•dol El•a•zar oo•ra va•tze•ah.

---

44. And he that was dead came forth, bound hand and foot with graveclothes: and his face was bound about with a napkin. Jesus saith unto them, Loose him, and let him go.

Greek/Transliteration

44. Καὶ ἐξῆλθεν ὁ τεθνηκώς, δεδεμένος τοὺς πόδας καὶ τὰς χεῖρας κειρίαις, καὶ ἡ ὄψις αὐτοῦ σουδαρίῳ περιεδέδετο. Λέγει αὐτοῖς ὁ Ἰησοῦς, Λύσατε αὐτόν, καὶ ἄφετε ὑπάγειν.

44. Kai exeilthen 'o tethneikos, dedemenos tous podas kai tas cheiras keiriais, kai 'ei opsis autou soudario periededeto. Legei autois 'o Yeisous, Lusate auton, kai aphete 'upagein.

Hebrew/Transliteration

מד. וַיֵּצֵא הַמֵּת וְיָדָיו וְרַגְלָיו אֲסוּרוֹת בְּתַכְרִיכִין וּפָנָיו קְשׁוּרִים בְּמִטְפַּחַת וַיֹּאמֶר יֵשׁוּעַ אֲלֵיהֶם הַתִּירֻהוּ וּתְנוּ לוֹ:לָלֶכֶת

44. Va•ye•tze ha•met ve•ya•dav ve•rag•lav a•soo•rot be•tach•ri•chin oo•fa•nav ke•shoo•rim be•mit•pa•chat va•yo•mer Yeshua aley•hem ha•ti•roo•hoo oot•noo lo la•la•chet.

Rabbinic Jewish Commentary
and his face was bound about with a napkin; the use of which was not only to tie up the chin and jaws, but to hide the grim and ghastly looks of a dead corpse; and one of the same price and value was used by rich and poor: for it is said (m),

"The wise men introduced a custom of using סודר, "a napkin", (the very word here used, which Nonnus says is Syriac,) of the same value, not exceeding a penny, that he might not be ashamed who had not one so good as another; and they cover the faces of the dead, that they might not shame the poor, whose faces were black with famine."

For it seems (n), "Formerly they used to uncover the faces of the rich, and cover the faces of the poor, because their faces were black through want, and the poor were ashamed; wherefore they ordered, that they should cover the faces of all, for the honour of the poor."

(m) Maimon. Hilchot Ebel, c. 4. sect. 1, (n) T. Bab. Moed Katon, fol. 27. 1.

---

45. Then many of the Jews which came to Mary, and had seen the things which Jesus did, believed on him.

Greek/Transliteration

45. Πολλοὶ οὖν ἐκ τῶν Ἰουδαίων, οἱ ἐλθόντες πρὸς τὴν Μαρίαν καὶ θεασάμενοι ἃ ἐποίησεν ὁ Ἰησοῦς, ἐπίστευσαν εἰς αὐτόν.

45. Polloi oun ek ton Youdaion, 'oi elthontes pros tein Marian kai theasamenoi 'a epoieisen 'o Yeisous, episteusan eis auton.

Hebrew/Transliteration

מה. וְרַבִּים מִן-הַיְּהוּדִים אֲשֶׁר בָּאוּ אֶל-מִרְיָם כִּרְאוֹתָם אֶת-אֲשֶׁר עָשָׂה יֵשׁוּעַ וַיַּאֲמִינוּ-בוֹ:

45. Ve•ra•bim min - ha•Ye•hoo•dim asher ba•oo el - Mir•yam kir•o•tam et - asher asa Yeshua va•ya•a•mi•noo - vo.

---

46. But some of them went their ways to the Pharisees, and told them what things Jesus had done.

Greek/Transliteration

46. Τινὲς δὲ ἐξ αὐτῶν ἀπῆλθον πρὸς τοὺς Φαρισαίους, καὶ εἶπον αὐτοῖς ἃ ἐποίησεν ὁ Ἰησοῦς.

46. Tines de ex auton apeilthon pros tous Pharisaious, kai eipon autois 'a epoieisen 'o Yeisous.

Hebrew/Transliteration

מו. וּמִקְצוֹתָם הָלְכוּ אֶל-הַפְּרוּשִׁים וַיַּגִּידוּ לָהֶם אֶת-אֲשֶׁר עָשָׂה יֵשׁוּעַ:

46. Oo•mik•tzo•tam hal•choo el - ha•P`roo•shim va•ya•gi•doo la•hem et - asher asa Yeshua.

---

47. Then gathered the chief priests and the Pharisees a council, and said, What do we? For this man doeth many miracles.

Greek/Transliteration

47. Συνήγαγον οὖν οἱ ἀρχιερεῖς καὶ οἱ Φαρισαῖοι συνέδριον, καὶ ἔλεγον, Τί ποιοῦμεν; Ὅτι οὗτος ὁ ἄνθρωπος πολλὰ σημεῖα ποιεῖ.

47. Suneigagon oun 'oi archiereis kai 'oi Pharisaioi sunedrion, kai elegon, Ti poioumen? 'Oti 'outos 'o anthropos polla seimeia poiei.

Hebrew/Transliteration

מז. וַיַּקְהִילוּ רָאשֵׁי הַכֹּהֲנִים וְהַפְּרוּשִׁים אֶת-הַסַּנְהֶדְרִין וַיֹּאמְרוּ מַה-נַּעֲשֶׂה הֲלֹא הָאִישׁ הַזֶּה עֹשֶׂה מוֹפְתִים רַבִּים:

47. Va•yak•hi•loo ra•shey ha•ko•ha•nim ve•haP`roo•shim et - ha•San•hed•rin va•yom•roo ma - na•a•se ha•lo ha•eesh ha•ze o•se mof•tim ra•bim.

---

48. If we let him thus alone, all men will believe on him: and the Romans shall come and take away both our place and nation.

Greek/Transliteration

48. Ἐὰν ἀφῶμεν αὐτὸν οὕτως, πάντες πιστεύσουσιν εἰς αὐτόν· καὶ ἐλεύσονται οἱ Ῥωμαῖοι καὶ ἀροῦσιν ἡμῶν καὶ τὸν τόπον καὶ τὸ ἔθνος.

48. Ean aphomen auton 'outos, pantes pisteusousin eis auton. kai eleusontai 'oi 'Romaioi kai arousin 'eimon kai ton topon kai to ethnos.

Hebrew/Transliteration

מח. וְאִם-נֶחְדַּל מִמֶּנּוּ כַּיּוֹם כֻּלָּם הֲלֹא יַאֲמִינוּ-בוֹ וּבָאוּ הָרוֹמִיִּים וְלָקְחוּ אֶת-מְקוֹמֵנוּ וְאֶת-עַמֵּנוּ:

48. Ve•eem - nech•dal mi•me•noo ka•yom ha•lo choo•lam ya•a•mi•noo - vo oo•va•oo ha•Ro•mi•yim ve•lak•choo et - me•ko•me•noo ve•et - ame•noo.

---

49. And one of them, named Caiaphas, being the high priest that same year, said unto them, Ye know nothing at all,

Greek/Transliteration

49. Εἷς δέ τις ἐξ αὐτῶν Καϊάφας, ἀρχιερεὺς ὢν τοῦ ἐνιαυτοῦ ἐκείνου, εἶπεν αὐτοῖς, Ὑμεῖς οὐκ οἴδατε οὐδέν,

49. 'Eis de tis ex auton Kaiaphas, archiereus on tou enyautou ekeinou, eipen autois, 'Umeis ouk oidate ouden,

Hebrew/Transliteration

מט. וְאֶחָד מֵהֶם קַיָּפָא שְׁמוֹ אֲשֶׁר הָיָה כֹהֵן גָּדוֹל בַּשָּׁנָה הַהִיא אָמַר אֲלֵיהֶם אַתֶּם לֹא-תָבִינוּ דָבָר:

49. Ve•e•chad me•hem Ka•ya•fa sh`mo asher ha•ya cho•hen ga•dol ba•sha•na ha•hee amar aley•hem atem lo - ta•vi•noo da•var.

Rabbinic Jewish Commentary

The high priesthood originally was not annual, but for life; but towards the close of the second temple, it came into the hands of the king, to appoint who would to be high priest (o); and it became venal; it was purchased with money; insomuch that they changed the priesthood once a twelve month, and every year a new high priest was made (p) now this man being in such an high office, and a man of no conscience, and of bad principles, being a Sadducee, as seems from Act_4:6, who denied the resurrection of the dead, and was unconcerned about a future state; and having no restraint upon him, in a bold, haughty, and blustering manner.

(o) Misn. Yebamot, c. 6. sect. 4. (p) T. Bab. Yoma, fol. 8. 2. Juchasin, fol. 139. 1.

---

50. Nor consider that it is expedient for us, that one man should die for the people, and that the whole nation perish not.

Greek/Transliteration

50. οὐδὲ διαλογίζεσθε ὅτι συμφέρει ἡμῖν ἵνα εἷς ἄνθρωπος ἀποθάνῃ ὑπὲρ τοῦ λαοῦ, καὶ μὴ ὅλον τὸ ἔθνος ἀπόληται.

50. oude dyalogizesthe 'oti sumpherei 'eimin 'ina 'eis anthropos apothanei 'uper tou laou, kai mei 'olon to ethnos apoleitai.

Hebrew/Transliteration

נ: וְגַם לֹא-תַשְׁכִּילוּ כִּי טוֹב לָכֶם אֲשֶׁר יָמוּת אִישׁ אֶחָד בְּעַד הָעָם מֵאַבְדַן הָעָם כֻּלּוֹ:

50. Ve•gam lo - tas•ki•loo ki tov la•chem asher ya•moot eesh e•chad be•ad ha•am me•ov•dan ha•am koo•lo.

---

51. And this spake he not of himself: but being high priest that year, he prophesied that Jesus should die for that nation;

Greek/Transliteration

51. Τοῦτο δὲ ἀφ᾽ ἑαυτοῦ οὐκ εἶπεν, ἀλλὰ ἀρχιερεὺς ὢν τοῦ ἐνιαυτοῦ ἐκείνου, προεφήτευσεν ὅτι ἔμελλεν Ἰησοῦς ἀποθνῄσκειν ὑπὲρ τοῦ ἔθνους,

51. Touto de aph 'eautou ouk eipen, alla archiereus on tou enyautou ekeinou, proepheiteusen 'oti emellen Yeisous apothneiskein 'uper tou ethnous,

Hebrew/Transliteration

נא. וְלֹא מִלִּבּוֹ דִּבֶּר כָּזֹאת כִּי אִם-בִּהְיוֹתוֹ כֹהֵן גָּדוֹל בַּשָּׁנָה הַהִיא נִבָּא בְפִיו כִּי-יֵשׁוּעַ יָמוּת בְּעַד הָעָם:

51. Ve•lo mi•li•bo di•ber ka•zot ki eem - bi•hee•yo•to co•hen ga•dol ba•sha•na ha•hee ni•ba ve•fiv ki - Yeshua ya•moot be•ad ha•am.

---

52. And not for that nation only, but that also he should gather together in one the children of God that were scattered abroad.

Greek/Transliteration
52. καὶ οὐχ ὑπὲρ τοῦ ἔθνους μόνον, ἀλλ᾽ ἵνα καὶ τὰ τέκνα τοῦ θεοῦ τὰ διεσκορπισμένα συναγάγῃ εἰς ἕν.

52. kai ouch 'uper tou ethnous monon, all 'ina kai ta tekna tou theou ta dieskorpismena sunagagei eis 'en.

Hebrew/Transliteration
‎נב. וְלֹא-לְבַד בְּעַד הָעָם כִּי אִם-גַּם-לְקַבֵּץ אֶת-בְּנֵי הָאֱלֹהִים הַנְּפֹצִים וְהָיוּ לַאֲחָדִים:

52. Ve•lo - le•vad be•ad ha•am ki eem - gam - le•ka•betz et - b`ney ha•Elohim ha•ne•fo•tzim ve•ha•yoo la•a•cha•dim.

Rabbinic Jewish Commentary
The Persic version renders it, "that he might gather them into one place": and in this, the red heifer was a type of Christ; whose blood was sprinkled directly before the tabernacle of the congregation, and without the camp; and which was done, as a Jewish writer says (q),

"To call to mind the design of the heifer, which was to bring ‎המרוחקים, "those that were afar off", from the camp of the Shekinah, to be near unto it."

(q) Abarbinel in Lev. xix. 3, 4.

---

53. Then from that day forth they took counsel together for to put him to death.

Greek/Transliteration
53. Ἀπ᾽ ἐκείνης οὖν τῆς ἡμέρας συνεβουλεύσαντο ἵνα ἀποκτείνωσιν αὐτόν.

53. Ap ekeineis oun teis 'eimeras sunebouleusanto 'ina apokteinosin auton.

Hebrew/Transliteration
‎נג. וּמִן-הַיּוֹם הַהוּא נוֹעֲצוּ עָלָיו יַחְדָּו לַהֲמִיתוֹ:

53. Oo•min - ha•yom ha•hoo no•a•tzoo alav yach•dav la•ha•mi•to.

---

54. Jesus therefore walked no more openly among the Jews; but went thence unto a country near to the wilderness, into a city called Ephraim, and there continued with his disciples.

Greek/Transliteration

54. Ἰησοῦς οὖν οὐκέτι παρρησίᾳ περιεπάτει ἐν τοῖς Ἰουδαίοις, ἀλλὰ ἀπῆλθεν ἐκεῖθεν εἰς τὴν χώραν ἐγγὺς τῆς ἐρήμου, εἰς Ἐφραῒμ λεγομένην πόλιν, κἀκεῖ διέτριβεν μετὰ τῶν μαθητῶν αὐτοῦ.

54. Yeisous oun ouketi parreisia periepatei en tois Youdaiois, alla apeilthen ekeithen eis tein choran engus teis ereimou, eis Ephraim legomenein polin, kakei dietriben meta ton matheiton autou.

Hebrew/Transliteration

נד. וְעַל-כֵּן לֹא-הִתְהַלֵּךְ יֵשׁוּעַ עוֹד בֵּין הַיְּהוּדִים בְּגָלוּי כִּי אִם-נָטָה מִשָּׁם עַד-הַכִּכָּר הַקְּרוֹבָה לַמִּדְבָּר אֶל-עִיר:וּשְׁמָהּ אֶפְרַיִם וַיֵּגֶר-שָׁם עִם-תַּלְמִידָיו

54. Ve•al - ken lo - hit•ha•lech Yeshua od bein ha•Ye•hoo•dim be•ga•looy ki eem - na•ta mi•sham ad - ha•ki•kar hak•ro•va la•mid•bar el - eer oosh•ma Eph•ra•yim va•ya•gar – sham eem - tal•mi•dav.

Rabbinic Jewish Commentary

into a city called Ephraim; the Vulgate Latin, Syriac, Arabic, and Persic versions, call it Ephren, and so some copies; it seems to be the same with the Ephraim of the Misnic and Talmudic Rabbi's; concerning which they say (r),

"Micmas and Mezonicha are the first for fine flour, and the next to them is Ephraim in the valley."

For it seems there were two Ephraims, one in the valley, and another in the mount (s) it was a place very fruitful for wheat; hence that saying of Jannes and Jambres, the magicians of Egypt, to Moses (t);

"Do you bring straw to Ephraim?"

Which was a proverbial expression, the same with ours of carrying coals to Newcastle: they seeing Moses do signs and wonders, supposed he did them by enchantment; and the sense of their proverb is, do you bring enchantments into Egypt, where there are so many already? This Ephraim, the Jews say (u), is the same with that in 2Ch_13:19, and as there Bethel is mentioned with it, it seems to have been in the tribe of Benjamin: and it may be observed, that Josephus (w) speaks of an Ephraim, along with Bethel likewise; so that they all seem to mean the same place; and according to the same writer, it was but a little city, and it may be an obscure one, for which reason Yeshua withdrew to it. Epiphanius (x) makes mention of the wilderness of Bethel and Ephraim, through which he travelled, accompanied by a Jew, as he came up from Jericho to the hill country; and is very likely the same wilderness which is here spoken of; and by some called Quarentana, and placed by the river Chereth, in the tribe of Benjamin, north east of

Jerusalem; and the same writer elsewhere calls (y) Ephraim, the city of the wilderness: according to Jerom (z), it was twenty miles from Aelia, or Jerusalem; though according to Eusebius, it was but eight miles, which is thought to be the truest account; and by them both is said to be a very large village, and in which they may not differ from Josephus; for it might be a large village, and yet a little city. Jerom (a) takes notice of a place called Aphra, in the tribe of Benjamin, which he says at that time was called the village Effrem, and was five miles from Bethel eastward; and of another called Aphraim, a city in the tribe of Issachar, which in his time went by the name of the village Affarea, six miles from the legion, northward; the former agrees best with this Ephraim.

And there continued with his disciples; spending his time in private conversation with them, teaching and instructing them in things concerning the kingdom of God, his time with them being now but short.

(r) Misn. Menachot, c. 8. sect. 1. (s) Barlenora in ib. (t) T. Bab. Menachot, fol. 85. 1. Gloss. in ib. Tzcror Hammor, fol. 170. 2. Bereshit Rabba, sect. 86. fol. 75. 4. (u) Yom. Tob. in Misn. Menachot, c. 8. sect. 1. & Gloss. in T. Bab. Menachot, fol. 83. 2. (w) De Bello Jud. l. 4. c. 9. sect. 9. (x) Adv. Haeres. l. 1. Tom. II. Haeres. 30. (y) Ib. Haeres. 29. (z) De locis Hebraicis, fol. 91. A. (a) lb. fol. 88. H. I.

---

55. And the Jews' passover was nigh at hand: and many went out of the country up to Jerusalem before the passover, to purify themselves.

Greek/Transliteration
55. ῏Ην δὲ ἐγγὺς τὸ Πάσχα τῶν ᾿Ιουδαίων· καὶ ἀνέβησαν πολλοὶ εἰς ᾿Ιεροσόλυμα ἐκ τῆς χώρας πρὸ τοῦ Πάσχα, ἵνα ἁγνίσωσιν ἑαυτούς.

55. Ein de engus to Pascha ton Youdaion. kai anebeisan polloi eis 'Yerosoluma ek teis choras pro tou Pascha, 'ina 'agnisosin 'eautous.

Hebrew/Transliteration
נה. וַיִּקְרַב חַג-הַפֶּסַח לַיְּהוּדִים וְרַבִּים מִן-הָאָרֶץ עָלוּ יְרוּשָׁלַיְמָה לִפְנֵי הַפֶּסַח לְהִתְקַדֵּשׁ שָׁמָּה:

55. Va•yik•rav chag - ha•Pe•sach la•Ye•hoo•dim ve•ra•bim min - ha•a•retz a•loo Ye•roo•sha•lai•ma lif•ney ha•Pe•sach le•hit•ka•desh sha•ma.

Rabbinic Jewish Commentary
to purify themselves; we read in 2Ch_30:18 of many that had not cleansed themselves, and yet ate the passover; for whom Hezekiah prayed, that they might be pardoned, which shows that they had done amiss: upon which place, Jarchi has this observation; that

"Judah (the men of Judah) were all clean, because they were near to Jerusalem, and could purify and sanctify themselves, and return to Jerusalem; but many of Ephraim, and Manasseh, and Issachar, and Zabulon, could not do so."

And this seems to be the case of these people, they were country people, that lived at a distance, and not having purified themselves from several uncleannesses, came up before the time, that they might cleanse themselves, and be ready at the time: in several cases purification was required; as with new mothers, menstruous and profluvious persons, and such that had touched a dead body, or any creeping thing, and in other cases; and which by reason of distance, might be neglected; wherefore it was necessary they should come up before the time of the passover, to fit themselves for it: the rule about defiled persons eating the passover, is this (b);

"If the congregation is polluted, or the greatest part of it, or the priests are unclean, and the congregation pure, it is kept in uncleanness; but if the lesser part of the congregation is defiled, the pure keep the first passover, and the unclean the second."

This, their commentators say (c), is to be understood of uncleanness, by touching the dead, which required seven days of purification; and it is very probable that this was the case of these persons, since it was about so many days before the passover, that they came up. The account Maimonides (d) gives of this matter is this;

"Who is a defiled person, that is put off to the second passover? everyone who cannot eat the passover, on the night of the fifteenth of Nisan, because of his uncleanness; as profluvious men and women, menstruous and new mothers, and the husbands of menstruous women; but he that toucheth the dead carcass of a beast, or a creeping thing, and the like, on the fourteenth, lo, he dips, and they slay for him (the passover) after he has dipped; and in the evening, when his sun is set, he eats the passover; he that is defiled by touching the dead, whose seventh day happens to be on the fourteenth, though he dips and is sprinkled on, and lo, he is fit to eat the holy things at evening, yet they do not kill for him, but he is put off to the second passover; as it is said, Num_9:6. "And there were certain men who were defiled by the dead body of a man, that they could not keep the passover on that day"; by tradition it is learned, that it was their seventh day, and therefore they asked if it should be killed for them, and they should eat at evening? and it was declared to them, that they should not kill for them: of what is this to be understood? when he is polluted with a defilement by the dead, which Nazarites shave for; but if he is polluted with other defilements by the dead, which the Nazarites do not shave for, they kill for him on his seventh day, after he has dipped, and is sprinkled upon; and when his sun is set, he eats his passover; a profluvious person, who sees two appearances, and reckons seven days, and dips on the seventh, they kill for him, and he eats at evening.--They do not kill for a menstruous woman on her seventh day, for lo, she does not dip till the eighth night, and she is not fit to eat holy things until the ninth night."

These, with many other cases there instanced, may serve to illustrate this passage.

(b) Misn. Pesachim, c. 7. sect. 6. Vid. Maimon. Korban Pesach. c. 7. sect. 1, 2, 3, 4, 5, 6. & Biah Hamikdash, c. 4. sect. 10-18. (c) Maimon. & Bartenora in Misn. ib. (d) Hilchot Korban Pesach. c. 6. sect. 1, 2, 3.

56. Then sought they for Jesus, and spake among themselves, as they stood in the temple, What think ye, that he will not come to the feast?

Greek/Transliteration

56. Ἐζήτουν οὖν τὸν Ἰησοῦν, καὶ ἔλεγον μετ' ἀλλήλων ἐν τῷ ἱερῷ ἑστηκότες, Τί δοκεῖ ὑμῖν; Ὅτι οὐ μὴ ἔλθῃ εἰς τὴν ἑορτήν;

56. Ezeitoun oun ton Yeisoun, kai elegon met alleilon en to 'iero 'esteikotes, Ti dokei 'umin? 'Oti ou mei elthei eis tein 'eortein?

Hebrew/Transliteration

נו. וַיְבַקְשׁוּ אֶת-יֵשׁוּעַ וַיֹּאמְרוּ אִישׁ אֶל-רֵעֵהוּ הָעֹמְדִים בְּבֵית הַמִּקְדָּשׁ מַה-יֶּהְגֶּה לִבְכֶם הַאִם לֹא-יָבֹא אֶל:הֶחָג -

56. Vay•vak•shoo et - Yeshua va•yom•roo eesh el - re•e•hoo ha•om•dim be•veit ha•mik•dash ma - ye•he•ge lib•chem ha•eem lo - ya•vo el - he•chag?

---

57. Now both the chief priests and the Pharisees had given a commandment, that, if any man knew where he were, he should shew it, that they might take him.

Greek/Transliteration

57. Δεδώκεισαν δὲ καὶ οἱ ἀρχιερεῖς καὶ οἱ Φαρισαῖοι ἐντολήν, ἵνα ἐάν τις γνῷ ποῦ ἐστιν, μηνύσῃ, ὅπως πιάσωσιν αὐτόν.

57. Dedokeisan de kai 'oi archiereis kai 'oi Pharisaioi entolein, 'ina ean tis gno pou estin, meinusei, 'opos pyasosin auton.

Hebrew/Transliteration

נז. וְרָאשֵׁי הַכֹּהֲנִים וְהַפְּרוּשִׁים נָתְנוּ פְקֻדָּה כִּי אִם-יֵדַע אִישׁ אֶת-מְקוֹמוֹ אַיּוֹ יָבֹא וְיַגִּיד לְמַעַן יִתְפְּשֵׂהוּ:

57. Ve•ra•shey ha•ko•ha•nim ve•haP`roo•shim nat•noo fe•koo•da ki eem - ye•da eesh et - me•ko•mo ayo ya•vo ve•ya•gid le•ma•an yit•pe•soo•hoo.

John, Chapter 12

1. Then Jesus six days before the passover came to Bethany, where Lazarus was which had been dead, whom he raised from the dead.

Greek/Transliteration
1. Ὁ οὖν Ἰησοῦς πρὸ ἓξ ἡμερῶν τοῦ Πάσχα ἦλθεν εἰς Βηθανίαν, ὅπου ἦν Λάζαρος ὁ τεθνηκώς, ὃν ἤγειρεν ἐκ νεκρῶν.

1. 'O oun Yeisous pro 'ex 'eimeron tou Pascha eilthen eis Beithanian, 'opou ein Lazaros 'o tethneikos, 'on eigeiren ek nekron.

Hebrew/Transliteration
א. וְשֵׁשֶׁת יָמִים לִפְנֵי חַג-הַפֶּסַח בָּא יֵשׁוּעַ אֶל-בֵּית-עַנְיָה וְשָׁם אֶלְעָזָר הַמֵּת אֲשֶׁר הֶחֱיָה מִן-הַמֵּתִים:

1. Ve•she•shet ya•mim lif•ney chag - ha•Pe•sach ba Yeshua el - Beit - An•ya ve•sham El•a•zar ha•met asher he•che•ya min - ha•me•tim.

Rabbinic Jewish Commentary
Or "before the six days of the passover"; not as designing the days of that feast, for they were seven; but as reckoning so many days back from it, that is, before the sixth day from the ensuing passover: if there were six complete days between this and the passover, as this way of speaking seems to imply; then this must be the day before the Jewish sabbath, and this is more likely, than that Yeshua should travel on the sabbath day: but if this was the sixth day before it, it was their sabbath day, and so at the going out of it in the evening, a supper was made for him, which with the Jews on that night, was a plentiful one; for they remembered the sabbath in its going out, as well as in its coming in (e), and this was to prevent grief at the going out of it: so some days before the passover, the lamb was separated from the flock, and kept up till the fourteenth day, Exo_12:3 particularly it may be observed, that seven days before the day of atonement, the high priest was separated from his own house, and had to the chamber Palhedrin (f); and much such a space of time there was, between the day of the great atonement by Yeshua, and his unction by Mary; which is said to be against the day of his burial, which being the same day with his sufferings, was the great day of atonement.

(e) Maimon. Hilchot Sabbat. c. 29. sect. 1. 11, 12, 29. (f) Misn. Yoma, c. 1. sect. 1.

---

2. There they made him a supper; and Martha served: but Lazarus was one of them that sat at the table with him.

Greek/Transliteration
2. Ἐποίησαν οὖν αὐτῷ δεῖπνον ἐκεῖ, καὶ ἡ Μάρθα διηκόνει· ὁ δὲ Λάζαρος εἷς ἦν τῶν ἀνακειμένων σὺν αὐτῷ.

2. Epoieisan oun auto deipnon ekei, kai 'ei Martha dieikonei. 'o de Lazaros 'eis ein ton anakeimenon sun auto.

Hebrew/Transliteration

:ב. וַיַּעֲשׂוּ-לוֹ שָׁם מִשְׁתֶּה בָּעֶרֶב וּמַרְתָא מְשָׁרֶתֶת אֹתוֹ וְאֶלְעָזָר הָיָה אֶחָד מִן-הַיֹּשְׁבִים אֶל-הַשֻּׁלְחָן

2. Va•ya•a•soo - lo sham mish•te ba•a•rev oo•Marta me•sha•re•tet o•to ve•El•azar ha•ya e•chad min - ha•yosh•vim el - ha•shool•chan.

---

3. Then took Mary a pound of ointment of spikenard, very costly, and anointed the feet of Jesus, and wiped his feet with her hair: and the house was filled with the odour of the ointment.

Greek/Transliteration

3. Ἡ οὖν Μαρία λαβοῦσα λίτραν μύρου νάρδου πιστικῆς πολυτίμου, ἤλειψεν τοὺς πόδας τοῦ Ἰησοῦ, καὶ ἐξέμαξεν ταῖς θριξὶν αὐτῆς τοὺς πόδας αὐτοῦ· ἡ δὲ οἰκία ἐπληρώθη ἐκ τῆς ὀσμῆς τοῦ μύρου.

3. 'Ei oun Maria labousa litran murou nardou pistikeis polutimou, eileipsen tous podas tou Yeisou, kai exemaxen tais thrixin auteis tous podas autou. 'ei de oikia epleirothei ek teis osmeis tou murou.

Herbrew/Transliteration

ג. וַתִּקַּח מִרְיָם מִרְקַחַת נֵרְךְ זַךְ וִיקַר-עֵרֶךְ מְאֹד לִטְרָא אַחַת מִשְׁקָלָהּ וַתִּמְשַׁח אֶת-רַגְלֵי יֵשׁוּעַ וּבְשַׂעֲרֹתֶיהָ נִגְּבָה:אֶת-רַגְלָיו וְהַבַּיִת מָלֵא רֵיחַ הַמִּרְקַחַת

3. Va•ti•kach Mir•yam mir•ka•chat nerd zach vi•kar - e•rech me•od lit•ra a•chat mish•ka•la va•tim•shach et - rag•ley Yeshua oov•sa•a•ro•te•ha nig•va et - rag•lav ve•ha•ba•yit ma•le re•ach ha•mir•ka•chat.

---

4. Then saith one of his disciples, Judas Iscariot, Simon's son, which should betray him,

Greek/Transliteration

4. Λέγει οὖν εἷς ἐκ τῶν μαθητῶν αὐτοῦ, Ἰούδας Σίμωνος Ἰσκαριώτης, ὁ μέλλων αὐτὸν παραδιδόναι,

4. Legei oun 'eis ek ton matheiton autou, Youdas Simonos Yskarioteis, 'o mellon auton paradidonai,

Hebrew/Transliteration

:ד. וְאֶחָד מִתַּלְמִידָיו הוּא יְהוּדָה בֶּן-שִׁמְעוֹן אִישׁ-קְרִיּוֹת אֲשֶׁר אַחֲרֵי-כֵן הִסְגִּירוֹ אָמַר לֵאמֹר

4. Ve•e•chad mi•tal•mi•dav hoo Yehooda ben - Shimon Eesh - K`ri•yot asher a•cha•rey - chen his•gi•ro amar le•mor.

5. Why was not this ointment sold for three hundred pence, and given to the poor?

Greek/Transliteration
5. Διὰ τί τοῦτο τὸ μύρον οὐκ ἐπράθη τριακοσίων δηναρίων, καὶ ἐδόθη πτωχοῖς;

5. Dya ti touto to muron ouk eprathei tryakosion deinarion, kai edothei ptochois?

Hebrew/Transliteration
ה. עַל-מֶה לֹא-תִמָּכֵר הַמִּרְקַחַת הַזֹּאת בִּשְׁלֹשׁ מֵאוֹת דִּינָר לָתֵת לָעֲנִיִּים:

5. Al - me lo - ti•ma•cher ha•mir•ka•chat ha•zot bish•losh me•ot di•nar la•tet la•a•ni•yim?

---

6. This he said, not that he cared for the poor; but because he was a thief, and had the bag, and bare what was put therein.

Greek/Transliteraton
6. Εἶπεν δὲ τοῦτο, οὐχ ὅτι περὶ τῶν πτωχῶν ἔμελεν αὐτῷ, ἀλλ᾽ ὅτι κλέπτης ἦν, καὶ τὸ γλωσσόκομον εἶχεν, καὶ τὰ βαλλόμενα ἐβάσταζεν.

6. Eipen de touto, ouch 'oti peri ton ptochon emelen auto, all 'oti klepteis ein, kai to glossokomon eichen, kai ta ballomena ebastazen.

Hebrew/Transliteration
ו. וְהוּא דִּבֶּר כָזֹאת לֹא מִדַּאֲגָתוֹ לָעֲנִיִּים רַק יַעַן כִּי-גַנָּב הָיָה וַאֲרוֹן אוֹצָרָם בְּיָדוֹ וְנָשָׂא מֵאֲשֶׁר נָתוּן בּוֹ:

6. Ve•hoo di•ber cha•zot lo mi•da•a•ga•to la•a•ni•yim rak ya•an ki - ga•nav ha•ya va•a•ron o•tza•ram be•ya•do ve•na•sa me•a•sher na•toon bo.

Rabbinic Jewish Commentary
The word rendered a "bag", is adopted by the Rabbinical Jews, into their language; and is sometimes read "Gloskema", and at other times "Dloskema", and is used by them for different things; sometimes (g) for a bier, or coffin, in which the dead was buried, which sense can have no place here; sometimes for a chest, or coffer (h); and so the Septuagint use the Greek word, in 2Ch_24:8, for the chest into which the people put their collection; and it may be so interpreted here, and so Nonnus renders it; it may signify the chest or coffer, which Judas had the care of, the keys of which were in his hands, and whatever were to be put into it, he bore, or carried thither: and it is also used by the Jewish writers, for a purse (i); it is asked,

"What is "Dloskema?" says Rabbah bar Samuel, טליקא דסבי, "the purse of old men";"

Or such as ancient men use; and this is the signification of it here: it may be the same with the "Loculi" of the Romans, and so the Vulgate Latin renders it here; which were different from a chest, or coffer, being moveable, and to be carried about, and which were carried by servants, as well as the purse (k). Judas had the purse, into which was put whatsoever was ministered to Yeshua, for the common supply of him and his disciples, and for the relief of the poor.

(g) Targum Jon. & Jerus. in Gen. l. 26. T. Bab. Moed Katon, fol. 24. 2. & Massech. Semacot, c. 3. sect. 2. (h) Misn. Meila, c. 6. sect. 1. T. Bab. Megilla, fol. 26. 2. (i) T. Bab. Gittin, fol. 28. 1. & Bava Metzia, fol. 20. 2. (k) Vid. Pignorium de Servis, p. 327, 328.

---

7. Then said Jesus, Let her alone: against the day of my burying hath she kept this.

Greek/Transliteration
7. Εἶπεν οὖν ὁ Ἰησοῦς, Ἄφες αὐτήν· εἰς τὴν ἡμέραν τοῦ ἐνταφιασμοῦ μου τετήρηκεν αὐτό.

7. Eipen oun 'o Yeisous, Aphes autein. eis tein 'eimeran tou entaphyasmou mou teteireiken auto.

Hebrew/Transliteration
ז. וַיֹּאמֶר יֵשׁוּעַ הַנַּח-לָהּ לְיוֹם קְבֻרָתִי הִכִּינָה זֹאת:

7. Va•yo•mer Yeshua ha•nach - la le•yom ke•voo•ra•ti he•chi•na zot.

---

8. For the poor always ye have with you; but me ye have not always.

Greek/Transliteration
8. Τοὺς πτωχοὺς γὰρ πάντοτε ἔχετε μεθ᾽ ἑαυτῶν, ἐμὲ δὲ οὐ πάντοτε ἔχετε.

8. Tous ptochous gar pantote echete meth 'eauton, eme de ou pantote echete.

Hebrew/Transliteration
ח. כִּי אֶת-הָעֲנִיִּים תִּמְצְאוּ לִפְנֵיכֶם תָּמִיד וְאוֹתִי לֹא תִמְצְאוּ תָּמִיד לִפְנֵיכֶם:

8. Ki et - ha•a•ni•yim tim•tze•oo lif•ney•chem ta•mid ve•o•ti lo tim•tze•oo ta•mid lif•ney•chem.

Rabbinic Jewish Commentary

For the Jews say (h), "There is no difference between this world (this present time) and the times of the Messiah, but the subduing of kingdoms only; as it is said, Deu_15:11, "for the poor shall never cease out of the land": the gloss on it is, from hence it may be concluded, that therefore, לעולם יש עניות, "for ever there will be poverty, and riches"."

The Jews also suppose cases, in which the collectors of alms may have no poor to distribute to, and direct what they shall do in such cases (l):

(h) T. Bab. Sabbat, fol. 63. 1. (l) T. Bab. Pesachim, fol. 13. 1. & Bava Metzia, fol. 38. 1. & Bava Bathra, fol. 8. 2.

---

9. Much people of the Jews therefore knew that he was there: and they came not for Jesus' sake only, but that they might see Lazarus also, whom he had raised from the dead.

Greek/Transliteration

9. Ἔγνω οὖν ὄχλος πολὺς ἐκ τῶν Ἰουδαίων ὅτι ἐκεῖ ἐστιν· καὶ ἦλθον οὐ διὰ τὸν Ἰησοῦν μόνον, ἀλλ᾽ ἵνα καὶ τὸν Λάζαρον ἴδωσιν, ὃν ἤγειρεν ἐκ νεκρῶν.

9. Egno oun ochlos polus ek ton Youdaion 'oti ekei estin. kai eilthon ou dya ton Yeisoun monon, all 'ina kai ton Lazaron idosin, 'on eigeiren ek nekron.

Hebrew/Transliteration

ט. וְרַבִּים מִן-הַיְּהוּדִים שָׁמְעוּ כִּי הוּא שָׁם וַיָּבֹאוּ לֹא-בַעֲבוּר יֵשׁוּעַ לְבַדּוֹ כִּי אִם-גַּם-לִרְאוֹת אֶת-אֶלְעָזָר אֲשֶׁר:הֶחֱיָה מִן-הַמֵּתִים

9. Ve•ra•bim min - ha•Ye•hoo•dim sham•oo ki hoo sham va•ya•vo•oo lo - va•a•voor Yeshua le•va•do ki eem - gam - lir•ot et - El•a•zar asher he•che•ya min - ha•me•tim.

---

10. But the chief priests consulted that they might put Lazarus also to death;

Greek/Transliteration
10. Ἐβουλεύσαντο δὲ οἱ ἀρχιερεῖς ἵνα καὶ τὸν Λάζαρον ἀποκτείνωσιν·

10. Ebouleusanto de 'oi archiereis 'ina kai ton Lazaron apokteinosin.

Hebrew/Transliteration
י. וַיִּוָּעֲצוּ רָאשֵׁי הַכֹּהֲנִים לַהֲרֹג גַּם אֶת-אֶלְעָזָר:

10. Va•yi•va•a•tzoo ra•shey ha•ko•ha•nim la•ha•rog gam et - El•a•zar.

11. Because that by reason of him many of the Jews went away, and believed on Jesus.

Greek/Transliteration
11. ὅτι πολλοὶ δι᾽ αὐτὸν ὑπῆγον τῶν Ἰουδαίων, καὶ ἐπίστευον εἰς τὸν Ἰησοῦν.

11. 'oti polloi di auton 'upeigon ton Youdaion, kai episteuon eis ton Yeisoun.

Hebrew/Transliteration
יא. כִּי בִּגְלָלוֹ אָזְלוּ יְהוּדִים רַבִּים וַיַּאֲמִינוּ בְּיֵשׁוּעַ:

11. Ki big•la•lo az•loo Ye•hoo•dim ra•bim va•ya•a•mi•noo be•Yeshua.

---

12. On the next day much people that were come to the feast, when they heard that Jesus was coming to Jerusalem,

Greek/Transliteration
12. Τῇ ἐπαύριον ὄχλος πολὺς ὁ ἐλθὼν εἰς τὴν ἑορτήν, ἀκούσαντες ὅτι ἔρχεται Ἰησοῦς εἰς Ἱεροσόλυμα,

12. Tei epaurion ochlos polus 'o elthon eis tein 'eortein, akousantes 'oti erchetai Yeisous eis 'Yerosoluma,

Hebrew/Transliteration
יב. וַיְהִי מִמָּחֳרַת כִּשְׁמֹעַ רַבִּים מִן-הָעָם מִן-עוֹלֵי הָרֶגֶל כִּי יֵשׁוּעַ בָּא יְרוּשָׁלָיְמָה:

12. Vay•hi mi•mo•cho•rat ki•sh`mo•a ra•bim min - ha•am min - o•ley ha•re•gel ki Yeshua ba Ye•roo•sha•lai•ma.

Rabbinic Jewish Commentary
Of the passover; and they were much people indeed, that came yearly to this feast, from all parts of the nation; for all the males in Israel, were obliged to appear at this time; and though the women were not obliged, yet multitudes of them came, and the fame of Yeshua might bring the more; add to which, that there was now a general expectation of the Messiah's coming, which brought the Jews from all parts of the world, to Jerusalem; so that this might be called indeed, פסח מעוכין, "a crowded passover": and though the following account is a stretching it too far, yet it may serve to illustrate this matter:

"Would you desire to know what multitudes were at Jerusalem of the priests, you may know, as it is written, 1Ki_8:63, and the tradition is, that an ox was offered for twenty four, and a sheep for eleven.--King Agrippa sought to know what was the number of the multitude, which were in Jerusalem; he said to the priests, lay by for me one kidney of every passover lamb; they laid by for him six hundred thousand pair of kidneys, double the number of those that came out of Egypt: and there is never a passover lamb, but there are more than ten numbered for it (m)."
(m) Echa Rabbati, fol. 42. 3, 4.

13. Took branches of palm trees, and went forth to meet him, and cried, Hosanna: Blessed is the King of Israel that cometh in the name of the Lord.

Greek/Transliteration

13. ἔλαβον τὰ βαΐα τῶν φοινίκων, καὶ ἐξῆλθον εἰς ὑπάντησιν αὐτῷ, καὶ ἔκραζον, Ὡσαννά· εὐλογημένος ὁ ἐρχόμενος ἐν ὀνόματι κυρίου, βασιλεὺς τοῦ Ἰσραήλ.

13. elabon ta baia ton phoinikon, kai exeilthon eis 'upanteisin auto, kai ekrazon, 'Osanna. eulogeimenos 'o erchomenos en onomati kuriou, basileus tou Ysraeil.

Hebrew/Transliteration

יג. וַיִּקְחוּ כַּפּוֹת תְּמָרִים בְּיָדָם וַיֵּצְאוּ לִקְרָאתוֹ וַיָּרִיעוּ הוֹשַׁע-נָא בָּרוּךְ הַבָּא בְּשֵׁם יְהוָֹה מֶלֶךְ יִשְׂרָאֵל:

13. Va•yik•choo cha•pot t`ma•rim be•ya•dam va•yetz•oo lik•ra•to va•ya•ri•oo Ho•sha - na Ba•rooch ha•ba be•shem Adonai Me•lech Israel.

Rabbinic Jewish Commentary

And as that tree was a sign of joy and victory, they carried branches of it in their hands, as they met the King Messiah, who was about to make his public entrance into Jerusalem, in triumph; and where by his sufferings and death, he should gain the victory over sin, Satan, the world, and death; and lay a solid foundation for joy and peace, to all that believe in him: the Jews say (n),

"If a man takes באיין, (the very Greek word here used,) palm tree branches in his hands, we know that he is victorious."

The Persic version reads, "branches of olives".

(n) Vajikra Rabba, sect. 30. fol. 170. 3.

---

14. And Jesus, when he had found a young ass, sat thereon; as it is written,

Greek/Transliteration

14. Εὑρὼν δὲ ὁ Ἰησοῦς ὀνάριον, ἐκάθισεν ἐπ᾽ αὐτό, καθώς ἐστιν γεγραμμένον,

14. 'Euron de 'o Yeisous onarion, ekathisen ep auto, kathos estin gegrammenon,

Hebrew/Transliteration

יד. וַיִּמְצָא יֵשׁוּעַ עַיִר וַיִּרְכַּב עָלָיו כַּכָּתוּב:

14. Va•yim•tza Yeshua a•yir va•yir•kav alav ka•ka•toov.

---

15. Fear not, daughter of Sion: behold, thy King cometh, sitting on an ass's colt.

Greek/Transliteration
15. Μὴ φοβοῦ, θύγατερ Σιών· ἰδού, ὁ βασιλεύς σου ἔρχεται, καθήμενος ἐπὶ πῶλον ὄνου.

15. Mei phobou, thugater Sion. idou, 'o basileus sou erchetai, katheimenos epi polon onou.

Hebrew/Transliteration
טו. אַל-תִּירְאִי בַּת-צִיּוֹן הִנֵּה מַלְכֵּךְ יָבוֹא לָךְ רֹכֵב עַל-עַיִר בֶּן-אֲתֹנוֹת:

15. Al - tir•ee bat - Tzi•yon hee•ne Mal•kech ya•vo lach ro•chev al - a•yir ben - ato•not.

Rabbinic Jewish Commentary
These words seem to be taken out of Isa_62:11 where it is said, "say ye to the daughter of Zion, behold thy salvation cometh", or "thy Saviour cometh"; meaning, without doubt, the Messiah: by the daughter of Zion is meant, not the city of Jerusalem, but the inhabitants thereof, the Jewish synagogue; or as the Targum renders it, כנישתא דציון, "the congregation of Zion", the people of the Jews; particularly the elect of God among them, those that embraced the true Messiah, and believed in him.

One of the Jewish commentators says (x), that interpreters are divided about the sense of this prophecy; but observes, that there are some that say this is the Messiah: and another (y) of them affirms, that it is impossible to explain it of any other than the king Messiah; and that it can be understood of no other, I have elsewhere (z) shown. "Meek"; in the prophecy of Zechariah it is, עני, "poor", as the Messiah Jesus was, in a temporal sense; but the word, both by the Septuagint, and our evangelist, is rendered

meek; as it is by the Targum, Jarchi, and Kimchi, who all explain it by ענותן, "lowly, humble, or meek": and a character it is, that well agrees with Yeshua, who, in the whole of his deportment, both in life and in death, was a pattern of meekness and lowliness of mind.

This is applied to the Messiah by the Jews, both ancient (a) and modern (v), who consider this as an instance and evidence of his humility: they suppose, this ass to be a very uncommon one, having an hundred spots on it; and say, that it was the foal of that which was created on the eve of the sabbath (w); and is the same that Abraham and Moses rode upon: and they own, as before observed, that Yeshua of Nazareth rode on one to Jerusalem, as is here related. Their ancient governors, patriarchs, princes, and judges, used to ride on asses, before the introduction and multiplication of horses in Solomon's time, forbidden by the law of God: wherefore, though this might seem mean and despicable at this present time, yet was suitable enough to Yeshua's character as a king, and as the son of David, and king of Israel; strictly observing the law given to the kings of Israel, and riding in such manner as they formerly did.

Jarchi affirms that it is impossible to interpret it of any other than the King Messiah; and this is the sense of many of their writers, both ancient and modern. It is applied to him in the Talmud; they say (r), he that sees an ass in his dream, let him look for salvation, as it is said, behold, thy king cometh unto thee, "riding on an ass". R. Alexander relates that R. Joshua ben Levi opposed these two phrases to each other, "in its time", and "I will hasten it", Isa_60:22 and gave this as the sense to reconcile them: if they (the Israelites) are worthy, i.e. of the coming of the Messiah, "I will hasten it"; if they are not worthy, it shall be "in its time"; and that he also put these Scriptures together, and compared them to that Scripture, "behold, one like the Son of man came with the clouds of heaven", Dan_7:13 and also what is written, "poor, and riding on an ass"; if they are worthy, he will come with the clouds of heaven; if they are not worthy, he will come poor and riding on an ass (s). In an ancient book (t) of theirs, at least so reckoned, it is said the King Messiah shall prevail over them all (the nations of the world, and the Israelites); as it is said, "poor, and riding on an ass, and on a colt, the foal of an ass": and in several other places of that work, and other treatises in it (u), the text is applied to the Messiah; as it likewise is in their ancient Midrashes or expositions. In one (w) it is observed,

"The Rabbi's say an ox; this is the anointed for war, as it is said, "his glory is like the firstling of his bullock", Deu_33:17 an ass; this is the King Messiah, as it is said, "poor, and riding on an ass";"

And again (x), on these words, "binding his foal to the vine, and his ass's colt unto the choice vine", Gen_49:11, this remark is made; this shall be when that shall come to pass which is written of him, "poor, and riding on an ass". And in another (y) of their expositions, the two Redeemers, Moses and the Messiah, are compared together; and, among the several things in which they agree, this is one; as it is said of the former redeemer, "and Moses took his wife and his sons, and set them on an ass", Exo_4:20 so it is said of the latter Redeemer (the Messiah), "poor, and riding on an ass". And thus it is interpreted by many of their more modern writers (z). This is to be understood of Yeshua's coming, not merely to Jerusalem, when he rode on an ass, after mentioned; but of his coming in the flesh, when he came to Zion, and for her good; and which was wonderful, and therefore a "behold" is prefixed to it; and is matter of great joy, which she is called to show, because of the birth of him who is her Saviour; and because of the good things that come by him; and because of his appearing as a King, and her King; for, as he was prophesied of as such, as such he came, though his kingdom was not of this world; and as Zion's King, being placed there by his Father, and to which he has a right by virtue of redemption, and is owned as such by his people in the effectual calling, and to whom all the following characters belong.

(x) Aben Ezra in Zech. ix. 9. (y) Jarchi in ib. (z) Prophecies of the Messiah literally fulfilled in Jesus, c. 9. p. 151, &c. (a) T. Bab. Sanhedrim, fol. 98. 1. & 99. 1. Bereshit Rabba, fol. 66. 2. & 85. 3. Midrash Kohelet, fol. 63. 2. Zohar in Gen.

fol. 127. 3. & in Num. fol. 83. 4. & in Deut. fol. 117. 1. & 118. 3. Raya Mehimna in Zohar. in Lev. fol. 38. 3. & in Num. fol. 97. 2. (v) Jarchi in Isa. xxvi 6. Baal Hatturim in Exod. fol. 88. 2. Abarbimel, Mashmia Jeshua, fol. 15. 4. (w) Pirke Eliezer, c. 31. Caphtor, fol. 81. 2.

(r) T. Bab. Beracot, fol. 56. 2. (s) T. Bab. Sanhedrin, fol. 98. 1. Vid. etiam ib. fol. 99. 10. (t) Zohar in Gen. fol. 127. 3. (u) Zohar in Numb. fol. 83. 4. & in Deut. fol. 117. 1. & 118. 3. Raya Mehimna apud ib. in Lev. fol. 38. 3. & in Numb. fol. 97. 2. (w) Bereshit Rabba, sect. 75. fol. 66. 2. (x) Bereshit Rabba, sect. 98. fol. 85. 3. (y) Midrash Kohelet, fol. 63. 2. (z) Jarchi in Isa. xxvi. 6. Baal hatturim on Exod. fol. 88. 2. Abarbinel, Mashmiah Jeshuah, fol. 15. 4. R. Abraham Seba, Tzeror Hammor, fol. 46. 2. Caphtor Uperah, fol. 81. 2.

---

16. These things understood not his disciples at the first: but when Jesus was glorified, then remembered they that these things were written of him, and that they had done these things unto him.

Greek/Translieration

16. Ταῦτα δὲ οὐκ ἔγνωσαν οἱ μαθηταὶ αὐτοῦ τὸ πρῶτον· ἀλλ᾽ ὅτε ἐδοξάσθη Ἰησοῦς, τότε ἐμνήσθησαν ὅτι ταῦτα ἦν ἐπ᾽ αὐτῷ γεγραμμένα, καὶ ταῦτα ἐποίησαν αὐτῷ.

16. Tauta de ouk egnosan 'oi matheitai autou to proton. all 'ote edoxasthei Yeisous, tote emneistheisan 'oti tauta ein ep auto gegrammena, kai tauta epoieisan auto.

Hebrew/Transliteration

טז. וְכָל-זֹאת לֹא-הֵבִינוּ תַלְמִידָיו בַּתְּחִילָה אַךְ כַּאֲשֶׁר לֻקַּח יֵשׁוּעַ אַחַר כָּבוֹד זָכְרוּ אָז כִּי-כֹה כָּתוּב עָלָיו וְכֹה:גַם-עָשׂוּ לֹו

16. Ve•chol - zot lo - he•vi•noo tal•mi•dav bat•chi•la ach ka•a•sher loo•kach Yeshua achar ka•vod zach•roo az ki - cho ka•toov alav ve•cho gam - a•soo lo.

---

17. The people therefore that was with him when he called Lazarus out of his grave, and raised him from the dead, bare record.

Greek/Transliteration

17. Ἐμαρτύρει οὖν ὁ ὄχλος ὁ ὢν μετ᾽ αὐτοῦ ὅτε τὸν Λάζαρον ἐφώνησεν ἐκ τοῦ μνημείου, καὶ ἤγειρεν αὐτὸν ἐκ νεκρῶν.

17. Emarturei oun 'o ochlos 'o on met autou 'ote ton Lazaron ephoneisen ek tou mneimeiou, kai eigeiren auton ek nekron.

Hebrew/Transliteration

:יז. וְהָעָם אֲשֶׁר הָיוּ אִתּוֹ הֵעִידוּ בְּפִיהֶם כִּי קָרָא אֶת-אֶלְעָזָר מִן-קִבְרוֹ וַיְחַיֵּהוּ מִן-הַמֵּתִים

17. Ve•ha•am asher ha•yoo ee•to he•ee•doo ve•fi•hem ki ka•ra et - El•a•zar
min - kiv•ro vay•cha•ye•hoo min - ha•me•tim.

---

18. For this cause the people also met him, for that they heard that he had
done this miracle.

Greek/Transliteration

18. Διὰ τοῦτο καὶ ὑπήντησεν αὐτῷ ὁ ὄχλος, ὅτι ἤκουσεν τοῦτο αὐτὸν
πεποιηκέναι τὸ σημεῖον.

18. Dya touto kai 'upeinteisen auto 'o ochlos, 'oti eikousen touto auton
pepoieikenai to seimeion.

Hebrew/Transliteration

:יח. וְעַל-כֵּן יָצְאוּ הָעָם לִקְרָאתוֹ אַחֲרֵי שָׁמְעָם כִּי עָשָׂה אֶת-הָאוֹת הַזֶּה

18. Ve•al - ken yatz•oo ha•am lik•ra•to a•cha•rey shom•am ki asa et - ha•ot
ha•ze.

---

19. The Pharisees therefore said among themselves, Perceive ye how ye
prevail nothing? behold, the world is gone after him.

Greek/Transliteration

19. Οἱ οὖν Φαρισαῖοι εἶπον πρὸς ἑαυτούς, Θεωρεῖτε ὅτι οὐκ ὠφελεῖτε οὐδέν·
ἴδε ὁ κόσμος ὀπίσω αὐτοῦ ἀπῆλθεν.

19. 'Oi oun Pharisaioi eipon pros 'eautous, Theoreite 'oti ouk opheleite ouden.
ide 'o kosmos opiso autou apeilthen.

Hebrew/Transliteration

יט. וְהַפְּרוּשִׁים אָמְרוּ אִישׁ אֶל-אָחִיו הַרְאִיתֶם כִּי יְדֵיכֶם לֹא תַעֲשֶׂינָה תּוּשִׁיָּה וְאַחֲרָיו כָּל-אָדָם
:יִמְשֹׁךְ

19. Ve•haP`roo•shim am•roo eesh el - a•chiv har•ee•tem ki ye•dey•chem lo
ta•a•sei•na too•shi•ya ve•a•cha•rav kol - adam yim•shoch.

Rabbinic Jewish Commentary

behold, the world is gone after him; the Vulgate Latin, Syriac, Arabic, and
Ethiopic versions read, "the whole world", and so Nonnus; the Persic version, "all
the people"; that is, a very great number of people; for they could not mean,

that all the inhabitants of the world, or every individual of mankind were followers of him, and became his disciples, nor even all in their own land; they themselves, with multitudes more of the same complexion, were an exception to this: but they speak in the common dialect of that nation, of which take two or three instances;

"Tt happened to a certain high priest, that he went out of the sanctuary, והוו אזלי כולי עלמא בתריה, "and the whole world went after him"; and when they saw Shemaiah and Abtalion, they left him, and went after them (o)."

And again (p), "R. Aba proclaimed, whoever seeks riches, and whoever seeks the way of life in the world to come, let him come and study in the law, and כולי עלמא, "the whole world" will gather together to him."

Once more (q), "Jonathan said to David, 1Sa_23:17, "Thou shall be king over Israel, and I will be next to thee"; what is the meaning of this? perhaps Jonathan the son of Saul saw עלמא, "the world" draw after David."

This shows the sense of those phrases, "the world", and "the whole world", when used in the article of redemption by Yeshua.

(o) T. Bab. Yoma, fol. 71. 2. (p) Zohar in Gen. fol. 60. 4. (q) T. Bab. Bava Metzia, fol. 85. 1.

---

20. And there were certain Greeks among them that came up to worship at the feast:

Greek/Transliteration
20. Ἦσαν δέ τινες Ἕλληνες ἐκ τῶν ἀναβαινόντων ἵνα προσκυνήσωσιν ἐν τῇ ἑορτῇ·

20. Eisan de tines 'Elleines ek ton anabainonton 'ina proskuneisosin en tei 'eortei.

Hebrew/Transliteration
כ. וּבְתוֹךְ עוֹלֵי הָרֶגֶל לְהִשְׁתַּחֲוֹת נִמְצְאוּ גַם-יְוָנִים:

20. Oov•toch o•ley ha•re•gel le•hish•ta•cha•vot nim•tze•oo gam - Ye•va•nim.

Rabbinic Jewish Commentary
"Hellenes", so called, from Hellen, a king of that name, as Pliny says (r) These were not Graecizing Jews, or Jews that dwelt in Greece, and spoke the Greek language; for they were called not Hellenes, but Hellenists; but these were, as the Vulgate Latin and Syriac versions render it, Gentiles; and were either mere Gentiles, and yet devout and religious men, who were allowed to offer sacrifice, and to worship, in the court of the Gentiles; or they were proselytes, either of righteousness, and so were circumcised, and had a right to eat of the passover,

as well as to worship at it; or of the gate, and so being uncircumcised, might not eat of the passover, yet might worship at it.

(r) Nat. His. l. 4. c. 7.

---

21. The same came therefore to Philip, which was of Bethsaida of Galilee, and desired him, saying, Sir, we would see Jesus.

Greek/Transliteration
21. οὗτοι οὖν προσῆλθον Φιλίππῳ τῷ ἀπὸ Βηθσαϊδὰ τῆς Γαλιλαίας, καὶ ἠρώτων αὐτὸν λέγοντες, Κύριε, θέλομεν τὸν Ἰησοῦν ἰδεῖν.

21. 'outoi oun proseilthon Philippo to apo Beithsaida teis Galilaias, kai eiroton auton legontes, Kurie, thelomen ton Yeisoun idein.

Hebrew/Transliteration
כא. וְהֵם בָּאוּ אֶל-פִּילִפּוֹס אִישׁ בֵּית-צַיְדָה מִן-הַגָּלִיל וַיְחַלּוּ אֶת-פָּנָיו לֵאמֹר אֲדֹנֵינוּ חֲפֵצִים אֲנַחְנוּ לִרְאוֹת אֶת:יֵשׁוּעַ -

21. Ve•hem ba•oo el - Pilipos eesh Beit - Tzai•da min - ha•Galil vay•cha•loo et - pa•nav le•mor ado•ney•noo cha•fe•tzim a•nach•noo lir•ot et - Yeshua.

---

22. Philip cometh and telleth Andrew: and again Andrew and Philip tell Jesus.

Greek/Transliteration
22. Ἔρχεται Φίλιππος καὶ λέγει τῷ Ἀνδρέᾳ· καὶ πάλιν Ἀνδρέας καὶ Φίλιππος λέγουσιν τῷ Ἰησοῦ.

22. Erchetai Philippos kai legei to Andrea. kai palin Andreas kai Philippos legousin to Yeisou.

Hebrew/Transliteration
כב. וַיָּבֹא פִילִפּוֹס וַיַּגֵּד לְאַנְדְּרָי וְאַנְדְּרַי וּפִילִיפּוֹס הִגִּידוּ הַדָּבָר לְיֵשׁוּעַ:

22. Va•ya•vo Filipos va•ya•ged le•An•derai ve•Ande•rai oo•Filipos hi•gi•doo ha•da•var le•Yeshua.

---

23. And Jesus answered them, saying, The hour is come, that the Son of man should be glorified.

23. Ὁ δὲ Ἰησοῦς ἀπεκρίνατο αὐτοῖς λέγων, Ἐλήλυθεν ἡ ὥρα ἵνα δοξασθῇ ὁ υἱὸς τοῦ ἀνθρώπου.

23. 'O de Yeisous apekrinato autois legon, Eleiluthen 'ei 'ora 'ina doxasthei 'o 'wios tou anthropou.

Hebrew/Transliteration
:כג. וַיַּעַן אֹתָם יֵשׁוּעַ לֵאמֹר הִנֵּה בָא הַמּוֹעֵד וּבֶן-הָאָדָם נֶאְדָּר יִהְיֶה בִּכְבוֹדוֹ

23. Va•ya•an o•tam Yeshua le•mor hee•ne ba ha•mo•ed oo•Ven - ha•adam ne•e•dar yi•hee•ye bich•vo•do.

---

24. Verily, verily, I say unto you, Except a corn of wheat fall into the ground and die, it abideth alone: but if it die, it bringeth forth much fruit.

Greek/Transliteration
24. Ἀμὴν ἀμὴν λέγω ὑμῖν, ἐὰν μὴ ὁ κόκκος τοῦ σίτου πεσὼν εἰς τὴν γῆν ἀποθάνῃ, αὐτὸς μόνος μένει· ἐὰν δὲ ἀποθάνῃ, πολὺν καρπὸν φέρει.

24. Amein amein lego 'umin, ean mei 'o kokkos tou sitou peson eis tein gein apothanei, autos monos menei. ean de apothanei, polun karpon pherei.

Hebrew/Transliteration
כד. אָמֵן אָמֵן אֲנִי אֹמֵר לָכֶם גַּרְגַּר דָּגָן אִם לֹא-יִפֹּל וָמֵת בְּתוֹךְ הָאָרֶץ יִשָּׁאֵר לְבַדּוֹ וְאִם יָמוּת יוֹצִיא זֶרַע רָב:

24. Amen amen ani o•mer la•chem gar•gar da•gan eem lo - yi•pol va•met be•toch ha•a•retz yi•sha•er le•va•do ve•eem ya•moot yo•tzi ze•ra rav.

Rabbinic Jewish Commentary
and die; or is corrupted, and putrefies; and which is done in three days time in moist land, but is longer in dry ground ere it perishes (z): and a corn of wheat is almost the only seed, that being cast into the earth, does die; and therefore is very aptly used by Yeshua.

(z) Rabbenu Samson & Bartenora in Misn. Celaim, c. 2. sect. 3.

---

25. He that loveth his life shall lose it; and he that hateth his life in this world shall keep it unto life eternal.

Greek/Transliteration
25. Ὁ φιλῶν τὴν ψυχὴν αὐτοῦ ἀπολέσει αὐτήν· καὶ ὁ μισῶν τὴν ψυχὴν αὐτοῦ ἐν τῷ κόσμῳ τούτῳ εἰς ζωὴν αἰώνιον φυλάξει αὐτήν.

25. 'O philon tein psuchein autou apolesei autein. kai 'o mison tein psuchein autou en to kosmo touto eis zoein aionion phulaxei autein.

Hebrew/Transliteration

:כה. הָאֹהֵב אֶת-נַפְשׁוֹ תְּכָרֶת-לוֹ וְהַשׂנֵא אֶת-נַפְשׁוֹ בָּעוֹלָם הַזֶּה שְׁמֶרָה תִהְיֶה-לוֹ לְחַיֵּי עַד

25. Ha•o•hev et - naf•sho ti•ka•ret - lo ve•ha•so•ne et - naf•sho ba•o•lam ha•ze
sh`moo•ra ti•hi•ye - lo le•cha•yey ad.

---

26. If any man serve me, let him follow me; and where I am, there shall also my servant be: if any man serve me, him will my Father honour.

Greek/Transliteration

26. Ἐὰν ἐμοὶ διακονῇ τις, ἐμοὶ ἀκολουθείτω· καὶ ὅπου εἰμὶ ἐγώ, ἐκεῖ καὶ ὁ διάκονος ὁ ἐμὸς ἔσται· καὶ ἐάν τις ἐμοὶ διακονῇ, τιμήσει αὐτὸν ὁ πατήρ.

26. Ean emoi dyakonei tis, emoi akoloutheito. kai 'opou eimi ego, ekei kai 'o dyakonos 'o emos estai. kai ean tis emoi dyakonei, timeisei auton 'o pateir.

Hebrew/Transliteration

כו. מִי-הֶחָפֵץ לְשָׁרְתֵנִי יֵלֵךְ בְּעִקְבוֹתַי וּבַאֲשֶׁר אֲהְיֶה אֲנִי שָׁם יִהְיֶה גַם-מְשָׁרְתִי וְכִי אִישׁ יְשָׁרֵת אֹתִי
אֹתוֹ יְכַבֵּד:הָאָב

26. Mee - he•cha•fetz le•shar•te•ni ye•lech be•eek•vo•tai oo•va•a•sher e•he•ye
ani sham yi•hee•ye gam - me•shar•ti ve•chi eesh ye•sha•ret o•ti o•to
ye•cha•bed ha•Av.

---

27. Now is my soul troubled; and what shall I say? Father, save me from this hour: but for this cause came I unto this hour.

Greek/Transliteration

27. Νῦν ἡ ψυχή μου τετάρακται· καὶ τί εἴπω; Πάτερ, σῶσόν με ἐκ τῆς ὥρας ταύτης. Ἀλλὰ διὰ τοῦτο ἦλθον εἰς τὴν ὥραν ταύτην.

27. Nun 'ei psuchei mou tetaraktai. kai ti eipo? Pater, soson me ek teis 'oras tauteis. Alla dya touto eilthon eis tein 'oran tautein.

Hebrew/Transliteration

:כז. עַתָּה נִבְהֲלָה נַפְשִׁי וּמָה אֹמַר הַצִּילֵנִי אָבִי מִן-עֵת הַמּוֹעֵד הַזֶּה אַךְ עַל-כֵּן בָּאתִי לַמּוֹעֵד הַזֶּה

27. Ata niv•ha•la naf•shi oo•ma o•mar ha•tzi•le•ni Avi min - et ha•mo•ed
ha•ze ach al - ken ba•ti la•mo•ed ha•ze.

---

28. Father, glorify thy name. Then came there a voice from heaven, saying, I have both glorified it, and will glorify it again.

Greek/Transliteration
28. Πάτερ, δόξασόν σου τὸ ὄνομα. Ἦλθεν οὖν φωνὴ ἐκ τοῦ οὐρανοῦ, Καὶ ἐδόξασα, καὶ πάλιν δοξάσω.

28. Pater, doxason sou to onoma. Eilthen oun phonei ek tou ouranou, Kai edoxasa, kai palin doxaso.

Hebrew/Transliteration
כח. אָבִי גַּדֵּל כְּבוֹד שְׁמֶךָ וְהִנֵּה קוֹל עֹנֶה מִשָּׁמַיִם גִּדַּלְתִּי כְבוֹדוֹ וְגַם-אֲגַדְּלֶנּוּ עוֹד:

28. Avi ga•del k`vod sh`me•cha ve•hee•ne kol o•ne mi•sha•ma•yim gi•dal•ti che•vo•do ve•gam - agad•le•noo od.

---

29. The people therefore, that stood by, and heard it, said that it thundered: others said, An angel spake to him.

Greek/Transliteration
29. Ὁ οὖν ὄχλος ὁ ἑστὼς καὶ ἀκούσας ἔλεγεν βροντὴν γεγονέναι· ἄλλοι ἔλεγον, Ἄγγελος αὐτῷ λελάληκεν.

29. 'O oun ochlos 'o 'estos kai akousas elegen brontein gegonenai. alloi elegon, Angelos auto lelaleiken.

Hebrew/Transliteration
כט. וְהָעָם הָעֹמְדִים שָׁם שָׁמְעוּ וְאָמְרוּ קוֹל רַעַם הוּא וְיֵשׁ מֵהֶם אָמְרוּ כִּי מַלְאָךְ דִּבֶּר אֵלָיו:

29. Ve•ha•am ha•om•dim sham sham•oo ve•am•roo kol ra•am hoo ve•yesh me•hem am•roo ki mal•ach di•ber elav.

Rabbinic Jewish Commentary
said that it thundered; as it used to do when "Bath Kol" was heard, which, as the Jews say (a),

"Is a voice that comes out of heaven proceeding from the midst of another voice,"

As thunder; wherefore some took this for thunder, and others for the voice of a messenger out of the thunder:

others said, an angel spoke to him; these being nearer, perceived it was an articulate voice, which expressed certain distinct words, which they thought were delivered by a messenger; for the Jews had a mighty notion of the discourse and conversation of messengers with men, which their Rabbi's pretended to understand; particularly R. Jochanan ben Zaccai, a Rabbi, who was living at this time, had learned their speech, and was well versed in it (b).

(a) Piske Tosephot in T. Bab. Sanhedrin, art. 30. (b) T. Bab. Succa, fol. 28. 1. & Bava Bathra, fol. 134. 1.

---

30. Jesus answered and said, This voice came not because of me, but for your sakes.

Greek/Transliteration

30. Ἀπεκρίθη Ἰησοῦς καὶ εἶπεν, Οὐ δι' ἐμὲ αὕτη ἡ φωνὴ γέγονεν, ἀλλὰ δι' ὑμᾶς.

30. Apekrithei Yeisous kai eipen, Ou di eme 'autei 'ei phonei gegonen, alla di 'umas.

Hebrew/Transliteration

:ל. וַיַּעַן יֵשׁוּעַ וַיֹּאמַר לֹא לְמַעֲנִי הָיָה הַקּוֹל הַזֶּה כִּי אִם-לְמַעַנְכֶם

30. Va•ya•an Yeshua va•yo•mar lo le•ma•a•ni ha•ya ha•kol ha•ze ki eem - le•ma•an•chem.

Rabbinic Jewish Commentary

but for your sakes; to convince them that he was the Messiah, and engage them to believe in him, or to leave them without excuse; since not only miracles were wrought before their eyes, but with their ears they heard God speaking to him, and which is the rule that they themselves prescribe; for according to them, no man is to be hearkened to, though he should do as many signs and wonders as Moses, the son of Amram, unless they hear with their ears, that the Lord speaks to him as he did to Moses (c).

(c) R. Mosis Kotsensis praefat. ad Mitzvot Tora, pr. Affirm.

---

31. Now is the judgment of this world: now shall the prince of this world be cast out.

Greek/Transliteration

31. Νῦν κρίσις ἐστὶν τοῦ κόσμου τούτου· νῦν ὁ ἄρχων τοῦ κόσμου τούτου ἐκβληθήσεται ἔξω.

31. Nun krisis estin tou kosmou toutou. nun 'o archon tou kosmou toutou ekbleitheisetai exo.

Hebrew/Transliteration

:לא. עַתָּה נֶחֱרַץ מִשְׁפַּט הָעוֹלָם הַזֶּה וְשַׂר הָעוֹלָם הַזֶּה נִדְחַף לְמַדְחֵפוֹת

31. Ata ne•che•ratz mish•pat ha•o•lam ha•ze ve•sar ha•o•lam ha•ze nid•chaf le•mad•che•fot.

Rabbinic Jewish Commentary

Now is the judgment of this world,.... That is, in a very short time will be the judgment of the Jewish world, when that shall be reproved, convinced, and condemned for their sin of rejecting Yeshua, and crucifying him, by the Spirit, in the ministration of the Gospel; and they still continuing in their impenitence and unbelief, in process of time wrath will come upon them, upon their nation, city, and temple, to the uttermost.

now shall the prince of this world be cast out. The phrase, שר העולם, "the prince of the world", is much used by Jewish writers (d), by whom a messenger is meant; and they seem to design the messenger of death, which is the devil: and it is certain, that he is here intended, and is so called, not because he has any legal power and authority over the world; but because he has usurped a dominion over it, and has great power and efficacy in the hearts of the children of disobedience, who yield a voluntary subjection to him, as if he was their proper lord and sovereign: now the time was at hand, when he should be cast out of the empire of the world he had assumed, and out of the temples of the Gentiles, and out of the hearts of God's elect among them.

(d) T. Bab. Yebamot, fol. 16. 2. & Sanhedrin, fol. 94. 1. & Cholin, fol. 60. 1.

---

32. And I, if I be lifted up from the earth, will draw all men unto me.

Greek/Transliteration
32. Κἀγὼ ἐὰν ὑψωθῶ ἐκ τῆς γῆς, πάντας ἑλκύσω πρὸς ἐμαυτόν.

32. Kago ean 'upsotho ek teis geis, pantas 'elkuso pros emauton.

Hebrew/Transliteration
לב. וַאֲנִי כַּאֲשֶׁר אֶנָּשֵׂא מֵעַל-הָאָרֶץ אֶמְשֹׁךְ כָּל-אָדָם אַחֲרַי:

32. Va•a•ni ka•a•sher e•na•se me•al - ha•a•retz em•shoch kol - adam a•cha•rai.

Rabbinic Jewish Commentary

Beza's most ancient copy, and some others, and the Vulgate Latin version read παντα, "all things"; and by "all" are meant, all the elect of God, all the children of God, "that were scattered abroad" The Jews say, that in the time to come, or in the days of the Messiah, all the proselytes shall be גרורים, "drawn", shall freely become proselytes (e). The allusion here, is to the setting up of a standard or ensign, to gather persons together. Yeshua's cross is the standard, his love is the banner, and he himself is the ensign, which draw souls to himself, and engage them to enlist themselves under him, and become his volunteers in the day his power; see Isa_11:10. (e) T. Bab. Avoda Zara, fol. 24. 1. & Gloss. in ib.

33. This he said, signifying what death he should die.

Greek/Transliteration
33. Τοῦτο δὲ ἔλεγεν, σημαίνων ποίῳ θανάτῳ ἔμελλεν ἀποθνῄσκειν.

33. Touto de elegen, seimainon poio thanato emellen apothneiskein.

Hebrew/Transliteration
לג. וְהַמִּלִין הָאֵלֶּה הוֹצִיא כִּי יִרְזְמוּן בְּאֵיזֶה מָוֶת יָמוּת:

33. Ve•ha•mi•lin ha•e•le ho•tzi ki yir•ze•moon be•ey•ze ma•vet ya•moot.

---

34. The people answered him, We have heard out of the law that Christ abideth for ever: and how sayest thou, The Son of man must be lifted up? who is this Son of man?

Greek/Transliteration
34. Ἀπεκρίθη αὐτῷ ὁ ὄχλος, Ἡμεῖς ἠκούσαμεν ἐκ τοῦ νόμου ὅτι ὁ χριστὸς μένει εἰς τὸν αἰῶνα· καὶ πῶς σὺ λέγεις, Δεῖ ὑψωθῆναι τὸν υἱὸν τοῦ ἀνθρώπου; Τίς ἐστιν οὗτος ὁ υἱὸς τοῦ ἀνθρώπου;

34. Apekrithei auto 'o ochlos, 'Eimeis eikousamen ek tou nomou 'oti 'o christos menei eis ton aiona. kai pos su legeis, Dei 'upsotheinai ton 'wion tou anthropou? Tis estin 'outos 'o 'wios tou anthropou?

Hebrew/Transliteration
לד. וַיַּעֲנוּ אֹתוֹ הָעָם שָׁמַעְנוּ מִפִּי הַתּוֹרָה כִּי הַמָּשִׁיחַ חַי הוּא לְעוֹלָם וְאֵיךְ תֹּאמַר אַתָּה כִּי נָשׂא יִנָּשֵׂא בֶּן-הָאָדָם:מִי הוּא זֶה בֶּן-הָאָדָם

34. Va•ya•a•noo o•to ha•am sha•ma•a•noo mi•pi ha•Torah ki ha•Ma•shi•ach chai hoo le•o•lam ve•eych to•mar ata ki na•so yi•na•se Ben - ha•adam mee hoo ze Ben - ha•adam?

Rabbinic Jewish Commentary

Jewish writers: in Zec_4:14 it is said "these are the two anointed ones, that stand by the LORD of the whole earth"; of which this interpretation is given (f).

"These are Aaron and the Messiah; and it would not be known which of them is (most) beloved, but that he says, Psa_110:4, "the LORD hath sworn, and will not repent, thou art a priest for ever"; from whence it is manifest that the Messiah is more beloved than Aaron the righteous priest."

And so another of them (g), speaking of Melchizedek, says,

"This is that which is written Psa_110:4, "the LORD hath sworn", who is this? this is he that is just, and having salvation, the King Messiah, as it is said, Zec_9:9."

So the 45th Psalm is understood by them of the Messiah; the King, in Psa_45:1, is by Ben Melech, said to be the King Messiah; Psa_45:2 is thus paraphrased by the Targum,

"Thy beauty, O King Messiah, is more excellent than the children of men."

And Aben Ezra observes, that this Psalm is either concerning David, or the Messiah his son, whose name is David, Eze_37:25 (h); and the passage in Psa_72:17 is frequently interpreted of the Messiah and his name, and is brought as a proof of the antiquity of it (i); and Psa_89:36 is also applied to him; and as for Dan_7:13, that is by many, both ancient and modern Jews, explained of the Messiah (k) and since then they understood these passages of him, it is easy to observe from whence they took this notion that the Messiah should abide for ever; but then they should have observed out of the same Torah, or Holy Scriptures, that the Messiah was to be stricken and cut off, was to be brought to the dust of death, and to pour out his soul unto death; all which is consistent with his abiding for ever, in his person and office; for though according to the said writings, he was to die and be buried, yet he was not to see corruption; he was to rise again, ascend on high, sit at the right hand of God, and rule till all his enemies became his footstool; his sufferings were to be in the way, and in order to his entrance into the glory that should always abide. The Jews have entertained a notion that Messiah the son of David shall not die, and they lay down this as a rule, that if anyone sets up for a Messiah, and does not prosper, but is slain, it is a plain case he is not the Messiah; so all the wise men at first thought that Ben Coziba was the Messiah, but when he was slain it was known to them that he was not (l). And upon this principle these Jews confront the Messiahship of Yeshua.

who is this son of man? is there any other son of man besides the Messiah? and can the son of man, that is the Messiah, be lifted up, or die, who is to abide for ever? and if thou art to be lifted up, or die, thou art not the Messiah or Daniel's son of man, whose kingdom is everlasting: but how come the Jews themselves to say, that the days of the Messiah, according to some, are but forty years, according to others seventy, according to others, three hundred and sixty five (m)? yea, they say, he shall be as other men, marry, have children, and then die (n). And how comes it to pass that Messiah ben Joseph shall be slain (o)? the truth of the matter is this, they having lost the true sense of the prophecies concerning the Messiah, and observing some that seem to differ, and which they know not how to reconcile, have fancied two Messiahs, the one that will be much distressed and be overcome and be slain; the other, who will be potent and victorious.

(f) Abot R. Nathan, c. 34. (g) R. Moses Hadarsan in Galatin. de cath. ver. l. 10. c. 6. (h) Vid. Tzeror Hammor, fol. 49. 2. (i) T. Bab. Pesachim, fol. 54. 1. Nedarim, fol. 39. 2. Bereshit Rabba, fol. 1, 2. Echa Rabbati, fol. 50. 2. Pirke Eliezer, c. 32. (k) Zohar in Gen. fol. 85. 4. Bemidbar Rabba, sect. 13. fol. 209. 4. Jarchi & Sandiah Gaon in Dan. vii. 13. & R. Jeshua in Aben Ezra in ib. (l) Maimon Hilchot

Melacim, c. 11. sect. 3, 4. Vid. Bereshit Rabba, sect. 98. fol. 86. 2. (m) T. Bab.
Sanhedrin, fol. 99. 1. (n) Maimon. in Misn. Sanhedrin, c. 11. sect. 1. (o) T. Bab.
Succa, fol. 52. 1.

---

35. Then Jesus said unto them, Yet a little while is the light with you. Walk while ye have the light, lest darkness come upon you: for he that walketh in darkness knoweth not whither he goeth.

Greek/Transliteration

35. Εἶπεν οὖν αὐτοῖς ὁ Ἰησοῦς, Ἔτι μικρὸν χρόνον τὸ φῶς μεθ᾽ ὑμῶν ἐστιν. Περιπατεῖτε ἕως τὸ φῶς ἔχετε, ἵνα μὴ σκοτία ὑμᾶς καταλάβῃ· καὶ ὁ περιπατῶν ἐν τῇ σκοτίᾳ οὐκ οἶδεν ποῦ ὑπάγει.

35. Eipen oun autois 'o Yeisous, Eti mikron chronon to phos meth 'umon estin. Peripateite 'eos to phos echete, 'ina mei skotia 'umas katalabei. kai 'o peripaton en tei skotia ouk oiden pou 'upagei.

Hebrew/Transliteration

לה. וַיֹּאמֶר אֲלֵיהֶם יֵשׁוּעַ עוֹד מְעַט מִזְעָר יָאִיר הָאוֹר לְעֵינֵיכֶם לְכוּ לְאוֹרוֹ בְּהִמָּצְאוֹ פֶּן-יְכַסֶּה אֶתְכֶם הַחֹשֶׁךְ:וְהַהֹלֵךְ בַּחֹשֶׁךְ יֵלֵךְ אֶל-אֲשֶׁר לֹא יֵדָע

35. Va•yo•mer aley•hem Yeshua od me•at miz•ar ya•eer ha•or le•ey•ne•chem le•choo le•o•ro be•hi•matz•oh pen - ye•cha•se et•chem ha•cho•shech ve•ha•ho•lech ba•cho•shech ye•lech el - asher lo ye•da.

---

36. While ye have light, believe in the light, that ye may be the children of light. These things spake Jesus, and departed, and did hide himself from them.

Greek/Transliteration

36. Ἕως τὸ φῶς ἔχετε, πιστεύετε εἰς τὸ φῶς, ἵνα υἱοὶ φωτὸς γένησθε. Ταῦτα ἐλάλησεν ὁ Ἰησοῦς, καὶ ἀπελθὼν ἐκρύβη ἀπ᾽ αὐτῶν.
36. 'Eos to phos echete, pisteuete eis to phos, 'ina 'wioi photos geneisthe. Tauta elaleisen 'o Yeisous, kai apelthon ekrubei ap auton.

Hebrew/Transliteration

לו. הַאֲמִינוּ בָאוֹר כָּל-עוֹד הוּא זֹרֵחַ עֲלֵיכֶם לְמַעַן תִּהְיוּ בְּנֵי הָאוֹר וְאַחֲרֵי הַדְּבָרִים הָאֵלֶּה הָלַךְ יֵשׁוּעַ וַיִּסָּתֵר:מִפְּנֵיהֶם

36. Ha•a•mi•noo va•or kol - od hoo zo•re•ach aley•chem le•ma•an ti•hi•yoo v`ney ha•or ve•a•cha•rey ha•d`va•rim ha•e•le ha•lach Yeshua va•yi•sa•ter mip•ney•hem.

---

37. But though he had done so many miracles before them, yet they believed not on him:

Greek/Transliteration
37. Τοσαῦτα δὲ αὐτοῦ σημεῖα πεποιηκότος ἔμπροσθεν αὐτῶν, οὐκ ἐπίστευον εἰς αὐτόν·

37. Tosauta de autou seimeia pepoieikotos emprosthen auton, ouk episteuon eis auton.

Hebrew/Transliteration
לז. וְהֵם לֹא הֶאֱמִינוּ לוֹ אַף כִּי-עָשָׂה אֹתוֹת רַבִּים לִפְנֵיהֶם:

37. Ve•hem lo he•e•mi•noo lo af ki - asa o•tot ra•bim lif•ney•hem.

---

38. That the saying of Esaias the prophet might be fulfilled, which he spake, Lord, who hath believed our report? and to whom hath the arm of the Lord been revealed?

Greek/Transliteration
38. ἵνα ὁ λόγος Ἡσαΐου τοῦ προφήτου πληρωθῇ, ὃν εἶπεν, Κύριε, τίς ἐπίστευσεν τῇ ἀκοῇ ἡμῶν; Καὶ ὁ βραχίων κυρίου τίνι ἀπεκαλύφθη;

38. 'ina 'o logos Eisaiou tou propheitou pleirothei, 'on eipen, Kurie, tis episteusen tei akoei 'eimon? Kai 'o brachion kuriou tini apekaluphthei?

Hebrew/Transliteration
לח. לְמַלֹּאת דְּבַר יְשַׁעְיָהוּ הַנָּבִיא אֲשֶׁר אָמַר יְהֹוָה מִי הֶאֱמִין לִשְׁמֻעָתֵנוּ וּזְרוֹעַ יְהֹוָה עַל-מִי נִגְלָתָה:

38. Le•ma•lot de•var Ye•sha•a•ya•hoo ha•na•vee asher amar Adonai mee he•e•min lish•moo•a•te•noo ooz•ro•a Adonai al - mee nig•la•ta?

---

39. Therefore they could not believe, because that Esaias said again,

Greek/Transliteration
39. Διὰ τοῦτο οὐκ ἠδύναντο πιστεύειν, ὅτι πάλιν εἶπεν Ἡσαΐας,

39. Dya touto ouk eidunanto pisteuein, 'oti palin eipen Eisaias,

Hebrew/Transliteration
לט. וְעַל-כֵּן לְהַאֲמִין לֹא יָכֹלוּ כִּי יְשַׁעְיָהוּ הוֹסִיף לֵאמֹר:

39. Ve•al - ken le•ha•a•min lo ya•cho•loo ki Ye•sha•a•ya•hoo ho•sif le•mor.

---

40. He hath blinded their eyes, and hardened their heart; that they should not see with their eyes, nor understand with their heart, and be converted, and I should heal them.

Greek/Transliteration
40. Τετύφλωκεν αὐτῶν τοὺς ὀφθαλμούς, καὶ πεπώρωκεν αὐτῶν τὴν καρδίαν· ἵνα μὴ ἴδωσιν τοῖς ὀφθαλμοῖς, καὶ νοήσωσιν τῇ καρδίᾳ, καὶ ἐπιστραφῶσιν, καὶ ἰάσωμαι αὐτούς.

40. Tetuphloken auton tous ophthalmous, kai peporoken auton tein kardian. 'ina mei idosin tois ophthalmois, kai noeisosin tei kardia, kai epistraphosin, kai iasomai autous.

Hebrew/Transliteration
מ. הֵשַׁע עֵינֵיהֶם וְהִשְׁמִין אֶת-לְבָבָם פֶּן-יִרְאוּ בְעֵינֵיהֶם וּלְבָבָם יָבִין וְשָׁבוּ וְרָפָאתִי לָהֶם:

40. He•sha ey•ne•hem ve•hish•min et - le•va•vam pen - yir•oo ve•ey•ney•hem ool•va•vam ya•vin ve•sha•voo ve•ri•pe•ti la•hem.

Rabbinic Jewish Commentary
The sense of the prophecy is, with respect to the times of the Messiah, that the Jews, whilst hearing the sermons preached by him, whether with, or without parables, should hear his voice, and the sound of it, but not understand his words internally, spiritually, and experimentally; and whilst they saw, with the eyes of their bodies, the miracles he wrought, they should see the facts done, which could not be denied and gainsayed by them, but should not take in the clear evidence, full proof, and certain demonstration given thereby, of his Messiahship. In the prophecy of Isaiah, the words run in the imperative, "hear ye, see ye", but are here rendered in the future, "shall hear, shall see", which rendering of the words is supported and established by the version of the Septuagint, by the Chaldee paraphrase, and by many Jewish commentators (l); who allow, that the words in Isaiah may be so understood, which is sufficient to vindicate the citation of them, by the evangelist, in this form of them.

For healing of diseases, and forgiveness of sins, are, in Scripture language, one and the same thing; and this sense of the phrase here, is justified by the Chaldee paraphrase, which renders it, וישתבק להון, "and they be forgiven", or "it be forgiven them", and by a Jewish commentator on the place; who interprets healing, of the healing of the soul, and adds והיא הסליחה, "and this is pardon" (m).

(l) In R. David Kimchi in Isa. vi. 9. (m) R. David Kimchi in loc.

---

41. These things said Esaias, when he saw his glory, and spake of him.

Greek/Transliteration
41. Ταῦτα εἶπεν Ἡσαΐας, ὅτε εἶδεν τὴν δόξαν αὐτοῦ, καὶ ἐλάλησεν περὶ αὐτοῦ.

41. Tauta eipen Eisaias, 'ote eiden tein doxan autou, kai elaleisen peri autou.

:מא. הַדְּבָרִים הָאֵלֶּה דִּבֶּר יְשַׁעְיָהוּ בַּחֲזוֹתוֹ אֶת-כְּבוֹדוֹ וַיִּנָּבֵא עָלָיו

41. Ha•d`va•rim ha•e•le di•ber Ye•sha•a•ya•hoo ba•cha•zo•to et - k`vo•do
va•yi•na•ve alav.

Rabbinic Jewish Commentary
These things said Esaias,.... Concerning the blinding and hardening of the Jews.

when he saw his glory, and spake of him; when he saw, in a visionary way, the
glory of the Messiah in the temple, and the hosts covering their faces with their
wings at the sight of him; and when he spake of him as the King, the LORD of
hosts, whom he had seen, Isa_6:1, from whence it is clear that he had respect to
the Jews in the times of the Messiah. The prophet says in Isa_6:1 that he "saw the
LORD": the Targumist renders it, "I saw", **יקרא דיי**, "the glory of YHWH"; and
in Isa_6:5 he says, "mine eyes have seen the King", YHWH, Zebaot, the LORD of
hosts; which the Chaldee paraphrase renders, "mine eyes have seen", **את יקר**, "the
glory" of the Shekinah, the King of the world, the LORD of hosts. Agreeably to
which Yeshua says here, that he saw his glory, the glory of his majesty, the glory
of his divine nature, the train of his divine perfections, filling the temple of the
human nature; and he spoke of him as the true YHWH, the LORD of hosts; and
which therefore is a very clear and strong proof of the proper divinity of Yeshua.

**42. Nevertheless among the chief rulers also many believed on him; but
because of the Pharisees they did not confess him, lest they should be put out
of the synagogue:**

Greek/Transliteration
42. Ὅμως μέντοι καὶ ἐκ τῶν ἀρχόντων πολλοὶ ἐπίστευσαν εἰς αὐτόν· ἀλλὰ διὰ
τοὺς Φαρισαίους οὐχ ὡμολόγουν, ἵνα μὴ ἀποσυνάγωγοι γένωνται.
42. 'Omos mentoi kai ek ton archonton polloi episteusan eis auton. alla dya
tous Pharisaious ouch 'omologoun, 'ina mei aposunagogoi genontai.

Hebrew/Transliteration
מב. אוּלָם גַּם מִן-הַשָּׂרִים הֶאֱמִינוּ-בוֹ רַבִּים אַךְ בַּעֲבוּר הַפְּרוּשִׁים לֹא הוֹדוּ בְפִיהֶם לְבִלְתִּי יְנֻדּוּ מִתּוֹךְ
:קְהָלָם

42. Oo•lam gam min - ha•sa•rim he•e•mi•noo - vo ra•bim ach ba•a•voor
ha•P`roo•shim lo ho•doo ve•fi•hem le•vil•ti ye•noo•doo mi•toch ke•ha•lam.

---

43. For they loved the praise of men more than the praise of God.

43. Ἠγάπησαν γὰρ τὴν δόξαν τῶν ἀνθρώπων μᾶλλον ἤπερ τὴν δόξαν τοῦ θεοῦ.

43. Eigapeisan gar tein doxan ton anthropon mallon eiper tein doxan tou theou.

מג. כִּי כְבוֹד אֲנָשִׁים יָקָר בְּעֵינֵיהֶם מִכְּבוֹד אֱלֹהִים:

43. Ki k`vod a•na•shim ya•kar be•ey•ne•hem mik•vod Elohim.

---

44. Jesus cried and said, He that believeth on me, believeth not on me, but on him that sent me.

44. Ἰησοῦς δὲ ἔκραξεν καὶ εἶπεν, Ὁ πιστεύων εἰς ἐμέ, οὐ πιστεύει εἰς ἐμέ, ἀλλ᾽ εἰς τὸν πέμψαντά με·

44. Yeisous de ekraxen kai eipen, 'O pisteuon eis eme, ou pisteuei eis eme, all eis ton pempsanta me.

מד. וַיִּקְרָא יֵשׁוּעַ וַיֹּאמַר הַמַּאֲמִין בִּי לֹא-בִי הוּא מַאֲמִין כִּי אִם-בְּשֹׁלְחִי:

44. Va•yik•ra Yeshua va•yo•mar ha•ma•a•min bi lo - vi hoo ma•a•min ki eem - be•shol•chi.

---

45. And he that seeth me seeth him that sent me.

45. καὶ ὁ θεωρῶν ἐμέ, θεωρεῖ τὸν πέμψαντά με.

45. kai 'o theoron eme, theorei ton pempsanta me.

מה. וְהָרֹאֶה אֹתִי הוּא רֹאֶה אֶת-שֹׁלְחִי:

45. Ve•ha•ro•eh o•ti hoo ro•eh et - shol•chi.

---

46. I am come a light into the world, that whosoever believeth on me should not abide in darkness.

Greek/Transliteration

46. Ἐγὼ φῶς εἰς τὸν κόσμον ἐλήλυθα, ἵνα πᾶς ὁ πιστεύων εἰς ἐμέ, ἐν τῇ σκοτίᾳ μὴ μείνῃ.

46. Ego phos eis ton kosmon eleilutha, 'ina pas 'o pisteuon eis eme, en tei skotia mei meinei.

Hebrew/Transliteration

מו. וַאֲנִי לְאוֹר בָּאתִי אֶל-הָעוֹלָם אֲשֶׁר כָּל-הַמַּאֲמִין בִּי לֹא יִשְׁכֹּן בַּחֲשֵׁכָה:

46. Va•a•ni le•or ba•ti el - ha•o•lam asher kol - ha•ma•a•min bi lo yish•kon ba•cha•she•cha.

---

47. And if any man hear my words, and believe not, I judge him not: for I came not to judge the world, but to save the world.

Greek/Transliteration

47. Καὶ ἐάν τίς μου ἀκούσῃ τῶν ῥημάτων καὶ μὴ πιστεύσῃ, ἐγὼ οὐ κρίνω αὐτόν· οὐ γὰρ ἦλθον ἵνα κρίνω τὸν κόσμον, ἀλλ᾽ ἵνα σώσω τὸν κόσμον.

47. Kai ean tis mou akousei ton 'reimaton kai mei pisteusei, ego ou krino auton. ou gar eilthon 'ina krino ton kosmon, all 'ina soso ton kosmon.

Hebrew/Transliteration

מז. וְאִישׁ כִּי יִשְׁמַע אֶת-דְּבָרַי וְלֹא יִשְׁמְרֵם אֲנִי לֹא אֶשְׁפֹּט אֹתוֹ כִּי לֹא-לִשְׁפֹּט אֶת-הָעוֹלָם בָּאתִי כִּי אִם-לְהוֹשִׁיעַ:אֶת-הָעוֹלָם

47. Ve•eesh ki yish•ma et - de•va•rai ve•lo yish•me•rem ani lo esh•pot o•to ki lo - lish•pot et - ha•o•lam ba•ti ki eem - le•ho•shi•a et - ha•o•lam.

---

48. He that rejecteth me, and receiveth not my words, hath one that judgeth him: the word that I have spoken, the same shall judge him in the last day.

Greek/Transliteration

48. Ὁ ἀθετῶν ἐμὲ καὶ μὴ λαμβάνων τὰ ῥήματά μου, ἔχει τὸν κρίνοντα αὐτόν· ὁ λόγος ὃν ἐλάλησα, ἐκεῖνος κρινεῖ αὐτὸν ἐν τῇ ἐσχάτῃ ἡμέρᾳ.

48. 'O atheton eme kai mei lambanon ta 'reimata mou, echei ton krinonta auton. 'o logos 'on elaleisa, ckcinos krinei auton en tei eschatei 'eimera.

Hebrew/Transliteration

מח. וְכִי יִמְאַס בִּי אִישׁ וְלֹא יִקַּח אֲמָרַי יֵשׁ שֹׁפֵט אֲשֶׁר-יִשְׁפְּטֶנּוּ הַדָּבָר אֲשֶׁר דִּבַּרְתִּי הוּא יִשְׁפְּטֶנּוּ בַּיּוֹם הָאַחֲרוֹן:

48. Ve•chi yim•as bi eesh ve•lo yi•kach ama•rai yesh sho•fet asher -
yish•pe•te•noo ha•da•var asher di•bar•ti hoo yish•pe•te•noo ba•yom
ha•a•cha•ron.

---

49. For I have not spoken of myself; but the Father which sent me, he gave me
a commandment, what I should say, and what I should speak.

Greek/Transliteration
49. Ὅτι ἐγὼ ἐξ ἐμαυτοῦ οὐκ ἐλάλησα· ἀλλ᾽ ὁ πέμψας με πατήρ, αὐτός μοι
ἐντολὴν ἔδωκεν, τί εἴπω καὶ τί λαλήσω.

49. 'Oti ego ex emautou ouk elaleisa. all 'o pempsas me pateir, autos moi
entolein edoken, ti eipo kai ti laleiso.

Hebrew/Transliteration
מט. כִּי אֲנִי לֹא מִלִּבִּי דִבַּרְתִּי כִּי אִם-הָאָב אֲשֶׁר שְׁלָחַנִי הוּא צִוַּנִי אֶת-אֲשֶׁר אֹמַר וְאֶת-אֲשֶׁר אֲדַבֵּר:

49. Ki ani lo mi•li•bi di•bar•ti chi eem - ha•Av asher sh`la•cha•ni hoo tzi•va•ni
et – asher o•mar ve•et - asher ada•ber.

---

50. And I know that his commandment is life everlasting: whatsoever I speak
therefore, even as the Father said unto me, so I speak.

Greek/Transliteration
50. Καὶ οἶδα ὅτι ἡ ἐντολὴ αὐτοῦ ζωὴ αἰώνιός ἐστιν· ἃ οὖν λαλῶ ἐγώ, καθὼς
εἴρηκέν μοι ὁ πατήρ, οὕτως λαλῶ.

50. Kai oida 'oti 'ei entolei autou zoei aionios estin. 'a oun lalo ego, kathos
eireiken moi 'o pateir, 'outos lalo.

Hebrew/Transliteration
נ. וְיָדַעְתִּי כִּי חַיֵּי עוֹלָם מִצְוָתוֹ וְעַל-כֵּן אֶת-אֲשֶׁר אָמַר אֵלַי הָאָב לְדַבֵּר אֹתוֹ אֶשְׁמֹר לְדַבֵּר:

50. Ve•ya•da•a•ti ki cha•yey o•lam mitz•va•to ve•al - ken et - asher amar e•lai
ha•Av le•da•ber o•to esh•mor le•da•ber.

John, Chapter 13

1. Now before the feast of the passover, when Jesus knew that his hour was come that he should depart out of this world unto the Father, having loved his own which were in the world, he loved them unto the end.

Greek/Transliteration

1. Πρὸ δὲ τῆς ἑορτῆς τοῦ Πάσχα, εἰδὼς ὁ Ἰησοῦς ὅτι ἐλήλυθεν αὐτοῦ ἡ ὥρα ἵνα μεταβῇ ἐκ τοῦ κόσμου τούτου πρὸς τὸν πατέρα, ἀγαπήσας τοὺς ἰδίους τοὺς ἐν τῷ κόσμῳ, εἰς τέλος ἠγάπησεν αὐτούς.

1. Pro de teis 'eorteis tou Pascha, eidos 'o Yeisous 'oti eleiluthen autou 'ei 'ora 'ina metabei ek tou kosmou toutou pros ton patera, agapeisas tous idious tous en to kosmo, eis telos eigapeisen autous.

Hebrew/Transliteration

א. וַיְהִי לִפְנֵי חַג-הַפֶּסַח וַיֵּדַע יֵשׁוּעַ כִּי בָא זְמַנּוֹ לַעֲלוֹת מִן-הָאָרֶץ אֶל-הָאָב וְאֶת-בְּחִירָיו אֲשֶׁר אָהֵב בָּאָרֶץ מֵאָז:כֵּן אֲהֵבָם עַד-אַחֲרִית

1. Vay•hi lif•ney chag - ha•Pe•sach va•ye•da Yeshua ki va z`ma•no la•a•lot min - ha•a•retz el - ha•Av ve•et - be•chi•rav asher ahev ba•a•retz me•az ken ahe•vam ad - acha•rit.

Rabbinic Jewish Commentary

Much such a phrase is made use of concerning Moses, of whom it is said (p), that the fourth song that was sung in the world, was sung by him

"When "his time was come", למפטר מן עלמא, "to depart out of the world".

A time or hour was fixed for this; for as there was a set time, called "the fulness of time", agreed upon for his coming into the world, so there was for his going out of it: and now this "his hour was come"; the time is now up, or at least very near at hand; and he "knew" it, being God omniscient, which gave him no uneasiness: nor did it in the least alienate his affections from his people.

"He loved them to the end": and which he showed by dying for them; and continues to show by interceding for them in heaven, by supplying them with all grace, and by preserving them from a final and total falling away; and he will at last introduce them into his kingdom and glory, when they shall be for ever with him; and so that love to them continues not only to the end of his own life, nor barely to the end of theirs, but to the end of the world, and for ever; and so εις τελος, signifies, and is rendered "continually", Luk_18:5, and in the Septuagint on Psa_9:6 answers to לנצח, which signifies "for ever"; and is so translated here by the Ethiopic version.

(p) Targum in Cant. i. 1, 7. Vid. Bereshit Rabba, sect. 96. fol. 84. 1. & Debarim Rabba, sect. 11. fol. 245. 2.

2. And supper being ended, the devil having now put into the heart of Judas Iscariot, Simon's son, to betray him;

Greek/Transliteration

2. Καὶ δείπνου γενομένου, τοῦ διαβόλου ἤδη βεβληκότος εἰς τὴν καρδίαν Ἰούδα Σίμωνος Ἰσκαριώτου ἵνα αὐτὸν παραδῷ,

2. Kai deipnou genomenou, tou dyabolou eidei bebleikotos eis tein kardian Youda Simonos Yskariotou 'ina auton parado,

Hebrew/Transliteration

ב. אַחֲרֵי סִיּוֹם סְעוּדַת הַמִּצְוָה וְאַחֲרֵי אֲשֶׁר נָתַן הַשָּׂטָן בְּלֵב יְהוּדָה בֶּן-שִׁמְעוֹן אִישׁ-קְרִיּוֹת לְהַסְגִּיר אֹתוֹ:

2. A•cha•rey si•yoom se•oo•dat ha•mitz•va ve•a•cha•rey asher na•tan ha•Satan be•lev Yehooda ben - Shimon Eesh - K`ri•yot le•has•gir o•to.

Rabbinic Jewish Commentary
Concerning Judas's surname, Iscariot, as that it may come from "Iscortia", which signifies a tanner's coat: for so it is said in the (q) Talmud,

"What is איסקורטיא, "Iscortia?" says Rabba bar Chanah, it is כיתונא דצלא, "a tanner's coat".

A sort of a leathern garment, as the gloss says, which tanners put over their clothes. However, this man was an apostle of Yeshua's whom Satan tempted to betray him; so that we see that the highest office, and greatest gifts, cannot secure men from the temptations of Satan.

(q) T. Bab. Nedarim, fol. 55. 2. Vid. Maimon. & Bartenora in Misn. Celim. c. 16. sect. 4. & Oholot, c. 8. sect. 1.

---

3. Jesus knowing that the Father had given all things into his hands, and that he was come from God, and went to God;

Greek/Transliteration

3. εἰδὼς ὁ Ἰησοῦς ὅτι πάντα δέδωκεν αὐτῷ ὁ πατὴρ εἰς τὰς χεῖρας, καὶ ὅτι ἀπὸ θεοῦ ἐξῆλθεν καὶ πρὸς τὸν θεὸν ὑπάγει,

3. eidos 'o Yeisous 'oti panta dedoken auto 'o pateir eis tas cheiras, kai 'oti apo theou exeilthen kai pros ton theon 'upagei,

Hebrew/Transliteration

ג. וַיֵּדַע יֵשׁוּעַ כִּי הָאָב נָתַן בְּיָדוֹ אֶת-כֹּל וְכִי הוּא מֵאֵת אֱלֹהִים יָצָא וְאֶל-אֱלֹהִים יָשׁוּב:

3. Va•ye•da Yeshua ki ha•Av na•tan be•ya•do et - kol ve•chi hoo me•et Elohim ya•tza ve•el - Elohim ya•shoov.

---

4. He riseth from supper, and laid aside his garments; and took a towel, and girded himself.

Greek/Transliteration
4. ἐγείρεται ἐκ τοῦ δείπνου, καὶ τίθησιν τὰ ἱμάτια, καὶ λαβὼν λέντιον διέζωσεν ἑαυτόν.

4. egeiretai ek tou deipnou, kai titheisin ta 'imatya, kai labon lention diezosen 'eauton.

Hebrew/Transliteration
:ד. וַיָּקָם מֵעַל הַשֻּׁלְחָן וַיִּפְשֹׁט אֶת-בְּגָדָיו וַיַּחְגֹּר מִטְפַּחַת עַל-מָתְנָיו

4. Va•ya•kom me•al ha•shool•chan va•yif•shot et - be•ga•dav va•yach•gor mit•pa•chat al - mot•nav.

Rabbinic Jewish Commentary
And took a towel; or "linen cloth", λεντιον, the same with לונטית in the Jerusalem Talmud (r):

and girded himself; with the towel, or linen cloth, which served both for a girdle, and after he had washed his disciples' feet, to wipe them with. This was a servile habit; so servants used to stand at the feet of their masters, girt about with a linen cloth (s); and shows, that the son of man came not to be ministered unto, but to minister.

(r) Sabbat, fol. 3. 1. & 12. 1. (s) Suetonius in Caligula, c. 26.

---

5. After that he poureth water into a bason, and began to wash the disciples' feet, and to wipe them with the towel wherewith he was girded.

Greek/Transliteration
5. Εἶτα βάλλει ὕδωρ εἰς τὸν νιπτῆρα, καὶ ἤρξατο νίπτειν τοὺς πόδας τῶν μαθητῶν, καὶ ἐκμάσσειν τῷ λεντίῳ ᾧ ἦν διεζωσμένος.

5. Eita ballei 'udor eis ton nipteira, kai eirxato niptein tous podas ton matheiton, kai ekmassein to lentio 'o ein diezosmenos.

Hebrew/Transliteration
:ה. וְאַחַר יָצַק מַיִם בְּכִיּוֹר וַיָּחֶל לִרְחֹץ רַגְלֵי תַלְמִידָיו וְלִמְחוֹתָן בַּמִּטְפַּחַת אֲשֶׁר-הוּא חָגוּר בָּהּ

5. Ve•a•char ya•tzak ma•yim be•chi•yor va•ya•chel lir•chotz rag•ley tal•mi•dav ve•lim•cho•tan ba•mit•pa•chat asher - hoo cha•goor ba.

Rabbinic Jewish Commentary

This custom of washing the feet was not used by the Jews at their passover, nor at their private entertainments, or common meals, but at the reception of strangers or travellers, which were just come off of a journey, whereby they had contracted dirt and filth, and was a servile work, never performed by superiors to their inferiors, but by inferiors to superiors; as by the wife to the husband, by the son to the father, and by the servant to his master; and was an instance of great humility in any others, as in Abigail, who said to David, "let thine handmaid be a servant to wash the feet of the servants of my Lord", 1Sa_25:41, upon which place some Jewish Rabbi's (u) have this note:

"This she said, **על צד הענוה,** "by way of humility", to show, that it would have been sufficient to her, if she became a wife to one of the servants of David, and washed his feet, as was the custom of a wife to her husband."

But what a surprising instance of humility and condescension is this, that Yeshua, the Lord and master, should wash the feet of his disciples, when it was their proper work and business to have washed his? Though we do not remember that this was expected from the disciple toward his master, unless included in that rule, "that the disciple is to honour his master, more than his father"; whereas it was a fixed point (w) with the Jews,

"That all works which a servant does to his master, a disciple does to his master, except unloosing his shoe."

Since therefore it was the work of a servant to wash his master's feet, a disciple was obliged to do this to his master likewise.

(u) R. Levi ben Gersom & R. Samuel Laniado in I Sam. xxv. 41. Vid. T. Bab. Cetubot, fol. 96. 1. & Maimon. Hilch. Ishot, c. 21. sect. 7. (w) T. Bab. Cetubot, fol. 96. 1.

---

6. Then cometh he to Simon Peter: and Peter saith unto him, Lord, dost thou wash my feet?

Greek/Transliteration
6. Ἔρχεται οὖν πρὸς Σίμωνα Πέτρον· καὶ λέγει αὐτῷ ἐκεῖνος, Κύριε, σύ μου νίπτεις τοὺς πόδας;

6. Erchetai oun pros Simona Petron. kai legei auto ekeinos, Kurie, su mou nipteis tous podas?

ו. וַיָּבֹא אֶל-שִׁמְעוֹן פֶּטְרוֹס וְהוּא אָמַר אֵלָיו הַאַתָּה אֲדֹנִי תִּרְחַץ אֶת-רַגְלָי:

6. Va•ya•vo el - Shimon Petros ve•hoo amar elav ha•a•ta Adoni tir•chatz et - rag•lai?

7. Jesus answered and said unto him, What I do thou knowest not now; but thou shalt know hereafter.

Greek/Transliteration

7. Ἀπεκρίθη Ἰησοῦς καὶ εἶπεν αὐτῷ, Ὃ ἐγὼ ποιῶ, σὺ οὐκ οἶδας ἄρτι, γνώσῃ δὲ μετὰ ταῦτα.

7. Apekrithei Yeisous kai eipen auto, 'O ego poio, su ouk oidas arti, gnosei de meta tauta.

Hebrew/Transliteration

ז. וַיַּעַן יֵשׁוּעַ וַיֹּאמֶר אֵלָיו אֵת אֲשֶׁר אֲנִי עֹשֶׂה בָּזֶה לֹא-תֵדַע עַתָּה אַךְ אַחֲרֵי-כֵן תַּשְׂכִּיל:

7. Va•ya•an Yeshua va•yo•mer elav et asher ani o•se va•ze lo - te•da ata ach a•cha•rey - chen tas•kil.

8. Peter saith unto him, Thou shalt never wash my feet. Jesus answered him, If I wash thee not, thou hast no part with me.

Greek/Transliteration

8. Λέγει αὐτῷ Πέτρος, Οὐ μὴ νίψῃς τοὺς πόδας μου εἰς τὸν αἰῶνα. Ἀπεκρίθη αὐτῷ ὁ Ἰησοῦς, Ἐὰν μὴ νίψω σε, οὐκ ἔχεις μέρος μετ᾽ ἐμοῦ.

8. Legei auto Petros, Ou mei nipseis tous podas mou eis ton aiona. Apekrithei auto 'o Yeisous, Ean mei nipso se, ouk echeis meros met emou.

Hebrew/Transliteration

ח. וַיֹּאמֶר אֵלָיו פֶּטְרוֹס לֹא-תִרְחַץ רַגְלַי לְעוֹלָם וַיַּעַן אֹתוֹ יֵשׁוּעַ אִם-לֹא אֶרְחָצְךָ אֵין-לְךָ חֵלֶק עִמָּדִי:

8. Va•yo•mer elav Petros lo - tir•chatz rag•lai le•o•lam va•ya•an o•to Yeshua eem – lo er•chatz•cha eyn - le•cha che•lek ee•ma•di.

9. Simon Peter saith unto him, Lord, not my feet only, but also my hands and my head.

9. Λέγει αὐτῷ Σίμων Πέτρος, Κύριε, μὴ τοὺς πόδας μου μόνον, ἀλλὰ καὶ τὰς χεῖρας καὶ τὴν κεφαλήν.

9. Legei auto Simon Petros, Kurie, mei tous podas mou monon, alla kai tas cheiras kai tein kephalein.

ט. וַיֹּאמֶר אֵלָיו שִׁמְעוֹן פֶּטְרוֹס בִּי אֲדֹנִי לֹא לְבַד אֶת-רַגְלַי כִּי אִם-גַּם אֶת-יָדַי וְאֶת-רֹאשִׁי:

9. Va•yo•mer elav Shimon Petros bi Adoni lo le•vad et - rag•lai ki eem - gam et - ya•dai ve•et - ro•shi.

---

10. Jesus saith to him, He that is washed needeth not save to wash his feet, but is clean every whit: and ye are clean, but not all.

10. Λέγει αὐτῷ ὁ Ἰησοῦς, Ὁ λελουμένος οὐ χρείαν ἔχει ἢ τοὺς πόδας νίψασθαι, ἀλλ᾽ ἔστιν καθαρὸς ὅλος· καὶ ὑμεῖς καθαροί ἐστε, ἀλλ᾽ οὐχὶ πάντες.

10. Legei auto 'o Yeisous, 'O leloumenos ou chreian echei ei tous podas nipsasthai, all estin katharos 'olos. kai 'umeis katharoi este, all ouchi pantes.

י. וַיֹּאמֶר אֵלָיו יֵשׁוּעַ הַמְרֻחָץ אֵין-לוֹ לִרְחֹץ עוֹד זוּלָתִי אֶת-רַגְלָיו כִּי כֻלּוֹ טָהוֹר הוּא וְאַתֶּם הִנְּכֶם טְהוֹרִים אֲבָל:לֹא כֻלְּכֶם

10. Va•yo•mer elav Yeshua ha•me•roo•chatz eyn - lo lir•chotz od zoo•la•tee et - rag•lav ki choo•lo ta•hor hoo ve•a•tem hin•chem te•ho•rim aval lo chool•chem.

Rabbinic Jewish Commentary
The allusion is either to persons washed all over in a bath, who have no need to wash again, unless their feet, which may contract some soil in coming out of it; or to travellers, who have often need to wash their feet, though no other part, and such is the case of the children of God in this life; or rather to the priests, who having bathed themselves in the morning, needed not to wash again all the day, except their hands and feet, on certain occasions (x).

(x) Misn. Yoma, c. 3. sect. 3.

---

11. For he knew who should betray him; therefore said he, Ye are not all clean.

11. ῞δει γὰρ τὸν παραδιδόντα αὐτόν· διὰ τοῦτο εἶπεν, Οὐχὶ πάντες καθαροί ἐστε.

11. dei gar ton paradidonta auton. dya touto eipen, Ouchi pantes katharoi este.

יא. כִּי יָדַע אֹתוֹ אֲשֶׁר יַסְגִּירֵנּוּ עַל-כֵּן אָמַר לֹא כֻלְּכֶם טְהוֹרִים:

11. Ki ya•da o•to asher yas•gi•re•noo al - ken amar lo chool•chem te•ho•rim.

---

12. So after he had washed their feet, and had taken his garments, and was set down again, he said unto them, Know ye what I have done to you?

12. ῞Οτε οὖν ἔνιψεν τοὺς πόδας αὐτῶν, καὶ ἔλαβεν τὰ ἱμάτια αὐτοῦ, ἀναπεσὼν πάλιν, εἶπεν αὐτοῖς, Γινώσκετε τί πεποίηκα ὑμῖν;

12. 'Ote oun enipsen tous podas auton, kai elaben ta 'imatya autou, anapeson palin, eipen autois, Ginoskete ti pepoieika 'umin?

יב. וְאַחֲרֵי אֲשֶׁר רָחַץ אֶת-רַגְלֵיהֶם וְלָבַשׁ אֶת-בְּגָדָיו שָׁב וַיֵּשֶׁב וַיֹּאמֶר אֲלֵיהֶם הַיְדַעְתֶּם מַה-זֹּאת עָשִׂיתִי לָכֶם:

12. Ve•a•cha•rey asher ra•chatz et - rag•ley•hem ve•la•vash et - be•ga•dav shav va•ye•shev va•yo•mer aley•hem hay•da•a•tem ma - zot a•si•ti la•chem?

---

13. Ye call me Master and Lord: and ye say well; for so I am.

13. ῾Υμεῖς φωνεῖτέ με, ῾Ο διδάσκαλος, καὶ ῾Ο κύριος· καὶ καλῶς λέγετε, εἰμὶ γάρ.

13. 'Umeis phoneite me, 'O didaskalos, kai 'O kurios. kai kalos legete, eimi gar.

יג. אַתֶּם קֹרְאִים-לִי רַבִּי וְאָדוֹן וְהֵיטַבְתֶּם לִקְרֹא-לִי כֵן כִּי-אֲנִי הוּא:

13. Atem kor•eem - li Rabbi ve•Adon ve•hey•tav•tem lik•ro - li chen ki - ani hoo.

Rabbinic Jewish Commentary

Ye call me Master and Lord,.... רבי, and מר, "Master" and "Lord", were dignified titles among the Jews, which they frequently (y) gave to their doctors and men of learning, and are often to be met with in their writings: hence the disciples called Yeshua by these names, not out of flattery, but reverence of him, and esteem for him; nor are they blamed, but commended for it:

and ye say well, for so I am; though he had acted the part of a servant in such a surprising manner, by washing their feet; yet he had not dropped and lost, but still maintains his place and authority as a "Master" to teach and instruct them, and as a "Lord" to rule and govern them.

(y) Vid. T. Bab. Beracot, fol. 3. 1. Derech Erets, c. 6. fol. 18. 2.

---

14. If I then, your Lord and Master, have washed your feet; ye also ought to wash one another's feet.

Greek/Transliteration
14. Εἰ οὖν ἐγὼ ἔνιψα ὑμῶν τοὺς πόδας, ὁ κύριος καὶ ὁ διδάσκαλος, καὶ ὑμεῖς ὀφείλετε ἀλλήλων νίπτειν τοὺς πόδας.

14. Ei oun ego enipsa 'umon tous podas, 'o kurios kai 'o didaskalos, kai 'umeis opheilete alleilon niptein tous podas.

Hebrew/Transliteration
יד. וְעַל-כֵּן אִם-אֲנִי הָאָדוֹן וְהָרַבִּי רָחַצְתִּי אֶת-רַגְלֵיכֶם עֲלֵיכֶם גַּם-אַתֶּם לִרְחֹץ אִישׁ אִישׁ אֶת-רַגְלֵי אָחִיו:

14. Ve•al - ken eem - ani ha•Adon ve•ha•Rabbi ra•chatz•ti et - rag•ley•chem aley•chem gam - atem lir•chotz eesh eesh et - rag•ley a•chiv.

---

15. For I have given you an example, that ye should do as I have done to you.

Greek/Transliteration
15. Ὑπόδειγμα γὰρ ἔδωκα ὑμῖν, ἵνα καθὼς ἐγὼ ἐποίησα ὑμῖν, καὶ ὑμεῖς ποιῆτε.

15. 'Upodeigma gar edoka 'umin, 'ina kathos ego epoiesa 'umin, kai 'umeis poieite.

Hebrew/Transliteration
טו. כִּי אֲנִי הוּא מוֹפֶתְכֶם לְמַעַן תַּעֲשׂוּן גַּם-אַתֶּם כַּאֲשֶׁר עָשִׂיתִי לָכֶם אָנִי:

15. Ki ani hoo mo•fet•chem le•ma•an ta•a•soon gam - atem ka•a•sher a•si•ti la•chem ani.

---

16. Verily, verily, I say unto you, The servant is not greater than his lord; neither he that is sent greater than he that sent him.

Greek/Transliteration
16. Ἀμὴν ἀμὴν λέγω ὑμῖν, Οὐκ ἔστιν δοῦλος μείζων τοῦ κυρίου αὐτοῦ, οὐδὲ ἀπόστολος μείζων τοῦ πέμψαντος αὐτόν.

16. Amein amein lego 'umin, Ouk estin doulos meizon tou kuriou autou, oude apostolos meizon tou pempsantos auton.

Hebrew/Transliteration
טז. אָמֵן אָמֵן אֲנִי אֹמֵר לָכֶם אֵין הָעֶבֶד גָּדוֹל מֵאֲדֹנָיו וְאֵין הַשָּׁלִיחַ רַב מִשֹׁלְחוֹ:

16. Amen amen ani o•mer la•chem eyn ha•e•ved ga•dol me•a•do•nav ve•eyn ha•sha•li•ach rav mi•shol•cho.

Rabbinic Jewish Commentary
neither he that is sent, is greater than he that sent him. This is also a way of speaking in use among the Jews;

"R. Meir says, (z) who is greatest, he that keeps, or he that is kept? from what is written in Psa_91:11, he that is kept, is greater than he that keeps: says R. Judah, which is greatest, he that carries, or he that is carried? from what is written in Psa_91:12, he that is carried, is greater than he that carries: says R. Simeon, from what is written, in Isa_6:8, הוי המשלח גדול מן המשתלח, "he that sends, is greater than he that is sent"."

Which is the very phrase here used by Yeshua; and his meaning is this, that if it was not below him, who had chose and called, and sent them forth as his apostles, to wash their feet, they who were sent by him, should not disdain to wash one another's.

(z) Bereshit Rabba, fol. 68. 1.

---

17. If ye know these things, happy are ye if ye do them.

Greek/Transliteration
17. Εἰ ταῦτα οἴδατε, μακάριοί ἐστε ἐὰν ποιῆτε αὐτά.

17. Ei tauta oidate, makarioi este ean poieite auta.

:יז. וְאִם-יְדַעְתֶּם זֹאת אַשְׁרֵיכֶם אִם-כֵּן תַּעֲשׂוּן

17. Ve•eem - ye•da•a•tem zot ash•rey•chem eem - ken ta•a•soon.

Rabbinic Jewish Commentary

There is an happiness "in" doing well, and which follows "on" it, though not "for" it, in a way of merit; on the other hand, persons who know and do not, are very unhappy; the Jews have a saying (a),

שהלמד שלא לעשות, "he that learns but not to do", it would have been better for him, if he had never been created; and says R. Jochanan, he that learns but not to do, it would have been better for him if his secundine had been turned upon his face, and he had never come into the world."

(a) Hieros. Beracot, fol. 3. 2.

---

18. I speak not of you all: I know whom I have chosen: but that the scripture may be fulfilled, He that eateth bread with me hath lifted up his heel against me.

Greek/Transliteration

18. Οὐ περὶ πάντων ὑμῶν λέγω· ἐγὼ οἶδα οὓς ἐξελεξάμην· ἀλλ᾽ ἵνα ἡ γραφὴ πληρωθῇ, Ὁ τρώγων μετ᾽ ἐμοῦ τὸν ἄρτον ἐπῆρεν ἐπ᾽ ἐμὲ τὴν πτέρναν αὐτοῦ.

18. Ou peri panton 'umon lego. ego oida 'ous exelexamein. all 'ina 'ei graphei pleirothei, 'O trogon met emou ton arton epeiren ep eme tein pternan autou.

Hebrew/Transliteration

יח. וְלֹא עַל-כֻּלְּכֶם דִּבַּרְתִּי כֵן כִּי יָדַעְתִּי אֶת-אֲשֶׁר בָּחַרְתִּי-בָם אַךְ לְמַעַן יָקוּם הַכָּתוּב אוֹכֵל לַחְמִי
:הִגְדִּיל עָלַי עָקֵב

18. Ve•lo al - kool•chem di•bar•ti chen ki ya•da•a•ti et - asher ba•char•ti - vam ach le•ma•an ya•koom ha•ka•toov o•chel lach•mi hig•dil a•lai a•kev.

---

19. Now I tell you before it come, that, when it is come to pass, ye may believe that I am he.

Greek/Transliteration

19. Ἀπ᾽ ἄρτι λέγω ὑμῖν πρὸ τοῦ γενέσθαι, ἵνα, ὅταν γένηται, πιστεύσητε ὅτι ἐγώ εἰμι.

19. Ap arti lego 'umin pro tou genesthai, 'ina, 'otan geneitai, pisteuseite 'oti ego eimi.

Hebrew/Transliteration

יט. מֵעַתָּה אֲנִי מַגִּיד לָכֶם דָּבָר טֶרֶם בֹּאוֹ לְמַעַן תַּאֲמִינוּ אַחֲרֵי בֹאוֹ כִּי אֲנִי הוּא:

19. Me•a•ta ani ma•gid la•chem da•var te•rem bo•oo le•ma•an ta•a•mi•noo
a•cha•rey vo•o ki ani hoo.

---

20. Verily, verily, I say unto you, He that receiveth whomsoever I send
receiveth me; and he that receiveth me receiveth him that sent me.

Greek/Transliteration

20. Ἀμὴν ἀμὴν λέγω ὑμῖν, Ὁ λαμβάνων ἐάν τινα πέμψω, ἐμὲ λαμβάνει· ὁ δὲ
ἐμὲ λαμβάνων, λαμβάνει τὸν πέμψαντά με.

20. Amein amein lego 'umin, 'O lambanon ean tina pempso, eme lambanei. 'o
de eme lambanon, lambanei ton pempsanta me.

Hebrew/Transliteration

כ. אָמֵן אָמֵן אֲנִי אֹמֵר לָכֶם הַמְקַבֵּל אֶת-מִי אֲשֶׁר אֶשְׁלַח פָּנַי הוּא מְקַבֵּל וְהַמְקַבֵּל פָּנַי הוּא מְקַבֵּל פְּנֵי שֹׁלְחִי:

20. Amen amen ani o•mer la•chem ha•m`ka•bel et - mee asher esh•lach pa•nai
hoo me•ka•bel ve•ha•m`ka•bel pa•nai hoo me•ka•bel p`ney shol•chi.

Rabbinic Jewish Commentary

It is a common saying among the Jews (c), ששלוחו של אדם כמותו, "that the
messenger of a man is as himself".

(c) T Bab. Beracot, fol. 34. 2. Kiddushin, fol. 41. 9. & 42. 1. & 43. 1. Bava Metzia,
fol. 96. 1.

---

21. When Jesus had thus said, he was troubled in spirit, and testified, and
said, Verily, verily, I say unto you, that one of you shall betray me.

Greek/Transliteration

21. Ταῦτα εἰπὼν ὁ Ἰησοῦς ἐταράχθη τῷ πνεύματι, καὶ ἐμαρτύρησεν καὶ εἶπεν,
Ἀμὴν ἀμὴν λέγω ὑμῖν ὅτι εἷς ἐξ ὑμῶν παραδώσει με.

21. Tauta eipon 'o Yeisous etarachthei to pneumati, kai emartureisen kai
eipen, Amein amein lego 'umin 'oti 'cis ex 'umon paradosei me.

Hebrew/Transliteration

כא. וַיְהִי כְּדַבֵּר יֵשׁוּעַ אֶת-הַדְּבָרִים הָאֵלֶּה וַתִּפָּעֶם רוּחוֹ בְּקִרְבּוֹ וַיַּגֵּד לָהֶם לֵאמֹר אָמֵן אָמֵן אֲנִי אֹמֵר
לָכֶם כִּי:אֶחָד מִכֶּם יַסְגִּיר אֹתִי

21. Vay•hi ke•da•ber Yeshua et - ha•d`va•rim ha•e•le va•ti•pa•em roo•cho
ve•kir•bo va•ya•ged la•hem le•mor Amen amen ani o•mer la•chem ki e•chad
mi•kem yas•gir o•ti.

---

22. Then the disciples looked one on another, doubting of whom he spake.

Greek/Transliteration
22. Ἔβλεπον οὖν εἰς ἀλλήλους οἱ μαθηταί, ἀπορούμενοι περὶ τίνος λέγει.

22. Eblepon oun eis alleilous 'oi matheitai, aporoumenoi peri tinos legei.

Hebrew/Transliteration
כב. וַיִּתְרָאוּ הַתַּלְמִידִים פָּנִים בְּפָנִים כִּי לֹא יָדְעוּ עַל-מִי דִבֵּר:

22. Va•yit•ra•oo ha•tal•mi•dim pa•nim be•fa•nim ki lo yad•oo al - mee di•ber.

---

23. Now there was leaning on Jesus' bosom one of his disciples, whom Jesus
loved.

Greek/Transliteration
23. Ἦν δὲ ἀνακείμενος εἷς τῶν μαθητῶν αὐτοῦ ἐν τῷ κόλπῳ τοῦ Ἰησοῦ, ὃν
ἠγάπα ὁ Ἰησοῦς·

23. Ein de anakeimenos 'eis ton matheiton autou en to kolpo tou Yeisou, 'on
eigapa 'o Yeisous.

Hebrew/Transliteration
כג. וְאֶחָד מִתַּלְמִידָיו אֲשֶׁר יֵשׁוּעַ אֲהֵבוֹ נִשְׁעָן עַל-חֵיקוֹ:

23. Ve•e•chad mi•tal•mi•dav asher Yeshua ahe•vo nish•an al - chey•ko.

Rabbinic Jewish Commentary
The posture of the Jews at table, was either "sitting" or "lying", and a difference
they make between these two;

"If, say they (d), היו יושבין, "they sat" to eat everyone asked a blessing for himself;
but if הסיבו, "they lay down", one asked a blessing for them all."

This lying down was not on their backs, nor on their right side, but on their left;
for they say (e), that

"Lying down on the back, is not called הסיבה, "lying down"; and lying on the right
side, is not called lying down."

And the reason given is (f), because they have need of the right hand to eat with; but as they elsewhere (g) observe,

"They used to eat lying along, leaning on the left side, their feet to the ground, and every man on a single couch."

Would you know the order in which they, lay, take the account as they have given it (h);

"When there were but two couches, the principal person lay first, and the second to him above him; and when there were three, the principal person lay in the middle, the second to him above him, and the third below him; and if he would talk with him, he raised himself upright, and sitting upright he talked with him; that is, as the gloss explains it, if the principal person was desirous to talk with him that was second to him, he must raise himself up from his lying down, and sit upright; for all the white he is leaning, he cannot talk with him, because he that is second to him, is behind the head of the principal person, and the face of the principal person is turned to the other side; and it is better for the second to sit below him, that he may hear his words, whilst he is leaning."

(d) Misn. Beracot, c. 6. sect. 6. (e) T. Bab. Pesachim, fol. 108. 1. (f) Gloss in ib. (g) Gloss in T. Bab. Beracot, fol. 46. 2. & Bartenora in Misn. Beracot, c. 6. sect. 6. (h) T. Bab. Beracot, fol. 46. 2.

---

24. Simon Peter therefore beckoned to him, that he should ask who it should be of whom he spake.

Greek/Transliteration
24. νεύει οὖν τούτῳ Σίμων Πέτρος πυθέσθαι τίς ἂν εἴη περὶ οὗ λέγει.

24. neuei oun touto Simon Petros puthesthai tis an eiei peri 'ou legei.

Hebrew/Transliteration
:כד. וַיִּרְמָז-לֹו שִׁמְעֹון פֶּטְרֹוס וַיֹּאמֶר אֵלָיו אֱמָר-נָא מִי-הוּא זֶה אֲשֶׁר דִּבֶּר עָלָיו

24. Va•yir•maz - lo Shimon Petros va•yo•mer elav emar - na mee - hoo ze asher di•ber alav.

Rabbinic Jewish Commentary
Peter perhaps lay at a distance from Christ, or in some such position, that he could not whisper to him himself; and besides, knew that John might use more freedom, as he was admitted to more familiarity with him; and being at some distance also from him, he beckoned to him; which was usually done at meals, when they could not, by reason of their posture, discourse together: this being the case, מחוי ליה במחוג, "they made signs", by nodding to one another (k); that is, as the gloss explains it, they pointed with their hands and fingers, and by nodding or

349

beckoning; such a method Peter took, signifying his desire to know who he spoke of.

(k) T. Bab. Beracot ib.

---

25. He then lying on Jesus' breast saith unto him, Lord, who is it?

Greek/Transliteration

25. Ἐπιπεσὼν δὲ ἐκεῖνος οὕτως ἐπὶ τὸ στῆθος τοῦ Ἰησοῦ, λέγει αὐτῷ, Κύριε, τίς ἐστιν;

25. Epipeson de ekeinos 'outos epi to steithos tou Yeisou, legei auto, Kurie, tis estin?

Hebrew/Transliteration

כה. וַיִּפֹּל עַל-צַוְּארֵי יֵשׁוּעַ וַיֹּאמֶר אֵלָיו אֲדֹנִי מִי הוּא:

25. Va•yi•pol al - tzav•rey Yeshua va•yo•mer elav Adoni mee hoo?

---

26. Jesus answered, He it is, to whom I shall give a sop, when I have dipped it. And when he had dipped the sop, he gave it to Judas Iscariot, the son of Simon.

Greek/Transliteration

26. Ἀποκρίνεται ὁ Ἰησοῦς, Ἐκεῖνός ἐστιν ᾧ ἐγὼ βάψας τὸ ψωμίον ἐπιδώσω. Καὶ ἐμβάψας τὸ ψωμίον, δίδωσιν Ἰούδᾳ Σίμωνος Ἰσκαριώτῃ.

26. Apokrinetai 'o Yeisous, Ekeinos estin 'o ego bapsas to psomion epidoso. Kai embapsas to psomion, didosin Youda Simonos Yskariotei.

Hebrew/Transliteration

כו. וַיַּעַן יֵשׁוּעַ זֶה הוּא אֲשֶׁר אֶטְבָּל-לוֹ פְרוּסָה וּנְתַתִּיהָ לוֹ וַיִּטְבֹּל אֶת-הַפְּרוּסָה וַיִּקָּחֶהָ וַיִּתְּנֶהָ אֶל- יְהוּדָה בֶּן-שִׁמְעוֹן אִישׁ-קְרִיּוֹת:

26. Va•ya•an Yeshua ze hoo asher et•bal - lo f`roo•sa oon•ta•ti•ha lo va•yit•bol et - ha•p`roo•sa va•yi•ka•che•ha va•yit•ne•ha el - Yehooda ben - Shimon Eesh - K`ri•yot.

Rabbinic Jewish Commentary

This was not the passover sop, which was dipped into a sauce made of various things, called by the Jews חרוסת; for this was not the "paschal" supper, but a common supper at a private house, two days before the feast of the passover; but this sop, or rather crust of bread, which whether dipped into a liquid, or only a piece of dry bread, which Yeshua dipped his hand into the dish for, and took, as some think, is not very material, was a piece of common bread, which Yeshua took up, without regard to any custom, or ceremony used at any feasts, and gave it to the betrayer, as a sign by which John might know him.

---

27. And after the sop Satan entered into him. Then said Jesus unto him, That thou doest, do quickly.

Greek/Transliteration
27. Καὶ μετὰ τὸ ψωμίον, τότε εἰσῆλθεν εἰς ἐκεῖνον ὁ Σατανᾶς. Λέγει οὖν αὐτῷ ὁ Ἰησοῦς, Ὃ ποιεῖς, ποίησον τάχιον.

27. Kai meta to psomion, tote eiseilthen eis ekeinon 'o Satanas. Legei oun auto 'o Yeisous, 'O poieis, poieison tachion.

Hebrew/Transliteration
כז. וְאַחֲרֵי אָכְלוֹ אֶת-הַפְּרוּסָה בָּא הַשָּׂטָן אֶל-קִרְבּוֹ וַיֹּאמֶר אֵלָיו יֵשׁוּעַ אֶת אֲשֶׁר-תַּעֲשֶׂה מַהֵר וַעֲשֵׂה:

27. Ve•a•cha•rey och•lo et - ha•p`roo•sa ba ha•Satan el - kir•bo va•yo•mer elav Yeshua et asher - ta•a•se ma•her va•a•se.

Rabbinic Jewish Commentary
The Jews have a saying (l), that

"No man commits a transgression, until נכנס בו רוח שטות, "a spirit of madness enters into him"."

Such an evil spirit entered into Judas, which pushed him on to commit this horrid iniquity.

(l) T. Bab. Sota, fol. 3. 1. Tzeror Hammor, fol. 112. 1. & 117. 3.

---

28. Now no man at the table knew for what intent he spake this unto him.

Greek/Transliteration
28. Τοῦτο δὲ οὐδεὶς ἔγνω τῶν ἀνακειμένων πρὸς τί εἶπεν αὐτῷ.

28. Touto de oudeis egno ton anakeimenon pros ti eipen auto.

Hebrew/Transliteration
כח. וְלֹא-יָדַע אִישׁ מִן-הַיֹּשְׁבִים שָׁם בַּמְּסִיבָּה עַל-מֶה דִּבֶּר אֵלָיו כָּזֹאת:

28. Ve•lo - ya•da eesh min - ha•yosh•vim sham bam•si•ba al - me di•ber elav ka•zot.

29. For some of them thought, because Judas had the bag, that Jesus had said unto him, Buy those things that we have need of against the feast; or, that he should give something to the poor.

Greek/Transliteration
29. Τινὲς γὰρ ἐδόκουν, ἐπεὶ τὸ γλωσσόκομον εἶχεν ὁ Ἰούδας, ὅτι λέγει αὐτῷ ὁ Ἰησοῦς, Ἀγόρασον ὧν χρείαν ἔχομεν εἰς τὴν ἑορτήν· ἢ τοῖς πτωχοῖς ἵνα τι δῷ.

29. Tines gar edokoun, epei to glossokomon eichen 'o Youdas, 'oti legei auto 'o Yeisous, Agorason 'on chreian echomen eis tein 'eortein. ei tois ptochois 'ina ti do.

Hebrew/Translitration
כט. כִּי יֵשׁ אֲשֶׁר חָשְׁבוּ בִּהְיוֹת צְרוֹר הַכֶּסֶף בְּיַד יְהוּדָה עַל-כֵּן אָמַר אֵלָיו יֵשׁוּעַ קְנֵה-נָא אֶת-אֲשֶׁר יֶחְסַר לָנוּ לֶחָג:אוֹ תְּנָא דָבָר לַעֲנִיִּים

29. Ki yesh asher chash•voo bi•hee•yot tze•ror ha•ke•sef be•yad Yehooda al - ken amar elav Yeshua k`ne - na et - asher yech•sar la•noo le•chag oh te•na da•var la•a•ni•yim.

---

30. He then having received the sop went immediately out: and it was night.

Greek/Transliteration
30. Λαβὼν οὖν τὸ ψωμίον ἐκεῖνος, εὐθέως ἐξῆλθεν· ἦν δὲ νύξ.

30. Labon oun to psomion ekeinos, eutheos exeilthen. ein de nux.

Hebrew/Transliteration
ל. וְהוּא בְּקַחְתּוֹ אֶת-הַפְּרוּסָה אֶל-פִּיו יָצָא פִתְאֹם וַיְהִי לָיְלָה:

30. Ve•hoo be•kach•to et - ha•p`roo•sa el - piv ya•tza fit•om vay•hi lai•la.

---

31. Therefore, when he was gone out, Jesus said, Now is the Son of man glorified, and God is glorified in him.

Greek/Transliteration
31. Ὅτε ἐξῆλθεν, λέγει ὁ Ἰησοῦς, Νῦν ἐδοξάσθη ὁ υἱὸς τοῦ ἀνθρώπου, καὶ ὁ θεὸς ἐδοξάσθη ἐν αὐτῷ.

31. 'Ote exeilthen, legei 'o Yeisous, Nun edoxasthei 'o 'wios tou anthropou, kai 'o theos edoxasthei en auto.

לא. וַיְהִי כַּאֲשֶׁר יָצָא וַיֹּאמֶר יֵשׁוּעַ עַתָּה נֶאְדָּר בֶּן-הָאָדָם בְּכָבוֹד וּבוֹ אֱלֹהִים בְּכָבוֹד נֶאְדָּר:

31. Vay•hi ka•a•sher ya•tza va•yo•mer Yeshua ata ne•e•dar Ben - ha•adam be•cha•vod oo•vo Elohim be•cha•vod ne•e•dar.

---

32. If God be glorified in him, God shall also glorify him in himself, and shall straightway glorify him.

32. Εἰ ὁ θεὸς ἐδοξάσθη ἐν αὐτῷ, καὶ ὁ θεὸς δοξάσει αὐτὸν ἐν ἑαυτῷ, καὶ εὐθὺς δοξάσει αὐτόν.

32. Ei 'o theos edoxasthei en auto, kai 'o theos doxasei auton en 'eauto, kai euthus doxasei auton.

לב. וֵאלֹהִים הוּא יַאֲדִיר אֹתוֹ בִּכְבוֹדוֹ וְגַם-יָחִישׁ לְהַאֲדִירוֹ:

32. Ve•Elohim hoo ya•a•dir o•to bich•vo•do ve•gam - ya•chish le•ha•a•di•ro.

---

33. Little children, yet a little while I am with you. Ye shall seek me: and as I said unto the Jews, Whither I go, ye cannot come; so now I say to you.

33. Τεκνία, ἔτι μικρὸν μεθ᾽ ὑμῶν εἰμι. Ζητήσετέ με, καὶ καθὼς εἶπον τοῖς Ἰουδαίοις ὅτι Ὅπου ὑπάγω ἐγώ, ὑμεῖς οὐ δύνασθε ἐλθεῖν, καὶ ὑμῖν λέγω ἄρτι.

33. Teknia, eti mikron meth 'umon eimi. Zeiteisete me, kai kathos eipon tois Youdaiois 'oti 'Opou 'upago ego, 'umeis ou dunasthe elthein, kai 'umin lego arti.

לג. בָּנַי הַיְקָרִים עוֹד-מְעַט מִזְעָר אֵשֵׁב עִמָּכֶם וְאַתֶּם תְּבַקְשׁוּנִי וְכַאֲשֶׁר אָמַרְתִּי אֶל-הַיְּהוּדִים כִּי אֶל-אֲשֶׁר אֲנִי הֹלֵךְ לֹא תוּכְלוּ לָבֹא שָׁמָּה כֵּן אֲנִי אֹמֵר עַתָּה גַּם-אֲלֵיכֶם:

33. Ba•nai hay•ka•rim od - me•at miz•ar e•shev ee•ma•chem ve•a•tem te•vak•shoo•ni ve•cha•a•sher amar•ti el - ha•Ye•hoo•dim ki el - asher ani ho•lech lo tooch•loo la•vo sha•ma ken ani o•mer ata gam - aley•chem.

---

34. A new commandment I give unto you, That ye love one another; as I have loved you, that ye also love one another.

34. Ἐντολὴν καινὴν δίδωμι ὑμῖν, ἵνα ἀγαπᾶτε ἀλλήλους· καθὼς ἠγάπησα ὑμᾶς, ἵνα καὶ ὑμεῖς ἀγαπᾶτε ἀλλήλους.

34. Entolein kainein didomi 'umin, 'ina agapate alleilous. kathos eigapeisa 'umas, 'ina kai 'umeis agapate alleilous.

Hebrew/Transliteration

לד. הִנֵּה מִצְוָה חֲדָשָׁה אֲנִי נֹתֵן לָכֶם לְאַהֲבָה אִישׁ אֶת-רֵעֵהוּ כַּאֲשֶׁר אֲהַבְתִּי אֶתְכֶם כֵּן גַּם-אַתֶּם אִישׁ - אֶת:רֵעֵהוּ תֶּאֱהָבוּן

34. Hee•ne mitz•va cha•da•sha ani no•ten la•chem le•a•ha•va eesh et - re•e•hoo ka•a•sher ahav•ti et•chem ken gam - atem eesh et - re•e•hoo te•e•ha•voon.

Rabbinic Jewish Commentary
The Yemenite Midrash says,
"In the future the Holy One, blessed is he, will seat the Messiah in the supernal Yeshiva, and they will call him, "YHWH" just as they call the Creator . . . and all those who walk on earth will come and sit before him to hear a *New Torah* and new commandments and the deep wisdom which he teaches Israel. . . and no person who hears a teaching from the mouth of the Messiah will ever forget it." (*Yemenite Midrash, cited in the Messiah Texts, Raphael Patai, pg. 256*)

The Jew has no reason to object as he does (m), to its being called a "new commandment": and its being "new", carries in it a reason or argument, why it should be observed.

Though this commandment, as to the matter of it, is the same with that of Moses, Lev_19:18; yet it takes in more, and "new" objects; since by "neighbour" there, seems to be meant "the children of their people", the Jews; and so they understood it only of their countrymen, and of proselytes at furthest, whereas this reaches to any "other" person.

(m) R. Isaac Chizzuk Emuna, l. 2. c. 54. p. 444.

---

35. By this shall all men know that ye are my disciples, if ye have love one to another.

Greek/Transliteration
35. Ἐν τούτῳ γνώσονται πάντες ὅτι ἐμοὶ μαθηταί ἐστε, ἐὰν ἀγάπην ἔχητε ἐν ἀλλήλοις.

35. En touto gnosontai pantes 'oti emoi matheitai este, ean agapein echeite en alleilois.

לה. בְּזֹאת יֵדְעוּ כֻלָּם כִּי תַלְמִידַי אַתֶּם אִם אַהֲבַת רֵעִים תָּלִין בֵּינֵיכֶם:

35. Ba•zot yed•oo choo•lam ki tal•mi•dai atem eem a•ha•vat re•eem ta•lin
bey•ney•chem.

---

36. Simon Peter said unto him, Lord, whither goest thou? Jesus answered
him, Whither I go, thou canst not follow me now; but thou shalt follow me
afterwards.

36. Λέγει αὐτῷ Σίμων Πέτρος, Κύριε, ποῦ ὑπάγεις; Ἀπεκρίθη αὐτῷ ὁ
Ἰησοῦς, Ὅπου ὑπάγω, οὐ δύνασαί μοι νῦν ἀκολουθῆσαι, ὕστερον δὲ
ἀκολουθήσεις μοι.

36. Legei auto Simon Petros, Kurie, pou 'upageis? Apekrithei auto 'o Yeisous,
'Opou 'upago, ou dunasai moi nun akoloutheisai, 'usteron de akoloutheiseis
moi.

לו. וַיֹּאמֶר אֵלָיו שִׁמְעוֹן פֶּטְרוֹס אֲדֹנִי אָנָה אַתָּה הֹלֵךְ וַיַּעַן יֵשׁוּעַ אֶל-אֲשֶׁר אֲנִי הֹלֵךְ לֹא-תוּכַל לָלֶכֶת
אַחֲרַי כַּיּוֹם:אַךְ הִנֵּה יָמִים בָּאִים וְהָלַכְתָּ אַחֲרָי

36. Va•yo•mer elav Shimon Petros Adoni ana ata ho•lech va•ya•an Yeshua el -
asher ani ho•lech lo - too•chal la•le•chet a•cha•rai ka•yom ach hee•ne ya•mim
ba•eem ve•ha•lach•ta a•cha•rai.

---

37. Peter said unto him, Lord, why cannot I follow thee now? I will lay down
my life for thy sake.

37. Λέγει αὐτῷ Πέτρος, Κύριε, διὰ τί οὐ δύναμαί σοι ἀκολουθῆσαι ἄρτι; Τὴν
ψυχήν μου ὑπὲρ σοῦ θήσω.

37. Legei auto Petros, Kurie, dya ti ou dunamai soi akoloutheisai arti? Tein
psuchein mou 'uper sou theiso.

לז. וַיֹּאמֶר אֵלָיו פֶּטְרוֹס אֲדֹנִי עַל-מֶה לֹא-אוּכַל לָלֶכֶת אַחֲרֶיךָ כַּיּוֹם הֲלֹא אֶת-נַפְשִׁי אֶתֵּן בַּעַדְךָ:

37. Va•yo•mer elav Fetros Adoni al - me lo - oo•chal la•le•chet a•cha•re•cha
ka•yom ha•lo et - naf•shi e•ten ba•a•de•cha.

---

38. Jesus answered him, Wilt thou lay down thy life for my sake? Verily, verily, I say unto thee, The cock shall not crow, till thou hast denied me thrice.

Greek/Transliteration

38. Ἀπεκρίθη αὐτῷ ὁ Ἰησοῦς, Τὴν ψυχήν σου ὑπὲρ ἐμοῦ θήσεις; Ἀμὴν ἀμὴν λέγω σοι, οὐ μὴ ἀλέκτωρ φωνήσῃ ἕως οὗ ἀπαρνήσῃ με τρίς.

38. Apekrithei auto 'o Yeisous, Tein psuchein sou 'uper emou theiseis? Amein amein lego soi, ou mei alektor phoneisei 'eos 'ou aparneisei me tris.

Hebrew/Transliteration

לח. וַיַּעַן יֵשׁוּעַ הֲתִתֵּן אֶת-נַפְשְׁךָ בַעֲדִי אָמֵן אָמֵן אֲנִי אֹמֵר לְךָ לֹא יִקְרָא הַתַּרְנְגֹל עַד-אֲשֶׁר תְּכַחֶשׁ-בִּי שָׁלֹשׁ פְּעָמִים:

38. Va•ya•an Yeshua ha•ti•ten et - naf•she•cha ba•a•di Amen amen ani o•mer lach lo yik•ra ha•tar•ne•gol ad - asher te•cha•chesh - bi sha•losh pe•a•mim.

John, Chapter 14

1. Let not your heart be troubled: ye believe in God, believe also in me.

Greek/Transliteration

1. Μὴ ταρασσέσθω ὑμῶν ἡ καρδία· πιστεύετε εἰς τὸν θεόν, καὶ εἰς ἐμὲ πιστεύετε.

1. Mei tarassestho 'umon 'ei kardia. pisteuete eis ton theon, kai eis eme pisteuete.

Hebrew/Transliteration

א. אַל-יֵחַת לִבְּכֶם הַאֲמִינוּ בֵאלֹהִים וּכְמוֹ-כֵן הַאֲמִינוּ בִּי:

1. Al - ye•chat lib•chem ha•a•mi•noo ve•Elohim ooch•mo - chen ha•a•mi•noo bi.

---

2. In my Father's house are many mansions: if it were not so, I would have told you. I go to prepare a place for you.

Greek/Transliteration

2. Ἐν τῇ οἰκίᾳ τοῦ πατρός μου μοναὶ πολλαί εἰσιν· εἰ δὲ μή, εἶπον ἂν ὑμῖν· Πορεύομαι ἑτοιμάσαι τόπον ὑμῖν.

2. En tei oikia tou patros mou monai pollai eisin. ei de mei, eipon an 'umin. Poreuomai 'etoimasai topon 'umin.

Hebrew/Transliteration

ב. מְעוֹנוֹת רַבּוֹת נִמְצָאוֹת בְּבֵית אָבִי כִּי לוּלֵא כֵן הָיִיתִי מַגִּיד לָכֶם וַאֲנִי הֹלֵךְ לְהָכִין לָכֶם מָקוֹם:

2. Me•o•not ra•bot nim•tza•ot be•veit Avi ki loo•le chen ha•yi•ti ma•gid la•chem va•a•ni ho•lech le•ha•chin la•chem ma•kom.

Rabbinic Jewish Commentary

Very agreeable to this way of speaking are many things in the Jewish writings:

"Says R. Isaack (o), how many מדורין על מדורין, "mansions upon mansions", are there for the righteous in that world? and the uppermost mansion of them all is the love of their Lord."

Moreover, they say (p), that

"In the world to come every righteous man shall have מדור, "a mansion", to himself."

Sometimes they (q) speak of "seven mansions" (a number of perfection) being prepared for the righteous in the other world, though entirely ignorant of the person by whom these mansions are prepared.

From the Greek μονή
monē; from *G3306; an abiding, an abode:* - abode (1), dwelling places (1).

---

3. And if I go and prepare a place for you, I will come again, and receive you unto myself; that where I am, there ye may be also.

Greek/Transliteration
3. Καὶ ἐὰν πορευθῶ, ἑτοιμάσω ὑμῖν τόπον· πάλιν ἔρχομαι καὶ παραλήψομαι ὑμᾶς πρὸς ἐμαυτόν, ἵνα ὅπου εἰμὶ ἐγώ, καὶ ὑμεῖς ἦτε.

3. Kai ean poreutho, 'etoimaso 'umin topon. palin erchomai kai paraleipsomai 'umas pros emauton, 'ina 'opou eimi ego, kai 'umeis eite.

Hebrew/Transliteration
ג. וְאַחֲרֵי אֲשֶׁר אֵלֵךְ וְאָכִין מָקוֹם לָכֶם שׁוֹב אָשׁוּב וְלָקַחְתִּי אֶתְכֶם אֵלָי לְמַעַן תִּהְיוּ עִמִּי שָׁם בַּאֲשֶׁר אֶהְיֶה:

3. Ve•a•cha•rey asher e•lech ve•a•chin ma•kom la•chem shov a•shoov ve•la•kach•ti et•chem e•lai le•ma•an ti•hi•yoo ee•mi sham ba•a•sher e•he•ye.

---

4. And whither I go ye know, and the way ye know.

Greek/Transliteration
4. Καὶ ὅπου ἐγὼ ὑπάγω οἴδατε, καὶ τὴν ὁδὸν οἴδατε.

4. Kai 'opou ego 'upago oidate, kai tein 'odon oidate.

Hebrew/Transliteration
ד. וְאַתֶּם יְדַעְתֶּם אָנָא אֲנִי הֹלֵךְ וְגַם אֶת-הַדֶּרֶךְ יְדַעְתֶּם:

4. Ve•a•tem ye•da•a•tem ana ani ho•lech ve•gam et - ha•de•rech ye•da•a•tem.

---

5. Thomas saith unto him, Lord, we know not whither thou goest; and how can we know the way?

Greek/Transliteration
5. Λέγει αὐτῷ Θωμᾶς, Κύριε, οὐκ οἴδαμεν ποῦ ὑπάγεις· καὶ πῶς δυνάμεθα τὴν ὁδὸν εἰδέναι;

5. Legei auto Thomas, Kurie, ouk oidamen pou 'upageis. kai pos dunametha tein 'odon eidenai?

ה. וַיֹּאמֶר אֵלָיו תּוֹמָא אֲדֹנִי לֹא יָדַעְנוּ אָנָה אַתָּה הֹלֵךְ וְאֵיכָה נֵדַע אֶת-הַדָּרֶךְ:

5. Va•yo•mer elav Toma Adoni lo ya•da•a•noo ana ata ho•lech ve•ey•cha ne•da et - ha•da•rech?

---

6. Jesus saith unto him, I am the way, the truth, and the life: no man cometh unto the Father, but by me.

Greek/Transliteration

6. Λέγει αὐτῷ ὁ Ἰησοῦς, Ἐγώ εἰμι ἡ ὁδὸς καὶ ἡ ἀλήθεια καὶ ἡ ζωή· οὐδεὶς ἔρχεται πρὸς τὸν πατέρα, εἰ μὴ δι᾽ ἐμοῦ.

6. Legei auto 'o Yeisous, Ego eimi 'ei 'odos kai 'ei aleitheya kai 'ei zoei. oudeis erchetai pros ton patera, ei mei di emou.

Hebrew/Transliteration

ו. וַיֹּאמֶר אֵלָיו יֵשׁוּעַ אָנֹכִי הַדֶּרֶךְ וְהָאֱמֶת וְהַחַיִּים וְאִישׁ לֹא-יָבֹא אֶל-הָאָב בִּלְתִּי עַל-יָדִי:

6. Va•yo•mer elav Yeshua ano•chi ha•de•rech ve•ha•e•met ve•ha•cha•yim ve•eesh lo - ya•vo el - ha•Av bil•tee al - ya•di.

Rabbinic Jewish Commentary

This phrase seems to be opposed to a notion of the Jews, that the Torah was the true way of life, and who confined truth to the Torah. They have a saying (r), that משה ותורתו אמת, "Moses and his Torah are the truth"; this they make Korah and his company say in gehenna, Numbers 16:35. That the Torah of Moses was truth, is certain; but it is too strong an expression to say of Moses himself, that he was truth; but well agrees with Yeshua, by whom grace and truth came in opposition to Moses, by whom came the Torah: but when they say (s), אין אמת אלא תורה, "there is no truth but the Torah", they do not speak truth. More truly do they speak, when, in answer to that question, מה אמת, "what is truth?" it is said, that he is the living God, and King of the world (t), characters that well agree with Yeshua.

(r) T. Bab. Bava Bathra. fol. 74. 1. Bemidbar Rabba, fol. 223. 2. (s) Hieros. Roshhashanah, fol. 59. 1. Praefat. Echa Rabbati, fol. 36. 2. (t) Ib. Sanhedrin, fol. 18. 1.

---

7. If ye had known me, ye should have known my Father also: and from henceforth ye know him, and have seen him.

7. Εἰ ἐγνώκειτέ με, καὶ τὸν πατέρα μου ἐγνώκειτε ἄν· καὶ ἀπ᾽ ἄρτι γινώσκετε αὐτόν, καὶ ἑωράκατε αὐτόν.

7. Ei egnokeite me, kai ton patera mou egnokeite an. kai ap arti ginoskete auton, kai 'eorakate auton.

ז. לוּ אֹתִי יְדַעְתֶּם יְדַעְתֶּם גַּם אֶת-אָבִי וּמֵעַתָּה יְדַעְתֶּם אֹתוֹ וְגַם-רְאִיתֶם אֹתוֹ:

7. Loo o•ti ye•da•a•tem ye•da•a•tem gam et - Avi oo•me•a•ta ye•da•a•tem o•to ve•gam - r`ee•tem o•to.

---

8. Philip saith unto him, Lord, shew us the Father, and it sufficeth us.

8. Λέγει αὐτῷ Φίλιππος, Κύριε, δεῖξον ἡμῖν τὸν πατέρα, καὶ ἀρκεῖ ἡμῖν.

8. Legei auto Philippos, Kurie, deixon 'eimin ton patera, kai arkei 'eimin.

ח. וַיֹּאמֶר אֵלָיו פִילִפּוֹס אֲדֹנִי הַרְאֵנוּ נָא אֶת-הָאָב וְרַב לָנוּ:

8• Va•yo•mer elav Filipos Adoni har•e•noo na et - ha•Av ve•rav la•noo.

---

9. Jesus saith unto him, Have I been so long time with you, and yet hast thou not known me, Philip? he that hath seen me hath seen the Father; and how sayest thou then, Shew us the Father?

9. Λέγει αὐτῷ ὁ Ἰησοῦς, Τοσοῦτον χρόνον μεθ᾽ ὑμῶν εἰμι, καὶ οὐκ ἔγνωκάς με, Φίλιππε; Ὁ ἑωρακὼς ἐμέ, ἑώρακεν τὸν πατέρα· καὶ πῶς σὺ λέγεις, Δεῖξον ἡμῖν τὸν πατέρα;

9. Legei auto 'o Yeisous, Tosouton chronon meth 'umon eimi, kai ouk egnokas me, Philippe? 'O 'eorakos eme, 'eoraken ton patera. kai pos su legeis, Deixon 'eimin ton patera?

ט. וַיֹּאמֶר אֵלָיו יֵשׁוּעַ הֲלֹא יָמִים רַבִּים הָיִיתִי עִמְּכֶם הֲטֶרֶם תֵּדַע אֹתִי פִילִפּוֹס הָרֹאֶה אֹתִי רֹאֶה אֶת-הָאָב:וְלָמָּה-זֶּה תֹאמַר הַרְאֵנוּ אֶת-הָאָב

9. Va•yo•mer elav Yeshua ha•lo ya•mim ra•bim ha•yi•ti ee•ma•chem
ha•te•rem te•da o•ti Pilipos? ha•ro•eh o•ti ro•eh et - ha•Av ve•la•ma - ze
to•mar har•e•noo et - ha•Av?

---

10. Believest thou not that I am in the Father, and the Father in me? the
words that I speak unto you I speak not of myself: but the Father that
dwelleth in me, he doeth the works.

Greek/Transliteration

10. Οὐ πιστεύεις ὅτι ἐγὼ ἐν τῷ πατρί, καὶ ὁ πατὴρ ἐν ἐμοί ἐστιν; Τὰ ῥήματα ἃ
ἐγὼ λαλῶ ὑμῖν, ἀπ᾽ ἐμαυτοῦ οὐ λαλῶ· ὁ δὲ πατὴρ ὁ ἐν ἐμοὶ μένων, αὐτὸς ποιεῖ
τὰ ἔργα.

10. Ou pisteueis 'oti ego en to patri, kai 'o pateir en emoi estin? Ta 'reimata 'a
ego lalo 'umin, ap emautou ou lalo. 'o de pateir 'o en emoi menon, autos poiei
ta erga.

Hebrew/Transliteration

י. הֲכִי לֹא תַאֲמִין כִּי אֲנִי בָאָב וְהָאָב בִּי הַדְּבָרִים אֲשֶׁר אֲנִי דֹבֵר אֲלֵיכֶם לֹא-מִלִּבִּי אֲנִי דֹבֵר כִּי הָאָב
הַשֹּׁכֵן בִּי:הוּא פֹעֵל בִּי פְּעֻלוֹתָיו

10. Ha•chi lo ta•a•min ki ani va•Av ve•ha•Av bi ha•d`va•rim asher ani do•ver
aley•chem lo - mi•li•bi ani do•ver ki ha•Av ha•sho•chen bi hoo fo•el bi
pe•oo•lo•tav.

---

11. Believe me that I am in the Father, and the Father in me: or else believe
me for the very works' sake.

Greek/Transliteration

11. Πιστεύετέ μοι ὅτι ἐγὼ ἐν τῷ πατρί, καὶ ὁ πατὴρ ἐν ἐμοί· εἰ δὲ μή, διὰ τὰ
ἔργα αὐτὰ πιστεύετέ μοι.

11. Pisteuete moi 'oti ego en to patri, kai 'o pateir en emoi. ei de mei, dya ta
erga auta pisteuete moi.

Hebrew/Transliteration

יא. הַאֲמִינוּ לִי כִּי-אֲנִי בָאָב וְהָאָב בִּי וְאִם-לֹא הַאֲמִינוּ לִי בִּגְלַל הַפְּעֻלוֹת הָאֵלֶּה:

11. Ha•a•mi•noo li ki - ani va•Av ve•ha•Av bi ve•eem - lo ha•a•mi•noo li
big•lal ha•pe•oo•lot ha•e•le.

---

12. Verily, verily, I say unto you, He that believeth on me, the works that I do shall he do also; and greater works than these shall he do; because I go unto my Father.

Greek/Transliteration

12. Ἀμὴν ἀμὴν λέγω ὑμῖν, ὁ πιστεύων εἰς ἐμέ, τὰ ἔργα ἃ ἐγὼ ποιῶ κἀκεῖνος ποιήσει, καὶ μείζονα τούτων ποιήσει· ὅτι ἐγὼ πρὸς τὸν πατέρα μου πορεύομαι.

12. Amein amein lego 'umin, 'o pisteuon eis eme, ta erga 'a ego poio kakeinos poieisei, kai meizona touton poieisei. 'oti ego pros ton patera mou poreuomai.

Hebrew/Transliteration

יב. אָמֵן אָמֵן אֲנִי אֹמֵר לָכֶם הַמַּאֲמִין בִּי אֶת-הַמַּעֲשִׂים אֲשֶׁר אֲנִי עֹשֶׂה יַעֲשֶׂה גַם-הוּא וּגְדֹלוֹת מֵאֵלֶּה יַעֲשֶׂה כִּי-אֶל-אָבִי אָנֹכִי הֹלֵךְ

12. Amen amen ani o•mer la•chem ha•ma•a•min bi et - ha•ma•a•sim asher ani o•se ya•a•se gam - hoo oog•do•lot me•e•le ya•a•se ki el - Avi ano•chi ho•lech.

---

13. And whatsoever ye shall ask in my name, that will I do, that the Father may be glorified in the Son.

Greek/Transliteration

13. Καὶ ὅ τι ἂν αἰτήσητε ἐν τῷ ὀνόματί μου, τοῦτο ποιήσω, ἵνα δοξασθῇ ὁ πατὴρ ἐν τῷ υἱῷ.

13. Kai 'o ti an aiteiseite en to onomati mou, touto poieiso, 'ina doxasthei 'o pateir en to 'wio.

Hebrew/Transliteration

יג. וְכָל-אֲשֶׁר תִּשְׁאֲלוּ בִשְׁמִי אֹתוֹ אֶעֱשֶׂה לְבַעֲבוּר יִגְדַּל כְּבוֹד הָאָב בִּבְנוֹ:

13. Ve•chol - asher tish•a•loo vish•mi o•to e•e•se le•va•a•voor yig•dal k`vod ha•Av bi•V`no.

---

14. If ye shall ask any thing in my name, I will do it.

Greek/Transliteration

14. Ἐάν τι αἰτήσητέ με ἐν τῷ ὀνόματί μου, ἐγὼ ποιήσω.

14. Ean ti aiteiseite me en to onomati mou, ego poieiso.

Hebrew/Transliteration

יד. כָּל-דָּבָר אֲשֶׁר תִּשְׁאֲלוּ בִשְׁמִי אֲנִי אֶעֱשֶׂנּוּ:

14. Kol - da•var asher tish•a•loo vish•mi ani e•e•se•noo.

---

15. If ye love me, keep my commandments.

Greek/Transliteration
15. Ἐὰν ἀγαπᾶτέ με, τὰς ἐντολὰς τὰς ἐμὰς τηρήσατε.

15. Ean agapate me, tas entolas tas emas teireisate.

Hebrew/Transliteration
טו. אִם-אֲהַבְתֶּם אֹתִי אֶת-מִצְוֹתַי תִּשְׁמֹרוּ:

15. Eem - ahav•tem o•ti et - mitz•vo•tai tish•mo•roo.

---

16. And I will pray the Father, and he shall give you another Comforter, that he may abide with you for ever;

Greek/Transliteration
16. Καὶ ἐγὼ ἐρωτήσω τὸν πατέρα, καὶ ἄλλον παράκλητον δώσει ὑμῖν, ἵνα μένῃ μεθ᾽ ὑμῶν εἰς τὸν αἰῶνα,

16. Kai ego eroteiso ton patera, kai allon parakleiton dosei 'umin, 'ina menei meth 'umon eis ton aiona,

Hebrew/Transliteration
טז. וַאֲנִי אֲחַלֶּה פְּנֵי הָאָב וְיִתֶּן לָכֶם מֵלִיץ אַחֵר אֲשֶׁר-יִשְׁכֹּן אִתְּכֶם עֲדֵי-עַד:

16. Va•a•ni a•cha•le f ney ha•Av ve•yi•ten la•chem me•litz a•cher asher - yish•kon eet•chem adey - ad.

Rabbinic Jewish Commentary

One of the names of the Messiah, with the Jews, is מנחם (u), "a Comforter"; such an one Yeshua had been to his disciples; and now he was about to leave them, and for their support under their sorrows, he promises to use his interest with his Father, that he would give them another Comforter, meaning the Spirit, who performs this his work and office, by taking of the things of Yeshua, and showing them to his people; by shedding abroad the love of the Father, and of the Son, into their hearts; by opening and applying the precious promises of the Gospel to them; by being a spirit of adoption in them; and by abiding with them as the seal, earnest, and pledge of their future glory.

When we consider these words, in connection with the preceding exhortation, to keep the commands of Yeshua, and as an encouragement so to do, it brings to mind a saying of R. Eliezer ben Jacob (w);

"He that does one commandment gets for himself פרקליט אחד, ενα παρακλητον, the very word here used, "one advocate", or "comforter"; and he that transgresses one command, gets for himself one accuser." (Pirkei Avot 4:15)

But though the word signifies both an advocate and a comforter, the latter seems to be the meaning of it here, as being more suited to the disconsolate condition of the disciples.

(u) T. Hieros. Beracot, fol. 5. 1. T. Bab. Sanhedrin, fol. 98. 2. Echa Rabbati, fol. 50. 2. (w) Pirke Abot, c. 4. sect. 11.

---

17. Even the Spirit of truth; whom the world cannot receive, because it seeth him not, neither knoweth him: but ye know him; for he dwelleth with you, and shall be in you.

Greek/Transliteration

17. τὸ πνεῦμα τῆς ἀληθείας, ὃ ὁ κόσμος οὐ δύναται λαβεῖν, ὅτι οὐ θεωρεῖ αὐτό, οὐδὲ γινώσκει αὐτό. Ὑμεῖς δὲ γινώσκετε αὐτό, ὅτι παρ᾽ ὑμῖν μένει, καὶ ἐν ὑμῖν ἔσται.

17. to pneuma teis aleitheias, 'o 'o kosmos ou dunatai labein, 'oti ou theorei auto, oude ginoskei auto. 'Umeis de ginoskete auto, 'oti par 'umin menei, kai en 'umin estai.

Hebrew/Transliteration

יז. הֲלֹא הוּא רוּחַ הָאֱמֶת אֲשֶׁר הָעוֹלָם לֹא-יָכֹל לְקַבְּלוֹ בַּאֲשֶׁר לֹא יִרְאָנּוּ וְלֹא יֵדָעֶנּוּ וְאַתֶּם יְדַעְתֶּם אֹתוֹ כִּי הוּא: שֹׁכֵן אִתְּכֶם וְאַף-הָיֹה יִהְיֶה בְּתוֹכְכֶם

17. Ha•lo hoo Roo•ach ha•e•met asher ha•o•lam lo - ya•chol le•kab•lo ba•a•sher lo yir•e•noo ve•lo ye•da•e•noo ve•a•tem ye•da•a•tem o•to ki hoo sho•chen eet•chem ve•af - ha•yo yi•hee•ye be•to•che•chem.

---

18. I will not leave you comfortless: I will come to you.

Greek/Transliteration
18. Οὐκ ἀφήσω ὑμᾶς ὀρφανούς· ἔρχομαι πρὸς ὑμᾶς.

18. Ouk apheiso 'umas orphanous. erchomai pros 'umas.

Hebrew/Transliteration
יח. וַאֲנִי לֹא אֶעֱזָבְכֶם יְתוֹמִים כִּי בֹא אָבֹא אֲלֵיכֶם:

18. Va•a•ni lo e•e•zov•chem ye•to•mim ki vo avo aley•chem.

Rabbinic Jewish Commentary

So among the Jews, disciples, and the world too, are represented as fatherless, when their Rabbi's and wise men are removed by death. Says R. Aba, (x) and so sometimes others, concerning R. Simeon ben Jochai,

"Woe to the world when thou shall go out of it, woe to the generation that shall be in the world when thou shall remove from them, וישתארון יתמין, "and they shall be left fatherless by thee"."

And in another place (y);

"Afterwards R. Akiba went out and cried, and his eyes flowed with water, and he said, woe Rabbi, woe Rabbi, for the world is left, יתום, "fatherless by thee"."

(x) Zohar in Num fol. 96. 3. & in Lev. fol. 42. 3. & in Exod. fol. 10. 3. & 28. 3. (y) Midrash Hannealam in Zohar in Gen. fol. 65. 4.

---

19. Yet a little while, and the world seeth me no more; but ye see me: because I live, ye shall live also.

Greek/Transliteration

19. Ἔτι μικρὸν καὶ ὁ κόσμος με οὐκέτι θεωρεῖ, ὑμεῖς δὲ θεωρεῖτέ με· ὅτι ἐγὼ ζῶ, καὶ ὑμεῖς ζήσεσθε.

19. Eti mikron kai 'o kosmos me ouketi theorei, 'umeis de theoreite me. 'oti ego zo, kai 'umeis zeisesthe.

Hebrew/Transliteration

יט. עוֹד מְעַט מִזְעָר וְהָעוֹלָם לֹא יוֹסִיף לִרְאוֹת אֹתִי וְאַתֶּם תִּרְאֻנִי כִּי-אָנִי חַי וְכֵן גַּם-אַתֶּם תִּחְיוּן:

19. Od me•at miz•ar ve•ha•olam lo yo•sif lir•ot o•ti ve•a•tem tir•oo•ni ki - ani chai ve•chen gam - atem tich•yoon.

---

20. At that day ye shall know that I am in my Father, and ye in me, and I in you.

Greek/Transliteration

20. Ἐν ἐκείνῃ τῇ ἡμέρᾳ γνώσεσθε ὑμεῖς ὅτι ἐγὼ ἐν τῷ πατρί μου, καὶ ὑμεῖς ἐν ἐμοί, καὶ ἐγὼ ἐν ὑμῖν.

20. En ekeinei tei 'eimera gnosesthe 'umeis 'oti ego en to patri mou, kai 'umeis en emoi, kai ego en 'umin.

:כ. בַּיּוֹם הַהוּא תֵּדְעוּ כִּי-אֲנִי בְאָבִי וְאַתֶּם בִּי וַאֲנִי בָכֶם

20. Ba•yom ha•hoo ted•oo ki - ani ve•Avi ve•a•tem bi va•a•ni va•chem.

---

21. He that hath my commandments, and keepeth them, he it is that loveth
me: and he that loveth me shall be loved of my Father, and I will love him,
and will manifest myself to him.

21. Ὁ ἔχων τὰς ἐντολάς μου καὶ τηρῶν αὐτάς, ἐκεῖνός ἐστιν ὁ ἀγαπῶν με· ὁ
δὲ ἀγαπῶν με, ἀγαπηθήσεται ὑπὸ τοῦ πατρός μου· καὶ ἐγὼ ἀγαπήσω αὐτόν,
καὶ ἐμφανίσω αὐτῷ ἐμαυτόν.

21. 'O echon tas entolas mou kai teiron autas, ekeinos estin 'o agapon me. 'o
de agapon me, agapeitheisetai 'upo tou patros mou. kai ego agapeiso auton,
kai emphaniso auto emauton.

כא. מִי אֲשֶׁר מִצְוֹתַי אִתּוֹ וְשֹׁמֵר לַעֲשׂוֹתָן זֶה הוּא אֲשֶׁר יֶאֱהָבַנִי וְאֹהֲבִי אָהוּב לְאָבִי וַאֲנִי אֹהֲבֵהוּ
:וְאֵלָיו אֶתְוַדָּע

21. Mee asher mitz•vo•tai ee•to ve•sho•mer la•a•so•tan ze hoo asher
ye•e•ha•va•ni ve•o•ha•vee a•hoov le•Avi va•a•ni o•ha•ve•hoo ve•e•lav et•va•da.

---

22. Judas saith unto him, not Iscariot, Lord, how is it that thou wilt manifest
thyself unto us, and not unto the world?

22. Λέγει αὐτῷ Ἰούδας, οὐχ ὁ Ἰσκαριώτης, Κύριε, καὶ τί γέγονεν ὅτι ἡμῖν
μέλλεις ἐμφανίζειν σεαυτόν, καὶ οὐχὶ τῷ κόσμῳ;

22. Legei auto Youdas, ouch 'o Yskarioteis, Kurie, kai ti gegonen 'oti 'eimin
melleis emphanizein seauton, kai ouchi to kosmo?

כב. וַיֹּאמֶר אֵלָיו יְהוּדָה לֹא אִישׁ-קְרִיּוֹת וְאֵיכָה אֲדֹנִי תִּקְרֶינָה כָּאֵלֶּה כִּי תָבֹא לְהִתְוַדַּע אֵלֵינוּ וְלֹא
:לְעוֹלָם

22. Va•yo•mer elav Yehooda lo Eesh - K`ri•yot ve•ey•cha Adoni tik•re•na
cha•e•le ki ta•vo le•hit•va•da e•ley•noo ve•lo la•o•lam?

---

23. Jesus answered and said unto him, If a man love me, he will keep my words: and my Father will love him, and we will come unto him, and make our abode with him.

Greek/Transliteration
23. Ἀπεκρίθη Ἰησοῦς καὶ εἶπεν αὐτῷ, Ἐάν τις ἀγαπᾷ με, τὸν λόγον μου τηρήσει, καὶ ὁ πατήρ μου ἀγαπήσει αὐτόν, καὶ πρὸς αὐτὸν ἐλευσόμεθα, καὶ μονὴν παρ᾽ αὐτῷ ποιήσομεν.

23. Apekrithei Yeisous kai eipen auto, Ean tis agapa me, ton logon mou teireisei, kai 'o pateir mou agapeisei auton, kai pros auton eleusometha, kai monein par auto poieisomen.

Hebrew/Transliteration
כג. וַיַּעַן יֵשׁוּעַ וַיֹּאמֶר אֵלָיו אִישׁ כִּי יֶאֱהָבַנִי יִשְׁמֹר אֶת-דְּבָרָי וְאָבִי יֶאֱהַב אֹתוֹ וְאֵלָיו נָבֹא וְשָׁכַנּוּ אִתּוֹ:

23. Va•ya•an Yeshua va•yo•mer elav eesh ki ye•e•ha•va•ni yish•mor et - de•va•rai ve•Avi ye•e•hav o•to ve•e•lav na•vo ve•sha•cha•noo ee•to.

---

24. He that loveth me not keepeth not my sayings: and the word which ye hear is not mine, but the Father's which sent me.

Greek/Transliteration
24. Ὁ μὴ ἀγαπῶν με, τοὺς λόγους μου οὐ τηρεῖ· καὶ ὁ λόγος ὃν ἀκούετε οὐκ ἔστιν ἐμός, ἀλλὰ τοῦ πέμψαντός με πατρός.

24. 'O mei agapon me, tous logous mou ou teirei. kai 'o logos 'on akouete ouk estin emos, alla tou pempsantos me patros.

Hebrew/Transliteration
כד. וְאִישׁ אֲשֶׁר לֹא יֶאֱהָבַנִי הוּא לֹא יִשְׁמֹר אֶת-דְּבָרָי וְהַדְּבָרִים אֲשֶׁר שְׁמַעְתֶּם לֹא מִלִּבִּי יָצָאוּ כִּי אִם-מִפִּי הָאָב:אֲשֶׁר שְׁלָחָנִי.

24. Ve•eesh asher lo ye•e•ha•va•ni hoo lo yish•mor et - de•va•rai ve•had•va•rim asher sh`ma•a•tem lo mi•li•bi ya•tza•oo ki eem - mi•pi ha•Av asher sh`la•cha•ni.

---

25. These things have I spoken unto you, being yet present with you.

Greek/Transliteration
25. Ταῦτα λελάληκα ὑμῖν παρ᾽ ὑμῖν μένων.

25. Tauta lelaleika 'umin par 'umin menon.

Hebrew/Transliteration

:כה. אֶת-אֵלֶּה דִּבַּרְתִּי אֲלֵיכֶם בְּעוֹד שִׁבְתִּי עִמָּכֶם

25. Et - ele di•bar•ti aley•chem be•od shiv•ti ee•ma•chem.

---

26. But the Comforter, which is the Holy Ghost, whom the Father will send in my name, he shall teach you all things, and bring all things to your remembrance, whatsoever I have said unto you.

Greek/Transliteration

26. Ὁ δὲ παράκλητος, τὸ πνεῦμα τὸ ἅγιον, ὃ πέμψει ὁ πατὴρ ἐν τῷ ὀνόματί μου, ἐκεῖνος ὑμᾶς διδάξει πάντα, καὶ ὑπομνήσει ὑμᾶς πάντα ἃ εἶπον ὑμῖν.

26. 'O de parakleitos, to pneuma to 'agion, 'o pempsei 'o pateir en to onomati mou, ekeinos 'umas didaxei panta, kai 'upomneisei 'umas panta 'a eipon 'umin.

Hebrew/Transliteration

כו. וְהַמֵּלִיץ הוּא רוּחַ הַקֹּדֶשׁ אֲשֶׁר-יִשְׁלָחֵהוּ הָאָב בִּשְׁמִי יְלַמֶּדְכֶם אֶת-כֹּל וְאָז תִּזְכְּרוּ כֹּל אֲשֶׁר-הִגַּדְתִּי
:לָכֶם

26. Ve•ha•me•litz hoo Roo•ach ha•Ko•desh asher - yish•la•che•hoo ha•Av bish•mi ye•la•med•chem et - kol ve•az tiz•ke•roo kol asher - hi•ga•d`ti la•chem.

Rabbinic Jewish Commentary

The word used there, as here, signifies an "advocate", and is so rendered, 1Jo_2:1, a patron, one that pleads and defends, the cause of another, before kings and princes; so the Jewish writers (z) use the word פרקליט, (advocate) same with παρακλητος, here, and give this as the sense of it: and which agrees well enough with the work and office of the Spirit of God, who has promised to the apostles to speak in them and for them, when they should be brought before kings and governors for Yeshua's sake.

(z) Maimon. & Bartenora in Pirke Abot, c. 4. sect. 11.

---

27. Peace I leave with you, my peace I give unto you: not as the world giveth, give I unto you. Let not your heart be troubled, neither let it be afraid.

Greek/Transliteration

27. Εἰρήνην ἀφίημι ὑμῖν, εἰρήνην τὴν ἐμὴν δίδωμι ὑμῖν· οὐ καθὼς ὁ κόσμος δίδωσιν, ἐγὼ δίδωμι ὑμῖν. Μὴ ταρασσέσθω ὑμῶν ἡ καρδία, μηδὲ δειλιάτω.

27. Eireinein aphieimi 'umin, eireinein tein emein didomi 'umin. ou kathos 'o kosmos didosin, ego didomi 'umin. Mei tarassestho 'umon 'ei kardia, meide deilyato.

Hebrew/Transliteration

כז. וְעַתָּה שָׁלוֹם אֲנִי מַגִּיחַ לָכֶם אֶת-שְׁלוֹמִי אֲנִי נֹתֵן לָכֶם לֹא כַאֲשֶׁר יִתֵּן הָעוֹלָם אֲנִי נֹתֵן לָכֶם אַל-
יִרְגַּז לִבְכֶם:וְאַל-יֵחָת.

27. Ve•a•ta sha•lom ani ma•ni•ach la•chem et - sh`lo•mi ani no•ten la•chem lo cha•a•sher yi•ten ha•o•lam ani no•ten la•chem al - yir•gaz lib•chem ve•al - ye•chat.

Rabbinic Jewish Commentary

Yeshua does not say "peace be to you"; which was the more usual form of salutation among the Jews, and which was used by them when they met, and not at parting; especially we have no instance of such a form as here used, by dying persons taking their leaves of their relations and friends. It must indeed be owned that the phrase, "to give peace", is with them the same as to salute, or wish health and prosperity. Take two or three of their rules as instances of it;

"Whoever knows his friend, that he is used לִיתֵן לוֹ שׁלוֹם (a), "to give him peace"; he shall prevent him with peace (i.e. salute him first), as it is said, "seek peace and pursue it"; but if he "gives" it to him, and he does not return it, he shall be called a robber."

Again, "(b) A man may not go into the house of a stranger, on his feast day, לִיתֵן לוֹ שׁלוֹם, "to give peace unto him" (or salute him); if he finds him in the street, he may give it to him with a low voice, and his head hanging down;"

Once (c) more, "A man לֹא יִתֵּן שׁלוֹם, "not give peace to", or salute his master, nor return peace to him in the way that they give it to friends, and they return it to one another."

Likewise it must be owned, that when they saluted persons of distinction, such as princes, nobles, and doctors, they repeated the word "peace" (d), though never to any strangers.

(a) T. Bab. Beracot, fol. 6. 2. (b) T. Bab. Gittin, fol. 62. 1. Maimon. Obede Cochabim, c. 10. sect. 5. (c) Maimon. Talmud Tora, c. 5. sect. 5. (d) T. Bab. Gittin, fol. 62. 1. Maimon. Hilch. Melacim. c. 10. sect. 12.

---

28. Ye have heard how I said unto you, I go away, and come again unto you. If ye loved me, ye would rejoice, because I said, I go unto the Father: for my Father is greater than I.

28. Ἠκούσατε ὅτι ἐγὼ εἶπον ὑμῖν, Ὑπάγω καὶ ἔρχομαι πρὸς ὑμᾶς. Εἰ ἠγαπᾶτέ με, ἐχάρητε ἂν ὅτι εἶπον, Πορεύομαι πρὸς τὸν πατέρα· ὅτι ὁ πατήρ μου μείζων μού ἐστιν.

28. Eikousate 'oti ego eipon 'umin, 'Upago kai erchomai pros 'umas. Ei eigapate me, echareite an 'oti eipon, Poreuomai pros ton patera. 'oti 'o pateir mou meizon mou estin.

כח. הֲלֹא שְׁמַעְתֶּם אֶת אֲשֶׁר-אָמַרְתִּי אֲלֵיכֶם כִּי אֵלֵךְ מִכֶּם וְעוֹד אֲשׁוּב אֲלֵיכֶם לוּ אֲהַבְתֶּם אֹתִי הֱיִיתֶם שְׂמֵחִים:בְּאָמְרִי לָכֶם כִּי-הֹלֵךְ אֲנִי אֶל-הָאָב כִּי הָאָב גָּדוֹל מִמֶּנִּי

28. Ha•lo sh`ma•a•tem et asher - amar•ti aley•chem ki e•lech mi•kem ve•od a•shoov aley•chem loo ahav•tem o•ti he•yi•tem s`me•chim be•om•ri la•chem ki - ho•lech ani el - ha•Av ki ha•Av ga•dol mi•me•ni.

---

29. And now I have told you before it come to pass, that, when it is come to pass, ye might believe.

29. Καὶ νῦν εἴρηκα ὑμῖν πρὶν γενέσθαι· ἵνα, ὅταν γένηται, πιστεύσητε.

29. Kai nun eireika 'umin prin genesthai. 'ina, 'otan geneitai, pisteuseite.

כט. וְעַתָּה הִגַּדְתִּי לָכֶם הַדָּבָר טֶרֶם בֹּאוֹ לְבַעֲבוּר תַּאֲמִינוּ אַחֲרֵי בֹאוֹ:

29. Ve•a•ta hi•ga•d`ti la•chem ha•da•var te•rem bo•oo le•va•a•voor ta•a•mi•noo a•cha•rey vo•o.

---

30. Hereafter I will not talk much with you: for the prince of this world cometh, and hath nothing in me.

30. Οὐκέτι πολλὰ λαλήσω μεθ᾽ ὑμῶν· ἔρχεται γὰρ ὁ τοῦ κόσμου ἄρχων, καὶ ἐν ἐμοὶ οὐκ ἔχει οὐδέν·

30. Ouketi polla laleiso meth 'umon. erchetai gar 'o tou kosmou archon, kai en emoi ouk echei ouden.

ל. וַאֲנִי לֹא-אוּכַל עוֹד לְהַרְבּוֹת אֲמָרִים עִמָּכֶם מִפְּנֵי שַׂר-הָעוֹלָם אֲשֶׁר יָבֹא וְהוּא אֵין-לוֹ חֵלֶק בִּי כָּל-מְאוּמָה:

30. Va•a•ni lo - oo•chal od le•har•bot ama•rim ee•ma•chem mip•ney sar - ha•o•lam asher ya•vo ve•hoo eyn - lo che•lek bi kol - me•oo•ma.

Rabbinic Jewish Commentary

The Jews say (e), that Samuel, by whom they mean the accuser, when he wrestled with Jacob, שלא מצא בו עון, "could not find any iniquity in him", he had committed; but this is only true of Jacob's antitype: for though his emissaries sought diligently for it, they could find none in him; though he had sin upon him, he had none in him; the sins of his people were imputed to him, but he had no sin inherent in him; hence, though he the Messiah was "cut off", according to Dan_9:26, "but not for himself"; which by the Septuagint is rendered και κριμα ουκ εστιν εν αυτω, "but there is no judgment" or "condemnation in him", i.e. no cause of condemnation; which agrees with what is here said.

(e) Tzeror Hammor, fol. 44. 2.

---

31. But that the world may know that I love the Father; and as the Father gave me commandment, even so I do. Arise, let us go hence.

Greek/Transliteration

31. ἀλλ᾽ ἵνα γνῷ ὁ κόσμος ὅτι ἀγαπῶ τὸν πατέρα, καὶ καθὼς ἐνετείλατό μοι ὁ πατήρ, οὕτως ποιῶ. Ἐγείρεσθε, ἄγωμεν ἐντεῦθεν.

31. all 'ina gno 'o kosmos 'oti agapo ton patera, kai kathos eneteilato moi 'o pateir, 'outos poio. Egeiresthe, agomen enteuthen.

Hebrew/Transliteration

לא. רַק לְבַעֲבוּר יֵדַע הָעוֹלָם כִּי אֲנִי אֹהֵב אֶת-הָאָב וְעֹשֶׂה אֲנִי כְּכֹל אֲשֶׁר צִוַּנִי הָאָב לְכוּ וְנֵלְכָה מִזֶּה:

31. Rak le•va•a•voor ye•da ha•o•lam ki ani o•hev et - ha•Av ve•o•se ani ke•chol asher tzi•va•ni ha•Av le•choo ve•nel•cha mi•ze.

Rabbinic Jewish Commentary

arise, let us go hence: The phrase is Jewish; so R. Jose and R. Chiyah say to one another as they sat, קום ונידך, "arise, and let us go hence" (f).

(f) Zohar in Exod. fol. 74. 1.

John, Chapter 15

1. I am the true vine, and my Father is the husbandman.

Greek/Transliteration
1. Ἐγώ εἰμι ἡ ἄμπελος ἡ ἀληθινή, καὶ ὁ πατήρ μου ὁ γεωργός ἐστιν.

1. Ego eimi 'ei ampelos 'ei aleithinei, kai 'o pateir mou 'o georgos estin.

Hebrew/Transliteration
א. אָנֹכִי הַגֶּפֶן גֶּפֶן אֱמֶת וְאָבִי הַכֹּרֵם:

1. Ano•chi ha•ge•fen ge•fen emet ve•Avi ha•ko•rem.

Rabbinic Jewish Commentary
Yeshua is the "true" vine; not that he is really and literally so, without a figure; but he is, as the Syriac renders it, נפתא דשררא, "the vine of truth". Just as Israel is called a noble vine, wholly a right seed, זרע אמת, "a seed of truth", Jer_2:21; right genuine seed; or, as the Septuagint render it, "a vine", bringing forth fruit, πασαν αληθινην, "wholly true"; to which the allusion may be here. Yeshua is the noble vine, the most excellent of vines, wholly a right seed, in opposition to, and distinction from, the wild and unfruitful, or degenerate plant of a strange vine: to him agree all the properties of a right and real vine; he really and truly communicates life, sap, juice, nourishment, and fruitfulness to the several branches which are in him.

The metaphor Yeshua makes use of was well known to the Jews; for not only the Jewish church is often compared to a vine, but the Messiah too, according to them: thus the Targumist explains the phrase in Psa_80:15, "the branch thou madest strong for thyself", of the King Messiah: and indeed, by comparing it with Psa_80:17 it seems to be the true sense of the passage (g). The Cabalistic Rabbi's say (h), that the Shekinah is called, גפן, "a vine"; see Gen_49:11; where the Jews observe (i), the King Messiah is so called. The Jews (k) say, there was a golden vine that stood over the gate of the temple, and it was set upon props; and whoever offered a leaf, or a grape, or a cluster, (that is, a piece of gold to the temple, in the form of either of these,) bought it, and hung it upon it. And of this vine also Josephus (l) makes mention, as being in Herod's temple; of which he says, that it was over the doors (of the temple), under the edges of the wall, having clusters hanging down from it on high, which filled spectators with wonder as for the size of it, so for the art with which it was made. And elsewhere he says (m), the inward door in the porch was all covered with gold, and the whole wall about it; and it had over it golden vines, from whence hung clusters as big as the stature of a man: now whether Yeshua may refer to this, being near the temple, and in view of it, and point to it, and call himself the true vine, in distinction from it, which was only the representation of one; or whether he might take occasion, from the sight of a real vine, to compare himself to one, nay be considered; since it was usual with Yeshua, upon sight or mention of natural things, to take the opportunity of treating of spiritual ones: though it may be rather this discourse of the vine and branches might be occasioned by his speaking of the fruit of the vine, at the time he ate the passover, and instituted the ordinance of the supper.

And my Father is the husbandman; or vinedresser. So God is called by Philo the Jew (n), γεωργος αγαθος, "a good husbandman"; and the same the Targumist says of The *Word* of the LORD (o),

"And my *Word* shall be unto them, כאכרא טבא, "as a good husbandman"."

Now Yeshua says this of his Father, both with respect to himself the vine, and with respect to the branches that were in him: he was the husbandman to him; he planted the vine of his human nature, and filled it with all the graces of the Spirit; he supported it, upheld it, and made it strong for himself, for the purposes of his grace, and for his own glory; and took infinite delight in it, being to him a pleasant plant, a plant of renown. The concern this husbandman has with the branches, is expressed in the following verse.

(g) Vid. R. Mosem Hadersan in Galatin. de Arcan. Cathol. verit, l. 8. c. 4. (h) Zohar in Exod. fol. 70. 2. & Cabala denudata, par. 1. p. 241. (i) Zohar in Gen fol. 127. 3. (k) Misn. Middot, c. 3. sect. 8. T. Bab. Cholin, fol. 90. 2. & Tamid, fol. 29. 1, 2. (l) Antiqu. l. 15. c. 11. sect. 3. (m) De Bello Jud. l. 5. c. 5. sect. 4. (n) Leg. Allegor. l. 1. p. 48. (o) Targum in Hos. 11. 4.

---

2. Every branch in me that beareth not fruit he taketh away: and every branch that beareth fruit, he purgeth it, that it may bring forth more fruit.

Greek/Transliteration
2. Πᾶν κλῆμα ἐν ἐμοὶ μὴ φέρον καρπόν, αἴρει αὐτό· καὶ πᾶν τὸ καρπὸν φέρον, καθαίρει αὐτό, ἵνα πλείονα καρπὸν φέρῃ.

2. Pan kleima en emoi mei pheron karpon, airei auto. kai pan to karpon pheron, kathairei auto, 'ina pleiona karpon pherei.

Hebrew/Transliteration
ב. כָּל-זְמוֹרָה מִמֶּנִּי אֲשֶׁר לֹא תַעֲשֶׂה עֲנָבִים יִכְרָתֶנָּה וַאֲשֶׁר תַּעֲשֶׂה עֲנָבִים יְקַיְּמֶנָּה לְהַרְבּוֹת אֶת-פִּרְיָה:

2. Kol - z`mo•ra mi•me•ni asher lo ta•a•se ana•vim yich•re•te•na va•a•sher ta•a•se ana•vim ye•kai•me•na le•har•bot et - pir•ya.

Rabbinic Jewish Commentary
These different acts of the vinedresser "taking away" some branches, and "purging" others, are expressed by the Misnic Rabbi's (p) by פיסולה, and זירודה.

The former, the commentators (q) say, signifies to cut off the branches that are withered and perished, and are good for nothing; and the latter signifies the pruning of the vine when it has a superfluity of branches, or these extend themselves too far; when some are left, and others taken off.

(p) Misn. Sheviith, c, 2. sect. 3. (q) Maimon. & Bartenora in ib.

---

3. Now ye are clean through the word which I have spoken unto you.

Greek/Transliteration
3. Ἤδη ὑμεῖς καθαροί ἐστε διὰ τὸν λόγον ὃν λελάληκα ὑμῖν.

3. Eidei 'umeis katharoi este dya ton logon 'on lelaleika 'umin.

Hebrew/Transliteration
ג. וְאַתֶּם זַכִּים הִנְּכֶם כַּיּוֹם עַל-פִּי דְבָרַי אֲשֶׁר דִּבַּרְתִּי אֲלֵיכֶם:

3. Ve•a•tem za•kim hin•chem ka•yom al - pi de•va•rai asher di•bar•ti aley•chem.

---

4. Abide in me, and I in you. As the branch cannot bear fruit of itself, except it abide in the vine; no more can ye, except ye abide in me.

Greek/Transliteration
4. Μείνατε ἐν ἐμοί, κἀγὼ ἐν ὑμῖν. Καθὼς τὸ κλῆμα οὐ δύναται καρπὸν φέρειν ἀφ᾽ ἑαυτοῦ, ἐὰν μὴ μείνῃ ἐν τῇ ἀμπέλῳ, οὕτως οὐδὲ ὑμεῖς, ἐὰν μὴ ἐν ἐμοὶ μείνητε.

4. Meinate en emoi, kago en 'umin. Kathos to kleima ou dunatai karpon pherein aph 'eautou, ean mei meinei en tei ampelo, 'outos oude 'umeis, ean mei en emoi meineite.

Hebrew/Transliteration
ד. הֱיוּ דְבֵקִים בִּי וַאֲנִי בָכֶם כִּי כַּאֲשֶׁר הַזְּמֹרָה פְּרִי בַל-תַּעֲשֶׂה מֵאֵלֶיהָ אִם-לֹא דָבְקָה בַגָּפֶן כֵּן גַּם- אַתֶּם אִם-לֹא:תִדְבְּקוּן בִּי

4. He•yoo d`ve•kim bi va•a•ni va•chem ki ka•a•sher ha•z`mo•ra p`ri val - ta•a•se me•e•le•ha eem - lo dav•ka va•ga•fen ken gam - atem eem - lo tid•be•koon bi.

---

5. I am the vine, ye are the branches: He that abideth in me, and I in him, the same bringeth forth much fruit: for without me ye can do nothing.

Greek/Transliteration
5. Ἐγώ εἰμι ἡ ἄμπελος, ὑμεῖς τὰ κλήματα. Ὁ μένων ἐν ἐμοί, κἀγὼ ἐν αὐτῷ, οὗτος φέρει καρπὸν πολύν· ὅτι χωρὶς ἐμοῦ οὐ δύνασθε ποιεῖν οὐδέν.

5. Ego eimi 'ei ampelos, 'umeis ta kleimata. 'O menon en emoi, kago en auto, 'outos pherei karpon polun. 'oti choris emou ou dunasthe poiein ouden.

Hebrew/Transliteration
ה. אָנֹכִי הַגֶּפֶן וְאַתֶּם הַזְּמֹרוֹת הַדָּבֵק בִּי וְאָנִי בּוֹ הוּא יְשַׁוֶּה רֹב פֶּרִי כִּי בִּלְעָדַי לֹא תוּכְלוּ עֲשׂוֹת מְאוּמָה:

5. Ano•chi ha•ge•fen ve•a•tem ha•z`mo•rot ha•da•vek bi ve•a•nee vo hoo ye•sha•ve rov p`ri ki bil•a•dai lo tooch•loo asot me•oo•ma.

---

6. If a man abide not in me, he is cast forth as a branch, and is withered; and men gather them, and cast them into the fire, and they are burned.

Greek/Transliteration
6. Ἐὰν μή τις μείνῃ ἐν ἐμοί, ἐβλήθη ἔξω ὡς τὸ κλῆμα, καὶ ἐξηράνθη, καὶ συνάγουσιν αὐτὰ καὶ εἰς τὸ πῦρ βάλλουσιν, καὶ καίεται.

6. Ean mei tis meinei en emoi, ebleithei exo 'os to kleima, kai exeiranthei, kai sunagousin auta kai eis to pur ballousin, kai kaietai.

Hebrew/Transliteration
ו. מִי אֲשֶׁר לֹא יִדְבַּק בִּי יַשְׁלִיכֵהוּ כַּנֵּצֶר אֲשֶׁר יִיבַשׁ וּמְקֹשֵׁשׁ יְקֹשְׁשׁוּ וּנְתָנוֹ לָאֵשׁ וְהָיָה לְבָעֵר:

6. Mee asher lo yid•bak vi yash•li•choo•hoo ke•ne•tzer asher yi•vash oom•ko•shesh ye•ko•she•she•noo oon•ta•no la•esh ve•ha•ya le•va•er.

Rabbinic Jewish Commentary
into the fire, and they are burned, or "it is burned"; for nothing else is such a branch good for. This may respect either the gnawings of conscience, that distress of mind, if not despair, that fearful looking for of judgment, and fiery indignation that will fall upon them as a people and a nation.

"Son of man, how is the vine tree more than any other tree, or than a branch that is among the trees of the forest?" (Eze_15:2)

The fruit of the vine tree is good, but its wood is of no use: a vine tree, if it bears fruit, is valuable; but if it does not, it is of no account. The people of the Jews are often compared to a vine, who, while they brought forth good fruit, were in esteem; but, when they became like an empty and fruitless vine, were rejected as good for nothing, Psa 80:8; they were originally no better than others; what they had were owing to the grace and goodness of God; and when they degenerated, they were the worst of all people.

So Jarchi paraphrases the words,

"Not of the vine in the vineyards, which bears fruit, speak I unto thee; but of the branch of the vine which grows in the forests;" (c)

And so Kimchi, "I do not ask thee of the vine tree which beareth fruit, for that is valuable; but of the branch (of the wild vine) which is among the trees of the forest, and is as they that do not bear fruit, concerning that I ask thee; for even it is not as the trees of the forest; for the trees of the forest, though they do not bear fruit, they are fit to do work of them, to make vessels of them, and to floor houses with them; but the wood of this vine is not so."

(c) הזמורה "surculus", Cocceius; "surculus vitis", Starckius; "vitis sylvestris", Munster. So Ben Melech interprets the branch, of a vine.

---

7. If ye abide in me, and my words abide in you, ye shall ask what ye will, and it shall be done unto you.

Greek/Transliteration
7. Ἐὰν μείνητε ἐν ἐμοί, καὶ τὰ ῥήματά μου ἐν ὑμῖν μείνῃ, ὃ ἐὰν θέλητε αἰτήσεσθε, καὶ γενήσεται ὑμῖν.

7. Ean meineite en emoi, kai ta 'reimata mou en 'umin meinei, 'o ean theleite aiteisesthe, kai geneisetai 'umin.

Hebrew/Transliteration
ז. אִם-בִּי אַתֶּם דְּבֵקִים וּדְבָרַי שְׁמֻרִים בָּכֶם תִּשְׁאָלוּ וְיֵעָשֶׂה לָכֶם כְּכָל-מִשְׁאֲלוֹת לִבְּכֶם:

7. Eem - bi atem d`ve•kim oo•d`va•rai sh`moo•rim ba•chem tish•a•loo ve•ye•a•se la•chem ke•chol - mish•a•lot lib•chem.

---

8. Herein is my Father glorified, that ye bear much fruit; so shall ye be my disciples.

Greek/Transliteration
8. Ἐν τούτῳ ἐδοξάσθη ὁ πατήρ μου, ἵνα καρπὸν πολὺν φέρητε· καὶ γενήσεσθε ἐμοὶ μαθηταί.

8. En touto edoxasthei 'o pateir mou, 'ina karpon polun phereite. kai geneisesthe emoi matheitai.

Hebrew/Transliteration
ח. בְּזֹאת יִגְדַּל כְּבוֹד אָבִי כִּי-תַעֲשׂוּ רֹב פֶּרִי וִהְיִיתֶם לִי לְתַלְמִידִים:

8. Be•zot yig•dal k`vod Avi ki - ta•a•soo rov p`ri vi•hi•yee•tem li le•tal•mi•dim.

---

9. As the Father hath loved me, so have I loved you: continue ye in my love.

9. Καθὼς ἠγάπησέν με ὁ πατήρ, κἀγὼ ἠγάπησα ὑμᾶς· μείνατε ἐν τῇ ἀγάπῃ τῇ ἐμῇ.

9. Kathos eigapeisen me 'o pateir, kago eigapeisa 'umas. meinate en tei agapei tei emei.

Hebrew/Transliteration
ט. כַּאֲשֶׁר אָהַב אֹתִי הָאָב כֵּן אֲהַבְתִּי אֶתְכֶם חֵסוּ בְּאַהֲבָתִי תָּמִיד:

9. Ka•a•sher ahav o•ti ha•Av ken ahav•ti et•chem cha•soo ve•a•ha•va•ti ta•mid.

---

10. If ye keep my commandments, ye shall abide in my love; even as I have kept my Father's commandments, and abide in his love.

Greek/Transliteration
10. Ἐὰν τὰς ἐντολάς μου τηρήσητε, μενεῖτε ἐν τῇ ἀγάπῃ μου· καθὼς ἐγὼ τὰς ἐντολὰς τοῦ πατρός μου τετήρηκα, καὶ μένω αὐτοῦ ἐν τῇ ἀγάπῃ.

10. Ean tas entolas mou teireiseite, meneite en tei agapei mou. kathos ego tas entolas tou patros mou teteireika, kai meno autou en tei agapei.

Hebrew/Transliteration
י. אִם אֶת-מִצְוֹתַי תִּשְׁמְרוּ תֵּחֲסוּ בְּאַהֲבָתִי תָּמִיד כַּאֲשֶׁר גַּם-אָנֹכִי מִצְוֹת אָבִי שָׁמַרְתִּי וְאֶחֱסֶה בְּאַהֲבָתוֹ תָּמִיד:

10. Eem et - mitz•vo•tai tish•me•roo te•che•soo ve•a•ha•va•ti ta•mid ka•a•sher gam - ano•chi mitz•vot Avi sha•mar•ti ve•e•che•se ve•a•ha•va•to ta•mid.

---

11. These things have I spoken unto you, that my joy might remain in you, and that your joy might be full.

Greek/Transliteration
11. Ταῦτα λελάληκα ὑμῖν, ἵνα ἡ χαρὰ ἡ ἐμὴ ἐν ὑμῖν μείνῃ, καὶ ἡ χαρὰ ὑμῶν πληρωθῇ.

11. Tauta lelaleika 'umin, 'ina 'ei chara 'ei emei en 'umin meinei, kai ei chara 'umon pleirothei.

Hebrew/Transliteration

יא. אֶת-הַדְּבָרִים הָאֵלֶּה דִּבַּרְתִּי אֲלֵיכֶם לְבַעֲבוּר תִּהְיֶה שִׂמְחָתִי עֲלֵיכֶם וְשִׂמְחַתְכֶם תִּמָּלֵא נַפְשְׁכֶם:

11. Et - ha•d`va•rim ha•e•le di•bar•ti aley•chem le•va•a•voor ti•hi•ye sim•cha•ti aley•chem ve•sim•chat•chem ti•ma•le naf•she•chem.

---

12. This is my commandment, That ye love one another, as I have loved you.

Greek/Transliteration

12. Αὕτη ἐστὶν ἡ ἐντολὴ ἡ ἐμή, ἵνα ἀγαπᾶτε ἀλλήλους, καθὼς ἠγάπησα ὑμᾶς.

12. 'Autei estin 'ei entolei 'ei emei, 'ina agapate alleilous, kathos eigapeisa 'umas.

Hebrew/Transliteration

יב. וְזֹאת הִיא מִצְוָתִי לְאַהֲבָה אִישׁ אֶת-אָחִיו כַּאֲשֶׁר אָנֹכִי אֲהַבְתִּי אֶתְכֶם:

12. Ve•zot hee mitze•va•ti le•a•ha•va eesh et - a•chiv ka•a•sher ano•chi ahav•ti et•chem.

---

13. Greater love hath no man than this, that a man lay down his life for his friends.

Greek/Transliteration

13. Μείζονα ταύτης ἀγάπην οὐδεὶς ἔχει, ἵνα τις τὴν ψυχὴν αὐτοῦ θῇ ὑπὲρ τῶν φίλων αὐτοῦ.

13. Meizona tauteis agapein oudeis echei, 'ina tis tein psuchein autou thei 'uper ton philon autou.

Hebrew/Transliteration

יג. אֵין לְאִישׁ אַהֲבָה רַבָּה מֵאֲשֶׁר אִם יִתֵּן אֶת-נַפְשׁוֹ בְּעַד יְדִידָיו:

13. Eyn le•eesh a•ha•va ra•ba me•a•sher eem yi•ten et - naf•sho be•ad ye•di•dav.

---

14. Ye are my friends, if ye do whatsoever I command you.

14. Ὑμεῖς φίλοι μου ἐστέ, ἐὰν ποιῆτε ὅσα ἐγὼ ἐντέλλομαι ὑμῖν.

14. 'Umeis philoi mou este, ean poieite 'osa ego entellomai 'umin.

יד. וְאַתֶּם יְדִידַי הִנְּכֶם רַק אִם-תַּעֲשׂוּ אֵת אֲשֶׁר-אָנֹכִי מְצַוֶּה אֶתְכֶם:

14. Ve•a•tem ye•di•dai hin•chem rak eem - ta•a•soo et asher - ano•chi me•tza•ve et•chem.

---

15. Henceforth I call you not servants; for the servant knoweth not what his lord doeth: but I have called you friends; for all things that I have heard of my Father I have made known unto you.

15. Οὐκέτι ὑμᾶς λέγω δούλους, ὅτι ὁ δοῦλος οὐκ οἶδεν τί ποιεῖ αὐτοῦ ὁ κύριος· ὑμᾶς δὲ εἴρηκα φίλους, ὅτι πάντα ἃ ἤκουσα παρὰ τοῦ πατρός μου ἐγνώρισα ὑμῖν.

15. Ouketi 'umas lego doulous, 'oti 'o doulos ouk oiden ti poiei autou 'o kurios. 'umas de eireika philous, 'oti panta 'a eikousa para tou patros mou egnorisa 'umin.

טו. לֹא עוֹד עֲבָדִים אֶקְרָא לָכֶם כִּי הָעֶבֶד אֵינֶנּוּ יֹדֵעַ אֶת-אֲשֶׁר אֲדֹנָיו עֹשֶׂה אַךְ לָכֶם קָרָאתִי יְדִידַי כִּי הוֹדַעְתִּי:אֶתְכֶם כֹּל אֲשֶׁר שָׁמַעְתִּי מִפִּי אָבִי

15. Lo od a•va•dim ek•ra la•chem ki ha•e•ved ey•ne•noo yo•de•a et - asher a•do•nav o•se ach la•chem ka•ra•ti ye•di•dai ki ho•da•a•ti et•chem kol asher sha•ma•a•ti mi•pi Avi.

---

16. Ye have not chosen me, but I have chosen you, and ordained you, that ye should go and bring forth fruit, and that your fruit should remain: that whatsoever ye shall ask of the Father in my name, he may give it you.

16. Οὐχ ὑμεῖς με ἐξελέξασθε, ἀλλ᾽ ἐγὼ ἐξελεξάμην ὑμᾶς, καὶ ἔθηκα ὑμᾶς, ἵνα ὑμεῖς ὑπάγητε καὶ καρπὸν φέρητε, καὶ ὁ καρπὸς ὑμῶν μένῃ· ἵνα ὅ τι ἂν αἰτήσητε τὸν πατέρα ἐν τῷ ὀνόματί μου, δῷ ὑμῖν.

16. Ouch 'umeis me exelexasthe, all ego exelexamein 'umas, kai etheika 'umas, 'ina 'umeis 'upageite kai karpon phereite, kai 'o karpos 'umon menei. 'ina 'o ti an aiteiseite ton patera en to onomati mou, do 'umin.

Hebrew/Transliteration

טז. לֹא אַתֶּם בְּחַרְתֶּם בִּי רַק-אֲנִי בָּחַרְתִּי בָּכֶם וַאֲנִי מִנִּיתִי אֶתְכֶם לָלֶכֶת וְלַעֲשׂוֹת פְּרִי וּפֶרְיְכֶם יַעֲמֹד - לָעַד וְכָל:דָּבָר אֲשֶׁר תִּשְׁאֲלוּ מֵאֵת הָאָב בִּשְׁמִי אֹתוֹ יִתֵּן לָכֶם

16. Lo atem be•char•tem bi rak - ani ba•char•ti ba•chem va•a•ni mi•ni•ti et•chem la•le•chet ve•la•a•sot p`ri oo•fer•ye•chem ya•a•mod la•ad ve•chol - da•var asher tish•a•loo me•et ha•Av bish•mi o•to yi•ten la•chem.

Rabbinic Jewish Commentary

Ye have not chosen me, but I have chosen you,.... Not but that they had made choice of him as their Lord and Master, Saviour and Redeemer; but not first, he was before hand with them; he chose them, before they chose him; so that his choice of them was entirely free, did not arise from any character, motive, or condition in them: the allusion is to a custom of the Jews, the reverse of which Yeshua acted; with whom it was usual for disciples to choose their own masters, and not masters their disciples: hence that advice of R. Joshuah ben Perachiah, said (r) to be the master of Yeshua of Nazareth,

עשה לך רב (s), "make", provide, or chose "thyself a master", and get thyself a companion."

Those words in Son_2:16; "My beloved is mine, and I am his", are thus paraphrased by the Jews (t);

"He hath chosen me, and I have chosen him".

(r) Ganz Tzemach David, fol. 24. 2. (s) Pirke Abot, c. 1. sect. 6. (t) Zohar in Exod. fol. 9. 1.

---

17. These things I command you, that ye love one another.

Greek/Transliteration
17. Ταῦτα ἐντέλλομαι ὑμῖν, ἵνα ἀγαπᾶτε ἀλλήλους.

17. Tauta entellomai 'umin, 'ina agapate alleilous.

Hebrew/Transliteration
:יז. וְזֹאת הִיא הַמִּצְוָה אֲשֶׁר אֲנִי מְצַוֶּה אֶתְכֶם כִּי אִישׁ אֶת-רֵעֵהוּ תֶּאֱהָבוּן

17. Ve•zot hee ha•mitz•va asher ani me•tza•ve et•chem ki eesh et - re•e•hoo te•e•ha•voon.

---

18. If the world hate you, ye know that it hated me before it hated you.

18. Εἰ ὁ κόσμος ὑμᾶς μισεῖ, γινώσκετε ὅτι ἐμὲ πρῶτον ὑμῶν μεμίσηκεν.

18. Ei 'o kosmos 'umas misei, ginoskete 'oti eme proton 'umon memiseiken.

יח. אִם-הָעוֹלָם יִשְׂנָא אֶתְכֶם הֲלֹא יְדַעְתֶּם כִּי אֹתִי שָׂנֵא לִפְנֵיכֶם:

18. Eem - ha•o•lam yis•na et•chem ha•lo ye•da•a•tem ki o•ti sa•ne lif•ney•chem.

---

19. If ye were of the world, the world would love his own: but because ye are not of the world, but I have chosen you out of the world, therefore the world hateth you.

19. Εἰ ἐκ τοῦ κόσμου ἦτε, ὁ κόσμος ἂν τὸ ἴδιον ἐφίλει· ὅτι δὲ ἐκ τοῦ κόσμου οὐκ ἐστέ, ἀλλ᾽ ἐγὼ ἐξελεξάμην ὑμᾶς ἐκ τοῦ κόσμου, διὰ τοῦτο μισεῖ ὑμᾶς ὁ κόσμος.

19. Ei ek tou kosmou eite, 'o kosmos an to idion ephilei. 'oti de ek tou kosmou ouk este, all ego exelexamein 'umas ek tou kosmou, dya touto misei 'umas 'o kosmos.

יט. לוּ הֱיִיתֶם מִן-הָעוֹלָם הָעוֹלָם יֶאֱהַב אֵת אֲשֶׁר-לוֹ אַךְ יַעַן כִּי-אֵין אַתֶּם מִן-הָעוֹלָם וַאֲנִי בָחַרְתִּי בָכֶם מִן-הָעוֹלָם עַל-כֵּן יִשְׂנָא אֶתְכֶם הָעוֹלָם -

19. Loo he•yi•tem min - ha•o•lam ha•o•lam ye•e•hav et asher - lo ach ya•an ki - eyn atem min - ha•o•lam va•a•ni va•char•ti va•chem min - ha•o•lam al - ken yis•na et•chem ha•o•lam.

Rabbinic Jewish Commentary
The Jews distinguish the disciples of the wise men, from אינשי דעלמא, "the men of the world" (u), pretending that they were not; but this is a character that only belongs to the disciples of Yeshua, in consequence of their being called by him out of it.

(u) T. Bab. Kiddushin, fol. 80. 2.

---

20. Remember the word that I said unto you, The servant is not greater than his lord. If they have persecuted me, they will also persecute you; if they have kept my saying, they will keep yours also.

20. Μνημονεύετε τοῦ λόγου οὗ ἐγὼ εἶπον ὑμῖν, Οὐκ ἔστιν δοῦλος μείζων τοῦ κυρίου αὐτοῦ. Εἰ ἐμὲ ἐδίωξαν, καὶ ὑμᾶς διώξουσιν· εἰ τὸν λόγον μου ἐτήρησαν, καὶ τὸν ὑμέτερον τηρήσουσιν.

20. Mneimoneuete tou logou 'ou ego eipon 'umin, Ouk estin doulos meizon tou kuriou autou. Ei eme edioxan, kai 'umas dioxousin. ei ton logon mou eteireisan, kai ton 'umeteron teireisousin.

כ. זִכְרוּ אֶת-הַדָּבָר אֲשֶׁר אָמַרְתִּי לָכֶם הָעֶבֶד אֵינֶנּוּ גָדוֹל מֵאֲדֹנָיו אִם-רָדְפוּ אֹתִי גַּם-אֶתְכֶם יִרְדֹּפוּ אִם-שָׁמְרוּ:אֶת-דְּבָרַי גַּם אֶת-דִּבְרֵיכֶם יִשְׁמֹרוּ

20. Zich•roo et - ha•da•var asher amar•ti la•chem ha•e•ved ey•ne•noo ga•dol me•a•do•nav eem - rad•foo o•ti gam - et•chem yir•do•foo eem - sham•roo et - de•va•rai gam et - div•rey•chem yish•mo•roo.

---

21. But all these things will they do unto you for my name's sake, because they know not him that sent me.

21. Ἀλλὰ ταῦτα πάντα ποιήσουσιν ὑμῖν διὰ τὸ ὄνομά μου, ὅτι οὐκ οἴδασιν τὸν πέμψαντά με.

21. Alla tauta panta poieisousin 'umin dya to onoma mou, 'oti ouk oidasin ton pempsanta me.

כא. אֲבָל כָּל-אֵלֶּה יַעֲשׂוּ לָכֶם בַּעֲבוּר שְׁמִי כִּי אֵינָם יֹדְעִים אֶת-שֹׁלְחִי:

21. Aval kol - ele ya•a•soo la•chem ba•a•voor sh`mi ki ey•nam yod•eem et - shol•chi.

---

22. If I had not come and spoken unto them, they had not had sin: but now they have no cloke for their sin.

22. Εἰ μὴ ἦλθον καὶ ἐλάλησα αὐτοῖς, ἁμαρτίαν οὐκ εἶχον· νῦν δὲ πρόφασιν οὐκ ἔχουσιν περὶ τῆς ἁμαρτίας αὐτῶν.

22. Ei mei eilthon kai elaleisa autois, 'amartian ouk eichon. nun de prophasin ouk echousin peri teis 'amartias auton.

כב. לוּלֵי בָאתִי וְהִגַּדְתִּי לָהֶם לֹא הוֹשַׁת עֲלֵיהֶם חֵטְא אֲבָל עַתָּה אֵין מַעֲנֶה בְּפִיהֶם עַל-חַטֹּאתָם:

22. Loo•ley va•ti ve•hi•ga•de•tee la•hem lo hoo•shat aley•hem chet aval ata
eyn ma•a•ne be•fi•hem al - cha•to•tam.

---

23. He that hateth me hateth my Father also.

Greek/Transliteration
23. Ὁ ἐμὲ μισῶν, καὶ τὸν πατέρα μου μισεῖ.

23. 'O eme mison, kai ton patera mou misei.

Hebrew/Transliteration
כג. הַשֹּׂנֵא אֹתִי הוּא שֹׂנֵא גַּם-אֶת-אָבִי:

23. Ha•so•ne o•ti hoo so•ne gam - et - Avi.

---

24. If I had not done among them the works which none other man did, they
had not had sin: but now have they both seen and hated both me and my
Father.

Greek/Transliteration
24. Εἰ τὰ ἔργα μὴ ἐποίησα ἐν αὐτοῖς ἃ οὐδεὶς ἄλλος πεποίηκεν, ἁμαρτίαν οὐκ
εἶχον· νῦν δὲ καὶ ἑωράκασιν καὶ μεμισήκασιν καὶ ἐμὲ καὶ τὸν πατέρα μου.

24. Ei ta erga mei epoieisa en autois 'a oudeis allos pepoieiken, 'amartian ouk
eichon. nun de kai 'eorakasin kai memiseikasin kai eme kai ton patera mou.

Hebrew/Transliteration
כד. לוּלֵי עָשִׂיתִי לִפְנֵיהֶם הַמַּעֲשִׂים אֲשֶׁר לֹא עָשָׂה אִישׁ אַחֵר לֹא-הוּשַׁת עֲלֵיהֶם חֵטְא אֲבָל עַתָּה רָאוּ
אֶת-מַעֲשַׂי:וַיִּשְׂנְאוּ גַם-אֹתִי וְגַם אֶת-אָבִי

24. Loo•ley a•si•ti lif•ney•hem ha•ma•a•sim asher lo asa eesh a•cher lo -
hoo•shat aley•hem chet aval ata ra•oo et - ma•a•sai va•yis•ne•oo gam - o•ti
ve•gam et - Avi.

---

25. But this cometh to pass, that the word might be fulfilled that is written in
their law, They hated me without a cause.

Greek/Transliteration
25. Ἀλλ᾽ ἵνα πληρωθῇ ὁ λόγος ὁ γεγραμμένος ἐν τῷ νόμῳ αὐτῶν ὅτι
Ἐμίσησάν με δωρεάν.

25. All 'ina pleirothei 'o logos 'o gegrammenos en to nomo auton 'oti Emiseisan me dorean.

:כה. אַךְ לְמַלֹּאת הַדָּבָר הַכָּתוּב בְּתוֹרָתָם וְשִׂינְאַת חִנָּם שְׂנֵאוּנִי

25. Ach le•ma•lot ha•da•var ha•ka•toov be•to•ra•tam ve•sin•at chi•nam s`ne•oo•ni.

Rabbinic Jewish Commentary

This sin of hating without a cause, is represented by the Jews as a very heinous one, and as the reason of the destruction of the second temple; under which they observe, that men studied in the law, and in the commandments, and in doing of good; and therefore ask why it was destroyed? the answer is, because there was under it, שנאת חנם, "hatred without a cause": to teach us, that hatred without a cause is equal to the three (capital) transgressions, idolatry, adultery, and murder, for which they say the first temple was destroyed (w). This is a tacit acknowledgment that the sin here mentioned was a reigning one, or that it much abounded in the time of Yeshua.

"Let not them that are mine enemies wrongfully rejoice over me: *neither* let them wink with the eye *that hate me without a cause*." (Psa_35:19)

"*They that hate me without a cause* are more than the hairs of mine head: they that would destroy me, *being* mine enemies wrongfully, are mighty: then I restored *that* which I took not away." (Psa_69:4)

(w) T. Bab, Yoma, fol. 9. 2. Hieros. Yoma, fol. 38. 3.

---

26. But when the Comforter is come, whom I will send unto you from the Father, even the Spirit of truth, which proceedeth from the Father, he shall testify of me:

Greek/Transliteration
26. Ὅταν δὲ ἔλθῃ ὁ παράκλητος, ὃν ἐγὼ πέμψω ὑμῖν παρὰ τοῦ πατρός, τὸ πνεῦμα τῆς ἀληθείας, ὃ παρὰ τοῦ πατρὸς ἐκπορεύεται, ἐκεῖνος μαρτυρήσει περὶ ἐμοῦ·

26. 'Otan de elthei 'o parakleitos, 'on ego pempso 'umin para tou patros, to pneuma teis aleitheias, 'o para tou patros ekporeuetai, ekeinos martureisei peri emou.

Hebrew/Transliteration
כו. אַךְ כַּאֲשֶׁר יָבֹא הַמֵּלִיץ אֲשֶׁר אֶשְׁלָחֵהוּ אֲלֵיכֶם מֵאֵת הָאָב הֲלֹא הוּא רוּחַ הָאֱמֶת הַיֹּצֵא מִמְּקוֹר הָאָב הוּא:יָעֵד-לִי

26. Ach ka•a•sher ya•vo ha•me•litz asher esh•la•che•noo aley•chem me•et ha•Av ha•lo hoo Roo•ach ha•e•met ha•yo•tze mim•kor ha•Av hoo ya•ed - li.

Rabbinic Jewish Commentary

The ancient Jews (x) spoke of the Comforter just in the same language; "The Spirit of God", in Gen_1:2; they say is the Holy Spirit, דנפיק מאלהים, "Which proceedeth from God": very pertinently does Yeshua take notice of this his character here, when he was about to speak of him as his testifier:

(x) Zohar in Gen. fol. 1. 4.

---

27. And ye also shall bear witness, because ye have been with me from the beginning.

Greek/Transliteration

27. καὶ ὑμεῖς δὲ μαρτυρεῖτε, ὅτι ἀπ᾽ ἀρχῆς μετ᾽ ἐμοῦ ἐστε.

27. kai 'umeis de martureite, 'oti ap archeis met emou este.

Hebrew/Transliteration

כז. וְגַם-אַתֶּם תָּעִידוּ לִי כִּי הֱיִיתֶם עִמָּדִי מֵרֹאשׁ:

27. Ve•gam - atem ta•ee•doo li ki he•yi•tem ee•ma•di me•rosh.

John, Chapter 16

1. These things have I spoken unto you, that ye should not be offended.

Greek/Transliteration
1. Ταῦτα λελάληκα ὑμῖν, ἵνα μὴ σκανδαλισθῆτε.

1. Tauta lelaleika 'umin, 'ina mei skandalistheite.

Hebrew/Transliteration
א. אֶת-אֵלֶּה דִּבַּרְתִּי אֲלֵיכֶם לְמַעַן לֹא תִכָּשֵׁלוּ:

1. Et - ele di•bar•ti aley•chem le•ma•an lo ti•ka•she•loo.

---

2. They shall put you out of the synagogues: yea, the time cometh, that whosoever killeth you will think that he doeth God service.

Greek/Transliteration
2. Ἀποσυναγώγους ποιήσουσιν ὑμᾶς· ἀλλ᾽ ἔρχεται ὥρα, ἵνα πᾶς ὁ ἀποκτείνας ὑμᾶς δόξῃ λατρείαν προσφέρειν τῷ θεῷ.

2. Aposunagogous poieisousin 'umas. all erchetai 'ora, 'ina pas 'o apokteinas 'umas doxei latreian prospherein to theo.

Hebrew/Transliteration
ב. הֵם יְנַדּוּ אֶתְכֶם מִתּוֹךְ הַקָּהָל וְאַף הִגִּיעַ הַזְּמָן אֲשֶׁר כָּל-הֹרֵג אֶתְכֶם יַחֲשֹׁב בְּלִבּוֹ כִּי קָרְבָּן הוּא מַקְרִיב:לֵאלֹהִים

2. Hem ye•na•doo et•chem mi•toch ha•ka•hal ve•af hi•gi•a haz•man asher kol - ho•reg et•chem ya•cha•shov be•li•bo ki kor•ban hoo mak•riv le•Elohim.

Rabbinic Jewish Commentary
The Jews had made a law already, that he that confessed that Yeshua was the Messiah, should be cast out of their synagogues; and they had put it in execution upon the blind man Yeshua restored to sight, for his profession of faith in him; which struck such a terror upon the people, that even many of the chief rulers who believed that Yeshua was the true Messiah, durst not confess him, because of this law; for it was what they could not bear the thoughts of, to be deemed and treated as heretics and apostates, and the vilest of wretches: for this putting out of the synagogue, was not the lesser excommunication, which was called נדוי "Niddui", and was a "separation" from a particular synagogue for a while; but the greater excommunication, either by חרם, "Cherem", or שמתא, "Shammatha"; when a person was cut out from the whole body of the Jewish church, called often the synagogue, or congregation of the people; and was devoted and consigned to utter destruction, which was the height of their ecclesiastical power, their rage and malice could carry them to; and this the apostles were to expect; nay, not only this,

but to have their lives taken away by ruffians, under a pretence of zeal for the service of God, and interest of religion:

yea, the time cometh, that whosoever killeth you, will think that he doth God service; (y) "With a zeal for God", his honour and glory; and valued themselves much upon such butcheries and inhumanity, and thought, as Yeshua here says, that they "did God service"; or as the Syriac renders it, דקורבנא מקרב, "offered a sacrifice to God", and so the Arabic and Ethiopic: and indeed this is a rule the Jews (z), and which they form upon the instance and example of Phinehas;

"That whoever sheds the blood of wicked men, (and such they reckoned the apostles and followers of Yeshua to be,) כאלו הקריב קרבן, "it is all one as if he offered a sacrifice".

(y) Jarchi & Bartenora in Misn. Sanhedrin, c. 9. sect. 6. (z) Bemidbar Rabbit, Parash, 21. fol. 229. 3.

---

3. And these things will they do unto you, because they have not known the Father, nor me.

Greek/Transliteration
3. Καὶ ταῦτα ποιήσουσιν, ὅτι οὐκ ἔγνωσαν τὸν πατέρα οὐδὲ ἐμέ.

3. Kai tauta poieisousin, 'oti ouk egnosan ton patera oude eme.

Hebrew/Transliteration
ג. וְאֶת-אֵלֶּה יַעֲשׂוּ לָכֶם כִּי גַּם-אֶת-אָבִי וְגַם-אֹתִי לֹא יָדָעוּ:

3. Ve•et - ele ya•a•soo la•chem ki gam - et - Avi ve•gam - o•ti lo ya•da•oo.

---

4. But these things have I told you, that when the time shall come, ye may remember that I told you of them. And these things I said not unto you at the beginning, because I was with you.

Greek/Transliteration
4. Ἀλλὰ ταῦτα λελάληκα ὑμῖν, ἵνα ὅταν ἔλθῃ ἡ ὥρα, μνημονεύητε αὐτῶν, ὅτι ἐγὼ εἶπον ὑμῖν. Ταῦτα δὲ ὑμῖν ἐξ ἀρχῆς οὐκ εἶπον, ὅτι μεθ᾽ ὑμῶν ἤμην.

4. Alla tauta lelaleika 'umin, 'ina 'otan elthei 'ei 'ora, mneimoneueite auton, 'oti ego eipon 'umin. Tauta de 'umin ex archeis ouk eipon, 'oti meth 'umon eimein.

ד. וָאַגִּיד לָכֶם אֶת-אֵלֶּה לְמַעַן תִּזְכְּרוּ אֹתָם בְּעִתָּם כִּי אֲנִי הַמְדַבֵּר אֲלֵיכֶם וְלֹא הִקְדַּמְתִּי לְהַגִּיד לָכֶם כָּל-זֶה:מֵרֹאשׁ בַּעֲבוּר כִּי הָיִיתִי עִמָּכֶם

4. Va•a•gid la•chem et - ele le•ma•an tiz•ke•roo o•tam be•ee•tam ki ani ha•me•da•ber aley•chem ve•lo hik•dam•ti le•ha•gid la•chem kol - ze me•rosh ba•a•voor ki ha•yi•ti ee•ma•chem.

---

5. But now I go my way to him that sent me; and none of you asketh me, Whither goest thou?

5. Νῦν δὲ ὑπάγω πρὸς τὸν πέμψαντά με, καὶ οὐδεὶς ἐξ ὑμῶν ἐρωτᾷ με, Ποῦ ὑπάγεις;

5. Nun de 'upago pros ton pempsanta me, kai oudeis ex 'umon erota me, Pou 'upageis?

ה. וְעַתָּה הִנְנִי הֹלֵךְ אֶל - שֹׁלְחִי וְאֵין עוֹד אִישׁ מִכֶּם שֹׁאֵל אֹתִי אָנָה אַתָּה הֹלֵךְ:

5. Ve•a•ta hi•ne•ni ho•lech el - shol•chi ve•eyn od eesh mi•kem sho•el o•ti ana ata ho•lech?

---

6. But because I have said these things unto you, sorrow hath filled your heart.

6. Ἀλλ᾽ ὅτι ταῦτα λελάληκα ὑμῖν, ἡ λύπη πεπλήρωκεν ὑμῶν τὴν καρδίαν.

6. All 'oti tauta lelaleika 'umin, 'ei lupei pepleiroken 'umon tein kardian.

ו. רַק לִבְכֶם מָלֵא עֶצֶב בְּדַבְּרִי אֲלֵיכֶם הַדְּבָרִים הָאֵלֶּה:

6. Rak lib•chem ma•le etzev be•dab•ri aley•chem ha•d`va•rim ha•e•le.

---

7. Nevertheless I tell you the truth; It is expedient for you that I go away: for if I go not away, the Comforter will not come unto you; but if I depart, I will send him unto you.

7. Ἀλλ᾽ ἐγὼ τὴν ἀλήθειαν λέγω ὑμῖν· συμφέρει ὑμῖν ἵνα ἐγὼ ἀπέλθω· ἐὰν γὰρ
ἐγὼ μὴ ἀπέλθω, ὁ παράκλητος οὐκ ἐλεύσεται πρὸς ὑμᾶς· ἐὰν δὲ πορευθῶ,
πέμψω αὐτὸν πρὸς ὑμᾶς.

7. All ego tein aleitheyan lego 'umin. sumpherei 'umin 'ina ego apeltho. ean
gar ego mei apeltho, 'o parakleitos ouk eleusetai pros 'umas. ean de poreutho,
pempso auton pros 'umas.

ז. אוּלָם אֱמֶת אַגִּיד לָכֶם כִּי טוֹב לָכֶם אֲשֶׁר אֵלֵךְ כִּי אִם-לֹא אֵלֵךְ לֹא-יָבֹא הַמֵּלִיץ אֲלֵיכֶם וְכִי-אֵלֵךְ
אֶשְׁלָחֶנּוּ:אֲלֵיכֶם

7. Oo•lam emet agid la•chem ki tov la•chem asher e•lech ki eem - lo e•lech lo -
ya•vo ha•me•litz aley•chem ve•chi - e•lech esh•la•che•noo aley•chem.

---

8. And when he is come, he will reprove the world of sin, and of righteousness,
and of judgment:

8. Καὶ ἐλθὼν ἐκεῖνος ἐλέγξει τὸν κόσμον περὶ ἁμαρτίας καὶ περὶ δικαιοσύνης
καὶ περὶ κρίσεως·

8. Kai elthon ekeinos elegxei ton kosmon peri 'amartias kai peri dikaiosuneis
kai peri kriseos.

ח. וְהוּא בְּבֹאוֹ יוֹכַח אֶת-הָעוֹלָם עַל-דְּבַר חֵטְא צְדָקָה וּמִשְׁפָּט:

8. Ve•hoo be•vo•o yo•chach et - ha•o•lam al - de•var chet tze•da•ka
oo•mish•pat.

---

9. Of sin, because they believe not on me;

9. περὶ ἁμαρτίας μέν, ὅτι οὐ πιστεύουσιν εἰς ἐμέ·

9. peri 'amartias men, 'oti ou pisteuousin eis eme.

ט. עַל-חֵטְא עַל-אֲשֶׁר לֹא הֶאֱמִינוּ בִי:

9. Al - chet al - asher lo he•e•mi•noo vi.

10. Of righteousness, because I go to my Father, and ye see me no more;

Greek/Transliteration
10. περὶ δικαιοσύνης δέ, ὅτι πρὸς τὸν πατέρα μου ὑπάγω, καὶ οὐκέτι θεωρεῖτέ με·

10. peri dikaiosuneis de, 'oti pros ton patera mou 'upago, kai ouketi theoreite me.

Hebrew/Transliteration
י. עַל-צְדָקָה עַל-כִּי הֹלֵךְ אֲנִי אֶל-אָבִי וְלֹא תִרְאֻנִי עוֹד:

10. Al - tze•da•ka al - ki ho•lech ani el - Avi ve•lo tir•oo•ni od.

---

11. Of judgment, because the prince of this world is judged.

Greek/Transliteration
11. περὶ δὲ κρίσεως, ὅτι ὁ ἄρχων τοῦ κόσμου τούτου κέκριται.

11. peri de kriseos, 'oti 'o archon tou kosmou toutou kekritai.

Hebrew/Transliteration
יא. וְעַל-מִשְׁפָּט עַל-כִּי יַרְשִׁיעַ אֶת-שַׂר הָעוֹלָם הַזֶּה בְּהִשָּׁפְטוֹ:

11. Ve•al - mish•pat al - ki yar•shi•a et - sar ha•o•lam ha•ze be•hi•shaf•to.

---

12. I have yet many things to say unto you, but ye cannot bear them now.

Greek/Transliteration
12. Ἔτι πολλὰ ἔχω λέγειν ὑμῖν, ἀλλ᾽ οὐ δύνασθε βαστάζειν ἄρτι.

12. Eti polla echo legein 'umin, all ou dunasthe bastazein arti.

Hebrew/Transliteration
יב. וְעוֹד לִי מִלִּין רַבּוֹת לְהוֹדִיעֲכֶם אַךְ לֹא-תוּכְלוּ שְׂאֵת אוֹתָן כַּיּוֹם:

12. Ve•od li mi•lin ra•bot le•ho•di•a•chem ach lo - tooch•loo s`et o•tan ka•yom.

---

13. Howbeit when he, the Spirit of truth, is come, he will guide you into all truth: for he shall not speak of himself; but whatsoever he shall hear, that shall he speak: and he will shew you things to come.

13. Ὅταν δὲ ἔλθῃ ἐκεῖνος, τὸ πνεῦμα τῆς ἀληθείας, ὁδηγήσει ὑμᾶς εἰς πᾶσαν τὴν ἀλήθειαν· οὐ γὰρ λαλήσει ἀφ᾽ ἑαυτοῦ, ἀλλ᾽ ὅσα ἂν ἀκούσῃ λαλήσει, καὶ τὰ ἐρχόμενα ἀναγγελεῖ ὑμῖν.

13. 'Otan de elthei ekeinos, to pneuma teis aleitheias, 'odeigeisei 'umas eis pasan tein aleitheyan. ou gar laleisei aph 'eautou, all 'osa an akousei laleisei, kai ta erchomena anangelei 'umin.

יג. וְרוּחַ הָאֱמֶת בְּבֹאוֹ יַנְחֶה אֶתְכֶם אֶל-הָאֱמֶת כֻּלָּהּ כִּי לֹא מִלִּבּוֹ יְדַבֵּר כִּי אִם אֶת-אֲשֶׁר יִשְׁמַע יַשְׁמִיעַ וְיַגִּיד:אֶת-הָאֹתִיּוֹת לְאָחוֹר

13. Ve•Roo•ach ha•e•met be•vo•o yan•che et•chem el - ha•e•met koo•la ki lo mi•li•bo ye•da•ber ki eem et - asher yish•ma yash•mi•a ve•ya•gid et - ha•o•ti•yot le•a•chor.

Rabbinic Jewish Commentary

The Jews (y) have a notion of the Holy Ghost being a guide into all wisdom and knowledge.

"R. Phinehas says, the Holy Spirit rested upon Joseph from his youth to the day of his death, and "guided him into all wisdom", as a shepherd leads his flock, according to Psa_80:1;"

(y) Pirke Eliezer, c. 39.

---

14. He shall glorify me: for he shall receive of mine, and shall shew it unto you.

14. Ἐκεῖνος ἐμὲ δοξάσει, ὅτι ἐκ τοῦ ἐμοῦ λήψεται, καὶ ἀναγγελεῖ ὑμῖν.

14. Ekeinos eme doxasei, 'oti ek tou emou leipsetai, kai anangelei 'umin.

יד. הוּא יְגַדֵּל כְּבוֹדִי כִּי יִקַּח מִשֶּׁלִּי וְהִגִּיד לָכֶם:

14. Hoo ye•ga•del ke•vo•di ki yi•kach mi•she•li ve•hi•gid la•chem.

---

15. All things that the Father hath are mine: therefore said I, that he shall take of mine, and shall shew it unto you.

15. Πάντα ὅσα ἔχει ὁ πατὴρ ἐμά ἐστιν· διὰ τοῦτο εἶπον, ὅτι ἐκ τοῦ ἐμοῦ λαμβάνει, καὶ ἀναγγελεῖ ὑμῖν.

15. Panta 'osa echei 'o pateir ema estin. dya touto eipon, 'oti ek tou emou lambanei, kai anangelei 'umin.

טז. כֹּל אֲשֶׁר לְאָבִי לִי הוּא עַל־כֵּן אָמַרְתִּי מִשֶּׁלִי יִקַּח וְהִגִּיד לָכֶם:

15. Kol asher le•Avi li hoo al - ken amar•ti mi•she•li yi•kach ve•hi•gid la•chem.

---

16. A little while, and ye shall not see me: and again, a little while, and ye shall see me, because I go to the Father.

16. Μικρὸν καὶ οὐ θεωρεῖτέ με, καὶ πάλιν μικρὸν καὶ ὄψεσθέ με, ὅτι ὑπάγω πρὸς τὸν πατέρα.

16. Mikron kai ou theoreite me, kai palin mikron kai opsesthe me, 'oti 'upago pros ton patera.

טז. עוֹד כִּמְעַט רֶגַע וְלֹא תִרְאֶנִי עוֹד וְעוֹד כִּמְעַט רֶגַע וְתִרְאֶנִי כִּי אֲנִי הֹלֵךְ אֶל־אָבִי:

16. Od kim•at re•ga ve•lo tir•oo•ni od ve•od kim•at re•ga ve•tir•oo•ni ki ani ho•lech el - Avi.

---

17. Then said some of his disciples among themselves, What is this that he saith unto us, A little while, and ye shall not see me: and again, a little while, and ye shall see me: and, Because I go to the Father?

17. Εἶπον οὖν ἐκ τῶν μαθητῶν αὐτοῦ πρὸς ἀλλήλους, Τί ἐστιν τοῦτο ὃ λέγει ἡμῖν, Μικρὸν καὶ οὐ θεωρεῖτέ με, καὶ πάλιν μικρὸν καὶ ὄψεσθέ με; καὶ ὅτι Ἐγὼ ὑπάγω πρὸς τὸν πατέρα;

17. Eipon oun ek ton matheiton autou pros alleilous, Ti estin touto 'o legei 'eimin, Mikron kai ou theoreite me, kai palin mikron kai opsesthe me? kai 'oti Ego 'upago pros ton patera?

יז. וְיֵשׁ מִתַּלְמִידָיו אֲשֶׁר נִדְבְּרוּ אָז אִישׁ אֶל-רֵעֵהוּ מַה-זֶּה אֲשֶׁר אָמַר אֵלֵינוּ עוֹד כִּמְעַט רֶגַע וְלֹא תִרְאוּנִי וְעוֹד:כִּמְעַט רֶגַע וְתִרְאוּנִי וְכִי אֲנִי הֹלֵךְ אֶל-הָאָב

17. Ve•yesh mi•tal•mi•dav asher nid•be•roo az eesh el - re•e•hoo ma - ze asher amar e•ley•noo od kim•at re•ga ve•lo tir•oo•ni ve•od kim•at re•ga ve•tir•oo•ni ve•chi ani ho•lech el - ha•Av?

---

18. They said therefore, What is this that he saith, A little while? we cannot tell what he saith.

18. Ἔλεγον οὖν, Τοῦτο τί ἐστιν ὃ λέγει, τὸ μικρόν; Οὐκ οἴδαμεν τί λαλεῖ.

18. Elegon oun, Touto ti estin 'o legei, to mikron? Ouk oidamen ti lalei.

יח. וַיֹּאמְרוּ מַה-זֶּה כִּמְעַט רֶגַע אֲשֶׁר אָמַר וַאֲנַחְנוּ לֹא נֵדַע מָה הוּא מְדַבֵּר:

18. Va•yom•roo ma - ze kim•at re•ga asher amar va•a•nach•noo lo ne•da ma hoo me•da•ber.

---

19. Now Jesus knew that they were desirous to ask him, and said unto them, Do ye inquire among yourselves of that I said, A little while, and ye shall not see me: and again, a little while, and ye shall see me?

19. Ἔγνω οὖν ὁ Ἰησοῦς ὅτι ἤθελον αὐτὸν ἐρωτᾶν, καὶ εἶπεν αὐτοῖς, Περὶ τούτου ζητεῖτε μετ᾽ ἀλλήλων, ὅτι εἶπον, Μικρὸν καὶ οὐ θεωρεῖτέ με, καὶ πάλιν μικρὸν καὶ ὄψεσθέ με;

19. Egno oun 'o Yeisous 'oti eithelon auton erotan, kai eipen autois, Peri toutou zeiteite met alleilon, 'oti eipon, Mikron kai ou theoreite me, kai palin mikron kai opsesthe me?

יט. וַיַּרְא יֵשׁוּעַ כִּי מְבַקְשִׁים הֵם לִשְׁאֹל אֶת-פִּיהוּ וַיֹּאמֶר אֲלֵיהֶם הֲתַחְקְרוּן זֶה אֶת-זֶה עַל כִּי-אָמַרְתִּי עוֹד כִּמְעַט רֶגַע:וְלֹא תִרְאֻנִי וְעוֹד כִּמְעַט רֶגַע וְתִרְאֻנִי

19. Va•yar Yeshua ki me•vak•shim hem lish•ol et - pi•hoo va•yo•mer aley•hem ha•tach•ke•roon ze et - ze al ki - amar•ti od kim•at re•ga ve•lo tir•oo•ni ve•od kim•at re•ga ve•tir•oo•ni?

---

20. Verily, verily, I say unto you, That ye shall weep and lament, but the world shall rejoice: and ye shall be sorrowful, but your sorrow shall be turned into joy.

20. Ἀμὴν ἀμὴν λέγω ὑμῖν ὅτι κλαύσετε καὶ θρηνήσετε ὑμεῖς, ὁ δὲ κόσμος χαρήσεται· ὑμεῖς δὲ λυπηθήσεσθε, ἀλλ᾽ ἡ λύπη ὑμῶν εἰς χαρὰν γενήσεται.

20. Amein amein lego 'umin 'oti klausete kai threineisete 'umeis, 'o de kosmos chareisetai. 'umeis de lupeitheisesthe, all 'ei lupei 'umon eis charan geneisetai.

Hebrew/Transliteration

כ. אָמֵן אָמֵן אֲנִי אֹמֵר לָכֶם כִּי אַתֶּם תִּבְכּוּ וְתֵילִילוּ וּבְנֵי הָעוֹלָם יָגִילוּ אַתֶּם תִּתְאַבְּלוּ אַךְ אֶבְלְכֶם יֵהָפֵךְ לְשָׂשׂוֹן:

20. Amen amen ani o•mer la•chem ki atem tiv•koo ve•tey•li•loo oov•ney ha•o•lam ya•gi•loo atem tit•ab•loo ach ev•le•chem ye•ha•fech le•sa•son.

---

21. A woman when she is in travail hath sorrow, because her hour is come: but as soon as she is delivered of the child, she remembereth no more the anguish, for joy that a man is born into the world.

21. Ἡ γυνὴ ὅταν τίκτῃ λύπην ἔχει, ὅτι ἦλθεν ἡ ὥρα αὐτῆς· ὅταν δὲ γεννήσῃ τὸ παιδίον, οὐκέτι μνημονεύει τῆς θλίψεως, διὰ τὴν χαρὰν ὅτι ἐγεννήθη ἄνθρωπος εἰς τὸν κόσμον.

21. 'Ei gunei 'otan tiktei lupein echei, 'oti eilthen 'ei 'ora auteis. 'otan de genneisei to paidion, ouketi mneimoneuei teis thlipseos, dya tein charan 'oti egenneithei anthropos eis ton kosmon.

Hebrew/Transliteration

כא. אִשָּׁה תָּחִיל בַּחֲבָלֶיהָ כִּי בָאָה עִתָּהּ וְאַחֲרֵי אֲשֶׁר הִמְלִיטָה אֶת-הַוָּלָד לֹא-תִזְכֹּר עוֹד חֶבְלָהּ - מִשִּׂמְחָתָהּ כִּי:אִישׁ נוֹלַד בָּעוֹלָם

21. Ee•sha ta•chil ba•cha•va•le•ha ki va•ah ee•ta ve•a•cha•rey asher him•li•ta et - ha•va•lad lo - tiz•kor od chev•la mi•sim•cha•ta ki - eesh no•lad ba•o•lam.

Rabbinic Jewish Commentary

Much such a way of speaking is used by the Jews (z), who observe,

"If a woman brings forth a male child, all is forgot, and she repents (i.e. of her impatience, or any unbecoming expression in the time of labour), בשמחת הזכר, "for the joy of a man child".

And Yeshua seems to have respect to a prevailing notion among them, as well as many others, of the felicity of male children: it is a common saying with them (a),

"Blessed is he whose children are males, and woe to him whose children are females:"

For they say (b), "When שבא זכר בעולם, "that a man child comes into the world", peace comes into the world."

Now Yeshua, by this instance, illustrates the sorrow his disciples should have by his departure, and the joy that they should be possessed of upon his return to them; that as the pains of a woman in travail are very sharp and severe, and the distress of her mind, about the issue of things respecting herself and offspring, is very great, so would be the grief and trouble of the disciples on account of the death of their Lord and master: but as when a woman is safely delivered of a man child, she is so filled with joy, that her sorrow is remembered no more so should it be with them, when Yeshua should appear to them; all their trouble, concern, anxiety of mind, and fears, that attended them, would all vanish away, and they be distressed with them no more.

(z) Tzeror Hammor, fol. 98. 2. (a) T. Bab. Pesachim, fol. 65. 1. Kiddushin, fol. 82. 2. Bava Bathra, fol. 16. 2. Sanhedrin, fol. 100. 2. (b) T. Bab. Nidda, fol. 31. 2.

---

22. And ye now therefore have sorrow: but I will see you again, and your heart shall rejoice, and your joy no man taketh from you.

Greek/Transliteration
22. Καὶ ὑμεῖς οὖν λύπην μὲν νῦν ἔχετε· πάλιν δὲ ὄψομαι ὑμᾶς, καὶ χαρήσεται ὑμῶν ἡ καρδία, καὶ τὴν χαρὰν ὑμῶν οὐδεὶς αἴρει ἀφ᾽ ὑμῶν.

22. Kai 'umeis oun lupein men nun echete. palin de opsomai 'umas, kai chareisetai 'umon 'ei kardia, kai tein charan 'umon oudeis airei aph 'umon.

Hebrew/Transliteration
כב. וְגַם-אַתֶּם מְלֵאִים יָגוֹן כַּיּוֹם אַךְ עוֹד אָשׁוּב אֶרְאֶה אֶתְכֶם וְשָׂשׂ לִבְּכֶם וְשִׂמְחַתְכֶם לֹא-יִקַּח מִכֶּם גָּבֶר:

22. Ve•gam - atem me•le•eem ya•gon ka•yom ach od a•shoov er•eh et•chem ve•sas lib•chem ve•sim•chat•chem lo - yi•kach mi•kem ga•ver.

---

23. And in that day ye shall ask me nothing. Verily, verily, I say unto you, Whatsoever ye shall ask the Father in my name, he will give it you.

---

23. Καὶ ἐν ἐκείνῃ τῇ ἡμέρᾳ ἐμὲ οὐκ ἐρωτήσετε οὐδέν. Ἀμὴν ἀμὴν λέγω ὑμῖν ὅτι ὅσα ἂν αἰτήσητε τὸν πατέρα ἐν τῷ ὀνόματί μου, δώσει ὑμῖν.

23. Kai en ekeinei tei 'eimera eme ouk eroteisete ouden. Amein amein lego 'umin 'oti 'osa an aiteiseite ton patera en to onomati mou, dosei 'umin.

כג. וּבַיּוֹם הַהוּא לֹא תִשְׁאָלוּ לִי כָל-שְׁאֵלָה אָמֵן אָמֵן אֲנִי אֹמֵר לָכֶם אִם תְּבַקְשׁוּ דָבָר מֵאֵת הָאָב יִתֵּן לָכֶם בִּשְׁמִי:

23. Oo•va•yom ha•hoo lo tish•a•loo li kol - sh`e•la Amen amen ani o•mer la•chem eem te•vak•shoo da•var me•et ha•Av yi•ten la•chem bish•mi.

---

24. Hitherto have ye asked nothing in my name: ask, and ye shall receive, that your joy may be full.

24. Ἕως ἄρτι οὐκ ᾐτήσατε οὐδὲν ἐν τῷ ὀνόματί μου· αἰτεῖτε, καὶ λήψεσθε, ἵνα ἡ χαρὰ ὑμῶν ᾖ πεπληρωμένη.

24. 'Eos arti ouk eiteisate ouden en to onomati mou. aiteite, kai leipsesthe, 'ina 'ei chara 'umon ei pepleiromenei.

כד. עַד-עַתָּה לֹא-בִקַשְׁתֶּם דָּבָר בִּשְׁמִי בַּקְשׁוּ וְתִקָּחוּ וְנַפְשְׁכֶם תִּמָּלֵא שִׂמְחָה:

24. Ad - ata lo - vi•kash•tem da•var bish•mi bak•shoo ve•tik•choo ve•naf•she•chem ti•ma•le sim•cha.

---

25. These things have I spoken unto you in proverbs: but the time cometh, when I shall no more speak unto you in proverbs, but I shall shew you plainly of the Father.

25. Ταῦτα ἐν παροιμίαις λελάληκα ὑμῖν· ἀλλ᾽ ἔρχεται ὥρα ὅτε οὐκέτι ἐν παροιμίαις λαλήσω ὑμῖν, ἀλλὰ παρρησίᾳ περὶ τοῦ πατρὸς ἀναγγελῶ ὑμῖν.

25. Tauta en paroimiais lelaleika 'umin. all erchetai 'ora 'ote ouketi en paroimiais laleiso 'umin, alla parreisia peri tou patros anangelo 'umin.

כה. אֶת-אֵלֶּה בִּמְשָׁלִים דִּבַּרְתִּי אֲלֵיכֶם אַךְ הִגִּיעַ הַמּוֹעֵד וְלֹא אֲדַבֵּר אֲלֵיכֶם עוֹד בִּמְשָׁלִים כִּי אִם-בְּמִלִּים בְּרֻרוֹת:אַגִּדְכֶם עַל-דְּבַר הָאָב

25. Et - ele bim•sha•lim di•bar•ti aley•chem ach hi•gi•a ha•mo•ed ve•lo ada•ber aley•chem od bim•sha•lim ki eem - be•mi•lim be•roo•rot aged•chem al - de•var ha•Av.

---

26. At that day ye shall ask in my name: and I say not unto you, that I will pray the Father for you:

26. Ἐν ἐκείνῃ τῇ ἡμέρᾳ ἐν τῷ ὀνόματί μου αἰτήσεσθε· καὶ οὐ λέγω ὑμῖν ὅτι ἐγὼ ἐρωτήσω τὸν πατέρα περὶ ὑμῶν·

26. En ekeinei tei 'eimera en to onomati mou aiteisesthe. kai ou lego 'umin 'oti ego eroteiso ton patera peri 'umon.

כו. בַּיּוֹם הַהוּא מִשְׁאֱלוֹתֵיכֶם בִּשְׁמִי תִּשְׁאָלוּ וְאֵינֶנִּי אֹמֵר לָכֶם כִּי אֲנִי אַעְתִּיר בַּעַדְכֶם אֶל-הָאָב:

26. Ba•yom ha•hoo mish•alo•tey•chem bish•mi tish•a•loo ve•ey•ne•ni o•mer la•chem ki ani a•a•tir ba•ad•chem el - ha•Av.

---

27. For the Father himself loveth you, because ye have loved me, and have believed that I came out from God.

27. αὐτὸς γὰρ ὁ πατὴρ φιλεῖ ὑμᾶς, ὅτι ὑμεῖς ἐμὲ πεφιλήκατε, καὶ πεπιστεύκατε ὅτι ἐγὼ παρὰ τοῦ θεοῦ ἐξῆλθον.

27. autos gar 'o pateir philei 'umas, 'oti 'umeis eme pephileikate, kai pepisteukate 'oti ego para tou theou exeilthon.

כז. כִּי-הָאָב גַּם-הוּא אֹהֵב אֶתְכֶם עֵקֶב אֲשֶׁר אֲהַבְתֶּם אֹתִי וַתַּאֲמִינוּ כִּי-מֵאֵת הָאָב יָצָאתִי:

27. Ki - ha•Av gam - hoo o•hev et•chem e•kev asher ahav•tem o•ti va•ta•a•mi•noo ki - me•et ha•Av ya•tza•ti.

---

28. I came forth from the Father, and am come into the world: again, I leave the world, and go to the Father.

28. Ἐξῆλθον παρὰ τοῦ πατρός, καὶ ἐλήλυθα εἰς τὸν κόσμον· πάλιν ἀφίημι τὸν κόσμον, καὶ πορεύομαι πρὸς τὸν πατέρα.

28. Exeilthon para tou patros, kai eleilutha eis ton kosmon. palin aphieimi ton kosmon, kai poreuomai pros ton patera.

Hebrew/Transliteration

כח. יָצָאתִי מֵאֵת הָאָב וּבָאתִי בָעוֹלָם וְעַתָּה אֶעֱזֹב אֶת-הָעוֹלָם וְאֵלֵךְ-לִי אֶל-הָאָב:

28. Ya•tza•ti me•et ha•Av oo•va•tee va•o•lam ve•a•ta a•shoov e•e•zov et - ha•o•lam ve•e•lech - li el - ha•Av.

---

29. His disciples said unto him, Lo, now speakest thou plainly, and speakest no proverb.

Greek/Transliteration

29. Λέγουσιν αὐτῷ οἱ μαθηταὶ αὐτοῦ, Ἴδε, νῦν παρρησίᾳ λαλεῖς, καὶ παροιμίαν οὐδεμίαν λέγεις.

29. Legousin auto 'oi matheitai autou, Yde, nun parreisia laleis, kai paroimian oudemian legeis.

Hebrew/Transliteration

כט. וַיֹּאמְרוּ תַלְמִידָיו הִנֵּה מִדַּבֵּר עַתָּה בְמִלִּים בְּרֵרוֹת וְלֹא תַבִּיעַ מָשָׁל:

29. Va•yom•roo tal•mi•dav hin•cha me•da•ber ata be•mi•lim be•roo•rot ve•lo ta•bi•ah ma•shal.

---

30. Now are we sure that thou knowest all things, and needest not that any man should ask thee: by this we believe that thou camest forth from God.

Greek/Transliteration

30. Νῦν οἴδαμεν ὅτι οἶδας πάντα, καὶ οὐ χρείαν ἔχεις ἵνα τίς σε ἐρωτᾷ· ἐν τούτῳ πιστεύομεν ὅτι ἀπὸ θεοῦ ἐξῆλθες.

30. Nun oidamen 'oti oidas panta, kai ou chreian echeis 'ina tis se erota. en touto pisteuomen 'oti apo theou exeilthes.

Hebrew/Transliteration

ל. עַתָּה יָדַעְנוּ כִּי-אַתָּה יֹדֵעַ כֹּל וְאֵין מַחְסֹר לְךָ אֲשֶׁר יִשְׁאָלְךָ אִישׁ בָּזֹאת נַאֲמִין כִּי מֵאֵת אֱלֹהִים יָצָאתָ:

30. Ata ya•da•a•noo ki - ata yo•de•a kol ve•eyn mach•sor le•cha asher yish•al•cha eesh ba•zot na•a•min ki me•et Elohim ya•tza•ta.

---

31. Jesus answered them, Do ye now believe?

Greek/Transliteration
31. Ἀπεκρίθη αὐτοῖς ὁ Ἰησοῦς, Ἄρτι πιστεύετε;

31. Apekrithei autois 'o Yeisous, Arti pisteuete?

Hebrew/Transliteration
לא. וַיַּעַן אֹתָם יֵשׁוּעַ הֲכִי תַאֲמִינוּ עָתָּה:

31. Va•ya•an o•tam Yeshua ha•chi ta•a•mi•noo ata?

---

32. Behold, the hour cometh, yea, is now come, that ye shall be scattered, every man to his own, and shall leave me alone: and yet I am not alone, because the Father is with me.

Greek/Transliteration
32. Ἰδού, ἔρχεται ὥρα καὶ νῦν ἐλήλυθεν, ἵνα σκορπισθῆτε ἕκαστος εἰς τὰ ἴδια, καὶ ἐμὲ μόνον ἀφῆτε· καὶ οὐκ εἰμὶ μόνος, ὅτι ὁ πατὴρ μετ᾽ ἐμοῦ ἐστιν.

32. Ydou, erchetai 'ora kai nun eleiluthen, 'ina skorpistheite 'ekastos eis ta idya, kai eme monon apheite. kai ouk eimi monos, 'oti 'o pateir met emou estin.

Hebrew/Transliteration
לב. הִנֵּה הַזְּמָן בָּא וּכְבָר הִגִּיעַ כִּי-תָפוּצוּ אִישׁ אִישׁ לְבֵיתוֹ וְאֹתִי תַעַזְבוּ לְבַדִּי אַךְ אֵינֶנִּי לְבַדִּי כִּי אָבִי עִמָּדִי:

32. Hee•ne haz•man ba ooch•var hi•gi•a ki - ta•foo•tzoo eesh eesh li•vey•to ve•o•ti ta•az•voo le•va•di ach ey•ne•ni le•va•di ki Avi ee•ma•di.

Rabbinic Jewish Commentary
"Awake, O sword, against my shepherd, and against the man *that is* my fellow, saith the LORD of hosts: smite the shepherd, and the sheep shall be scattered: and I will turn mine hand upon the little ones." (Zec_13:7)

Aben Ezra says this prophecy refers to the great wars which shall be in all the earth in the times of Messiah ben Joseph; but they regard the times of Yeshua the son of David, who is already come. The Targum is,

"Be revealed, O sword, against the king, and against the ruler his companion, who is like unto him."

And very remarkable, are the words of R. Samuel Marochianus (b), who, writing of the coming of the Messiah, says,

"I fear, O my Lord, that that which Zechariah the prophet said, "I will smite the Shepherd, and the sheep of the flock shall be scattered", was fulfilled when we smote the Shepherd of those little ones and holy apostles."

(b) Apud Burkium in loc. e Mullero.

---

33. These things I have spoken unto you, that in me ye might have peace. In the world ye shall have tribulation: but be of good cheer; I have overcome the world.

Greek/Transliteration

33. Ταῦτα λελάληκα ὑμῖν, ἵνα ἐν ἐμοὶ εἰρήνην ἔχητε. Ἐν τῷ κόσμῳ θλίψιν ἔχετε· ἀλλὰ θαρσεῖτε, ἐγὼ νενίκηκα τὸν κόσμον.

33. Tauta lelaleika 'umin, 'ina en emoi eireinein echeite. En to kosmo thlipsin echete. Alla tharseite, ego nenikeika ton kosmon.

Hebrew/Transliteration

לג. וַאֲנִי בַּדְּבָרִים הָאֵלֶּה בָּאתִי לְהַגִּיד לָכֶם כִּי בִי שָׁלוֹם יִהְיֶה-לָכֶם בָּעוֹלָם צָרָה תְּבוֹאַתְכֶם אַךְ- הִתְאַזְּרוּ עֹז אֲנִי:נִצַחְתִּי אֶת-הָעוֹלָם

33. Va•a•ni bad•va•rim ha•e•le ba•ti le•ha•gid la•chem ki vi sha•lom yi•hee•ye - la•chem ba•o•lam tza•ra t`vo•at•chem ach - hit•az•roo oz ani ni•tzach•ti et - ha•o•lam.

John, Chapter 17

1. These words spake Jesus, and lifted up his eyes to heaven, and said, Father, the hour is come; glorify thy Son, that thy Son also may glorify thee:

Greek/Transliteration

1. Ταῦτα ἐλάλησεν ὁ Ἰησοῦς, καὶ ἐπῆρεν τοὺς ὀφθαλμοὺς αὐτοῦ εἰς τὸν οὐρανόν, καὶ εἶπεν, Πάτερ, ἐλήλυθεν ἡ ὥρα· δόξασόν σου τὸν υἱόν, ἵνα καὶ ὁ υἱός σου δοξάσῃ σε·

1. Tauta elaleisen 'o Yeisous, kai epeiren tous ophthalmous autou eis ton ouranon, kai eipen, Pater, eleiluthen 'ei 'ora. doxason sou ton 'wion, 'ina kai 'o 'wios sou doxasei se.

Hebrew/Transliteration

א. אֶת-אֵלֶּה דִּבֶּר יֵשׁוּעַ וַיִּשָּׂא עֵינָיו לַמָּרוֹם וַיֹּאמַר אָבִי גַּדֵּל כְּבוֹד בִּנְךָ כִּי בָא מוֹעֵד וּבִנְךָ יְגַדֵּל כְּבוֹדֶךָ:

1. Et - ele di•ber Yeshua va•yi•sa ey•nav la•ma•rom va•yo•mar Avi ga•del k`vod Bin•cha ki va mo•ed oo•Vin•cha ye•ga•del k`vo•de•cha.

Rabbinic Jewish Commentary

and lift up his eyes to heaven; the seat of the divine majesty, the throne of his Father. This is a prayer gesture. It is said (c) of R. Tanchuma, that הגביה פניו לשמים, "He lift up his face to heaven", and said before the holy blessed God, Lord of the world, and this is expressive of the ardency and affection of the mind of Yeshua, and of his confidence of the divine favour: it shows that his mind was filled with devotion and faith, and was devoid of shame and fear, and was possessed of great freedom, boldness, and intrepidity.

(c) Vajikra Rabba, sect. 34. fol. 174. 4.

---

2. As thou hast given him power over all flesh, that he should give eternal life to as many as thou hast given him.

Greek/Transliteration

2. καθὼς ἔδωκας αὐτῷ ἐξουσίαν πάσης σαρκός, ἵνα πᾶν ὃ δέδωκας αὐτῷ, δώσει αὐτοῖς ζωὴν αἰώνιον.

2. kathos edokas auto exousian paseis sarkos, 'ina pan 'o dedokas auto, dosei autois zoein aionion.

Hebrew/Transliteration

ב. כַּאֲשֶׁר אַתָּה תִמְשִׁילֵהוּ בְּכָל-בָּשָׂר לָתֵת חַיֵּי עוֹלָם לְכֹל אֲשֶׁר-נָתַתָּה לּוֹ:

2. Ka•a•sher ata tam•shi•le•hoo be•chol - va•sar la•tet cha•yey o•lam le•chol asher - na•ta•ta lo.

---

3. And this is life eternal, that they might know thee the only true God, and Jesus Christ, whom thou hast sent.

Greek/Transliteration
3. Αὕτη δέ ἐστιν ἡ αἰώνιος ζωή, ἵνα γινώσκωσίν σε τὸν μόνον ἀληθινὸν θεόν, καὶ ὃν ἀπέστειλας Ἰησοῦν χριστόν.

3. 'Autei de estin 'ei aionios zoei, 'ina ginoskosin se ton monon aleithinon theon, kai 'on apesteilas Yeisoun christon.

Hebrew/Transliteration
ג. וּמַה חַיֵּי עוֹלָם אֲשֶׁר יֵדְעוּ אֹתְךָ כִּי אַתָּה לְבַדְּךָ אֵל-אֶמֶת וְאֶת-יֵשׁוּעַ הַמָּשִׁיחַ אֲשֶׁר שָׁלָחְתָּ:

3. Oo•ma cha•yey o•lam asher yed•oo ot•cha ki ata le•vad•cha el - emet ve•et – Yeshua ha•Ma•shi•ach asher sha•lach•ta.

Rabbinic Jewish Commentary
The Jews say of the Torah (d), "One man said to his friend, let us dash them against that wall and kill them, because they have left חיי עולם הבא, "eternal life"; (the gloss upon it is, תורה, "the Torah";) and employ themselves in a temporary life, the gloss says of this world, which is merchandise."

More truly does Philo the Jew say (e), that "fleeing to the Divine Being, "is eternal life"; and running front him is death."

The Arians and Unitarians urge this text, against the true and proper deity of our Lord Yeshua, and his equality with the Father, but without success; since the Father is called the only true God, in opposition to the many false gods of the Heathens, but not to the exclusion of the Son or Spirit; for Yeshua is also styled the one Lord, and only Lord God, but not to the exclusion of the Father; yea the true God and eternal life; was he not, he would never, as here, join himself with the only true God; and besides, eternal life is made to depend as much upon the knowledge of him, as of the Father.

"And we know that the Son of God is come, and hath given us an understanding, that we may know him that is true, and we are in him that is true, in his Son Yeshua the Messiah. He is the true God, and eternal life." (1Joh_5:20)

(d) T. Bab. Taanith, fol. 21. 1. (e) De profugis, p. 461.

---

4. I have glorified thee on the earth: I have finished the work which thou gavest me to do.

Greek/Translieration
4. Ἐγώ σε ἐδόξασα ἐπὶ τῆς γῆς· τὸ ἔργον ἐτελείωσα ὃ δέδωκάς μοι ἵνα ποιήσω.

4. Ego se edoxasa epi teis geis. to ergon eteleiosa 'o dedokas moi 'ina poieiso.

Hebrew/Transliteration
:ד. אֶת-כְּבוֹדְךָ גִּדַּלְתִּי בָאָרֶץ כִּלִּיתִי אֶת-הַמְּלָאכָה אֲשֶׁר נָתַתָּה לִי לַעֲשׂוֹתָהּ

4. Et - k`vod•cha gi•dal•ti va•a•retz ki•li•ti et - ha•m`la•cha asher na•ta•ta li la•a•so•ta.

---

5. And now, O Father, glorify thou me with thine own self with the glory which I had with thee before the world was.

Greek/Transliteration
5. Καὶ νῦν δόξασόν με σύ, πάτερ, παρὰ σεαυτῷ τῇ δόξῃ ᾗ εἶχον πρὸ τοῦ τὸν κόσμον εἶναι παρὰ σοί.

5. Kai nun doxason me su, pater, para seauto tei doxei eichon pro tou ton kosmon einai para soi.

Hebrew/Transliteration
:ה. וְעַתָּה כַּבְּדֵנִי-נָא עִמְּךָ אָבִי בַּכָּבוֹד אֲשֶׁר הָיָה-לִי עִמְּךָ טֶרֶם נַעֲשׂוֹ שָׁמַיִם וָאָרֶץ

5. Ve•a•ta kab•de•ni - na eem•cha Avi ba•ka•vod asher ha•ya - li eem•cha te•rem na•a•soo sha•ma•yim va•a•retz.

Rabbinic Jewish Commentary
The Jews have a notion that God will give to the King Messiah, מן הכבוד של מעלה, "Of the supreme glory" (g)

the glory which I had with thee before the world was; the same phrase with לעולם, or קודם העולם, used by the Jews (h). This is not to be understood of the glory of the human nature of Yeshua, abstractly considered.

(g) Midrash Tillim in Psal. 20 apud Galatin. de Arcan. Cathol. Ver. l. 3. c. 9. (h) Gloss in T. Bab Pesachim, fol. 54. 1.

---

6. I have manifested thy name unto the men which thou gavest me out of the world: thine they were, and thou gavest them me; and they have kept thy word.

6. Ἐφανέρωσά σου τὸ ὄνομα τοῖς ἀνθρώποις οὓς δέδωκάς μοι ἐκ τοῦ κόσμου· σοὶ ἦσαν, καὶ ἐμοὶ αὐτοὺς δέδωκας· καὶ τὸν λόγον σου τετηρήκασιν.

6. Ephanerosa sou to onoma tois anthropois 'ous dedokas moi ek tou kosmou. soi eisan, kai emoi autous dedokas. kai ton logon sou teteireikasin.

ו. הוֹדַעְתִּי אֶת-שְׁמְךָ לַאֲנָשִׁים אֲשֶׁר אֹתָם נָתַתָּ-לִי מִן-הָעוֹלָם לְךָ הָיוּ וְאַתָּה נְתַתָּם לִי וְהֵם אִמְרָתְךָ יִנְצֹרוּ:

6. Ho•da•a•ti et - shim•cha la•a•na•shim asher o•tam na•ta•ta - li min - ha•o•lam le•cha ha•yoo ve•a•ta n`ta•tam li ve•hem eem•rat•cha yin•tzo•roo.

---

7. Now they have known that all things whatsoever thou hast given me are of thee.

7. Νῦν ἔγνωκαν ὅτι πάντα ὅσα δέδωκάς μοι, παρὰ σοῦ ἐστιν·

7. Nun egnokan 'oti panta 'osa dedokas moi, para sou estin.

ז. יֹדְעִים הֵם כַּיוֹם כִּי-כֻלָּם אֲשֶׁר נָתַתָּה לִי מֵאִתְּךָ הֵמָּה:

7. Yod•eem hem ka•yom ki - choo•lam asher na•ta•ta li me•eet•cha he•ma.

---

8. For I have given unto them the words which thou gavest me; and they have received them, and have known surely that I came out from thee, and they have believed that thou didst send me.

8. ὅτι τὰ ῥήματα ἃ δέδωκάς μοι, δέδωκα αὐτοῖς· καὶ αὐτοὶ ἔλαβον, καὶ ἔγνωσαν ἀληθῶς ὅτι παρὰ σοῦ ἐξῆλθον, καὶ ἐπίστευσαν ὅτι σύ με ἀπέστειλας.

8. 'oti ta 'reimata 'a dedokas moi, dedoka autois. kai autoi elabon, kai egnosan aleithos 'oti para sou exeilthon, kai episteusan 'oti su me apesteilas.

ח. כִּי שַׂמְתִּי לִפְנֵיהֶם אֶת-הַדְּבָרִים אֲשֶׁר שַׂמְתָּ בְּפִי וְהֵם שָׁמְעוּ וַיַּכִּירוּ בֶאֱמֶת כִּי מֵאִתְּךָ יָצָאתִי וַיַּאֲמִינוּ כִּי אַתָּה שְׁלַחְתָּנִי:

8. Ki sam•ti lif•ney•hem et - ha•d`va•rim asher sam•ta be•fi ve•hem sham•oo va•ya•ki•roo ve•e•met ki me•eet•cha ya•tza•ti va•ya•a•mi•noo ki ata sh`lach•ta•ni.

Rabbinic Jewish Commentary

Jonathan ben Uzziel (l) paraphrases the text in Deu_18:18; concerning that prophet, the Messiah, God would raise up, after this manner;

"A prophet will I raise up unto them from among their brethren by the Holy Spirit like unto thee; ‏ואיתן פתגמי‏, "And I will give the words", of my prophecy into his mouth, and he shall speak with them all that I have commanded."

(l) Targum Jon. in Deut. xviii. 18.

---

9. I pray for them: I pray not for the world, but for them which thou hast given me; for they are thine.

Greek/Transliteration
9. Ἐγὼ περὶ αὐτῶν ἐρωτῶ· οὐ περὶ τοῦ κόσμου ἐρωτῶ, ἀλλὰ περὶ ὧν δέδωκάς μοι, ὅτι σοί εἰσιν·

9. Ego peri auton eroto. ou peri tou kosmou eroto, alla peri 'on dedokas moi, 'oti soi eisin.

Hebrew/Transliteration
‏ט. וַאֲנִי בַּעֲדָם מַפְגִיעַ לֹא בְעַד הָעוֹלָם אֶפְגַּע בְּךָ כִּי אִם-בְּעַד אֵלֶּה אֲשֶׁר נָתַתָּה לִי כִּי-לְךָ הֵמָּה:‏

9. Va•a•ni ba•a•dam maf•gi•a lo ve•ad ha•o•lam ef•ga be•cha ki eem - be•ad ele asher na•ta•ta li ki - le•cha he•ma.

---

10. And all mine are thine, and thine are mine; and I am glorified in them.

Greek/Transliteration
10. καὶ τὰ ἐμὰ πάντα σά ἐστιν, καὶ τὰ σὰ ἐμά· καὶ δεδόξασμαι ἐν αὐτοῖς.

10. kai ta ema panta sa estin, kai ta sa ema. kai dedoxasmai en autois.

Hebrew/Transliteration
‏י. וְכָל-שֶׁלִּי שֶׁלָּךְ וְשֶׁלָּךְ שֶׁלִּי אֲשֶׁר בָּם אֶתְפָּאָר:‏

10. Ve•chol - she•li she•lach ve•she•lach she•li asher bam et•pa•ar.

---

11. And now I am no more in the world, but these are in the world, and I come to thee. Holy Father, keep through thine own name those whom thou hast given me, that they may be one, as we are.

Greek/Transliteration

11. Καὶ οὐκέτι εἰμὶ ἐν τῷ κόσμῳ, καὶ οὗτοι ἐν τῷ κόσμῳ εἰσίν, καὶ ἐγὼ πρός σε ἔρχομαι. Πάτερ ἅγιε, τήρησον αὐτοὺς ἐν τῷ ὀνόματί σου, ᾧ δέδωκάς μοι, ἵνα ὦσιν ἕν, καθὼς ἡμεῖς.

11. Kai ouketi eimi en to kosmo, kai 'outoi en to kosmo eisin, kai ego pros se erchomai. Pater 'agie, teireison autous en to onomati sou, 'o dedokas moi, 'ina osin 'en, kathos 'eimeis.

Hebrew/Transliteration

יא. לֹא אָגוּר עוֹד בָּאָרֶץ וְהֵם גֵּרִים בָּאָרֶץ וַאֲנִי בָא אֵלֶיךָ אָבִי קְדֹשִׁי שְׁמֹר בְּשִׁמְךָ אֶת-אֵלֶּה אֲשֶׁר נָתַתָּה לִי לְמַעַן:יִהְיוּ אֶחָד כָּמֹנוּ

11. Lo agoor od ba•a•retz ve•hem ga•rim ba•a•retz va•a•ni va e•le•cha Avi K`do•shi sh`mor be•shim•cha et - ele asher na•ta•ta li le•ma•an yi•hee•yoo e•chad ka•mo•noo.

---

12. While I was with them in the world, I kept them in thy name: those that thou gavest me I have kept, and none of them is lost, but the son of perdition; that the scripture might be fulfilled.

Greek/Transliteration

12. Ὅτε ἤμην μετ᾽ αὐτῶν ἐν τῷ κόσμῳ, ἐγὼ ἐτήρουν αὐτοὺς ἐν τῷ ὀνόματί σου· οὓς δέδωκάς μοι, ἐφύλαξα, καὶ οὐδεὶς ἐξ αὐτῶν ἀπώλετο, εἰ μὴ ὁ υἱὸς τῆς ἀπωλείας, ἵνα ἡ γραφὴ πληρωθῇ.

12. 'Ote eimein met auton en to kosmo, ego eteiroun autous en to onomati sou. 'ous dedokas moi, ephulaxa, kai oudeis ex auton apoleto, ei mei 'o 'wios teis apoleias, 'ina 'ei graphei pleirothei.

Hebrew/Transliteration

יב. בִּהְיוֹתִי עִמָּהֶם בָּעוֹלָם אֹתָם בִּשְׁמְךָ כֹּל אֲשֶׁר נָתַתָּה לִי שְׁמַרְתִּי וְלֹא-אָבַד אֶחָד מֵהֶם - זוּלָתִי בֶן:הָאֲבַדּוֹן לְמַלֹּאת דְּבַר-הַכָּתוּב

12. Bi•hi•yo•ti ee•ma•hem ba•o•lam sha•mar•ti o•tam bish•me•cha kol asher na•ta•ta li sha•mar•ti ve•lo - avad e•chad me•hem zoo•la•tee ben - ha•a•va•don le•ma•lot de•var - ha•ka•toov.

Rabbinic Jewish Commentary

Some have thought that this only refers to the general sense of the Scriptures, both the Torah and prophets; that some are chosen to everlasting life, and others are appointed to wrath; that some are saved, and others lost; some sons of God, and others sons of perdition; but it rather seems to regard some particular passage or passages of Scripture relating to Judas, his character, condition and end, and which are very manifestly pointed at, in the Psalm 109:8 referred to;

"As for the servants whom I have given thee, there shall not one of them perish; for I will require them from among thy number." (2 Esdras 2:26)

---

13. And now come I to thee; and these things I speak in the world, that they might have my joy fulfilled in themselves.

Greek/Transliteration
13. Νῦν δὲ πρός σε ἔρχομαι, καὶ ταῦτα λαλῶ ἐν τῷ κόσμῳ, ἵνα ἔχωσιν τὴν χαρὰν τὴν ἐμὴν πεπληρωμένην ἐν αὐτοῖς.

13. Nun de pros se erchomai, kai tauta lalo en to kosmo, 'ina echosin tein charan tein emein pepleiromenein en autois.

Hebrew/Transliteration
יג. וְעַתָּה הִנְנִי בָא אֵלֶיךָ וְהַדְּבָרִים הָאֵלֶּה דִּבַּרְתִּי בָאָרֶץ לְמַלֹּאת נַפְשָׁם שִׂמְחָתִי:

13. Ve•a•ta hi•ne•ni va e•le•cha ve•had•va•rim ha•e•le di•bar•ti va•a•retz le•ma•lot naf•sham sim•cha•ti.

---

14. I have given them thy word; and the world hath hated them, because they are not of the world, even as I am not of the world.

Greek/Transliteration
14. Ἐγὼ δέδωκα αὐτοῖς τὸν λόγον σου, καὶ ὁ κόσμος ἐμίσησεν αὐτούς, ὅτι οὐκ εἰσὶν ἐκ τοῦ κόσμου, καθὼς ἐγὼ οὐκ εἰμὶ ἐκ τοῦ κόσμου.

14. Ego dedoka autois ton logon sou, kai 'o kosmos emiseisen autous, 'oti ouk eisin ek tou kosmou, kathos ego ouk eimi ek tou kosmou.

Hebrew/Transliteration
יד. אֲנִי נָתַתִּי לָהֶם דְּבָרְךָ וְהָעוֹלָם שָׂנֵא אֹתָם יַעַן כִּי לֹא מִן-הָעוֹלָם הֵם כַּאֲשֶׁר גַּם-אֲנִי לֹא מִן-הָעוֹלָם אָנִי:

14. Ani na•ta•ti la•hem d`var•cha ve•ha•olam so•ne o•tam ya•an ki lo min - ha•o•lam hem ka•a•sher gam - ani lo min - ha•o•lam ani.

---

15. I pray not that thou shouldest take them out of the world, but that thou shouldest keep them from the evil.

15. Οὐκ ἐρωτῶ ἵνα ἄρῃς αὐτοὺς ἐκ τοῦ κόσμου, ἀλλ᾽ ἵνα τηρήσῃς αὐτοὺς ἐκ τοῦ πονηροῦ.

15. Ouk eroto 'ina areis autous ek tou kosmou, all 'ina teireiseis autous ek tou poneirou.

טו. וַאֲנִי אֵינֶנִּי מַפְגִּיעַ בַּעֲדָם כִּי תִקָּחֵם מִן-הָעוֹלָם רַק כִּי אִם-תַּצִּילֵם מִן-הָרָע:

15. Va•a•ni ey•ne•ni maf•gi•a ba•a•dam ki ti•ka•chem min - ha•o•lam rak ki eem - ta•tzi•lem min - ha•ra.

---

16. They are not of the world, even as I am not of the world.

16. Ἐκ τοῦ κόσμου οὐκ εἰσίν, καθὼς ἐγὼ ἐκ τοῦ κόσμου οὐκ εἰμί.

16. Ek tou kosmou ouk eisin, kathos ego ek tou kosmou ouk eimi.

טז. לֹא מִן-הָעוֹלָם הֵם כַּאֲשֶׁר גַּם-אֲנִי לֹא מִן-הָעוֹלָם אָנִי:

16. Lo min - ha•o•lam hem ka•a•sher gam - ani lo min - ha•o•lam ani.

---

17. Sanctify them through thy truth: thy word is truth.

17. Ἁγίασον αὐτοὺς ἐν τῇ ἀληθείᾳ σου· ὁ λόγος ὁ σὸς ἀλήθειά ἐστιν.

17. 'Agiason autous en tei aleitheia sou. 'o logos 'o sos aleitheya estin.

יז. קַדֵּשׁ אֹתָם בַּאֲמִתֶּךָ דְּבָרְךָ אֱמֶת:

17. Ka•desh o•tam ba•a•mi•te•cha d`var•cha emet.

---

18. As thou hast sent me into the world, even so have I also sent them into the world.

18. Καθὼς ἐμὲ ἀπέστειλας εἰς τὸν κόσμον, κἀγὼ ἀπέστειλα αὐτοὺς εἰς τὸν κόσμον.

18. Kathos eme apesteilas eis ton kosmon, kago apesteila autous eis ton kosmon.

Hebrew/Transliteration

יח. כַּאֲשֶׁר אַתָּה שְׁלַחְתַּנִי בָעוֹלָם כֵּן אֲנִי שְׁלַחְתִּים בָּעוֹלָם:

18. Ka•a•sher ata sh`lach•ta•ni va•o•lam ken ani sh`lach•tim ba•o•lam.

---

19. And for their sakes I sanctify myself, that they also might be sanctified through the truth.

Greek/Transliteration
19. Καὶ ὑπὲρ αὐτῶν ἐγὼ ἁγιάζω ἐμαυτόν, ἵνα καὶ αὐτοὶ ὦσιν ἡγιασμένοι ἐν ἀληθείᾳ.

19. Kai 'uper auton ego 'agyazo emauton, 'ina kai autoi osin 'eigyasmenoi en aleitheia.

Hebrew/Transliteration
יט. וּבַעֲדָם הִקְדַּשְׁתִּי אֶת-נַפְשִׁי וְכֵן גַּם-הֵם אֶת-נַפְשָׁם בֶּאֱמֶת יַקְדִּישׁוּ:

19. Oo•va•a•dam hik•dash•ti et - naf•shi ve•chen gam - hem et - naf•sham be•e•met yak•di•shoo.

---

20. Neither pray I for these alone, but for them also which shall believe on me through their word;

Greek/Transliteration
20. Οὐ περὶ τούτων δὲ ἐρωτῶ μόνον, ἀλλὰ καὶ περὶ τῶν πιστευόντων διὰ τοῦ λόγου αὐτῶν εἰς ἐμέ·

20. Ou peri touton de eroto monon, alla kai peri ton pisteuonton dya tou logou auton eis eme.

Hebrew/Transliteration
כ. אוּלָם לֹא בְעַד-אֵלֶּה לְבַדָּם אֲנִי מַעְתִּיר לָךְ כִּי אִם-גַּם-בְּעַד אֵלֶּה אֲשֶׁר יַאֲמִינוּ בִי עַל-פִּי דְבָרָם:

20. Oo•lam lo be•ad - ele le•va•dam ani ma•a•tir lach ki eem - gam - be•ad ele asher ya•a•mi•noo vi al - pi d`va•ram.

---

21. That they all may be one; as thou, Father, art in me, and I in thee, that they also may be one in us: that the world may believe that thou hast sent me.

---

21. ἵνα πάντες ἓν ὦσιν· καθὼς σύ, πάτερ, ἐν ἐμοί, κἀγὼ ἐν σοί, ἵνα καὶ αὐτοὶ ἐν ἡμῖν ἓν ὦσιν· ἵνα ὁ κόσμος πιστεύσῃ ὅτι σύ με ἀπέστειλας.

21. 'ina pantes 'en osin. kathos su, pater, en emoi, kago en soi, 'ina kai autoi en 'eimin 'en osin. 'ina 'o kosmos pisteusei 'oti su me apesteilas.

כא. לְמַעַן יִהְיוּ כֻלָּם לְאֶחָד כַּאֲשֶׁר אַתָּה אָבִי בִּי וַאֲנִי בָּךְ כֵּן יִהְיוּ גַם-הֵם בָּנוּ לְבַעֲבוּר יַאֲמִין הָעוֹלָם כִּי אַתָּה שְׁלַחְתָּנִי:

21. Le•ma•an yi•hee•yoo choo•lam le•e•chad ka•a•sher ata Avi bi va•a•ni bach ken yi•hee•yoo gam - hem ba•noo le•va•a•voor ya•a•min ha•o•lam ki ata sh`lach•ta•ni.

---

22. And the glory which thou gavest me I have given them; that they may be one, even as we are one:

22. Καὶ ἐγὼ τὴν δόξαν ἣν δέδωκάς μοι, δέδωκα αὐτοῖς, ἵνα ὦσιν ἕν, καθὼς ἡμεῖς ἕν ἐσμεν.

22. Kai ego tein doxan 'ein dedokas moi, dedoka autois, 'ina osin 'en, kathos 'eimeis 'en esmen.

כב. וַאֲנִי נָתַתִּי לָהֶם אֶת-הַכָּבוֹד אֲשֶׁר נָתַתָּה לִי לְבַעֲבוּר יִהְיוּ לְאֶחָד כַּאֲשֶׁר גַּם אֲנַחְנוּ אֶחָד:

22. Va•a•ni na•ta•ti la•hem et - ha•ka•vod asher na•ta•ta li le•va•a•voor yi•hee•yoo le•e•chad ka•a•sher gam a•nach•noo e•chad.

---

23. I in them, and thou in me, that they may be made perfect in one; and that the world may know that thou hast sent me, and hast loved them, as thou hast loved me.

23. Ἐγὼ ἐν αὐτοῖς, καὶ σὺ ἐν ἐμοί, ἵνα ὦσιν τετελειωμένοι εἰς ἕν, καὶ ἵνα γινώσκῃ ὁ κόσμος ὅτι σύ με ἀπέστειλας, καὶ ἠγάπησας αὐτούς, καθὼς ἐμὲ ἠγάπησας.

23. Ego en autois, kai su en emoi, 'ina osin teteleiomenoi eis 'en, kai 'ina ginoskei 'o kosmos 'oti su me apesteilas, kai eigapeisas autous, kathos eme eigapeisas.

Hebrew/Transliteration

כג. אֲנִי בָהֶם וְאַתָּה בִּי לְמַעַן יִהְיוּ תַמִּים בְּאֶחָד וּלְמַעַן יֵדַע הָעוֹלָם כִּי אַתָּה שְׁלַחְתַּנִי וְכִי אֲהַבְתָּ אֹתָם כַּאֲשֶׁר:אֲהַבְתָּנִי

23. Ani ba•hem ve•a•ta bi le•ma•an yi•hee•yoo ta•mim be•e•chad ool•ma•an ye•da ha•o•lam ki ata sh`lach•ta•ni ve•chi ahav•ta o•tam ka•a•sher a•hav•ta•ni.

---

24. Father, I will that they also, whom thou hast given me, be with me where I am; that they may behold my glory, which thou hast given me: for thou lovedst me before the foundation of the world.

Greek/Transliteration

24. Πάτερ, οὓς δέδωκάς μοι, θέλω ἵνα ὅπου εἰμὶ ἐγώ, κἀκεῖνοι ὦσιν μετ᾽ ἐμοῦ· ἵνα θεωρῶσιν τὴν δόξαν τὴν ἐμήν, ἣν ἔδωκάς μοι, ὅτι ἠγάπησάς με πρὸ καταβολῆς κόσμου.

24. Pater, 'ous dedokas moi, thelo 'ina 'opou eimi ego, kakeinoi osin met emou. 'ina theorosin tein doxan tein emein, 'ein edokas moi, 'oti eigapeisas me pro kataboleis kosmou.

Hebrew/Transliteration

כד. וַאֲנִי חָפַצְתִּי אָבִי כִּי אֵלֶּה אֲשֶׁר נָתַתָּה לִּי יִהְיוּ עִמִּי גַּם - הֵם בַּאֲשֶׁר אֶהְיֶה לְמַעַן יִרְאוּ אֶת-כְּבוֹדִי אֲשֶׁר נָתַתָּה:לִּי כִּי אֲהַבְתָּ אֹתִי טֶרֶם הִוָּסֵד אָרֶץ

24. Va•a•ni cha•fatz•ti Avi ki ele asher na•ta•ta li yi•hee•yoo ee•mi gam - hem ba•a•sher e•he•ye le•ma•an yir•oo et - ke•vo•di asher na•ta•ta li ki ahav•ta o•ti te•rem hi•va•sed a•retz.

---

25. O righteous Father, the world hath not known thee: but I have known thee, and these have known that thou hast sent me.

Greek/Transliteration

25. Πάτερ δίκαιε, καὶ ὁ κόσμος σε οὐκ ἔγνω, ἐγὼ δέ σε ἔγνων, καὶ οὗτοι ἔγνωσαν ὅτι σύ με ἀπέστειλας·

25. Pater dikaie, kai 'o kosmos se ouk egno, ego de se egnon, kai 'outoi egnosan 'oti su me apesteilas.

Hebrew/Transliteration

כה. אָבִי הַצַּדִּיק הֵן הָעוֹלָם אֵינֶנּוּ יֹדֵעַ אֹתְךָ וַאֲנִי יְדַעְתִּיךָ וְאֵלֶּה יֹדְעִים כִּי אַתָּה שְׁלַחְתָּנִי:

25. Avi ha•tza•dik hen ha•o•lam ey•ne•noo yo•de•a ot•cha va•a•ni ye•da•a•ti•cha ve•e•le yod•eem ki ata sh`lach•ta•ni.

26. And I have declared unto them thy name, and will declare it: that the love wherewith thou hast loved me may be in them, and I in them.

Greek/Transliteration

26. καὶ ἐγνώρισα αὐτοῖς τὸ ὄνομά σου, καὶ γνωρίσω· ἵνα ἡ ἀγάπη, ἣν ἠγάπησάς με, ἐν αὐτοῖς ᾖ, κἀγὼ ἐν αὐτοῖς.

26. kai egnorisa autois to onoma sou, kai gnoriso. 'ina 'ei agapei, 'ein eigapeisas me, en autois ei, kago en autois.

Hebrew/Transliteration

כו. הוֹדַעְתִּי לָהֶם אֶת-שִׁמְךָ וְכֵן אוֹסִיף לְהוֹדִיעָם לְמַעַן תִּהְיֶה-בָּם הָאַהֲבָה אֲשֶׁר אֲהַבְתָּנִי וְגַם-אֲנִי אֶהְיֶה בְּתוֹכָם:

26. Ho•da•a•ti la•hem et - shim•cha ve•chen o•sif le•ho•di•am le•ma•an ti•hi•ye – bam ha•a•ha•va asher a•hav•ta•ni ve•gam - ani e•he•ye be•to•cham.

John, Chapter 18

1. When Jesus had spoken these words, he went forth with his disciples over the brook Cedron, where was a garden, into the which he entered, and his disciples.

Greek/Transliteration

1. Ταῦτα εἰπὼν ὁ Ἰησοῦς ἐξῆλθεν σὺν τοῖς μαθηταῖς αὐτοῦ πέραν τοῦ χειμάρρου τῶν Κέδρων, ὅπου ἦν κῆπος, εἰς ὃν εἰσῆλθεν αὐτὸς καὶ οἱ μαθηταὶ αὐτοῦ.

1. Tauta eipon 'o Yeisous exeilthen sun tois matheitais autou peran tou cheimarrou ton Kedron, 'opou ein keipos, eis 'on eiseilthen autos kai 'oi matheitai autou.

Hebrew/Transliteration

א. וַיְכַל יֵשׁוּעַ לְדַבֵּר אֶת-הַדְּבָרִים הָאֵלֶּה וַיֵּצֵא עִם-תַּלְמִידָיו אֶל-עֵבֶר לַנַחַל קִדְרוֹן וַיָּבֹא לַגָּן אֲשֶׁר שָׁם הוּא:וְתַלְמִידָיו

1. Vay•chal Yeshua le•da•ber et - ha•d`va•rim ha•e•le va•ye•tze eem - tal•mi•dav el – ever la•na•chal Kid•ron va•ya•vo la•gan asher sham hoo ve•tal•mi•dav.

Rabbinic Jewish Commentary

The same with "Kidron" in 2Sa_15:23; and elsewhere: it had its name, not from cedars, for not cedars but olives chiefly grew upon the mount, which was near it; and besides the name is not Greek, but Hebrew, though the Arabic version renders it, "the brook" אל ארז, "of Cedar": it had its name either from the darkness of the valley in which it ran, being between high mountains, and having gardens in it, and set with trees; or from the blackness of the water through the soil that ran into it, being a kind of a common sewer, into which the Jews cast everything that was unclean and defiling; see 2Ch_29:16.

Particularly there was a canal which led from the altar in the temple to it, by which the blood and soil of the sacrifices were carried into it (m). This brook was but about three feet over from bank to bank, and in the summer time was quite dry, and might be walked over dry shod; and is therefore by Josephus sometimes called the brook of Kidron (n), and sometimes the valley of Kidron (o): in this valley were corn fields; for hither the sanhedrim sent their messengers to reap the sheaf of the firstfruits, which always was to be brought from a place near to Jerusalem (p); and it is very likely that willows grew by the brook, from whence they might fetch their willow branches at the feast of tabernacles; for the Jews say (q), there is a place below Jerusalem called Motza, (in the Gemara it is said to be Klamia or Colonia,) whither they went down and gathered willow branches; it seems to be the valley of Kidron, which lay on the east of Jerusalem, between that and the Mount of Olives (r); it had fields and gardens adjoining to it; see 2Ki_23:4. So we read of a garden here, into which Yeshua immediately went, when he passed over this brook. The blood, the filth and soil of it, which so discoloured the water, as to give it the name of the Black Brook, used to be sold to the gardeners to dung their gardens with (s). It was an emblem of this world, and the darkness and filthiness of it, and of the exercises and troubles of the people of God in it, which lie in the way to the heavenly paradise and Mount of Zion, through which Yeshua himself went, drinking "of the brook in the way", Psa_110:7; and through which also all his disciples and followers enter into the kingdom of heaven: it may also be a figure of the dark valley of the shadow of death, through which Yeshua and all his members pass to the heavenly glory. And I see not why this black and unclean brook may not be a representation of the pollutions and defilements of sin; which being laid on Yeshua when he passed over it, made him so heavy and sore amazed in the human nature, as to desire the cup might pass from him. Once more let it be observed, that it was the brook David passed over when he fled from his son Absalom; in this David was a type of Messiah, as in other things: Absalom represented the people of the Jews, who rejected the Messiah, and rebelled against him; Ahithophel, Judas, who betrayed him; and the people that went with David over it, the disciples of Yeshua; only there was this difference; there was a father fleeing from a son, here a son going to meet his father's wrath; David and his people wept when they went over this brook, but so did not Yeshua and his disciples; the sorrowful scene to them both began afterwards in the garden. This black brook and dark valley, and it being very late at night when it was passed over, all add to that dark dispensation, that hour of darkness, which now came upon Yeshua; yet he went forth over it of his own accord, willingly and cheerfully; not being forced or compelled by any; and his disciples with him, not to be partners of his sufferings, but to be witnesses of them, and to receive some knowledge and instruction from what they should see and hear.

(m) Misn. Middot, c. 3. sect. 2. Meila, c. 3. sect. 3. & Bartenora in ib. Maimon. & Bartenora in Misn. Zebachim, c. 8. 7. & Temura, c. 7. sect. 6. (n) Antiqu. l. 8. c. 1. sect. 5. (o) Ib. l. 9. c. 7. sect. 3. & de Bello Jud. l. 5. c. 4. sect. 2. & c. 6. sect. 1. (p) Misna Menachot, c. 10. sect. 2, 3. (q) Misna Succa, c. 4. sect. 5. (r) Jerom de locis Hebraicis, fol. 92. C. (s) Misn. Yoma, c. 5. sect 6. Maimon. Meila, c. 2. sect. 11.

---

2. And Judas also, which betrayed him, knew the place: for Jesus ofttimes resorted thither with his disciples.

Greek/Transliteration
2. Ἄδει δὲ καὶ Ἰούδας, ὁ παραδιδοὺς αὐτόν, τὸν τόπον· ὅτι πολλάκις συνήχθη ὁ Ἰησοῦς ἐκεῖ μετὰ τῶν μαθητῶν αὐτοῦ.

2. dei de kai Youdas, 'o paradidous auton, ton topon. 'oti pollakis suneichthei 'o Yeisous ekei meta ton matheiton autou.

Hebrew/Transliteration
ב. וִיהוּדָה הַמַּסְגִּיר יָדַע אֶת-הַמָּקוֹם הַהוּא כִּי יֵשׁוּעַ וְתַלְמִידָיו פְּעָמִים רַבּוֹת נוֹעֲדוּ שָׁם:

2. Vi•Y`hoo•da ha•mas•gir ya•da et - ha•ma•kom ha•hoo ki Yeshua
ve•tal•mi•dav pe•a•mim ra•bot no•a•doo sham.

---

3. Judas then, having received a band of men and officers from the chief
priests and Pharisees, cometh thither with lanterns and torches and weapons.

Greek/Transliteration
3. Ὁ οὖν Ἰούδας, λαβὼν τὴν σπεῖραν, καὶ ἐκ τῶν ἀρχιερέων καὶ Φαρισαίων
ὑπηρέτας, ἔρχεται ἐκεῖ μετὰ φανῶν καὶ λαμπάδων καὶ ὅπλων.

3. 'O oun Youdas, labon tein speiran, kai ek ton archiereon kai Pharisaion
'upeiretas, erchetai ekei meta phanon kai lampadon kai 'oplon.

Hebrew/Transliteration
ג. וַיִּקַּח יְהוּדָה אֶת-הַגְדוּד וְאֶת-הַמְשָׁרְתִים אֲשֶׁר לְרָאשֵׁי הַכֹּהֲנִים וְהַפְּרוּשִׁים וַיָּבֹא שָׁם בְּנֵרוֹת
וְלַפִּידִים וּכְלֵי-נָשֶׁק -

3. Va•yi•kach Yehooda et - ha•g`dood ve•et - ha•me•shar•tim asher le•ra•shey
ha•ko•ha•nim ve•haP`roo•shim va•ya•vo sham be•ne•rot ve•la•pi•dim
ooch•ley - na•shek.

Rabbinic Jewish Commentary
cometh thither with lanterns, and torches, and weapons: פנס, which is no other
than the Greek word here used for a lantern, the Jews tell us (u), was an earthen
vessel, in which a candle was put and covered, that the wind might not put it out,
and it had holes in the sides of it, through which light was let out; their לפיד, or
"lamp", here rendered "torch", they say (w), was also an earthen vessel in the form
of a reed, at the top of which was a proper receptacle, in which they burnt old rags
dipped in oil: now though it was full moon, being the time of the passover, they
brought these along with them to discover him by the light of, and find him out
with them, if he should hide himself among the trees, or in any of the more shady
places in the garden; and they took warlike instruments, as swords, spears, and
staves, as if they had a thief or a murderer to apprehend, or a little army of men to
encounter with; whereas there were only Yeshua, and his eleven disciples; and
these in no condition, nor had any design, to defend themselves in an hostile
manner.

(u) Maimon. & Bartenora in Misn. Celim, c. 2. sect. 4. (w) Ib. in sect. 8.

---

4. Jesus therefore, knowing all things that should come upon him, went forth,
and said unto them, Whom seek ye?

Greek/Transliteration
4. Ἰησοῦς οὖν, εἰδὼς πάντα τὰ ἐρχόμενα ἐπ᾽ αὐτόν, ἐξελθὼν εἶπεν αὐτοῖς,
Τίνα ζητεῖτε;

4. Yeisous oun, eidos panta ta erchomena ep auton, exelthon eipen autois,
Tina zeiteite?

Hebrew/Transliteration

:ד. וְיֵשׁוּעַ יָדַע אֶת כָּל-אֲשֶׁר יְבֹאוּ וַיֵּצֵא וַיֹּאמֶר אֲלֵיהֶם אֶת-מִי תְבַקֵּשׁוּן

4. Ve•Yeshua ya•da et kol - asher ye•vo•e•noo va•ye•tze va•yo•mer aley•hem
et – mee te•va•ke•shoon?

---

5. They answered him, Jesus of Nazareth. Jesus saith unto them, I am he. And
Judas also, which betrayed him, stood with them.

Greek/Transliteration

5. Ἀπεκρίθησαν αὐτῷ, Ἰησοῦν τὸν Ναζωραῖον. Λέγει αὐτοῖς ὁ Ἰησοῦς, Ἐγώ
εἰμι. Εἱστήκει δὲ καὶ Ἰούδας ὁ παραδιδοὺς αὐτὸν μετ᾽ αὐτῶν.

5. Apekritheisan auto, Yeisoun ton Nazoraion. Legei autois 'o Yeisous, Ego
eimi. 'Eisteikei de kai Youdas 'o paradidous auton met auton.

Hebrew/Transliteration

:ה. וַיַּעֲנוּ אֹתוֹ אֶת-יֵשׁוּעַ הַנָּצְרִי וַיֹּאמֶר אֲלֵיהֶם יֵשׁוּעַ אֲנִי הוּא וִיהוּדָה הַמַּסְגִּיר עֹמֵד אֶצְלָם

5. Va•ya•a•noo o•to et - Yeshua ha•Notz•ri va•yo•mer aley•hem Yeshua ani
hoo vi•Y`hoo•da ha•mas•gir o•med etz•lam.

---

6. As soon then as he had said unto them, I am he, they went backward, and
fell to the ground.

Greek/Transliteration

6. Ὡς οὖν εἶπεν αὐτοῖς ὅτι Ἐγώ εἰμι, ἀπῆλθον εἰς τὰ ὀπίσω, καὶ ἔπεσον χαμαί.

6. 'Os oun eipen autois 'oti Ego eimi, apeilthon eis ta opiso, kai epeson
chamai.

Hebrew/Transliteration

:ו. וַיְהִי כַּאֲשֶׁר אָמַר אֲלֵיהֶם יֵשׁוּעַ אֲנִי הוּא וַיִּסֹּגוּ אָחוֹר וַיִּפְּלוּ אָרְצָה

6. Vay•hi ka•a•sher amar aley•hem Yeshua ani hoo va•yi•so•goo achor
va•yip•loo ar•tza.

Rabbinic Jewish Commentary

This was done, not to make his escape from them; but to give proof of his deity,
and a specimen of his power at the great day; and to let them know, that if he had
not thought fit to have surrendered himself voluntarily to them, though he was an

unarmed person, they, with all their men and arms, could never have laid hold on him; and to show them, that he could as easily have struck them dead, as to cause them to fall to the ground: and sometimes striking a person dead immediately, is expressed by this phrase of striking to the ground; and is ascribed to God, who does it by the ministry of angels: says R. Simeon ben Shetach (z), to some persons at variance,

"Let the master of thoughts come, (i.e. the blessed God,) and take vengeance on you; immediately Gabriel came, **והבטן בקרקע**, "and smote them to the ground"; and they died immediately."

The like is elsewhere said (a), "If thou transgresseth thy father's command, immediately comes Gabriel, and "smites to the ground"."

(z) F. Bab. Sanhedrin, fol. 19. 2. (a) Shemot Rabba, sect. 1. fol. 91. 2.

---

7. Then asked he them again, Whom seek ye? And they said, Jesus of Nazareth.

Greek/Transliteration
7. Πάλιν οὖν αὐτοὺς ἐπηρώτησεν, Τίνα ζητεῖτε; Οἱ δὲ εἶπον, Ἰησοῦν τὸν Ναζωραῖον.

7. Palin oun autous epeiroteisen, Tina zeiteite? 'Oi de eipon, Yeisoun ton Nazoraion.

Hebrew/Transliteration
:ז. וַיּוֹסֶף וַיִּשְׁאַל אֹתָם אֶת-מִי תְבַקֵּשׁוּ וַיֹּאמְרוּ אֶת-יֵשׁוּעַ הַנָּצְרִי

7. Va•yo•sef va•yish•al o•tam et - mee te•va•ke•shoo va•yom•roo et - Yeshua ha•Notz•ri.

Rabbinic Jewish Commentary
Something like this Josephus (b) reports concerning Elisha the prophet, though not repeated as here, nor attended with the like effect: he relates that Elisha having requested of God that he would smite his enemies with blindness, and that being granted he went into the midst of them, and asked them, τινα επιζητουντες ηλθον, "whom do ye come to seek?" they say Elisha the prophet: he promised them to deliver him to them, if they would follow him into the city, where he was; and so they being blinded by God, both in their sight and in their mind, followed the prophet.

(b) Antiqu. l. 9. c. 4. sect. 3.

---

8. Jesus answered, I have told you that I am he: if therefore ye seek me, let these go their way:

Greek/Transliteration
8. Ἀπεκρίθη Ἰησοῦς, Εἶπον ὑμῖν ὅτι ἐγώ εἰμι· εἰ οὖν ἐμὲ ζητεῖτε, ἄφετε τούτους ὑπάγειν·

8. Apekrithei Yeisous, Eipon 'umin 'oti ego eimi. ei oun eme zeiteite, aphete toutous 'upagein.

Hebrew/Transliteration

:ח. וַיַּעַן יֵשׁוּעַ הֲלֹא אָמַרְתִּי לָכֶם כִּי אֲנִי הוּא עַל-כֵּן אִם-אֹתִי תְבַקְשׁוּ הַנִּיחוּ לָאֵלֶּה וְיֵלֵכוּ

8. Va•ya•an Yeshua ha•lo amar•ti la•chem ki ani hoo al - ken eem - o•ti te•vak•shoo ha•ni•choo la•e•le ve•ye•le•choo.

---

9. That the saying might be fulfilled, which he spake, Of them which thou gavest me have I lost none.

Greek/Transliteration
9. ἵνα πληρωθῇ ὁ λόγος ὃν εἶπεν ὅτι Οὓς δέδωκάς μοι, οὐκ ἀπώλεσα ἐξ αὐτῶν οὐδένα.

9. 'ina pleirothei 'o logos 'on eipen 'oti 'Ous dedokas moi, ouk apolesa ex auton oudena.

Hebrew/Transliteration

:ט. לְהָקִים הַדָּבָר אֲשֶׁר אָמַר מֵאֵלֶּה אֲשֶׁר נָתַתָּה לִי לֹא-אָבַד לִי אַף-אֶחָד

9. Le•ha•kim ha•da•var asher amar me•e•le asher na•ta•ta li lo - avad li af - e•chad.

---

10. Then Simon Peter having a sword drew it, and smote the high priest's servant, and cut off his right ear. The servant's name was Malchus.

Greek/Transliteration
10. Σίμων οὖν Πέτρος ἔχων μάχαιραν εἵλκυσεν αὐτήν, καὶ ἔπαισεν τὸν τοῦ ἀρχιερέως δοῦλον, καὶ ἀπέκοψεν αὐτοῦ τὸ ὠτίον τὸ δεξιόν. Ἦν δὲ ὄνομα τῷ δούλῳ Μάλχος.

10. Simon oun Petros echon machairan 'eilkusen autein, kai epaisen ton tou archiereos doulon, kai apekopsen autou to otion to dexion. Ein de onoma to doulo Malchos.

Hebrew/Transliteration

י. וְחֶרֶב הָיְתָה בִּידֵי שִׁמְעוֹן פֶּטְרוֹס אֹתָהּ וַיַּד הַפֹּהֵן הַגָּדוֹל וַיְקַצֵּץ אֶת-אָזְנוֹ הַיְמָנִית אֶת-עֶבֶד הַפֹּהֵן וַיִּשְׁלֹף אֹתָהּ וְשֵׁם הָעֶבֶד:מַלְכּוֹס

10. Ve•che•rev hai•ta biy•dey Shimon Petros va•yish•lof o•ta va•yach et - eved ha•ko•hen ha•ga•dol vay•ka•tzetz et - oz•no hay`ma•nit ve•shem ha•e•ved Mal•chos.

Rabbinic Jewish Commentary

This was a name frequent with the Syrians, Phoenicians, and Hebrews. Jerom (c) wrote the life of one Malchus, a monk or Eremite, who was by nation a Syrian; and Porphyry, that great enemy of Christianity, who was by birth a Tyrian, his original name was Malchus, as was his father's; and "which", in the Syrian, and his country dialect, as he himself (d) and others (e) say, signifies a "king". Josephus (f) speaks of one Cleodemus, whose name was Malchus, that wrote a history of the Hebrews. And some Jewish Rabbi's were of this name; hence we read of רב מלוך, "R. Maluc" (g), and of רב מלכיו, "R. Malcio" (h); the name is the same with Malluch, Neh_10:4.

(c) Tom. I. fol. 87. (d) Porphyr. vita in Plotin. c. 17. (e) Eunapius in vita Porphyr. p. 16. (f) Antiqu. l. 1. c. 15. (g) T. Hieros. Succa, fol. 53. 3. & Bab. Bathra, fol. 16. 1. (h) T. Bab. Nidda, fol. 52. 1.

---

11. Then said Jesus unto Peter, Put up thy sword into the sheath: the cup which my Father hath given me, shall I not drink it?

Greek/Transliteration

11. Εἶπεν οὖν ὁ Ἰησοῦς τῷ Πέτρῳ, Βάλε τὴν μάχαιράν σου εἰς τὴν θήκην· τὸ ποτήριον ὃ δέδωκέν μοι ὁ πατήρ, οὐ μὴ πίω αὐτό;

11. Eipen oun 'o Yeisous to Petro, Bale tein machairan sou eis tein theikein. to poteirion 'o dedoken moi 'o pateir, ou mei pio auto?

Hebrew/Transliteration

יא. וַיֹּאמֶר יֵשׁוּעַ אֶל - פֶּטְרוֹס חָשֵׁב חַרְבְּךָ אֶל - נְדָנָה הַאֵם אֶת-כּוֹס אֲשֶׁר נָתַן-לִי אָבִי אֲנִי לֹא-אֶשְׁתֶּנָּה:

11. Va•yo•mer Yeshua el - Petros cha•shev char•be•cha el - n`da•na ha•eem et - kos asher na•tan - li Avi ani lo - esh•te•na?

---

12. Then the band and the captain and officers of the Jews took Jesus, and bound him,

Greek/Transliteration

12. Ἡ οὖν σπεῖρα καὶ ὁ χιλίαρχος καὶ οἱ ὑπηρέται τῶν Ἰουδαίων συνέλαβον τὸν Ἰησοῦν, καὶ ἔδησαν αὐτόν,

12. 'Ei oun speira kai 'o chiliarchos kai 'oi 'upeiretai ton Youdaion sunelabon ton Yeisoun, kai edeisan auton,

Hebrew/Transliteration

יב. וְהַגְּדוּד וְשַׂר הָאֶלֶף וּמְשָׁרְתֵי הַיְּהוּדִים תָּפְשׂוּ אָז אֶת-יֵשׁוּעַ וַיַּאַסְרֻהוּ:

12. Ve•hag•dood ve•sar ha•e•lef oom•shar•tey ha•Ye•hoo•dim taf•soo az et – Yeshua va•ya•as•roo•hoo.

Rabbinic Jewish Commentary

Hereby the types of him were fulfilled, as the binding of Isaac, when his father was going to offer him up, and the binding of the sacrifice with cords to the horns of the altar: who that has read the ceremonies of the sheaf of the firstfruits, but must call them to mind, upon reading this account of the apprehension and binding of Christ, and leading him to the high priest? This sheaf was fetched from places the nearest to Jerusalem, particularly from the fields of Kidron: the manner was this (i):

"The messengers of the sanhedrim went out (from Jerusalem) on the evening of the feast day (the sixteenth of Nisan, and over the brook Kidron to the adjacent fields), and bound the standing corn in bundles, that it might be the easier reaped; and all the neighbouring cities gathered together there, that it might be reaped in great pomp; and when it was dark, one (of the reapers) says to them, is the sun set? they say, yes; and again, is the sun set? they say, yes: with this sickle (shall I reap?) they say, yes; again, with this sickle (shall I reap?) they say, yes; in this basket (shall I put it?) they say, yes; again, in this basket (shall I put it?) they say, yes; if on the sabbath day he says to them, is this sabbath day? they say, yes; again, is this sabbath day? they say, yes; (it was sabbath day this year;) Shall I reap? they say to him reap, shall I reap? they say to him reap; three times upon everything; then they reap it, and put it into the baskets, and, bring it to the court, where they dry it at the fire."

Whoever reads this, will easily observe a likeness: the messengers of the great sanhedrim go to the fields of Kidron, in the evening, with their sickles and baskets; bind the standing corn; questions and answers pass between them and the people before they reap; and when they have done, they bring the sheaf in their basket to the court, to be dried at the fire. So the officers of the high priest, with others, pass over the brook Kidron, with lanterns, torches, and weapons; in the night go into a garden; there apprehend Yeshua; questions and answers pass between them there; then they lay hold on him, bind him, and bring him to the high, priest.

(i) Misn. Menachot, c. 10. sect. 2, 3, 4.

---

13. And led him away to Annas first; for he was father in law to Caiaphas, which was the high priest that same year.

Greek/Transliteration

13. καὶ ἀπήγαγον αὐτὸν πρὸς Ἄνναν πρῶτον· ἦν γὰρ πενθερὸς τοῦ Καϊάφα, ὃς ἦν ἀρχιερεὺς τοῦ ἐνιαυτοῦ ἐκείνου.

13. kai apeigagon auton pros Annan proton. ein gar pentheros tou Kaiapha, 'os ein archiereus tou enyautou ekeinou.

Hebrew/Transliteration

:יג. וַיּוֹלִיכֻהוּ בָּרִאשׁוֹנָה אֶל-חָנָן כִּי הוּא הָיָה חֹתֵן קַיָּפָא הַכֹּהֵן הַגָּדוֹל בַּשָּׁנָה הַהִיא

13. Va•yo•li•choo•hoo va•ri•sho•na el - Chanan ki hoo ha•ya cho•ten Ka•ya•fa ha•ko•hen ha•ga•dol ba•sha•na ha•hee.

Rabbinic Jewish Commentary

And led him away to Annas first,.... Who is elsewhere mentioned with Caiaphas as an high priest also, Luk_3:2. He was the "sagan" of the high priest; he and Caiaphas seem to have had the high priesthood alternately; and either now, because his house lay first in the way, or rather, because he was a man of age, learning, and experience, as these men usually were, that they might supply the deficiencies of the high priests, who were sometimes very weak and unlearned men (k); therefore they first lead him to him, to have his advice how to proceed, and to take him along with them to his son-in-law, where the great council was convened, and that he might use his interest and authority, in taking proper measures, in order to put Yeshua to death; and especially they led him to him, for the reason here assigned.

(k) Misn. Yoma, c. 1. sect. 3, 6.

---

14. Now Caiaphas was he, which gave counsel to the Jews, that it was expedient that one man should die for the people.

Greek/Transliteration

14. Ἦν δὲ Καϊάφας ὁ συμβουλεύσας τοῖς Ἰουδαίοις, ὅτι συμφέρει ἕνα ἄνθρωπον ἀπολέσθαι ὑπὲρ τοῦ λαοῦ.

14. Ein de Kaiaphas 'o sumbouleusas tois Youdaiois, 'oti sumpherei 'ena anthropon apolesthai 'uper tou laou.

Hebrew/Transliteration

:יד. הוּא קַיָּפָא אֲשֶׁר בַּעֲצָתוֹ לַיְהוּדִים הִגִּיד כִּי טוֹב אֲשֶׁר יֹאבַד אִישׁ-אֶחָד בְּעַד כָּל-הָעָם

14. Hoo Ka•ya•fa asher ba•a•tza•to la•Ye•hoo•dim hi•gid ki tov asher yo•vad eesh - e•chad be•ad kol - ha•am.

---

15. And Simon Peter followed Jesus, and so did another disciple: that disciple was known unto the high priest, and went in with Jesus into the palace of the high priest.

Greek/Transliteration

15. Ἠκολούθει δὲ τῷ Ἰησοῦ Σίμων Πέτρος, καὶ ὁ ἄλλος μαθητής. Ὁ δὲ μαθητὴς ἐκεῖνος ἦν γνωστὸς τῷ ἀρχιερεῖ, καὶ συνεισῆλθεν τῷ Ἰησοῦ εἰς τὴν αὐλὴν τοῦ ἀρχιερέως·

15. Eikolouthei de to Yeisou Simon Petros, kai 'o allos matheiteis. 'O de matheiteis ekeinos ein gnostos to archierei, kai suneiseilthen to Yeisou eis tein aulein tou archiereos.

Hebrew/Transliteration

טו. וְשִׁמְעוֹן פֶּטְרוֹס וְתַלְמִיד אַחֵר הָלְכוּ אַחֲרֵי יֵשׁוּעַ וְהַתַּלְמִיד הַהוּא נוֹדָע הָיָה לַכֹּהֵן הַגָּדוֹל וַיָּבֹא עִם-יֵשׁוּעַ:לַחֲצַר הַכֹּהֵן הַגָּדוֹל

15. Ve•Shimon Petros ve•tal•mid a•cher hal•choo a•cha•rey Yeshua ve•ha•tal•mid ha•hoo no•da ha•ya la•ko•hen ha•ga•dol va•ya•vo eem - Yeshua la•cha•tzar ha•ko•hen ha•ga•dol.

---

16. But Peter stood at the door without. Then went out that other disciple, which was known unto the high priest, and spake unto her that kept the door, and brought in Peter.

Greek/Transliteration

16. ὁ δὲ Πέτρος εἱστήκει πρὸς τῇ θύρᾳ ἔξω. Ἐξῆλθεν οὖν ὁ μαθητὴς ὁ ἄλλος ὃς ἦν γνωστὸς τῷ ἀρχιερεῖ, καὶ εἶπεν τῇ θυρωρῷ, καὶ εἰσήγαγεν τὸν Πέτρον.

16. 'o de Petros 'eisteikei pros tei thura exo. Exeilthen oun 'o matheiteis 'o allos 'os ein gnostos to archierei, kai eipen tei thuroro, kai eiseigagen ton Petron.

Hebrew/Transliteration

טז. וּפֶטְרוֹס עָמַד מִחוּץ לַשָּׁעַר וַיֵּצֵא הַתַּלְמִיד הָאַחֵר הַנּוֹדָע לַכֹּהֵן הַגָּדוֹל וַיְדַבֵּר אֶל-הַשֹּׁעֶרֶת וַיָּבֵא אֶת-פֶּטְרוֹס:הַבָּיְתָה

16. Oo•Fetros amad mi•choo•tz la•sha•ar va•ye•tze ha•tal•mid ha•a•cher ha•no•da la•ko•hen ha•ga•dol va•y`da•ber el - ha•sho•e•ret va•ya•ve et - Pe•taros ha•bai•ta.

---

17. Then saith the damsel that kept the door unto Peter, Art not thou also one of this man's disciples? He saith, I am not.

17. Λέγει οὖν ἡ παιδίσκη ἡ θυρωρὸς τῷ Πέτρῳ, Μὴ καὶ σὺ ἐκ τῶν μαθητῶν εἶ τοῦ ἀνθρώπου τούτου; Λέγει ἐκεῖνος, Οὐκ εἰμί.

17. Legei oun 'ei paidiskei 'ei thuroros to Petro, Mei kai su ek ton matheiton ei tou anthropou toutou? Legei ekeinos, Ouk eimi.

יז. וַתֹּאמֶר הָאָמָה הַשֹּׁעֶרֶת אֶל-פֶּטְרוֹס הֲלֹא גַם-אַתָּה מִתַּלְמִידֵי הָאִישׁ הַזֶּה וַיֹּאמֶר לֹא אָנִי:

17. Va•to•mer ha•a•ma ha•sho•e•ret el - Petros ha•lo gam - ata mi•tal•mi•dey ha•eesh ha•ze va•yo•mer lo ani.

---

18. And the servants and officers stood there, who had made a fire of coals; for it was cold: and they warmed themselves: and Peter stood with them, and warmed himself.

18. Εἱστήκεισαν δὲ οἱ δοῦλοι καὶ οἱ ὑπηρέται ἀνθρακιὰν πεποιηκότες, ὅτι ψύχος ἦν, καὶ ἐθερμαίνοντο· ἦν δὲ μετ᾽ αὐτῶν ὁ Πέτρος ἑστὼς καὶ θερμαινόμενος.

18. 'Eisteikeisan de 'oi douloi kai 'oi 'upeiretai anthrakyan pepoieikotes, 'oti psuchos ein, kai ethermainonto. ein de met auton 'o Petros 'estos kai thermainomenos.

יח. וְשָׁם עָמְדוּ הָעֲבָדִים וְהַמְשָׁרְתִים וַיְבַעֲרוּ גֶחָלִים לְהִתְחַמֵּם מִפְּנֵי הַקֹּר וַיַּעֲמֹד גַּם-פֶּטְרוֹס עִמָּהֶם וַיִּתְחַמָּם:

18. Ve•sham am•doo ha•a•va•dim ve•ham•shar•tim vay•va•a•roo ge•cha•lim le•hit•cha•mem mip•ney ha•kor va•ya•a•mod gam - Petros ee•ma•hem va•yit•cha•mam.

Rabbinic Jewish Commentary

Such very great dews fell as made it very cold, especially in the night; and from one of the Jewish canons (m), that the year was not intercalated, (which when done was chiefly on account of the passover,) neither for snow nor frost; which, as he justly remarks, supposes there might be frost and snow at the time of the passover. The same is observed in the Talmud (n), where the gloss upon it is,

"That they might not desist, on that account, from coming to the passover."

The passover was always in the spring of the year, when nights are commonly cold, as they are generally observed to be at the vernal equinox: this night might be remarkably cold; which seems to be suggested by the Persic version, which reads, "for it was cold that night"; and the Ethiopic version, "for the cold of that night was great"; and adds what is neither in the text, nor true, "for the country was cold". The Arabic version, as it should seem, very wrongly renders it, "for it was winter"; since the passover was never kept in the winter season, but always in the spring, in the month Nisan: the winter season, with the Jews, were half the month of Chisleu, all Tebeth, and half Shebet (o); though this is to be observed in favour of that version, that the Jews distinguish their winter into two parts; the one they call חורף, which, as the gloss says, is the strength of winter, the coldest part of it, and which lasts the time before mentioned; and the other they call קור, which is the end of winter, and when the cold is not so strong; and half Nisan is taken into this; for they say that half Shebat, all Adar, and half Nisan, are reckoned to this part of winter: so that, according to this account, the fourteenth of Nisan, which was the day on which the passover was killed; or at least the fifteenth, which was now begun, was the last day of winter, and so just secures the credit of the above version.

(m) Maimon. Hilch. Kiddush Chodesh, c. 4. sect. 6. (n) T. Bab. Sanhedrin, fol. 11. 1. (o) T. Bab. Bava Metzia, fol. 106. 2.

---

19. The high priest then asked Jesus of his disciples, and of his doctrine.

Greek/Transliteration
19. Ὁ οὖν ἀρχιερεὺς ἠρώτησεν τὸν Ἰησοῦν περὶ τῶν μαθητῶν αὐτοῦ, καὶ περὶ τῆς διδαχῆς αὐτοῦ.

19. 'O oun archiereus eiroteisen ton Yeisoun peri ton matheiton autou, kai peri teis didacheis autou.

Hebrew/Transliteration
יט. וַיִּשְׁאַל הַכֹּהֵן הַגָּדוֹל אֶת-יֵשׁוּעַ עַל-תַּלְמִידָיו וְעַל-תּוֹרָתוֹ:

19. Va•yish•al ha•ko•hen ha•ga•dol et - Yeshua al - tal•mi•dav ve•al - to•ra•to.

Rabbinic Jewish Commentary
By their canons (p), was allowed and encouraged: "If any of the disciples (of the person accused) says, I have a crime to lay to his charge, they silence him; but if one of the disciples says, I have something to say in his favour, they bring him up, and place him between them; nor does he go down from thence all the day; and if there is anything in what he says, שומעין לו, "they hearken to him".

The Jews indeed pretend (q) that after Yeshua was found guilty, a herald went before him forty days declaring his crime, and signifying, that if anyone knew anything worthy in him, to come and declare it; but none were found: but this is all lies and falsehood, to cover their wickedness;no disciple of his was allowed to speak for him.

20. Jesus answered him, I spake openly to the world; I ever taught in the synagogue, and in the temple, whither the Jews always resort; and in secret have I said nothing.

Greek/Transliteration

20. Ἀπεκρίθη αὐτῷ ὁ Ἰησοῦς, Ἐγὼ παρρησίᾳ ἐλάλησα τῷ κόσμῳ· ἐγὼ πάντοτε ἐδίδαξα ἐν συναγωγῇ καὶ ἐν τῷ ἱερῷ, ὅπου πάντοτε οἱ Ἰουδαῖοι συνέρχονται, καὶ ἐν κρυπτῷ ἐλάλησα οὐδέν.

20. Apekrithei auto 'o Yeisous, Ego parreisia elaleisa to kosmo. ego pantote edidaxa en sunagogei kai en to 'iero, 'opou pantote 'oi Youdaioi sunerchontai, kai en krupto elaleisa ouden.

Hebrew/Transliteration

כ. וַיַּעַן אֹתוֹ יֵשׁוּעַ אָנֹכִי לְעֵין הַשֶּׁמֶשׁ דִּבַּרְתִּי אֶל-הָעוֹלָם וְתָמִיד לִמַּדְתִּי בְּבֵית-הַכְּנֶסֶת וּבְבֵית הַמִּקְדָּשׁ אֲשֶׁר שָׁם:כָּל-הַיְּהוּדִים נִקְהָלִים וְלֹא-דִבַּרְתִּי דָבָר בַּסָּתֶר

20. Va•ya•an o•to Yeshua ano•chi le•ein ha•she•mesh di•bar•ti el - ha•o•lam ve•ta•mid li•ma•de•ti be•veit - ha•k`ne•set oo•ve•veit ha•mik•dash asher sham kol - ha•Ye•hoo•dim nik•ha•lim ve•lo - di•bar•ti da•var ba•sa•ter.

Rabbinic Jewish Commentary

The phrase Yeshua speaks, "I said nothing in secret," וְלֹא-דִבַּרְתִּי דָבָר בַּסָּתֶר, echoes the words of Isaiah 48,

"Come near to me and hear this: From the beginning I have not spoken in secret (לֹא מֵרֹאשׁ בַּסֵּתֶר דִּבַּרְתִּי); from the time that it was, there am I. Now the Lord YHWH has sent me, with his Spirit. (Isaiah 48:16)

---

21. Why askest thou me? ask them which heard me, what I have said unto them: behold, they know what I said.

Greek/Transliteration

21. Τί με ἐπερωτᾷς; Ἐπερώτησον τοὺς ἀκηκοότας, τί ἐλάλησα αὐτοῖς· ἴδε, οὗτοι οἴδασιν ἃ εἶπον ἐγώ.

21. Ti me eperotas? Eperoteison tous akeiko'otas, ti elaleisa autois. ide, 'outoi oidasin 'a eipon ego.

Hebrew/Transliteration

כא. וְלָמָּה-זֶּה תִּשְׁאָלֵנִי שְׁאַל-נָא אֶת-הָאֲנָשִׁים אֲשֶׁר שָׁמְעוּ דְבָרַי הֲנָם יֹדְעִים אֶת-אֲשֶׁר הוֹרֵיתִי:

425

21. Ve•la•ma - ze tish•a•le•ni sh`al - na et - ha•a•na•shim asher sham•oo
de•va•rai hi•nam yod•eem et - asher ho•rey•ti.

---

22. And when he had thus spoken, one of the officers which stood by struck
Jesus with the palm of his hand, saying, Answerest thou the high priest so?

Greek/Transliteration

22. Ταῦτα δὲ αὐτοῦ εἰπόντος, εἷς τῶν ὑπηρετῶν παρεστηκὼς ἔδωκεν ῥάπισμα
τῷ Ἰησοῦ, εἰπών, Οὕτως ἀποκρίνῃ τῷ ἀρχιερεῖ;

22. Tauta de autou eipontos, 'eis ton 'upeireton paresteikos edoken 'rapisma
to Yeisou, eipon, 'Outos apokrinei to archierei?

Hebrew/Transliteration

כב. וַיְהִי כְדַבְּרוֹ אֶת-הַדְּבָרִים הָאֵלֶּה וַיַּךְ אֶחָד הַמְשָׁרְתִים הָעֹמֵד שָׁם אֶת-יֵשׁוּעַ עַל-הַלְּחִי וַיֹּאמַר
הֲכָזֹאת תַּעֲנֶה:אֶת-הַכֹּהֵן הַגָּדוֹל

22. Vay•hi ke•dab•ro et - ha•d`va•rim ha•e•le va•yach e•chad ha•me•shar•tim
ha•o•med sham et - Yeshua al - hal•chi va•yo•mar ha•cha•zot ta•a•ne et -
ha•ko•hen ha•ga•dol?

---

23. Jesus answered him, If I have spoken evil, bear witness of the evil: but if
well, why smitest thou me?

Greek/Transliteration

23. Ἀπεκρίθη αὐτῷ ὁ Ἰησοῦς, Εἰ κακῶς ἐλάλησα, μαρτύρησον περὶ τοῦ
κακοῦ· εἰ δὲ καλῶς, τί με δέρεις;

23. Apekrithei auto 'o Yeisous, Ei kakos elaleisa, martureison peri tou kakou.
ei de kalos, ti me dereis?

Hebrew/Transliteration

כג. וַיַּעַן אֹתוֹ יֵשׁוּעַ אִם-רָעָה דִבַּרְתִּי עֲנֵה בִּי אֶת-הָרָעָה וְאִם-נְכוֹנָה עַל-מֶה הִכִּיתָנִי:

23. Va•ya•an o•to Yeshua eem - ra•ah di•bar•ti a•ne vi et - ha•ra•ah ve•eem -
n`cho•na al - me hi•ki•ta•ni?

Rabbinic Jewish Commentary

If he had said nothing contrary to truth, reason, and good manners, then he ought
not to be used and treated in such an injurious way. And moreover, the officer
ought to have been corrected by the Council, and have been made to pay the two
hundred "zuzim", or pence, the line for such an affront, according to the Jewish
canon, or more, according to the dignity of the person abused (r).

(r) Misn. Bava Kama, c. 8. sect. 6.

24. Now Annas had sent him bound unto Caiaphas the high priest.

Greek/Transliteration
24. Ἀπέστειλεν αὐτὸν ὁ Ἅννας δεδεμένον πρὸς Καϊάφαν τὸν ἀρχιερέα.

24. Apesteilen auton 'o Annas dedemenon pros Kaiaphan ton archierea.

Hebrew/Transliteration
:כד. וְחָנָן שָׁלַח אֹתוֹ אָסוּר אֶל-קַיָּפָא הַכֹּהֵן הַגָּדוֹל

24. Ve•Chanan sha•lach o•to a•soor el - Ka•ya•fa ha•ko•hen ha•ga•dol.

---

25. And Simon Peter stood and warmed himself. They said therefore unto him, Art not thou also one of his disciples? He denied it, and said, I am not.

Greek/Transliteration
25. Ἦν δὲ Σίμων Πέτρος ἑστὼς καὶ θερμαινόμενος· εἶπον οὖν αὐτῷ, Μὴ καὶ σὺ ἐκ τῶν μαθητῶν αὐτοῦ εἶ; Ἡρνήσατο οὖν ἐκεῖνος, καὶ εἶπεν, Οὐκ εἰμί.

25. Ein de Simon Petros 'estos kai thermainomenos. eipon oun auto, Mei kai su ek ton matheiton autou ei? Eirneisato oun ekeinos, kai eipen, Ouk eimi.

Hebrew/Transliteration
:כה. וְשִׁמְעוֹן פֶּטְרוֹס עֹמֵד וּמִתְחַמֵּם וַיֹּאמְרוּ אֵלָיו הֲלֹא גַם-אַתָּה מִתַּלְמִידָיו וַיְכַחֵשׁ וַיֹּאמֶר לֹא אָנִי

25. Ve•Shimon Petros o•med oo•mit•cha•mem va•yom•roo elav ha•lo gam –
ata mi•tal•mi•dav vay•cha•chesh va•yo•mer lo ani.

---

26. One of the servants of the high priest, being his kinsman whose ear Peter cut off, saith, Did not I see thee in the garden with him?

Greek/Transliteration
26. Λέγει εἷς ἐκ τῶν δούλων τοῦ ἀρχιερέως, συγγενὴς ὢν οὗ ἀπέκοψεν Πέτρος τὸ ὠτίον, Οὐκ ἐγώ σε εἶδον ἐν τῷ κήπῳ μετ᾿ αὐτοῦ;

26. Legei 'eis ek ton doulon tou archiereos, sungeneis on 'ou apekopsen Petros to otion, Ouk ego se eidon en to keipo met autou?

Hebrew/Transliteration
כו. וְאֶחָד מֵעַבְדֵי הַכֹּהֵן הַגָּדוֹל מוֹדָע לָאִישׁ הַהוּא אֲשֶׁר קִצֵּץ פֶּטְרוֹס אֶת-אָזְנוֹ אָמַר אֵלָיו הֲלֹא אֲנִי
רְאִיתִיךָ עִמּוֹ:בַּגָּן

26. Ve•e•chad me•av•dey ha•ko•hen ha•ga•dol mo•da la•eesh ha•hoo asher ki•tzetz Petros et - oz•no amar elav ha•lo ani r`ee•ti•cha ee•mo ba•gan?

27. Peter then denied again: and immediately the cock crew.

Greek/Transliteration
27. Πάλιν οὖν ἠρνήσατο ὁ Πέτρος, καὶ εὐθέως ἀλέκτωρ ἐφώνησεν.

27. Palin oun eirneisato 'o Petros, kai eutheos alektor ephoneisen.

Hebrew/Transliteration
כז. וַיּוֹסֶף פֶּטְרוֹס וַיְכַחֵשׁ וּבְרֶגַע זֶה קָרָא הַתַּרְנְגֹל:

27. Va•yo•sef Petros vay•cha•chesh oov•re•ga ze ka•ra ha•tar•ne•gol.

Rabbinic Jewish Commentary
The fine for plucking a man's ears, and which some understand of plucking them off, was four hundred "zuzim" (s), or, pence; which, as they answer to Roman pence, amount to twelve pounds ten shillings; a sum of money Peter perhaps could not have raised, without great difficulty: and therefore, that it might be believed he was not a disciple of Yeshua, so not the man; he swears in a profane manner, and imprecates the judgments of God upon him.

(s) Misn. Bava Kama, c. 8, sect. 6. Vid. L'Empereur in ib.

---

28. Then led they Jesus from Caiaphas unto the hall of judgment: and it was early; and they themselves went not into the judgment hall, lest they should be defiled; but that they might eat the passover.

Greek/Transliteration
28. ῎Αγουσιν οὖν τὸν ᾿Ιησοῦν ἀπὸ τοῦ Καϊάφα εἰς τὸ πραιτώριον· ἦν δὲ πρωΐ, καὶ αὐτοὶ οὐκ εἰσῆλθον εἰς τὸ πραιτώριον, ἵνα μὴ μιανθῶσιν, ἀλλ᾿ ἵνα φάγωσιν τὸ Πάσχα.

28. Agousin oun ton Yeisoun apo tou Kaiapha eis to praitorion. ein de proi, kai autoi ouk eiseilthon eis to praitorion, 'ina mei myanthosin, all 'ina phagosin to Pascha.

Hebrew/Transliteration
כח. וַיּוֹלִיכוּ אֶת-יֵשׁוּעַ מִבֵּית קַיָּפָא אֶל-בֵּית הַמִּשְׁפָּט כַּעֲלוֹת הַבֹּקֶר וְהֵם לֹא בָאוּ לְתוֹךְ בֵּית הַמִּשְׁפָּט לְבִלְתִּי יִטַּמָּאוּ וְלֹא יוּכְלוּ לֶאֱכֹל אֶת-הַפָּסַח:

28. Va•yo•li•choo et - Yeshua mi•beit Ka•ya•fa el - beit ha•mish•pat ka•a•lot ha•bo•ker ve•hem lo va•oo le•toch beit ha•mish•pat le•vil•ti yi•tam•oo ve•lo yooch•loo le•e•chol et - ha•Pa•sach.

Rabbinic Jewish Commentary

and they themselves went not into the judgment hall, lest they should be defiled; that is, the Jews, only the band of Roman soldiers went in; the reason of this was, because it was the house of a Gentile, and with them, מדורות העכום טמאים, "the dwelling houses of Gentiles", or idolaters, "are unclean" (t); yea, if they were the houses of Israelites, and Gentiles were admitted to dwell in them, they were defiled, and all that were in them; for so they say (u),

"If the collectors for the government enter into a house to dwell in, all in the house are defiled."

They did not think it lawful to rent out a house in Judea to an Heathen (w), or to assist in building a Basilica for them; which they explain to be a palace, in which judges sit to judge men (x): hence the reason of their caution, and which they were the more observant of,

that they might eat the passover; pure and undefiled; not the passover lamb, for that they had eaten the night before; but the "Chagigah", or feast on the fifteenth day of the month. Many Christian writers, both ancient and modern, have concluded from hence, that Yeshua did not keep his last passover, at the same time the Jews did; and many things are said to illustrate this matter, and justify Yeshua in it: some observe the distinction of a sacrificial, and commemorative passover; the sacrificial passover is that, in which the lamb was slain, and was fixed to a certain time and place, and there was no altering it; the commemorative passover is that, in which no lamb is slain and eaten, only a commemoration made of the deliverance of the people of Israel out of Egypt; such as is now kept by the Jews, being out of their own land, where sacrifice with them is not lawful; and this it is supposed Yeshua kept, and not the former: but it does not appear that there was such a commemorative passover kept by the Jews, in Yeshua's time, and whilst the temple stood: and supposing there was such an one allowed, and appointed for those that were at a distance from Jerusalem, and could not come up thither, (which was not the case of Yeshua and his disciples,) it is reasonable to conclude, that it was to be kept, and was kept at the time the sacrificial passover was, in the room of which it was substituted, as it is by the Jews to this day; so that this will by no means clear the matter, nor solve the difficulty; besides it is very manifest, that the passover Yeshua kept was sacrificial; and such an one the disciples proposed to get ready for him, and did, of which he and they are said to eat: "and the first day of unleavened bread, when they KILLED the passover, his disciples said to him, where wilt thou that we go and prepare, that thou mayest EAT the passover?" Mar_14:12 and again, "then came the day of unleavened bread, when the passover MUST be KILLED", Luk_22:7. "They made ready the passover", Luk_22:13 "and he sat down, and the twelve apostles with him", Luk_22:14 "and he said unto them, with desire I have desired to eat this passover", Luk_22:15.

Others suggest, that this difference of observing the passover by Yeshua and the Jews arose from fixing the beginning of the month, and so accordingly the feasts in it, by the φασις, or appearance of the moon; and that Yeshua went according to the true appearance of it, and the Jews according to a false account: but of this, as a fact, there is no proof; besides, though the feasts were regulated and fixed according to the appearance of the moon, yet this was not left to the arbitrary will, pleasure, and judgment of particular persons, to determine as they should think proper; but the sanhedrim, or chief council of the nation sat, at a proper time, to hear and examine witnesses about the appearance of the moon; and accordingly determined, and none might fix but them (y); and as this was doubtless the case at this time, it is not very reasonable to think, that Yeshua would differ from them: besides, it was either a clear case, or a doubtful one; if the former, then there would be no room nor reason to keep another day; and if it was the latter, then two days were observed, that they might be sure they were right (z); but then both were kept by all the Jews: and that the time of this passover was well known, is clear from various circumstances; such and such facts were done, so many days before it; six days before it, Yeshua came to Bethany, Joh_12:1 and two days before it, he was in the same place, Mat_26:2 and says to his disciples, "ye know that after two days is the feast of the passover". Others taking it for granted, that Yeshua kept the passover a day before the usual and precise time, defend it, by observing the despotic and legislative power of Yeshua, who had a right to dispense with the time of this feast, and could at his pleasure anticipate it, because the betraying of him and his death were so near at hand: that he had such a power will not be disputed; but that he should use it in this way, does not seem necessary, on account of his death, seeing none but the living were obliged to it; nor so consistent with his wisdom, since hereby the mouths of his enemies would be opened against him, for acting not agreeably to the law of God: moreover, when it is considered that the passover, according to the Jews, was always kept במועדו, "in its set time" (a), and was not put off on the account of the sabbath, or anything else, to another day; and that though when it was put off for particular persons, on account of uncleanness, to another month, yet still it was to be kept on the fourteenth day at even, in that month, Num_9:10 it will not easily be received that Yeshua observed it a day before the time: besides, the passover lamb was not killed in a private house, but in the temple, in the court of it, and that always on the fourteenth of Nisan, after noon: so says Maimonides (b),

"It is an affirmative command to slay the passover on the fourteenth of the month Nisan, after the middle of the day. The passover is not slain but in the court, as the rest of the holy things; even in the time that altars were lawful, they did not offer the passover on a private altar; and whoever offers the passover on a private altar, is to be beaten; as it is said, "thou mayest not sacrifice the passover within any of thy gates, which the Lord thy God giveth thee", Deu_16:5.".

And seeing therefore a passover lamb was not to be killed at home, but in the court of the priests, in the temple, it does not seem probable, that a single lamb should be suffered to be killed there, for Yeshua and his disciples, on a day not observed by the Jews, contrary to the sense of the sanhedrim, and of the whole nation: add to this, that the sacred text is express for it, that it was at the exact time of this feast, when it was come according to general computation, that the disciples moved to Yeshua to prepare the passover for him, and did, and they with him kept it: the account Matthew gives is very full; "now the first day of the feast of unleavened bread"; that is, when that was come in its proper time and course, "the disciples came to Yeshua"; saying unto him, where wilt "thou that we prepare for thee to eat the passover?" He bids them go to the city to such a man, and say, "I will keep the passover at thy house with my disciples, and the disciples did as Yeshua had appointed, and they made ready the passover; now when the even was come", the time of eating the passover, according to the law of God, "he sat down with the twelve, and as they did eat". Mat_26:17 and Mark is still more particular, who says, "and the first day of unleavened bread, when they killed the passover"; that is, when the Jews killed the passover, on the very day the lamb was slain, and eaten by them; and then follows much the same account as before, Mar_14:12 and Luke yet more clearly expresses it, "then came the day of unleavened bread, when the passover must be killed"; according to the law of God, and the common usage of the people of the Jews; yea, he not only observes, that Yeshua kept the usual day, but the very hour, the precise time of eating it; for he says, "and when the hour was come, he sat down, and the twelve apostles with him", Luk_22:7. Nor is there anything in this text, that is an objection to Yeshua and the Jews keeping the passover at the same time; since by the passover here is meant, the "Chagigah", or feast kept on the fifteenth day of the month, as it is sometimes called: in Deu_16:2 it is said, "thou shalt therefore sacrifice the passover unto the Lord thy God, of the flock and the herd": now the passover of the herd, can never mean the passover lamb, but the passover "Chagigah"; and so the Jewish commentators explain it; "of the herd", says Jarchi, thou shalt sacrifice for the "Chagigah"; and says Aben Ezra, for the peace offerings; so Josiah the king is said to give for the passovers three thousand bullocks, and the priests three hundred oxen, and the Levites five hundred oxen, 2Ch_35:7 which Jarchi interprets of the peace offerings of the "Chagigah", there called passovers; and so in 1 Esdres 1:7-9 mention is made of three thousand calves, besides lambs, that Josias gave for the passover; and three hundred by some other persons, and seven hundred by others: the passage in Deuteronomy, is explained of the "Chagigah", in both Talmuds (c), and in other writings (d); so besides the passover lamb, we read of sacrifices slain, לשום פסח, "in the name of" the passover, or on account of it (e); and particularly of the calf and the young bullock, slain for the sake of the passover (f): and now this is the passover which these men were to eat that day, and therefore were careful not to defile themselves, that so they might not be unfit for it; otherwise had it been the passover lamb in the evening, they might have washed themselves in the evening, according to the rules of טבול יום, or "the daily washing", and been clean enough to have eat it: besides, it may be observed, that all the seven days were called the passover; and he that ate the unleavened bread, is said by eating that, to eat the passover; and thus they invite their guests daily to eat the bread, saying (g),

"Everyone that is hungry, let him come and eat all that he needs, ויפסח, "and keep the passover".

It is easy to observe the consciences of these men, who were always wont to strain at a gnat and swallow a camel; they scruple going into the judgment hall, which belonged to an Heathen governor, and where was a large number of Heathen soldiers; but they could go along with these into the garden to apprehend Yeshua, and spend a whole night in consulting to shed innocent blood: no wonder that God should be weary of their sacrifices and ceremonious performances, when, trusting to these, they had no regard to moral precepts: however, this may be teaching to us, in what manner we should keep the feast, and eat of the true passover, Yeshua; not with malice and wickedness, as these Jews ate theirs, but with sincerity and truth: besides, a sanhedrim, when they had condemned anyone to death, were forbidden to eat anything all that day (h); and so whilst scrupling one thing, they broke through another.

(t) Misn. Oholot, c. 18. sect. 7. (u) Maimon. Mishcab & Mosheb, c. 12. sect. 12. (w) Misn. Avoda Zara, c. 1. sect. 8. (x) Jarchi & Bartenora in ib. sect. 7. (y) Maimon. Kiddush Hachodesh, c. 2. sect. 7, 8. (z) Ib. c. 5. sect. 6, 7, 8. (a) Maimon. in Misn. Pesachim, c. 7. sect. 4. & Bartenora in ib. c. 5. sect. 4. (b) Hilchot Korban Pesacb. c. 1. sect. 1, 3. (c) T. Hieros. Pesacb. fol. 33. 1. T. Bab. Pesachim, fol. 70. 2. (d) Maimon. Korban Pesach. c. 10. sect. 12. Moses Kotsensis Mitzvot Tora, pr. neg. 349. (e) Misn. Pesachim, c. 6. sect. 5. (f) T. Bab. Menachot, fol. 3. 1. (g) Haggadah Shel Pesach. p. 4. Ed. Rittangel. (h) T. Bab. Sanhedrin, fol. 63. 1. Maimon. Hilch. Sanhedrin, c. 13. sect. 4.

---

29. Pilate then went out unto them, and said, What accusation bring ye against this man?

Greek/Transliteration

29. Ἐξῆλθεν οὖν ὁ Πιλᾶτος πρὸς αὐτούς, καὶ εἶπεν, Τίνα κατηγορίαν φέρετε κατὰ τοῦ ἀνθρώπου τούτου;

29. Exeilthen oun 'o Pilatos pros autous, kai eipen, Tina kateigorian pherete kata tou anthropou toutou?

Hebrew/Transliteration

כט. וַיֵּצֵא פִילָטוֹס אֲלֵיהֶם וַיֹּאמַר מַה-שִׂיטְנָה תָבִיאוּ עַל-הָאִישׁ הַזֶּה:

29. Va•ye•tze Filatos aley•hem va•yo•mar ma - sit•na ta•vi•oo al - ha•eesh ha•ze?

---

30. They answered and said unto him, If he were not a malefactor, we would not have delivered him up unto thee.

Greek/Transliteration

30. Ἀπεκρίθησαν καὶ εἶπον αὐτῷ, Εἰ μὴ ἦν οὗτος κακοποιός, οὐκ ἄν σοι παρεδώκαμεν αὐτόν.

30. Apekritheisan kai eipon auto, Ei mei ein 'outos kakopoios, ouk an soi paredokamen auton.

Hebrew/Transliteration

ל. וַיַּעֲנוּ וַיֹּאמְרוּ אֵלָיו לוּלֵא הָיָה זֶה פֹּעֵל אָוֶן לֹא הִסְגַּרְנוּ אֹתוֹ בְּיָדֶיךָ:

---

30. Va•ya•a•noo va•yom•roo elav loo•le ha•ya ze po•el - aven lo his•gar•noo o•to be•ya•de•cha.

---

31. Then said Pilate unto them, Take ye him, and judge him according to your law. The Jews therefore said unto him, It is not lawful for us to put any man to death:

31. Εἶπεν οὖν αὐτοῖς ὁ Πιλάτος, Λάβετε αὐτὸν ὑμεῖς, καὶ κατὰ τὸν νόμον ὑμῶν κρίνατε αὐτόν. Εἶπον οὖν αὐτῷ οἱ Ἰουδαῖοι, Ἡμῖν οὐκ ἔξεστιν ἀποκτεῖναι οὐδένα·

31. Eipen oun autois 'o Pilatos, Labete auton 'umeis, kai kata ton nomon 'umon krinate auton. Eipon oun auto 'oi Youdaioi, 'Eimin ouk exestin apokteinai oudena.

לא. וַיֹּאמֶר אֲלֵיהֶם פִּילָטוֹס קְחוּ אֹתוֹ אַתֶּם וְשִׁיפְטֻהוּ עַל-פִּי תוֹרַתְכֶם וַיֹּאמְרוּ אֵלָיו הַיְהוּדִים אֵין-לָנוּ כֹּח:לְהָמִית נֶפֶשׁ אָדָם

31. Va•yo•mer aley•hem Pilatos ke•choo o•to atem ve•shif•too•hoo al - pi to•rat•chem va•yom•roo elav ha•Ye•hoo•dim eyn - la•noo cho•ach le•ha•mit ne•fesh adam.

Rabbinic Jewish Commentary
the Jews therefore said unto him, it is not lawful for us to put any man to death; Thereby insinuating, that he was guilty of a crime, which deserved death, and which they could not inflict; not that they were of such tender consciences, that they could not put him to death, or that they had no law to punish him with death, provided he was guilty; but because judgments in capital cases had ceased among them; nor did they try causes relating to life and death, the date of which they often make to be forty years before the destruction of the temple (i); and which was much about, or a little before the time these words were spoken: not that this power was taken away wholly from them by the Romans; though since their subjection to the empire, they had not that full and free exercise of it as before; but through the great increase of iniquity, particularly murder, which caused such frequent executions, that they were weary of them (k); and through the negligence and indolence of the Jewish sanhedrim, and their removal from the room Gazith, where they only judged capital causes (l): as for the stoning of Stephen, and the putting of some to death against whom Saul gave his voice, these were the outrages of the zealots, and were not according to a formal process in any court of judicature. Two executions are mentioned in their Talmud; the one is of a priest's daughter that was burnt for a harlot (m), and the other of the stoning of Ben Stada in Lydda (n); the one, according to them, seems to be before, the other after the destruction of the temple; but these dates are not certain, nor to be depended upon: for since the destruction of their city and temple, and their being carried captive

into other lands, it is certain that the power of life and death has been wholly taken from them; by which it appears, that the sceptre is removed from Judah, and a lawgiver from between his feet; and this they own almost in the same words as here expressed; for they say (o) of a certain man worthy of death,

"Why dost thou scourge him? he replies, because he lay with a beast; they say to him, hast thou any witnesses? he answers, yes; Elijah came in the form of a man, and witnessed; they say, if it be so, he deserves to die; to which he answers, "from the day we have been carried captive out of our land, לית לן רשותא למקטל, we have no power to put to death".

But at this time, their power was not entirely gone; but the true reason of their saying these words is, that they might wholly give up Yeshua to the Roman power, and throw off the reproach of his death from themselves; and particularly they were desirous he should die the reproachful and painful death of the cross, which was a Roman punishment: had they took him and judged him according to their law, which must have been as a false prophet, or for blasphemy or idolatry, the death they must have condemned him to, would have been stoning; but it was crucifixion they were set upon; and therefore deliver him up as a traitor, and a seditious person, in order thereunto.

(i) T. Bab. Sabbat, fol. 15. 1. Sanhedrin, fol. 41. 1. T. Hieros. Sanhedrin, fol. 18. 1. & 24. 2. Juchasin, fol. 51. 1. Moses Kotsensis pr. affirm. 99. (k) T. Bab. Avoda Zara fol. 8. 2. Juchasin, fol. 21. 1. (l) Gloss. in T. Bab. Avoda Zara, fol. 8, 2. (m) T. Hieros. Sanhedrin, fol. 24. 2. (n) Ib. fol. 25. 4. (o) T. Bab. Beracot, fol. 58. 1.

---

32. That the saying of Jesus might be fulfilled, which he spake, signifying what death he should die.

Greek/Transliteration
32. ἵνα ὁ λόγος τοῦ ᾽Ιησοῦ πληρωθῇ, ὃν εἶπεν, σημαίνων ποίῳ θανάτῳ ἤμελλεν ἀποθνῄσκειν.

32. 'ina 'o logos tou Yeisou pleirothei, 'on eipen, seimainon poio thanato eimellen apothneiskein.

Hebrew/Transliteration
:לב. לְמַלֹּאת דְּבַר יֵשׁוּעַ אֲשֶׁר הִגִּיד מַה-יִּהְיֶה מוֹתוֹ אֲשֶׁר יוּמָת

32. Le•ma•lot de•var Yeshua asher hi•gid ma - yi•hee•ye mo•to asher yoo•mat.

---

33. Then Pilate entered into the judgment hall again, and called Jesus, and said unto him, Art thou the King of the Jews?

33. Εἰσῆλθεν οὖν εἰς τὸ πραιτώριον πάλιν ὁ Πιλᾶτος, καὶ ἐφώνησεν τὸν Ἰησοῦν, καὶ εἶπεν αὐτῷ, Σὺ εἶ ὁ βασιλεὺς τῶν Ἰουδαίων;

33. Eiseilthen oun eis to praitorion palin 'o Pilatos, kai ephoneisen ton Yeisoun, kai eipen auto, Su ei 'o basileus ton Youdaion?

לג. וַיָּשָׁב פִּילָטוֹס אֶל-בֵּית הַמִּשְׁפָּט וַיִּקְרָא אֶל-יֵשׁוּעַ וַיֹּאמֶר אֵלָיו הַאַתָּה הוּא מֶלֶךְ הַיְּהוּדִים:

33. Va•ya•shov Pilatos el - beit ha•mish•pat va•yik•ra el - Yeshua va•yo•mer elav ha•a•ta hoo Me•lech ha•Ye•hoo•dim?

---

34. Jesus answered him, Sayest thou this thing of thyself, or did others tell it thee of me?

34. Ἀπεκρίθη αὐτῷ ὁ Ἰησοῦς, Ἀφ᾽ ἑαυτοῦ σὺ τοῦτο λέγεις, ἢ ἄλλοι σοι εἶπον περὶ ἐμοῦ;

34. Apekrithei auto 'o Yeisous, Aph 'eautou su touto legeis, ei alloi soi eipon peri emou?

לד. וַיַּעַן יֵשׁוּעַ הֲמִלִּבְּךָ אַתָּה דֹבֵר כֵּן אוֹ כֵן הִגִּידוּ-לְךָ עָלַי אֲחֵרִים:

34. Va•ya•an Yeshua ha•mi•lib•cha ata do•ver ken oh chen hi•gi•doo - le•cha a•lai a•che•rim?

---

35. Pilate answered, Am I a Jew? Thine own nation and the chief priests have delivered thee unto me: what hast thou done?

35. Ἀπεκρίθη ὁ Πιλᾶτος, Μήτι ἐγὼ Ἰουδαῖός εἰμι; Τὸ ἔθνος τὸ σὸν καὶ οἱ ἀρχιερεῖς παρέδωκάν σε ἐμοί· τί ἐποίησας;

35. Apekrithei 'o Pilatos, Meiti ego Youdaios eimi? To ethnos to son kai 'oi archiereis paredokan se emoi. ti epoieisas?

לה. וַיַּעַן פִּילָטוֹס הֲכִי יְהוּדִי אָנֹכִי הֵן עַמְּךָ וְרָאשֵׁי הַכֹּהֲנִים הִסְגִּירוּךָ בְיָדִי מֶה עָשִׂיתָ:

35. Va•ya•an Pilatos ha•chi Ye•hoo•di ano•chi hen am•cha ve•ra•shey ha•ko•ha•nim his•gi•roo•cha ve•ya•di me a•si•ta?

36. Jesus answered, My kingdom is not of this world: if my kingdom were of this world, then would my servants fight, that I should not be delivered to the Jews: but now is my kingdom not from hence.

Greek/Transliteration

36. Ἀπεκρίθη Ἰησοῦς, Ἡ βασιλεία ἡ ἐμὴ οὐκ ἔστιν ἐκ τοῦ κόσμου τούτου· εἰ ἐκ τοῦ κόσμου τούτου ἦν ἡ βασιλεία ἡ ἐμή, οἱ ὑπηρέται ἂν οἱ ἐμοὶ ἠγωνίζοντο, ἵνα μὴ παραδοθῶ τοῖς Ἰουδαίοις· νῦν δὲ ἡ βασιλεία ἡ ἐμὴ οὐκ ἔστιν ἐντεῦθεν.

36. Apekrithei Yeisous, 'Ei basileia 'ei emei ouk estin ek tou kosmou toutou. ei ek tou kosmou toutou ein 'ei basileia 'ei emei, 'oi 'upeiretai an 'oi emoi eigonizonto, 'ina mei paradotho tois Youdaiois. nun de 'ei basileia 'ei emei ouk estin enteuthen.

Hebrew/Transliteration

לו. וַיַּעַן יֵשׁוּעַ מַלְכוּתִי אֵינֶנָּה מִן-הָעוֹלָם הַזֶּה אִלּוּ מִן-הָעוֹלָם הַזֶּה הָיְתָה מַלְכוּתִי מְשָׁרְתַי יִלָּחֲמוּ לִי לְבִלְתִּי:אֲנָתֵן בִּידֵי הַיְּהוּדִים אַךְ עַתָּה מַלְכוּתִי אֵינֶנָּה מִפֹּה

36. Va•ya•an Yeshua mal•choo•ti ey•ne•na min - ha•o•lam ha•ze ee•loo min - ha•o•lam ha•ze hai•ta mal•choo•ti me•shar•tai yi•la•cha•moo li le•vil•ti e•na•ten biy•dey ha•Ye•hoo•dim ach ata mal•choo•ti ey•ne•na mi•po.

Rabbinic Jewish Commentary
Every thing that is carnal, sensual, and worldly, must be removed from our conceptions of Yeshua's kingdom, here or hereafter: and to this agrees what some Jewish writers say of the Messiah, and his affairs;

"The Messiah (they say (o)) is separated from the world, because he is absolutely intellectual; but the world is corporeal; how then should the Messiah be in this world, when the world is corporeal, and ענין המשיח הוא אלהי לא גשמי, "The business of the Messiah is divine, and not corporeal?""

And since this was the case, Caesar, or any civil government, had no reason to be uneasy on account of his being a king, and having a kingdom; since his kingdom and interests did not in the least break in upon, or injure any others: and that this was the nature of his kingdom, he proves by the following reason.

(o) R. Juda Bezaleel Nizeach Israel, fol. 48.

---

37. Pilate therefore said unto him, Art thou a king then? Jesus answered, Thou sayest that I am a king. To this end was I born, and for this cause came I into the world, that I should bear witness unto the truth. Every one that is of the truth heareth my voice.

37. Εἶπεν οὖν αὐτῷ ὁ Πιλᾶτος, Οὐκοῦν βασιλεὺς εἶ σύ; Ἀπεκρίθη Ἰησοῦς, Σὺ λέγεις, ὅτι βασιλεύς εἰμι ἐγώ. Ἐγὼ εἰς τοῦτο γεγέννημαι, καὶ εἰς τοῦτο ἐλήλυθα εἰς τὸν κόσμον, ἵνα μαρτυρήσω τῇ ἀληθείᾳ. Πᾶς ὁ ὢν ἐκ τῆς ἀληθείας ἀκούει μου τῆς φωνῆς.

37. Eipen oun auto 'o Pilatos, Oukoun basileus ei su? Apekrithei Yeisous, Su legeis, 'oti basileus eimi ego. Ego eis touto gegenneimai, kai eis touto eleilutha eis ton kosmon, 'ina martureiso tei aleitheia. Pas 'o on ek teis aleitheias akouei mou teis phoneis.

לז. וַיֹּאמֶר אֵלָיו פִּילָטוֹס אִם-כֵּן מֶלֶךְ אַתָּה וַיַּעַן יֵשׁוּעַ אַתָּה אָמַרְתָּ כִּי-מֶלֶךְ אֲנִי לָזֹאת נוֹלַדְתִּי וְלָזֹאת בָּאתִי:בָּעוֹלָם לְהָעִיד עַל-הָאֱמֶת מִי אֲשֶׁר לָאֱמֶת יִשְׁמַע אֶת-קוֹלִי

37. Va•yo•mer elav Pilatos eem - ken me•lech ata va•ya•an Yeshua ata amar•ta ki - me•lech ani la•zot no•la•de•ti ve•la•zot ba•ti va•o•lam le•ha•eed al - ha•e•met mee asher la•e•met yish•ma et - ko•li.

---

38. Pilate saith unto him, What is truth? And when he had said this, he went out again unto the Jews, and saith unto them, I find in him no fault at all.

38. Λέγει αὐτῷ ὁ Πιλᾶτος, Τί ἐστιν ἀλήθεια; Καὶ τοῦτο εἰπών, πάλιν ἐξῆλθεν πρὸς τοὺς Ἰουδαίους, καὶ λέγει αὐτοῖς, Ἐγὼ οὐδεμίαν αἰτίαν εὑρίσκω ἐν αὐτῷ.

38. Legei auto 'o Pilatos, Ti estin aleitheya? Kai touto eipon, palin exeilthen pros tous Youdaious, kai legei autois, Ego oudemian aitian 'eurisko en auto.

לח. וַיֹּאמֶר אֵלָיו פִּילָטוֹס מַה הִיא הָאֱמֶת וְאַחֲרֵי דַבְּרוֹ כָזֹאת שָׁב אֶל-הַיְּהוּדִים וַיֹּאמֶר אֲלֵיהֶם אֲנִי לֹא-מָצָאתִי:בּוֹ עָוֹן

38. Va•yo•mer elav Pilatos ma hee ha•e•met ve•a•cha•rey dab•ro cha•zot shav el - ha•Ye•hoo•dim va•yo•mer aley•hem ani lo - ma•tza•ti vo a•von.

Rabbinic Jewish Commentary

The same question is put in the Talmud (p), מה אמת, "what is truth?" and it is answered, that he is the living God, and the King of the World: we do not find that Yeshua gave any answer to this question, which might be put in a scornful, jeering way; nor did Pilate wait for one. (p) T. Hieros. Sanhedrin, fol. 18. 1.

---

39. But ye have a custom, that I should release unto you one at the passover: will ye therefore that I release unto you the King of the Jews?

---

39. Ἔστιν δὲ συνήθεια ὑμῖν, ἵνα ἕνα ὑμῖν ἀπολύσω ἐν τῷ Πάσχα· βούλεσθε οὖν ὑμῖν ἀπολύσω τὸν βασιλέα τῶν Ἰουδαίων;

39. Estin de suneitheya 'umin, 'ina 'ena 'umin apoluso en to Pascha. boulesthe oun 'umin apoluso ton basilea ton Youdaion?

לט. וְהִנֵּה זֶה הַחֹק מֵאָז לְשַׁלַּח לָכֶם בַּפֶּסַח אֶחָד מֵהָאֲסִירִים לַחָפְשִׁי וְעַתָּה אִם־טוֹב בְּעֵינֵיכֶם אֲשַׁלַּח לָכֶם:אֶת־מֶלֶךְ הַיְּהוּדִים

39. Ve•hee•ne ze ha•chok me•az le•sha•lach la•chem ba•Pe•sach e•chad me•ha•a•si•rim la•chof•shi ve•a•ta eem - tov be•ey•ne•chem a•sha•lach la•chem et - Me•lech ha•Ye•hoo•dim?

---

40. Then cried they all again, saying, Not this man, but Barabbas. Now Barabbas was a robber.

40. Ἐκραύγασαν οὖν πάλιν πάντες, λέγοντες, Μὴ τοῦτον, ἀλλὰ τὸν Βαραββᾶν· ἦν δὲ ὁ Βαραββᾶς λῃστής.

40. Ekraugasan oun palin pantes, legontes, Mei touton, alla ton Barabban. ein de 'o Barabbas leisteis.

מ. וַיּוֹסִיפוּ וַיִּצְעֲקוּ לֵאמֹר לֹא אֶת־זֶה כִּי אִם אֶת־בַּר־אַבָּא וּבַר־אַבָּא הָיָה שׁוֹדֵד:

40. Va•yo•si•foo va•yitz•a•koo le•mor lo et - ze ki eem et - Bar - Aba oo•Var - Aba ha•ya sho•ded.

John, Chapter 19

1. Then Pilate therefore took Jesus, and scourged him.

Greek/Transliteration
1. Τότε οὖν ἔλαβεν ὁ Πιλᾶτος τὸν Ἰησοῦν, καὶ ἐμαστίγωσεν.

1. Tote oun elaben 'o Pilatos ton Yeisoun, kai emastigosen.

Hebrew/Transliteration
א. אָז יִקַּח פִּילָטוֹס אֶת-יֵשׁוּעַ וַיְיַסֵּר אֹתוֹ בַּשּׁוֹטִים:

1. Az yi•kach Pilatos et - Yeshua va•ye•ya•ser o•to ba•sho•tim.

---

2. And the soldiers platted a crown of thorns, and put it on his head, and they put on him a purple robe,

Greek/Transliteration
2. Καὶ οἱ στρατιῶται πλέξαντες στέφανον ἐξ ἀκανθῶν ἐπέθηκαν αὐτοῦ τῇ κεφαλῇ, καὶ ἱμάτιον πορφυροῦν περιέβαλον αὐτόν,

2. Kai 'oi stratiotai plexantes stephanon ex akanthon epetheikan autou tei kephalei, kai 'imation porphuroun periebalon auton,

Hebrew/Transliteration
ב. וְאַנְשֵׁי הַצָּבָא שָׂרְגוּ כֶתֶר קוֹצִים וַיָּשִׂימוּ עַל-רֹאשׁוֹ וַיַּלְבִּישֻׁהוּ מְעִיל אַרְגָּמָן:

2. Ve•an•shey ha•tza•va sar•goo che•ter ko•tzim va•ya•si•moo al - ro•sho va•yal•bi•shoo•hoo me•eel ar•ga•man.

Rabbinic Jewish Commentary
In one of the most incredible moments in history, Moshe came face to face with YHWH,

"The Messenger of YHWH appeared to him in a flame of fire out of the midst of a thorn bush (סְנֶה). He looked, and behold, the bush burned with fire, and the bush was not consumed." (Exodus 3:2)

The Targum identifies the 'Messenger' in the Bush as *Zagnugael*, which is one of the 70 names of Metatron, who Kol HaTor identifies as the "Mashiach ben Yosef from above,"

"But Mosheh was keeping the flock of Jethro his father-in-law, the rabba of Midian; and he had led the flock to a pleasant place of pasturage which is behind the desert, and had come to the mountain on which was revealed the glory of the LORD, even Horeb. And Zagnugael, the messenger of the LORD, appeared to him in a fame of fire in the midst of the thorn bush. And he gazed, and, behold, the bush burned with fire, yet the bush was neither burned nor consumed with fire." (Targum Onkelos on Exodus 3)

YHWH instructs Moshe to take off his sandals,
"He said, 'Do not come close. Take your sandals off of your feet, for the place you are standing on is holy ground." (Exodus 3:5)

A similiar event happens to Joshua,
"It happened, when Joshua was by Jericho, that he lifted up his eyes and looked, and behold, a man stood in front of him with his sword drawn in his hand. Joshua went to him, and said to him, 'Are you for us, or for our adversaries?' He said, 'No, but I have come now as commander of the HaShem's army. Joshua fell on his face to the earth, and worshipped, and said to him, 'What does my lord say to his servant? The prince of HaShem's army said to Joshua, 'Take your shoes off of your feet; for the place on which you stand is holy. Joshua did so." (Joshua 5:13-15)

However, why would the Messenger of YHWH appear in a thornbush? Thorns are related to the curse upon Adam,

"To Adam he said, Because you have listened to your wifes voice, and have eaten of the tree, of which I commanded you, saying, You shall not eat of it, cursed is the ground for your sake. In toil you will eat of it all the days of your life." (Genesis 3:17)

Would it not be more appropriate to appear in the midst of a towering Cedar of Lebanon? Rashi explains,

"And the messenger of YHWH appeared to him in a flame of fire out of the midst of a thornbush (3:2)" Why in a thornbush and not some other tree? In order to demonstrate that "I am with them in their affliction." (Rashi, cited at Chabad.org)

Isaiah 63 says,
"In all their affliction he was afflicted, and the messenger of his presence saved them; in his love and in his pity he redeemed them; he lifted them up and carried them all the days of old." (Isaiah 63:9, ESV)

---

3. And said, Hail, King of the Jews! and they smote him with their hands.

Greek/Transliteration
3. καὶ ἔλεγον, Χαῖρε, ὁ βασιλεὺς τῶν Ἰουδαίων· καὶ ἐδίδουν αὐτῷ ῥαπίσματα.

3. kai elegon, Chaire, 'o basileus ton Youdaion. kai edidoun auto 'rapismata.

Hebrew/Transliteration

ג. וַיִּגְּשׁוּ אֵלָיו וַיִּקְרְאוּ יְחִי מֶלֶךְ הַיְּהוּדִים וַיַּכֻּהוּ עַל-הַלֶּחִי:

3. Va•yig•shoo elav va•yik•re•oo Ye•chi Me•lech ha•Ye•hoo•dim
va•ya•koo•hoo al - ha•le•chi.

---

4. Pilate therefore went forth again, and saith unto them, Behold, I bring him forth to you, that ye may know that I find no fault in him.

Greek/Transliteration

4. Ἐξῆλθεν οὖν πάλιν ἔξω ὁ Πιλάτος, καὶ λέγει αὐτοῖς, Ἴδε, ἄγω ὑμῖν αὐτὸν ἔξω, ἵνα γνῶτε ὅτι ἐν αὐτῷ οὐδεμίαν αἰτίαν εὑρίσκω.

4. Exeilthen oun palin exo 'o Pilatos, kai legei autois, Yde, ago 'umin auton exo, 'ina gnote 'oti en auto oudemian aitian 'eurisko.

Hebrew/Transliteration

ד. וַיָּשָׁב פִּילָטוֹס וַיֵּצֵא הַחוּצָה וַיֹּאמֶר אֲלֵיהֶם הִנֵּה אוֹצִיאֶנּוּ לִפְנֵיכֶם לְבַעֲבוּר תֵּדְעוּ כִּי לֹא-מָצָאתִי בוֹ עָוֹן:

4. Va•ya•shov Pilatos va•ye•tze ha•choo•tza va•yo•mer aley•hem hee•ne o•tzi•e•noo lif•ney•chem le•va•a•voor ted•oo ki lo - ma•tza•ti vo a•von.

---

5. Then came Jesus forth, wearing the crown of thorns, and the purple robe. And Pilate saith unto them, Behold the man!

Greek/Transliteration

5. Ἐξῆλθεν οὖν ὁ Ἰησοῦς ἔξω, φορῶν τὸν ἀκάνθινον στέφανον καὶ τὸ πορφυροῦν ἱμάτιον. Καὶ λέγει αὐτοῖς, Ἴδε, ὁ ἄνθρωπος.

5. Exeilthen oun 'o Yeisous exo, phoron ton akanthinon stephanon kai to porphuroun 'imation. Kai legei autois, Yde, 'o Anthropos!

Hebrew/Transliteration

ה. וַיֵּצֵא יֵשׁוּעַ הַחוּצָה נֹשֵׂא כֶּתֶר הַקּוֹצִים וּמְעִיל הָאַרְגָּמָן עָלָיו וַיֹּאמֶר אֲלֵיהֶם פִּילָטוֹס הִנֵּה הַגֶּבֶר:

5. Va•ye•tze Yeshua ha•choo•tza no•se che•ter ha•ko•tzim oom•eel ha•ar•ga•man alav va•yo•mer aley•hem Pilatos hee•ne ha•ga•ver!

---

6. When the chief priests therefore and officers saw him, they cried out, saying, Crucify him, crucify him. Pilate saith unto them, Take ye him, and crucify him: for I find no fault in him.

6. Ὅτε οὖν εἶδον αὐτὸν οἱ ἀρχιερεῖς καὶ οἱ ὑπηρέται, ἐκραύγασαν λέγοντες, Σταύρωσον, σταύρωσον αὐτόν. Λέγει αὐτοῖς ὁ Πιλάτος, Λάβετε αὐτὸν ὑμεῖς καὶ σταυρώσατε· ἐγὼ γὰρ οὐχ εὑρίσκω ἐν αὐτῷ αἰτίαν.

6. 'Ote oun eidon auton 'oi archiereis kai 'oi 'upeiretai, ekraugasan legontes, Stauroson, stauroson auton. Legei autois 'o Pilatos, Labete auton 'umeis kai staurosate. ego gar ouch 'eurisko en auto aitian.

Hebrew/Transliteration

ו. וְרָאשֵׁי הַכֹּהֲנִים וְהַמְשָׁרְתִים כִּרְאוֹתָם אֹתוֹ צָעֲקוּ לֵאמֹר הַצְלֵב הַצְלֵב אֹתוֹ וַיֹּאמֶר אֲלֵיהֶם פִּילָטוֹס קְחוּ אֹתוֹ:אַתֶּם וְהַצְלִיבֻהוּ כִּי אֲנִי לֹא-מָצָאתִי בוֹ עָוֹן

6. Ve•ra•shey ha•ko•ha•nim ve•ham•shar•tim kir•o•tam o•to tza•a•koo le•mor hatz•lev hatz•lev o•to va•yo•mer aley•hem Pilatos ke•choo o•to atem ve•hatz•li•voo•hoo ki ani lo - ma•tza•ti vo a•von.

---

7. The Jews answered him, We have a law, and by our law he ought to die, because he made himself the Son of God.

Greek/Transliteration

7. Ἀπεκρίθησαν αὐτῷ οἱ Ἰουδαῖοι, Ἡμεῖς νόμον ἔχομεν, καὶ κατὰ τὸν νόμον ἡμῶν ὀφείλει ἀποθανεῖν, ὅτι ἑαυτὸν υἱὸν θεοῦ ἐποίησεν.

7. Apekritheisan auto 'oi Youdaioi, 'Eimeis nomon echomen, kai kata ton nomon 'eimon opheilei apothanein, 'oti 'eauton 'wion theou epoieisen.

Hebrew/Transliteration

ז. וַיַּעֲנוּ אֹתוֹ הַיְּהוּדִים הִנֵּה יֶשׁ-לָנוּ תוֹרָה וּלְפִי תוֹרָתֵנוּ מִשְׁפָּט-מָוֶת לוֹ כִּי-מִתְאַמֵּר לֵאמֹר בֶּן-הָאֱלֹהִים הוּא:

7. Va•ya•a•noo o•to ha•Ye•hoo•dim hee•ne yesh - la•noo To•rah ool•fi To•ra•te•noo mish•pat - ma•vet lo ki - mit•a•mer le•mor Ben - ha•Elohim hoo.

Rabbinic Jewish Commentary

This he had often asserted in his ministry, or what was equivalent to it, and which they so understood; and indeed had said that very morning, before the high priest in his palace, what amounted thereunto, and which he so interpreted; upon which he rent his garments, and charged him with blasphemy: for that God has a son, is denied by the Jews, since Yeshua asserted himself to be so, though formerly believed by them; nor was it now denied that there was a Son of God, or that he was expected; but the blasphemy with them was, that Yeshua set up himself to be he: but now it is vehemently opposed by them, that God has a son; so from Ecc_4:8 they endeavour to prove (q), that God has neither a brother, ולא בן, "nor a son"; but, "Hear, O Israel, they observe, the Lord our God is one Lord". And elsewhere (r),

"There is one"; this is the holy blessed God; "and not a second"; for he has no partner or equal in his world; "yea, he hath neither child nor brother"; he hath no brother, nor hath he a son; but the holy blessed God loves Israel, and calls them his children, and his brethren.".

All which is opposed to the Judeo-Christain doctrine, relating to the sonship of Yeshua and the powers in heaven teaching. The conduct of these men, at this time, deserves notice, as their craft in imposing on Pilate's ignorance of their laws; and the little regard that they themselves had to them, in calling for crucifixion instead of stoning; and their inconsistency with themselves, pretending before it was not lawful for them to put any man to death; and now they have a law, and by that law, in their judgment, he ought to die.

(q) Debarim Rabba, sect. 2. fol. 237. 3. (r) Midrash Kohelet, fol. 70. 1.

---

8. When Pilate therefore heard that saying, he was the more afraid;

Greek/Transliteration
8. ῞Οτε οὖν ἤκουσεν ὁ Πιλάτος τοῦτον τὸν λόγον, μᾶλλον ἐφοβήθη,

8. 'Ote oun eikousen 'o Pilatos touton ton logon, mallon ephobeithei,

Hebrew/Transliteration
ח. כְּשָׁמֹעַ פִּילָטוֹס אֶת-הַדָּבָר הַזֶּה וַיִּירָא יֶתֶר מְאֹד:

8. Ki•sh`mo•a Pilatos et - ha•da•var ha•ze va•yi•ra ye•ter me•od.

---

9. And went again into the judgment hall, and saith unto Jesus, Whence art thou? But Jesus gave him no answer.

Greek/Transliteration
9. καὶ εἰσῆλθεν εἰς τὸ πραιτώριον πάλιν, καὶ λέγει τῷ Ἰησοῦ, Πόθεν εἶ σύ; Ὁ δὲ Ἰησοῦς ἀπόκρισιν οὐκ ἔδωκεν αὐτῷ.

9. kai eiseilthen eis to praitorion palin, kai legei to Yeisou, Pothen ei su? 'O de Yeisous apokrisin ouk edoken auto.

Hebrew/Transliteration
ט. וַיָּשָׁב וַיָּבֹא אֶל-בֵּית הַמִּשְׁפָּט וַיֹּאמֶר אֶל-יֵשׁוּעַ אֵי מִזֶּה אָתָּה וְיֵשׁוּעַ לֹא-עָנָה אֹתוֹ מְאוּמָה:

9. Va•ya•shov va•ya•vo el - beit ha•mish•pat va•yo•mer el - Yeshua ey mi•ze ata ve•Yeshua lo - ana o•to me•oo•ma.

---

10. Then saith Pilate unto him, Speakest thou not unto me? knowest thou not that I have power to crucify thee, and have power to release thee?

Greek/Transliteration

10. Λέγει οὖν αὐτῷ ὁ Πιλάτος, Ἐμοὶ οὐ λαλεῖς; Οὐκ οἶδας ὅτι ἐξουσίαν ἔχω σταυρῶσαί σε, καὶ ἐξουσίαν ἔχω ἀπολῦσαί σε;

10. Legei oun auto 'o Pilatos, Emoi ou laleis? Ouk oidas 'oti exousian echo staurosai se, kai exousian echo apolusai se?

Hebrew/Transliteration

י. וַיֹּאמֶר אֵלָיו פִּילָטוֹס הַאֵלַי לֹא תְדַבֵּר הֲלֹא תֵדַע כִּי יָדִי רַב-לִי לְשַׁלְּחֶךָ וְרַב-לִי לִצְלָבֶךָ:

10. Va•yo•mer elav Pilatos ha•e•lai lo te•da•ber ha•lo te•da ki ya•di rav - li le•sha•le•cha•cha ve•rav - li litz•la•ve•cha?

---

11. Jesus answered, Thou couldest have no power at all against me, except it were given thee from above: therefore he that delivered me unto thee hath the greater sin.

Greek/Transliteration

11. Ἀπεκρίθη Ἰησοῦς, Οὐκ εἶχες ἐξουσίαν οὐδεμίαν κατ᾽ ἐμοῦ, εἰ μὴ ἦν σοι δεδομένον ἄνωθεν· διὰ τοῦτο ὁ παραδιδούς μέ σοι μείζονα ἁμαρτίαν ἔχει.

11. Apekrithei Yeisous, Ouk eiches exousian oudemian kat emou, ei mei ein soi dedomenon anothen. dya touto 'o paradidous me soi meizona 'amartian echei.

Hebrew/Transliteration

יא. וַיַּעַן אֹתוֹ יֵשׁוּעַ אֵין - לְךָ כֹּחַ עָלַי לוּלֵא נִתַּן - לְךָ מֵעָל עַל-כֵּן עֲוֹן מַסְגִּירִי בְּיָדֶיךָ גָּדוֹל מֵעֲוֹנֶךָ:

11. Va•ya•an o•to Yeshua eyn - le•cha cho•ach a•lai loo•le ni•tan - le•cha me•al al – ken a•von mas•gi•rai be•ya•de•cha ga•dol me•a•vo•ne•cha.

Rabbinic Jewish Commentary

The Jews themselves agree in general, "That all the things of this world depend on above; and when they agree above first, (they say (s),) they agree below; and that there is no power below, until that דאתייהיב שולטנותא לעילא, "power is given from above".

(s) Zohar in Gen. fol. 99. 1.

---

12. And from thenceforth Pilate sought to release him: but the Jews cried out, saying, If thou let this man go, thou art not Caesar's friend: whosoever maketh himself a king speaketh against Caesar.

Greek/Transliteration

12. Ἐκ τούτου ἐζήτει ὁ Πιλάτος ἀπολῦσαι αὐτόν. Οἱ δὲ Ἰουδαῖοι ἔκραζον λέγοντες, Ἐὰν τοῦτον ἀπολύσῃς, οὐκ εἶ φίλος τοῦ Καίσαρος· πᾶς ὁ βασιλέα ἑαυτὸν ποιῶν, ἀντιλέγει τῷ Καίσαρι.

12. Ek toutou ezeitei 'o Pilatos apolusai auton. 'Oi de Youdaioi ekrazon legontes, Ean touton apoluseis, ouk ei philos tou Kaisaros. pas 'o basilea 'eauton poion, antilegei to Kaisari.

Hebrew/Transliteration

יב. וְעַל-זֹאת בִּקֵּשׁ פִּילָטוֹס לְשַׁלְּחוֹ וְהַיְּהוּדִים צָעֲקוּ וְאָמְרוּ אִם-תְּשַׁלַּח אֶת-הָאִישׁ הַזֶּה אֵינְךָ אֹהֵב אֶת-הַקֵּיסָר: כִּי הַמִּתְקוֹמֵם לִהְיוֹת לְמֶלֶךְ הוּא מִתְקוֹמֵם עַל-הַקֵּיסָר

12. Ve•al - zot bi•kesh Pilatos le•shal•cho ve•ha•Ye•hoo•dim tza•a•koo ve•am•roo eem - te•sha•lach et - ha•eesh ha•ze eyn•cha o•hev et - ha•Key•sar ki ha•mit•ko•mem li•hee•yot le•me•lech hoo mit•ko•mem al - ha•Key•sar.

---

13. When Pilate therefore heard that saying, he brought Jesus forth, and sat down in the judgment seat in a place that is called the Pavement, but in the Hebrew, Gabbatha.

Greek/Transliteration

13. Ὁ οὖν Πιλάτος ἀκούσας τοῦτον τὸν λόγον ἤγαγεν ἔξω τὸν Ἰησοῦν, καὶ ἐκάθισεν ἐπὶ τοῦ βήματος, εἰς τόπον λεγόμενον Λιθόστρωτον, Ἑβραϊστὶ δὲ Γαββαθᾶ·

13. 'O oun Pilatos akousas touton ton logon eigagen exo ton Yeisoun, kai ekathisen epi tou beimatos, eis topon legomenon Lithostroton, 'Ebraisti de Gabbatha.

Hebrew/Transliteration

יג. כְּשָׁמֹעַ פִּילָטוֹס אֶת-הַדְּבָרִים הָאֵלֶּה הוֹצִיא אֶת-יֵשׁוּעַ הַחוּצָה וַיֵּשֶׁב עַל-כִּסֵּא הַמִּשְׁפָּט בְּמָקוֹם הַנִּקְרָא: מַרְצֶפֶת אֲבָנִים וּבְעִבְרִית גַּבְּתָא

13. Ki•sh`mo•a Piltos et - ha•d`va•rim ha•e•le ho•tzi et - Yeshua ha•choo•tza va•ye•shev al - ki•se ha•mish•pat ba•ma•kom ha•nik•ra Mar•tze•fet Ava•nim oov•Eev•rit Gab•ta.

Rabbinic Jewish Commentary

This place, in the Greek tongue, was called "Lithostrotos"; or "the pavement of stones", as the Syriac version renders it: it is thought to be the room "Gazith", in which the sanhedrim sat in the temple when they tried capital causes (t); and it was so called, because it was paved with smooth, square, hewn stones:

"It was in the north part; half of it was holy, and half of it common; and it had two doors, one for that part which was holy, and another for that which was common;

And in that half which was common the sanhedrim sat (u)."

So that into this part of it, and by this door, Pilate, though a Gentile, might enter. This place, in the language of the Jews, who at this time spoke Syriac, was "Gabbatha", front its height, as it should seem; though the Syriac and Persic versions read "Gaphiphtha", which signifies a fence, or an enclosure. Mention is made in the Talmud (w) of the upper "Gab" in the mountain of the house; but whether the same with this "Gabbaths", and whether this is the same with the chamber "Gazith", is not certain. The Septuagint use the same word as John here does, and call by the same name the pavement of the temple on which the Israelites felt and worshipped God, 2Ch_7:3.

(t) Gloss. in T. Bab. Avoda Zara, fol. 8. 2. (u) T. Bab. Yoma, fol. 25. 1. Maimon. Hilch. Beth Habbechira, c. 5. sect. 17. Bartenora in Misn. Middot, c. 5. sect. 3. (w) T. Bab. Sabbat, fol. 115. 1.

---

14. And it was the preparation of the passover, and about the sixth hour: and he saith unto the Jews, Behold your King!

Greek/Transliteration
14. ἦν δὲ Παρασκευὴ τοῦ Πάσχα, ὥρα δὲ ὡσεὶ ἕκτη· καὶ λέγει τοῖς Ἰουδαίοις, Ἴδε, ὁ βασιλεὺς ὑμῶν.

14. ein de Paraskeuei tou Pascha, 'ora de 'osei 'ektei. kai legei tois Youdaiois, Yde, 'o basileus 'umon.

Hebrew/Transliteration
יד. וַיֹּאמֶר אֶל-הַיְּהוּדִים בְּעֶרֶב הַפֶּסַח הַהוּא כַּשָּׁעָה הַשְּׁשִׁית הִנֵּה מַלְכְּכֶם:

14. Va•yo•mar el - ha•Ye•hoo•dim ba•e•rev ha•Pe•sach ha•hoo ka•sha•ah ha•shi•sheet hee•ne Mal•ke•chem.

Rabbinic Jewish Commentary
And it was the preparation of the passover,.... So the Jews (x) say, that Yeshua suffered on the eve of the passover; and the author of the blasphemous account of his life says (y), it was the eve both of the passover and the sabbath; which account so far agrees with the evangelic history; but then this preparation of the passover was not of the passover lamb, for that had been prepared and eaten the night before. Nor do I find that there was any particular day which was called "the preparation of the passover" in such sense, and much less that this day was the day before the eating of the passover. According to the law in Exo_12:3 the lamb for the passover was to be separated from the rest of the flock on the tenth day of the month, and to be kept up till the fourteenth; but this is never called the preparation of the passover; and was it so called, it cannot be intended here; the preparing and making ready the passover the evangelists speak of, were on the same day it was eaten, and design the getting ready a place to eat it in, and things convenient for

that purpose, and the killing the lamb, and dressing it, and the like, Mat_26:17 there is what the Jews call פרוס הפסח, which was a space of fifteen days before the passover, and began at the middle of the thirty days before the feast, in which they used to ask questions, and explain the traditions concerning the passover (z): but this is never called the preparation of the passover: and on the night of the fourteenth month they sought diligently, in every hole and corner of their houses, for leavened bread, in order to remove it (a); but this also never went by any such name: wherefore, if any respect is had to the preparation for the passover, it must either design the preparation of the "Chagigah", which was a grand festival, commonly kept on the fifteenth day, and which was sometimes called the passover; or else the preparation for the whole feast all the remaining days of it; but it seems best of all to understand it only of the preparation for the sabbath, which, because it was in the passover week, is called the passover preparation day: and it may be observed, that it is sometimes only called "the day of the preparation", and "the preparation", Mat_27:62 and sometimes the "Jews' preparation day", Joh_19:42 and it is explained by the Evangelist Mar_15:42. "It was the preparation, that is, the day before the sabbath"; on which they both prepared themselves for the sabbath, and food to eat on that day; and this being the time of the passover likewise, the preparation was the greater: and therefore to distinguish this preparation day for the sabbath, from others, it is called the passover preparation; nor have I observed that any other day is called the preparation but that before the sabbath: the Jews dispute about preparing food for the sabbath on a feast day, as this was; they seem to forbid it, but afterwards soften their words, and allow it with some provisos: their canon runs thus (b);

"A feast day which falls on the eve of the sabbath, a man may not boil (anything) at the beginning of the feast day for the sabbath; but he may boil for the feast day; and if there is any left, it may be left for the sabbath; and he may make a boiling on the eve of a feast day, and depend on it for the sabbath: the house of Shamtoni say two boilings; and the house of Hillell say one boiling."

Bartenora on the passage observes, that some say the reason of this boiling on the evening of a feast day, is for the honour of the sabbath; for because from the evening of the feast day, the sabbath is remembered, that which is best is chosen for the sabbath, that the sabbath may not be forgotten through the business of the feast day. The account Maimonides (c) gives of this matter is,

"On a common day they "prepare" for the sabbath, and on a common day they prepare for a feast day; but they do not prepare on a feast day for the sabbath, nor is the sabbath, מכינה, "a preparation" for a feast day."

This seems to be contrary to the practice of the Jews in the time of Yeshua, as related by the evangelists, understanding by the preparation they speak of, a preparation of food for the sabbath; but what he afterwards says (d) makes some allowance for it:

"A feast day, which happens to be on the eve of the sabbath, (Friday,) they neither bake nor boil, on a feast day what is eaten on the morrow, on the sabbath; and this prohibition is from the words of the Scribes, (not from the word of God,) that a man should not boil any thing on a feast day for a common day, and much less for the sabbath; but if he makes a boiling (or prepares food) on the evening of a feast day on which he depends and boils and bakes on a feast day for the sabbath, lo, this is lawful; and that on which he depends is called the mingling of food."

And this food, so called, was a small portion of food prepared on a feast for the sabbath, though not less than the quantity of an olive, whether for one man or a thousand (e); by virtue of which, they depending on it for the sabbath, they might prepare whatever they would, after having asked a blessing over it, and saying (f),

"By this mixture it is free for me to bake and boil on a feast day what is for the morrow, the sabbath; and if a man prepares for others, he must say for me, and for such an one, and such an one; or for the men of the city, and then all of them may bake and boil on a feast day for the sabbath."

And about the sixth hour; to which agrees the account in Mat_27:45, Luk_23:44 but Mar_15:25 says that "it was the third hour, and they crucified him"; and Beza says, he found it so written in one copy; and so read Peter of Alexandria, Beza's ancient copy, and some others, and Nonnus: but the copies in general agree in, and confirm the common reading, and which is differently accounted for; some by the different computations of the Jews and Romans; others by observing that the day was divided into four parts, each part containing three hours, and were called the third, the sixth, the ninth, and the twelfth hours; and not only that time, when one of these hours came, was called by that name, but also from that all the space of the three hours, till the next came, was called by the name of the former: for instance, all the space from nine o'clock till twelve was called "the third hour"; and all from twelve till three in the afternoon "the sixth hour": hence the time of Yeshua's crucifixion being supposed to be somewhat before, but yet near our twelve of the clock, it may be truly here said that it was about the sixth hour; and as truly by Mark the third hour; that space, which was called by the name of the third hour, being not yet passed, though it drew toward an end. This way go Godwin and Hammond, whose words I have expressed, and bids fair for the true solution of the difficulty: though it should be observed, that Mark agrees with the other evangelists about the darkness which was at the sixth hour, the time of Yeshua's crucifixion, Mar_15:33 and it is to be remarked, that he does not say that it was the third hour "when" they crucified him, or that they crucified him at the third hour; but it was the third hour, "and" they crucified him. It was the time of day when they should have been at the daily sacrifice, and preparing for the solemnity of that day particularly, which was their Chagigah, or grand feast; but instead of this they were prosecuting his crucifixion, which they brought about by the sixth hour. And about this time Pilate said, and did the following things:

and he saith unto the Jews, behold your king; whom some of your people, it seems, have owned for their king, and you charge as setting up himself as one; see what a figure he makes; does he look like a king? this he said, in order to move upon their affections, that, if possible, they might agree to release him, and to shame them out of putting such a poor despicable creature to death;

and as upbraiding them for their folly, in fearing anything from so mean and contemptible a man.

(x) T. Bab. Sanhedrin, fol. 43. 1. & 67. 1. (y) Toldos Jesu, p. 18. (z) Misn. Shekalim, c. 3. sect. 1. & Bartenora in ib. T. Bab. Pesachim, fol. 6. 1. (a) Misn. Pesachim, c. 1. sect. 1, 2, 3. (b) Misn. Betza, c. 2. sect. 1. (c) Hilchot Yom Tob. c. 1. sect. 19. (d) Ib. c. 6. sect. 1. (e) Maimon. & Bartenora in Misn. Betza, c. 2. sect. 1. (f) Maimon. Hilchot Yom Tob, c. 6. sect. 8.

---

15. But they cried out, Away with him, away with him, crucify him. Pilate saith unto them, Shall I crucify your King? The chief priest answered, We have no king but Caesar.

Greek/Transliteration

15. Οἱ δὲ ἐκραύγασαν, Ἆρον, ἆρον, σταύρωσον αὐτόν. Λέγει αὐτοῖς ὁ Πιλάτος, Τὸν βασιλέα ὑμῶν σταυρώσω; Ἀπεκρίθησαν οἱ ἀρχιερεῖς, Οὐκ ἔχομεν βασιλέα εἰ μὴ Καίσαρα.

15. 'Oi de ekraugasan, Aron, aron, stauroson auton. Legei autois 'o Pilatos, Ton basilea 'umon stauroso? Apekritheisan 'oi archiereis, Ouk echomen basilea ei mei Kaisara.

Hebrew/Transliteration

טו. וַיִּצְעֲקוּ הֵיְצֵא הֵיְצֵא אֹתוֹ צְלֹב אֹתוֹ וַיֹּאמֶר אֲלֵיהֶם פִּילָטוֹס הֲצָלֹב אֶצְלֹב אֶת-מַלְכְּכֶם וַיַּעֲנוּ רָאשֵׁי הַכֹּהֲנִים:אֵין-לָנוּ מֶלֶךְ כִּי אִם-הַקֵּיסָר

15. Va•yitz•a•koo hay•tze hay•tze o•to tze•lov o•to va•yo•mer aley•hem Pilatos ha•tza•lov etz•lov et - Mal•ke•chem va•ya•a•noo ra•shey ha•ko•ha•nim eyn - la•noo me•lech ki eem - ha•Key•sar.

Rabbinic Jewish Commentary

Whereby they denied God to be their king, though they used to say, and still say in their prayers; "We have no king but God" (g): they rejected the government of the King Messiah, and tacitly confessed that the sceptre was departed from Judah; and what they now said, came quickly upon them, and still continues; for according to prophecy, Hos_3:4 they have been many days and years "Without a king": and this they said in spite to Yeshua, and not in respect to Caesar, whose government they would have been glad to have had an opportunity to shake off. They could name no one as king but Yeshua, or Caesar; the former they rejected, and were obliged to own the latter: it is a poor observation of the Jew (h) upon this passage, that it

"Shows that before the crucifixion of Jesus, the Roman Caesars ruled over Israel; and that this Caesar was Tiberius, who had set Pilate over Jerusalem, as is clear from Luk_3:1. Wherefore here is an answer to the objection of the Nazarenes, who say that the Jews, for the sin of crucifying Jesus, lost their kingdom."

To which may be replied, that this is not said by any of the writers of the New Testament, that the kingdom of the Jews was taken away from them for their sin of crucifying Jesus; and therefore this is no contradiction to anything said by them.

(g) T. Bab. Taanith, fol. 25. 2. Seder Tephillot, fol. 46. 2. Ed. Basil. fol. 71. 2. Ed. Amsterd. (h) R. Isaac Chizzuk Emuna, par. 2. c. 57. p. 446.

---

16. Then delivered he him therefore unto them to be crucified. And they took Jesus, and led him away.

Greek/Transliteration
16. Τότε οὖν παρέδωκεν αὐτὸν αὐτοῖς, ἵνα σταυρωθῇ. Παρέλαβον δὲ τὸν Ἰησοῦν καὶ ἤγαγον·

16. Tote oun paredoken auton autois, 'ina staurothei. Parelabon de ton Yeisoun kai eigagon.

Hebrew/Transliteration
‏טז. אָז נְתָנוֹ בְיָדָם לִצְלֹב אֹתוֹ וַיִּקְחוּ אֶת-יֵשׁוּעַ וַיּוֹלִיכֻהוּ:

16. Az n`ta•no ve•ya•dam litz•lov o•to va•yik•choo et - Yeshua va•yo•li•choo•hoo.

---

17. And he bearing his cross went forth into a place called the place of a skull, which is called in the Hebrew Golgotha:

Greek/Transliteration
17. καὶ βαστάζων τὸν σταυρὸν αὐτοῦ ἐξῆλθεν εἰς τόπον λεγόμενον Κρανίου Τόπον, ὃς λέγεται Ἑβραϊστὶ Γολγοθᾶ·

17. kai bastazon ton stauron autou exeilthen eis topon legomenon Kraniou Topon, 'os legetai 'Ebraisti Golgotha.

Hebrew/Transliteration
‏יז. וַיִּשָּׂאוּ אֹתוֹ אֶת-עֵץ צְלָבוֹ וַיְבִיאֻהוּ אֶל-הַמָּקוֹם הַנִּקְרָא מְקוֹם הַגֻּלְגֹּלֶת וּבְעִבְרִית גָּלְגָּלְתָּא:

17. Va•ya•si•oo o•to et - etz tze•la•vo vay•vi•oo•hoo el - ha•ma•kom ha•nik•ra me•kom ha•gool•go•let oov•Eev•rit Gol•gal•ta.

Rabbinic Jewish Commentary
The Zohar says, "From the dew in this skull (Gulgalta) manna is ground for the righteous for the World to Come, and through it the dead shall be revived."
(Zohar, Ha'azinu 117)

And he bearing his cross,.... Which was usual for malefactors to do, as Lipsius (i) shows out of Artemidorus, and Plutarch; the former says,

"The cross is like to death, and he that is to be fixed to it, first bears it;"

And the latter says, "And everyone of the malefactors that are punished in body, "carries out his own cross"."

The Syriac writers have it (k), who say,

"When Noah went out of the ark there was made a distribution of the bones of Adam; to Shem, his head was given, and the place in which he was buried is called "Karkaphta": where likewise Christ was crucified;"

Which word signifies a skull, as Golgotha does: and so likewise the Arabic writers (l); who affirm that Shem said these words to Melchizedek,

"Noah commanded that thou shouldst take the body of Adam, and bury it in the middle of the earth; therefore let us go, I and thou, and bury it; wherefore Shem and Melchizedek went to take the body of Adam, and the angel of the Lord appeared to them and went before them, till they came to the place Calvary, where they buried him, as the angel of the Lord commanded them:"

The same also had the ancient fathers of the Christian church; Cyprian (m) says, that it is a tradition of the ancients, that Adam was buried in Calvary under the place where the cross of Yeshua was fixed; and Jerom makes mention of it more than once; so Paula and Eustochium, in an epistle supposed to be dictated by him, or in which he was assisting, say (n), in this city, meaning Jerusalem, yea in this place, Adam is said to dwell, and to die; from whence the place where Yeshua was crucified is called Calvary, because there the skull of the ancient man was buried: and in another place he himself says (o), that he heard one disputing in the church and explaining, Eph_5:14 of Adam buried in Calvary, where Yeshua was crucified, and therefore was so called. Ambrose (p) also takes notice of it; the place of the cross, says he, is either in the midst of the land, that it might be conspicuous to all, or over the grave of Adam, as the Hebrews dispute: others say that the hill itself was in the form of a man's skull, and therefore was so called; it was situated, as Jerom says (q), on the north of Mount Zion, and is thought by some to be the same with the hill Gareb, in Jer_31:39. It was usual to crucify on high hills, so Polycrates was crucified upon the highest top of Mount Mycale (r).

(i) De Cruce, l. 2. c. 5. p. 76. (k) Bar Bahluli apud Castel. Lexic. Polyglot. col. 3466. (l) Elmacinus, p. 13. Patricides, p. 12. apud Hottinger. Smegma Oriental. l. 1. c. 8. p. 257. (m) De Resurrectione Christi, p. 479. (n) Epist. Marcellae, fol. 42. L. Tom. I. (o) Comment. in Eph. v. 14. (p) Comment. in Luc. xx. 33. (q) De locis Hebraicis, fol. 92. F. (r) Valer. Maxim. l. 6. c. ult.

18. Where they crucified him, and two other with him, on either side one, and Jesus in the midst.

Greek/Transliteration

18. ὅπου αὐτὸν ἐσταύρωσαν, καὶ μετ᾽ αὐτοῦ ἄλλους δύο, ἐντεῦθεν καὶ ἐντεῦθεν, μέσον δὲ τὸν Ἰησοῦν.

18. 'opou auton estaurosan, kai met autou allous duo, enteuthen kai enteuthen, meson de ton Yeisoun.

Hebrew/Transliteration

יח. וַיִּצְלְבוּ אֹתוֹ שָׁם וּשְׁנֵי אֲנָשִׁים אֲחֵרִים עִמּוֹ מֵעֵבֶר מִזֶּה וּמִזֶּה וְיֵשׁוּעַ בֵּין שְׁנֵיהֶם:

18. Va•yitz•le•voo o•to sham oosh•ney a•na•shim a•che•rim ee•mo me•e•ver mi•ze oo•mi•ze ve`Yeshua bein sh`ney•hem.

---

19. And Pilate wrote a title, and put it on the cross. And the writing was, JESUS OF NAZARETH THE KING OF THE JEWS.

Greek/Transliteration

19. Ἔγραψεν δὲ καὶ τίτλον ὁ Πιλάτος, καὶ ἔθηκεν ἐπὶ τοῦ σταυροῦ· ἦν δὲ γεγραμμένον, Ἰησοῦς ὁ Ναζωραῖος ὁ βασιλεὺς τῶν Ἰουδαίων.

19. Egrapsen de kai titlon 'o Pilatos, kai etheiken epi tou staurou. ein de gegrammenon, Yeisous 'o Nazoraios 'o basileus ton Youdaion.

Hebrew/Transliteration

יט. וַיִּכְתֹּב פִּילָטוֹס כְּתֹבֶת עַל-לוּחַ וַיְשִׂימֵהוּ עַל-הַצְּלָב יֵשׁוּעַ הַנָּצְרִי מֶלֶךְ הַיְּהוּדִים:

19. Va•yich•tov Pilatos k`to•vet al - loo•ach va•yi•si•me•hoo al - hatz•lav Yeshua ha•Notz•ri Me•lech ha•Ye•hoo•dim.

---

20. This title then read many of the Jews: for the place where Jesus was crucified was nigh to the city: and it was written in Hebrew, and Greek, and Latin.

Greek/Transliteration

20. Τοῦτον οὖν τὸν τίτλον πολλοὶ ἀνέγνωσαν τῶν Ἰουδαίων, ὅτι ἐγγὺς ἦν ὁ τόπος τῆς πόλεως ὅπου ἐσταυρώθη ὁ Ἰησοῦς· καὶ ἦν γεγραμμένον Ἑβραϊστί, Ἑλληνιστί, Ῥωμαϊστί.

20. Touton oun ton titlon polloi anegnosan ton Youdaion, 'oti engus ein 'o topos teis poleos 'opou estaurothei 'o Yeisous. kai ein gegrammenon 'Ebraisti, 'Elleinisti, 'Romaisti.

כ. וְיהוּדִים רַבִּים קָרְאוּ אֶת-הַכְּתֹבֶת כִּי הַמָּקוֹם אֲשֶׁר נִצְלַב-שָׁם יֵשׁוּעַ קָרוֹב לָעִיר וְהַכְּתֹבֶת כְּתוּבָה עִבְרִית:רוֹמִית וִיוָנִית

20. Vi•Yehoo•dim ra•bim kar•oo et - ha•k`to•vet ki ha•ma•kom asher nitz•lav
– sham Yeshua ka•rov la•eer ve•ha•k`to•vet k`too•va Eev•rit Ro•mit
vi•Ye•va•nit.

---

21. Then said the chief priests of the Jews to Pilate, Write not, The King of the Jews; but that he said, I am King of the Jews.

21. Ἔλεγον οὖν τῷ Πιλάτῳ οἱ ἀρχιερεῖς τῶν Ἰουδαίων, Μὴ γράφε, Ὁ βασιλεὺς τῶν Ἰουδαίων· ἀλλ᾿ ὅτι Ἐκεῖνος εἶπεν, Βασιλεύς εἰμι τῶν Ἰουδαίων.

21. Elegon oun to Pilato 'oi archiereis ton Youdaion, Mei graphe, 'O basileus ton Youdaion. all 'oti Ekeinos eipen, Basileus eimi ton Youdaion.

כא. וַיֹּאמְרוּ רָאשֵׁי כֹהֲנֵי הַיְּהוּדִים אֶל-פִּילָטוֹס אַל-תִּכְתֹּב מֶלֶךְ הַיְּהוּדִים רַק כִּי אָמַר אֲנִי מֶלֶךְ הַיְּהוּדִים:

21. Va•yom•roo ra•shey cho•ha•ney ha•Ye•hoo•dim el - Pilatos al - tich•tov Me•lech ha•Ye•hoo•dim rak ki amar ani Me•lech ha•Ye•hoo•dim.

---

22. Pilate answered, What I have written I have written.

22. Ἀπεκρίθη ὁ Πιλάτος, Ὃ γέγραφα, γέγραφα.

22. Apekrithei 'o Pilatos, 'O gegrapha, gegrapha.

כב. וַיַּעַן פִּילָטוֹס אֶת-אֲשֶׁר כָּתַבְתִּי כָּתַבְתִּי:

22. Va•ya•an Pilatos et - asher ka•tav•ti ka•tav•ti.

Rabbinic Jewish Commentary
This he said, either because he could not alter it after it was written, for it is said (w), that "A proconsul's table is his sentence, which being once read, not one letter can either be increased or diminished; but as it is recited, so it is related in the instrument of the province;" (w) Apulei Florid. c. 9.

23. Then the soldiers, when they had crucified Jesus, took his garments, and made four parts, to every soldier a part; and also his coat: now the coat was without seam, woven from the top throughout.

Greek/Transliteration
23. Οἱ οὖν στρατιῶται, ὅτε ἐσταύρωσαν τὸν Ἰησοῦν, ἔλαβον τὰ ἱμάτια αὐτοῦ, καὶ ἐποίησαν τέσσαρα μέρη, ἑκάστῳ στρατιώτῃ μέρος, καὶ τὸν χιτῶνα. Ἦν δὲ ὁ χιτὼν ἄραφος, ἐκ τῶν ἄνωθεν ὑφαντὸς δι' ὅλου.

23. 'Oi oun stratiotai, 'ote estaurosan ton Yeisoun, elabon ta 'imatya autou, kai epoieisan tessara merei, 'ekasto stratiotei meros, kai ton chitona. Ein de 'o chiton araphos, ek ton anothen 'uphantos di 'olou.

Hebrew/Transliteration
כג. וַיְהִי כַּאֲשֶׁר צָלְבוּ אַנְשֵׁי הַצָּבָא אֶת-יֵשׁוּעַ וַיִּקְחוּ אֶת-בְּגָדָיו וַיְחַלְּקוּם אַרְבָּעָה רֹבַע לְאִישׁ אִישׁ - וְגַם אֶת:כֻּתָּנְתּוֹ וְהַכֻּתֹּנֶת לֹא הָיְתָה תְּפוּרָה כִּי אִם-מַעֲשֵׂה אֹרֵג מִשָּׂפָה עַד-הַשָּׂפָה

23. Vay•hi ka•a•sher tzal•voo an•shey ha•tza•va et - Yeshua va•yik•choo et - be•ga•dav vay•chal•koom ar•ba•ah ro•va le•eesh eesh ve•gam et - koo•tan•to ve•hak•to•net lo hai•ta t`foo•ra ki eem - ma•a•se o•reg mi•sa•fa ad - ha•sa•fa.

Rabbinic Jewish Commentary
now the coat was without seam, woven from the top throughout: in such an one the Jews say (b) Moses ministered: and of this sort and make was the robe of the high priest, said to be of "woven work", Exo_28:32 upon which Jarchi remarks, ולא במחט, "and not with a needle"; it was all woven, and without any seam: and so the Jews say (c) in general of the garments of the priests:

"The garments of the priests are not made of needlework, but of woven work; as it is said, Exo_28:32. Abai says, it is not necessary (i.e. the use of the needle) but for their sleeves; according to the tradition, the sleeve of the garments of the priests is woven by itself, and is joined to the garment, and reaches to the palm of the hand."

So that this was an entire woven garment from top to bottom, excepting the sleeves, which were wove separately and sewed to it; of this kind also was his coat, which Jacob Iehudah Leon says (d),

"Was a stately woollen coat of a sky colour, wholly woven, all of one piece, without seam, without sleeves;"

Such a garment Yeshua our great High Priest wore, which had no seam in it, but was a curious piece of texture from top to bottom. The very learned Braunius (e) says, he has seen such garments in Holland, and has given fine cuts of them, and also of the frame in which they are wrought. What authority Nonnus had to call this coat a black one, or others for saying it was the work of the Virgin Mary, I know not.

(b) T. Bab. Taanith, fol. 11. 2. Gloss in ib. (c) T. Bab. Yoma, c. 7. foi. 72. 2. Maimon. Hilch. Cele Hamikdash, c. 8. sect. 16. (d) Relation of Memorable Things in the Tabernacle, &c. c. 5. p. 23. (e) De vestitu Sacerdot. Heb. l. 1. c. 16. p. 346, 360, 361.

---

24. They said therefore among themselves, Let us not rend it, but cast lots for it, whose it shall be: that the scripture might be fulfilled, which saith, They parted my raiment among them, and for my vesture they did cast lots. These things therefore the soldiers did.

Greek/Transliteration
24. Εἶπον οὖν πρὸς ἀλλήλους, Μὴ σχίσωμεν αὐτόν, ἀλλὰ λάχωμεν περὶ αὐτοῦ, τίνος ἔσται· ἵνα ἡ γραφὴ πληρωθῇ ἡ λέγουσα, Διεμερίσαντο τὰ ἱμάτιά μου ἑαυτοῖς, καὶ ἐπὶ τὸν ἱματισμόν μου ἔβαλον κλῆρον. Οἱ μὲν οὖν στρατιῶται ταῦτα ἐποίησαν.

24. Eipon oun pros alleilous, Mei schisomen auton, alla lachomen peri autou, tinos estai. 'ina 'ei graphei pleirothei 'ei legousa, Diemerisanto ta 'imatya mou 'eautois, kai epi ton 'imatismon mou ebalon kleiron. 'Oi men oun stratiotai tauta epoieisan.

Hebrew/Transliteration
כד. וַיֹּאמְרוּ אִישׁ אֶל-רֵעֵהוּ לֹא נִקְרָעֶהָ אֹתָהּ אַךְ נַפִּילָה עָלֶיהָ גּוֹרָל לְמִי תִהְיֶה לְהָקִים דְּבַר הַכָּתוּב יְחַלְּקוּ בְגָדַי:לָהֶם וְעַל-לְבוּשִׁי יַפִּילוּ גוֹרָל וַיַּעֲשׂוּ-כֵן אַנְשֵׁי הַצָּבָא

24. Va•yom•roo eesh el - re•e•hoo lo nik•re•ah o•ta ach na•pi•la a•le•ha go•ral le•mi ti•hi•ye le•ha•kim de•var ha•ka•toov ye•chal•koo ve•ga•dai la•hem ve•al - le•voo•shi ya•pi•loo go•ral va•ya•a•soo - chen an•shey ha•tza•va.

Rabbinic Jewish Commentary
The whole psalm is to be understood of the Messiah, not of David, as some do (f); many passages in it cannot be applied to him, such as speak of the dislocation of his bones, the piercing of his hands and feet, and this of parting his garments, and casting lots for his vesture: all which had their literal accomplishment in Jesus: nor can it be understood of Esther, as it is by some Jewish (g) interpreters; there is not one word in it that agrees with her, and particularly, not the clause here cited; and there are some things in it which are manifestly spoken of a man, and not of a woman, as Psa_22:8 nor can the whole body of the Jewish nation, or the congregation of Israel be intended, as others say (h); since it is clear, that a single person is spoken of throughout the psalm, and who is distinguished from others, from his brethren, from the congregation, from the seed of Jacob and Israel, Psa_22:22 and indeed, no other than the Messiah can be meant; he is pointed at in the very title of it, Aijeleth Shahar, which words, in what way soever they are rendered, agree with him: if by "the morning daily sacrifice", as they are by the Targum; he is the Lamb of God, who continually takes away the sins of the world; and very fitly is he so called in the title of a psalm, which speaks so much of his

sufferings and death, which were a propitiatory sacrifice for the sins of his people: or by the morning star, as others (i) interpret them; Yeshua is the bright and morning star, the day spring from on high, the sun of righteousness, and light of the world: or by "the morning help", as by the Septuagint; Yeshua had early help from God in the morning of his infancy, when Herod sought his life, and in the day of salvation of his people; and early in the morning was he raised from the dead, and had glory given him: or by "the morning hind", which seems best of all, to which he may be compared, as to a roe or hart, in Son_2:9 for his love and loveliness, and for his swiftness and readiness in appearing for the salvation of his people; and for his being hunted by Herod in the morning of his days; and being encompassed by those dogs, the Scribes and Pharisees, Judas and the band of soldiers; see Psa_22:16. The first words of the psalm were spoken by Yeshua the true Messiah, when he hung upon the cross, and are truly applied to himself; his reproaches and sufferings endured by him there, are particularly and exactly described in it, and agree with no other; the benefits which the people of God were to enjoy, in consequence of his sufferings, and the conversion of the Gentiles spoken of in it, which is peculiar to the days of the Messiah, show to whom it belongs. The Jews "themselves" are obliged to interpret some parts of it concerning him; they sometimes say (k), that by Aijeleth Shahar is meant the Shekinah, a name that well suits with the Messiah Yeshua, who tabernacled in our nature; the Psa_22:26 is applied by Jarchi to the time of the redemption, and the days of the Messiah; so that upon the whole, this passage is rightly cited with respect to the Messiah, and is truly said to be fulfilled by this circumstance, of the soldiers doing with his garments as they did:

(f) R. R. in Kimchi in Psal. 22. (g) R. R. in Jarchi in Psal. 22. (h) Kimchi & Ben Meleeh in ib. (i) Vid. Kimchi & Abendana in ib. (k) Zohar in Lev. fol. 5. 4. & Imre Bina in ib.

---

25. Now there stood by the cross of Jesus his mother, and his mother's sister, Mary the wife of Cleophas, and Mary Magdalene.

Greek/Transliteration

25. Εἰστήκεισαν δὲ παρὰ τῷ σταυρῷ τοῦ Ἰησοῦ ἡ μήτηρ αὐτοῦ, καὶ ἡ ἀδελφὴ τῆς μητρὸς αὐτοῦ, Μαρία ἡ τοῦ Κλωπᾶ, καὶ Μαρία ἡ Μαγδαληνή.

25. 'Eisteikeisan de para to stauro tou Yeisou 'ei meiteir autou, kai 'ei adelphei teis meitros autou, Maria 'ei tou Klopa, kai Maria 'ei Magdaleinei.

Hebrew/Transliteration

כה. וְעַל-יַד צְלַב יֵשׁוּעַ עָמְדוּ אִמּוֹ וַאֲחוֹת אִמּוֹ וּמִרְיָם אֵשֶׁת קְלוֹפָס וּמִרְיָם הַמַּגְדָּלִית:

25. Ve•al - yad tz`lav Yeshua am•doo ee•mo va•a•chot ee•mo oo•Miryam eshet K`lofas oo•Miryam ha•Mag•da•lit.

---

26. When Jesus therefore saw his mother, and the disciple standing by, whom he loved, he saith unto his mother, Woman, behold thy son!

Greek/Transliteration
26. Ἰησοῦς οὖν ἰδὼν τὴν μητέρα, καὶ τὸν μαθητὴν παρεστῶτα ὃν ἠγάπα, λέγει τῇ μητρὶ αὐτοῦ, Γύναι, ἰδοὺ ὁ υἱός σου.

26. Yeisous oun idon tein meitera, kai ton matheitein parestota 'on eigapa, legei tei meitri autou, Gunai, idou 'o 'wios sou.

Hebrew/Transliteration
:כו. וַיַּרְא יֵשׁוּעַ אֶת-אִמּוֹ וְאֶת-תַּלְמִידוֹ אֲשֶׁר אָהַב עֹמְדִים אֶצְלוֹ וַיֹּאמֶר אֶל-אִמּוֹ אִשָׁה רְאִי זֶה בְּנֵךְ

26. Va•yar Yeshua et - ee•mo ve•et - tal•mi•do asher ahav om•dim etz•lo va•yo•mer el - ee•mo ee•sha r`ee ze be•nech?

---

27. Then saith he to the disciple, Behold thy mother! And from that hour that disciple took her unto his own home.

Greek/Transliteration
27. Εἶτα λέγει τῷ μαθητῇ, Ἰδοὺ ἡ μήτηρ σου. Καὶ ἀπ᾽ ἐκείνης τῆς ὥρας ἔλαβεν ὁ μαθητὴς αὐτὴν εἰς τὰ ἴδια.

27. Eita legei to matheitei, Ydou 'ei meiteir sou. Kai ap ekeineis teis 'oras elaben 'o matheiteis autein eis ta idya.

Hebrew/Transliteration
:כז. וְאַחַר אָמַר אֶל-תַּלְמִידוֹ רְאֵה זֹאת אִמֶּךָ וַיַּאַסְפָה הַתַּלְמִיד אֶל-בֵּיתוֹ מֵהַיּוֹם הַהוּא וָמָעְלָה

27. Ve•a•char amar el - tal•mi•do r`•eh zot ee•me•cha va•ya•as•fa ha•tal•mid el - bei•to me•ha•yom ha•hoo va•ma•ala.

---

28. After this, Jesus knowing that all things were now accomplished, that the scripture might be fulfilled, saith, I thirst.

Greek/Transliteration
28. Μετὰ τοῦτο ἰδὼν ὁ Ἰησοῦς ὅτι πάντα ἤδη τετέλεσται, ἵνα τελειωθῇ ἡ γραφή, λέγει, Διψῶ.

28. Meta touto idon 'o Yeisous 'oti panta eidei tetelestai, 'ina teleiothei 'ei graphei, legei, Dipso.

Hebrew/Transliteration
:כח. וְיֵשׁוּעַ בְּדַעְתּוֹ אַחֲרֵי-כֵן כִּי נִשְׁלַם כָּל-דָּבָר אַךְ לְמַלֹּאת אֶת-הַכָּתוּב אָמַר צָמֵאתִי

457

28. Ve•Yeshua be•da•a•to a•cha•rey - chen ki nish•lam kol - da•var ach le•ma•lot et - ha•ka•toov amar tza•me•ti.

TaNaKh-Old Testament
that the Scripture might be fulfilled: might appear to have its accomplishment, which predicted the great drought and thirst that should be on him, Psa_22:15 and that his enemies at such a time would give him vinegar to drink, Psa_69:21.

"They gave me also gall for my meat; and in my thirst they gave me vinegar to drink." (Psa_69:21)

---

29. **Now there was set a vessel full of vinegar: and they filled a spunge with vinegar, and put it upon hyssop, and put it to his mouth.**

Greek/Transliteration
29. Σκεῦος οὖν ἔκειτο ὄξους μεστόν· οἱ δέ, πλήσαντες σπόγγον ὄξους, καὶ ὑσσώπῳ περιθέντες, προσήνεγκαν αὐτοῦ τῷ στόματι.

29. Skeuos oun ekeito oxous meston. 'oi de, pleisantes spongon oxous, kai 'ussopo perithentes, proseinegkan autou to stomati.

Hebrew/Transliteration
כט. וְשָׁם עָמַד כְּלִי מָלֵא חֹמֶץ וַיְמַלְאוּ סְפוֹג בַּחֹמֶץ וַיָּשִׂימוּ עַל-רֹאשׁ אֵזוֹב וַיַּגִּיעוּהוּ אֶל-פִּיו:

29. Ve•sham amad k`li ma•le cho•metz va•yit•be•loo se•fog ba•cho•metz va•ya•si•moo al - rosh ezov va•ya•gi•oo•hoo el - piv.

Rabbinic Jewish Commentary
Whether Yeshua drank of it or no is not certain; it seems by what follows as if he did; at least he took it, being offered to him: the Jews themselves say (b), that Yeshua said, give me a little water to drink, and they gave him חומץ חזק, "sharp vinegar"; which so far confirms the evangelic history.

(b) Toklos Jesu, p. 17.

---

30. **When Jesus therefore had received the vinegar, he said, It is finished: and he bowed his head, and gave up the ghost.**

Greek/Transliteration
30. Ὅτε οὖν ἔλαβεν τὸ ὄξος ὁ Ἰησοῦς, εἶπεν, Τετέλεσται· καὶ κλίνας τὴν κεφαλήν, παρέδωκεν τὸ πνεῦμα.

30. 'Ote oun elaben to oxos 'o Yeisous, eipen, Tetelestai. kai klinas tein kephalein, paredoken to pneuma.

ל. וַיִּטְעַם יֵשׁוּעַ מִן-הַחֹמֶץ וַיֹּאמֶר נִשְׁלָם וַיֵּט אֶת-רֹאשׁוֹ וַיַּפְקֵד אֶת-רוּחוֹ:

30. Va•yit•am Yeshua min - ha•cho•metz va•yo•mer nish•lam va•yet et -
ro•sho va•yaf•ked et - roo•cho.

**31. The Jews therefore, because it was the preparation, that the bodies should
not remain upon the cross on the Sabbath day, (for that Sabbath day was an
high day,) besought Pilate that their legs might be broken, and that they
might be taken away.**

Greek/Transliteration

31. Οἱ οὖν Ἰουδαῖοι, ἵνα μὴ μείνῃ ἐπὶ τοῦ σταυροῦ τὰ σώματα ἐν τῷ σαββάτῳ
ἐπεὶ Παρασκευὴ ἦν- ἦν γὰρ μεγάλη ἡ ἡμέρα ἐκείνου τοῦ σαββάτου-
ἠρώτησαν τὸν Πιλάτον ἵνα κατεαγῶσιν αὐτῶν τὰ σκέλη, καὶ ἀρθῶσιν.

31. 'Oi oun Youdaioi, 'ina mei meinei epi tou staurou ta somata en to sabbato
epei Paraskeuei ein- ein gar megalei 'ei 'eimera ekeinou tou sabbatou-
eiroteisan ton Pilaton 'ina kateagosin auton ta skelei, kai arthosin.

Hebrew/Transliteration

לא. וְהַיְּהוּדִים חָשׁוּ לְבִלְתִּי הִשָּׁאֵר אֶת-הַפְּגָרִים עַל-הָעֵץ בְּיוֹם הַשַּׁבָּת כִּי-עֶרֶב שַׁבָּת הָיָה וְהַשַּׁבָּת
הַהוּא גָּדוֹל:הוּא עַל-כֵּן שָׁאֲלוּ מִפִּילָטוֹס לְשַׁבֵּר אֶת-שׁוֹקֵיהֶם כִּי יָמוּתוּ וּלְהוֹרִידָם מִן-הָעֵץ

31. Ve•haye•hoo•dim cha•shoo le•vil•ti hash•er et - ha•p`ga•rim al - ha•etz
be•yom ha•Sha•bat ki - erev Sha•bat ha•ya ve•ha•Sha•bat ha•hoo ga•dol hoo
al - ken sha•a•loo mi•Pilatos le•sha•ber et - sho•key•hem ki ya•moo•too
ool•ho•ri•dam min - ha•etz.

Rabbinic Jewish Commentary

It was not only a sabbath, and a sabbath in the passover week, but it was the day in
which all the people appeared and presented themselves before the LORD in the
temple, and the sheaf of the first fruits was offered up; all which solemnities
meeting together made it a very celebrated day: it is in the original text, "it was the
great day of the sabbath"; which is the language of the Talmudists, and who say

נקרא שבת הגדול "Is called the great sabbath", on account of the miracle or sign of
the passover;" (d),

And in the Jewish Liturgy (e) there is a collect for the "great sabbath": hence the
Jews pretending a great concern lest that day should be polluted, though they made
no conscience of shedding innocent blood.

(d) Piske Tosephot Sabbat, art. 314. (e) Seder Tephillot, fol. 183. 2. &c. Ed. Basil.

459

32. Then came the soldiers, and brake the legs of the first, and of the other which was crucified with him.

Greek/Transliteration

32. ᾿Ηλθον οὖν οἱ στρατιῶται, καὶ τοῦ μὲν πρώτου κατέαξαν τὰ σκέλη καὶ τοῦ ἄλλου τοῦ συσταυρωθέντος αὐτῷ·

32. Eilthon oun 'oi stratiotai, kai tou men protou kateaxan ta skelei kai tou allou tou sustaurothentos auto.

Hebrew/Transliteration

:לב. וַיָּבֹאוּ אַנְשֵׁי הַצָּבָא וַיְשַׁבְּרוּ אֶת-שׁוֹקֵי הָאֶחָד וְאֶת-שׁוֹקֵי הַשֵּׁנִי אֲשֶׁר נִצְלְבוּ עִמּוֹ

32. Va•ya•vo•oo an•shey ha•tza•va vay•shab•roo et - sho•key ha•e•chad ve•et - sho•key ha•she•ni asher nitz•le•voo ee•mo.

---

33. But when they came to Jesus, and saw that he was dead already, they brake not his legs:

Greek/Transliteration

33. ἐπὶ δὲ τὸν ᾿Ιησοῦν ἐλθόντες, ὡς εἶδον αὐτὸν ἤδη τεθνηκότα, οὐ κατέαξαν αὐτοῦ τὰ σκέλη·

33. epi de ton Yeisoun elthontes, 'os eidon auton eidei tethneikota, ou kateaxan autou ta skelei.

Hebrew/Transliteration

:לג. וַיָּבֹאוּ אֶל-יֵשׁוּעַ וַיִּרְאוּ כִּי-כְבָר מֵת וְלֹא שִׁבְּרוּ אֶת-שׁוֹקָיו

33. Va•ya•vo•oo el - Yeshua va•yir•oo ki - che•var met ve•lo shib•roo et - sho•kav.

---

34. But one of the soldiers with a spear pierced his side, and forthwith came there out blood and water.

Greek/Transliteration

34. ἀλλ᾿ εἷς τῶν στρατιωτῶν λόγχῃ αὐτοῦ τὴν πλευρὰν ἔνυξεν, καὶ εὐθέως ἐξῆλθεν αἷμα καὶ ὕδωρ.

34. all 'eis ton stratioton logchei autou tein pleuran enuxen, kai eutheos exeilthen 'aima kai 'udor.

Hebrew/Transliteration

:לד. אַךְ אֶחָד מֵאַנְשֵׁי הַצָּבָא דְקָרוֹ בַחֲנִית בְּצִדּוֹ וַיֵּצֵא דָם וָמָיִם

---

34. Ach e•chad me•an•shey ha•tza•va d`ka•ro va•cha•nit be•tzi•do va•ye•tze dam va•ma•yim.

Rabbinic Jewish Commentary

This water and blood some make to signify baptism and the Lord's supper, which are both of Yeshua's appointing, and spring from him, and refer to his sufferings and death; rather they signify the blessings of sanctification and justification, the grace of the one being represented by water, as it frequently is in the Old and New Testament, and the other by blood, and both from Yeshua: that Yeshua was the antitype of the rock in the wilderness, the apostle assures us, in 1Co_10:4 and if the Jews are to be believed, he was so in this instance; Jonathan ben Uzziel, in his Targum on Num_20:11 says that,

"Moses smote the rock twice, at the first time אטיפת אדמא, "blood dropped out": and at the second time abundance of waters flowed out."

The same is affirmed by others (h) elsewhere in much the same words and order.

(h) Shemot Rabba, sect. 3. fol. 94. 1. Zohar in Num. fol. 102. 4.

---

35. And he that saw it bare record, and his record is true: and he knoweth that he saith true, that ye might believe.

Greek/Transliteration

35. Καὶ ὁ ἑωρακὼς μεμαρτύρηκεν, καὶ ἀληθινή ἐστιν αὐτοῦ ἡ μαρτυρία, κἀκεῖνος οἶδεν ὅτι ἀληθῆ λέγει, ἵνα ὑμεῖς πιστεύσητε.

35. Kai 'o 'eorakos memartureiken, kai aleithinei estin autou 'ei marturia, kakeinos oiden 'oti aleithei legei, 'ina 'umeis pisteuseite.

Hebrew/Transliteration

לה. וְהַמֵּעִיד עַל-זֶה רָאָה אֶת-הַדָּבָר וְעֵדוּתוֹ נֶאֱמָנָה וְהוּא יֹדֵעַ כִּי אֱמֶת יֶהְגֶּה חִכּוֹ לְבַעֲבוּר תַּאֲמִינוּ גַּם-אַתֶּם:

35. Ve•ha•me•eed al - ze ra•ah et - ha•da•var ve•e•doo•to ne•e•ma•na ve•hoo yo•de•a ki emet ye•he•ge chi•ko le•va•a•voor ta•a•mi•noo gam - atem.

---

36. For these things were done, that the scripture should be fulfilled, A bone of him shall not be broken.

Greek/Transliteration

36. Ἐγένετο γὰρ ταῦτα ἵνα ἡ γραφὴ πληρωθῇ, Ὀστοῦν οὐ συντριβήσεται ἀπ᾽ αὐτοῦ.

36. Egeneto gar tauta 'ina 'ei graphei pleirothei, Ostoun ou suntribeisetai ap autou.

Hebrew/Transliteration
:לוֹ. וְכָל-זֶה הָיָה לְקַיֵּם אֶת-הַכָּתוּב וְעֶצֶם לֹא-תִשְׁבְּרוּ בוֹ

36. Ve•chol - ze ha•ya le•ka•yem et - ha•ka•toov ve•e•tzem lo - tish•be•roo vo.

Rabbinic Jewish Commentary

For this will be true of the wicked, as well as of the righteous: and much less is the meaning of the words, one of his bones shall not be broken, namely, the bone "luz", the Jews speak of; which, they say (i), remains uncorrupted in the grave, and is so hard that it cannot be softened by water, nor burnt in the fire, nor ground in the mill, nor broke with an hammer; by and from which God will raise the whole body at the last day.

Maimonides (k) says, "He that breaks a bone in a pure passover, lo, he is to be beaten, as it is said, "and a bone ye shall not break in it": and so it is said of the second passover, "and a bone ye shall not break in it"; but a passover which comes with uncleanness, if a man breaks a bone in it, he is not to be beaten: from the literal sense it may be learned, that a bone is not to be broken, whether in a pure or defiled passover: one that breaks a bone on the night of the fifteenth, or that breaks a bone in it within the day, or that breaks one after many days, lo, he is to be beaten; wherefore they burn the bones of the passover in general, with what is left of its flesh, that they may not come to damage: none are guilty but for the breaking of a bone on which there is flesh of the quantity of an olive, or in which there is marrow; but a bone in which there is no marrow, and on which there is no flesh of the quantity of an olive, a man is not guilty for breaking it; and if there is flesh upon it of such a quantity, and he breaks the bone in the place where there is no flesh, he is guilty, although the place which he breaks is quite bare of its flesh: he that breaks after (another) has broken, is to be beaten."

And with these rules agree the following canons (l),

"The bones and sinews, and what is left, they burn on the sixteenth day, but if that falls on the sabbath, they burn them on the seventeenth, because these do not drive away the sabbath or a feast day."

And so it fell out this year in which Yeshua suffered, for the sixteenth was the sabbath day: again,

"He that breaks a bone in a pure passover, lo, he is to be beaten with forty stripes; but he that leaves anything in a pure one, and breaks in an impure one, is not to be beaten with forty stripes;"

Yea, they say (m), though

"It was a little kid and tender, and whose bones are tender, they may not eat them; for this is breaking of the bone, and if he eats he is to be beaten, for it is the same thing whether a hard or a tender bone be broken."

Now in this as in many other respects the paschal lamb was a type of Messiah, whose bones were none of them to be broken, to show that his life was not taken away by men, but was laid down freely by himself; and also the unbroken strength of Yeshua under the weight of sin, the curse of the law, and wrath of God, and conflict with Satan, when he obtained eternal redemption for us: and also this was on account of his resurrection from the dead, which was to be in a few days; though had his bones been broken he could easily have restored them, but it was the will of God it should be otherwise. Moreover, as none of the bones of his natural body were to be broken, so none that are members of him in a spiritual sense, who are bone of his bone and flesh of his flesh, shall ever be lost.

(i) Bereshit Rabba, sect. 28. fol. 23. 3. Vajikra Rabba, sect. 18. fol. 159. 3. Zohar in Gen. fol. 51. 1. & 82. 1. (k) Hilchot Korban Pesach. c. 10. sect. 1, 2, 3, 4. (l) Misn. Pesachim, c. 7. sect. 10, 11. (m) Maimon. Korban Pesach. c. 10. sect. 9.

---

37. And again another scripture saith, They shall look on him whom they pierced.

Greek/Transliteration
37. Καὶ πάλιν ἑτέρα γραφὴ λέγει, Ὄψονται εἰς ὃν ἐξεκέντησαν.

37. Kai palin 'etera graphei legei, Opsontai eis 'on exekenteisan.

Hebrew/Transliteration
:לז. וְעוֹד כָּתוּב לֵאמֹר וְהִבִּטוּ אֵלָיו אֵת אֲשֶׁר-דָּקָרוּ

37. Ve•od ka•toov le•mor ve•hi•bi•too elav et asher - da•ka•roo.

Rabbinic Jewish Commentary
The Jewish Rabbi's (n) themselves own that these words respect the Messiah, though they pretend that Messiah ben Joseph is meant, who shall be slain in the wars of Gog and Magog; for since their disappointment, and the blindness and hardness of heart which have followed it, they feign two Messiahs as expected by them; one Messiah ben David, who they suppose will be prosperous and victorious; and the other Messiah ben Joseph, who will suffer much, and at last be killed.

"'They will look upon him whom they pierced' means literally that Israel pierced him, although legally speaking he did not deserve to die…since his generation was not clean; however, he had to be killed in order to atone for the people of Israel" (Rabbi Tzadok Hacohen of Lublin; *Poked Akarim, letter he*: The Concealed Light, Tsvi Sadan pg.48)

38. And after this Joseph of Arimathaea, being a disciple of Jesus, but secretly for fear of the Jews, besought Pilate that he might take away the body of Jesus: and Pilate gave him leave. He came therefore, and took the body of Jesus.

Greek/Transliteration

38. Μετὰ ταῦτα ἠρώτησεν τὸν Πιλάτον Ἰωσὴφ ὁ ἀπὸ Ἀριμαθαίας, ὢν μαθητὴς τοῦ Ἰησοῦ, κεκρυμμένος δὲ διὰ τὸν φόβον τῶν Ἰουδαίων, ἵνα ἄρῃ τὸ σῶμα τοῦ Ἰησοῦ· καὶ ἐπέτρεψεν ὁ Πιλάτος. Ἦλθεν οὖν καὶ ἦρεν τὸ σῶμα τοῦ Ἰησοῦ.

38. Meta tauta eiroteisen ton Pilaton Yoseiph 'o apo Arimathaias, on matheiteis tou Yeisou, kekrummenos de dya ton phobon ton Youdaion, 'ina arei to soma tou Yeisou. kai epetrepsen 'o Pilatos. Eilthen oun kai eiren to soma tou Yeisou.

Hebrew/Transliteration

לח. וַיְהִי אַחַר הַדְּבָרִים הָאֵלֶּה יוֹסֵף מִן-הָרָמָתַיִם הוּא אֲשֶׁר הָיָה תַלְמִיד יֵשׁוּעַ בַּסֵּתֶר מִיִּרְאָתוֹ אֶת-הַיְּהוּדִים:וַיִּשְׁאַל מֵאֵת פִּילָטוֹס לָתֶת-לוֹ לָשֵׂאת אֶת-גּוּפַת יֵשׁוּעַ

38. Vay•hi achar ha•d`va•rim ha•e•le Yo•sef min - ha•Ra•ma•ta•yim hoo asher ha•ya tal•mid Yeshua ba•se•ter mi•yir•a•to et - ha•Ye•hoo•dim va•yish•al me•et Pilatos la•tet – lo la•set et - goo•fat Yeshua.

39. And there came also Nicodemus, which at the first came to Jesus by night, and brought a mixture of myrrh and aloes, about an hundred pound weight.

Greek/Transliteration

39. Ἦλθεν δὲ καὶ Νικόδημος, ὁ ἐλθὼν πρὸς τὸν Ἰησοῦν νυκτὸς τὸ πρῶτον, φέρων μίγμα σμύρνης καὶ ἀλόης ὡς λίτρας ἑκατόν.

39. Eilthen de kai Nikodeimos, 'o elthon pros ton Yeisoun nuktos to proton, pheron magma smurneis kai aloeis 'os litras 'ekaton.

Hebrew/Transliteration

לט. וַיִּתֶּן-לוֹ פִּילָטוֹס רִשְׁיוֹן וַיָּבֹא וַיִּשָּׂא אֶת-גּוּפַת יֵשׁוּעַ וְנַקְדִּימוֹן אֲשֶׁר לְפָנִים בָּא אֶל-יֵשׁוּעַ בַּלַּיְלָה בָּא גַם-הוּא:וְהֵבִיא סַמִּים בְּלוּלִים מֹר-וַאֲהָלוֹת כְּמֵאָה לִיטְרִין

39. Va•yi•ten - lo Pilatos rish•yon va•ya•vo va•yi•sa et - goo•fat Yeshua ve•Nak•dimon asher le•fa•nim ba el - Yeshua ba•lai•la ba gam - hoo ve•he•vee sa•mim be•loo•lim mor - va•a•ho•lot ke•me•ah li•ta•rin.

Rabbinic Jewish Commentary
This Nicodemus is thought to be the same with Nicodemus ben Gorion, the Talmudists speaks of, who, they say (u), was one of the three rich men in Jerusalem; as this appears to be a rich man, from the large quantity of myrrh and aloes he brought with him, and which must be very costly. Moreover, they say (w), that he had another name, which was Boni; and they themselves observe (x), that Boni was one of the disciples of Yeshua, as this Nicodemus was, though a secret one, as Joseph.

(u) T. Bab. Gittin, fol. 56. 1. (w) T. Bab. Taanith, fol. 20. 1. (x) T. Bab. Sanhedrin, fol. 43. 1.

---

40. Then took they the body of Jesus, and wound it in linen clothes with the spices, as the manner of the Jews is to bury.

Greek/Transliteration
40. Ἔλαβον οὖν τὸ σῶμα τοῦ Ἰησοῦ, καὶ ἔδησαν αὐτὸ ἐν ὀθονίοις μετὰ τῶν ἀρωμάτων, καθὼς ἔθος ἐστὶν τοῖς Ἰουδαίοις ἐνταφιάζειν.

40. Elabon oun to soma tou Yeisou, kai edeisan auto en othoniois meta ton aromaton, kathos ethos estin tois Youdaiois entaphyazein.

Hebrew/Transliteration
מ. וַיִּקְחוּ אֶת-גּוּפַת יֵשׁוּעַ וַיַּעַטוּהָ בְתַכְרִיכִים אֲשֶׁר מִלְאוּ בְשָׂמִים כְּדֶרֶךְ קְבוּרַת הַיְּהוּדִים:

40. Va•yik•choo et - goo•fat Yeshua va•ya•a•too•ha ve•tach•ri•chim asher mil•oo ve•sa•mim ke•de•rech ke•voo•rat ha•Ye•hoo•dim.

Rabbinic Jewish Commentary
as the manner of the Jews is to bury; Both was usual with them; both to wind up the dead in linen; hence R. Jonathan, alluding to this custom, when R. Isai was taken, and others would have delivered him, said, יכרך המת בסדינו, "let the dead be wrapped in his own linen (d)"; and also to bury them with spices; hence we read of "the spices of the dead" in a Jewish canon (e):

"They do not say a blessing over a lamp, nor over the spices of idolaters; nor over a lamp, nor over הבשמים של מתים, "the spices of the dead".

(d) T. Hieros. Ternmot, fol. 46. 2. (e) Misn. Beracot. c. 8. sect. 6.

---

41. Now in the place where he was crucified there was a garden; and in the garden a new sepulchre, wherein was never man yet laid.

41. Ἦν δὲ ἐν τῷ τόπῳ ὅπου ἐσταυρώθη κῆπος, καὶ ἐν τῷ κήπῳ μνημεῖον καινόν, ἐν ᾧ οὐδέπω οὐδεὶς ἐτέθη.

41. Ein de en to topo 'opou estaurothei keipos, kai en to keipo mneimeion kainon, en 'o oudepo oudeis etethei.

מא. וּבַמָּקוֹם אֲשֶׁר נִצְלַב-שָׁם הָיָה גָן וּבוֹ קֶבֶר חָדָשׁ אֲשֶׁר עוֹד לֹא-נִקְבַּר בּוֹ אִישׁ:

41. Oo•va•ma•kom asher nitz•lav - sham ha•ya gan oo•vo kever cha•dash asher od lo - nik•bar bo eesh.

Rabbinic Jewish Commentary
and in the garden a new sepulchre; They might not bury within the city. Some chose to make their sepulchres in their gardens, to put them in mind of their mortality, when they took their walks there; so R. Dustai, R. Janhal, and R. Nehurai, were buried, בפרדס, "in a garden", or orchard (f); and so were Manasseh and Amon, kings of Judah, 2Ki_21:18. Here Joseph had one, hewn out in a rock, for himself and family, and was newly made. The Jews distinguish between an old, and a new sepulchre; they say (g),

קבר חדש, "A new sepulchre" may be measured and sold, and divided, but an old one might not be measured, nor sold, nor divided."

Wherein was never man yet laid; This is not improperly, nor impertinently added, though the evangelist had before said, that it was a new sepulchre; for that it might be, and yet bodies have been lain in it; for according to the Jewish canons (h),

"There is as a new sepulchre, which is an old one; and there is an old one, which is as a new one; an old sepulchre, in which lie ten dead bodies, which are not in the power of the owners, הריזה כקבר חדש, "lo, this is as a new sepulchre"."

Now Yeshua was laid in such an one, where no man had been laid, that it might appear certainly that it was he, and not another, that was risen from the dead.

(f) Jechus haabot, p. 43. Ed. Hottinger. (g) Massech. Sernacot, c. 24. fol. 16. 3. (h) Ib.

---

42. There laid they Jesus therefore because of the Jews' preparation day; for the sepulcher was nigh at hand.

42. Ἐκεῖ οὖν διὰ τὴν Παρασκευὴν τῶν Ἰουδαίων, ὅτι ἐγγὺς ἦν τὸ μνημεῖον, ἔθηκαν τὸν Ἰησοῦν.

42. Ekei oun dya tein Paraskeuein ton Youdaion, 'oti engus ein to mneimeion, etheikan ton Yeisoun.

Hebrew/Transliteration

מב. וּבִהְיוֹת הַיּוֹם עֶרֶב שַׁבָּת לַיְּהוּדִים וְהַקֶּבֶר קָרוֹב קָבְרוּ בוֹ אֶת-יֵשׁוּעַ:

42. Oo•vi•hi•yot ha•yom erev Sha•bat la•Ye•hoo•dim ve•ha•ke•ver ka•rov kav•roo vo et - Yeshua.

Rabbinic Jewish Commentary

Because of the Jews' preparation day; either for the Chagigah, or the sabbath, which was just at hand; the Persic version reads, "the night of the sabbath": for this reason, they could not dig a grave purposely for him; for it was forbidden on feast days; and therefore they put him into a tomb ready made: the canon runs (i),

"They may not dig pits, וקברות, "nor graves", on a solemn feast day."

The former of these, the commentators say (k), are graves dug in the earth, and the latter edifices built over graves; and for the same reason, because it was such a day, they did not take his body to any of their houses, and embalm and anoint it, as they otherwise would have done; but this being a solemn day, and the sabbath drawing on apace, they hastened the interment, and took the most opportune place that offered.

(i) Misn. Moed Katon, c. 1. sect. 6. (k) Maimon. & Bartenora in ib.

John, Chapter 20

1. The first day of the week cometh Mary Magdalene early, when it was yet dark, unto the sepulchre, and seeth the stone taken away from the sepulchre.

Greek/Transliteration

1. Τῇ δὲ μιᾷ τῶν σαββάτων Μαρία ἡ Μαγδαληνὴ ἔρχεται πρωΐ, σκοτίας ἔτι οὔσης, εἰς τὸ μνημεῖον, καὶ βλέπει τὸν λίθον ἠρμένον ἐκ τοῦ μνημείου.

1. Tei de mya ton sabbaton Maria 'ei Magdaleinei erchetai proi, skotias eti ouseis, eis to mneimeion, kai blepei ton lithon eirmenon ek tou mneimeiou.

Hebrew/Transliteration

א. וַיְהִי בְּאֶחָד בַּשַּׁבָּת וַתָּבֹא מִרְיָם הַמַּגְדָּלִית לִפְנוֹת בֹּקֶר בַּחֲשֵׁכָה אֶל-הַקָּבֶר וַתֵּרֶא אֶת-הָאֶבֶן מְגוֹלָלָה מֵעַל-הַקָּבֶר:

1. Vay•hi ba•e•chad ba•Sha•bat va•ta•vo Mir•yam ha•Mag•da•lit lif•not bo•ker ba•cha•she•cha el - ha•ka•ver va•te•re et - ha•e•ven me•go•la•la me•al - ha•ka•ver.

Rabbinic Jewish Commentary
The Tabernacle was raised on the first day,
"It happened on the eighth day, that Moses called Aaron and his sons, and the elders of Israel." (Leviticus 9:1)

Chabad.org comments,
"It was "the eighth day" because it followed a seven-day "training" period, during which the Mishkan was erected each morning and and disassembled each evening, and Aaron and his four sons were initiated into the *kehunah* (priesthood). But it was also a day which our Sages describe as possessing many "firsts": it was a Sunday, the first day of the week; it was the 1st of Nissan, marking the beginning of a new year; it was the first day that the Divine Presence came to dwell in the Sanctuary; the first day of the *kehunah*; the first day of the service in the Sanctuary; and so on. There is even an opinion that this was the anniversary of the creation of the universe." (Chabad.org, The Eighth Dimension)

Chabad.org continues,
"If the number seven defines the natural reality, eight represents that which is higher than nature…In contrast, eight represents the introduction of a reality that is beyond all nature and definition, including the definition transcendence. This eighth dimension (if we can call it a dimension) has no limitations at all: it transcends and pervades, being beyond nature yet also fully present within it, being equally beyond matter and spirit and equally within them. . the messianic seventh millennium of history will be followed by the ultimate "eight": the supra-historical World to Come (*Olam Ha-ba*), in which the divine reality will unite with the created reality in ways that we cannot even speculate upon in a world in which finite and infinite are mutually exclusive." (Chabad.org, The Eighth Dimension)

2. Then she runneth, and cometh to Simon Peter, and to the other disciple, whom Jesus loved, and saith unto them, They have taken away the Lord out of the sepulchre, and we know not where they have laid him.

Greek/Transliteration
2. Τρέχει οὖν καὶ ἔρχεται πρὸς Σίμωνα Πέτρον καὶ πρὸς τὸν ἄλλον μαθητὴν ὃν ἐφίλει ὁ Ἰησοῦς, καὶ λέγει αὐτοῖς, Ἦραν τὸν κύριον ἐκ τοῦ μνημείου, καὶ οὐκ οἴδαμεν ποῦ ἔθηκαν αὐτόν.

2. Trechei oun kai erchetai pros Simona Petron kai pros ton allon matheitein 'on ephilei 'o Yeisous, kai legei autois, Eiran ton kurion ek tou mneimeiou, kai ouk oidamen pou etheikan auton.

Hebrew/Transliteration
ב. וַתָּרָץ וַתָּבֹא אֶל-שִׁמְעוֹן פֶּטְרוֹס וְאֶל-הַתַּלְמִיד הָאַחֵר אֲשֶׁר אָהַב אֹתוֹ יֵשׁוּעַ וַתֹּאמֶר אֲלֵיהֶם הִנֵּה - נָשְׂאוּ אֶת:אֲדֹנֵינוּ מִן-הַקֶּבֶר וַאֲנַחְנוּ לֹא נֵדַע אָנָה שָׂמוּ אֹתוֹ

2. Va•ta•rotz va•ta•vo el - Shimon Pet•roos ve•el - ha•tal•mid ha•a•cher asher ahav o•to Yeshua va•to•mer aley•hem hee•ne nas•oo et - Ado•ney•noo min - ha•ke•ver va•a•nach•noo lo ne•da ana sa•moo o•to.

---

3. Peter therefore went forth, and that other disciple, and came to the sepulchre.

Greek/Transliteration
3. Ἐξῆλθεν οὖν ὁ Πέτρος καὶ ὁ ἄλλος μαθητής, καὶ ἤρχοντο εἰς τὸ μνημεῖον.

3. Exeilthen oun 'o Petros kai 'o allos matheiteis, kai eirchonto eis to mneimeion.

Hebrew/Transliteration
ג. וַיֵּצֵא פֶטְרוֹס וְהַתַּלְמִיד הָאַחֵר וַיֵּלְכוּ אֶל-הַקֶּבֶר:

3. Va•ye•tze Fetros ve•ha•tal•mid ha•a•cher va•yel•choo el - ha•ka•ver.

---

4. So they ran both together: and the other disciple did outrun Peter, and came first to the sepulchre.

Greek/Transliteration
4. Ἔτρεχον δὲ οἱ δύο ὁμοῦ· καὶ ὁ ἄλλος μαθητὴς προέδραμεν τάχιον τοῦ Πέτρου, καὶ ἦλθεν πρῶτος εἰς τὸ μνημεῖον,

4. Etrechon de 'oi duo 'omou. kai 'o allos matheiteis proedramen tachion tou Petrou, kai eilthen protos eis to mneimeion,

ד. וּשְׁנֵיהֶם רָצוּ יַחְדָּו וַיְמַהֵר הַתַּלְמִיד הָאַחֵר לָרוּץ וַיַּעֲבֹר אֶת-פֶּטְרוֹס וַיָּבֹא רִאשׁוֹן אֶל-הַקֶּבֶר:

4. Oosh•ney•hem ra•tzoo yach•dav vay•ma•her ha•tal•mid ha•a•cher la•rootz va•ya•a•vor et - Petros va•ya•vo ri•shon el - ha•ka•ver.

---

5. And he stooping down, and looking in, saw the linen clothes lying; yet went he not in.

Greek/Transliteration

5. καὶ παρακύψας βλέπει κείμενα τὰ ὀθόνια, οὐ μέντοι εἰσῆλθεν.

5. kai parakupsas blepei keimena ta othonya, ou mentoi eiseilthen.

Hebrew/Transliteration

ה. וַיִּשַּׁח וַיַּשְׁקֵף אֶל-תּוֹכוֹ וַיַּרְא אֶת-הַתַּכְרִיכִים מֻנָּחִים לְבַדָּם וְלֹא יָרַד פְּנִימָה:

5. Va•yi•shach va•yash•kef el - to•cho va•yar et - ha•tach•ri•chim moo•na•chim le•va•dam ve•lo ya•rad p`ni•ma.

---

6. Then cometh Simon Peter following him, and went into the sepulchre, and seeth the linen clothes lie,

Greek/Transliteration

6. Ἔρχεται οὖν Σίμων Πέτρος ἀκολουθῶν αὐτῷ, καὶ εἰσῆλθεν εἰς τὸ μνημεῖον, καὶ θεωρεῖ τὰ ὀθόνια κείμενα,

6. Erchetai oun Simon Petros akolouthon auto, kai eiseilthen eis to mneimeion, kai theorei ta othonya keimena,

Hebrew/Transliteration

ו. וְגַם-שִׁמְעוֹן פֶּטְרוֹס בָּא אַחֲרָיו וַיֵּרֶד אֶל-הַקֶּבֶר וַיַּרְא אֶת-הַתַּכְרִיכִים מֻנָּחִים לְבַדָּם:

6. Ve•gam - Shimon Petros ba a•cha•rav va•ye•red el - ha•ka•ver va•yar et - ha•tach•ri•chim moo•na•chim le•va•dam.

---

7. And the napkin, that was about his head, not lying with the linen clothes, but wrapped together in a place by itself.

Greek/Transliteration

7. καὶ τὸ σουδάριον ὃ ἦν ἐπὶ τῆς κεφαλῆς αὐτοῦ, οὐ μετὰ τῶν ὀθονίων κείμενον, ἀλλὰ χωρὶς ἐντετυλιγμένον εἰς ἕνα τόπον.

7. kai to soudarion 'o ein epi teis kephaleis autou, ou meta ton othonion keimenon, alla choris entetuligmenon eis 'ena topon.

Hebrew/Transliteration

ז. וְהַמִּטְפַּחַת אֲשֶׁר הָיְתָה עַל-רֹאשׁוֹ אֵינֶנָּה עִם-הַתַּכְרִיכִים כִּי אִם-צְנוּפָה לְבַדָּהּ בְּמָקוֹם אַחֵר:

7. Ve•ha•mit•pa•chat asher hai•ta al - ro•sho ey•ne•na eem - ha•tach•ri•chim ki eem - tze•noo•fa le•va•da be•ma•kom a•cher.

---

8. Then went in also that other disciple, which came first to the sepulchre, and he saw, and believed.

Greek/Transliteration
8. Τότε οὖν εἰσῆλθεν καὶ ὁ ἄλλος μαθητὴς ὁ ἐλθὼν πρῶτος εἰς τὸ μνημεῖον, καὶ εἶδεν, καὶ ἐπίστευσεν·

8. Tote oun eiseilthen kai 'o allos matheiteis 'o elthon protos eis to mneimeion, kai eiden, kai episteusen.

Hebrew/Transliteration
ח. וַיֵּרֶד שָׁם גַּם-הַתַּלְמִיד הָאַחֵר אֲשֶׁר-בָּא רִאשׁוֹן אֶל-הַקֶּבֶר וַיַּרְא וַיַּאֲמֵן:

8. Va•ye•red sham gam - ha•tal•mid ha•a•cher asher - ba ri•shon el - ha•ke•ver va•yar va•ya•a•men.

---

9. For as yet they knew not the scripture, that he must rise again from the dead.

Greek/Transliteration
9. οὐδέπω γὰρ ᾔδεισαν τὴν γραφήν, ὅτι δεῖ αὐτὸν ἐκ νεκρῶν ἀναστῆναι.

9. oudepo gar eideisan tein graphein, 'oti dei auton ek nekron anasteinai.

Hebrew/Transliteration
ט. כִּי עַד-עַתָּה לֹא-הֵבִינוּ עוֹד אֶת-הַכְּתוּבִים כִּי נָכוֹן לוֹ לָקוּם מִן-הַמֵּתִים:

9. Ki ad - ata lo - he•vi•noo od et - ha•k`too•vim ki na•chon lo la•koom min - ha•me•tim.

---

10. Then the disciples went away again unto their own home.

Greek/Transliteration
10. Ἀπῆλθον οὖν πάλιν πρὸς ἑαυτοὺς οἱ μαθηταί.

10. Apeilthon oun palin pros 'eautous 'oi matheitai.

י. וַיָּשֻׁבוּ הַתַּלְמִידִים וַיֵּלְכוּ אֶל-בֵּיתָם:

10. Va•ya•shoo•voo ha•tal•mi•dim va•yel•choo el - bey•tam.

---

11. But Mary stood without at the sepulchre weeping: and as she wept, she stooped down, and looked into the sepulchre,

Greek/Transliteration
11. Μαρία δὲ εἱστήκει πρὸς τὸ μνημεῖον κλαίουσα ἔξω· ὡς οὖν ἔκλαιεν, παρέκυψεν εἰς τὸ μνημεῖον,

11. Maria de 'eisteikei pros to mneimeion klaiousa exo. 'os oun eklaien, parekupsen eis to mneimeion,

Hebrew/Transliteration
יא. וּמִרְיָם עָמְדָה מִחוּץ לַקֶּבֶר וַתֵּבְךְ וַיְהִי בִּבְכּוֹתָהּ וַתִּשַּׁח וַתַּשְׁקֵף אֶל-תּוֹךְ הַקָּבֶר:

11. Oo•Mir•yam am•da mi•choo•tz la•ke•ver va•tevch vay•hi biv•ko•ta va•ti•shach va•tash•kef el - toch ha•ka•ver.

---

12. And seeth two angels in white sitting, the one at the head, and the other at the feet, where the body of Jesus had lain.

Greek/Transliteration
12. καὶ θεωρεῖ δύο ἀγγέλους ἐν λευκοῖς καθεζομένους, ἕνα πρὸς τῇ κεφαλῇ, καὶ ἕνα πρὸς τοῖς ποσίν, ὅπου ἔκειτο τὸ σῶμα τοῦ Ἰησοῦ.

12. kai theorei duo angelous en leukois kathezomenous, 'ena pros tei kephalei, kai 'ena pros tois posin, 'opou ekeito to soma tou Yeisou.

Hebrew/Transliteration
יב. וַתֵּרֶא שְׁנֵי מַלְאָכִים עֹטִים לְבָנִים וְיֹשְׁבִים בַּמָּקוֹם אֲשֶׁר שָׂמוּ אֶת-גּוּפַת יֵשׁוּעַ אֶחָד מְרַאֲשֹׁתָיו וְאֶחָד מַרְגְּלֹתָיו:

12. Va•te•re sh`ney mal•a•chim o•tim le•va•nim ve•yosh•vim ba•ma•kom asher sa•moo et - goo•fat Yeshua e•chad me•ra•a•sho•tav ve•e•chad mar•ge•lo•tav.

Rabbinic Jewish Commentary
Matthew and Mark speak but of one, but Luke of two, as here; whom he calls men, because they appeared in an human form, and in shining garments, or white

apparel; and which appearance is entirely agreeable to the received notion of the Jews, that as evil angels or devils are clothed in black, so good angels, or ministering spirits, לבושי לבנים, "are clothed in white" (l), expressive of their spotless purity and innocence.

(l) Gloss. in T. Bab. Kiddushin, fol. 72. 1.

---

13. And they say unto her, Woman, why weepest thou? She saith unto them, Because they have taken away my Lord, and I know not where they have laid him.

Greek/Transliteration
13. Καὶ λέγουσιν αὐτῇ ἐκεῖνοι, Γύναι, τί κλαίεις; Λέγει αὐτοῖς, ὅτι Ἦραν τὸν κύριόν μου, καὶ οὐκ οἶδα ποῦ ἔθηκαν αὐτόν.

13. Kai legousin autei ekeinoi, Gunai, ti klaieis? Legei autois, 'oti Eiran ton kurion mou, kai ouk oida pou etheikan auton.

Hebrew/Transliteration
:יג. וַיֹּאמְרוּ אֵלֶיהָ אִשָּׁה לָמֶה תִבְכִּי אֲלֵיהֶם כִּי נָשְׂאוּ אֶת-אֲדֹנִי מִזֶּה וְלֹא אֵדַע אָנָה שָׂמֻהוּ

13. Va•yom•roo e•le•ha ee•sha la•me tiv•ki aley•hem ki nas•oo et - Adoni mi•ze ve•lo eda ana sa•moo•hoo.

---

14. And when she had thus said, she turned herself back, and saw Jesus standing, and knew not that it was Jesus.

Greek/Transliteration
14. Καὶ ταῦτα εἰποῦσα ἐστράφη εἰς τὰ ὀπίσω, καὶ θεωρεῖ τὸν Ἰησοῦν ἑστῶτα, καὶ οὐκ ᾔδει ὅτι Ἰησοῦς ἐστιν.

14. Kai tauta eipousa estraphei eis ta opiso, kai theorei ton Yeisoun 'estota, kai ouk eidei 'oti Yeisous estin.

Hebrew/Transliteration
:יד. עוֹד הִיא מְדַבֶּרֶת כָּזֹאת וַתֵּפֶן מֵאַחֲרֶיהָ וַתֵּרֶא אֶת-יֵשׁוּעַ עֹמֵד וְלֹא יָדְעָה כִּי הוּא יֵשׁוּעַ

14. Od hee me•da•be•ret ka•zot va•te•fen me•a•cha•re•ha va•te•re et - Yeshua o•med ve•lo yad•ah ki hoo Yeshua.

---

15. Jesus saith unto her, Woman, why weepest thou? whom seekest thou? She, supposing him to be the gardener, saith unto him, Sir, if thou have borne him hence, tell me where thou hast laid him, and I will take him away.

Greek/Transliteration
15. Λέγει αὐτῇ ὁ Ἰησοῦς, Γύναι, τί κλαίεις; Τίνα ζητεῖς; Ἐκείνη, δοκοῦσα ὅτι ὁ κηπουρός ἐστιν, λέγει αὐτῷ, Κύριε, εἰ σὺ ἐβάστασας αὐτόν, εἰπέ μοι ποῦ ἔθηκας αὐτόν, κἀγὼ αὐτὸν ἀρῶ.

15. Legei autei 'o Yeisous, Gunai, ti klaieis? Tina zeiteis? Ekeinei, dokousa 'oti 'o keipouros estin, legei auto, Kurie, ei su ebastasas auton, eipe moi pou etheikas auton, kago auton aro.

Hebrew/Transliteration
טו. וַיֹּאמֶר אֵלֶיהָ יֵשׁוּעַ אִשָּׁה לָמֶה תִבְכִּי אֶת-מִי תְבַקֵּשִׁי וְהִיא חָשְׁבָה כִּי-נֹטֵר הַגָּן הוּא וַתֹּאמֶר אֵלָיו - אֲדֹנִי אִם:אַתָּה נָשָׂאתָ אֹתוֹ מִזֶּה הַגִּידָה-נָּא לִי אֵיפֹא שַׂמְתָּ אֹתוֹ וַאֲנִי אֵלֵךְ וְאֶשָּׂאֶנּוּ

15. Va•yo•mer e•le•ha Yeshua ee•sha la•me tiv•ki et - mee te•va•ke•shi ve•hee chash•va ki - no•ter ha•gan hoo va•to•er elav Adoni eem - ata na•sa•ta o•to mi•ze ha•gi•da - na li ey•fo sam•ta o•to va•a•ni e•lech ve•e•sa•e•noo.

Rabbinic Jewish Commentary
Why does John include the unusual detail that she supposed him to be the "gardener"? The answer is found in Genesis,

"YHWH God planted a garden eastward (mi'kedem), in Eden, and there he put the man whom he had formed." (Genesis 2:8)

As Adam is formed from the dust of the earth, so is the Son of Man raised from the dust. The Messiah is the 'Gardener' who desires to be close to us, and walk with us again. The Messiah speaks with the woman alone in the garden to bring tikkun for the snake speaking with the first woman in the garden. Now The Holy Mashiach has reversed the curse and will return us to the Garden of Eden. The Holy Snake has crushed the head of the primeval serpent, and he has destroyed death.

---

16. Jesus saith unto her, Mary. She turned herself, and saith unto him, Rabboni; which is to say, Master.

Greek/Transliteration
16. Λέγει αὐτῇ ὁ Ἰησοῦς, Μαρία. Στραφεῖσα ἐκείνη λέγει αὐτῷ, Ῥαββουνί- ὃ λέγεται, Διδάσκαλε.

16. Legei autei 'o Yeisous, Maria. Strapheisa ekeinei legei auto, 'Rabbouni- 'o legetai, Didaskale.

Hebrew/Transliteration

טז. וַיֹּאמֶר אֵלֶיהָ יֵשׁוּעַ מִרְיָם וַתֵּפֶן וַתֹּאמֶר אֵלָיו עִבְרִית רַבּוּנִי אֲשֶׁר יֵאָמֵר רַבִּי:

16. Va•yo•mer e•le•ha Yeshua Mir•yam va•te•fen va•to•mer elav Eev•rit
Ra•boo•ni asher ye•a•mer Rabbi.

Rabbinic Jewish Commentary

The word Rabboni, is of the Chaldee and Syriac form, and signifies "my Lord, or master"; and is commonly applied to one that has a despotic power over another; though all the Oriental versions say, that she spoke to him in Hebrew. The Syriac and Ethiopic, "Rabboni", but the Arabic and Persic, "Rabbi". The titles of Rab, Rabbi, and Rabban, are frequent with the Jewish Rabbi's; who say (m), that Rabbi is greater than Rab, and Rabban is greater than Rabbi; and a man's own name greater than Rabban: but the word in the form here used Rabbon, I do not remember ever to have observed applied to any of the Rabbi's; but is frequently used of the Divine Being, who, in their prayers, is often addressed in this manner, רבונו של עולם "Lord of the world" (n).

(m) Halichot Olam Tract. 1. c. 3. p. 25. (n) T. Bab. Taanith, fol. 20. 1. Sanhedrin, fol. 94. 1. Abot R. Nathan, c. 9. Bereshit Rabba, sect. 8. fol. 6. 4.

---

17. Jesus saith unto her, Touch me not; for I am not yet ascended to my Father: but go to my brethren, and say unto them, I ascend unto my Father, and your Father; and to my God, and your God.

Greek/Transliteration

17. Λέγει αὐτῇ ὁ Ἰησοῦς, Μή μου ἅπτου, οὔπω γὰρ ἀναβέβηκα πρὸς τὸν πατέρα μου· πορεύου δὲ πρὸς τοὺς ἀδελφούς μου, καὶ εἰπὲ αὐτοῖς, Ἀναβαίνω πρὸς τὸν πατέρα μου καὶ πατέρα ὑμῶν, καὶ θεόν μου καὶ θεὸν ὑμῶν.

17. Legei autei 'o Yeisous, Mei mou 'aptou, oupo gar anabebeika pros ton patera mou. poreuou de pros tous adelphous mou, kai eipe autois, Anabaino pros ton patera mou kai patera 'umon, kai theon mou kai theon 'umon.

Hebrew/Transliteration

יז. וַיֹּאמֶר אֵלֶיהָ יֵשׁוּעַ אַל-תִּגְּעִי בִי כִּי עוֹד לֹא עָלִיתִי אֶל-הָאָב אַךְ לְכִי אֶל-אַחַי וְאִמְרִי אֲלֵיהֶם הִנְנִי - עֹלֶה אֶל-אָבִי וַאֲבִיכֶם אֶל-אֱלֹהַי וֵאלֹהֵיכֶם

17. Va•yo•mer e•le•ha Yeshua al - tig•ee vi ki od lo ali•ti el - ha•Av ach le•chi el - a•chai ve•eem•ree aley•hem hi•ne•ni o•le el - Avi va•Avi•chem el - Elohai ve•Elohey•chem.

---

18. Mary Magdalene came and told the disciples that she had seen the Lord, and that he had spoken these things unto her.

Greek/Transliteration

18. Ἔρχεται Μαρία ἡ Μαγδαληνὴ ἀπαγγέλλουσα τοῖς μαθηταῖς ὅτι ἑώρακεν τὸν κύριον, καὶ ταῦτα εἶπεν αὐτῇ.

18. Erchetai Maria 'ei Magdaleinei apangellousa tois matheitais 'oti 'eoraken ton kurion, kai tauta eipen autei.

Hebrew/Transliteration

יח. וַתָּבֹא מִרְיָם הַמַּגְדָּלִית וַתַּגֵּד לַתַּלְמִידִים כִּי-רָאֲתָה אֶת-הָאָדוֹן וְכִי כָזֹאת דִּבֶּר אֵלֶיהָ:

18. Va•ta•vo Mir•yam ha•Mag•da•lit va•ta•ged la•tal•mi•dim ki - ra•a•ta et - ha•Adon ve•chi ka•zot di•ber e•le•ha.

---

19. Then the same day at evening, being the first day of the week, when the doors were shut where the disciples were assembled for fear of the Jews, came Jesus and stood in the midst, and saith unto them, Peace be unto you.

Greek/Transliteration

19. Οὔσης οὖν ὀψίας, τῇ ἡμέρᾳ ἐκείνῃ τῇ μιᾷ τῶν σαββάτων, καὶ τῶν θυρῶν κεκλεισμένων ὅπου ἦσαν οἱ μαθηταὶ συνηγμένοι, διὰ τὸν φόβον τῶν Ἰουδαίων, ἦλθεν ὁ Ἰησοῦς καὶ ἔστη εἰς τὸ μέσον, καὶ λέγει αὐτοῖς, Εἰρήνη ὑμῖν.

19. Ouseis oun opsias, tei 'eimera ekeinei tei mya ton sabbaton, kai ton thuron kekleismenon 'opou eisan 'oi matheitai suneigmenoi, dya ton phobon ton Youdaion, eilthen 'o Yeisous kai estei eis to meson, kai legei autois, Eireinei 'umin.

Hebrew/Transliteration

יט. וַיְהִי בָעֶרֶב בַּשַּׁבָּת הַהוּא כַּאֲשֶׁר נִסְגְּרוּ דַלְתוֹת הַבַּיִת אֲשֶׁר נִקְבְּצוּ שָׁם הַתַּלְמִידִים מִיִּרְאָתָם אֶת-הַיְּהוּדִים:וַיָּבֹא יֵשׁוּעַ וַיַּעֲמֹד בְּתוֹכָם וַיֹּאמֶר אֲלֵיהֶם שָׁלוֹם עֲלֵיכֶם

19. Vay•hi ba•e•rev ba•Sha•bat ha•hoo ka•a•sher nis•ge•roo dal•tot ha•ba•yit asher nik•be•tzoo sham ha•tal•mi•dim mi•yir•a•tam et - ha•Ye•hoo•dim va•ya•vo Yeshua va•ya•a•mod be•to•cham va•yo•mer aley•hem sha•lom aley•chem.

---

20. And when he had so said, he shewed unto them his hands and his side. Then were the disciples glad, when they saw the Lord.

Greek/Transliteration

20. Καὶ τοῦτο εἰπὼν ἔδειξεν αὐτοῖς τὰς χεῖρας καὶ τὴν πλευρὰν αὐτοῦ. Ἐχάρησαν οὖν οἱ μαθηταὶ ἰδόντες τὸν κύριον.

20. Kai touto eipon edeixen autois tas cheiras kai tein pleuran autou. Echareisan oun 'oi matheitai idontes ton kurion.

Hebrew/Transliteration
:כ. וְאַחֲרֵי דַבְּרוֹ כָזֹאת הֶרְאָם אֶת־יָדָיו וְאֶת־צִדּוֹ וַיִּשְׂמְחוּ הַתַּלְמִידִים בִּרְאוֹתָם אֶת־הָאָדוֹן

20. Ve•a•cha•rey dab•ro cha•zot her•am et - ya•dav ve•et - tzi•do
va•yis•me•choo ha•tal•mi•dim bir•o•tam et - ha•Adon.

---

21. Then said Jesus to them again, Peace be unto you: as my Father hath sent me, even so send I you.

Greek/Transliteration
21. Εἶπεν οὖν αὐτοῖς ὁ Ἰησοῦς πάλιν, Εἰρήνη ὑμῖν· καθὼς ἀπέσταλκέν με ὁ πατήρ, κἀγὼ πέμπω ὑμᾶς.

21. Eipen oun autois 'o Yeisous palin, Eireinei 'umin. kathos apestalken me 'o pateir, kago pempo 'umas.

Hebrew/Transliteration
:כא. וַיּוֹסֶף יֵשׁוּעַ וַיֹּאמֶר אֲלֵיהֶם שָׁלוֹם לָכֶם כַּאֲשֶׁר שָׁלַח אֹתִי הָאָב כֵּן הִנְנִי שֹׁלֵחַ אֶתְכֶם

21. Va•yo•sef Yeshua va•yo•mer aley•hem sha•lom la•chem ka•a•sher sha•lach o•ti ha•Av ken hi•ne•ni sho•le•ach et•chem.

---

22. And when he had said this, he breathed on them, and saith unto them, Receive ye the Holy Ghost:

Greek/Transliteration
22. Καὶ τοῦτο εἰπὼν ἐνεφύσησεν καὶ λέγει αὐτοῖς, Λάβετε πνεῦμα ἅγιον.

22. Kai touto eipon enephuseisen kai legei autois, Labete pneuma 'agion.

Hebrew/Transliteration
:כב. וְאַחֲרֵי דַבְּרוֹ כָזֹאת וַיִּפַּח בָּהֶם וַיֹּאמֶר אֲלֵיהֶם קְחוּ לָכֶם אֶת־רוּחַ הַקֹּדֶשׁ

22. Ve•a•cha•rey dab•ro cha•zot va•yi•pach ba•hem va•yo•mer aley•hem ke•choo la•chem et - Roo•ach ha•Ko•desh.

Rabbinic Jewish Commentary
"YHWH Elohim formed man from the dust of the ground, and breathed into his nostrils the breath of life; and man became a living soul." (Genesis 2:7)

Where does the Breath of Life enter? Into the nostrils! In Lamentations, it reveals the secret of the Breath of Life

"The breath of our nostrils, the Messiah of the YHWH, was taken in their pits; Of whom we said, Under his shadow we shall live among the nations."
(Lamentations 4:20)

The breath of our nostrils is the Messiah. The Mashiach is the one who resurrects the dead. Chaim Kramer, of the Breslov Research Institute writes,

"Mashiach is represented by the "nose," our source of life and breath. . . As long as we breathe the breath of hope – the breath of prayer and reliance upon God – there is hope that Mashiach will come and fully purify our lives. The verse states (Lamentations 4:2), "The breath of our nostrils [is] the Mashiach of God."
(Mashiach, Who, What Why, How Where, When, Chaim Kramer, Breslov Research Institute, pg. 71)

Amazingly, the breath breathed into Adam occurred on Rosh HaShanah, the day of Resurrection:

"Man becomes a living, sentient being when God breathes His breath into him, transforming him from physical matter into a living hybrid of the physical and spiritual. When we blow the shofar on the day of Man's creation, it serves as a memorial to that first breath, the divine breath of life blown at the dawn of Creation, on Rosh Hashana."
(Aish.com, M'oray HaAish, R. Ari Kahn: The Sound of the Shofar)

R' Chaim Kramer then makes an astonishing statement:
"...just as breathing sustains each person, whether one is conscious of it or not, so too, Mashiach, the world's ultimate rectification, has sustained the world from its inception, whether we are conscious of it or not."
(Mashiach, Who, What Why, How Where, When, Chaim Kramer, Breslov Research Institute, pg. 44)

Just as prayer links to the incense, Kramer notes,
"Mashiach will "breathe the fear of God," since his soul is rooted in the place of breathing, the nose. And this "nose," the source of life of the Mashiach, alludes to prayer. Rebbe Nachman thus taught: Mashiach's main weapon is prayer..." Thus prayer is represented by the nose. And the nose is breathing, life itself."
(Mashiach, Who, What Why, How Where, When, Chaim Kramer, Breslov Research Institute, pg. 42)

He continues,
"...[Mashiach's] "breathing" will have a very positive effect upon mankind. . . The breath that Mashiach will breathe will emanate from the Torah and its 613 mitzvot. This is "The spirit of God [that] hovered over the waters." The spirit is Mashiach and the waters are the Torah. Mashiach's spirit is embedded in the Torah and he will draw his breath, the awe of God, from it. With this spirit, he will

be able to "breathe into others" filing them with an awe and respect for God."
(Mashiach, Who, What, Why, How, Where, When, Chaim Kramer, Breslov
Research Institute, pg.63)

The Jews have of the Spirit of the Messiah, who say (p), that

"The Spirit went from between the wings of the cherubim, ונשביה, "and breathed
upon him" (Menasseh) by the decree, or order of the *Word* of YHWH."

(p) Targum in 2 Chron. xxxiii. 13.

**23. Whose soever sins ye remit, they are remitted unto them; and whose
soever sins ye retain, they are retained.**

Greek/Transliteration
23. Ἄν τινων ἀφῆτε τὰς ἁμαρτίας, ἀφίενται αὐτοῖς· ἄν τινων κρατῆτε,
κεκράτηνται.

23. An tinon apheite tas 'amartias, aphientai autois. an tinon krateite,
kekrateintai.

Hebrew/Transliteration
כג. אִישׁ אִישׁ אֲשֶׁר תִּסְלְחוּ לוֹ אֶת-חֲטָאָיו וְנִסְלַח לוֹ וְאִם תְּשִׂיתוּם עָלָיו עָלָיו יִהְיוּ:

23. Eesh eesh asher tis•le•choo lo et - cha•ta•av ve•nis•lach lo ve•eem
te•shi•toom alav alav yi•hee•yoo.

**24. But Thomas, one of the twelve, called Didymus, was not with them when
Jesus came.**

Greek/Transliteration
24. Θωμᾶς δέ, εἷς ἐκ τῶν δώδεκα, ὁ λεγόμενος Δίδυμος, οὐκ ἦν μετ᾽ αὐτῶν
ὅτε ἦλθεν ὁ Ἰησοῦς.

24. Thomas de, 'eis ek ton dodeka, 'o legomenos Didumos, ouk ein met auton
'ote eilthen 'o Yeisous.

Hebrew/Transliteration
כד. וְתוֹמָא הַנִּקְרָא דִידוּמוֹס אֶחָד מִשְׁנֵים הֶעָשָׂר לֹא-הָיָה עִמָּהֶם בְּבֹא יֵשׁוּעַ:

24. Ve•Toma ha•nik•ra Di•doo•mos e•chad mi•sh`neim he•a•sar lo - ha•ya
ee•ma•hem be•vo Yeshua.

Rabbinic Jewish Commentary

The person here spoken of, is described by his Hebrew name Thomas, and his Greek one Didymus, which both signify a twin; and perhaps he was one. It was common with the Jews to have two names, a Jewish and a Gentile one; by the one they went in the land of Israel, and by the other when without the land (q); nay, they often went by one name in Judea, and by another in Galilee (r); where Thomas might go by the name of Didymus with the Greeks, that might live with the Jews in some of those parts: he is also said to be "one of the twelve" apostles, which was their number at first, though Judas now was gone off from them, and therefore are sometimes only called the "eleven".

(q) T. Hieros. Gittin, fol. 43. 2. (r) T. Hieros. Gittin, fol. 45. 3.

---

25. The other disciples therefore said unto him, We have seen the Lord. But he said unto them, Except I shall see in his hands the print of the nails, and put my finger into the print of the nails, and thrust my hand into his side, I will not believe.

Greek/Transliteration

25. Ἔλεγον οὖν αὐτῷ οἱ ἄλλοι μαθηταί, Ἑωράκαμεν τὸν κύριον. Ὁ δὲ εἶπεν αὐτοῖς, Ἐὰν μὴ ἴδω ἐν ταῖς χερσὶν αὐτοῦ τὸν τύπον τῶν ἥλων, καὶ βάλω τὸν δάκτυλόν μου εἰς τὸν τύπον τῶν ἥλων, καὶ βάλω τὴν χεῖρά μου εἰς τὴν πλευρὰν αὐτοῦ, οὐ μὴ πιστεύσω.

25. Elegon oun auto 'oi alloi matheitai, 'Eorakamen ton kurion. 'O de eipen autois, Ean mei ido en tais chersin autou ton tupon ton 'eilon, kai balo ton daktulon mou eis ton tupon ton 'eilon, kai balo tein cheira mou eis tein pleuran autou, ou mei pisteuso.

Hebrew/Transliteration

כה. וַיֹּאמְרוּ אֵלָיו יֶתֶר הַתַּלְמִידִים רָאִינוּ אֶת-הָאָדוֹן וַיֹּאמֶר אֲלֵיהֶם אִם-לֹא אֶרְאֶה אֶת-מַדְקְרוֹת הַמַּסְמְרִים:בְּיָדָיו וְלֹא אֶתְקַע אֶת-אֶצְבָּעִי בְּנִקְבֵי הַמַּסְמְרִים הָאֵלֶּה וּבְיָדִי לֹא אֶגַּע בְּצִדּוֹ לֹא אַאֲמִינָה

25. Va•yom•roo elav ye•ter ha•tal•mi•dim ra•ee•noo et - ha•Adon va•yo•mer aley•hem eem - lo er•eh et - mad•ke•rot ha•mas•me•rim be•ya•dav ve•lo et•ka et - etz•ba•ee be•nik•vey ha•mas•me•rim ha•e•le vv•ya•dee lo ega be•tzi•do lo a•a•mi•na.

Rabbinic Jewish Commentary

The bodies of men were sometimes fastened to the cross with cords, and not nails (s). How many were used, whether three, as some, or four, as others, or more, as were sometimes used (t), is not certain, nor material to know. The Alexandrian copy, and some others, and the Vulgate Latin, Syriac, and Persic versions read, "the place of the nails"; that is, the place where the nails were drove. Thomas knew that Yeshua was fastened to the cross with nails, and that his side was pierced with a spear; which he, though not present, might have had from John, who was an eyewitness thereof; but though they had all seen him alive, he will not trust to their testimony; nay, he was determined not to believe his own eyes; unless he put his finger into, as well as saw, the print of the nails, and thrust his hand into his side, as well as beheld the wound made by the spear, he is resolved not to believe. And his sin of unbelief is the more aggravated, inasmuch as this disciple was present at the raising of Lazarus from the dead by Yeshua, and had heard Yeshua himself say, that he should rise from the dead the third day. We may learn from hence how great is the sin of unbelief; that the best of men are subject to it; and that though this was over ruled by divine providence to bring out another proof Yeshua's resurrection, yet this did not excuse the sin of Thomas: and it may be observed, that as Thomas would not believe without seeing the marks of the nails and spear in Yeshua's flesh; so many will not believe, unless they find such and such marks in themselves, which often prove very ensnaring and distressing. Just such an unbeliever as Thomas was, the Jews make Moses to be, when Israel sinned: they say,

"He did not believe that Israel had sinned, but said, אם איני רואה איני מאמין, "If I do not see, I will not believe" (u)."

(s) Vid. Lipsium de Cruce, l. 2. c. 8. p. 87. (t) Ib. c. 9. p. 91. (u) Shemot Rabba, sect. 46. fol. 142. 2.

---

26. And after eight days again his disciples were within, and Thomas with them: then came Jesus, the doors being shut, and stood in the midst, and said, Peace be unto you.

Greek/Transliteration
26. Καὶ μεθ᾽ ἡμέρας ὀκτὼ πάλιν ἦσαν ἔσω οἱ μαθηταὶ αὐτοῦ, καὶ Θωμᾶς μετ᾽ αὐτῶν. Ἔρχεται ὁ Ἰησοῦς, τῶν θυρῶν κεκλεισμένων, καὶ ἔστη εἰς τὸ μέσον καὶ εἶπεν, Εἰρήνη ὑμῖν.

26. Kai meth 'eimeras okto palin eisan eso 'oi matheitai autou, kai Thomas met auton. Erchetai 'o Yeisous, ton thuron kekleismenon, kai estei eis to meson kai eipen, Eireinei 'umin.

Hebrew/Transliteration
כו. וּמִקְצֵה שְׁמֹנַת יָמִים נִקְהֲלוּ הַתַּלְמִידִים בַּבַּיִת פְּנִימָה עוֹד הַפַּעַם וְתוֹמָא עִמָּהֶם וַיָּבֹא יֵשׁוּעַ כַּאֲשֶׁר סֻגְרוּ:הַדְּלָתוֹת וַיַּעֲמֹד בְּתוֹכָם וַיֹּאמֶר שָׁלוֹם עֲלֵיכֶם.

26. Oo•mik•tze sh`mo•nat ya•mim nik•ha•loo ha•tal•mi•dim ba•ba•yit p`ni•ma od ha•pa•am ve•Toma ee•ma•hem va•ya•vo Yeshua ka•a•sher soog•roo had•la•tot va•ya•a•mod be•to•cham va•yo•mer sha•lom aley•chem.

Rabbinic Jewish Commentary
It has been proven from Josephus (w), that the Jews used to express a week by eight days. (w) Antiqu. l. 7. c. 9. And;

"Imagine being able to walk through walls. You wouldn't bother with opening doors; you could pass right through them…Imagine being able to disappear or reappear at will. Instead of driving to school or work, you would just vanish and rematerialize in your classroom or office…You would be hailed as a master surgeon, with the ability to repair the internal organs of patients without ever cutting the skin…No secrets could be kept from us. No treasures could be hidden from us. No obstructions could stop us. We would truly be miracle workers, performing feats beyond the comprehension of mortals. We would also be omnipotent. What being could possess such God-like power? The answer: a being from a higher dimensional world."

(Michio Kaku, Hyperspace, Chapter 2, Anchor Books, pg. 46)

---

27. Then saith he to Thomas, reach hither thy finger, and behold my hands; and reach hither thy hand, and thrust it into my side: and be not faithless, but believing.

Greek/Transliteration
27. Εἶτα λέγει τῷ Θωμᾷ, Φέρε τὸν δάκτυλόν σου ὧδε, καὶ ἴδε τὰς χεῖράς μου· καὶ φέρε τὴν χεῖρά σου, καὶ βάλε εἰς τὴν πλευράν μου· καὶ μὴ γίνου ἄπιστος, ἀλλὰ πιστός.

27. Eita legei to Thoma, Phere ton daktulon sou 'ode, kai ide tas cheiras mou. kai phere tein cheira sou, kai bale eis tein pleuran mou. kai mei ginou apistos, alla pistos.

Hebrew/Transliteration
כז. וְאַחַר אָמַר אֶל-תּוֹמָא הוֹשֵׁט אֶת-אָצְבָּעֲךָ הֵנָּה וּרְאֵה אֶת-יָדַי וְהוֹשֵׁט אֶת-יָדְךָ וּמֶשֵׁנִי בְּצִדִּי וְאַל-תְּהִי חָסֵר:אֱמוּנָה כִּי אִם-הַאֲמֵן תַּאֲמִין

27. Ve•a•char amar el - Toma ho•shet et - etz•ba•a•cha he•na oor•eh et - ya•dai ve•ho•shet et - yad•cha oo•moo•she•nee ve•tzi•di ve•al - te•hi cha•sar e•moo•na ki eem - ha•a•men ta•a•min.

---

28. And Thomas answered and said unto him, My Lord and my God.

Greek/Transliteration
28. Καὶ ἀπεκρίθη Θωμᾶς, καὶ εἶπεν αὐτῷ, Ὁ κύριός μου καὶ ὁ θεός μου.

28. Kai apekrithei Thomas, kai eipen auto, 'O kurios mou kai 'o theos mou.

Hebrew/Transliteration
כח. וַיַּעַן תּוֹמָא וַיֹּאמֶר אֵלָיו אֲדֹנִי וֵאלֹהָי:

---

28. Va•ya•an Toma va•yo•mer elav Adoni ve•Elohai.

Rabbinic Jewish Commentary

my Lord and my God; He owns him to be LORD, as he was both by creation and redemption; and God, of which he was fully assured from his omniscience, which he had given a full proof of, and from the power that went along with his words to his heart, and from a full conviction he now had of his resurrection from the dead.

He asserts his interest in him as his LORD and his God; which denotes his subjection to him, his affection for him, and faith in him; so the divine *Word* is called in Philo the Jew, κυριος μου, "my Lord" (x).

(x) Lib. Allegor. l. 2. p. 101.

---

29. Jesus saith unto him, Thomas, because thou hast seen me, thou hast believed: blessed are they that have not seen, and yet have believed.

Greek/Transliteration

29. Λέγει αὐτῷ ὁ Ἰησοῦς, Ὅτι ἑώρακάς με, πεπίστευκας; Μακάριοι οἱ μὴ ἰδόντες, καὶ πιστεύσαντες.

29. Legei auto 'o Yeisous, 'Oti 'eorakas me, pepisteukas? Makarioi 'oi mei idontes, kai pisteusantes.

Hebrew/Transliteration

כט. וַיֹּאמֶר אֵלָיו יֵשׁוּעַ יַעַן אֲשֶׁר רְאִיתַנִי הֶאֱמַנְתָּ תּוֹמָא אַשְׁרֵי אֵלֶּה הַמַּאֲמִינִים וְרָאוֹ לֹא רָאוּ:

29. Va•yo•mer elav Yeshua ya•an asher r`ee•ta•ni he•e•man•ta Toma ash•rey ele ha•ma•a•mi•nim ve•ra•o lo ra•oo.

Rabbinic Jewish Commentary

The word Thomas is omitted in the Alexandrian copy, and in Beza's ancient copy, and in some others, and in the Syriac, Arabic, and Ethiopic versions.

"One said to R. Jochanan, expound Rabbi; for it is beautiful for thee to expound: for as thou sayest, so I see: he replied to him, Raka, אלמלא לא ראית לא האמנת, "if thou seest not, thou wilt not believe?".

(y) T. Bab. Bava Bathra, fol. 75. 1. & Sanhedrin, fol. 100. 1.

---

30. And many other signs truly did Jesus in the presence of his disciples, which are not written in this book:

Greek/Transliteration

30. Πολλὰ μὲν οὖν καὶ ἄλλα σημεῖα ἐποίησεν ὁ Ἰησοῦς ἐνώπιον τῶν μαθητῶν αὐτοῦ, ἃ οὐκ ἔστιν γεγραμμένα ἐν τῷ βιβλίῳ τούτῳ.

30. Polla men oun kai alla seimeia epoieisen 'o Yeisous enopion ton matheiton autou, 'a ouk estin gegrammena en to biblio touto.

Hebrew/Transliteration

ל. וְגַם-מוֹפְתִים אֲחֵרִים רַבִּים עָשָׂה יֵשׁוּעַ לְעֵינֵי תַלְמִידָיו אֲשֶׁר לֹא-נִכְתְּבוּ בַּסֵּפֶר הַזֶּה:

30. Ve•gam - mof•tim a•che•rim ra•bim asa Yeshua le•ei•ney tal•mi•dav asher lo - nich•te•voo ba•se•fer ha•ze.

---

31. But these are written, that ye might believe that Jesus is the Christ, the Son of God; and that believing ye might have life through his name.

Greek/Transliteration

31. Ταῦτα δὲ γέγραπται, ἵνα πιστεύσητε ὅτι Ἰησοῦς ἐστιν ὁ χριστὸς ὁ υἱὸς τοῦ θεοῦ, καὶ ἵνα πιστεύοντες ζωὴν ἔχητε ἐν τῷ ὀνόματι αὐτοῦ.

31. Tauta de gegraptai, 'ina pisteuseite 'oti Yeisous estin 'o christos 'o 'wios tou theou, kai 'ina pisteuontes zoein echeite en to onomati autou.

Hebrew/Transliteration

לא. אַךְ-אֵלֶּה נִכְתְּבוּ לְבַעֲבוּר תַּאֲמִינוּ כִּי יֵשׁוּעַ הוּא הַמָּשִׁיחַ בֶּן-הָאֱלֹהִים וּלְבַעֲבוּר יִהְיוּ לָכֶם חַיִּים עֵקֶב:אֱמוּנַתְכֶם בִּשְׁמוֹ

31. Ach - ele nich•te•voo le•va•a•voor ta•a•mi•noo ki Yeshua hoo ha•Ma•shi•ach Ben - ha•Elohim ool•va•a•voor yi•hee•yoo la•chem cha•yim e•kev emoo•nat•chem bish•mo.

John, Chapter 21

1. After these things Jesus shewed himself again to the disciples at the sea of Tiberias; and on this wise shewed he himself.

Greek/Transliteration
1. Μετὰ ταῦτα ἐφανέρωσεν ἑαυτὸν πάλιν ὁ Ἰησοῦς τοῖς μαθηταῖς ἐπὶ τῆς θαλάσσης τῆς Τιβεριάδος· ἐφανέρωσεν δὲ οὕτως.

1. Meta tauta ephanerosen 'eauton palin 'o Yeisous tois matheitais epi teis thalasseis teis Tiberyados. ephanerosen de 'outos.

Hebrew/Transliteration
א. וַיְהִי אַחֲרֵי-כֵן וַיּוֹסֶף יֵשׁוּעַ לְהֵרָאוֹת אֶל-תַּלְמִידָיו עַל-יַם טְבַרְיָה וְכֹה נִרְאָה אֲלֵיהֶם:

1. Vay•hi a•cha•rey - chen va•yo•sef Yeshua le•he•ra•ot el - tal•mi•dav al - yam Te•var•ya ve•cho nir•ah aley•hem.

---

2. There were together Simon Peter, and Thomas called Didymus, and Nathanael of Cana in Galilee, and the sons of Zebedee, and two other of his disciples.

Greek/Transliteration
2. Ἦσαν ὁμοῦ Σίμων Πέτρος, καὶ Θωμᾶς ὁ λεγόμενος Δίδυμος, καὶ Ναθαναὴλ ὁ ἀπὸ Κανᾶ τῆς Γαλιλαίας, καὶ οἱ τοῦ Ζεβεδαίου, καὶ ἄλλοι ἐκ τῶν μαθητῶν αὐτοῦ δύο.

2. Eisan 'omou Simon Petros, kai Thomas 'o legomenos Didumos, kai Nathanaeil 'o apo Kana teis Galilaias, kai 'oi tou Zebedaiou, kai alloi ek ton matheiton autou duo.

Hebrew/Transliteration
ב. כַּאֲשֶׁר יָשְׁבוּ יַחְדָּו שִׁמְעוֹן פֶּטְרוֹס וְתוֹמָא הַנִּקְרָא דִידוּמוֹס וּנְתַנְאֵל מִקָּנֵה אֲשֶׁר בַּגָּלִיל וּבְנֵי זַבְדִּי וּשְׁנַיִם אֲחֵרִים:מִתַּלְמִידָיו

2. Ka•a•sher yash•voo yach•dav Shimon Petros ve•Toma ha•nik•ra Di•doo•mos oo•N`tan•el mi•Kana asher ba•Ga•lil oov•ney Zav•di oosh•na•yim a•che•rim mi•tal•mi•dav.

---

3. Simon Peter saith unto them, I go a fishing. They say unto him, We also go with thee. They went forth, and entered into a ship immediately; and that night they caught nothing.

3. Λέγει αὐτοῖς Σίμων Πέτρος, Ὑπάγω ἁλιεύειν. Λέγουσιν αὐτῷ, Ἐρχόμεθα
καὶ ἡμεῖς σὺν σοί. Ἐξῆλθον καὶ ἐνέβησαν εἰς τὸ πλοῖον εὐθύς, καὶ ἐν ἐκείνῃ
τῇ νυκτὶ ἐπίασαν οὐδέν.

3. Legei autois Simon Petros, 'Upago 'alieuein. Legousin auto, Erchometha
kai 'eimeis sun soi. Exeilthon kai enebeisan eis to ploion euthus, kai en ekeinei
tei nukti epiasan ouden.

Hebrew/Transliteration

ג. וַיֹּאמֶר אֲלֵיהֶם שִׁמְעוֹן פֶּטְרוֹס הִנְנִי הֹלֵךְ לָדוּג וַיֹּאמְרוּ אֵלָיו עִמְּךָ גַּם-אֲנַחְנוּ וַיֵּצְאוּ מִיָּד וַיֵּרְדוּ
אֶל-הָאֳנִיָּה:וְלֹא לָכְדוּ מְאוּמָה בַּלַּיְלָה הוּא

3. Va•yo•mer aley•hem Shimon Petros hi•ne•ni ho•lech la•doog va•yom•roo
elav ee•mach ne•lech gam - a•nach•noo va•yetz•oo mi•yad va•yer•doo el -
ha•o•ni•ya ve•lo lach•doo me•oo•ma ba•lai•la hoo.

Rabbinic Jewish Commentary

This is said to be one of the ten traditions which Joshua delivered to the children
of Israel, when he divided the land among them (z):

"That any man should be free to catch fish in the waters (or sea) of Tiberias; and
he might fish with an hook only; but he might not spread a net, or place a ship
there, except the children of the tribe to whom that sea belonged in their division."

But now these disciples, or the greater part of them at least, belonging to the tribe
and division in which the sea was, had a right to carry a ship or boat thither, and
make use of a net, as they did. Besides, there was another reason for fishing here,
because there were no unclean fish; for the Jews say (a), that

"In a place of running water no clean fish goes along with unclean fish, and lo, the
sea of Tiberias is כגון המים מהלכין הן, "as running waters".

(z) Maimon. Hilch. Nezike Maramon, c. 5. sect. 3. Vid. T. Bab. Bava Kama, fol.
81. 1. (a) T. Hieros. Avoda Zara, fol. 42. 1.

**4. But when the morning was now come, Jesus stood on the shore: but the
disciples knew not that it was Jesus.**

Greek/Transliteration

4. Πρωΐας δὲ ἤδη γενομένης ἔστη ὁ Ἰησοῦς εἰς τὸν αἰγιαλόν· οὐ μέντοι
ἤδεισαν οἱ μαθηταὶ ὅτι Ἰησοῦς ἐστιν.

4. Proias de eidei genomeneis estei 'o Yeisous eis ton aigyalon. ou mentoi
eideisan 'oi matheitai 'oti Yeisous estin.

:ד. הַבֹּקֶר אוֹר וְהִנֵּה יֵשׁוּעַ עֹמֵד עַל-שְׂפַת הַיָּם וְהַתַּלְמִידִים לֹא יָדְעוּ כִּי יֵשׁוּעַ הוּא

4. Ha•bo•ker or ve•hee•ne Yeshua o•med al - s`fat ha•yam ve•ha•tal•mi•dim lo
yad•oo ki Yeshua hoo.

---

5. Then Jesus saith unto them, Children, have ye any meat? They answered
him, No.

5. Λέγει οὖν αὐτοῖς ὁ Ἰησοῦς, Παιδία, μή τι προσφάγιον ἔχετε; Ἀπεκρίθησαν
αὐτῷ, Οὔ.

5. Legei oun autois 'o Yeisous, Paidia, mei ti prosphagion echete?
Apekritheisan auto, Ou.

:ה. וַיֹּאמֶר אֲלֵיהֶם יֵשׁוּעַ בָּנַי הֲיֵשׁ-לָכֶם דָּבָר לֶאֱכֹל וַיַּעֲנוּ וַיֹּמְרוּ אָיִן

5. Va•yo•mer aley•hem Yeshua ba•nai ha•yesh - la•chem da•var le•e•chol
va•ya•a•noo va•yom•roo a•yin.

---

6. And he said unto them, Cast the net on the right side of the ship, and ye
shall find. They cast therefore, and now they were not able to draw it for the
multitude of fishes.

6. Ὁ δὲ εἶπεν αὐτοῖς, Βάλετε εἰς τὰ δεξιὰ μέρη τοῦ πλοίου τὸ δίκτυον, καὶ
εὑρήσετε. Ἔβαλον οὖν, καὶ οὐκέτι αὐτὸ ἑλκύσαι ἴσχυσαν ἀπὸ τοῦ πλήθους
τῶν ἰχθύων.

6. 'O de eipen autois, Balete eis ta dexya merei tou ploiou to diktuon, kai
'eureisete. Ebalon oun, kai ouketi auto 'elkusai ischusan apo tou pleithous ton
ichthuon.

ו. וַיֹּאמֶר אֲלֵיהֶם פִּרְשׂוּ אֶת-הַמִּכְמֹרֶת מִימִין לָאֳנִיָּה וּמְצָאתֶם וַיִּפְרְשׂוּ וְלֹא-יָכְלוּ עוֹד לְמָשְׁכָהּ מֵרֹב
דָּגִים:

6. Va•yo•mer aley•hem pir•soo et - ha•mich•mo•ret miy•min la•o•ni•ya
oom•tza•tem va•yif•re•soo ve•lo - yach•loo od le•mosh•cha merov da•gim.

---

7. Therefore that disciple whom Jesus loved saith unto Peter, It is the Lord. Now when Simon Peter heard that it was the Lord, he girt his fisher's coat unto him, (for he was naked,) and did cast himself into the sea.

Greek/Transliteration

7. Λέγει οὖν ὁ μαθητὴς ἐκεῖνος ὃν ἠγάπα ὁ Ἰησοῦς τῷ Πέτρῳ, Ὁ κύριός ἐστιν. Σίμων οὖν Πέτρος, ἀκούσας ὅτι ὁ κύριός ἐστιν, τὸν ἐπενδύτην διεζώσατο- ἦν γὰρ γυμνός- καὶ ἔβαλεν ἑαυτὸν εἰς τὴν θάλασσαν.

7. Legei oun 'o matheiteis ekeinos 'on eigapa 'o Yeisous to Petro, 'O kurios estin. Simon oun Petros, akousas 'oti 'o kurios estin, ton ependutein diezosato- ein gar gumnos- kai ebalen 'eauton eis tein thalassan.

Hebrew/Transliteration

ז. וְהַתַּלְמִיד הַהוּא אֲשֶׁר יֵשׁוּעַ אֲהֵבוֹ אָמַר אֶל-פֶּטְרוֹס הָאָדוֹן הוּא וְכִשְׁמֹעַ שִׁמְעוֹן פֶּטְרוֹס כִּי הוּא הָאָדוֹן וַיַּעֲט:אֶת-מְעִילוֹ כִּי עֵרֹם הָיָה וַיִּתְנַפֵּל אֶל-הַיָּם

7. Ve•ha•tal•mid ha•hoo asher Yeshua ahe•vo amar el - Petros ha•Adon hoo ve•chish•mo•a Shimon Petros ki hoo ha•Adon va•ya•at et - me•ee•lo ki erom ha•ya va•yit•na•pel el - ha•yam.

Rabbinic Jewish Commentary

The Greek word επενδυτης, here used, is manifestly the אפונדת of the Hebrews; and which, the Jewish writers say (b), was a strait garment, which a man put on next his flesh to dry up the sweat; and a very proper one for Peter, who had been toiling all night, and very fit for him to swim in; and, by what follows, appears to be put on him next his flesh: for he was naked; for to suppose him entirely naked, whilst fishing, being only in company with men, and those parts of nature having a covering, which always require one, was not at all indecent and unbecoming.

(b) Maimon. & Bartenora in Misn. Sabbat, c. 10. sect. 3.

---

8. And the other disciples came in a little ship; (for they were not far from land, but as it were two hundred cubits,) dragging the net with fishes.

Greek/Transliteration

8. Οἱ δὲ ἄλλοι μαθηταὶ τῷ πλοιαρίῳ ἦλθον- οὐ γὰρ ἦσαν μακρὰν ἀπὸ τῆς γῆς, ἀλλ᾽ ὡς ἀπὸ πηχῶν διακοσίων- σύροντες τὸ δίκτυον τῶν ἰχθύων.

8. 'Oi de alloi matheitai to ployario eilthon- ou gar eisan makran apo teis geis, all 'os apo peichon dyakosion- surontes to diktuon ton ichthuon.

Hebrew/Transliteration

ח. וְיֶתֶר הַתַּלְמִידִים בָּאוּ בָאֳנִיָּתָם כִּי לֹא הִרְחִיקוּ מִן-הַיַּבָּשָׁה כִּי אִם-כְּמָאתַיִם אַמָּה וַיִּמְשְׁכוּ אֶת-הַמִּכְמֹרֶת עִם-הַדָּגִים:

8. Ve•ye•ter ha•tal•mi•dim ba•oo va•o•ni•yatam ki lo hir•chi•koo min -
ha•ya•ba•sha ki eem - ke•ma•ta•yim ama va•yim•she•choo et -
ha•mich•mo•ret eem - ha•da•gim.

---

9. As soon then as they were come to land, they saw a fire of coals there, and
fish laid thereon, and bread.

Greek/Transliteration
9. Ὡς οὖν ἀπέβησαν εἰς τὴν γῆν, βλέπουσιν ἀνθρακιὰν κειμένην καὶ ὀψάριον
ἐπικείμενον, καὶ ἄρτον.

9. 'Os oun apebeisan eis tein gein, blepousin anthrakyan keimenein kai
opsarion epikeimenon, kai arton.

Hebrew/Transliteration
:ט. וַיֵּצְאוּ אֶל-הַיַּבָּשָׁה וַיִּרְאוּ גַּחֲלֵי-אֵשׁ עֲרוּכִים שָׁם וְדָג עֲלֵיהֶם וְכִכַּר לָחֶם

9. Va•yetz•oo el - ha•ya•ba•sha va•yir•oo ga•cha•ley - esh aroo•chim sham
ve•dag aley•hem ve•chi•kar la•chem.

---

10. Jesus saith unto them, Bring of the fish which ye have now caught.

Greek/Transliteration
10. Λέγει αὐτοῖς ὁ Ἰησοῦς, Ἐνέγκατε ἀπὸ τῶν ὀψαρίων ὧν ἐπιάσατε νῦν.

10. Legei autois 'o Yeisous, Enegkate apo ton opsarion 'on epyasate nun.

Hebrew/Transliteration
:י. וַיֹּאמֶר אֲלֵיהֶם יֵשׁוּעַ הָבִיאוּ הֲלֹם מִן-הַדָּגִים אֲשֶׁר לְכַדְתֶּם עָתָּה

10. Va•yo•mer aley•hem Yeshua ha•vi•oo ha•lom min - ha•da•gim asher
le•cha•de•tem ata.

---

11. Simon Peter went up, and drew the net to land full of great fishes, and
hundred and fifty and three: and for all there were so many, yet was not the
net broken.

Greek/Transliteration
11. Ἀνέβη Σίμων Πέτρος, καὶ εἵλκυσεν τὸ δίκτυον ἐπὶ τῆς γῆς, μεστὸν ἰχθύων
μεγάλων ἑκατὸν πεντήκοντα τριῶν· καὶ τοσούτων ὄντων, οὐκ ἐσχίσθη τὸ
δίκτυον.

11. Anebei Simon Petros, kai 'eilkusen to diktuon epi teis geis, meston ichthuon megalon 'ekaton penteikonta trion. kai tosouton onton, ouk eschisthei to diktuon.

יא. וַיַּעַל שִׁמְעוֹן פֶּטְרוֹס וַיִּמְשֹׁךְ אֶת-הַמִּכְמֹרֶת אֶל-הַיַּבָּשָׁה וְהִיא מְלֵאָה דָגִים גְּדוֹלִים מֵאָה וַחֲמִשִּׁים וּשְׁלֹשָׁה:וּבְכָל-זֹאת לֹא נִקְרְעָה הַמִּכְמֹרֶת מֵרֹב הַדָּגִים

11. Va•ya•al Shimon Petros va•yim•shoch et - ha•mich•mo•ret el - ha•ya•ba•sha ve•hee me•le•ah da•gim ge•do•lim me•ah va•cha•mi•shim oosh•lo•sha oov•chol - zot lo nik•re•ah ha•mich•mo•ret merov ha•da•gim.

---

12. Jesus saith unto them, Come and dine. And none of the disciples durst ask him, Who art thou? knowing that it was the Lord.

Greek/Transliteration

12. Λέγει αὐτοῖς ὁ Ἰησοῦς, Δεῦτε ἀριστήσατε. Οὐδεὶς δὲ ἐτόλμα τῶν μαθητῶν ἐξετάσαι αὐτόν, Σὺ τίς εἶ; εἰδότες ὅτι ὁ κύριός ἐστιν.

12. Legei autois 'o Yeisous, Deute aristeisate. Oudeis de etolma ton matheiton exetasai auton, Su tis ei? eidotes 'oti 'o kurios estin.

Hebrew/Transliteration

יב. וַיֹּאמֶר אֲלֵיהֶם יֵשׁוּעַ בֹּאוּ אִכְלוּ אֲרֻחַת הַבֹּקֶר וְאֵין גַּם-אֶחָד בַּתַּלְמִידִים אֲשֶׁר מְלָאוֹ לִבּוֹ לִשְׁאֹל מִי אַתָּה כִּי:יָדְעוּ אֲשֶׁר הוּא הָאָדוֹן

12. Va•yo•mer aley•hem Yeshua bo•oo eech•loo aroo•chat ha•bo•ker ve•eyn gam - e•chad ba•tal•mi•dim asher me•lao li•bo lish•ol mee ata ki yad•oo asher hoo ha•Adon.

---

13. Jesus then cometh, and taketh bread, and giveth them, and fish likewise.

Greek/Transliteration

13. Ἔρχεται οὖν ὁ Ἰησοῦς, καὶ λαμβάνει τὸν ἄρτον, καὶ δίδωσιν αὐτοῖς, καὶ τὸ ὀψάριον ὁμοίως.

13. Erchetai oun 'o Yeisous, kai lambanei ton arton, kai didosin autois, kai to opsarion 'omoios.

Hebrew/Transliteration

יג. וַיָּבֹא יֵשׁוּעַ וַיִּקַּח אֶת-הַלֶּחֶם וַיִּתֵּן לָהֶם וְגַם אֶת-הַדָּגָה:

13. Va•ya•vo Yeshua va•yi•kach et - ha•le•chem va•yi•ten la•hem ve•gam et - ha•da•ga.

14. This is now the third time that Jesus shewed himself to his disciples, after that he was risen from the dead.

14. Τοῦτο ἤδη τρίτον ἐφανερώθη ὁ Ἰησοῦς τοῖς μαθηταῖς αὐτοῦ, ἐγερθεὶς ἐκ νεκρῶν.

14. Touto eidei triton ephanerothei 'o Yeisous tois matheitais autou, egertheis ek nekron.

יד. וְזֹאת הַפַּעַם הַשְּׁלִישִׁית אֲשֶׁר-נִרְאָה יֵשׁוּעַ אֶל-תַּלְמִידָיו אַחֲרֵי קוּמוֹ מִן-הַמֵּתִים:

14. Ve•zot ha•pa•am hash`li•sheet asher - nir•ah Yeshua el - tal•mi•dav a•cha•rey koo•mo min - ha•me•tim.

---

15. So when they had dined, Jesus saith to Simon Peter, Simon, son of Jonas, lovest thou me more than these? He saith unto him, Yea, Lord; thou knowest that I love thee. He saith unto him, Feed my lambs.

15. Ὅτε οὖν ἠρίστησαν, λέγει τῷ Σίμωνι Πέτρῳ ὁ Ἰησοῦς, Σίμων Ἰωνᾶ, ἀγαπᾷς με πλεῖον τούτων; Λέγει αὐτῷ, Ναὶ κύριε· σὺ οἶδας ὅτι φιλῶ σε. Λέγει αὐτῷ, Βόσκε τὰ ἀρνία μου.

15. 'Ote oun eiristeisan, legei to Simoni Petro 'o Yeisous, Simon Yona, agapas me pleion touton? Legei auto, Nai kurie. su oidas 'oti philo se. Legei auto, Boske ta arnia mou.

טו. וַיְהִי אַחֲרֵי אָרְחָתָם וַיֹּאמֶר יֵשׁוּעַ אֶל-שִׁמְעוֹן פֶּטְרוֹס שִׁמְעוֹן בַּר-יוֹנָה הַאֹהֵב אַתָּה אֹתִי יֶתֶר מֵאֵלֶּה וַיֹּאמֶר אֵלָיו:אֲדֹנִי אַתָּה יָדַעְתָּ כִּי אֲהַבְתִּיךָ וַיֹּאמֶר אֵלָיו נַהֵל אֶת-עֲלֹתָי

15. Vay•hi a•cha•rey aroo•cha•tam va•yo•mer Yeshua el - Shimon Petros Shimon Bar - Yona ha•o•hev ata o•ti ye•ter me•e•le va•yo•mer elav hen Adoni ata ya•da•ata ki ahav•ti•cha va•yo•mer elav na•hel et - a•lo•tai.

---

16. He saith to him again the second time, Simon, son of Jonas, lovest thou me? He saith unto him, Yea, Lord; thou knowest that I love thee. He saith unto him, Feed my sheep.

16. Λέγει αὐτῷ πάλιν δεύτερον, Σίμων Ἰωνᾶ, ἀγαπᾷς με; Λέγει αὐτῷ, Ναὶ κύριε· σὺ οἶδας ὅτι φιλῶ σε. Λέγει αὐτῷ, Ποίμαινε τὰ πρόβατά μου.

16. Legei auto palin deuteron, Simon Yona, agapas me? Legei auto, Nai kurie. su oidas 'oti philo se. Legei auto, Poimaine ta probata mou.

Hebrew/Transliteration

טז. וַיֹּאמֶר אֵלָיו פַּעַם שֵׁנִית שִׁמְעוֹן בַּר-יוֹנָה הַאֹהֵב אַתָּה אֹתִי וַיֹּאמֶר אֵלָיו הֵן אֲדֹנִי אַתָּה יָדַעְתָּ כִּי
אֲהַבְתִּיךָ:וַיֹּאמֶר אֵלָיו נְחֵה אֶת-צֹאנִי

16. Va•yo•mer elav pa•am she•nit Shimon Bar - Yona ha•o•hev ata o•ti va•yo•mer elav hen Adoni ata ya•da•ata ki ahav•ti•cha va•yo•mer elav n`che et - tzo•ni.

---

17. He saith unto him the third time, Simon, son of Jonas, lovest thou me? Peter was grieved because he said unto him the third time, Lovest thou me? And he said unto him, Lord, thou knowest all things; thou knowest that I love thee. Jesus saith unto him, Feed my sheep.

Greek/Transliteration
17. Λέγει αὐτῷ τὸ τρίτον, Σίμων Ἰωνᾶ, φιλεῖς με; Ἐλυπήθη ὁ Πέτρος ὅτι εἶπεν αὐτῷ τὸ τρίτον, Φιλεῖς με; Καὶ εἶπεν αὐτῷ, Κύριε, σὺ πάντα οἶδας· σὺ γινώσκεις ὅτι φιλῶ σε. Λέγει αὐτῷ ὁ Ἰησοῦς, Βόσκε τὰ πρόβατά μου.

17. Legei auto to triton, Simon Yona, phileis me? Elupeithei 'o Petros 'oti eipen auto to triton, Phileis me? Kai eipen auto, Kurie, su panta oidas. su ginoskeis 'oti philo se. Legei auto 'o Yeisous, Boske ta probata mou.

Hebrew/Transliteration
יז. וַיֹּאמֶר אֵלָיו פַּעַם שְׁלִישִׁית שִׁמְעוֹן בַּר-יוֹנָה הַאֹהֵב אַתָּה אֹתִי וַיִּתְעַצֵּב פֶּטְרוֹס אֶל-לִבּוֹ כִּי אָמַר
שְׁלִישִׁית הַאֹהֵב אַתָּה אֹתִי וַיֹּאמֶר אֵלָיו אֲדֹנִי אַתָּה אֶל-כֹּל יָדַעְתָּ אַתָּה יָדַעְתָּ כִּי אֲהַבְתִּיךָ אֵלָיו פַּעַם
יֵשׁוּעַ רְעֵה וַיֹּאמֶר אֵלָיו:אֶת-צֹאנִי

17. Va•yo•mer elav pa•am sh`li•sheet Shimon Bar - Yona ha•o•hev ata o•ti va•yit•a•tzev Petros el - li•bo ki amar elav pa•am sh`li•sheet ha•o•hev ata o•ti va•yo•mer elav Adoni ata el - kol ya•da•ata ata ya•da•ata ki ahav•ti•cha va•yo•mer elav Yeshua r`•eh et - tzo•ni.

---

18. Verily, verily, I say unto thee, When thou wast young, thou girdedst thyself, and walkedst whither thou wouldest: but when thou shalt be old, thou shalt stretch forth thy hands, and another shall gird thee, and carry thee whither thou wouldest not.

Greek/Transliteration
18. Ἀμὴν ἀμὴν λέγω σοι, ὅτε ἦς νεώτερος, ἐζώννυες σεαυτόν, καὶ περιεπάτεις ὅπου ἤθελες· ὅταν δὲ γηράσῃς, ἐκτενεῖς τὰς χεῖράς σου, καὶ ἄλλος σε ζώσει, καὶ οἴσει ὅπου οὐ θέλεις.

18. Amein amein lego soi, 'ote eis neoteros, ezonnues seauton, kai periepateis 'opou eitheles. 'otan de geiraseis, ekteneis tas cheiras sou, kai allos se zosei, kai oisei 'opou ou theleis.

Hebrew/Transliteration

יח. אָמֵן אָמֵן אֲנִי אֹמֵר לָךְ בְּעוֹד נַעַר הָיִיתָ בְּיָדְךָ חָגַרְתָּ אֶת־מָתְנֶיךָ וַתֵּלֶךְ אֶל־אֲשֶׁר חָפַצְתָּ וְכִי תִזְקַן
תִּפְרֹשׂ כַּפֶּיךָ:וְאַחֵר יַחְגָּרְךָ וּנְשָׂאָךָ אֶל־אֲשֶׁר לֹא תַחְפֹּץ

18. Amen amen ani o•mer lach be•od na•ar ha•yi•ta be•yad•cha cha•gar•ta et - mot•ne•cha va•te•lech el - asher cha•fatz•ta ve•chi tiz•kan tif•ros ka•pe•cha ve•a•cher yach•gor•cha oon•sa•a•cha el - asher lo tach•potz.

Rabbinic Jewish Commentary

Peter lived to the times of Nero (c), under whom he suffered, about forty years after this.

This refers not so much to an inability through old age to gird himself, and therefore should stretch forth his hands, that another might with more ease do it for him, and which would be the reverse of his former and present case; for the word gird is used in another sense than before, and signifies the binding of him as, a prisoner with cords, or chains; so "girding", with the Jews, is the same as הקשירה והאסירה, "tying and binding" (d): but either to the stretching out of his hands upon the cross, when he should be girt and bound to that; for persons were sometimes fastened to the cross with cords, and not always with nails (e): or, as others think, to his carrying of his cross on his shoulders, with his hands stretched out and bound to the piece of wood which went across; though his being girded or bound may as well be thought to follow the former, as this.

(c) Euseb. Eccl. Hist. l. 2. c. 25. (d) R. David Kimchi, Sepher Shorash. rad. חגר (e) Lipsius de Cruce, l. 2. c. 8. Bartholinus de Cruce, p. 57. 112.

---

19. This spake he, signifying by what death he should glorify God. And when he had spoken this, he saith unto him, Follow me.

Greek/Transliteration

19. Τοῦτο δὲ εἶπεν, σημαίνων ποίῳ θανάτῳ δοξάσει τὸν θεόν. Καὶ τοῦτο εἰπὼν λέγει αὐτῷ, ᾿Ακολούθει μοι.

19. Touto de eipen, seimainon poio thanato doxasei ton theon. Kai touto eipon legei auto, Akolouthei moi.

Hebrew/Transliteration

יט. וְאוּלָם כָּזֹאת הוּא דִבֶּר בְּרָמְזוֹ לוֹ בְּאֵיזֶה מָוֶת הוּא יָמוּת אֲשֶׁר יְגַדֵּל בּוֹ כְּבוֹד אֱלֹהִים וְאַחֲרֵי דַבְּרוֹ
כָּזֹאת אָמַר:אֵלָיו לֵךְ אַחֲרָי

19. Ve•oo•lam ka•zot hoo di•ber be••rom•zo lo be•ey•ze ma•vet hoo ya•moot asher yig•dal bo k`vod Elohim ve•a•cha•rey dab•ro cha•zot amar elav lech a•cha•rai.

Rabbinic Jewish Commentary

signifying by what death he should glorify God; for by the above words Christ not only intimated that Peter should die, not a natural, but a violent death, or that he should die a martyr in his cause, but the very kind of death he should die, namely, by crucifixion; and that Peter was crucified at Rome, ecclesiastical history confirms (f), when Yeshua was magnified, and God was glorified by his zeal and courage, faith and patience, constancy and perseverance to the end.

(f) Euseb. Eccl. Hist. l. 2. c 25.

---

20. Then Peter, turning about, seeth the disciple whom Jesus loved following; which also leaned on his breast at supper, and said, Lord, which is he that betrayeth thee?

Greek/Transliteration

20. Ἐπιστραφεὶς δὲ ὁ Πέτρος βλέπει τὸν μαθητὴν ὃν ἠγάπα ὁ Ἰησοῦς ἀκολουθοῦντα, ὃς καὶ ἀνέπεσεν ἐν τῷ δείπνῳ ἐπὶ τὸ στῆθος αὐτοῦ καὶ εἶπεν, Κύριε, τίς ἐστιν ὁ παραδιδούς σε;

20. Epistrapheis de 'o Petros blepei ton matheitein 'on eigapa 'o Yeisous akolouthounta, 'os kai anepesen en to deipno epi to steithos autou kai eipen, Kurie, tis estin 'o paradidous se?

Hebrew/Transliteration

כ. וַיִּפֶן פֶּטְרוֹס וַיַּרְא אֶת-הַתַּלְמִיד אֲשֶׁר יֵשׁוּעַ אֲהֵבוֹ הֹלֵךְ אַחֲרֵיהֶם וְהוּא אֲשֶׁר נָפַל עַל-צַוָּארוֹ בְּמִשְׁתֵּה הָעֶרֶב:וְאָמַר אֲדֹנִי מִי הוּא-זֶה אֲשֶׁר יַסְגִּירֶךָ

20. Va•yi•fen Petros va•yar et - ha•tal•mid asher Yeshua ahe•vo ho•lech a•cha•rey•hem ve•hoo asher na•fal al - tza•va•ro be•mish•te ha•e•rev ve•a•mar Adoni mee hoo – ze asher yas•gi•re•cha?

---

21. Peter seeing him saith to Jesus, Lord, and what shall this man do?

Greek/Transliteration

21. Τοῦτον ἰδὼν ὁ Πέτρος λέγει τῷ Ἰησοῦ, κύριε, οὗτος δὲ τί;

21. Touton idon 'o Petros legei to Yeisou, kurie, 'outos de ti?

Hebrew/Transliteration

כא. וַיְהִי בִּרְאוֹת אֹתוֹ פֶּטְרוֹס וַיֹּאמֶר אֶל-יֵשׁוּעַ אֲדֹנִי מָה אַחֲרִיתוֹ:

21. Vay•hi bir•ot o•to Petros va•yo•mer el - Yeshua Adoni ve•ze ma
acha•ri•to?

---

22. Jesus saith unto him, If I will that he tarry till I come, what is that to thee?
follow thou me.

Greek/Transliteration
22. Λέγει αὐτῷ ὁ Ἰησοῦς, Ἐὰν αὐτὸν θέλω μένειν ἕως ἔρχομαι, τί πρός σε; Σὺ
ἀκολούθει μοι.

22. Legei auto 'o Yeisous, Ean auton thelo menein 'eos erchomai, ti pros se?
Su akolouthei moi.

Hebrew/Transliteration
כב. וַיֹּאמֶר אֵלָיו יֵשׁוּעַ אִם-חָפַצְתִּי כִּי יִשָּׁאֵר עַד-אֲשֶׁר אָבֹא אַךְ מַה-לָּךְ לֵךְ אַחֲרֵי:

22. Va•yo•mer elav Yeshua eem - cha•fatz•ti ki yi•sha•er ad - asher avo ach
ma - lach lech a•cha•rai.

---

23. Then went this saying abroad among the brethren, that that disciple
should not die: yet Jesus said not unto him, He shall not die; but, If I will that
he tarry till I come, what is that to thee?

Greek/Transliteration
23. Ἐξῆλθεν οὖν ὁ λόγος οὗτος εἰς τοὺς ἀδελφούς, ὅτι ὁ μαθητὴς ἐκεῖνος οὐκ
ἀποθνήσκει· καὶ οὐκ εἶπεν αὐτῷ ὁ Ἰησοῦς, ὅτι οὐκ ἀποθνήσκει· ἀλλ᾽, Ἐὰν
αὐτὸν θέλω μένειν ἕως ἔρχομαι, τί πρός σε;

23. Exeilthen oun 'o logos 'outos eis tous adelphous, 'oti 'o matheiteis ekeinos
ouk apothneiskei. kai ouk eipen auto 'o Yeisous, 'oti ouk apothneiskei. all,
Ean auton thelo menein 'eos erchomai, ti pros se?

Hebrew/Transliteration
כג. עַל-כֵּן יָצָא הַדָּבָר הַזֶּה בֵּין הָאַחִים כִּי הַתַּלְמִיד הַהוּא לֹא יָמוּת וְיֵשׁוּעַ לֹא אָמַר-לוֹ כִּי לֹא-יָמוּת
רַק אָמַר:אִם-חָפַצְתִּי כִּי-יִשָּׁאֵר עַד-אֲשֶׁר אָבֹא אַךְ מַה-לָּךְ

23. Al - ken ya•tza ha•da•var ha•ze bein ha•a•chim ki ha•tal•mid ha•hoo lo
ya•moot ve•Yeshua lo amar - lo ki lo - ya•moot rak amar eem - cha•fatz•ti ki -
yi•sha•er ad – asher avo ach ma – lach?

---

24. This is the disciple which testifieth of these things, and wrote these things:
and we know that his testimony is true.

---

24. Οὗτός ἐστιν ὁ μαθητὴς ὁ μαρτυρῶν περὶ τούτων, καὶ γράψας ταῦτα· καὶ οἴδαμεν ὅτι ἀληθής ἐστιν ἡ μαρτυρία αὐτοῦ.

24. 'Outos estin 'o matheiteis 'o marturon peri touton, kai grapsas tauta. kai oidamen 'oti aleitheis estin 'ei marturia autou.

כד. זֶה הוּא הַתַּלְמִיד הַנֹּתֵן אֶת-עֵדוּתוֹ לָאֵלֶּה וְהוּא אֲשֶׁר כָּתַב כָּל-אֵלֶּה וְיָדַעְנוּ כִּי עֵדוּתוֹ נֶאֱמָנָה:

24. Ze hoo ha•tal•mid ha•no•ten et - e•doo•to la•e•le ve•hoo asher ka•tav kol – ele ve•ya•da•a•noo ki e•doo•to ne•e•ma•na.

---

25. And there are also many other things which Jesus did, the which, if they should be written every one, I suppose that even the world itself could not contain the books that should be written. Amen.

25. Ἔστιν δὲ καὶ ἄλλα πολλὰ ὅσα ἐποίησεν ὁ Ἰησοῦς, ἅτινα ἐὰν γράφηται καθ᾽ ἕν, οὐδὲ αὐτὸν οἶμαι τὸν κόσμον χωρῆσαι τὰ γραφόμενα βιβλία. Ἀμήν.

25. Estin de kai alla polla 'osa epoieisen 'o Yeisous, 'atina ean grapheitai kath 'en, oude auton oimai ton kosmon choreisai ta graphomena biblia. Amein.

כה. וְעוֹד יֵשׁ מַעֲשִׂים רַבִּים אֲחֵרִים אֲשֶׁר עָשָׂה יֵשׁוּעַ אַךְ אִם-יִכָּתְבוּ כֻלָּם אֶחָד אַחַר אֶחָד יַחְשֹׁב לְבָבִי כִּי לֹא:תָכִיל כָּל-הָעוֹלָם אֶת-הַסְּפָרִים אֲשֶׁר יִכָּתֵבוּן אָמֵן

25. Ve•od yesh ma•a•sim ra•bim a•che•rim asher asa Yeshua ach eem - yi•kat•voo choo•lam e•chad achar e•chad ya•cha•shov le•va•vi ki lo ta•chil kol - ha•o•lam et - has•fa•rim asher yi•ka•te•voon Amen.

Rabbinic Jewish Commentary
One of their Rabbi's says (h), "If all the seas were ink, and the bulrushes pens, and the heavens and the earth volumes, and all the children of men Scribes, אין מספיקין לכתוב תורה, "they would not be sufficient to write the Torah", which have learned."

And it is commonly said (i) by them, if this, or that, or the other thing was done, לא יכיל עלמא למסבל, "the world would not be able to bear them". And a later writer (k) of theirs, speaking of the different interpretations given by some of their Rabbi's of a certain passage, says, they are so many, that an ass is not able to carry their books. And the intention of this expression, supposing it hyperbolical, is to show, that but a few of the wonderful things done by Yeshua were recorded by the evangelist, in comparison of the many which he every day did, in all places where he came; for he was continually going about doing good, and healing all manner of diseases; but these that were written are sufficient to prove him to be the true

Messiah, and to require faith in him as such. To all which the evangelist sets his "Amen", as attesting and confirming the truth of all he had written; and which may be depended upon, and assented to, as truth, by all that read this Gospel. The Alexandrian copy, and Beza's Cambridge copy, have not the word "Amen"; nor have the Vulgate Latin, Syriac, Arabic, and Persic versions. In some copies the following words are added,

"The Gospel according to John was given out thirty two years after the ascension of Yeshua".

Which would fall on the year of Yeshua 66, and so before the destruction of Jerusalem; which is contrary to the common opinion of learned men, some placing it in the year 97, others in the year 99.

(John starts his Gospel by stating: "All things were made by him". If one were to attempt to even summarise the works of creation, there is no way the world could contain the resulting volumes! Editor.)

(g) Jacob Aben ben Amram, porta veritatis, No. 1094. apud Kidder, Demonstration of the Messiah, par. 3. p. 67. Ed. fol. (h) Shirhashirim Rabba, fol. 4. 2. (i) Zohar in Exod. fol. 106. 4. & in Lev. fol. 26. 2. & 49. 3. & in Num. fol. 52. 2. & 59. 3. & 63. 3. & 64. 4. & 82. 3, 4. (k) R. Abraham Seba in Tzeror Hammor, fol. 79. 1.

---

^end^

JEWISH INTERTESTAMENTAL AND EARLY RABBINIC
LITERATURE: BIBLIOGRAPHY

Berenbaum, Michael and Fred Skolnik. *Encyclopaedia Judaica.* 2d ed.; 22 vols.;
Detroit: Macmillan Reference USA and Keter, 2007. Also available elec-

* David Chapman is associate professor of New Testament and Archaeology at
Covenant Theological
Seminary, 12330 Conway Road, St. Louis, MO 63141. Andreas Köstenberger is
research professor of
New Testament and Biblical Theology at Southeastern Baptist Theological
Seminary, 120 S. Wingate St.,
Wake Forest, NC 27587.

1 *JETS* 43 (2000): 577–618. Appreciation is again expressed to friends at Tyndale
House and to the
university and seminary libraries in Cambridge, Tübingen, and St. Louis.
236 JOURNAL OF THE EVANGELICAL THEOLOGICAL SOCIETY
tronically from Gale Virtual Reference Library. A fine substantial update
of the original and still useful 16 volume *Encyclopaedia Judaica* (Jerusalem:
Keter, 1972), which originally received several annual yearbooks and
two update volumes (1982, 1994) and was issued on CD-ROM in 1997.
Both editions were preceded by an incomplete 10-volume German set
entitled *Encyclopaedia Judaica: das Judentum in Geschichte und Gegenwart*
(Berlin:
Eschkol, 1928–34), which only covered articles beginning with the
letters A–L but often contained longer treatments than the 1972 version.
[*EncJud*]
Collins, John J. and Daniel C. Harlow, eds. *The Eerdmans Dictionary of Early
Judaism.*
Grand Rapids/Cambridge: Eerdmans, 2010. Brief survey articles
introduce "Early Judaism" (pp. 1–290) followed by dictionary entries on
more specific matters (pp. 291–1360). Quite helpful. [*EDEJ*]
Evans, Craig A. and Stanley E. Porter, eds. *Dictionary of New Testament
Background.*
Downers Grove/Leicester: InterVarsity, 2000. Helpful articles
with good bibliography. [*DNTB*]
Freedman, David Noel, ed. *The Anchor Bible Dictionary.* 6 vols. New York:
Doubleday, 1992. Includes useful introductory articles on much intertestamental
literature. Also on CD-ROM. [*ABD*]
Neusner, Jacob and Alan J. Avery-Peck, eds. *Encyclopaedia of Midrash: Biblical
Interpretation in Formative Judaism.* 2 vols. Leiden: Brill, 2005.
Neusner, Jacob, Alan J. Avery-Peck, and William Scott Green, eds. *The
Encyclopedia
of Judaism.* 5 vols. New York: Continuum/Leiden: Brill, 1999–
2003. 3 initial volumes plus 2 supplement volumes. Some articles with
bibliography.
Neusner, Jacob and William Scott Green, eds. *Dictionary of Judaism in the
Biblical
Period: 450 B.C.E. to 600 C.E.* 2 vols. New York: Macmillan, 1996; repr.

Peabody, MA: Hendrickson, 1999. Relatively short articles with no bibliography.

Singer, Isidore et al., eds. *The Jewish Encyclopedia.* 12 vols. New York/London: Funk & Wagnalls, 1901–1906. Older than *EncJud* but often has fuller articles. Available online at http://www.jewishencyclopedia.com and scanned images at http://archive.org. [*JE*]

Werblowsky, R. J. Zwi and Geoffrey Wigoder, eds. *The Oxford Dictionary of the Jewish Religion.* Oxford: OUP, 1997. Competent (but very concise) articles with limited bibliography. [*ODJR*]

1.2 Works Containing Surveys of Jewish Literature

Davies, W. D., Louis Finkelstein, John Sturdy, William Horbury, and Steven T. Katz, eds. *Cambridge History of Judaism.* 4 vols. Cambridge: CUP, 1984–2006. [*CHJ*]

Evans, Craig A. *Ancient Texts for New Testament Studies: A Guide to the Background Literature.* Peabody, MA: Hendrickson, 2005. Update of his *Noncanonical Writings and New Testament Interpretation* (1992).

Grabbe, Lester L. *A History of the Jews and Judaism in the Second Temple Period.* 4 vols. London/New York: T & T Clark, 2004–. Emphasis on discussing sources, with a tendency toward some skepticism and late dating.

Haase, Wolfgang, ed. *Aufstieg und Niedergang der Römischen Welt* II.19.1–2, II.20.1–2, and II.21.1–2. Berlin: de Gruyter, 1979–1987. [*ANRW*]

Helyer, Larry R. *Exploring Jewish Literature of the Second Temple Period: A Guide for New Testament Students.* Downers Grove: InterVarsity, 2002.

Kraft, Robert A. and George W. E. Nickelsburg, eds. *Early Judaism and Its Modern Interpreters.* Philadelphia: Fortress/Atlanta: Scholars, 1986.

McNamara, Martin. *Intertestamental Literature.* Wilmington, DE: Michael Glazier, 1983.

Mulder, Martin Jan, ed. *Mikra: Text, Translation, Reading and Interpretation of the Hebrew Bible in Ancient Judaism and Early Christianity.* CRINT 2.1. Assen/ Maastricht: Van Gorcum, 1988; Philadelphia: Fortress, 1988. Very helpful, especially on LXX, Targums, and other versions of the OT. [*Mikra*]

Neusner, Jacob, ed. *Judaism in Late Antiquity, Vol. 1: The Literary and Archaeological Sources.* Handbuch der Orientalistik 1.16; Leiden: Brill, 1995. [*JLA*]

Nickelsburg, George W. E. *Jewish Literature Between the Bible and the Mishnah.* 2d ed. Philadelphia: Fortress, 2005. Principally discusses DSS, Apocrypha, and Pseudepigrapha. With CD-ROM of entire book, plus images and a study guide. [Nickelsburg, *Jewish Literature*]

Sæbø, Magne, ed. *Hebrew Bible, Old Testament: The History of its Interpretation: Vol. 1 From the beginnings to the Middle Ages (until 1300).* Part 1: Antiquity. Göttingen: Vandenhoeck & Ruprecht, 1996.

Schürer, Emil. *The History of the Jewish People in the Age of Jesus Christ (175 B.C.– A.D. 135).* Ed. Geza Vermes et al. Rev. English ed. 3 vols. in 4. Edinburgh: T & T Clark, 1973–1987. For decades the standard work in the field (not to be confused with Hendrickson's reprinted translation of the original German edition, which is now out of date). [*HJPAJC*]

Stemberger, Günter. *Introduction to the Talmud and Midrash.* Fine work; see full bibliography under Rabbinic Literature. [Stemberger, *Introduction*]

Stone, Michael E., ed. *Jewish Writings of the Second Temple Period.* CRINT 2.2. Assen: Van Gorcum; Philadelphia: Fortress, 1984. See further CRINT volumes under Rabbinic Literature below. [*JWSTP*]

VanderKam, James C. *An Introduction to Early Judaism.* Grand Rapids: Eerdmans, 2001. Esp. pp. 53–173.

1.3 Sourcebooks

Barrett, C. K. *The New Testament Background: Writings from Ancient Greece and the Roman Empire that Illuminate Christian Origins.* San Francisco: Harper, 1987. A more recent edition (with different subtitle) of this classic sourcebook.

Chilton, Bruce D., gen. ed. *A Comparative Handbook to the Gospel of Mark: Comparisons with Pseudepigrapha, the Qumran Scrolls, and Rabbinic Literature.* The New Testament Gospels in their Judaic Contexts 1. Leiden: Brill, 2009. After each pericope in Mark, an extensive array of comparable Jewish sources are quoted and followed by a very brief commentary on those sources.

De Lange, Nicholas. *Apocrypha: Jewish Literature of the Hellenistic Age.* New York: Viking, 1978. Excerpts Apocrypha and Pseudepigrapha writings in thematic categories.

238 JOURNAL OF THE EVANGELICAL THEOLOGICAL SOCIETY

Elwell, Walter A. and Robert W. Yarbrough, eds. *Readings from the First-Century World: Primary Sources for New Testament Study.* Encountering Biblical Studies. Grand Rapids: Baker, 1998. Intended for college students. First part topical, second part quotes illuminating Jewish and Graeco-Roman sources in NT canonical order.

Feldman, Louis H. and Meyer Reinhold. *Jewish Life and Thought among Greeks and Romans: Primary Readings.* Minneapolis: Augsburg Fortress, 1996; Edinburgh: T & T Clark, 1996. A fine collection covering a broad array of key topics.

Fitzmyer, Joseph A. and Daniel J. Harrington. *A Manual of Palestinian Aramaic Texts (second century B.C.–second century A.D.).* BibOr 34. Rome: Biblical

Institute Press, 1978. Highly significant collection of texts with translations and introduction (includes many Qumran documents).

Ginzberg, Louis. *The Legends of the Jews.* 7 vols. Jewish Publication Society of America, 1909–1938; repr. Baltimore: Johns Hopkins, 1998. Puts in narrative form the various rabbinic and apocryphal stories about OT heroes. Vols. 5–6 notes; vol. 7 index. Currently available online at several sites, though often without the vital endnotes and index volumes (see http://archive.org).

Hayward, C. T. R. *The Jewish Temple: A non-biblical sourcebook.* London/New York: Routledge, 1996.

Instone-Brewer, David. *Traditions of the Rabbis from the Era of the New Testament.* Grand Rapid: Eerdmans, 2004–. Following the order of Mishnah, excerpts selections from the Mishnah and the Tosefta that likely predate the year 70; provides text, translation, and brief commentary. [*TRENT*]

Nadich, Judah. *The Legends of the Rabbis.* 2 vols. London: Jason Aronson, 1994. Puts in narrative form the various rabbinic stories about early rabbis (Neusner's *Rabbinic Traditions about the Pharisees* is to be preferred for academic use).

Neusner, Jacob. *The Rabbinic Traditions about the Pharisees before 70.* 3 vols. Leiden: Brill, 1971. An enormously helpful source book with commentary and summary analysis (reprints from University of South Florida and Wipf & Stock).

Runesson, Anders, Donald D. Binder, and Birger Olsson. *The Ancient Synagogue from its Origin to 200 C.E.: A Source Book.* Leiden: Brill, 2008; paperback Brill, 2010. Ancient literary sources, inscriptions and archaeological remains for both the land of Israel and the diaspora. Also includes a chapter on Jewish temples outside Jerusalem (e.g. Leontopolis).

Schiffman, Lawrence H. *Texts and Traditions: A Source Reader for the Study of Second Temple and Rabbinic Judaism.* Hoboken: Ktav, 1998. Complements his history of early Judaism.

Williams, Margaret H, ed. *The Jews among the Greeks and Romans: A Diasporan Sourcebook.* Baltimore: Johns Hopkins, 1998; London: Duckworth, 1998.

1.4 Bibliography

Anderson, Norman Elliott. *Tools for Bibliographical and Backgrounds Research on the New Testament.* 2d ed. South Hamilton, MA: Gordon-Conwell Theological Seminary, 1987.

Delling, Gerhard. *Bibliographie zur Jüdisch-Hellenistischen und Intertestamentarischen Literatur 1900–1965.* TU 106. Berlin: Akademie, 1969.

Noll, Stephen F. *The Intertestamental Period: A Study Guide.* Inter-Varsity

Christian
Fellowship of the United States of America, 1985.
1.5 General Computer Programs and English-based Websites (current at
time of writing)
Dinur Center for Research in Jewish History of the Hebrew University in
Jerusalem
(useful web links under "Second Temple and Talmudic Era"):
http://jewishhistory.huji.ac.il/links/texts.htm.
Early Jewish Writings by Peter Kirby (links to older translations and introductions
to Apocrypha, Pseudepigrapha, Philo and Josephus; currently
many broken links but still useful): http://www.earlyjewishwritings.com.
*4 Enoch: The Online Encyclopedia of Second Temple Judaism and Christian
Origins* by
the Enoch Seminar (edited wiki that is still in process):
http://www.4enoch.org.
HebrewBooks.org (classical Hebrew books for free download; website in
Hebrew):
http://www.hebrewbooks.org.
Internet Sacred Text Archive (older English translations of Jewish literature;
primarily
rabbinic works): http://www.sacred-texts.com/jud/index.htm.
The Judaic Classics Deluxe Edition: CD-ROM from Davka Software available for
Windows or Mac (see below under Rabbinic Literature).
New Testament Gateway (Judaica page): http://www.ntgateway.com/tools-
andresources/
judaica.
Paleojudaica by James R. Davila: http://paleojudaica.blogspot.com.
Princeton University Library Jewish Studies Resources: http://www.princeton.edu
/~pressman/jewsub.htm.
Resource Pages for Biblical Studies by Torrey Seland: http://torreys.org/bible.
Second Temple Synagogues by Donald Binder (includes links to introductions,
texts, and photos of early Jewish literature): http://www.pohick.org/sts.
Thesaurus Linguae Graecae (searchable database of ancient Greek literature
available on CD-ROM or via internet subscription; includes Philo, Josephus,
Greek Apocrypha and Pseudepigrapha). Website at
http://www.tlg.uci.edu.
Tyndale House (helpful links for Biblical Studies): http://www.tyndale.
cam.ac.uk/index.php?page=weblinks.
Virtual Religion Index: http://virtualreligion.net/vri/judaic.html (note links to
Biblical Studies and to Jewish Studies).
2. Old Testament Versions
2.1 Greek Versions
2.1.1 Septuagint
The term "Septuagint" is properly attributed only to the Old Greek
Pentateuch (translated c. 3d cent. BC), but common parlance labels the whole Old
Greek OT and Apocrypha as Septuagint (LXX). It represents the earliest extant
240 JOURNAL OF THE EVANGELICAL THEOLOGICAL SOCIETY
Jewish Greek translation of the OT. However, since the major LXX manuscripts

are Christian, the possibility exists of Christian tampering with the text at some junctures. While earlier studies frequently focused on the LXX as a textual witness to its Hebrew *Vorlage*, a significant trend now also views its renderings of the OT as representing traditional Jewish interpretation. The individual biblical books vary in their translation style, indicating a plurality of translators and dates of translation. Some biblical books differ significantly from the MT (e.g. Jeremiah, Samuel), and others exist in double recensions (e.g. Judges, Esther, Tobit, Daniel). The LXX also provides a major witness to all the Apocrypha except 4 Ezra [= 2 Esdras] (including also 3–4 Maccabees and Odes, which are not in the traditional English Apocrypha).

Bibliographies:

Dogniez, Cécile. *Bibliography of the Septuagint (1970–1993)*. VTSup 60. Leiden: Brill, 1995.

Brock, Sebastian P., Charles T. Fritsch, and Sidney Jellicoe. *A Classified Bibliography of the Septuagint*. ALGHJ 6. Leiden: Brill, 1973.

See also: bibliographic updates in *The Bulletin of the International Organization for Septuagint and Cognate Studies* (webpage at http://ccat.sas.upenn.edu /ioscs); also note the Septuagint Online webpage at http:// www.kalvesmaki.com/LXX and the bibliography to the Septuaginta Deutsch at http://www.septuagintaforschung.de/files/WUNT-219-Bibilographie.pdf.

Critical and Diplomatic Texts:

Septuaginta: Vetus Testamentum Graecum Auctoritate Academiae Scientiarum Gottingensis editum. 16 vols. Göttingen: Vandenhoeck & Ruprecht, 1931–. The standard scholarly critical edition, but incomplete. Known as the "Göttingen edition." Some volumes are divided into separate "parts."

Barthélemy, Dominique. *Les Devanciers D'Aquila: Première Publication Intégrale du Texte des Fragments du Dodécaprophéton*. VTSup 10. Leiden: Brill, 1963. Greek Minor Prophets scroll from Na☐al ☐ever (8HevXIIgr). Also see DJD 8, and Lifshitz in *IEJ* 12 (1962) 201–207 and in *Yedio☐ t* 26 (1962) 183–90.

Brooke, Alan England, Norman McLean, and Henry St. John Thackeray, eds. *The Old Testament in Greek*. London: Cambridge University Press, 1906–1940. Text of Codex Vaticanus with extensive apparatus. Since the Göttingen edition is incomplete, this still provides the best critical apparatus for the Former Prophets and Chronicles. Available online at http://archive.org.

Handbook Text:

Rahlfs, Alfred and Robert Hanhart, eds. *Septuaginta*. Rev. ed. 2 vols. in 1. Stuttgart: Deutsche Bibelgesellschaft, 2006. An eclectic text, but without adequate critical apparatus to evaluate editorial decisions (with a "moderate revision" from Rahlfs's 1935 edition). Rahlfs's original text is frequently found in Bible software (e.g. Accordance, BibleWorks, etc.) and online.

Text and Translation:
Brenton, Lancelot C. L. *The Septuagint with Apocrypha: Greek and English.* London:
Samuel Bagster & Sons, 1851; repr. Peabody, MA: Hendrickson, 1992. Now dated in comparison to the NETS translation (see below), but has the advantage of a facing Greek text. Digitized pages available free online at http://www.archive.org and at http://www.ccel.org /ccel/brenton/lxx.html and English text of Brenton at http://www.ecclesia.org/truth/septuagint-hyperlinked.html.

Translation:
Pietersma, Albert and Benjamin G. Wright, eds. *A New English Translation of the Septuagint.* Oxford/New York: Oxford University Press, 2007. Fine translation by a team of Septuagint scholars. Abbreviated NETS. Available for some Bible software, and free online access at http://ccat.sas.upenn.edu /nets/edition.

Concordance:
Hatch, Edwin and Henry A. Redpath. *A Concordance to the Septuagint and the Other Greek Versions of the Old Testament.* 3 vols. Oxford: Clarendon, 1897–1906. Available online at http://archive.org. "Second edition" (Grand Rapids: Baker, 1998) contains a Hebrew-Greek reverse index by Muraoka.
A number of volumes have been released in the Computer Bible Series (series editors J. Arthur Baird, David Noel Freedman, and Watson E. Mills) published by Biblical Research Associates or by Edwin Mellen Press. These have been produced by J. David Thompson and are entitled similar to *A Critical Concordance to the Septuagint Genesis* or to *A Critical Concordance to the Apocrypha: 1 Maccabees.* Each provides book-by-book concordances of the LXX with a number of statistical aides.
Many computer programs also contain tagged Septuagint texts (e.g. BibleWorks, Accordance).

Lexicons:
Chamberlain, Gary Alan. *The Greek of the Septuagint: A Supplemental Lexicon.* Peabody, MA: Hendrickson, 2011. Includes all words not in BDAG, and otherwise only supplements BDAG on words when Septuagintal Greek meanings differ from standard NT definitions (thus this book by itself does not include all LXX vocabulary).
Lust, Johan, Erik Eynikel, and Katrin Hauspie. *A Greek-English Lexicon of the Septuagint.* Rev. ed. Stuttgart: Deutsche Bibelgesellschaft, 2003. First edition issued in two volumes (1992, 1996). Helpful glosses of all LXX vocabulary.
Muraoka, T. *A Greek-English Lexicon of the Septuagint.* Louvain: Peeters, 2009. Now complete, whereas previous iterations just focused on the Twelve Prophets (1993) or the Twelve Prophets and the Pentateuch (2002). A fine work by a careful lexicographer; should be consulted regularly.
Muraoka, T. *A Greek-Hebrew-Aramaic Two-way Index to the Septuagint.* Louvain:

Peeters, 2010. Allows one to see what Greek words are used to translate
the Hebrew/Aramaic OT, and vice versa. Previous parts of this tool
were published in his earlier LXX lexicons (1993 and 2002) and in the
Baker edition of Hatch's LXX concordance; but with the publication of
his 2009 lexicon, this is now a stand-alone document.

Rehkopf, Friedrich. *Septuaginta-Vokabular.* Göttingen: Vandenhoeck &
Ruprecht, 1989. Provides a single German gloss for each Greek word.
For each entry he lists some LXX texts and compares with word count
usage in the NT.

Taylor, Bernard A. *Analytical Lexicon to the Septuagint: Expanded edition.*
Peabody,
MA: Hendrickson; Stuttgart: Deutsche Bibelgesellschaft, 2009. Revision
of his 1994 Zondervan edition, listing every word form found in Rahlfs's
edition and employing glosses from the Lust/Eynikel/Hauspie lexicon;
especially helpful for difficult parsings.

Grammars:

Conybeare, F. C. and St. George Stock. *Grammar of Septuagint Greek.* Boston:
Ginn & Co., 1905; repr. Peabody, MA: Hendrickson, 1995. Introductory,
but with section on syntax not in Thackeray (or in the German
grammar by Helbing). Available online at http://archive.org and at
http://www.ccel.org/c/conybeare /greekgrammar.

Thackeray, Henry St. John. *A Grammar of the Old Testament in Greek*, Vol. 1:
Introduction,
Orthography and Accidence. Cambridge: CUP, 1909; repr.
Hildesheim: Olms, 1987. Available online at http://archive.org.

Introductions:

Dines, Jennifer M. *The Septuagint.* Understanding the Bible and its World.
London: T & T Clark, 2004. Good short survey, especially helpful for
first exposure to LXX studies.

Fernández Marcos, Natalio. *The Septuagint in Context: Introduction to the Greek
Versions of the Bible.* Trans. Wilfred G. E. Watson from 2d Spanish ed.
Atlanta: Society of Biblical Literature, 2009. Useful introduction from
standpoint of Spanish scholarship (previous English edition published
by Leiden: Brill, 2000).

Harl, Marguerite, Gilles Dorival, and Olivier Munnich. *La Bible Grecque des
Septante: Du judaïsme hellénistique au christianisme ancient.* Initiations au
christianisme
ancien; Paris: Cerf, 1988. Introduction by important French
scholars.

Jellicoe, Sidney. *The Septuagint and Modern Study.* Oxford: Clarendon, 1968;
repr. Winona Lake: Eisenbrauns, 1993. Assumes the earlier *Introduction*
by Swete.

Jobes, Karen H. and Moisés Silva. *Invitation to the Septuagint.* Grand Rapids:
Baker, 2000. Fine volume providing overall orientation to Septuagint
study.

Siegert, Folker. *Zwischen Hebräischer Bibel und Altem Testament: Eine
Einführung in*

die Septuaginta. Münsteraner Judaistische Studien 9. Münster: LIT, 2001.
Additional volume provides index and "Wirkungsgeschichte" of the
LXX in antiquity (see *Register zur "Einführung in die Septuaginta"*; Münster:
LIT, 2003).
Swete, Henry Barclay. *An Introduction to the Old Testament in Greek.* Rev.
Richard
Rusden Ottley. Cambridge: CUP, 1914; repr. Peabody, MA: Hendrickson,
1989. Classic textbook available online at http://archive.org and at
http://www.ccel.org/s/ swete/greekot.
Also see *HJPAJC* 3.1:474–493; *Mikra* 161–88; *CHJ* 2:534–562; *ABD* 5:1093–
1104.
Commentaries:
Harl, Marguerite, et al. *La Bible d'Alexandrie.* 17+ vols. Paris: Cerf, 1986–.
Focuses
on how the LXX would have been read by Greek speakers in Jewish
and Christian antiquity.
Septuagint Commentary Series. Leiden: Brill, 2005–. Edited by S. E. Porter,
R. Hess, and J. Jarick.
Wevers, John William. *Notes on the Greek Text of Genesis.* SBLSCS 35. Atlanta:
Scholars, 1993. Discusses textual and philological issues. Wevers has
produced similar volumes for the rest of the Pentateuch.
The International Organization for Septuagint and Cognate Studies (IOSCS)
announced plans in 2005 to publish the SBL Commentary on the Septuagint
(though no volumes have appeared at time of writing).
2.1.2 Aquila, Symmachus, Theodotion
Known primarily from the fragmentary sources of Origen's Hexapla, "the
Three" represent Jewish Greek translations from the early Common Era (though
there are some early traditions that Symmachus and even Theodotion were
Ebionite Christians). Extensive Syro-Hexaplaric fragments and remnants of the
Three exist in other languages (notably Armenian). Bibliographies, concordances,
and introductions on the Three are also listed in works on the LXX above (see also
HJPAJC 3.1:493–504).
Text:
Field, Fridericus. *Origenis Hexaplorum quae supersunt.* 2 vols. Oxford:
Clarendon,
1875. Available online at http://archive.org. Other fragments have surfaced
since Field, thus see the bibliographies and introductions noted
under LXX. Also note that Göttingen LXX volumes list Hexaplaric traditions
in the bottom apparatus. An English translation of Field's own
Latin prolegomena to this work has been produced by Gérard J. Norton
(Paris: Gabalda, 2005). The "Hexapla Institute" has announced plans to
publish a new critical edition of Hexapla fragments (see
http://www.hexapla.org).
Concordance:
Reider, Joseph and Nigel Turner. *An Index to Aquila.* VTSup 12. Leiden: Brill,
1966. Use in addition to the listing in Hatch and Redpath, Vol. 3 (see
under LXX).
Commentary:

Salvesen, Alison. *Symmachus in the Pentateuch.* JSS Monograph 15. Manchester: University of Manchester, 1991.

2.2 Targumim

Aramaic translations and paraphrases of the OT are known from as early as the Qumran community. The targumim appear to originate from liturgical use in the synagogue, when a *meturgeman* would compose an (occasionally paraphrastic or expansive) Aramaic rendering of the biblical text to be read in the service. Such targumim can testify to how the biblical text was interpreted in Judaism. "Official" targumim on the Pentateuch (*Tg. Onqelos*) and the Prophets (*Tg. Jonathan*) have been passed down from Babylonian rabbinic circles, while parallel traditions are also known from Palestine. There are additional targumic traditions for each of the non-Aramaic books of the Writings. Besides MSS and printed editions devoted to targumim, the official targumim are printed with the MT in Rabbinic Bibles alongside traditional rabbinic commentaries. Targumic texts also occur in Polyglot editions (e.g. those printed in Antwerp, Paris, and London [=Walton's]) in parallel with the MT and other translations. The issues of dating and transmission history of the various targumim are often quite complex.

2.2.1 General Bibliography

Bibliography:

Grossfeld, Bernard. *A Bibliography of Targum Literature.* Vols. 1 and 2: Bibliographica Judaica 3 and 8. New York: Ktav, 1972, 1977. Vol. 3: New York: Sepher-Hermon, 1990.

Forestell, J. T. *Targumic Traditions and the New Testament: An Annotated Bibliography with a New Testament Index.* SBL Aramaic Studies 4. Chico, CA: Scholars, 1979.

Nickels, Peter. *Targum and New Testament: A Bibliography together with a New Testament Index.* Scripta Pontificii Instituti Biblici 117. Rome: Pontifical Biblical Institute, 1967. Updated in Forestell.

Ongoing listing of publications in the *Newsletter for Targumic and Cognate Studies* (now with its own website, including some targum translations at http://targum.info). Note also the bibliographic articles by Díez Macho in Vols. 4 and 5 of *Neophyti 1* (listed below).

Critical Texts:

Sperber, Alexander. *The Bible in Aramaic: Based on Old Manuscripts and Printed Texts.* 4 vols. in 5. Leiden: Brill, 1959–1973. Vol. 4b presents a series of helpful studies on the preceding volumes. Major critical text of *Targums Onqelos* and *Jonathan*; less reliable on the Writings.

Translations:

McNamara, Martin, gen. ed. *The Aramaic Bible.* 22 vols. Edinburgh: T & T Clark, 1987–2007. Standard contemporary translation series, with typically good introductions and notes.

Also see: Etheridge under Pentateuch. Some translations are also being made available online (see http://targum.info/targumic-texts). Eldon Clem is producing English translations for Accordance Bible Software of Targums Onkelos, Jonathan, Neofiti, and Pseudo-Jonathan; see http://www.accordancebible.com and note the review in *Aramaic Studies* 5 (2007) 151–58.

Concordances:

Searchable morphologically tagged Aramaic texts are currently available for Accordance, BibleWorks, and Logos software packages. These are based on texts from the Comprehensive Aramaic Lexicon Project (sometimes drawing on older editions, such as those by Lagarde).

Lexicons:

Cook, Edward M. *A Glossary of Targum Onkelos: According to Alexander Sperber's*
Edition. Studies in the Aramaic Interpretation of Scripture. Leiden: Brill, 2008.

Dalman, Gustav. *Aramäisch-neuhebräisches Wörterbuch zu Targum, Talmud, und Midrasch.* Göttingen, 1938. Available online at http://archive.org.

Jastrow, Marcus. *A Dictionary of the Targumim, the Talmud Babli and Yerushalmi,*
and the Midrashic Literature. 2 vols. New York: Pardes, 1950; singlevolume repr. New York: Judaica, 1971 and Peabody, MA: Hendrickson, 2005. Convenient resource for translating all targumic and early rabbinic literature. Available online at http://www.tyndalearchive.com/tabs /jastrow.

Levy, J. *Chaldäisches Wörterbuch über die Targumim und einen grossen Theil des rabbinischen*
Schriftthums. 2 vols. Leipzig: Baumgärtner, 1867–1868; repr. Köln: Joseph Melzer, 1959. Available online at http://archive.org.

Sokoloff, Michael. *A Dictionary of Jewish Babylonian Aramaic of the Talmudic and*
Geonic Periods. Dictionaries of Talmud, Midrash and Targum 3. Ramat-Gan, Israel: Bar Ilan University Press; Baltimore: Johns Hopkins, 2002. Sokoloff's dictionaries generally employ better informed lexicography than Jastrow.

Sokoloff, Michael. *A Dictionary of Jewish Palestinian Aramaic of the Byzantine Period.*
2d ed. Dictionaries of Talmud, Midrash and Targum 2; Ramat-Gan, Israel: Bar Ilan University Press; Baltimore: Johns Hopkins, 2002. Also contains a marvelous set of indexes to the passages cited.

Also see: Comprehensive Aramaic Lexicon Project of Hebrew Union College at http://call.cn.huc.edu. This website includes a searchable database of Aramaic lexical information and of Aramaic texts through the 13th century. It also houses a bibliographic database, and lists "Addenda et Corrigenda" to the two Sokoloff dictionaries above.

Grammars:

Dalman, Gustaf. *Grammatik des Jüdisch-Palästinischen Aramäisch: Nach den Idiomen des Palästinischen Talmud des Onkelostargum und Prophetentargum und der Jerusalemischen Targume.* 2d ed. Leipzig: Hinrichs, 1905; repr. Darmstadt: Wissenschaftliche Buchgesellschaft, 1960. Available online at http://archive.org.

Fassberg, Steven E. *A Grammar of the Palestinian Targum Fragments from the Cairo Genizah.* HSS 38. Atlanta: Scholars, 1991. Focuses primarily on phonology and morphology.

Golomb, David M. *A Grammar of Targum Neofiti.* HSM 34. Chico, CA: Scholars, 1985. Attends primarily to morphology, but contains a final chapter reviewing matters of verbal and nominal syntax.

Kuty, Renaud J. *Studies in the Syntax of Targum Jonathan to Samuel.* Ancient Near Eastern Studies Supplements 30. Leuven: Peeters, 2010. Whereas other studies focus on morphology, this highlights key syntactical matters.

Stevenson, William B. *Grammar of Palestinian Jewish Aramaic.* 2d ed. Oxford: Clarendon, 1962. Beginning grammar (though without exercises) introducing the language of both Palestinian and Babylonian post-biblical Jewish Aramaic. Includes syntactical notes missing in Dalman. Second edition reprint of 1924 with a new "Appendix on Numerals" by J. A. Emerton.

Some beginning grammars of Biblical Aramaic also touch on Targumic Aramaic (and other works of rabbinic origin); e.g. F. E. Greenspahn, *An Introduction to Aramaic.* 2d ed. Atlanta: SBL, 2003. Also see Y. Frank, *Grammar for Gemara* (below under Babylonian Talmud).

Introductions:

Bowker, John. *The Targums and Rabbinic Literature.* Cambridge: CUP, 1969. An introduction to the targumim in relation to other rabbinic literature. Also contains a translation of a substantial portion of *Tg. Ps.-J.* to Genesis.

Díez Macho, Alejandro. *El Targum: Introducción a las traducciones aramaicas de la Biblia.* Textos y Estudios 21. Madrid: Consejo Superior de Investigaciones Científicas, 1982. The classic introduction by the foremost member of the "Spanish school."

Flesher, Paul V. M., and Bruce Chilton. *The Targums: A Critical Introduction.* Studies in the Aramaic Interpretation of Scripture 12; Leiden: Brill, 2011; Waco, TX: Baylor University Press, 2011. Significant recent introduction that covers a wide array of academic topics.

Gleßmer, Uwe. *Einleitung in die Targume zum Pentateuch.* TSAJ 48. Tübingen: J. C. B. Mohr [Paul Siebeck], 1995.

Grelot, Pierre. *What Are the Targums? Selected Texts.* Trans. Salvator Attanasio; Old Testament Studies 7; Collegeville, MN: Liturgical, 1992. Selections of expansive targumic passages with introduction. Caution is required since Grelot combines different targumic traditions.

Le Déaut, Roger. *Introduction à la Littérature Targumique.* Rome: Institut
Biblique
Pontifical, 1966. "Premiere partie" and thus incomplete, but quite helpful.
Also see his brief article in *CHJ* 2:563–90; and his more substantial
treatment of "Targum" in L. Pirot and A. Robert, *Supplément au Dictionnaire
de la Bible.* Paris: Letouzey, 2005, 13:1*–344*.
Levine, Etan. *The Aramaic Version of the Bible: Contents and Context.* BZAW
174.
Berlin: de Gruyter, 1988. Addresses the targumim as a whole, focusing
on targumic themes.
McNamara, Martin. *Targum and Testament Revisited: Aramaic Paraphrases of
the*
Hebrew Bible. 2d ed. Grand Rapids: Eerdmans, 2010. Also contains a
helpful appendix that introduces all extant targums.
See also: the useful articles by P. S. Alexander in *Mikra* 217–53 and in *ABD*
6:320–331; also note *HJPAJC* 1:99–114; *CHJ* 2:563–590.

2.2.2 Targumim on the Pentateuch
Divided into the following categories:
(1) Official Targum of Babylonia = Onqelos (text in Sperber above).
(2) "Palestinian Targumim" (editions noted below)
(a) Neofiti 1
(b) Pseudo-Jonathan
(c) Fragment Targum
(d) Cairo Genizah Fragments
(e) Toseftot
(f) Festival Collections
(g) Targumic Poems
For texts and bibliography on the last three categories see: Sperber, *Bible in
Aramaic* 1:354–57 (above); *Mikra* 251; and Klein, *Genizah Manuscripts* Vol. 1:
xxviii–
xxxix (below).

Texts:

Diez Macho, Alexander, L. Diez Merino, E. Martinez Borobio, and Teresa
Martinez Saiz, eds. *Biblia Polyglotta Matritensia IV: Targum Palaestinense in
Pentateuchum.* 5 vols. Madrid: Consejo Superior de Investigaciones
Científicas, 1977–88. Contains Palestinian Targumim in parallel columns
(Neofiti, Pseudo-Jonathan, Fragment Targum, Cairo Genizah fragments)
along with a Spanish translation of Pseudo-Jonathan. Very helpful.
Díez Macho, Alejandro, ed. *Neophyti 1: Targum Palestinense MS de la Biblioteca
Vaticana.* 6 vols. Textos y Estudios 7–11 and 20; Madrid-Barcelona:
Consejo Superior de Investigaciones Científicas, 1968–1979. Text of *Tg.
Neof.* with facing Spanish translation and appended French and English
translations. Each volume is prefaced with extensive introductory essays
by Díez Macho. Volumes 2–5 also include verse-by-verse listings of
(mostly rabbinic, but also pseudepigraphic and Christian) parallels to the
interpretive elements in *Tg. Ps.-J.* and *Tg. Neof.* Volume 6 contains addenda,
corrigenda, and indexes. A photocopy edition of the manuscript
also exists (Jerusalem: Makor, 1970).

Ginsburger, M. *Pseudo-Jonathan (Thargum Jonathan ben Usiël zum Pentateuch). Nach*
der Londoner Handschrift (Brit. Mus. add. 27031). Berlin: S. Calvary, 1903;
repr. New York: Hildesheim, 1971. Editor's name can also be spelled
Ginsberger in catalogs. There is another edition of this manuscript by
D. Rieder (Jerusalem, 1974), reprinted with Modern Hebrew translation
in 2 vols. in 1984–85. Also note the edition by Clarke (below under
Concordances).
Klein, Michael L. *Genizah Manuscripts of Palestinian Targum to the Pentateuch.*
2
vols. Cincinnati: Hebrew Union College, 1986. Vol. 1 contains introduction,
text, and translation of Genizah MSS of Pentateuchal targumim, also
of festival collections, toseftot and targumic poems (additionally listing
helpful bibliography for locating other toseftot, festival collections
and targumic poems). Vol. 2 includes notes, glossary of vocabulary, and
plates.

248 JOURNAL OF THE EVANGELICAL THEOLOGICAL SOCIETY

Klein, Michael L. *The Fragment-Targums of the Pentateuch: According to their Extant*
Sources. 2 vols. AnBib 76. Rome: Biblical Institute Press, 1980. Vol. 1
introduction,
text and indexes; Vol. 2 translation. Strongly preferred over
Ginsburger's 1899 edition.
For Onqelos see Sperber (§2.2.1 above). Note also Masorah in Michael L.
Klein, *The Masorah to Targum Onqelos: as preserved in MSS Vatican Ebreo*
448, Rome Angelica Or. 7, Fragments from the Cairo Genizah and in Earlier
Editions by A. Berliner and S. Landauer. Targum Studies 1. Academic Studies
in the History of Judaism; Binghamton, NY: Global Publications,
SUNY Binghamton, 2000.

Translation:
Etheridge, J. W. *The Targums of Onkelos and Jonathan ben Uzziel on the Pentateuch*
with the Fragments of the Jerusalem Targum. 1862; repr. New York: Ktav,
1968. Available online at http://targum.info/targumic-texts
/pentateuchal-targumim and at http://archive.org. Also available for
BibleWorks and Logos software. The McNamara *Aramaic Bible* series
above is now generally preferred.
Le Déaut, Roger, with collaboration by Jacques Robert. *Targum du Pentateuque.*
5 vols. SC; Paris: Cerf, 1978–1981. French translation of Targum
Neofiti and Targum Pseudo-Jonathan in parallel pages, with brief translational
notes. The fifth volume serves as a topical index.
Also see: *The Aramaic Bible* series (above under 2.2.1 Targumim General
Bibliography).

Concordances:
Brederek, Emil. *Konkordanz zum Targum Onkelos.* BZAW 9. Giessen: Alfred
Töpelmann, 1906. Available online at http://archive.org.
Clarke, E. G., W. E. Aufrecht, J. C. Hurd, and F. Spitzer. *Targum Pseudo-*
Jonathan of the Pentateuch: Text and Concordance. Hoboken: Ktav, 1984.

Contains the same manuscript as Ginsberger and Rieder with KWIC concordance; on the concordance see M. Bernstein's cautious review in *JQR* 79 (1988) 227–30.

Kassovsky,. 5 vols. in 1. Jerusalem: Kiriath Moshe, 1933–40. For Onqelos.

Kaufman, Stephen A., Michael Sokoloff, and with the assistance of Edward M. Cook. *A Key-Word-in-Context Concordance to Targum Neofiti.* Publications of the Comprehensive Aramaic Lexicon Project 2. Baltimore: John Hopkins University Press, 1993. Also presents English glosses of the Aramaic words.

Note also some rabbinic search software contain searchable targumic texts (see under Rabbinic Literature).

Commentaries:

Aberbach, Moses and Bernard Grossfeld. *Targum Onkelos to Genesis: A Critical Analysis together with an English Translation of the Text.* New York: Ktav, 1982. Text of A. Berliner with English translation and comments (based on Sperber's edition).

Drazin, Israel. *Targum Onkelos to Exodus: An English Translation of the Text With Analysis and Commentary.* New York: Ktav, 1990. Text of A. Berliner with English translation and comments (based on Sperber's edition). Drazin has produced similar commentaries for *Tg. Onq.* to Leviticus (1994), Numbers (1998), and Deuteronomy (1982). Drazin emphasizes the literal translational elements of the Targum rather than seeing it as a full rabbinic interpretation. Note the cautious reviews by Emerton in *VT* 43 (1993) 280–81 and by Levine in *CBQ* 57 (1995) 766–67.

Grossfeld, Bernard. *Targum Neofiti 1: An Exegetical Commentary to Genesis, Including Full Rabbinic Parallels.* New York: Sepher-Hermon, 2000. Includes transcription of text and commentary with emphasis on rabbinic texts that parallel the Targum.

2.2.3 Targumim on the Prophets

Targum Jonathan forms the "official" targum to the Former and Latter Prophets (text in Sperber, *Bible in Aramaic*, Vols. 2 and 3). There are also Palestinian Toseftot (marginal comments of other targumic traditions alongside Targum Jonathan in the MSS). On the Toseftot: see pp. vi–xlii of De Lagarde, *Prophetae Chaldaice* (below); see also Sperber, *Bible in Aramaic*, descriptions on pp. ix–x of Vol. 2 and p. xi of Vol. 3; further bibliography in *Mikra* 252. Translation (with notes) in McNamara, *The Aramaic Bible* (see above).

Text:

De Lagarde, Paul. *Prophetae Chaldaice.* Leipzig: Teubner, 1872. Standard edition before Sperber (on which see §2.2.1 above). Available online at http://archive.org.

Stenning, J. F. *The Targum of Isaiah.* Oxford: Clarendon, 1949. A pointed critical text of Targum Jonathan to Isaiah with translation; Palestinian

Toseftot to the Targum on pp. 224–28.

Concordances:

Moor, Johannes C. de, et al., eds. *A Bilingual Concordance to the Targum of the Prophets.* 21 vols. Leiden: Brill, 1995–2005. A concordance of the individual books of *Tg. Jon.* to the Former and Latter Prophets. Also lists Hebrew equivalents to the Aramaic vocabulary (providing English glosses to both the Aramaic and Hebrew terms).

Van Zijl, J. B. *A Concordance to the Targum of Isaiah: Based on the Brit. Mus. Or. MS. 2211.* SBLAS 3. Missoula, MT: Scholars, 1979.

Commentaries:

Levine, Etan. *The Aramaic Version of Jonah.* New York: Sepher-Hermon, 1975. Introduction, text, translation, and commentary of *Tg. Jon.* to Jonah.

Smelik, Willem F. *The Targum of Judges.* OTS 36. Leiden: Brill, 1995. Extensive introduction and commentary.

Van Staalduine-Sulman, Eveline. *The Targum of Samuel.* Studies in the Aramaic Interpretation of Scripture 1. Leiden: Brill, 2002. Commentary, translation, and study.

250 JOURNAL OF THE EVANGELICAL THEOLOGICAL SOCIETY

2.2.4 Targumim on the Writings

No known rabbinic targumic traditions exist for Daniel or for Ezra-Nehemiah (note these books already employ Aramaic). The study of the targumim to the Writings necessitates caution since frequently several targumic recensions exist for any one OT book (for overview see *ABD* 6:320–331). Note that Targum Job is different than the Qumran Job Targum (=11QtgJob =11Q10; see DJD 23 and further bibliography below under "Dead Sea Scrolls"). Two targumic traditions to Esther are recognized (Targum Rishon and Targum Sheni = *Tg. Esth I and II*). A so-called "Third Targum to Esther" exists in the Antwerp Polyglot, but it is disputed whether this Third Targum is essentially a condensation of Targum Rishon, the predecessor of Rishon, or properly a targum at all.

General Texts:

Sperber, Alexander. *The Bible in Aramaic: Based on Old Manuscripts and Printed Texts.* Vol. 4a. Leiden: Brill, 1968. Contains *Tg. Chron* (MS Berlin 125) and *Tg. Ruth* as in the De Lagarde edition, and includes from Brit. Mus. Or. 2375: *Tg. Cant, Tg. Lam, Tg. Eccl, and Tg. Esth* (mixed text type of Esther, due to the manuscript used).

De Lagarde, Paul. *Hagiographa Chaldaice.* Leipzig: Teubner, 1873. Text of targumim to the Writings, including those not in Sperber (Psalms, Job, Proverbs, and both Esther Rishon and Esther Sheni). Available online at http://books.google.com.

Individual Texts:

Díez Merino, Luis. *Targum de Salmos: Edición Príncipe del Ms. Villa-Amil n. 5 de Alfonso de Zamora.* Bibliotheca Hispana Biblica 6. Madrid: Consejo Superior de Investigaciones Científicas, 1982. Introduction, text, Latin translation

(by Alfonso de Zamora) and studies on this manuscript of *Tg.*
Psalms.

Stec, David M. *The Text of the Targum of Job: An Introduction and Critical Edition.*
AGJU 20. Leiden: Brill, 1994. A fine edition.

Díez Merino, Luis. *Targum de Job: Edición Principe del Ms. Villa-Amil n° 5 de Alfonso de Zamora.* Bibliotheca Hispana Biblica 8. Madrid: Consejo Superior de Investigaciones Científicas, 1984.

Díez Merino, Luis. *Targum de Proverbios. Edición Principe del Ms. Villa-Amil n° 5 de Alfonso de Zamora.* Madrid: Consejo Superior de Investigaciones Científicas, 1984. The next major edition of *Tg. Proverbs* since De Lagarde, *Hagiographa Chaldaice* (above).

Levine, Etan. *The Aramaic Version of Ruth.* AnBib 58. Rome: Biblical Institute Press, 1973. Introduction, text, translation, and commentary.

Jerusalmi, Isaac. *The Song of Songs in the Targumic Tradition: Vocalized Aramaic Text with Facing English Translation and Ladino Versions.* Cincinnati: Ladino, 1993.

Alonso Fontela, Carlos. *El Targum al Cantar de los Cantares (Edición Critica).* Collección Tesis Doctorales. Madrid: Editorial de la Universidad Complutense de Madrid, 1987.

Melamed, R. H. *The Targum to Canticles according to Six Yemenite MSS.* PhiladelJEWISH phia: Dropsie College, 1921. Covers the Yemenite recension, which differs from the Western texts at points. Reprinted from a series of articles in *JQR* n.s. 10–12 (1919–1921). Available online at http://archive.org.

Díez Merino, Luis. *Targum de Qohelet: Edición Principe del Ms. Villa-Amil n° 5 de Alfonso de Zamora.* Bibliotheca Hispana Biblica 13. Madrid: Consejo Superior de Investigaciones Científicas, 1987. An important edition of a manuscript otherwise unavailable.

Levine, Etan. *The Aramaic Version of Qohelet.* New York: Sepher-Hermon, 1978. Photocopy of MS Urb. 1 with translation and "conceptual analysis."

Levy, A. *Das Targum zu Qohelet nach sudarabischen Handschriften herausgegeben.* Breslau, 1905. Critical edition of *Tg. Eccl.*

Brady, Christian M. M. *The Rabbinic Targum of Lamentations: Vindicating God.* Studies in the Aramaic Interpretation of Scripture 3. Leiden: Brill, 2003. Study of this targum that includes a transcription of Codex Urbinas Hebr. 1 and translation.

Heide, Albert van der. *The Yemenite Tradition of the Targum of Lamentations: Critical Text and Analysis of the Variant Readings.* Leiden: Brill, 1981. The Yemenite tradition is significantly different from the Western text tradition.

Levine, Etan. *The Aramaic Version of Lamentations.* New York: Hermon, 1976. Introduction, text, translation, and commentary.

Ego, Beate. *Targum Scheni zu Ester: Übersetzung, Kommentar und theologische*

Deutung. TSAJ 54. Tübingen: Mohr Siebeck, 1996.

Grossfeld, Bernard. *The Targum Sheni to the Book of Esther: A Critical Edition based on MS. Sassoon 282 with Critical Apparatus.* New York: Sepher-Hermon, 1994. Includes a full-length concordance and a photocopy of this manuscript.

Grossfeld, Bernard. *The First Targum to Esther: According to the MS Paris Hebrew 110 of the Bibliotheque Nationale.* New York: Sepher-Hermon, 1983. Critical text, translation, and commentary with introduction to Targum Rishon to Esther. Includes plates.

Le Déaut, R., and J. Robert. *Targum des Chroniques (Cod. Vat. Urb. Ebr. 1).* 2 vols. AnBib 51. Rome: Biblical Institute Press, 1971. Vol. 1 introduction and (French) translation; Vol. 2 text, indexes, and a glossary of vocabulary in Aramaic, French, and English.

Concordance:

Grossfeld, Bernard. *Concordance of the First Targum to the Book of Esther.* SBLAS 5. Chico, CA: Scholars, 1984. For the Second Targum (Targum Sheni) see the KWIC concordance in Grossfeld's edition noted above.

2.3 Other (Latin and Syriac)

Whereas the Vulgate is clearly Christian (translated by Jerome), the lineage of the Old Latin is more obscure. A frequent dependence on the LXX, and occasional portions that agree with Jewish tradition over the LXX, make it possible that the Old Latin contains some certifiable Jewish passages. The Peshi☐ta, though ultimately a Christian Bible, may originally have been allied with Jewish tradition, especially

252 JOURNAL OF THE EVANGELICAL THEOLOGICAL SOCIETY

when it agrees with the targumim. For sake of space, standard Latin and Syriac grammars and lexicons are not listed below. Other early translations that appear largely dependent on the Septuagint, such as Bohairic Coptic or Christian Palestinian Aramaic, are not represented below. For introductions see *Mikra* 255–97, 299–313; *ABD* 6:794–803.

Old Latin Texts:

Vetus Latina: Die Reste der altlateinischen Bibel. Freiburg: Herder, 1951–. Critical edition currently covering Genesis, Canticles, Wisdom, Ecclesiasticus, and Isaiah from the OT and Apocrypha. Projected 26 volumes (with multiple parts).

Sabatier, Petri, ed. *Bibliorum Sacrorum Latinae Versiones Antiquae.* 3 vols. Rheims: Reginald Florentain, 1743–1749. Vulgate and Old Latin in parallel columns. Some volumes available on http://archive.org.

Peshi☐ta Bibliography:

Dirksen, P. B. *An Annotated Bibliography of the Peshi☐ta of the Old Testament.* Monographs of the Peshi☐ta Institute 5. Leiden: Brill, 1989.

Syriac Peshi☐ta Text:

Vetus Testamentum Syriace Iuxta Simplicem Syrorum Versionem [= *The Old Testament*

in Syriac According to the Peshita Version]. Leiden: Brill, 1973–. In four
parts, with multiple fascicles.

Peshita Translation:

Lamsa, George M. *The Holy Bible from Ancient Eastern Manuscripts: Containing
the
Old and New Testaments, translated from the Peshitta, the authorized Bible of the
church of the East.* Philadelphia: Holman, 1957; repr. San Francisco: Harper
& Row, 1985. Not fully reliable. Available online at
http://www.aramaicpeshitta.com/OTtools/LamsaOT.htm.
Gorgias Press has inaugurated its Surath Ktobh series (overseen by George A.
Kiraz, projected to be 30 volumes), featuring facing pages of the Peshi☐ta
(without textual apparatus) and a literal English translation.

Peshita Concordances:

Borbone, P. G. and K. D. Jenner, eds. *The Old Testament in Syriac According to
the Peshitta Version: Part 5 Concordance.* Vetus Testamentum Syriace. Leiden:
Brill, 1997–.
Strothmann, Werner, Kurt Johannes, and Manfred Zumpe. *Konkordanz zur
Syrischen Bibel: Die Propheten.* 4 vols. GOF Reihe 1, Syriaca 25. Wiesbaden:
Otto Harrassowitz, 1984. They also produced a four volume 1986 concordance
for *Der Pentateuch* (GOF Reihe 1, Syriaca 26).
Peshi☐ta texts are increasingly coming available for Bible software (e.g.
Accordance
and BibleWorks).

Peshita Introduction:

Weitzman, M. P. *The Syriac Version of the Old Testament: An Introduction.*
University
of Cambridge Oriental Publications 56. Cambridge: CUP, 1999.

See also: Pp. 1057–59 in *EDEJ.*

3. Apocrypha

Various Christian OT manuscripts (Greek, Latin, Syriac, etc.) contain books
not found in the Masoretic tradition. Translations may be found in some English
Bibles (e.g. RSV, NRSV, NEB, REB) of the Greek (LXX) apocrypha as well as
Latin "2 Esdras." Other translations may be found in the editions edited by
Charles,
by Charlesworth (for 4 Ezra), and by Kümmel listed under General
Pseudepigrapha
Bibliography below (cf. esp. Charlesworth, *OTP* 2:609–24 for apocryphal Psalms).
English "2 Esdras" is listed in the Vulgate as 4 Ezra and should not be
confused with LXX 2 Esdras (which is the Greek version of OT Ezra and
Nehemiah). Most modern scholars believe 4 Ezra is a compilation, often
designating (the probably Christian) chapters 1–2 and chapters 15–16 as 5 Ezra
and
6 Ezra respectively. Thus the name "4 Ezra" in much modern scholarship has been
reserved for Vulgate 4 Ezra 3–14.
The above listed LXX editions and concordances serve for the Greek
Apocrypha. Greek fragments of 4 Ezra have been discovered (see Denis,
Fragmenta

pseudepigraphorum below under Pseudepigrapha). Latin versions of these books as well as the whole of 4 Ezra are also known in the Old Latin (see above) and Vulgate (for concordances to Latin 4 Ezra, see Denis or Lechner-Schmidt under General Pseudepigrapha Bibliography below). For Syriac editions, see the Peshi☐ta bibliography above. Many books of the Apocrypha are thought to stem from Semitic originals. Prior to the DSS, fragments in Hebrew were known of Ben Sira (= Sirach = Ecclesiasticus). Hebrew and Aramaic texts have been found in the DSS for Tobit (4Q196–200 in DJD XIX), Sirach (2Q18 in DJD III; 11QPsa [=11Q5] xxi–xxii in DJD IV; some Masada texts) and some of the apocryphal Psalms (11QPsa in DJD IV; for 4Q380–381 see Schuller, *Non-Canonical Psalms from Qumran* below under "Dead Sea Scrolls"); for a list see Peter W. Flint "Appendix II," in Flint & Vanderkam, eds., *The Dead Sea Scrolls After Fifty Years*, pp. 666–68 (see "Introductions" under Dead Sea Scrolls below).

Other Bibliography:

Reiterer, Friedrich Vinzenz, ed. *Bibliographie zu Ben Sira.* BZAW 266. Berlin: de Gruyter, 1998. Not well indexed or annotated.

See also: Bibelwissenschaft by Franz Böhmisch (http://www.animabit.de /bibel/sir.htm).

Other Texts (Ordered by apocryphal book):

Beentjes, Pancratius C. *The Book of Ben Sira in Hebrew: A Text Edition of all Extant Hebrew Manuscripts and a Synopsis.* VTSup 68. Leiden: Brill, 1997. Paperback repr. Society of Biblical Literature (2006).

254 JOURNAL OF THE EVANGELICAL THEOLOGICAL SOCIETY

The Book of Ben Sira: Text, Concordance and an Analysis of the Vocabulary. The Historical Dictionary of the Hebrew Language. Jerusalem: Academy of the Hebrew Language and Shrine of the Book, 1973. Synoptic edition of Hebrew MSS with concordance.

Yadin, Yigael. *The Ben Sira Scroll from Masada.* Jerusalem: Israel Exploration Society, 1965. Repr. from *Eretz-Israel* vol. 8.

Schechter, S. and C. Taylor. *The Wisdom of Ben Sira: Portions of the Book of Ecclesiasticus from Hebrew Manuscripts in the Cairo Genizah Collection Presented to the University of Cambridge by the Editors.* Cambridge: CUP, 1899.

Klijn, Albertus Frederik J. *Die Esra-Apokalypse (IV. Esra): Nach dem lateinischen Text unter Benutzung der anderen Versionen übersetzt.* GCS. Berlin: de Gruyter, 1992.

Stone, Michael E. *The Armenian Version of IV Ezra.* University of Pennsylvania Armenian Texts and Studies. Missoula, MT: Scholars Press, 1979.

Sievers, Joseph. *Synopsis of the Greek Sources for the Hasmonean Period: 1–2 Maccabees and Josephus War 1 and Antiquities 12–14.* Rome: Editrice Pontificio Istituto Biblico, 2001. Useful for comparative and historical studies.

Texts are only presented in Greek.
Weeks, S. D. E., S. J. Gathercole, L. T. Stuckenbruck. *The Book of Tobit: Texts from the Principal Ancient and Medieval Traditions. With Synopsis, Concordances, and Annotated Texts in Aramaic, Hebrew, Greek, Latin, and Syriac.* Fontes et subsidia ad Bibliam pertinentes 3. Berlin: de Gruyter, 2004.
Wagner, Christian J. *Polyglotte Tobit-Synopse: Griechisch, Lateinisch, Syrisch, Hebräisch, Aramäisch: mit einem Index zu den Tobit-Fragmenten vom Toten Meer.* Mitteilungen des Septuaginta-Unternehmens 28. Göttingen: Vandenhoeck & Ruprecht, 2003. Greek, Latin, and Syriac in parallel columns, with separate section on Hebrew and Aramaic fragments.
See also: Berger synopsis of 4 Ezra with 2 Baruch (below under Pseudepigrapha: 2 Baruch).

Other Concordances:
Barthélemy, D. and O. Rickenbacher. *Konkordanz zum hebräischen Sirach mit syrisch-hebräischem Index.* Göttingen: Vandenhoeck & Ruprecht, 1973. Also see concordance in *The Book of Ben Sira* (above).
Muraoka, T. *A Greek-Hebrew/Aramaic Index to I Esdras.* SBLSCS 11. Chico, CA: Scholars Press, 1984.
Strothmann, Werner, ed. *Wörterverzeichnis der apokryphen-deuterokanonischen Schriften des Alten Testaments in der Peshitta.* Göttinger Orientforschungen Reihe 1, Syriaca 27. Wiesbaden: Otto Harrassowitz, 1988. Also provides a Latin gloss for each Syriac word.
Winter, Michael M. *A Concordance to the Peshi☐ta Version of Ben Sira.* Monographs of the Peshitta Institute 2. Leiden: Brill, 1976.

Lexicon:
For Greek see above under Septuagint and below under General Pseudepigrapha Bibliography. For Hebrew text of Ben Sira see Clines, ed., *Dictionary of Classical Hebrew* (below under Dead Sea Scrolls).

Introductions:
Brockington, L. H. *A Critical Introduction to the Apocrypha.* London: Gerald Duckworth, 1961.
DeSilva, David A. *Introducing the Apocrypha: Message, Context, and Significance.* Grand Rapids: Baker, 2002.
Harrington, Daniel J. *Invitation to the Apocrypha.* Grand Rapids: Eerdmans, 1999.
Kaiser, Otto. *The Old Testament Apocrypha: An Introduction.* Peabody, MA: Hendrickson, 2004. Translation of his 2000 German edition.
Longenecker, Bruce W. *2 Esdras.* Guides to the Apocrypha and Pseudepigrapha; Sheffield: Sheffield Academic Press, 1995. Other helpful introductions have also appeared in this series, including Bartlett on *1 Maccabees*, DeSilva on *4 Maccabees*, Coggins on *Sirach*, Grabbe on *Wisdom of Solomon*, Otzen on *Tobit and Judith*.
Metzger, Bruce M. *An Introduction to the Apocrypha.* Oxford: OUP, 1957.

Oesterley, W. O. E. *An Introduction to the Books of the Apocrypha.* New York: Macmillan, 1935.

Torrey, Charles Cutler. *The Apocryphal Literature: A Brief Introduction.* New Haven:

Yale University Press, 1945. Also introduces many books of the Pseudepigrapha.

See also: Nickelsburg, *Jewish Literature*; *JWSTP*; *HJPAJC* Vol. 3; *CHJ* 2:409–503; *ABD* 1:292–94 and s.v. by book; *EDEJ* 143–62 and s.v. by book.

Commentaries:

Abel, P. F.-M. *Les Livres des Maccabées.* Études Bibliques. Paris: J. Gabalda, 1949.

Larcher, C. *Le Livre de la Sagesse ou La Sagesse de Salomon.* Études Bibliques n.s.

1; 3 vols. Paris: J. Gabalda, 1983–1985.

Scarpat, Giuseppe. *Libro della Sapienza: Testo, traduzione, introduzione e comment.* 3

vols. Biblica Testi e studi 1, 3, 6. Brescia: Paideia, 1989–1999.

Talshir, Zipora. *1 Esdras: A Text Critical Commentary.* SBLSCS 50. Atlanta: Society

of Biblical Literature, 2001.

Commentaries exist on each book in some biblical commentary series. In English note especially Septuagint Commentary Series (Brill), Commentaries on Early Jewish Literature series (de Gruyter), Anchor Bible series (Doubleday), Jewish

Apocryphal Literature series from Dropsie University (Harper), and Stone on *Fourth Ezra* in the Hermeneia series (Fortress). Shorter but still helpful are the volumes in the Cambridge Bible Commentary series (CUP) and the OT Message series (Michael Glazier). Also see the UBS Handbook Series (United Bible Societies)

for translation comments. In German note the Herders Theologischer Kommentar zum Alten Testament series (Herder), Das Alte Testament Deutsch: Apokryphen, Neuer Stuttgarter Kommentar Altes Testament (Katholisches Bibelwerk), and Die Neue Echter Bibel (Echter). Some one-volume commentaries also include the Apocrypha; e.g. *Eerdmans Commentary on the Bible* (Eerdmans, 2003).

256 JOURNAL OF THE EVANGELICAL THEOLOGICAL SOCIETY

4. Pseudepigrapha (Jewish)

The term "pseudepigrapha" properly refers to literature written under an assumed name (generally of some famous OT person). However, "the Pseudepigrapha" has become almost a catch-all category for intertestamental works

which do not fit elsewhere. The translation volume edited by Charlesworth, while focusing on works of primarily Jewish origin, also includes some Christian works. Below are listed the most important pseudepigraphal works for the study of Judaism. Since some Christian pseudepigrapha may include original Jewish material,

a few of these are also noted. For bibliography of other Christian pseudepigrapha and some lesser known works see Haelewyck, *Clavis Apocryphorum* (noted below).

Pseudo-Philo and named Jewish authors are listed later in this bibliography.

4.1 General Pseudepigrapha Bibliography

Bibliography:

Orlov, Andrei A. *Selected Studies in the Slavonic Pseudepigrapha.* SVTP 23. Leiden/
Boston: Brill, 2009. Note the "Selected Bibliography on the
Transmission of the Jewish Pseudepigrapha in the Slavic Milieux" on
pp. 201–434.

DiTommaso, Lorenzo. *A Bibliography of Pseudepigrapha Research 1850–1999.*
JSPSup 39. Sheffield: Sheffield Academic Press, 2001. 1067 very helpful
pages.

Lehnardt, Andreas. *Bibliographie zu den jüdischen Schriften aus hellenistisch-römischer
Zeit. JSHRZ* VI/2. Gütersloh: Gütersloher Verlagshaus, 1999. Very useful.

Haelewyck, J.-C. *Clavis Apocryphorum Veteris Testamenti.* CChr. Turnhout:
Brepols, 1998. Valuable list of texts, translations, and concordances for
each pseudepigraphal book.

Charlesworth, James H. *The Pseudepigrapha and Modern Research with a Supplement.*
New ed. SBLCS. Chico, CA: Scholars, 1981. Dated, but also contains
competent brief introductions.

See also: Arbeitshilfen für das Studium der Pseudepigraphen
(http://www.unileipzig.
de/~nt/asp/index.htm).

Texts (general):

Stone, Michael E. *Armenian Apocrypha Relating to Adam and Eve.* SVTP 14.
Leiden:
Brill, 1996. Not all of this material is early. Also see W. Lowndes
Lipscomb, *The Armenian Apocryphal Adam Literature.* University of
Pennsylvania
Armenian Texts and Studies 8. Scholars Press, 1990.

Stone, Michael E. *Armenian Apocrypha Relating to the Patriarchs and Prophets.*
Jerusalem:
Israel Academy of Sciences and Humanities, 1982.

Denis, Albert-Marie. *Fragmenta pseudepigraphorum quae supersunt graeca.*
PVTG 3.
Leiden: Brill, 1970. The standard edition of Greek fragments. Bound
with Black's edition of Greek 1 Enoch.

See also: Online Critical Pseudepigrapha (http://ocp.tyndale.ca), which provides
introductions (with bibliography on modern editions of texts) and
original language texts for many works.

Translations:

Charles, R. H., ed. *The Apocrypha and Pseudepigrapha of the Old Testament in English.*
2 vols. Oxford: Clarendon, 1913. Still quite useful, though supplanted
by Charlesworth and Sparks. Available online at http://archive.org
or at http://www.ccel.org/c/charles/otpseudepig.

Charlesworth, James H., ed. *The Old Testament Pseudepigrapha.* 2 vols. New

York: Doubleday, 1983–1985; paperback repr. Peabody, MA: Hendrickson, 2009. The current most common English translation; includes helpful introductions and notes (see also Scripture Index listed below). Many contributions are excellent, but some have been critiqued for poor textual basis or for inadequacies in the notes and introductions; cf. the detailed reviews by S. P. Brock in *JJS* 35 (1984) 200–209 and *JJS* 38 (1987) 107–14. [=*OTP*]

Kümmel, Werner Georg, et al., gen. eds. *Jüdische Schriften aus hellenistischrömischer Zeit.* Gütersloh: G. Mohn/Gütersloher Verlagshaus, 1973–2005. A highly respected multi-volume German translation series with fine introductions and commentary. [= JSHRZ]

Lichtenberger, Hermann and Gerbern S. Oegema, gen. eds. *Jüdische Schriften aus hellenistisch-römischer Zeit Neue Folge.* Gütersloh: Gütersloher Verlagshaus, 2005–. Multi-volume continuation of *JSHRZ.* [=*JSHRZNF*]

Sparks, H. F. D., ed. *The Apocryphal Old Testament.* Oxford: Clarendon, 1984. A useful one-volume edition with succinct introductions of a subset of works also found in Charlesworth's *OTP*; for comparison with *OTP* see review by G. W. E. Nickelsburg in *CBQ* 50 (1988) 288–91 and those by M. E. Stone and R. A. Kraft in *Religious Studies Review* 14 (1988) 111–17. [= AOT]

Further important translations appear in Spanish (Alejandro Díez Macho, et al., eds., *Apocrifos del Antiguo Testamento.* 5 vols. Madrid: Ediciones Cristiandad, 1982–1987) and in Italian (Paulo Sacchi, et al., eds., *Apocrifi Dell'Antico Testamento.* 5 vols. Turin: Unione Tipografico-Editrice Torinese/ Brescia: Paideia, 1981–1997).

A new two-volume collection of lesser known pseudepigrapha is due out soon, published by Eerdmans and edited by Richard Bauckham and James R. Davila under the auspices of the More Old Testament Pseudepigrapha Project (see http://www.st-andrews.ac.uk/divinity/rt/ moreoldtestamentpseudepigrapha).

Also see: Translations of varying qualities available online at http://sacredtexts. com/chr/apo/index.htm and at http://www.piney.com/ ApocalypticIndex. html and at http://jewishchristianlit.com/Texts.

Concordances:

Bauer, Johannes B. *Clavis Apocryphorum supplementum: complectens voces versionis Germanicae Libri Henoch Slavici, Libri Jubilaeorum, Odarum Salomonis.* Grazer theologische Studien 4. Graz: Institut für Ökumenische Theologie und Patrologie an der Universität Graz, 1980. Not a concordance to the original languages but to German translations. For his book-by-book concordance of Greek pseudepigrapha, see below under "Lexicon."

Denis, Albert-Marie. *Concordance grecque des Pseudépigraphes d'Ancien Testament:*

Concordance, Corpus des textes, Indices. Louvain-la-Neuve: Institut Orientaliste, 1987. Very useful. Denis produced an earlier concordance of the Greek version of Baruch (Leuven: Peeters, 1970).

Denis, Albert-Marie. *Concordance latine des Pseudépigraphes d'Ancien Testament:*
Concordance, Corpus des textes, Indices. Turnhout: Brepols, 1993. A fine work. Denis released an earlier concordance of the Latin version of Jubilees (Université catholique de Louvain, 1973; repr. Turnhout: Brepols, 2002).

Lechner-Schmidt, Wilfried. *Wortindex der lateinisch erhaltenen Pseudepigraphen zum*
Alten Testament. TANZ 3. Tübingen: Francke, 1990. Also contains some texts.

See also: the *Thesaurus Linguae Graecae* database for searchable Greek texts, as well as tagged Greek modules available for Accordance, BibleWorks, and Logos software.

Scripture Index:

Delamarter, Steve. *A Scripure Index to Charlesworth's The Old Testament Pseudepigrapha.*
London/New York: Sheffield Academic Press, 2002. Indexes all references to OT and NT books in the introductions, notes and margins of *OTP*; necessarily dependent on the work of the original translators (which varies "in terms of quantity and focus" from book to book).

Lexicon:

Wahl, Christian Abraham. *Clavis Librorum Veteris Testamenti Apocryphorum Philologica.*
Leipzig: Johannes Ambrosius Barth, 1853; repr. Graz: Akademische Druck, 1972. Repr. contains Wahl's lexicon of the Greek Apocrypha and Pseudepigrapha, and J. B. Bauer's book-by-book concordance of the Greek Pseudepigrapha.

Introductions:

De Jonge, M., ed. *Outside the Old Testament.* Cambridge: CUP, 1985. Selected Jewish Pseudepigrapha excerpts with commentary.

Denis, Albert-Marie, et al. *Introduction à la littérature religieuse judéo-hellénistique.* 2
vols. Turnhout: Brepols, 2000. Also note his previous *Introduction aux Pseudépigraphes grecs d'Ancien Testament.* SVTP 1. Leiden: Brill, 1970.

Díez Macho, Alejandro. *Apocrifos del Antiguo Testamento.* Vol. 1: Introduccion General a Los Apocrifos del Antiguo Testamento. Madrid: Ediciones Cristiandad, 1984.

Turdeanu, Emile. *Apocryphes slaves et roumains de l'Ancien Testament.* SVTP 5. Leiden: Brill, 1981.

See also: Nickelsburg, *Jewish Literature*; Helyer, *Exploring Jewish Literature*; *JWSTP*; *HJPAJC* Vol. 3; *CHJ* 2:409–503; *EDEJ* 143–62 and s.v. by book. Older introduction by Torrey (see under Apocrypha). Individual introductions are appearing in the "Guides to the Apocrypha and Pseudepigrapha" series from Sheffield Academic Press (some are noted below).

4.2 Special Pseudepigrapha Bibliography (alphabetical by book)

This list contains the best-known books with likely Jewish lineage in collections of "Old Testament Pseudepigrapha." The principal languages of extant

MSS for each book are noted below. Dates largely concur with those in Charlesworth *OTP*. If the texts available are clearly Christian (with an assumed Jewish substratum), this is indicated. Not included are some highly fragmented texts and those unlikely to be of Jewish provenance. Pseudo-Philo and other individual writers are found later in this bibliography. Consult also the General Pseudepigrapha Bibliography above (especially Lehnardt's *Bibliographie* and the introductions and translations in *OTP* and *JSHRZ*). More detailed bibliography of texts (including fragments and later versions) in Haelewyck, *Clavis Apocryphorum* and
DiTommaso, *Bibliography*.

AHIQAR (Aramaic; 7th–6th cent. BC).
In the Elephantine papyri, with later recensions in many languages; thought to be related to the (Greek) Life of Aesop and so listed in Denis, *Fragmenta pseudepigraphorum* (see above).

Text and Translation:
Porten, Bezalel, and Ada Yardeni. *Textbook of Aramaic Documents from Ancient Egypt.* Vol. 3: Literature, Accounts, Lists. Winona Lake: Eisenbrauns, 1986–1993, 23–53.
Cowley, A. *Aramaic Papyri of the Fifth Century B.C.* Oxford: Clarendon, 1923, 204–48. Widely known edition with translation and extensive notes. Available online at http://archive.org.
Conybeare, F. C., J. Rendel Harris, and Agnes Smith Lewis. *The Story of A☐i☐ar from the Syriac, Arabic, Armenian, Ethiopic, Greek and Slavonic Versions.* London:
C. J. Clay & Sons, 1898. Extensive introduction with translations of versions listed in the title plus texts of Greek (Life of Aesop), Armenian, Syriac, and Arabic. Available online at http://archive.org.

Commentary:
Lindenberger, James M. *The Aramaic Proverbs of Ahiqar.* JHNES. Baltimore: Johns Hopkins University Press, 1983.

Grammar:
Muraoka, Takamitsu and Bezalel Porten. *A Grammar of Egyptian Aramaic.* 2d rev. ed. Leiden: Brill, 2003.

Concordance:
Porten, Bezalel and Jerome A. Lund. *Aramaic Documents from Egypt: A Key-Word-in-Context Concordance.* Winona Lake: Eisenbrauns, 2002.

APOCALYPSE OF ABRAHAM (Old Slavonic; 1st–2d cent. AD)
Text, Translation, and Commentary:
Rubinkiewicz, Ryszard. *L'Apocalypse d' Abraham en vieux slave: Introduction, texte critique, traduction et commentaire.* Lublin: Société des Lettres et des Sciences de l'Université Catholique de Lublin, 1987. Apparently edited without reference to the Philonenko edition.
Philonenko-Sayar, Belkis and Marc Philonenko. "L'Apocalypse d'Abraham:
260 JOURNAL OF THE EVANGELICAL THEOLOGICAL SOCIETY
Introduction, texte slave, traduction et notes." *Sem* 31 (1981) 1–119.

APOCALYPSE OF ADAM (Coptic; 1st–4th cent. AD)

Found among Nag Hammadi gnostic texts, yet considered to be Jewish in origin. Consult Nag Hammadi scholarship for further translations (e.g. J. M. Robinson, ed., *Nag Hammadi Library in English*) and concordances (e.g. Folker Siegert, *Nag-Hammadi-Register*). Another possible Jewish gnostic text is *Poimandres* in the *Corpus Hermeticum* (see further *JWSTP* 443–81).

Text and Translation:

Parrott, Douglas M., ed. *Nag Hammadi Codices V,2–5 and VI with Papyrus Berolinensis 8502, 1 and 4.* NHS 11. Leiden: Brill, 1979, 151–95. Text edited by G. W. MacRae.

Text, Translation, and Commentary:

Morard, Françoise. *L'Apocalypse d' Adam (NH V, 5).* Bibliothèque copte de Nag Hammadi: Section textes 15. Québec: Les Presses de l'Université Laval, 1985.

APOCALYPSE OF ELIJAH (Coptic, Greek; 1st–4th cent. AD) Christian text with likely Jewish substratum.

Text and Translation:

Pietersma, Albert, Susan Turner Comstock, and Harold W. Attridge. *The Apocalypse of Elijah based on P. Chester Beatty 2018.* SBLTT 19. Chico, CA, Scholars, 1981. Coptic text and translation, includes appendix on Greek fragment. Also in Denis, *Fragmenta pseudepigraphorum* (above). *See also* material in *HJPAJC* 3.2:799–803.

APOCALYPSE OF MOSES (*see* Life of Adam and Eve)

APOCALYPSE OF SEDRACH (*see note below* under 4 Ezra)

APOCALYPSE OF ZEPHANIAH (Coptic and Greek fragments; 1st cent. BC–1st cent. AD) Christian with possible Jewish substratum.

Text and Discussion:

Steindorff, Georg. *Die Apokalypse des Elias, eine unbekannte Apokalypse und Bruchstücke der Sophonias Apokalypse.* TU 17.3. Leipzig: Hinrichs, 1899. Available online at http://archive.org. Also see Denis, *Fragmenta pseudepigraphorum.*

APOCRYPHON OF EZEKIEL (Greek and Hebrew fragments; 1st cent. BC–1st cent. AD) Probable Jewish work with possible Christian influence in extant fragments.

Text, Translation and Discussion:

Stone, Michael E., Benjamin G. Wright, and David Satran, eds. *The Apocryphal Ezekiel.* SBLEJL 18. Atlanta: Society of Biblical Literature, 2000. Includes the five fragments previously published by Mueller plus other possible contenders. Also studies later Christian traditions about Ezekiel.

Mueller, James R. *The Five Fragments of the Apocryphon of Ezekiel: A Critical Study.* Journal for the Study of the Pseudepigrapha Supplement Series 5. Sheffield: Sheffield Academic Press, 1994. Also see Denis, *Fragmenta pseudepigraphorum.*

(PSEUDO-) ARISTEAS, [LETTER OF] (Greek; 2nd cent. BC, possibly later)

Critical Text, Translation, Notes, and Concordance:
Pelletier, André. *Lettre D'Aristée à Philocrate: Introduction, texte critique, traduction et*
notes, index complet des mots grecs. SC 89. Paris: Cerf, 1962. Best current critical
text. A text can also be found appended to Swete's *Introduction to the
Old Testament in Greek.*
Critical Text:
Wendland, Paul. *Aristeae ad Philocratem Epistula cum Ceteris de Origine Versionis*
LXX Interpretum Testimoniis. Leipzig: Teubner, 1900. Available online at
http://archive.org.
Text and Notes:
Hadas, Moses. *Aristeas to Philocrates (Letter of Aristeas).* New York: Harper &
Brothers, 1951. Includes text, lengthy introduction, and brief notes.
Meecham, Henry G. *The Letter of Aristeas: A Linguistic Study with Special Reference*
to the Greek Bible. Manchester: Manchester University Press, 1935. Notes
focus on use of Greek language.
Online see http://www.voskrese.info/spl/miller-arist.pdf (Greek text and
translation) and http://www.ccel.org/c/charles/otpseudepig/
aristeas.htm (Charles, ed., translation).
Introduction:
See Jellicoe, *Septuagint and Modern Study* 29–58 (under Septuagint); Bartlett, *Jews*
in the Hellenistic World 11–34 (under Josephus).
ASCENSION OF ISAIAH (Ethiopic, Latin, Greek fragments, etc.; 2d
cent. BC–4th cent. AD)
Christian with a probable Jewish section known as "Martyrdom of Isaiah" in
1:1–3:12 [omit 1:2b–6a] and 5:1b–14.
Texts:
Bettiolo, Paolo, et al. *Ascensio Isaiae: Textus.* CChr.SA 7. Turnhout: Brepols,
1995. Contains Ethiopic, Greek, Coptic, Latin, and Slavonic texts (with
Italian translation). Earlier edition of Ethiopic and Latin texts by Dillmann
(*Ascencio Isaiae: Aethiopice et Latine*, Leipzig: Brockhaus, 1877) available
free at http://books.google.com. Greek text also in Denis, *Fragmenta
pseudepigraphorum.*
Translation and Commentary:
Charles, R. H. *The Ascension of Isaiah.* London: Adam & Charles Black, 1900.
Also includes Ethiopic, Latin, and Slavonic (transcribed) texts in parallel
columns. Available online at http://archive.org.
Tisserant, Eugène. *Ascension d'Isaie.* Paris: Letouzey et Ané, 1909. Available
online at http://archive.org.
262 JOURNAL OF THE EVANGELICAL THEOLOGICAL SOCIETY
Introduction:
Knight, Jonathan. *The Ascension of Isaiah.* Sheffield: Sheffield Academic Press,
1995.
Commentary:
Norelli, Enrico. *Ascensio Isaiae: Commentarius.* CChr.SA 8. Turnhout: Brepols,

1995. In Italian.
Assumption (Testament) of Moses (Latin; 1st cent. AD)
Text, Translation, and Commentary:
Tromp, Johannes. *The Assumption of Moses: A Critical Edition with Commentary.*
SVTP 10. Leiden: Brill, 1993. Supplants R. H. Charles, *Assumption of Moses.*
London: Black, 1897. Abraham Schalit also began a commentary on
chapter one before his death which was later published as *Untersuchungen
zur Assumptio Moses* (Leiden: Brill, 1989).
2 BARUCH (=Syriac Apocalypse of Baruch; also Greek fragments and Arabic
version; 2nd cent. AD)
Text:
Gurtner, Daniel M. *Second Baruch: A Critical Edition of the Syriac Text With
Greek
and Latin Fragments, English Translation, Introduction, and Concordances.*
Jewish
and Christian Texts in Contexts and Related Studies 5. London: T &
T Clark, 2009.
Leemhuis, F., A. F. J. Klijn, and G. J. H. Van Gelder. *The Arabic Text of the
Apocalypse of Baruch: Edited and Translated with a Parallel Translation of the
Syriac Text.* Leiden: Brill, 1986.
Dedering, S., ed. *Apocalypse of Baruch.* Vetus Testamentum Syriace IV, 3.
Leiden:
Brill, 1973. For the final *Epistle* the Leiden edition remains forthcoming,
use M. Kmoskó, *Epistola Baruch filii Neriae*, in R. Graffin, *Patrologia
Syriaca* 1,2 (Paris: Firmin-Didot, 1907) col. 1208–1237. For Greek
fragments see Denis, *Fragmenta pseudepigraphorum* in general bibliography.
Translation and Commentary:
Bogaert, Pierre. *Apocalypse de Baruch: Introduction, traduction du syriaque et
commentaire.*
2 vols. SC 144–45. Paris: Cerf, 1969.
Also see: Berger, Klaus, Gabriele Fassbeck, and Heiner Reinhard. *Synopse des
Vierten Buches Esra und der Syrischen Baruch-Apokalypse.* TANZ 8. Tübingen:
Francke, 1992. Based on German translation.
3 BARUCH (= Greek Apocalypse of Baruch; Slavonic version in two recensions;
1st–3rd cent. AD)
Christian with Jewish substratum.
Text:
Picard, J.-C. *Apocalypsis Baruchi Graece.* PVTG 2. Leiden: Brill, 1967.
Commentary:
Kulik, Alexander. *3 Baruch: Greek-Slavonic Apocalypse of Baruch.* CEJL. Berlin:
de
Gruyter, 2010.
4 BARUCH (*see* Paraleipomena Jeremiou)
1 ENOCH (Ethiopic Enoch; also in Greek, Aramaic fragments, and other
versional fragments; 2d cent. BC–1st cent. AD)
Texts (and Translations):
Knibb, Michael A., in consultation with Edward Ullendorff. *The Ethiopic Book
of Enoch: A New Edition in the Light of the Aramaic Dead Sea Fragments.* 2

vols. Oxford: Clarendon, 1978. Vol. 1: Text and Apparatus; Vol. 2: Introduction, Translation, and Commentary. Supplants previous editions by R. H. Charles (1906) and A. Dillmann (1851).

Milik, J. T. and Matthew Black. *The Books of Enoch: Aramaic Fragments of Qumrân Cave 4*. Oxford: Clarendon, 1976. Texts, translations, plates, and extensive comments.

Black, M. *Apocalypsis Henochi Graece*. PVTG 3. Leiden: Brill, 1970. Edition of Greek text; bound with Denis, *Fragmenta pseudepigraphorum*. For addenda and corrigenda see Black and Vanderkam, *The Book of Enoch or 1 Enoch* (below).

Commentaries:

Black, Matthew, in consultation with James C. Vanderkam. *The Book of Enoch or 1 Enoch: A New English Edition with Commentary and Textual Notes.* SVTP 7. Leiden: Brill, 1985. Extensive commentary, consciously revising Charles's 1912 commentary. With Otto Neugebauer on chaps. 72–82.

Charles, R. H. *The Book of Enoch or 1 Enoch.* Oxford: Clarendon, 1912. Translation with extensive commentary. The author prefers this (what amounts to a 2d edition) over his earlier *The Book of Enoch* (1893). Available online at http://archive.org.

Nickelsburg, George W. E. *1 Enoch 1: A Commentary on the Book of 1 Enoch, Chapters 1–36; 81–108.* Hermeneia; Minneapolis: Fortress, 2001.

Nickelsburg, George W. E. and James C. Vanderkam. *1 Enoch 2: A Commentary on the Book of 1 Enoch, Chapters 37–82.* Hermeneia. Minneapolis: Fortress, 2012. Nickelsburg and Vanderkam have also produced *1 Enoch: A New Translation.* Philadelphia: Fortress, 2004.

Stuckenbruck, Loren T. *1 Enoch 91–108.* CEJL. Berlin: de Gruyter, 2007.

Tiller, Patrick A. *A Commentary on the Animal Apocalypse of 1 Enoch.* SBL Early Judaism and Its Literature 4. Atlanta: Scholars, 1993.

Earlier important commentaries by A. Dillmann (Vogel, 1853) and François Martin (Letouzey, 1906). Short commentary article by Daniel C. Olson in J. D. G. Dunn, gen. ed., *Eerdmans Commentary to the Bible.* Grand Rapids: Eerdmans, 2003.

2 ENOCH (Slavonic Enoch, in two recensions; 1st cent. AD)

Text and Translation:

Vaillant, A. *Le Livre des secrets d'Hénoch.* Paris: Institut d'Etudes Slaves, 1952.

Translation and Commentary:

Morfill, W. R. and R. H. Charles. *The Book of the Secrets of Enoch.* Oxford: Clarendon, 1896.

Concordance to German Translation:

See above Bauer, *Clavis Apocryphorum Supplementum.*

264 JOURNAL OF THE EVANGELICAL THEOLOGICAL SOCIETY

3 ENOCH (Hebrew Enoch; 5th – 6th cent. AD): *See below* under Hekhalot literature.

4 EZRA (*see above* under Apocrypha)

Several Christian pseudepigraphic works also draw on Ezra as a central figure and may be indebted to Jewish sources (e.g. Greek Apocalypse of Ezra, Vision of Ezra, and Apocalypse of Sedrach); *see* Charlesworth *OTP* 1:561–613; text of some in Otto Wahl, ed. *Apocalypsis Esdrae—Apocalypsis Sedrach—Visio beati Esdrae.* PVTG 4. Leiden: Brill, 1977.

HISTORY OF JOSEPH (*see* Charlesworth, ed., *OTP* 2:467–75)

HISTORY OF THE RECHABITES (Greek, Syriac, and many versions; 1st–4th cent. AD)

Substantially Christian, possible Jewish substratum.

Text and Translation:

Charlesworth, James H. *The History of the Rechabites. Volume I: The Greek Recension.*

SBLTT 17. Chico, CA: Scholars, 1982. Critical Greek text; an edition of the Syriac text is still desired. Brief commentary by Chris H. Knights in *JSJ* 28 (1997) 413–36.

JANNES AND JAMBRES (Greek and Latin fragments)

Text, Translation, and Commentary:

Pietersma, Albert. *The Apocryphon of Jannes and Jambres the Magicians.* Religions in the Graeco-Roman World 119. Leiden: Brill, 1994. Includes facsimile plates.

JOSEPH AND ASENETH (Greek and Latin versions in two recensions, also Armenian, and other versions; 1st cent. BC–2d cent. AD)

Text and Translation:

Burchard, Christoph. *A Minor Edition of the Armenian Version of Joseph and Aseneth.*

Hebrew University Armenian Studies 10. Leuven: Peeters, 2010. Diplomatic text supplemented with 12 other important manuscripts.

Fink, Uta Barbara. *Joseph und Aseneth: Revision des griechischen Textes und Edition der zweiten lateinischen Übersetzung.* Fontes et subsidia ad Bibliam pertinentes 5. Berlin/New York: de Gruyter, 2008. Important revision of Burchard's provisional Greek text of the long recension (though without a full textual apparatus), with a synoptic edition of Latin "L2" manuscripts. Includes study of manuscript stemma. See review in *BBR* 20 (2010) 110–12.

Burchard, Christoph with Carsten Burfeind and Uta Barbara Fink. *Joseph und Aseneth: Kritisch Herausgegeben.* PVTG 5. Leiden/Boston: Brill, 2003. Critical edition focusing on the longer Greek recension (which Burchard believes is earlier than the short recension). While the apparatus is excellent, the text itself remains the same as Burchard's "provisional" Greek text. Burchard himself translated this longer recension into English in Charlesworth, *OTP*.

Philonenko, Marc. *Joseph et Aséneth: Introduction, texte critique, traduction et notes.*

SPB 13. Leiden: Brill, 1968. Standard edition of the shorter Greek reJEWISH cension plus word index. ET of this shorter recension in H. F. D. Sparks, *Apocryphal Old Testament.*

Introduction:
Humphrey, Edith M. *Joseph and Aseneth*. Guides to the Apocrypha and Pseudepigrapha
8. Sheffield: Sheffield Academic Press, 2000.
Other:
Burchard, Christoph. *Gesammelte Studien zu Joseph und Aseneth*. SVTP 13. Leiden:
Brill, 1996. Collection of significant articles on the text, importance, and state of study (including bibliography). Includes a reprint of Burchard's Vorläufiger Text ("provisional text") of the long recension (pp. 161–209).
Reinmuth, Eckart, ed. *Joseph und Aseneth: Eingeleitet, ediert, übersetzt und mit interpretierenden*
Essays. Scripta Antiquitatis Posterioris ad Ethicam Religionemque pertinentia 15. Tübingen: Mohr-Siebeck, 2009).
Note also "The Aseneth Home Page" at http://markgoodacre.org/aseneth /index.htm.
JUBILEES (Hebrew fragments; Ethiopic Versions; Latin, Greek, and Syriac fragments; 2d cent. BC)
Hebrew Texts:
For extensive Qumran cave 4 fragments (4Q216–228) see DJD 13; other fragments in DJD 1, 3, and 7. Also cf. *RevQ* 12.4 [= 48] (1987) 529–36; *RevQ* 14.1 [= 53] (1989) 129–30. For possible Masada fragments see *Er-Isr* 20 (1989) 278–86.
Texts:
Vanderkam, James C., ed. *The Book of Jubilees: A Critical Text*. CSCO 510. Leuven:
Peeters, 1989. A critical text of the Ethiopic, supplanting the older edition by R. H. Charles (Oxford, 1895); also with Greek, Syriac, Latin, and some Hebrew fragments (though not the bulk of 4Q216–228). Not all Greek and Syriac fragments are included (cf. Denis, *Fragmenta pseudepigraphorum* above).
Translation and Textual Notes:
Vanderkam, James C. *The Book of Jubilees*. CSCO 511. Leuven: Peeters, 1989.
Translates his critical text (including the fragments), with extensive notes on text and translation.
Translation and Commentary:
Charles, R. H. *The Book of Jubilees or The Little Genesis*. London: Adam & Charles Black, 1902. Available online at http://archive.org.
Concordance to German Translation:
See above Bauer, *Clavis Apocryphorum Supplementum*.
Introduction:
Vanderkam, James C. *The Book of Jubilees*. Guides to Apocrypha and Pseudepigrapha.
Sheffield: Sheffield Academic Press, 2001.
LADDER OF JACOB (Slavonic)
Only known from Slavonic Christian excerpts, H. G. Lunt (in *OTP* 2:401–411)
266 JOURNAL OF THE EVANGELICAL THEOLOGICAL SOCIETY

suggests a possible 1st-cent. date and potential Jewish Greek substratum. Cf. *HJPAJC* 3.2:805.

LIFE OF ADAM AND EVE

The subject of Adam and Eve appears in different manuscript traditions: Greek (= Apocalypse of Moses; also Armenian and other versions; 1st cent. AD), Latin, two Slavonic recensions, the Armenian "Penitence of Adam," and other recensions.

Textual Synopsis:

Anderson, Gary A., and Michael E. Stone, eds. *A Synopsis of the Books of Adam and Eve.* 2d rev. ed. SBL Early Judaism and Its Literature 5. Atlanta: Scholars, 1999. Armenian, Georgian, Greek, Latin, and Slavonic texts. Also see their website with translations (http://jefferson.village.virginia.edu/anderson, which links to http://www2.iath.virginia.edu/anderson).

Text:

Tromp, Johannes. *The Life of Adam and Eve in Greek: A Critical Edition.* PVTG 6. Leiden: Brill, 2005.

Stone, Michael E. *Texts and Concordances of the Armenian Adam Literature.* Volume 1. SBLEJL 12. Atlanta: Scholars Press, 1996. Volume 1 includes the Penitence of Adam, the Book of Adam, and Genesis 1–4 in Armenian (with concordances to each and a non-critical text of each). Volume 2 has been published as *A Concordance of the Armenian Apocryphal Adam Books* (Leuven: Peeters, 2001). For a critical edition of the Armenian texts see above works by Stone and by Lipscomb under General Pseudepigrapha Bibliography; also M. E. Stone, *The Penitence of Adam.* 2 vols. CSCO 429–430. Leuven: Peeters, 1981.

Text, Translation, and Commentary:

Dochhorn, Jan. *Die Apokalypse des Mose: Text, Übersetzung, Kommentar.* TSAJ 106. Tübingen: Mohr-Siebeck, 2005.

Bertrand, Daniel A. *La vie grecque d'Adam et Eve: Introduction, texte, traduction et commentaire.* Recherches intertestamentaires 1. Paris: Maisonneuve, 1987.

Introductions:

De Jonge, Marinus and Johannes Tromp. *The Life of Adam and Eve and Related Literature.* Guides to the Apocrypha and Pseudepigrapha 4. Sheffield: Sheffield Academic Press, 1997.

Stone, Michael E. *A History of the Literature of Adam and Eve.* SBL Early Judaism and Its Literature 3. Atlanta: Scholars, 1992.

LIVES OF THE PROPHETS (Greek, Latin, Syriac, Armenian, Ethiopic, and other versions; 1st cent. AD). Christian with Jewish substratum.

Text, Translation, and Commentary:

Schwemer, Anna Maria. *Studien zu den frühjüdischen Prophetenlegenden* Vitae Prophetarum: *Einleitung, Übersetzung und Kommentar.* 2 vols. TSAJ 49–50; Tübingen: Mohr-Siebeck, 1995–1996. Based on the Greek text, which is edited in a synoptic edition at the end of Vol. 2 (this edition has also been published separately as *Synopse zu den Vitae Prophetarum*). Previous edition by C. C. Torrey (SBLMS 1; Philadelphia: Scholars Press, 1946). For other versions see listing in Schwemer's Vol. 1, pp. 18–22 (cf. Haelewyck, *Clavis Apocryphorum* 167–73).

3–4 Maccabees (Greek, Syriac, and other versions)

3 Maccabees (1st cent. BC) is edited in the Göttingen LXX, and 4 Maccabees (1st cent. AD) is found in Rahlfs's LXX; both appear in the LXX concordances; translations in *OTP* 2:509–64. See also LXX bibliography above.

Introduction:

DeSilva, David A. *4 Maccabees.* Guides to the Apocrypha and Pseudepigrapha 7. Sheffield: Sheffield Academic Press, 1998.

Commentaries:

Commentaries can be found in the Jewish Apocryphal Literature series (Dropsie/Harper) by Hadas, and in the Septuagint Commentary Series (Brill) on 3 Maccabees (by N. Clayton Croy) and 4 Maccabees (by David A. deSilva).

MARTYRDOM OF ISAIAH (*see* Ascension of Isaiah)

(PSEUDO-) MENANDER (Syriac; 3d cent. AD)

Traditionally included with Jewish corpus, though actual provenance is unsure. See discussion and translation in *OTP* 2:583–606; also *HJPAJC* 3.1:692–94.

ODES (*see* Septuagint)

ODES OF SOLOMON (Syriac, also portions in Greek and Coptic; 1st–2d cent. AD)

Christian, though some propose a Jewish origin.

Texts, Translations, Concordance, and Bibliography:

Lattke, Michael. *Die Oden Salomos in ihrer Bedeutung für Neues Testament und Gnosis.*

4 vols. OBO 25. Fribourg Suisse: Editions Universitaires/Göttingen: Vandenhoeck & Ruprecht, 1979–1986. Band I contains texts (with a separate part Ia printing a Syriac facsimile with plates). Band II includes a concordance of each language. Band III is an extensive annotated bibliography of studies on Odes (from 1799 to 1984). Band IV is a collection of articles by Lattke (note he extends his bibliography list to 1997 on pp. 233–51).

Text and Translation:

Charlesworth, James Hamilton. *The Odes of Solomon: The Syriac Texts.* SBLTT 13. Missoula, MT: Scholars Press, 1977. Corrected repr. of 1973 OUP edition. See also facsimile edition *Papyri and Leather Manuscripts of the Odes of Solomon* (Duke University, 1981). Charlesworth also released a translation under the title *The Earliest Christian Hymnbook* (Eugene, OR: Cascade, 2009).

Also see the Rendell Harris items listed under the Psalms of Solomon. An older text with German translation by Walter Bauer. *Die Oden Salomos.* Berlin: de Gruyter, 1933.

Translation and Commentary:

Lattke, Michael. *Odes of Solomon.* Trans. Marianne Ehrhardt. Hermeneia. Minneapolis: Fortress, 2009. Translates his 3 volume German commentary

originally in NTOA 41. Göttingen: Vandenhoeck & Ruprecht, 1999–
2005. Lattke produced a German translation with shorter notes for Fontes
Christiani. FC 19. Freiburg: Herder, 1995.
Pierre, Marie-Joseph, with the collaboration of Jean-Marie Martin. *Les Odes de
Salomon.* Apocryphes 4. Turnhout: Brepols, 1994.
Concordance to German Translation:
See above Bauer, *Clavis Apocryphorum Supplementum.*
PARALEIPOMENA JEREMIOU (also called 4 Baruch; Greek in two recensions,
Ethiopic and other versions; 1st–3d cent. AD)
Text, Translation and Commentary:
Herzer, Jens. *4 Baruch (Paraleipomena Jeremiou).* SBLWAW 22. Atlanta:
Society
of Biblical Literature, 2005. Fine critical text.
Riaud, Jean. *Les Paralipomènes du Prophète Jérémie: Présentation, texte original,
traduction
et commentaries.* Université Catholique de l'Ouest, 1994.
Text and Translation:
Kraft, Robert A. and Ann-Elizabeth Purintun. *Paraleipomena Jeremiou.* SBLTT
1. Missoula, MT: Society of Biblical Literature, 1972.
PRAYER OF JACOB and PRAYER OF JOSEPH (*see* Charlesworth, ed.,
OTP 2:699–723; cf. *HJPAJC* 3.2:798–99)
PRAYER OF MANASSEH (*see* Septuagint; also in Charlesworth, ed., *OTP*
2:625–37)
PSALMS OF SOLOMON (Greek and Syriac; 1st cent. BC)
Greek Text:
Wright, Robert B. *The Psalms of Solomon: A Critical Edition of the Greek Text.*
Jewish and Christian Texts in Contexts and Related Studies 1. London:
T & T Clark, 2007. Wright also offers a CD-ROM with color images of
extant Greek and Syriac manuscripts (see p. 224).
Gebhardt, Oscar von. *Die Psalmen Salomos.* TU 13/2. Leipzig: Hinrichs, 1895.
Earlier critical text of Greek that only collates 8 of the 12 available MSS.
Available online at http://archive.org. A handy Greek text can be found
in Rahlfs's LXX edition (based on Gebhardt).
Syriac Critical Text:
See above "Syriac Peshi□ta Text" (Vol. IV, 6).
Greek and Syriac texts:
Trafton, Joseph L. *The Syriac Version of the Psalms of Solomon: A Critical
Evaluation.*
SBLSCS 11. Atlanta: Scholars, 1985. Comes with a separate fascicle
of facing Greek and Syriac texts (with apparatus). See review in *JSS* 32
(1987) 204–207.
Translation:
Also translated in the NETS LXX translation (see above under Septuagint
and http://ccat.sas.upenn.edu/nets/edition/31-pssal-nets.pdf).
Commentaries:
Atkinson, Kenneth. *An Intertextual Study of the Psalms of Solomon.* Studies in the
Bible and Early Christianity 49. Lewiston, NY: Edwin Mellen, 2001. Includes
Greek text, translation, parallel passages in other Jewish literature

(esp. OT and Apocrypha), and commentary.

Rendell Harris, J. and A. Mingana. *The Odes and Psalms of Solomon Re-edited.* 2 vols. Manchester: John Rylands University Library, 1916–1920. Also note Rendell Harris's earlier *The Odes and Psalms of Solomon: Now First Published from the Syriac Version.* Cambridge: CUP, 1909. Both are available online at http://archive.org.

Ryle, Herbert Edward, and Montague Rhodes James. *Psalms of the Pharisees Commonly Called The Psalms of Solomon.* Cambridge: CUP, 1891. Classic edition with text, translation, introduction, and extensive notes. The Pharisaic identification is not accepted by all. Available at http://archive.org.

Viteau, J. *Les Psaumes de Salomon: Introduction, texte grec et traduction.* Paris: Letouzey et Ané, 1911. With extensive notes. Available online at http://archive.org.

SENTENCES OF (PSEUDO-) PHOCYLIDES (Greek; 1st cent. BC–1st cent. AD)

Wisdom poetry of Jewish origin, but with muted OT references and written under a pagan Greek pseudonym.

Text:

Young, D. *Theognis, Ps-Pythagoras, Ps-Phocylides, Chares, Anonymi Aulodia, fragmentum teleiambicum.* 2 vols.; Leipzig, 1961, 1971. Volume 2 includes the critical text of Ps.-Phocylides.

Text, Translation, and Commentary:

Horst, P. W. van der. *The Sentences of Pseudo-Phocylides: With Introduction and Commentary.* SVTP 4. Leiden: Brill, 1978. Also includes a concordance.

Wilson, Walter T. *The Sentences of Pseudo-Phocylides.* CEJL. Berlin: de Gruyter, 2005.

SIBYLLINE ORACLES (Greek with Latin fragments; 2d cent. BC–7th cent. AD)

Large portions of Books 3 and 5 are considered Jewish; book 4 may have been ultimately redacted by a Jewish editor, and books 11–14 may have a later Jewish origin (this is disputed).

Greek Text:

Geffcken, Johannes. *Die Oracula Sibyllina.* GCS. Leipzig: Hinrichs, 1902. Available online at http://archive.org.

Introductions and Studies on Jewish Sections:

Buitenwerf, Rieuwerd. *Book III of the Sibylline Oracles and its Social Setting: with an Introduction, Translation, and Commentary.* SVTP 17. Leiden: Brill, 2003.

Collins, John J. *The Sibylline Oracles of Egyptian Judaism.* SBLDS 13. Missoula, MT: Society of Biblical Literature, 1974.

Nikiprowetzky, Valentin. *La troisième Sibylle.* Ecole pratique des hautes Etudes270 JOURNAL OF THE EVANGELICAL THEOLOGICAL SOCIETY Sorbonne; Etudes juives 9; Paris: Mouton, 1970. Includes text, translation, notes, and extensive introduction.

Parke, H. W. *Sibyls and Sibylline Prophecy in Classical Antiquity.* Ed. B. C.

McGing. London/New York: Routledge, 1988.
See also: Bartlett, *Jews in the Hellenistic World* 35–55 (under Josephus); older translation of Books 3–5 by H. N. Bate (SPCK, 1918).
TESTAMENT OF ABRAHAM (Greek, also Coptic and other versions; 1st–2nd cent. AD)
Exists in both a long and short recension, with likely common ancestry.
Critical Text:
Roddy, Nicolae. *The Romanian Version of the Testament of Abraham: Text, Translation,*
and Cultural Context. SBLEJL 19. Atlanta: SBL, 2001.
Schmidt, Francis. *Le Testament grec d'Abraham: Introduction, édition critique des deux*
recensions grecques, traduction. TSAJ 11. Tübingen: Mohr-Siebeck, 1986.
Text and Translation:
Stone, Michael E. *The Testament of Abraham: The Greek Recensions.* SBLTT 2.
Missoula, MT: Society of Biblical Literature, 1972. Based on M. R.
James's (1892) edition of Greek texts. An older translation by G. H. Box (London: SPCK, 1927) exists of both recensions along with Gaselee's translation of the Testaments of Isaac and Jacob.
Commentary:
Allison, Dale C. Jr. *Testament of Abraham.* CEJL. Berlin: de Gruyter, 2003.
Delcor, Mathias. *Le Testament d' Abraham: Introduction, Traduction du texte grec, et*
Commentaire de la recension grecque longue. SVTP 2. Leiden: Brill, 1973.
Bibliography:
Nickelsburg, George W. E. Jr. "Review of the Literature." In *Studies on the Testament*
of Abraham, ed. George W. E. Nickelsburg Jr. SBLSCS 6. Missoula, MT: Scholars Press, 1976, 9–22. The same volume also contains translations of the Church Slavonic and Coptic versions.
TESTAMENT OF ADAM (Several recensions in Syriac, Greek, Armenian, and other versions; 2d–5th cent. AD). Christian, with possible Jewish substratum.
Texts and Translations:
Robinson, Stephen Edward. *The Testament of Adam: An Examination of the Syriac and Greek Traditions.* SBLDS 52. Chico, CA: Scholars, 1982. For Armenian editions, see Stone volumes in General bibliography of Pseudepigrapha.
See further Haelewyck, *Clavis Apocryphorum* 8–12.
TESTAMENT OF ISAAC and TESTAMENT OF JACOB (both Coptic, Arabic, Ethiopic; 2d–3d cent. AD). Christian, with some possible Jewish elements; see both Delcor and Box under *Testament of Abraham*, and note *OTP* 1:903–18; *JTS* n.s. 8 (1957) 225–39.
TESTAMENT OF JOB (Greek, also Coptic and Slavonic; 1st cent. BC–1st cent. AD)
Bibliography:
Spittler, Russell P. "The Testament of Job: a history of research and interpretation."
In *Studies on the Testament of Job*, ed. Michael A. Knibb and Pieter

W. Van Der Horst. SNTSMS 66. Cambridge: CUP, 1989, 7–32. The
same volume also has an edition of the Coptic text.
Text:
Brock, S. P., ed. *Testamentum Iobi.* PVTG 2. Leiden: Brill, 1967.
Text and Translation:
Kraft, Robert A., et al., eds. *The Testament of Job: According to the SV Text.*
SBLTT 5. Missoula, MT: SBL, 1974.
TESTAMENT OF MOSES (*see* Assumption of Moses)
TESTAMENT OF SOLOMON (Greek; 1st–3d cent. AD)
Christian, with possible Jewish substratum.
Text:
McCown, Chester Charlton. *The Testament of Solomon.* Leipzig: Hinrichs, 1922.
Available online at http://archive.org. For translation and introduction
see *OTP* 1:935–87.
Commentary:
Busch, Peter. *Das Testament Salomos: Die älteste christliche Dämonologie,*
kommentiert
und in deutscher Erstübersetzung. TU 153. Berlin/New York: de Gruyter,
2006.
TESTAMENTS OF THE TWELVE PATRIARCHS (Aramaic and Hebrew
fragments; two Greek recensions; Syriac, Armenian, and other
versions; 2d cent. BC with later interpolations [disputed]). Christian,
with Jewish substratum. Cf. with 1Q21 (in DJD 1), 3Q7 (in DJD 3),
4Q213–215 (in DJD 22); 4Q484, and 4Q537–541.
Bibliography:
Slingerland, H. Dixon. *The Testaments of the Twelve Patriarchs: A Critical*
History of
Research. SBLMS 21. Missoula, MT: Scholars Press, 1977.
Text:
Stone, Michael E. *An Editio Minor of the Armenian Version of the Testaments of*
the
Twelve Patriarchs. Hebrew University Armenian Studies 11. Leuven:
Peeters, 2012. Text (based on 11 selected extant MSS), translation and
commentary.
De Jonge, M., et al. *The Testaments of the Twelve Patriarchs: A Critical Edition of*
the
Greek Text. PVTG I,2. Leiden: Brill, 1978. Updates Charles's 1908 edition
and De Jonge's own shorter Brill edition of a single Cambridge UL
manuscript from 1964 (entitled *Testamenta XII Patriarcharum*). Includes
word index and partial listing of Armenian variants (note bibliography
on p. 193).
Stone, Michael E. *The Armenian Version of the Testament of Joseph: Introduction,*
Critical Edition, and Translation. SBLTT 6. Missoula, MT: Scholars Press,
1975.
Stone, Michael E. *The Testament of Levi: A First Study of the Armenian MSS of*
the
272 JOURNAL OF THE EVANGELICAL THEOLOGICAL SOCIETY

Testaments of the XII Patriarchs in the Convent of St. James, Jerusalem: with Text,
Critical Apparatus, Notes and Translation. Jerusalem: St. James, 1969.
Charles, Robert Henry. *The Greek Versions of the Testaments of the Twelve Patriarchs:*
Edited from nine MSS together with the Variants of the Armenian and Slavonic versions and some Hebrew Fragments. Oxford: Clarendon, 1908; repr. Darmstadt: Wissenschaftliche Buchgesellschaft, 1966. Available online at http://archive.org. Versional materials are unfortunately only in retroverted Greek. Aramaic fragments from Cairo Genizah.
Commentary:
Charles, R. H. *The Testaments of the Twelve Patriarchs: Translated from the Editor's*
Greek Text and Edited, with Introduction, Notes, and Indices. London: Adam & Charles Black, 1908. Available online at http://archive.org.
Hollander, H. W., and M. de Jonge. *The Testaments of the Twelve Patriarchs: A Commentary.* SVTP 8. Leiden: Brill, 1985.
Introduction:
Kugler, Robert A. *The Testaments of the Twelve Patriarchs.* Guides to Apocrypha and Pseudepigrapha. Sheffield: Sheffield Academic Press, 2001.
TREATISE OF SHEM (Syriac; 1st cent. BC [disputed])
Text and Translation:
Charlesworth, James H. "Die 'Schrift des Sem': Einführung, Text und Übersetzung," in *ANRW* II.20.2. Berlin: de Gruyter, 1987, 951–87.

END

.

CPSIA information can be obtained
at www.ICGtesting.com
Printed in the USA
LVOW05s1118110617
537717LV00014B/910/P